EBAN

EBAN

ROBERT ST. JOHN

W. H. Allen
London and New York
A division of Howard and Wyndham Ltd
1973

AUTHOR'S NOTE

While this book is not authorized or commissioned, Abba Eban did make available his archives and files, without restriction, except that certain letters and documents cannot be directly quoted while the principals are still alive. During the preparation of this book Abba Eban participated in a considerable number of tape-recorded sessions in Jerusalem, Tel Aviv and Washington, as did many of his friends, members of his family and professional associates, as well as some of his critics and political opponents in Israel, the United States and Europe. The sources of all major passages are cited, but in the interest of brevity no mention is made of the hundreds of newspaper and magazine articles in British, Israeli and American publications used as source material, after careful checking. Because the Hebrew language has its own alphabet, there is no standard English-language spelling of Hebrew words. The spellings herein are in conformity with the Standard Jewish Encyclopedia, Cecil Roth, editor-in-chief, Doubleday, 1966.

PHOTO CREDITS

Personal collection of Abba Eban: 1–8, 19, 20, 27; Courtesy of Israel Office of Information: 9, 11–15, 18, 21, 23–26, 29, 30; Howell's Photo Studio: 10; United Nations Photo: 16; United Press Photo: 17; Wide World Photos, Inc.: 22.

Printed in Great Britain by
Fletcher & Son Ltd, Norwich
for the publishers W. H. Allen & Co Ltd,
43 Essex Street, London WC2R 3JG
Bound by Richard Clay (The Chaucer Press) Ltd,
Bungay, Suffolk

ISBN 0 491 01310 8

To Alida Eban

APPRECIATION

These are the people on five continents who supplied the stories, checked the facts, gave of their time and deserve thanks:

ISRAEL

Abba Eban	Moshe Medzini	Benad Avital
Suzy Eban	Arthur Lourie	Meron Medzini
David Ben-Gurion	Etyan Ben-Tzur	Dov Sinai
David Horowitz	David Rivlin	Morris Rosetti
David Hacohon	Gidoon Rafael	Dan Pattir
Simcha Dinitz	Regina Medzini	Israel Schen
Teddy Kollek	Avraham Avidar	Haim Zohar
Michael Arnon	Gershon Avner	Leo Crown
Yacov Herzog	Pinhas Eliav	B. S. Barkai
Chaim Herzog	Nahum Astar	Betty Shiloah
Lord Edwin Samuel	Hava Bitan	Chanock Rinnot
	Lady Samuel	Jeannette Lourie

ENGLAND

Alida Eban	Richard Crossman	Lady Waley Cohen
Dr. I. Eban	Lina Halper	Dr. David Tabor
Carmel Eban	Victor Mishcon	Prof. Bernard Lewis
Gershon Ellenbogen	Frank Singleton	Rita Lipton Levy
Eileen Ellenbogen	Joseph Linton	Tom Pocock
Ruth Lynn	Michael Comay	Nathan Goldenberg
Dr. Robin Lynn	David Carrington	Ruth Lush Cree
Norman Bentwich	Dr. Sam Sacks	John Shaftsley
Dr. Elsie Sacks	R. S. Thompson	S. A. Elwood
Dr. Neville Halper	Dr. Raphael Eban	Nackdemon Doniach

UNITED STATES

Sen. Abraham Ribicoff	Stanley Rabinowitz	Moshe Raviv
Dr. Maurice Shapiro	I. L. Kenen	Shaul Ben-Haim
Martin Agronsky	Florence Wellins	Leopold Freudberg
Zvi Brosh	Vera Honig	Peter Jessup
Hana Raviv	Ludwig Rosenberg	Phillip Slomovitz
David Zysman	Dewey Stone	Anne Stone
Nelson Glueck	Dr. Helen Glueck	Edna Ruth Johnson
		Isaac Don Levine

OTHERS

Matthew Pamm, Cape Town, South
  Africa
G. Saron, Cape Town, South Africa
Ben Sacks, Lisbon, Portugal

David Zuckerman, Cape Town,
  South Africa
José Jesús Montoya, Bogotá,
  Colombia

CONTENTS

1

The People with the Big Ears

SMOKE FROM THE CHIMNEYS of a hundred dwelling places in Yanishki[1] rose in precisely perpendicular lines for a hundred feet or so, and then billowed out to form a great gray cloud that hung over the town as if to protect it from celestial harm. Snow in the roadways, already there for months, had become so hard packed that the runners of sleighs and sledges glided along swiftly, making horse power seem hardly necessary. Even a deaf man, observing the townspeople coming and going, could tell when they talked to one another by watching the white frost that puffed from their mouths. It was a normal winter day in Yanishki, which was a normal Lithuanian town except for the bells of the great Russian Orthodox church, with its onion-shaped dome. The church bells of Yanishki had a wide reputation; they were the loudest church bells anyone in that part of Lithuania had ever heard. When Yanishki's church bells were ringing it took a powerful voice and an acute sense of hearing to carry on a conversation above the din. That was how the people of Yanishki came to be known as "those with the big ears." Also, Yanishki had a reputation as a place inhabited by an unduly large number of horse thieves.

Not far from the church stood the shop of Eliahu Velva (Wolf) Sacks, general merchant. The living quarters were small—just two rooms—but the business establishment was extensive and every square meter of space was crowded with merchandise: silks from France, silverware from England, men's, women's and children's garments from Vilna and Warsaw, but mainly bolts of cloth. There was a saying in Yanishki: "If you want a really good piece of cloth, go and see Elievelva Sacks!"

Eliahu was his proper Hebrew name and Velva (Wolf) his middle name, but the people of Yanishki called him "Elievelva" for short and everyone spoke of him with affection. "One of the noblest men a woman ever had in her womb," was the way one of his wife's friends used to express it.

As a boy Eliahu had been a *yeshivah-bokher*, which is to say, his family, considering him cut out for a life of prayer and study, sent him to a school in which Jewish boys were given advanced education, mostly of a religious nature. These pious students in many ways resembled medieval monks. Some were as young as thirteen, others as old as thirty. They lived in poverty, sleeping on hard benches in poorly heated synagogues, which they used as study halls as well as dormitories. The yeshivah-bokher would often eat in a different home each day of the week—if he was lucky enough to find hospitality that frequently.

The yeshivah to which Eliahu's parents sent him was in Neustadt, a short distance by horse and carriage from the famous city of Tilsit on the Nieman River. One of the homes to which he was most frequently invited for meals was that of Moshe Lieb Hirshowitz, an extremely religious Jew as well as a successful merchant, who decided the boy had qualities that would make him more successful in business than he might be in the pursuit of religious learning, so he began training him in the ways of commerce.

Marriage was important in the life of a yeshivah-bokher. The caprice of emotion was seldom involved. The primary question was whether there was good rapport between the young man and the prospective father-in-law, for habitually the yeshivah-bokher after the marriage went to live in the home of the bride's parents.

It became a fable in the Sacks home that Eliahu caught his first glimpse of Bassa, the daughter of Shana and Moshe Hirshowitz, just twenty-four hours before the marriage. Eliahu was nineteen, Bassa slightly younger. Under the guidance of his father-in-law the boy began training for a business career, yet he never abandoned his interest in Hebrew learning, which had been and would always remain his greatest love.

After it was thought that Eliahu had learned enough about retailing to be trusted alone with the store, both parents would occasionally go to Tilsit for the day. As soon as the door closed behind them, Eliahu would take out his Hebrew books and be lost in study even before they were out of sight down the road.

Within a year after the marriage Bassa gave birth to a girl she named Lina, fair like the mother and of good health, although a majority of the children that followed died either before, during, or soon after birth. Of the eleven Bassa conceived, only four survived.

Lina was still a small girl when the Sacks family moved from Neustadt to the town with the loud bells and there Eliahu went into business for himself. Yanishki was a typical *shtetl* or small town, in the Pale of Settlement, that vast area of Czarist Russia, including Lithuania, in which Jews were permitted to have permanent residence. In such communities, isolated from the surrounding peasant population, the Jews spoke their own language, developed their own institutions, maintained a certain independence of outlook and formed a coherent ethnic group. Although victims of economic and social injustice, poverty and squalor, their sense of Jewishness was strong and their moral and spiritual integrity great.[2]

A considerable percentage of the population of Yanishki was composed of Jews, who, by Russian law, were forbidden to engage in any agricultural pursuits, so they became the merchants, tailors, shoemakers, metalworkers, cabinetmakers, coppersmiths and bakers of Yanishki. Several who owned horses and wagons were in the hauling business—transporting people as well as things—and there were two enterprising Jews who filled great wooden vats with water from the river and sold it from house to house. There were also Jewish musicians and a locksmith who wore, wherever he went, a massive collar hung with keys of every imaginable shape and description, and a few *luftmenschen*. The word literally meant "men of the air." They were brokers or commission merchants who acquired the nickname either because they were always talking about the "big deals" they were about to consummate or because sometimes it was so long between deals that they had to "live on air."[3]

In Yanishki many more children were born to the Sacks family—and died. One of the three others who did survive was a tiny girl who came into the world so frail that no one expected her to live out the first week. Putting all their hope into the name they gave her, the parents called her Altenka, meaning "the old one." Some of the superstitious people of Yanishki insisted that it was giving her this name that was responsible for what happened; Altenka not only lived but soon lost her frailty and grew into a strong, healthy child. Quite understandably, when she was old enough to comprehend the meaning of her name she found it so distasteful she decided to pick one of her own. After much thought she chose Alida, not because it had any special meaning but because "it sounds so beautiful whenever I say it."

While Bassa raised the children and tended shop, Eliahu often traveled extensively around Russia on business trips and several times went to South Africa where he established a commission house that was chiefly concerned with importing eggs from such distant places as China and Denmark. Each time he returned home his English was more polished than ever. Before long it became his favorite language—after Hebrew— and he taught all four children to converse in English. To encourage them he promised them that someday they might go to England to live.

Eliahu often told his children: "I want all of you to become acquainted with the wise and important people of the world."

Everyone agreed—his wife, his children and even his best friends— that Eliahu Wolf Sacks was a better scholar than a businessman. He was what they called in Lithuania a *maskil*—not a professional scholar yet one whose chief interest actually is in scholarship—knowledge for its own sake, unpolluted by practical considerations. He was a member of what was then a small band of men who believed in the revival of Hebrew as a national language and so he drilled his children not only in how to pray in Hebrew but to engage in everyday conversation in the tongue of the prophets.

One of Alida's earliest memories was of sitting at her father's feet while she recited her *alef, bet, gimel* and sounded out simple Hebrew words. Although she was only four or five she showed great aptitude for languages and her father took pride in showing her off to his learned friends.

"Listen, now, to *Mein Kind!*" he would say. This was one Yiddish expression he always used. His wife, his children and later his favorite grandchild were invariably called mein kind.

Eliahu's consuming interest was Hebrew literature and Hebrew tradition, and he taught the four young ones to revere scholarship. Although he held no academic or religious position, the people of Yanishki called on him continuously for advice, aware of his wealth of knowledge and respectful of his wisdom.

Eliahu's one relaxation, when he was not studying, teaching or advising, was playing chess. Customers would come into the store, select an article of clothing or perhaps even a whole bolt of cloth, but after waiting interminably to be heeded would finally leave with their purchases, saying:

"Don't forget to put it on the books."

Eliahu, hardly looking up, would nod and wave a hand, but the entry was seldom made. Sometimes Bassa, checking over the accounts, would discover that some customer was greatly behind in making payments and would ask Eliahu to send for him. When the man appeared Eliahu was more than likely to engage him in a game of chess or half an hour of philosophical discussion, forgetting completely the purpose of the call.

In 1903, when Lina was nineteen, Alida twelve and the sons, Ben and Sam, eleven and seven, Eliahu Sacks came into the living quarters one cold winter day with the moisture of melted snow still glistening on his red beard and announced they were leaving Yanishki.

"We are going to England. For good."

In London Eliahu, after considerable searching, finally took a twelve-room house at 211 Amhurst Road in the Jewish section of a suburb called Stoke Newington, on the north side of the city. One attraction was that nearby were several bookshops that sold not only the London Yiddish newspaper and a weekly Hebrew paper called *Ha Yehudi* (The Jew) but even sometimes papers from eastern Europe.

The London house was so big that for the first time there was a separate room for each member of the family. Eliahu, in his bedroom, had a table on which he kept his newspapers in orderly piles. When any one pile got too big he would tie it with string and put it away in the bedroom closet, pile upon pile. No newspaper in the Sacks home was ever thrown away or even used to start a fire. There was a dining room with a table so large it could seat twenty-eight comfortably, the most impressive piece of furniture in the house.

The first thing Eliahu Sacks did in London after moving his family into the new house was to establish a branch of his South African business.

One day *Ha Yehudi* carried a small ad signed Benzion Halper, which announced that a proficient young scholar was willing to give Hebrew lessons for a modest sum per hour. Eliahu hired him at once and he was given a room in the Stoke Newington house, his task to give all four children intensive Hebrew instruction and also imbue them with a love of the culture. It was, Mr. Sacks explained, a very fortuitous situation, because he himself was about to go off to South Africa for an extended stay and it would be good to have in the house a young man who could be trusted.

The one member of the family happy with the new situation was Lina, now a coquettish honey-blonde. First she acquired respect for her Hebrew teacher, who was just two years her senior; then she fell excitingly in love with him. In proposing to her he said:

"That is, if you are not afraid to share the life of a poor scholar, for, as Solomon Schechter has so well pointed out, anti-Semitics can be a very profitable business; Semitics do not pay nearly so well."

Soon after the marriage Halper received an appointment as lecturer in a newly opened institution in Philadelphia called the Dropsie College for Hebrew and Cognate Learning, so he and Lina left Stoke Newington for America.

During these years Alida had mastered a number of languages and was especially fluent in French. Her father, who spent much time managing his business in South Africa, one day wrote from Cape Town that he had taken into his firm as bookkeeper a bright man who had emigrated to South Africa at the age of eighteen and was now one of the leaders of the Zionist movement there. It was not strange, Mr. Sacks wrote, that the man came from Lithuania, because South Africa at that time was the favorite place of immigration for Litvaks, "but isn't it a coincidence that he comes from our old shtetl, Yanishki?" Even more than that, Eliahu remembered having gone to "either his *bris* [ceremony of circumcision] or his *barmitzvah;* I am not sure which."

The next time Eliahu Sacks arrived home from Cape Town he announced that he had chosen a husband for Alida and then presented to his wife and daughter his new business associate, Abraham Meir Solomon, a handsome man of medium height, with brown hair and eyes, whose whole face smiled when he talked.

Alida was not impressed—she was only twenty-two; he was thirty-four —so she did not immediately accept his proposal of marriage.

"Think it over," he told her. Then he set off for Germany on a business trip. While he was gone he barraged her with letters.

"I am sure they were the most beautiful love letters any man ever wrote to a woman," Alida said. "It was his letters I fell in love with."

The wedding took place in London soon after Solomon returned. Then they left for South Africa aboard the *Edinburgh Castle.* The voyage took three weeks. There was much about Cape Town that Alida liked. She had never seen such immense and beautiful flowers. "And Cape Town has such very nice Jews," she wrote to a friend in London. She also was impressed that no one ever locked doors.

Until now Alida had had little exposure to Zionism, for her father was not at all convinced that there could ever be a re-creation of the Jewish state. His favorite comment on Zionism, which Alida knew by heart from hearing it so often, was:

"Can you see hair on the palm of my hand?"

But as soon as Alida put foot to South African soil she found herself in the vortex of Zionist agitation and organization. At the dock they were met by a party of her husband's Zionist associates and the night after their arrival the Dorshei Zion Association, of which Mr. Solomon was an officer, held a public meeting to greet them and wish them "a long and happy life in the South African Jewish community."

"Avromeir," as Solomon was called by his friends, had talent as both a speaker and a writer. He represented Cape Zionists at almost all Zionist conferences held in the country, was well known as a lecturer on a variety of Jewish subjects and contributed frequent articles to the *Zionist Record*.[4]

That same year Alida's first child, Ruth, was born, followed just fourteen months later, on February 2, 1915, by a boy, who at his *bris* according to Jewish custom was given a Hebrew name, Abba, the common noun for "father." Alida picked the name because her favorite grandfather had been Abba Tobias Sacks, Eliahu's father, known in his native village as "Witzly," the Yiddish word for "the village wit." But Alida was afraid that when her son went to school the boys would nickname him "Abie," a name she disliked. As it is customary for a Jewish child to have an "everyday name," in addition to his Hebrew name, the father suggested Aubrey.

"I know two Aubreys who are simply awful!" Alida replied.

Nevertheless it was finally agreed he should be called Aubrey.

"He weighed only five pounds at birth," the mother reported, "and he had a very small body but a beautiful large head."

He had twinkling brown eyes and his mother insisted he was born with a great sense of humor. "You could tell just by looking at him as he lay in his crib."

A few weeks before Aubrey's conception World War I had commenced. On the day of his birth Von Hindenburg hurled fifty thousand men at the Russian lines near Warsaw. Aubrey was only sixteen days old when Germany ordered a submarine blockade of the British Isles, which made Alida feel frighteningly cut off from London, the place she still considered home.

Shortly before Aubrey's birth his father became seriously ill. Cape Town doctors were not in agreement, so some of Alida's friends thought she should take her husband to London as quickly as possible.

As her husband's condition continued to deteriorate friends interceded for her with a member of the South African Parliament, Morris Alexander, who finally arranged passage for the mother, father and two children.

Aubrey was then six months old; Ruth twenty months. They went on a troopship taking about five hundred South African soldiers to England to help protect the British Isles against an expected German invasion.

The voyage took two days short of a month. While they were at sea Italy declared war on Germany. Severe fighting was going on in the part of Lithuania from which both Mr. and Mrs. Solomon had come.

From Cape Town Alida had written to her father telling him how worried she was about Aubrey; how frail he was; how delicate. When they stepped from the Portsmouth-London train Eliahu Sacks, without even bothering to embrace his daughter, took Aubrey from her arms, looked into the baby's face and exclaimed: "Why did you write me such nonsense? Mein Kind is a prince!"

It was the name by which he would henceforth always call him.

The illness that had mystified Cape Town doctors was diagnosed in London as terminal cancer of the liver and pancreas. When the patient was told, he looked up from a newspaper full of war news and said:

"There are soldiers dying every day, every minute. What right do I have to grumble?"

One week before Aubrey's first birthday Solomon asked those attending him:

"What is the date today?"

They told him January 25.

"This is the day on which I will be dying," he said. Then his face brightened and he asked, very seriously:

"I wonder if I have time to read the morning paper? Yes, please someone go out and get the morning paper for me. Quickly!"

After finishing a perusal of the news Solomon lay back on his pillow and fell into a deep sleep from which he never awoke.

Early in 1917 the Zionist offices at 175 Piccadilly needed someone to take charge of their archives who was proficient in English, Russian, German and French, and Alida Sacks Solomon was recommended. She began work soon after Aubrey's second birthday. Her immediate superior was Nahum Sokolow, the well-known Zionist leader, upon whom she looked with awe. He was in his fifties then, a sharp-minded man with a small mustache and a closely trimmed goatee already beginning to turn gray.

The young widow was suddenly in daily contact with distinguished members of London's Jewish hierarchy, for this was the year of the Balfour Declaration and in the months immediately preceding its promulgation there was intensive activity behind the scenes. Balfour himself went to the United States and met with President Wilson, who gave his support. Sokolow conferred frequently with Balfour and Herbert Louis Samuel, the British statesman and philosopher who had been the first professing Jew to become a member of a British Cabinet and whose memorandum to the Cabinet in 1914 had paved the way for the eventual Declaration. But the man she came to know best, because he was the central figure in the entire cataclysmic drama, was Chaim Weizmann, whose little mustache and pointed beard made him look like Sokolow, except that Weizmann was taller and already almost bald, although he was only forty-three. She naturally had no idea that this man, who was at the same time a celebrated chemist and an ardent Zionist leader, would have more to do with influencing the career of her first-born son than she herself would have.

The atmosphere of the Zionist headquarters was contagious and when Alida returned home each night she tried unsuccessfully to enthuse her father. It was no longer necessary for him to repeat his favorite figure of speech. If he just looked down at the palm of his hand the whole family knew what he meant.

Then came the memorable day of November 2, 1917, when a one-page letter headed "Foreign Office" and signed simply "Arthur James Balfour" was sent to Lord Rothschild for transmission to the Zionist Federation. That evening Sokolow telephoned the Sacks home and asked Alida to come down quickly to headquarters to help with the translation of the Balfour letter into Russian, French and German.

"Aubrey was lying in his crib fretting," she later said, "and I hated to leave him. But I had to make a choice: to stay home with my baby or play a small part in the events of this important moment. It didn't take me long to decide. After all, my mother could care for the baby, maybe even better than I could, and so I went down to Piccadilly and when I saw how short the Declaration was—can you believe it, it was only sixty-eight words!—I knew I would not be unfaithful to my child for very long."

To celebrate the accomplishment that the Declaration represented, a mass meeting was held at the Stoll Theatre in Kingsway and Alida persuaded her father to go with her. The building was packed. Most of the important British Zionist leaders were on the platform. The speeches were a mixture of wild emotionalism and precise logic. Rarely were public utterances so frequently interrupted by applause. Alida remembered how Chaim Weizmann stood at the front of the platform with both hands high above his head in a gesture of triumph. She also never forgot how her father sat upright, almost rigid, through much of the evening and then, overcome by the spirit of the occasion, finally put his head in his hands and began to weep.

The younger Sacks son, Sam, had become a doctor. He was a bachelor and used one part of the Sacks home as an office and another part as a dispensary. At this time in England most doctors, instead of sending their patients to a pharmacy with a prescription for the medicine they needed, set up their own drug departments. Because many London doctors had gone into the armed forces, Dr. Sam Sacks in a short time built up such a large practice that he needed someone to run his dispensary and Alida was drafted. Now she had three jobs: mother to two small children, work at Zionist headquarters and what she called "dispensing." All three were in conflict. If she was at the office in Piccadilly, she would often get an emergency call from her brother: "You must come! There are a hundred patients—more or less—and I can't possibly see them all and handle the dispensing, too." When she would argue that the Zionists needed her, he would shout into the phone, "Tell them they'll get Palestine just as quickly without you!" In the dispensary she was more valuable than anyone else would have been because she had learned so much from her brother about diagnosing physical ailments that she often gave medicine to patients without the doctor ever seeing them. Dr. Sacks had a simple system which his sister memorized: "The white medicine for the stomach, the red medicine for a cough, the black pills for the bowels and the blue liquid to gargle." As long as she kept her colors straight she had no problem.[5]

Often when there was a long queue of patients waiting for her to fill their prescriptions she would get a telephone call from Piccadilly asking where on earth she had filed a certain paper that Mr. Sokolow or Dr. Weizmann urgently needed.

After spending much of her time rushing back and forth between her home and Piccadilly, a not inconsiderable distance, she finally persuaded Simon Marks and Sokolow to let her advertise for a replacement.

It was zeppelin raids on London and the telephone calls that came at all hours of the night from Dr. Sacks's patients and the impossibility of giving any attention to the children that resulted in the decision to send Ruth, Aubrey and their grandmother to live with relatives in Ireland for the duration of the war.

One day Aubrey, then less than four years old, came running into the house and announced to his sister:

"Ruthie! Ruthie! The war's over! Now we can go home to London."

His sister responded by saying:

"What was the war, Aubrey?"

Several months later the grandmother took the two children back to London and the grandfather decided it was time for Aubrey, having passed his fourth birthday, to start learning Hebrew. But the Sacks home was hardly a place for concentration. A worldwide epidemic of influenza had broken out, London was badly hit and Dr. Sacks was working night and day. Often twenty-four hours would go by without a chance to take off his clothes. His sister was just as busy, for every patient required some form of medication. And now she had two children under her feet again. Aubrey gave her little trouble, but Ruth was boisterous and would run through the house, from living quarters to the doctor's office to the dispensary, filling the air with Irish songs at a wild Irish pitch. In this atmosphere the grandfather had some difficulty trying to explain the intricacies of Hebrew to Aubrey, attentive though the boy was, so late one night, after the last patient had left, he said to his daughter:

"Don't you think you had better send one of the children back to Ireland?"

"Which?"

Without an instant's hesitation he said:

"It will have to be Ruth, for I have already started the instruction of Mein Kind."

At this time the education of Aubrey Solomon began in earnest. In a shop on Whitechapel Road the grandfather bought large sheets of brown wrapping paper and with a pair of manicuring scissors cut out immense Hebrew letters. This was the way Aubrey memorized the alphabet.

Because of the war domestic help was difficult to come by, but finally, somehow, they found Sarah. She was almost seventy, was inconceivably ugly and had only one tooth and few qualifications for the job, but Aubrey loved her because she recited nursery rhymes to him by the hour.

One day when the grandfather was out Aubrey ran through the house with a piece of brown paper clutched in each hand until he found Sarah.

"Which is the *gimel* and which is the *nun?*"

To Sarah the two pieces of paper seemed identical. They both looked like a letter *C* backward.

"I don't know," she finally confessed.

Hours later Alida Solomon found her son sitting disconsolately looking out the window.

"What's the matter, darling?" she asked as she took him in her arms.

"Sarah doesn't know something."

"Doesn't know what?"

"She doesn't know the difference between a gimel and a nun."

The mother tried to explain that Sarah was not Jewish; that Sarah's alphabet was different; that Sarah was not stupid. But Aubrey refused to be consoled. He was four years old and his first idol had crashed. Sarah didn't know something.

As soon as the war was over Alida's friends in South Africa began writing to her about the possessions she had left behind when she so hurriedly sailed off to England. Also, there were several minor legal matters to be settled so, please, would she come as soon as possible. First she had to go to Ireland to be sure her daughter would be all right during her absence.

It was January of 1920. Ruth, who had just celebrated her sixth birthday, greeted her mother by telling her, excitedly, about "my friend." The two sons of the family with whom she was staying—the Elliotts—were studying to be doctors and they were often helped with their medical assignments by a young man who came almost every evening to the Elliott house. Often, after he and Ruth had had a long chat, he would give her a ha'penny to buy "something wonderful." Before starting to study medicine he had been a lecturer in physics at St. Andrews in Scotland and he had told Ruth many stories of that famous university.

"His name is Dr. Isaac Eban," Ruth explained, "but everyone calls him Ickie. You *will* let me take you over to meet him, won't you?"

The meeting took place the next day, but Alida's thoughts were on her trip. In February of 1920 she sailed for Cape Town.

"I didn't have the courage to tell my son I was going far away and possibly for a long time, so I just said, 'Darling, I am going off for a few days to see a friend.' I know it was a terrible thing to do. He made me feel, even before I was out the door, that everything was going out of his life."

Aubrey was more pensive than usual after his mother left, but he enjoyed the hours he spent each day studying under his grandfather's direction, and his grandmother took good care of him until she became seriously ill. Then Aubrey was sent to Kent Coast College, a Jewish boys' school at Herne Bay run by a man named Hockbaum. Grandfather Sacks chose it because the students were required to study Hebrew.

This was not a period Aubrey remembered with pleasure. Those in school with him observed that he rarely took part in the games the other boys played and seldom smiled. To escape from the loneliness, he read incessantly. Circumstances had begun to shape his character.[6]

Alida Solomon was gone exactly a year. The first thing she did when she returned was to take a train to Herne Bay, arriving late in the evening. A fierce winter wind was blowing and the temperature inside the school buildings seemed not much different than outside. Someone who went to Aubrey's room to look for him reported he was nowhere to be found. Finally the distraught mother discovered him in one of the public rooms sitting on top of a radiator to keep warm, while he read aloud to a circle of boys on the floor at his feet, huddled as close to the heat as they could get.

Alida had come back from this second sojourn in South Africa with a strange little accent she would retain the rest of her life. It was not the normal South African pronunciation; it was just her own unique way of speaking English. Sometimes her voice actually seemed to ripple. When she wasn't laughing she was at least smiling and she seemed to be constantly enveloped in a glow. Her friends found her liveliness contagious.

Upon her return Alida was astonished to find that "Ruth's friend," as Dr. Isaac Eban was called, was now a professional associate of her brother and had been completely accepted by her father as a member of the Sacks household. The explanation was that soon after her departure from London a scarlet fever epidemic broke out and Dr. Sacks sent a telegram to Belfast asking if either of his cousins could come to assist him with his severe case load. The Elliott boys were otherwise committed but Dr. Eban was available and willing. When he arrived a few days later Dr. Sacks offered him living quarters in addition to a well-paying position. The whole family liked him. The nickname he soon acquired was "The Goy," the Hebrew word for a non-Jew, because he spoke Scottish, a "foreign language."

Shortly after Alida's return she began to agree with her daughter's estimate of the bachelor from Belfast, who was just one year her senior. Four months later they were married.

The three-story house at 12 Kennington Park Road into which the Eban family moved was in the Elephant and Castle area, which takes its name from a public house or pub which Shakespeare mentioned in one of his plays. Kennington Park Road is one of the principal thoroughfares of South London, cutting through a section in which few if any Jews lived. It was a strange, mixed neighborhood of Georgian and Regency houses, some in various degrees of decay. Poverty and shabby gentility lived side by side. A few houses of architectural merit were still occupied in Aubrey's boyhood by doctors like his stepfather, or by successful merchants, or by theatrical people. Others had been turned into cheap rooming houses or boardinghouses. It was an area thick with pubs, such as the Tankard, the Three Stags, the White Horse and the Horns. It was also dotted with London music halls. At 287 Kennington Park Road there was a derelict house in which Charlie Chaplin had once lived, close by a pickle factory and a slaughterhouse. Along Kennington Park Road Chaplin spent his boyhood, just as Aubrey would be doing. It was on Kennington Park Road that Chaplin used to watch a cabby with feet that hurt him so badly that he wore oversized shoes and slithered along in the painful manner that the boy learned to imitate so ludicrously. Not far from the Eban home were music halls in which Chaplin's father and mother at one time sang together and which gave their son his chance to become famous.[7]

Kennington Park Road in the early 1920s was a vital, pulsating place. Most of the now drab houses were attached to each other by a common wall and had a few square feet of green in front—a bush or a few flowers, usually covered with soft coal soot. When Alida gave a friend the new address the friend said:

"What a strange place for a Jewish family to live! Don't you realize, my dear, that you will be isolated, Jewishly?"

Alida explained that her husband had been assigned to the Elephant and Castle area as a panel doctor under the Health Services, which had a rule that a general practitioner had to live within two miles of his patients so as to be available day and night. Being obliged to live among the poor, most doctors had their homes and their offices in the same building.

The Eban house stood back a little from the street. To get to the garden in the rear one had to go through the house. The garden was long and narrow and for many years was in the care of a most unusual gardener. His name was Brewer and he was on the gardening staff at Buckingham Palace, but he augmented his government wages by working off-hours for people other than the Royal Family. He would appear for work dressed like a clerk in a countinghouse, with an attaché case in hand and a bowler hat on his head. He always took off his jacket, folded it and placed it gently on a chair. Then he would go to work in his spotless white shirt and black braces. He and Mrs. Eban specialized in dahlias that grew to an immense size and were the pride of the family.[8]

On the ground floor at 12 Kennington Park Road Dr. Eban had his waiting room, surgery and dispensary. On the next floor there was a happy family living room as well as a small kitchen, and on the top floors the bedrooms. Aubrey's room faced onto Kennington Park Road and as a small boy he spent much time standing in the window watching the buses, trams and cars speeding by. But his real love was reading, at first simple English stories. One day he went to his mother and said: "Mummy, you must listen to this!"

The story was about a red hen that hatched ten eggs, nine of which produced chickens and the tenth a duckling. The nine made life so unhappy for the duckling that as soon as it learned to flutter its wings a little it took off and never returned. When he reached the end of the story Aubrey was in tears. His mother took him in her arms but he was not easily consoled. The story seemed to have bitter significance for him.

With an uncle and a stepfather both doctors, Aubrey became accustomed to a great deal of medical reviewing. One day he asked his mother what had happened to his own father and when he was told that Mr. Solomon had died shortly after arriving in England from South Africa Aubrey was silent for a moment, then wryly commented: "He must have had a very high temperature."[9]

Several Englishmen who have known Aubrey from childhood are convinced that his love of cricket had something to do with forming his character and shaping his mind. London has two world-famous cricket grounds. Lord's is across the river and miles to the northwest, but equally celebrated is The Oval, less than a mile down Kennington Park Road from the Eban house. Although cricket is a man's game, Ruth and Aubrey developed an equal fondness for it and spent many afternoons at The Oval together.

Although Ruth was the elder of the two, Aubrey was more proficient in reading. He liked to read aloud and especially enjoyed it if he had an audience. Knowing this, whenever Ruth saw him with a book in his hands she would run after him and say: "Read it to me, please!" And he never refused.

In the summer of 1922 Alida gained one child permanently and lost another temporarily. A daughter, Carmel, was born in July and about the same time Grandfather Sacks decided it was time Aubrey went to a good grammar school. He picked St. Olave's and St. Savior's Grammar School for Boys, commonly known simply as St. Olave's. It was a school with an impressive history, founded in 1571 during the thirteenth year of

the reign of Elizabeth I. The school occupied a set of neo-Tudor buildings with twin towers in Bermondsey close by the docks and not far
from Tower Bridge, in a neighborhood of warehouses, granaries and factories—a dreary part of London. Yet St. Olave's had a reputation of being one of the strictest and best grammar schools in the city.

In Yanishki the Sacks family had lived an autonomous, self-contained
Jewish life, isolated from the mainstream of Russian thought and culture.
In London Aubrey now began to live in two worlds. Through his schoolboy associations he became part of the general environment, yet with
his family he continued to live in an atmosphere of Jewish ideas, values
and aspirations.

2

Mind in the Making

FOR FIVE DAYS each week in St. Olave's School Aubrey Solomon studied the subjects that all English schoolboys were expected to pursue: Latin, English grammar, British history, the geography of the Empire, simple arithmetic and science. But on Friday afternoon, when religious Jews were preparing to start their celebration of the Sabbath, Aubrey would take a bus to the home of his grandfather, who now lived on Lodgges Road in Hackney, on the opposite side of London from the Elephant and Castle. There for the next forty-eight hours Aubrey lived in a different world and underwent quite a different course of instruction.

Eliahu Sacks, by now approaching his sixtieth year, had acquired an almost fanatical ambition: to create an exceptional Hebrew scholar. He was certain that in Aubrey he had the proper raw material, for the boy was respectful, attentive, alert of mind, retained everything he was taught and actually seemed to enjoy learning something new, whether it was a Hebrew word he had never heard before or some strange verbal construction. For a child not yet eight he was amazingly philosophical and already had not only respect for the written word but an almost physical love of books.

In these days Eliahu Sacks was a tall, distinguished-looking man who carried himself with dignity, his shoulders erect, his step firm. He and George V, who had been on the British throne for about thirteen years, were within a few months of being the same age and bore a resemblance to each other. At least Aubrey thought so, for in later years he often likened his grandfather to the Hanoverian monarch. The Sacks beard and mustache, now streaked with gray, were trimmed much in the George V manner. His hair was so closely cropped that he appeared in photographs to be almost bald. His eyes were dark brown, the eyes of a gentle man. Although he was quiet of manner and scholarly in mien, he could become quite intense over anything he considered vital. On the street he was frequently mistaken by strangers for a judge because of his frock coat, top hat and large gold watch chain across his waistcoat. But most of his own people recognized him for what he was: a learned Jew of the old school, who had a love of Jewish culture for its own sake. He was not fanatically religious, his interest in Hebrew matters being rooted in neither religious nor political Zionism.

Eliahu Sacks was constitutionally unable to utter an untruth, no matter what the provocation, and if anyone told him a lie he was more hurt than angry. He had the capacity for patience that a good pedagogue needs and a love of knowledge that was contagious, at least for Aubrey. Also, he seemed never to forget anything.

This was the man who was going to have more to do with shaping the mind and affecting the destiny of his grandson than anyone else, alive or dead. During the next few years the forty-eight hours a week that Aubrey spent with him turned out to be more important than all the other influences combined.

They worked in the grandfather's own room, which was a combination study, library and bedroom. Against one wall stood an immense bed with a brass headboard. Because he liked to do his reading horizontally, the grandfather often remained in his pajamas and robe all day, getting out of bed only for meals. The other walls were lined with bookshelves. The room had two large closets in which he kept his bundles of old Hebrew and Yiddish newspapers. When the family moved from the Stoke Newington house he brought with him his entire newspaper file. He was occasionally chided about the futility of saving newspapers, until one day a family friend came to call and was introduced to the grandfather as Robin Lynn.

"Are you a Jew?" Mr. Sacks asked. "That's not a Jewish name."

The visitor explained he was a Jew; his name originally had been Naftalin until he changed it.

"Yes," said Mr. Sacks. "I know that name very well. Your family came from Lithuania, didn't they?"

When Mr. Lynn appeared at the house some days later the grandfather came from his study with a Yiddish newspaper in his hand. It was dated 1878 and contained a picture of a man named Naftalin, who at the time was city treasurer of Telz, Lithuania, and who turned out to have been the great-great-uncle of Mr. Lynn. The story was often quoted in the Eban family as an example of what a memory the grandfather had and also of how well organized both his mind and his newspaper files were.

Mr. Sacks had one absolute rule: no one was permitted to smoke in his room. His one eccentricity was that whenever he was invited any- where for a meal he took with him in one pocket of his coat a package of smoked salmon and roast duck. If the food that was served failed to please him, he would send his wife or one of his children to the hallway to "bring me something from my coat pocket."

Bassa was tolerant of her husband's lack of practicality, of his business ventures, which often turned out something less than successful, and of the way he indulged his grandson. He was cautious about spending money for anything else, but when it came to books he was almost reckless. He had an enormous library, covering a wide variety of subjects, and wanted Aubrey to have his own library, too.

Mr. Sacks rarely came home from a book-shopping expedition with just a single volume; often he would be weighted down with his purchases. Once in his own room he would push the newspapers on the table aside and arrange the newly acquired books in two piles: one for himself, the other for Aubrey. There was a rule that anyone was free to read his books, to study them, to refer to them, but no one could take a book out of his room. The single exception was his grand- son.

For six years Aubrey spent weekends with his grandfather. While other boys were playing he was memorizing, studying, learning. While other boys' minds were on frivolities his was on the conjugation of irregular verbs, the Talmudic arguments of medieval rabbis, the beauty of ancient Hebrew literature. It was no wonder he became even more shy and sensitive and that introversion developed. During these two days a week with his grandfather he was in a world apart, totally cut off from London and the twentieth century, immersed in timeless, placeless scholasticism. The grandfather devoted himself wholeheartedly to his self-assumed task, with no thought of how his grandson might ever make use of all the knowledge he was acquiring. That was the whole point of the culture he represented: it was there for its own sake. Yet he would not have been human had he not been pleased at the love he saw his grandson acquiring for both the Hebrew language and ancient Hebrew culture.

The entire family often went on holidays together and at such times Aubrey seemed less introspective. Sometimes it was to France or Belgium, or to distant parts of England. Aubrey's favorite spot was

Droitwich in the Shakespeare country only a few miles west of Strat-
ford on Avon, celebrated for its saline-saturated water. In the public
gardens there was a band concert every night. Aubrey would work his
way to a vantage point as close to the bandstand as possible and
stand for an hour or more intently watching the conductor. Mother
Eban was pleased because she thought it indicated a budding interest
in music and she had always had musical ambitions for her son. What
Mother Eban did not know was what Aubrey whispered to Ruth their
first night in Droitwich:

"That's just what I want to be when I grow up—a band conductor!"

In later years Ruth speculated that what apparently appealed to him
about the role of band conductor was that he was directing people.[1]

One evening at the family dinner table Mother Eban brought up the
matter of names. Carmel, of course, would be Carmel Eban, whereas
Aubrey and Ruth still bore the name of Solomon. Neither of them
remembered anything about their own father and both had developed
great affection for their mother's second husband, whom they called
"Daddy."

"I think it would be good if all my children had the same name,"
the mother suggested.

The matter was put to a family vote and there being no dissent
Aubrey and Ruth Solomon became Aubrey and Ruth Eban.

When Aubrey was nine his aunt, Lina Halper, returned disconsolate
from Philadelphia. Her husband, after winning acclaim as a Hebrew and
Arabic scholar, had suddenly died of pneumonia at the age of forty.
The widow and her two small sons moved in with Mr. and Mrs. Sacks.
Neville, the younger, was only a few months older than Aubrey yet
they had little in common, for Neville was tempestuous compared with
his quiet, gentle cousin. Neville and Ruth, however, got along well
together. Often Ruth would accompany Aubrey when he went to the
Sacks home on Friday afternoon and she and Neville would devise
innumerable ways to get Aubrey out of his grandfather's study.

"He used to read and study, read and study until the tears fell into
his voice," Ruth has said. "It went on hour after hour. I couldn't bear
it. I used to thump on the study door. Neville and I would make as
much noise as we could, playing ball. We would hit the ball on the door
and kick up a fearful racket to distract Grandpa and make him realize
Aubrey had had enough and that we wanted him to come out and
play."[2]

Neville's best recollection of his cousin was of how one day he told

Aubrey he had a ten-page essay to write for school and would Aubrey give him a little help. Aubrey made no reply but the next morning presented Neville with an essay exactly ten pages long, written in his usual neat calligraphy. Neville painstakingly copied it and turned it in. When it came back it bore a failing grade and this notation in the teacher's handwriting:

"Excellent, but the author forgot to sign his name."[3]

Although Ruth was so much unlike her brother, she appreciated the qualities that made him different. She never remembered his growing angry, regardless of the provocation. He never hit out at anyone or anything, even in self-defense. He never lost his temper or committed a violent act. He was intellectually but not physically aggressive.[4]

In 1924 Mrs. Eban gave birth to a fourth child, Raphael.

Late in 1927, as Aubrey approached thirteen, his grandfather announced it was time he started preparing for his barmitzvah. Mr. Sacks was a member of the South Hackney Synagogue, whose rabbi, Dr. Louis Rabinowitz,[5] wanted to instruct the boy, but the grandfather insisted that he himself would take on the responsibility.

For his barmitzvah Aubrey wrote a discourse in a seven- by nine-inch hardcover notebook he bought in Snell's Stationery Store on Mare Street. In mature calligraphy, with no misspellings or grammatical errors and very few corrections, he wrote:

"For the last couple of months prior to my barmitzvah my dear grandfather took up with me a religious course of study . . . and I may say it highly interested me. . . . [His grandfather in red ink on a blank facing page suggested the phrase be worded "it interested me exceedingly."] I felt greatly desirous to be more fully enlightened on the subject of the reception of the Torah by Moses from God. Under the able guidance of my dear learned grandfather and taking advantage of his valuable library, I have been assisted to it."

He then told of all the books he and his grandfather had "eagerly and wholeheartedly" read and the encyclopedias they had consulted.

"It was my intention at first to deliver my speech in Hebrew, but I have considered the possible difficulties of the Sephardic and the Ashkenazi pronunciations which may arouse complications to our respectable friends who have honored us today by taking part in my barmitzvah celebration. On reflection, however, it occurred to me that there might be many of our guests who might prefer to hear it in English, so I have decided . . . to make up a collection of extracts of the Prologues of the Talmud for delivery in Hebrew and then go more fully into translation."

The address itself was a brief history of the Torah and the Talmud; who wrote them, how, why and when. It ran to eighteen handwritten pages. On one of the blank pages at the back of the notebook Aubrey drew two caricatures of a woman with exaggeratedly large eyes, a tailored suit and no ears, which he labeled "Miss Maenain"—perhaps a schoolteacher. On the last page he wrote his own name as "Aubrey Solomon Eban" and under it "Carmel Eban." His baby sister was then hardly six but in his shy way he had already developed affection for her and she looked up to him as if he were an ancient Hebrew prophet.[6]

On the day of the barmitzvah early in 1928 Carmel and Raphael both had measles and needed their mother's attention. (One of the reasons Aubrey was often neglected as a child was because Carmel had serious mastoid trouble until she underwent an operation at the age of six and Raphael was frail and underweight, so between them they kept the mother busy.) Although Mrs. Eban was unable to hear her elder son deliver the first formal address of his life and see him go through the ceremony that officially admitted him to manhood, she did manage to prepare refreshments for the small party of friends who came to the house afterward.[7]

Soon after his barmitzvah Aubrey was taken to a meeting at which a distinguished Zionist delivered a long address. By custom after such a talk some member of the audience was designated to stand up and make a short speech of thanks and appreciation. This evening, when the chairman called on "Mr. Eban" everyone in the audience turned to see who this man was. To their surprise they saw a small boy stand up and then heard him deliver a congratulatory speech in faultless Hebrew. Because it was an impromptu talk, no record was kept of it, but it was a milestone in the boy's life, for whereas his barmitzvah speech had been the first prepared talk of his career, this was his first attempt at an unwritten, unrehearsed expression of opinion. Those in the audience who understood Hebrew were greatly impressed.

Aubrey had few illnesses in his youth, but he had an accident that the family long remembered. He was coming home from school one day engrossed in reading a book. Neither he nor anyone else remembered what the book was, but he was holding it at arm's length, his eyes fixed on the print and his mind so occupied with the story that he walked head on into a lamppost with such force that he knocked out his four front teeth and sustained a great many cuts and bruises about the face. He was in great pain by the time he reached home, his face so swollen that he could hardly see to climb the stairs, yet he seemed more chagrined by what had happened than physically pained.

"You were lucky, darling, that you didn't walk into an automobile or a railroad train," his mother told him.

It was weeks before his face and mouth looked normal again.[8]

Aubrey was about fifteen when he came home from St. Olave's one day in a fit of despondency. He paced the house, his head hung low, a puzzled frown on his face. His mother decided to follow her practice of not asking questions, but after dinner, when he still volunteered nothing, she said:

"Is everything all right at school, darling?"

Then he blurted it out. The headmaster had made a remark that troubled him. In front of the whole class he said that Aubrey had an obligation to excel, because "you are a Jew and Jews have a special mission—a special place; they must be better than the rest."

Aubrey said this suggested inequality. He saw no reason why he and other Jews had to be judged by different standards. Why should they be expected to be better? What the headmaster was implying was that whatever a single Jew does, individually, engages all Jews, commits all Jews, reflects on all Jews. If Wilson Smith, a non-Jew, does something, the public reaction is to Wilson Smith. If Aubrey Eban or some other Jew does something good it reflects credit on all Jews; if he does something reprehensible it reflects discredit on all Jews. It was this collectivization of responsibility that bothered him.

The Sacks-Eban family formed a perfect Greek chorus for Aubrey. With each member he had an entirely different relationship. Eliahu Sacks, as he had said in his barmitzvah speech, was his "dear learned grandfather" whom he deeply revered. The stepfather, Dr. Eban, respected and loved by Aubrey, was seldom critical. His mother could make Aubrey laugh with her flashes of wit and it was to her he always went in times of trouble. From Ruth he was beginning to grow apart, as their interests branched off, but until now she had been his closest companion and greatest admirer. As Carmel grew older she was taking Ruth's place. She and Aubrey had much in common, intellectually if not temperamentally. Aunt Lina was volatile and unpredictable, much more Russian than British or American, often guilty of hyperbole but as convinced as her father that there was something special about Aubrey. There was no question about which of these diverse characters dominated the scene. When there was conflict Alida Sacks Eban made the decision that was ultimately followed. She was still young—under forty. Although the mother of four she once said:

"I wasn't aware of them all the time. Only when they were ill or upset or unhappy or cross or angry. If they were sick I was all a mother should have been, but at other times it seemed to me that it didn't matter. I didn't bring them up. I let them grow up. I had just one rule. If they did something wrong they must own up to it, no matter what it was. I would say to them, 'If you want me to be on your side, you must tell the truth. If you've spilt the ink, or lost your money, it doesn't matter. Tell it! Then you can look people in the face.'"[9]

In 1930 Eliahu Sacks was only seventy-three, but he seemed to sense that his time was nearly up. What disturbed him most about the prospect of dying was who would carry on the instruction of his grandson, so he began looking for a qualified substitute, but before he was able to engage a teacher he became seriously ill. It began with a cold he caught going to the funeral of a friend. Complications developed and in a short time he was very weak. One Saturday afternoon when his daughter came to see him he said:

"Let me have the Kind. Send him to me tonight."

Aubrey, by then fifteen, went by bus, spent a long evening with his grandfather, slept the night in the Sacks home and returned to Kennington Park Road the next day. Most of the following week the grandfather was desperately ill. On Friday, with little strength left, he again asked that Aubrey be sent to him, "Quickly!" Aubrey was taken by taxi from his school to the Sacks home just in time for his grandfather to put his hand feebly on the boy's head before he died.

After the funeral Alida Eban faced the problem of what to do about Aubrey's Hebrew education.

"Papa will turn over in his grave," she told the family, "unless I do something quickly."

She remembered that of all the men he had interviewed her father had preferred Isaac Wartski, a lecturer at the School for Oriental Studies, who agreed to teach the boy for several hours every Sunday at ten shillings a lesson.

The death of Eliahu Sacks ended one chapter of Aubrey's life and began another. He never forgot all that his grandfather had taught him and he never contested the theory that it was his grandfather more than anyone else who had molded his thinking and ultimately shaped his career. But now his weekends were free and he began to lead a more normal young man's life.

3

Dominated by the Dilemma

THERE WAS NOTHING particularly privileged or advantaged in the upbringing of Aubrey Eban, so that whatever he would achieve in competition with his contemporaries would be the result of his intellectual
capacity, his character and his persistence. In later life some of his
Israeli political critics, ignorant of his background, would argue that he
was born with a silver spoon in his mouth and therefore acquired
talents and capacities beyond the reach of others. Such was far from
the truth. His family had no particular lineage, no prominent social
position and little money. The weapon he took into the battle of life
was a sharp intellectual capacity, polished and honed by the best that
British humanistic education could provide and by the Hebrew dimension his grandfather added. He also had the good fortune of being a
member of a family in which intellectual achievement was given a
higher value than material wealth or any kind of pretension.

Aubrey's feeling about Jewish destiny was not born out of close
contact with Jewish misery, as with so many of Europe's Zionist
leaders. No near relatives had suffered in pogroms in Russia or anywhere
else. He never came face to face with drastic examples of the Jewish
predicament, as Herzl did in the Dreyfus case. In his personal life there
was no evidence of any volcanic aspect of being Jewish. But in his
inner world—in the world of his aspirations and imagination—he was
dominated by the dilemma of the Jewish people. Abstractly, from his
reading, he discovered the pathos of Jewish suffering, the humiliation
of his own people, their inability to achieve any dignified sense of
identity. Although in the England of his day Jews were living relatively untroubled lives, Aubrey was sharply aware of the fragility of
existence in a world in which Jews had no homeland and therefore no

assurance of collective survival. Early in life he seemed to feel a sense of Jewish mission.

In the Eban home there was much discussion of philosophy, morals, ethics, Hebrew history and the Bible, yet little attention was paid to the dietary laws and other traditional Jewish religious practices. It was what is commonly called by Jews a "non-observant home." Usually on Friday evenings when more conventionally religious Jews were in their synagogues attending prayer services, Aubrey had been with his grandfather studying the Hebrew language and culture. But now after his grandfather's death he often attended the strictly orthodox Brixton Synagogue, which had a membership of some three hundred families, among them the Ebans. There he came under the spell of the synagogue's founder, Rabbi Arnold Mishcon, a distinguished-looking Russian emigrant with a short goatee and clerical collar, who had taught himself Arabic as well as English and Hebrew, and had a reputation as a scholar of the classics.

Aubrey was greatly influenced by Rabbi Mishcon's passionate Zionism, which appealed to the boy's reason as well as to his emotions. He was fascinated not only by the content of the rabbi's sermons but also by the oratorical skill with which he held the attention of his congregants. Instead of confining his preaching to conventional interpretations of Mosaic Law, the rabbi would quote Greek, Latin and English literature and often gave profound philosophical expositions that kept the agile young Eban mind well exercised. Rabbi Mishcon's breadth of vision was contagious and Aubrey, even though young, became infected with it. Contrawise, the rabbi became interested in the intellectual potentialities of this quiet, scholarly youth. He was impressed by Aubrey's cold logic, a quality which the rabbi thought might lead him to a career in higher mathematics.[1]

Often they discussed Zionism and when the rabbi formed a Young Zionist society called Heatid, the Hebrew word for "the future," Aubrey became one of its first members, along with Victor Mishcon, the rabbi's son, who was six months Aubrey's junior. There were twenty or thirty members at the start, almost half girls. They elected Aubrey their first vice-chairman and later chairman. As they got to know Aubrey, these young colleagues found him likable but diffident and shy yet always exuberant when he was asked to "say a few words." In his orderly mind he had every fact about Zionism he had ever heard or read neatly catalogued and organized. For anyone impressed by syllogisms, his addresses were persuasive. If he knew in advance he was going to be asked to speak he would prepare his talk sentence by sentence, thought by thought, paragraph by paragraph, then would memorize it in its entirety so when he was called on he could speak without notes. Thus, whatever his speeches lacked in spontaneity they gained in perfection of language and organization, so if they were taken down in shorthand and reproduced they read as well as they sounded; they were brilliant literary exercises as well as convincing oratory. Everyone who listened to him—even those who disagreed with his position—was aware he was a person of scholastic probity.

Physically he was tall for his age and slim. One of his friends said: "He looked already like a young university don." His voice at that age was not especially compelling and he had a habit of letting it rise and fall in cadences, much like those of an English clergyman. One of his favorite phrases was "And I would ask you to reflect upon it. . . ." with his voice always dropping on the last three words.[2]

About this time Alida Eban heard that David Ben-Gurion, general secretary of Histadrut, the Jewish labor organization in Palestine, was in London for a parliamentary debate on the Middle East and so she went to a Zionist friend, Benzion Kounine, a medical doctor who always took care of Ben-Gurion when he came to London, and suggested he try to arrange for Ben-Gurion to see "my very talented young Zionist son." Several weeks later Ben-Gurion left London and went back to Palestine without having met Aubrey. Hiding her great disappointment Mrs. Eban told a friend:

"Never mind! Someday Ben-Gurion will hear of my son anyway."[3]

It was Aubrey's early Zionist activities that brought about his first contact with girls his own age. Because of his attendance at an all-boys school since the age of seven and a half and because for years he had spent his weekends in cloistered study with his grandfather, he had had little normal social intercourse. But now at Zionist meetings he met teen-age girls who shared his intellectual interests, were as enthusiastic as he was about Zionism and also introduced him to the world of dancing, parties, films, plays, recitals, concerts, picnics and the other divertisements of their age group. His new friends soon discovered that if they made conversational advances Aubrey would respond, often brilliantly. He had a ripe sense of humor, yet his greatest bursts of laughter were over his *own* bon mots. Many of the young women found this rather handsome yet quite modest boy masculinely attractive.

Late in the 1920s the Association of Young Zionist Societies inaugurated an annual summer school, taking over a boarding school in some scenically attractive part of the country for two weeks each year. In that holiday atmosphere young Zionists from London, Liverpool, Leeds and even Ireland and Scotland were put through an intensive course of instruction, with speakers brought in from as far away as the United States and various parts of Europe. In 1931 the summer school was held at Rhuddlan in Wales, the next year at Rossall, a famous school near Blackpool. The summer school organizers persuaded Aubrey not only to attend but to give a series of lectures. For the occasion he outfitted himself with a wardrobe of very modish sports clothes. In the group pictures he stood out because of his sartorial elegance.

Back in London they all plunged into intense Zionist activity. A speakers' school was set up and professional elocution teachers were brought in to instruct the young people in platform techniques. Aubrey by now was adroit enough as a speaker to *give* lessons rather than take them. But he did attend a school at Zionist headquarters in which he was trained in how to handle hecklers.

As soon as the leadership decided the young people were qualified they were given a baptism of fire by being sent into Hyde Park to mount a soapbox and address the men and women who were certain to congregate. In every crowd there were Arabs with questions intended to embarrass. Aubrey became a master at handling such hecklers.

Aubrey had an early introduction to fund raising, for one of the tasks of the Young Zionists was to hold functions, such as dances, to raise money for the work, or to make fund-raising talks to audiences of young and old alike. He early developed an effective fund-raising technique.

Although he had a single-mindedness about Zionism, his friends, especially the girls, tried to persuade him to take an interest in less serious matters. They taught him to play table tennis. They urged him to talk about his favorite sport, cricket. When he invited them to his home, Alida would serve refreshments and Dr. Eban would give them a classical record concert. Occasionally they would discuss Richard Aldington, who was Aubrey's favorite writer of the moment because of Aldington's fascination with the imagery and unrhymed cadence of Greek poetry. He had just published his second satirical novel, *The Colonel's Daughter,* which they had all read and enjoyed.

Aubrey was the leader of a movement among the Young Zionists to conduct at least some of their meetings entirely in Hebrew, but he had great opposition. A compromise was finally reached; all speakers were asked to deliver the first few sentences of every talk in Hebrew.

Chaim Weizmann, Dr. Selig Brodetsky, a member of the World Zionist Executive and of the Jewish Agency Executive, and other Zionist leaders had their eyes open for talented young people to use in their campaign for a Jewish state.[4] Among those recruited at this time, who became Aubrey's close associates in the Young Zionist movement, were Abe Herman, later known as Avraham Harman, who became Eban's successor as Israel's ambassador to the United States; David Tabor, later professor at Cambridge; and Nathan Goldenberg, who became one of the principal Zionist leaders of Great Britain.

In the early 1930s Aubrey worked closely with Goldenberg in creating a new Zionist society called Avodah for those between seventeen and twenty-five, which would lay primary stress on the Hebrew language and on serious service in the cause of Zionism. Aubrey's greatest contribution to the Young Zionist movement was as one of the editors of *The Young Zionist*, official organ of the Association of Young Zionist Societies. As early as 1931, when he was still only sixteen, he was not only writing a monthly article for the magazine and helping to edit it, but was sending innumerable letters in his precise calligraphy to world-famous Zionists asking them for literary contributions. In a letter to Goldenberg dated December 30, 1931 (he was then only sixteen), commenting on the fact that thirteen hundred persons had attended a Zionist ball, Aubrey remarked with almost adult bitterness that "if half the time, publicity, organization, circularization, advertising, etc. that was put into the annual ball were devoted for a couple of months to the business position of the magazine we should never have to lose a penny on the YE again. I intend to bring this matter up at the next Executive meeting, so I will contain my indignation until then."[5]

Carmel was eight years old now, the dreamer of the family. Although they had different fathers, she and Aubrey had many characteristics in common, especially their excessive sensitivity. Aubrey became Carmel's idol. Whatever Aubrey said must be true. Whatever Aubrey thought must be important. Whatever Aubrey did, of course, was perfect. Carmel shared Aubrey's feeling for words. Behind 12 Kennington Park Road there was a garden house in which the older members of the family had their afternoon tea when the weather was pleasant. Carmel called it "my Poetry House" and there she would often go alone to write fragile verse, which she would timidly read to her older brother, always hoping for his approval, which meant more to her than anything else in the world. She had her own room in the Kennington Park Road house, directly under Aubrey's, and one of her earliest memories is of his pacing. Sometimes when she was reading or studying or trying to sleep she would hear the rhythmic sound of his feet, from one end of the room to the other, then a pause, and then back again, then another slight pause, then more steps. It often went on for hours. Carmel was sure he paced this way because it helped him memorize, or maybe because it helped him work out his intellectual problems— the intellectual problems that a girl of eight obviously knew nothing about, but which a man of fifteen or sixteen had to face.[6]

During school holidays Aubrey did odd jobs at the Zionist offices, which had moved from Piccadilly to 77 Great Russell Street, directly across Montague Street from the British Museum in a four-story building with an ornate ironwork balcony that made it look more like a restaurant in the Latin Quarter of New Orleans than the headquarters of Zionist politicians. It was there in the summer of 1929 that Aubrey shared the excitement when an enlarged Jewish Agency was formed, including a whole galaxy of non-Zionist Jews holding high positions in the world at large who now publicly identified themselves with the chief purpose of Zionism—working for a homeland.

Young Eban was fifteen years old when he had a brief musical career quite by accident. His sister Ruth, who had been taking piano lessons, decided she no longer was interested in becoming a pianist. When her mother objected, because the lessons had been paid for in advance, a compromise was reached: Aubrey would take the remaining lessons. Because he rarely questioned a decision made by his mother, he agreed, although his attitude toward a piano was quite unlike his attitude toward books. Yet he persisted long enough to take part in a concert given by a group of pupils in the parlor of the teacher's home. Someone in the audience reported that "he played something quite simple, but it was his courage rather than his musicianship that commanded approval." A short time later Aubrey gave up music as a participant art.[7]

Some of the Eban children's happiest family memories were of Birchington, a seaside town in Kent not far from Canterbury. There in 1930 they rented a house some distance from the village, so there was much walking to get provisions, mail and newspapers. Although Aubrey would always walk to the village or go swimming if Ruth or Carmel asked him to, he seemed to enjoy best remaining alone with his books. "He was always so quiet, so unobtrusive; he almost seemed lonely," Ruth explained.[8]

Alida's mother, Bassa Sacks, died two years after Eliahu. On her deathbed she asked her daughter:

"How is Aubele?" This was the Yiddish diminutive she often used for her grandson.

"He's all right, Mother. Just fine."

"But how is he getting along with the new teacher who took Eliahu's place?"

"Fine! Mr. Wartski likes Aubrey very much."

"Never mind how the teacher likes the boy," snapped back the grandmother. "The question is, how does the boy like the teacher?"[9]

When Aubrey was in the fifth form at St. Olave's Mrs. Eban received an urgent call from Headmaster Abel to come to the school at once. From the tone of his voice it was clear some grave situation had arisen. When she arrived he shut the door so his secretary would not be able to overhear their conversation and began by saying:

"To put it bluntly, your son has been caught in an outright lie!"

Painfully Mr. Abel explained there had been a debate between the sixth form and the fifth form, and Aubrey had spoken brilliantly and had helped win the debate for his side, but when the headmaster later inquired where Aubrey had obtained the material he had read—in what book or other publication he had found it—"the boy had the audacity to tell me he had written it himself.

"Of course," continued Mr. Abel, "this couldn't possibly be the truth, and so I ask you, my dear Mrs. Eban, just how do you think we should discipline your son?"

The mother smiled and replied:

"Mr. Abel, may I suggest that at the earliest possible opportunity you arrange another debate—an impromptu debate. Don't announce the subject until the members of the two teams are assembled. Then just see what happens. I can tell you in advance, for I know my son. He will give just as brilliant an exposition on the subject, whatever it is, as he did on the last occasion."[10]

When Aubrey was fifteen he received the school's annual English prize. When he was sixteen he passed the school examination with such high honors he was excused from taking any future examinations. During his last year at St. Olave's he won a greatly coveted poetry prize for writing Latin hexameters.[11]

In his pre-university days Aubrey had several other teachers besides those at St. Olave's, his grandfather and Mr. Wartski, among them Professor Taubenhaus, who taught him German and who, after a few lessons, commented to Mrs. Eban:

"Frau Eban, a new star is risen in the Jewish firmament."

Then there was Nackdemon Doniach, son of longtime friends of Dr. and Mrs. Eban, who had made a brilliant record at Oxford, graduating at twenty-one with high honors. By now he was twenty-five or twenty-six but still interested only in scholarly matters. One day Mrs. Eban and Mrs. Doniach were talking in the manner of proud Jewish mothers about their sons.

"I have a very bright boy," Mrs. Eban said. "The only trouble is that since Papa died . . ."

"I have a very bright boy, too," Mrs. Doniach interrupted. "Why not have my bright boy teach your bright boy?"

The Doniach son, known by family and friends as Nacki, had recently been married and lived in a very small gardener's house in the area of London called Swiss Cottage, and so one day Aubrey, his mother and Mrs. Doniach paid a call on him, Mrs. Eban explaining that Aubrey had already had years of training under her father and needed "only a few additional touches."

"Just teach him anything and everything he might need to know to take the scholarship examinations a year from now for Cambridge." Then as an afterthought she added: "He already excels in Latin and knows German, some Greek and a little French. And of course Hebrew."

A bargain was finally struck. Aubrey would come to the Doniach cottage once a week for several hours of intensive work. But the teacher soon discovered that there was little the pupil needed to know about biblical or modern Hebrew, so they branched into Arabic, with which Aubrey had no difficulty because of its close relationship with Hebrew. The three qualifications that made him such an excellent language student, in Doniach's opinion, were "instant recall, a photographic memory and rapid perception." The theory on which Doniach operated was that "schools teach less and less about more and more, while I tried to teach young Eban more and more about less and less."

Mrs. Doniach was more puzzled than impressed by her husband's young pupil. To her he seemed pathetically incapable of casual human contacts. Even though he was eighteen and she was only twenty-four, she was unable to communicate with him on any level. He was concerned, she decided, only with The Idea. "He seemed removed from the world of human beings. Each week when he came for his lesson and I would open the door for him he would blush to the roots of his hair,"

In preparation for the Cambridge examinations Doniach would go to the British Museum and look up obscure Greek and Latin quotations and give them to Aubrey to translate and memorize and thus sharpen his classical mind.[12]

During the early 1930s the young Scottish-Jewish doctor, Robin Lynn, was a frequent visitor at the Eban home. At first he came to see only the parents, but later to court Ruth. When Ruth was nineteen he said to her: "I've been waiting seven years, you know." So they were married. That was in 1933. That same year Aubrey had his eighteenth birthday and the question was debated in the family whether he was ready to take the examinations for a university scholarship. Dr. Eban voted "yes." If Aubrey waited "he will just lose a year of his life." Mrs. Eban voted "no." Aubrey settled it by insisting he was eager to go before the scholarship board. When he did appear he was told that the choice was between himself and a nineteen-year-old applicant.

"For the other fellow this is his only chance. If we give the scholarship to you he will never get into Cambridge. But if you were to stand aside this time and come back again next year . . ."

So Aubrey returned to St. Olave's for the busiest year of his life thus far, because in addition to his studies and work with outside language teachers he was now more active than ever in Zionist affairs.

London's young Jews were in a state of ferment. Just a few years earlier Vladimir Jabotinsky had formed Ha-Tzohar (The Revisionists), advocating a Jewish state on both sides of the Jordan River and opposing official Zionist policy as lacking in purpose and firmness. Jabotinsky's youth organization, the Joseph Trumpeldor League, commonly called Betar, had held its first world congress in Danzig and was attracting followers from among the young Jews of London. Zionists and non-Zionists, Revisionists and non-Revisionists met in crowded halls and their conflicts overflowed into the streets. Youth was no disqualification in this war of words. The weapons were fast repartee and a skillful pen. Aubrey used both in arguing for the conventional Zionist concept of a Jewish state. Sometimes he would take Carmel to Zionist meetings. If he did not she would learn the time and place and go alone, just to be able to hear her brother. Coming home from one of these meetings she expostulated to her mother:

"You really *must* hear him! It will make you so proud, Mummy. Please promise that the next time I find out about a meeting you'll go with me."

Mrs. Eban agreed and a week or two later she and Carmel went to a gathering presided over by Sir Leon Simon, who was later knighted for his work as director of telegraphs and telephones in the British Post Office. The hall was filled by the time they arrived. Mrs. Eban stood behind a post to avoid being seen by her son. After the meeting she agreed Aubrey had been forceful in the presentation of his arguments and brilliant in his manner of delivery. She waited up until her son finally came home and then said to him in her uninhibited manner:

"Look, darling, I went to your meeting tonight and I stood behind a post and heard you speak. But there was one thing that bothered me. I saw a boy sitting in the audience who, all the time you were talking, was holding his head in his hands as if he had a headache. Whatever you were saying must have been making him very unhappy."

Without an instant's hesitation Aubrey replied:

"Maybe that boy didn't know what I was talking about, but the others did. That boy's reaction was not important to me. I was addressing the chair, not him."

Telling the story years later Mrs. Eban said:

"How typical of him! He never did have any time for minor matters. It was always the big issue that was important. Even when he was a boy."[13]

One of Aubrey's young Zionist friends who was courting a Christian girl thought she might be impressed if he took her to a Zionist meeting at which Eban was to speak. On the way home he asked her how she had liked the address by his friend. Her reply:

"He talks beautifully. Just like a *Times* editorial."[14]

This same year—1933—Haim Arlosoroff, the brilliant young head of the political department of the Jewish Agency Executive in Jerusalem, then only thirty-four years old, was murdered by unknown assailants on the Tel Aviv seafront, a crime for which several members of the Revisionist movement were arrested. Although all defendants were later acquitted in court, the case increased the conflicts among Zionists everywhere, especially among the young members of the movement in London. Aubrey was deeply affected by the tragedy. He had read Arlosoroff's writings and had come to feel that he almost knew him personally. It was the first time a death had ever affected him this deeply, except, of course, the death of his grandfather. But it had an intensifying influence on his Zionism.[15]

Arlosoroff was succeeded by a man a few years his senior, Moshe Shertok, who later changed his name to Sharett and who in those days almost commuted between London and Tel Aviv. He was a friend of the Eban family and several times came to the house on Kennington Park Road to call. Once he brought with him Berl Katznelson, who was known as the ideologist of the Palestinian labor movement and who just three years earlier had helped found the political party called Mapai, and as editor of the Histadrut daily *Davar* had a reputation as a brilliant journalist. Thus Aubrey for the first time met two men who in a few years would greatly affect his life. Both were fishermen, being always on the lookout for likely young people to draw into their Zionist net. With Katznelson it was an avocation. With Sharett it was something even more. Although Aubrey was just nineteen and had only begun to distinguish himself, he made a deep impression on both men.[16]

While he was still a pupil at St. Olave's Aubrey had his first experience with organizational politics. The mother organization of young people's clubs like Heatid and Halapid was the Association of Young Zionist Societies, which stressed social activities and fund raising. The leader of the opposition was Goldenberg, who argued that time, money and energy should be concentrated instead on educational, cultural and political work. One of his chief supporters was David ("Dod") Tabor, then a brilliant young student at London University.[17] He also enlisted the help of Eban, Abe Herman and others.

In the early days of the organizational struggle, Aubrey, during a talk in which he was trying to be very gentle in his criticism of Young Zionist officers, told a meeting:

"As the cock said to the hen, when showing her an ostrich egg, 'This is not by way of comparison, my dear, but merely by way of illustrating what goes on elsewhere!'"

The young rebels, who called themselves the New Look Group, eventually were successful in packing the executive of the AYZS and after obtaining control reversed the association's policies. While Aubrey was an eager conspirator, he told his confederates he had little interest in holding office so he was named editor of *The Young Zionist*, the organization's monthly. Then the AYZS was amalgamated with the University Zionist Federation and the new organization became the Federation of Zionist Youth, with Goldenberg as its first president. In a short time it had nearly three thousand members.[18]

Already, even at this young age, Aubrey had an impeccable command of the English language, could address a gathering equally well in English or Hebrew, always seemed to use exactly the correct words to express his meaning, approached every subject analytically and structured his remarks, however informal, as an architect might structure a baroque building.

He and Dod Tabor often held vigorous discussion over whether Zionism's function was to create cultural islands in the diaspora, such as a university and other places where Jews could speak Hebrew, or whether all energies should be concentrated on working for the creation of a Jewish state. They agreed that events of the 1930s would probably have a greater effect in deciding the question than anyone's intellectual convictions.[19]

The Cambridge examinations were no problem for young Eban, but he was so eager to know the precise results that each morning he got up at 5 A.M. and walked from his parents' seaside cottage to the village of Birchington to buy the *Times* and hurriedly scan it from front to back looking for an announcement of the results. Carmel well remembered the day he finally learned he had been awarded the scholarship. He said nothing as he came through the front door, but his young sister knew by the expression on his face he had found in the paper he carried under his arm the news that in October he would become a Cambridge undergraduate. He had been awarded the Kennett Scholarship in Hebrew and the classics at Queens' College.

A few days later a letter arrived from Herbert Martin James Loewe, celebrated orientalist scholar and reader in rabbinics at Queens', who suggested that if Aubrey would forget Hebrew and concentrate on classical languages for a year or two, the other beginning Cambridge students might—just *might*—catch up with him in the oriental languages.

One of the first people Alida Eban told was her friend Mrs. Doniach and then she went to see Mrs. Doniach's brilliant son and said to him:

"What can we give you as a reward for what you have done for our boy?"

Modestly the young teacher replied:

"I did nothing. He did it himself. But if you think that I am deserving of some reward, then let me continue to teach him once a week until he actually has to leave for Cambridge."

The mother readily agreed. In these months teacher and pupil concentrated on Arabic, especially the Syrian dialect.

The last time Mrs. Eban and Mrs. Doniach ever talked together about their sons Mrs. Doniach said:

"Alida, I do not want to embarrass you, but would you like to know what my son told me about your son? He said that of the many, many pupils he has taught, Aubrey was the most brilliant one of all. Would you believe it?"

Mrs. Eban said she would.[20]

The fall of 1934 saw the breakup, at least temporarily, of the closely knit group of young people with whom Aubrey had been having such a pleasureful association during the past several years. Abe Herman went off to Oxford, Aubrey and David Tabor to Cambridge.

4

Sharpening of the Wit

CAMBRIDGE IS one hour and eighteen minutes north of London by express train. Its twenty-four colleges in the 1930s were providing elite education for fewer than five thousand carefully selected male students. In addition there were about five hundred females in the two women's colleges. (These facts and figures have changed considerably in the past four decades. There are now more than ten thousand students and four colleges for women.)

Queens' College was founded in 1448 and had the reputation of being among the most beautiful of the twenty-four. Its orange-colored brick buildings lie directly on the Cam, the river lined with weeping willows that flows the length of the city and on Sundays and holidays is crowded with watercraft of all sorts: punts, canoes, rowboats and skiffs. Across the river, reached from Queens' by an ancient rustic bridge, is a shaded area called the Backs, a wide-open green stretching past a number of colleges, where students can loll on the grass, dogs are exercised and there is a degree of sylvan serenity. By American standards Queens' was an exceedingly small college, with fewer than three hundred undergraduates, all male.

Aubrey Solomon Eban entered Queens' in October of 1934, the very week that Mao Tse-tung and a hundred thousand Chinese Communists began their six-thousand-mile trek from the south to the north of China and two months after Paul von Hindenburg died in Germany and Adolf Hitler, abolishing the presidency, took for himself the title of Führer.

Since undergraduates were required to live in college lodgings or approved boardinghouses, Aubrey found modest quarters in a building on Silver Street. His scholarship covered tuition and major expenses, but his bills for the first Michaelmas term listed these items: assessed room rent, £15, 5s ($80.64); breakfasts with tea, 8s ($2.01); books, £2, 5s, 10d ($11.54); hire of plates and crockery, 7s, 6d ($1.78); hire of linens, 10s ($2.52); hot baths, 10s, 6d ($2.65); meals, £2, 3s, 7d ($10.97); mending, 5s ($1.26); electrical current, 16s, 6d ($4.05); gas for fires, according to the meter, £2, 1s, 1d ($10.35); storing of bicycle, 4s ($1.01); cleaning of boots, 3s ($.75); cleaning of suit, 2s, 6d ($.52). (The official rate in 1934 was $5.0393 to the pound sterling.)

The total for the term came to slightly over $130. The next term's bills showed no charge for cleaning of boots, but this was balanced by a slight fee for "replacement of electric light bulbs."[1]

Aubrey took the advice of Mr. Loewe about concentrating first on classical studies, but his interest in oriental languages and cultures remained primary. Loewe was the grandson of Louis L. Loewe, a distinguished nineteenth-century orientalist who had been secretary to Sir Moses Montefiore and had written Montefiore's biography. At Cambridge Mr. Loewe and his wife, Ethel, were looked upon as the godparents of the Jewish community. They held open house for Jewish students and tried to make them feel at ease in what for some was an alien atmosphere. It was the Loewes who helped Aubrey make the transition between London and Cambridge; between the Elephant and Castle and Queens'; between the rather restricted world in which he had lived thus far and the elite, sophisticated milieu in which he now found himself. There was one thing about Mr. Loewe that bothered Aubrey. As he later put it:

"He had one abnormality; he was the most passionate anti-Zionist one could imagine. He thought the idea of a national homeland was a wild and eccentric dream. It was, in fact, an almost subversive thought to him. He made this quite clear to me, although he knew Zionism was the central passion of my life. As a Hebraist he objected to the idea of the language being revived, because he preferred it dead and neatly classified. He was one of a great many academic Hebraists who resented the idea of Hebrew ever being spoken again, because by being spoken it would break the barriers of his own grammatical methodology."[2]

Early in his Cambridge career Aubrey met at the Loewe home Gershon Ellenbogen, a King's College undergraduate from Liverpool with whom he discovered he had much in common. They were both Jews, both Zionists, both classical scholars, both liked to write and each had deep respect for those qualities the other possessed that he himself lacked, so a strong friendship developed which lasted for many years.

Unlike Aubrey, Gershon had been brought up in a home that was extremely observant but he himself became less and less so as time went by. Aubrey made a practice of skipping the Friday evening prayer service at Cambridge Synagogue, as did Gershon in his later undergraduate days. But they both attended the dinner which followed. The menu never varied, from week to week, month to month, year to year. The principal dish was thick pea soup and those who patronized the dinners called themselves "the soup-spillers."

Even before coming to Cambridge Aubrey had joined Poale Zion, the Socialist Zion party, for he held to the thesis there could be no Zionism unless it was socialist in character. From childhood he had had an acute sense of social responsibility. In his life on Kennington Park Road he had seen plenty of dinginess, shabbiness and some want, yet his tendency in all things was to get excited not by what he saw or personally experienced but by what he knew was happening, by his historic knowledge. Thus it was with his socialism.

Once Berl Katznelson came to Cambridge to see Aubrey and several other young men whom he considered his "young hopefuls." As Eban described the visit later:

"His hair was tousled, his mustache shaggy and he wore a sort of workman's hat. Sitting with us there in Cambridge, amid all the pomp and tradition of the ancient university town, he seemed a most improbable figure."[3]

Aubrey was described by a girl acquaintance at this time:

"He was always very proper. Never flashy. Never dandified. Always just right. A complete person, eager to live his own life. He was very catholic in his tastes. He was quite tall and as I remember him rather slim. He was very selective in every way. He had reserve and dignity such as I had seldom ever before seen in anyone so young."[4]

During his second year Aubrey again concentrated on Latin and Greek and by the end of that year had taken ten years of Latin and five of Greek, counting his studies at St. Olave's. With the oriental languages in which he would eventually specialize, he was laying the foundation for an understanding of the logic and structure of language that would someday make him a master of both the written and spoken word. Although he had the intellectual and emotional makeup of a scholar and spent most of his waking hours concentrating on books, and although by nature an introvert, his interest in Zionism propelled him into organizational work, sometimes perhaps against his will. He joined the Cambridge University Zionist Society and eventually became its president.

He was an officer of the Zionist Federation and vice-president of the Federation of Zionist Youth. When the Jewish Society and Hebrew Congregation was reorganized he became its first president. He also served on the executive committee of the Cambridge branch of the League of Nations Union. Whenever he took the floor at a meeting of any of these organizations to propose a motion, plead a cause or fight for a principle, he was articulate and convincing. Often he took a minority position on the matter under discussion and had the task of trying to win over a hostile majority. The greater the odds, the more brilliantly he would argue. In those meetings he began to learn the art of forensic give-and-take, for it was not always possible for him to prepare in advance the statements he delivered.

In these early university days he also continued to use the written word to further his ideas about politics in general and the Middle East in particular. By the time he was twenty-one his articles had appeared in the *Zionist Review,* the *New Palestine,* the *Cambridge Review,* the *South African Jewish Chronicle* and *The Young Zionist.* He never used his full name, always signing himself A. S. Eban.[5]

As a Socialist Zionist Aubrey quite naturally became identified with Socialist groups at Cambridge. He was a member of the Cambridge University Socialist Club and attended meetings at which reports were read on such subjects as the French Popular Front, freedom of the press, the Spanish Civil War and the International Brigade. The Cambridge Socialists and Communists had a loose working agreement. For example, the Socialist paper listed all Communist meetings and lectures, pointing out that Socialists were welcome to attend.[6]

Many of his new colleagues at the university who knew nothing of his background considered him aloof. At the university he acquired admirers but few intimate friends. Those who did know him well realized he was a person of talent and immense integrity, but at the same time criticized him for being "always weighty, physically as well as in subject matter" and for his extreme unpunctuality. "We could always rely upon him to be late, whatever the occasion." His fastidiousness was often commented on. He was fastidious about his appearance, his dress and his behavior, as well as about his relationship with other people. In his Cambridge days he developed a strange quality of secretiveness. As one colleague put it: "He would often be secretive when there was nothing whatsoever to be secretive about." Another said: "I am sure he was even secretive with himself. He seemed to some of us to be running away from himself." A Cantabrigian who has known him all his life said that in Eban "we watched the ferment of an unhappy childhood working through a noble imagination." Another friend put it differently: "At Queens' we saw his personality receiving its final polish, his wit being sharpened, his mind developing its great brilliance."[7]

Each summer Aubrey went to Europe with his family. In this way he mastered French. One summer he took courses at the Sorbonne. Thus he added one more language to those he could already speak fluently.

In the autumn of his second year at the university he joined the Cambridge Union, one of the university's several extracurricular societies. It had its own red brick, two-story building just off Bridge Street. Heavy, red velour draperies hung at all the windows. Inside there was a well-stocked library, a well-stocked bar, game rooms and lounges.[8]

The Cambridge Union brought together students from all the male colleges for various intellectual divertisements, the most important a debate held each Tuesday evening. The subject was announced long in advance and those taking part often worked for weeks on their presentations. An opportunity was provided by the variety of the subjects for the speakers to develop their ability at serious argument, intellectual entertainment, satire or barbed rebuttal. At least half the debates were on frivolous matters. One of the first that Aubrey heard was on the proposition: "That this house would rather have its tongue in its cheek than a bee in its bonnet." Because so many men who later became brilliant public speakers, trial lawyers or political debaters received their first forensic experience at the Cambridge Union the society became known as "the cradle of British oratory."

The president of the society occupied an elevated "throne" at the far side of the Great Hall; directly below him sat the secretary. When a debater was speaking he stood at a wooden stand called, as in the House of Commons, "the dispatch box." Members of the society took places on black, leather-covered benches arranged as nearly as possible like the benches in the House of Commons. Any overflow went into balconies on all four sides of the room. The benches and balconies seated seven hundred, but on those occasions when the subject was especially provocative or the speakers especially popular, students would sometimes stand three or four deep around the walls, or would sit on their haunches in the aisles, or in warm weather crowd on a fire escape. The debates were always called for eight o'clock and would occasionally last almost until midnight.

Sometimes the two speakers on each side of the question were students, but often after one student had spoken pro and one contra, two distinguished outsiders would take the floor—members of the House of Commons or the House of Lords, noted barristers, Cabinet members, Fleet Street editors or celebrated foreigners—men from whom the Cantabrigians might learn something about the art of public speaking.

Union members were generally assigned to speak for or against a motion and so the point of view they expressed did not necessarily reflect their own opinions. Only on political and religious questions was one entitled to speak in favor of one's own viewpoint.

As far as possible the students seated themselves according to their advance opinion on the subject being debated, those on the affirmative occupying benches to the right, those opposed to the left. During the evening anyone who changed his mind could "cross over." After the four prepared presentations had been made, the secretary would call for short comments from other Union members who had signified their desire to be heard, first from the right, then from the left. The clerk kept a careful record of everyone who spoke, noting the time each started and finished. Whereas each of the principal speakers would talk for perhaps half an hour, the subsequent remarks were generally limited to four or five minutes.

The voting was done in an interesting manner—as in the House of Commons. Each Union member chose which of two doors he would use in leaving the hall, one marked "AYES" and the other "NOES." The tellers counted them as they filed through, although the counting did not begin until one speaker had been heard on each side of the question.

In order to interrupt a speaker a member had to raise a formal point of order or point of information. Speakers were permitted to use notes but not to read a prepared speech. There was no public address system (and there still isn't) so the young orators had to project their voices to the far corners of the room.

No smoking was permitted during debates. Dignity and decorum were the rule, but occasionally groups of students would stomp their feet or walk out en masse to show their reaction to a speaker—good preparation for anyone who might at some future date have to talk to an audience of UN delegates.

Cambridge activities were reported in the columns of five local publications, the city's daily newspaper and four university weeklies, the *Cambridge Review*, the *Guardsman* and *Granta*, each with a magazine format, and the *Varsity Weekly*, looking like a newspaper. Short of becoming involved in a scandal—and the Cambridge press loved scandals —there was nothing an undergraduate could do that could possibly get him more publicity than to take a prominent part in Union debates. All five papers gave more space and larger headlines to the debates than to Rugby, lacrosse or even cricket. The *Varsity Weekly* carried a report of each debate on its front page, always under a large headline. Often it was the lead story of the week. The university papers were ruthless in their treatment of Union speakers. Those who put on a poor performance were castigated as "ill-prepared," "boring," "impossible" or worse. This made any compliments rather meaningful.

The first time Aubrey asked to be heard was on October 29, 1935, shortly after he joined the society. The debate that evening was on whether the Union should welcome women students into full membership in the society. Until now no female had even been permitted to listen to the debates, except in the public gallery. Aubrey spoke for five minutes, vigorously defending the rights of females. However, the vote at the end of the evening was 193 for, 274 against. It was not until eleven years later that a young woman was finally permitted to attend a debate and eighteen years before the Union amended its bylaws to admit women members, indicating, perhaps, how far ahead of his time Eban had been.

Cambridge students at the start of their academic career can choose to go out for an honors degree in some specific subject. The examination is called a tripos. The word, peculiar to Cambridge, is of odd origin. In the early days of the university some levity was provided at commencement exercises by an official who recited a humorous poem about each student who was about to get his degree. Because he sat on a three-legged stool or tripod as he made his rhymed jokes, he was called a tripos. The word then somehow came to be used for the honors examination a student took in mathematics, and finally for any honors examination. In the spring of 1936 Aubrey was one of thirty-six Cambridge students to receive a First Class, Part 1 tripos in classical studies, winning special credit for Latin verse composition. Still an undergraduate, he then went on to work for a second tripos in oriental languages.[9]

During 1936 Eban attended nearly all the Union debates, but most of the time he sat in silence, listening to a wide variety of subjects being debated by students and distinguished visitors, studying closely their style and learning much by observation. Then, for the first time, the Union decided to deal with the Palestine issue in open debate, with an Arab speaker and a Jewish speaker opposing each other. The subject was: "That the Government's use of force in Palestine is a confession of its failure to grasp and solve the country's problems." The Arab position was taken by E. A. Ghory of Harvard University and the Jewish position by Sir Robert Waley Cohen, a leader of the Anglo-Jewish community, who later became founder of the Society of Christians and Jews. Of the five thousand or more students in the men's colleges there were then only a few more than a hundred Jews—2 percent—and only thirty or forty were interested in Zionism. With several other Jewish students Aubrey that night seated himself on the "aye" side of the hall. He followed closely the arguments of the principal speakers. After seven other students had spoken from the floor, he took his place behind the dispatch box and for nine minutes, in words that commanded the close attention of the entire large audience, ably supported the affirmative.

Just a few months earlier, Arab rioting in Palestine, encouraged by the Fascist governments of both Italy and Germany, had turned into guerrilla warfare against the 384,000 Jewish settlers there. Hundreds of innocent Jewish men, women and children had already been killed. Yet Aubrey argued with conviction that Arabs and Jews could still live peaceably together in Palestine if the British Government would just revise its policies. As an example he told of their cooperation in forming labor unions. Some students, because of his compelling presentation, switched sides during the evening. Yet the final vote was 149 for, 163 against. Not enough pro-Arab or pro-British students had been converted.

Aubrey gained one devoted admirer with his early Union appearances. The anonymous Cambridge correspondent of the *Olavian*, school paper of St. Olave's, wrote in the December, 1936, issue:

"Eban has plunged into the study of oriental languages and is rarely seen except on the road to the Union, where he occasionally bursts out with a speech of meteoric brilliance."[10]

That term Aubrey was appointed one of the principal speakers on the affirmative of the question: "That the public school system is a disgrace to twentieth century England."[11] He was supported by Charles Fletcher-Cooke, who later became a member of Parliament, and one of his opponents was his good friend the Honorable Patrick Theobald Tower Butler of Trinity, son of the twenty-seventh Baron of Dunboyne, who was known in the streets of Cambridge as Paddy, but who would eventually succeed his father and become the twenty-eighth Lord Dunboyne.[12]

The debate was on January 26, 1937, and Aubrey talked for fourteen minutes—from 8:20 until 8:34. He spoke of the futility and uselessness of public schools and said they enabled the wealthy to get rid of their children "and thus are able to devote too much time to politics."

He attacked England's ruling class as being estranged from the life of the people "by luck, heredity and commercial prosperity." Declaring public schools "hotbeds of a snobbish, aristocratic society which is a disgrace to the twentieth century," he concluded by calling for the overthrow of the entire British public school system "and I have no desire to build anything on the ruins." It was obvious that the audience appreciated his sardonic technique, for the vote was: ayes, 118; nays, 89.

The next day one newspaper critic said it was "an excellent and very witty maiden speech," while another commented on his "creative and entertaining wit." A third said Eban had not hesitated to employ his talents in criticism of the public school system from which he himself had emerged and complimented him on his "rapid sentences and dialectical style."

In the spring of 1937 Aubrey was one of only two students to be placed in the First Class of the oriental languages tripos Part 1. He now had gained First Classes in two Part 1 triposes.[13]

In its July, 1937, issue the *Olavian* said:

"For Eban Cambridge has come to be as vital a part of his existence as is the huge pipe which always droops from his mouth, emitting the most pungent odours. No doubt he will soon be resigning himself to a lifetime to be spent in this burgh."[14]

From now on Aubrey never missed a Tuesday night at the Union and rarely passed up an opportunity to express an opinion. The atmosphere of the day needs to be understood. This was 1936–38. Gandhi was active in India, but India was thousands of miles away and only a few students showed awareness of the campaign for India's independence. Hitler had sent his Nazi troops charging into the Rhineland in violation of the Versailles Treaty, but the Rhine was a great distance from the Cam. The movie houses of Cambridge were crowded as never before. Most of the films were from America. Students stood in queues to watch Ginger Rogers and Fred Astaire in *The Gay Divorcée*, Merle Oberon and Leslie Howard in *The Scarlet Pimpernel*, Joan Crawford, Robert Montgomery, Gracie Fields, Marlene Dietrich, Greta Garbo, Clark Gable, Miriam Hopkins. The *Varsity Weekly* recommended that everyone see Crosby in *Tea for Two*. One night Paul Robeson sang to a packed house at the Regal. The students heard Ruth Draper perform. Horowitz gave a concert. Rubenstein played. C. P. Snow and T. S. Eliot were being read and the avant-garde was becoming enthusiastic over abstract art. There was widespread use of benzedrine by students preparing for exams. Franco had set up his revolutionary government at

Burgos and Spain was being torn by bloody civil war. A few Cambridge students took part in a drive for "Milk for Spanish Loyalists," but only a few.[15]

At teas and sherry parties, which were popular, the talk was generally idle. For the majority there were no intense hatreds and no fierce loves of anybody or anything. The Cantabrigians gossiped, exchanged frustrations and speculated on what they would do—someday. The *Varsity Weekly* editorialized about bad manners in cinema houses and sex orgies on weekends. When Jewish students were forced to leave Germany if they wished to continue their education, the *Varsity Weekly* proposed that Cambridge open its doors to them, but the suggestion created little reaction.

That was the spirit of the day. Aubrey belonged to a minority that had little in common with the others. He did speak during most of the Union's frivolous debates. And he did sharpen his sense of humor by writing amusing letters to friends about inconsequential matters. Yet, young though he was, he seemed more aware than most of his colleagues of the seriousness of the times.

During his college days he often said he disliked political labels, yet he was well known in Cambridge as a Socialist, a Zionist, a supporter of Loyalist Spain, an articulate critic of Chamberlain and his appeasement policy and an implacable enemy of the several Fascist dictatorships by now firmly established in Europe. This was the time of the Popular Front of all left parties in England and so Aubrey was thrown into intimate contact with Communists as well as Socialists. He and his friend Gershon were members of the Left Book Club and read masses of radical literature. They belonged to several Socialist organizations and both asked to be heard whenever the debates at the Union concerned Spain, the Nazis, Chamberlain, Palestine or any other controversial subject.[16]

In 1937 Winston Churchill held no office except as a Conservative Member of Parliament. He had spent recent years painting happy landscapes and writing a six-volume study of his famous ancestor, Marlborough. But now he was deeply concerned about the build-up of Germany's military machine and was taking every opportunity to plead for a more powerful British air force. One weekend he came to Cambridge and met with a group of students, full of dark foreboding. For the first time Aubrey was able to study at close range Churchill's ability to stir an audience.

"We shall all be destroyed: death and destruction will rain down upon us!"

Thirty-five years later Aubrey still remembered every nuance of the voice and would be able to repeat the sentence with all the full-mouthed Churchillian pomposity. Already an admirer of unconventional phraseology, he never forgot hearing Churchill speak of those running the government at that time as "a group of restless epileptics."[17]

Ordinarily *Granta*, like most college papers, brought its readers little that was not already known, but when Aubrey picked up the issue of February 3, 1937, he was shocked to read a two-page account of the death of a close friend, John Cornford, son of the poetess Frances Cornford and Professor Cornford. He had been at Trinity, while Aubrey was at Queens', but both were members of the Cambridge University Socialist Club and the Cambridge Union, where Aubrey had often heard his friend deliver brilliant speeches. A scholar with a bright future, Cornford had dropped out of Cambridge when Italy began sending war planes to Franco and the issue in Spain became apparent. At first he served in the International Brigade and then returned to England to form a British section of the Spanish People's Army. He was killed the day after his twenty-first birthday on the Córdoba front while leading his compatriots in battle. For the next few days Aubrey was quieter than usual. News of the death apparently had a profound effect on him, both intellectually and emotionally.

The Union announced as the subject of its next debate: "That this house deplores His Majesty's Government's policy of non-intervention in Spain." Aubrey was not chosen as one of the principal speakers, but as soon as it was possible for those on the benches to be heard he asked for the floor and spoke brilliantly for eight minutes in favor of the resolution, helping to win an overwhelming vote for intervention and against His Majesty's Government. He also organized meetings in support of the Spanish Loyalists.

One of the Union's most controversial debates in the winter of 1937 was on the motion: "That this house recognizes that the only hope for civilization lies in the victory of the working class over capitalism and that this victory can only be secured if the working class forces are led according to the principles of the parties affiliated with the Communist International." As a supporter of the Popular Front, Aubrey argued for the affirmative, but the vote showed Union members overwhelmingly for capitalism.

That same spring he rose in a Union debate to argue against the idea that "American isolation is splendid." The *Varsity Weekly*, after calling all the other speakers "incompetents," said, "Aubrey Eban was a positive oasis."

"Resolved that work is the curse of the drinking classes." The Union had planned it as an evening of entertainment rather than erudition, so Aubrey kept his arguments for the most part bantering. He began by admitting that he spoke with the voice of inexperience. His only knowledge of the drinking class had been acquired at a banquet one evening, where he watched the behavior of the officers, "from the president's epicurean discrimination, to the secretary's reckless abandon, to the vice-president's sordid emphasis on quantity." Striking one of the evening's few serious chords he said: "When a man earns thirty shillings a week and has to lay aside fifty million for rearmament, what else is there to do but work?"

The reporter who covered the debate for *Granta* commented: "Eban has a genius for misquotation and secures his effects by exaggeration." But in the next paragraph he wrote: "His speeches always have a number of neat cracks and I would sooner listen to him than to most speakers at the Union."

During the 1936 summer vacation Aubrey was engaged by the press department of the Zionist Federation to prepare a pamphlet in answer to a pro-Arab tract entitled *Who Is Prospering in Palestine?* which had been widely circulated in Great Britain and the United States with devastating effects.

That same year the New Look Group moved from the Zionist youth organization into the senior organization, the Zionist Federation, and Aubrey eventually became a member of the Federation's council, as well as chairman of the educational committee. Meetings of these two bodies were held each month at 77 Great Russell Street and no matter what the weather, nor how occupied he was with studies at the university, Aubrey always made the trip from Cambridge to London to be present for these discussions of Zionist strategy and activity.[18]

One memorable evening Aubrey walked into the Federation's council meeting accompanied by a stranger whom he introduced as Viscount Erleigh, grandson of the head of Imperial Chemical Industries and a member of one of Britain's wealthiest Jewish families, which had shown little interest until now in Zionism. Aubrey had met the Viscount at Cambridge and had persuaded him to give Zionism some consideration.

The young man, who later became Marquess of Reading, was thus converted to Zionism.[19]

In the spring of 1937 Zionists all over the world—but especially in Britain—were energized by the report of a commission headed by Lord Peel, which had gone to Palestine to investigate the Arab riots and had issued a four-hundred-page document recommending that Britain continue to hold under its Mandate Jerusalem, Haifa, Nazareth, Bethlehem and a corridor from Jerusalem to the sea, and that the rest of Palestine be partitioned, with the Arabs receiving 75 percent including the Negev desert, and the Jews receiving only Galilee and a narrow coastal strip as their long-awaited national homeland.

Hitler was closing the doors of Germany. Franco and Fascism were winning in Spain. And now world Jewry began to fragment over Partition. At Cambridge Zionist students debated the issue just as vociferously as their elders. The twentieth World Zionist Congress was held that summer (1937) in Zurich, Switzerland, and although Aubrey was not yet twenty-four, the minimum age for a delegate, he decided to go as an observer, which meant he could see and hear but neither speak nor vote.

At the nineteenth Congress Chaim Weizmann, Aubrey's idol, had been elected president to succeed Nahum Sokolow. Years later Aubrey described how Weizmann was separated from the masses of Jews "by the range and distinction of his contacts, by his taste for elegance, order and sophistication in daily life, and by the broad scope of his cultural experience. . . ."[20] He knew that Weizmann was gripped by a single theme and he felt awe and respect for him because of his total consecration. Their backgrounds were entirely different, for Aubrey was peculiarly British in every way; a Jew, to be sure, but a distinctly British Jew, while Weizmann was the gifted son of a timber merchant of Pinsk, and his language, voice and mannerisms never ceased to convey that rich and solid culture of the Pale of Settlement. Yet they were both Zionists, with the same hope, the same dream.[21]

Sitting in a balcony at Zurich, Aubrey watched the clash of personalities on the Congress platform. One of the dominant characters in the drama was David Ben-Gurion, at this time fifty-one years old, who had for the past six years held a position of power as chairman of the Zionist Executive. Like Weizmann, Ben-Gurion was in favor of Partition, but Katznelson was not. It was the first time the black-mustached editor had ever opposed his close friend in public. Also against the Peel plan were the two great rabbis from the United States, Stephen

Wise and Abba Hillel Silver. So, also, was Golda Meyerson (later Meir) whom Ben-Gurion would someday choose as his Foreign Minister. So, also, were the Revisionists and Jabotinsky. The opponents all made brilliant speeches and to some it seemed that their logic was irrefutable.[22]

Ben-Gurion's argument was that the Partition plan was "the beginning of the redemption for which we have waited for two thousand years."

Aubrey followed the debate as excitedly as if it were a cricket match. In a way he was disappointed when a resolution was finally passed that saved everyone's face but settled nothing. It instructed Congress leaders to get more details from the British about what they had in mind.

Back in Cambridge, Aubrey reported to his fellow Zionists on all that had happened and then began preparing for the next Union debate. The subject seemed inconsequential after Zurich: "That this house, declining alike optimism and pessimism, affirms its belief in meliorism." Announcement of the debate sent many a Cambridge student to his dictionary to discover what the seldom-used word means: "The doctrine or belief, fundamental to some systems of ethics, that the world tends naturally to become better, or is capable of being made better by human efforts; a mean between pessimism and optimism."

The affirmative position was taken by Paddy Butler. Aubrey was assigned the negative. The two visiting speakers were Viscount Herbert Louis Samuel, then sixty-seven, who had been first High Commissioner for Palestine, and Lord Ponsonby, who defended.[23]

The Union hall was crowded as Butler began by taking the optimistic viewpoint that "man definitely is able to better his world." Aubrey followed by arguing:

"There have been far reaching improvements in the life of the people of the country, but has this improvement been in proportion to the increase in the potential? Has the actual improvement kept pace with the possibility of improvement?"

Lord Samuel turned his fire on young Eban, declaring his surprise that the previous speaker had defended optimism against meliorism, for he would have thought it would be enough just to look at the state of the world today—to look, for example at Spain and China— and to recall the memories of the last war (World War I).

Lord Ponsonby, who had recently resigned his leadership in the House of Lords because of his pacifism, compared an optimist and a pessimist thus: "I find that an optimist is being continually disappointed at finding he is wrong, while a pessimist, who may find himself wrong just as often, is very glad."

The duel between the two visitors was a lesson in brilliant repartee that Aubrey enjoyed. After the votes were counted it was announced that the meliorism motion had been lost, 194 to 159, meaning that Aubrey's side had won.[24]

The next month Aubrey spoke for the affirmative in a debate entitled: "That the Soviet Union is a new civilization." He was quoted as having said: "Civilization is a monopoly here in England, whereas in Russia it is more reasonably distributed." What most people remembered from the evening was an Eban bon mot. Extemporaneously he accused one of his opponents of "working himself up into his usual state of self-strangulation." Years later Eban revived the phrase, using it to describe a UN opponent.

In another debate that term, while denouncing Mussolini, Aubrey said:

"In Rome a book has just been printed with only one word in it. The title of the book is, *Who's Who in Italy.*"

By now reporters for all five Cambridge papers had discovered that young Eban's remarks made good copy, even if he spoke for only a few minutes from the floor, so they gave him extensive coverage and quoted all his quips. Although still an undergraduate, he grew accustomed to seeing whatever he said in public on the front pages of newspapers. This was heady fare for so young a man and he was not immune to its intoxicating effect.

The first debate of 1938 found Aubrey taking the position that Socialism would be the most desirable form of government for the United Kingdom. Perhaps it was the subject that drew so large a crowd, or Eban's growing reputation as a skilled and entertaining debater, or the appearance on the program of Professor Harold Laski, teacher of political science at the University of London, who had recently been made a member of the executive committee of the Labour party and was at the height of his popularity with young college rebels. Whatever it was, the Union hall was crowded to the doors when the debate began. Eban opened his prepared statement with what a reporter next day called "a barrage of wisecracks, almost epigrams." Then he turned withering fire on the capitalistic system, declaring he did not wish to deprecate capitalism's achievements, "but it is ridiculous to make these past achievements capitalism's title to eternal respect." As to national defense—a subject uppermost in many minds, for this was 1938—

Eban said "a Socialist Britain would not be impeded by foreign investments from intervening in Spain and China in her own true interests." He attacked Prime Minister Neville Chamberlain for his "orgies of self-congratulation" and described the statesmanship of Chamberlain's government as "largely an exercise in self-euphemism."

Eban was brilliantly supported by Laski, who defined a Communist as "a Socialist who means what he says." It was the young student's first personal encounter with the distinguished political scientist and before the evening was over each had acquired respect for the other. Privately Laski told Eban he ought to consider British politics as a career. Aubrey smiled and replied:

"The thought had occurred to me."

The next day the press gave the debate extensive coverage. *Granta* said: "Eban just drips wisecracks," but then the reporter added: "He has the most flexible use of language I know. I am getting tired of having to report each term that he is the best speaker in the Union."

Another reporter commented on Eban's "unceasing flow of racy epithets" and added: "He is the incarnation of the *mot juste* and his style is as brilliant as we have learned to expect from him."

In between preparing for debates and pursuing his study of oriental languages Aubrey intensified his Zionist activities. He became one of the six men on the committee that actually ran the Cambridge University Jewish Society and in a meeting early in 1938 at the synagogue on Thompson's Lane he discussed for more than one hour before a large audience the subject: "Palestine What Now?"

On March 7, 1938, a thousand Spaniards were killed in a Franco air raid on the Loyalist-held city of Barcelona, the most murderous the world had yet known, a foretaste of what was to come if World War II broke out. Four days later Hitler ordered the invasion of Austria. Resistance was slight and in another two days Arthur Seyss-Inquart, Austria's leading Nazi, who would be hanged years later at Nuremberg as a war criminal, in his new capacity as Chancellor proclaimed the political and geographical union of Germany and Austria under Hitler.

At this moment of intense world nervousness, twelve young English students set out from London for Paris at the invitation of left-wing French students to make their own observations about the progress of Socialism in France. The trip was arranged by the Cambridge University Liberal Club, which invited representatives of the important

university societies to go along. Aubrey, his close friend Gershon Ellenbogen and Paddy Butler went as representatives of the Union.

In Paris they met Premier Pierre-Étienne Flandin, Léon Blum, who
preceded Flandin as Premier and would soon succeed him in that office,
and many other distinguished Frenchmen. Aubrey was especially impressed by Blum, who had been head of the French Socialist party
for eighteen years and who as a Jew took keen interest in the Jewish
labor movement. (In just two years Blum would be imprisoned by
Pétain, placed on trial by his own people, handed over to the Germans
and deported to the Buchenwald extermination camp.) They also visited
the St. Cyr Military School and talked with trade union leaders, all in
the course of a few days. In a report called *Politics in Paris* the Cambridge students recorded their impressions. Derek Ezra, who was destined for eminence in British public administration, as secretary of the
delegation wrote:

"We did not confine our political discussions to the Hotel Matignon
or the Quai d'Orsay. We talked with taxi drivers, shopkeepers and
waiters. We learned as much from them as we did in exalted circles."

Aubrey, given the right to report on any phase of French life, wrote
his piece on *French Democracy*.

"Tourists are always surprised and not a little diverted to see the
grandiloquent slogans of the French revolution on the coins, tram
tickets, public buildings and postoffices of the modern republic. . . . A
casual reference to *liberté* in a speech of courtesy still evokes immediate
and ardent applause. All the dates which commemorate the origins of
French democracy are observed with careful zeal. The revolutionary
tradition is an important factor in determining the social outlook of the
French people. Only when this is realized can the foreigner begin to
understand the resilience of French democracy and its sudden capacity
for unified action whenever danger threatens. . . . We saw Fascist
posters liberally spread about Paris. These invariably used anti-Jewish
prejudice as a stick with which to beat the leader of the Front Popu-
laire."

Aubrey had been to Paris before, but for many in the delegation this
was their first time so far from home and they wanted to sample
everything for which Paris is noted, especially its night life. By majority
vote they decided one evening to patronize a nightclub in the Champs-
Elysées called Mimi Pinson's, which advertised *"Danseuses Absolument
Nues."* Actually the dancers were not absolutely nude, but there was
enough bare flesh to excite most of the young Cantabrigians. The

effect of the wine they drank added to the feeling that they were having a riotous time. As far as Aubrey could remember they all left together for their hotel without anyone having succumbed to the enticements of Mimi Pinson's girls. Long after they had forgotten about the almost nude dancers Gershon and Aubrey remembered something that happened as they were about to go through the doorway and out into the Champs-Elysées. One of the young men, Raymond Le Goy, who would later become an important British civil servant, seeing that one of his colleagues had left his glass of wine undrunk, suddenly rushed back to the table shouting *"Gaspillage!* (Waste!)" and quickly emptied the glass before rejoining the party, still gurgling *"Gaspillage!"*

In March of 1938 the union of Germany and Austria was approved by the Italian Grand Assembly at Mussolini's directions. Two weeks later the Cambridge Union debated: "That this house condemns His Majesty's Government for their failure effectively to uphold the interest of this country in preserving the freedom of Czechoslovakia and of the other independent and non-Germanic nations of Central and South-eastern Europe." Aubrey, supported by the distinguished London editor Wickham Steed, took the affirmative.

It would be another five months before Chamberlain would sell out Czechoslovakia at Munich, but the prescient young Eban already had fears. Brilliantly he sketched the history of appeasement and with discerning foresight warned that Hitler would not be satisfied even with Czechoslovakia, were he to get it. "Beyond are the rich minerals and oil fields of Rumania and Yugoslavia. But this is not all." He told his intent listeners that after taking Central Europe Germany's next aim, according to her own admission, would be the British colonies. Hitting out at members of his audience, he said the British were the only people who had not taken Hitler's book, *Mein Kampf,* literally and seriously. British foreign policy had for too long been dictated "by fear of bolshevism—a German word for democracy." Then, in what the papers next day called "a great peroration," he said:

"Has Britain anymore control over its own destiny? It is not too late for collective resistance to the demands and actions of the Fascist powers. Spain is the key to the situation. A victory of the Spanish government would mean strengthening the forces working for peace in the world. I invoke the self-interest of the house, as well as its idealism."

Aubrey Solomon Eban was just twenty-three years old when he made these remarks to several hundred fellow students and faculty members in the debating hall of the Cambridge Union, yet he was being more politically perspicacious and more prophetic than many world leaders of the day. The next issue of the *Cambridge Review* called it "the brilliant speech which we are used to hearing from Eban." *Granta* gave him the title of "the Union's most fluent debater." He had been largely instrumental in obtaining a vote of 143 to 79.

If those who made a practice of attending the Union debates were getting used to hearing brilliant speeches by Eban, Eban himself was getting used to reading eulogistic reviews by the reporters who covered the debates. And yet the day after each event he would buy the newspapers and hurriedly scan their columns with the nervous anticipation of an actor the morning after opening night looking for the judgment of the critics. Already he was beginning to develop supreme self-confidence in his ability as a public speaker, although he had many nervous habits and perspiration would often stand in beads on his forehead as he rose to speak. Even before the final burst of applause he was able to judge, himself, whether he had made an effective presentation, yet what was most important to him was the next-morning journalistic appraisal.

The last debate of the spring term was supposed to have offered an opportunity for the sort of playful banter that many Union members enjoyed. The proposition was: "That society is better analyzed by Groucho Marx than by Karl Marx." But Aubrey decided to take the matter seriously, supporting Karl Against Groucho, and he helped get a slight majority for the negative.

In the spring of 1938 Aubrey was one of only two students to pass the Part 2 oriental languages tripos in Hebrew and Arabic, after being examined by a number of distinguished Oxford and Cambridge professors.[25] Thus he graduated with a triple first, making him a rarity in academic circles. Nothing like this had happened at Cambridge in eleven years. He also was elected to the Wright Scholarship, awarded for the study of Arabic languages and literature.

A few years later, looking back on his undergraduate days, he wrote a friend about his only regret:

"I am sorry that we sowed so few wild oats."

The summer after his graduation Aubrey received a call to come to Zionist headquarters at Great Russell Street. Weizmann's secretary, Arthur Lourie, had been compelled to go to America suddenly, because of the illness of his wife. Someone was needed urgently to fill in for him while he was gone and Weizmann himself, remembering "Alida's very bright son," asked them to send for Aubrey. The man who interviewed him was Lewis Bernstein Namier, fifty-year-old historian, who at one time had been political secretary of the Jewish Agency and now was professor of modern history at Manchester, but still was a close associate and adviser of Weizmann. Aubrey was flattered. Most of the intellectual Young Zionists knew about Namier, for he had already written fundamental studies on eighteenth-century English political history, as well as on international relations in the nineteenth and twentieth centuries.[26]

"Dr. Weizmann knows a great deal about you," he explained, "both through his association with your mother and also from his observation of your academic work and your activity with the Young Zionists. He would like you to assist us until Mr. Lourie returns."

Aubrey tried not to show his eagerness. He was already torn about what he wanted to do with his life. Zionism was his passion, but the idea of a career in British politics also intrigued him. Then there was the love he had already acquired for things academic. He was certain he could be happy spending the rest of his life on the grounds and in the buildings of a great university like Cambridge. But the chance to work in close association with Weizmann—to help in the realization of The Great Dream—now drove everything else from his mind, at least temporarily. Weizmann maintained a suite of rooms at the Dorchester, where he lived as if he were the president of a sovereign state, at a time when there was neither a sovereign state nor a president. But Weizmann ignored this small detail. By acting the role he infected others with the pretense. He had his own Rolls-Royce and enjoyed the life of a London gentleman. Even the contempt he seemed to have for lesser men had a certain quality of regality. Since watching him in action at Zurich, Aubrey had made him the central character of his fantasies.

"May I assume that you will help us?" Professor Namier was asking.

"Certainly!" Aubrey came out of his reverie. "Of course. Certainly!"

It was a summer to be remembered. Aubrey was treated as one of the inner circle and he was privy to much inside information. One day he was shown a letter that had come to Weizmann from his good friend Orde Wingate, a non-Jewish British Army officer stationed in Palestine, who had learned a thousand words of Hebrew and was attempting to read the Bible from start to finish in the ancient language. In the letter Wingate wrote at length about the need to form a Jewish Palestine defense force and offered his own services as an officer in such an army. Later that year Weizmann cabled Wingate asking him to come to London for a conference. It was then that Aubrey met the fanatically pro-Jewish officer for the first time.

"I listened to him as he cursed the Chamberlain Government for what he called the betrayal of the Jews. There was a strange wildness in his eyes. I thought he was a little mad, but the Chief had great respect for him." (Those who were closely associated with Weizmann generally referred to him as the Chief.)

Once when Aubrey expressed surprise to Weizmann that he discussed the Zionists' top secrets with or in front of Wingate, the Chief replied sharply:

"If I live another twenty years [he actually lived only another fourteen] I might become as much of a Zionist as Wingate is."[27]

5

The Cataclysm Begins

IN THE AUTUMN of 1938 Aubrey migrated from Queens' to Pembroke College, Cambridge, as a research fellow and tutor in oriental languages. Now that he was a graduate student he was no longer compelled to live in college lodging houses, so he found unlicensed rooms on a short thoroughfare, Corn Exchange Street, in the heart of Cambridge only a few hundred yards from Pembroke. The two prim spinsters who were his landladies had an innate suspicion of all students in general, but seemed to consider Aubrey especially peculiar. They provided him with the bare essentials of living—nothing more. The two rooms were an improvement over his undergraduate quarters but they were dingy by almost any standards. The furnishings consisted of an iron bedstead and a night table in one room, and in the other a bare wooden worktable and two armchairs covered with a frayed corduroy material that apparently had originally been tan but now was slightly off-black. Other students brightened up their quarters with posters, pictures, draperies, but Gershon Ellenbogen observed that months after Aubrey moved in he had made only one minor improvement: he had taken down an aquatint of the coronation of Queen Victoria and had substituted a cheap print of the *Mona Lisa*. Pointing to this new wall decoration Aubrey told his friend:

"That print celebrates my initial victory over my Board of Landladies when I refused to inhabit the same room as the Coronation of Victoria, an event which, according to the picture, took place in a thick fog in the presence of five thousand bloated dignitaries and two fat and naked cherubim bearing the royal standard."

Except for his instant reaction to the coronation scene, Aubrey apparently was impervious to his new surroundings.

Pembroke, founded in 1346, is housed in buildings of deep red brick with a turret at each corner and a noble entrance gateway. Early in the sixteenth century Erasmus occupied one of the south turret rooms. It was the college of many other celebrated Englishmen, among them Thomas Gray, author of "Elegy Written in a Country Churchyard." More important to Aubrey, this was the college of William Pitt the Younger, who entered Cambridge at the age of fourteen. Aubrey had read many of his speeches and knew he had been one of the great political orators of the eighteenth century and had been named Britain's Chancellor of the Exchequer at twenty-three (exactly Eban's age when he entered Pembroke) and at twenty-four had become Prime Minister. In the courtyard of Pembroke there is a bronze statue of Pitt as a young man, a scroll in his left hand, his right hand extended. Once when Eban was standing in the courtyard looking up into the face of the bronze figure a passerby stopped and remarked on how much they resembled each other, a comparison Aubrey found not at all distasteful.

In the December, 1938, issue of the *Olavian* there was this news note:

"Is not Eban still a power in the land? Does not the Press believe him to be the Union's most fluent speaker in recent years and perhaps the most well-informed Young Zionist in the country? 'Tis true he is hardly seen by mortal eye, but we must hasten to explode the rumor that the eclipse of the moon was really Aubrey being caught up in a cloud from the tip of Parnassus or somewhere."[1]

By this time Eban and Ellenbogen were close friends, sharing many of the same ideas and interests. Both were now active journalists, Gershon a member of the editorial board of *Granta* and Aubrey editor of *The Young Zionist*. At one of Mr. Loewe's Saturday night open house receptions Gershon introduced Aubrey to a young woman who was to play different but important roles in their lives: Eileen Alexander, student for the past two years at Girton, one of the women's colleges of Cambridge; short, rather plump, with brown eyes, dark brown hair and a positive manner of speaking. A friend once said of her: "Eileen was always slightly exotic. Always noticeable. Very unusual."[2] Her father, Aaron Alexander, was born in South Africa to a Jewish family of modest means. After graduating from a South African university he went to Cambridge, where he became friendly with a wealthy young student, Lionel Mosseri, son of a family of Jewish bankers in Cairo, Egypt, who had lived there since the eighteenth century, after emigrating from Leghorn, Italy. Young Alexander eventually married the sister of Mosseri and settled in Cairo, where before long he became a successful international lawyer. This young Cambridge student, Eileen, was the eldest of his children, born just twenty-one years ago in Cairo, where she lived until she was eighteen. By coincidence it had been one of Eileen's uncles, Morris Alexander, who had arranged passage during World War I from South Africa to England for Aubrey, his mother, his father and his sister Ruth.

Eileen was a combination of Europe and the Middle East, of Italy and Egypt. Plus being Jewish. It was obvious she had been brought up in surroundings of culture and affluence. She talked (without trying to impress anyone) of how since childhood she had spent six months of every year touring Europe by private limousine with her parents, two brothers, their chauffeur and a governess; of the Alexanders' second home, in Scotland; of the lavish style in which they lived in Cairo; of the important people they entertained; of her father's intimate connection with numerous members of the British aristocracy.

On the surface there was nothing in common between Eileen and Aubrey. She had not the slightest interest in Zionism, a subject which by silent agreement they never discussed. In her childhood she had known some Hebrew, but by now she had forgotten it almost entirely, while to him Hebrew had become extremely important. She lived in a perpetual state of passionate emotion, as one friend put it, "several keys higher than is tolerable to the human ear," while Aubrey seemed to have his emotions under absolute control at all times. She was doing her graduate work in English, concentrating on the Arthurian legend, which seemed about as far in the limbo of remote matters as anyone could possibly get, whereas Aubrey was primarily concerned with the language and problems of the twentieth-century Middle East. She liked to share confidences, while he seemed constitutionally unable to confide deeply in anyone. Yet there was great compatibility of mind. Eileen, Gershon and Aubrey were all deeply rooted in the classic European cultural tradition, with its rich heritage of literature and philosophy. Also, they all spoke the same language—the language of "Oxbridge" liberal arts students. Above all they could make one another laugh. They were not only witty in themselves but were the cause of wit in each other, especially in their exchange of letters in which it pleased them to keep up a bantering tone, even when discussing the grimmest matters.

There was a difference, however, between Gershon's and Aubrey's relationship with Eileen. With Gershon it was a normal male-female affinity and eventually he and Eileen fell in love and were married. The relationship that developed between Aubrey and Eileen was more subtle, more unusual. One incident was typical. They both used the immense Cambridge University Library, one of the largest libraries in the world with two or three million volumes in its stacks. One morning as Aubrey came into the reading room with its high, painted-wood ceiling and large oval windows, he saw Eileen sitting in a deep blue leather armchair at one of the long tables, so he took a vacant place opposite her. They smiled recognition at each other and then she went back to reading some book pertaining to brave knights and fair ladies, while he opened a volume on peculiar Arabic conjugations. After lunch they were both back at the same table, again opposite each other. Late in the afternoon Eileen pushed across the table a piece of stationery on which she had written:

"I was *very* shocked to see you biting your nails this morning, Aubrey. Do you often do this? Oh! You're doing it *now*. Why?"

Aubrey read, smiled, then wrote an answer:

"No, not often. Only in the stress of complex and exceptional emotions, cares, solicitude, ecstasies, preoccupations or famine."

This was an example of the peculiar correspondence that would go on for many years. From his Corn Exchange rooms, from army camps, from France, Switzerland, Egypt, Palestine, from wherever they were they would write sometimes short notes or sometimes extremely long letters to each other in which they would express themselves with apparently no restraint.

During the next few years Aubrey wrote to Eileen about the impending war, then about the actual start of the Nazi sweep across Europe, the plight of the Jews and about some of his own not too pleasant experiences, yet in all his letters he never once abandoned the tone set in that first written conversation about nail biting. As Eileen later put it:

"I think we got the cream of Aubrey's fun, because this was before he had assumed any of the burdens and responsibilities of a diplomat or a statesman. We saw him as few others ever did. We saw the gayest of him."[3]

Because speaking even in a whisper was prohibited in the university library, they communicated by written notes all that year, exercising their literary inventiveness, chiding each other, sometimes even engaging in sharp insults on small bits of paper. As their relationship developed and Aubrey realized that Eileen appreciated his abrasive wit enough not to be easily offended by anything he said or wrote, he practiced on her his love of ridicule and made her the butt of what others might have considered almost insults. On one occasion, referring to her tendency to keep the floor once she had obtained it, he said:

"Conversations with Eileen tend to be unilateral."

Another time he said:

"Eileen has her feet firmly planted in the clouds."

Eileen herself gave this explanation of their relationship:

"I was a foil for him. Even with me, after we had known each other for years, he still displayed his innate shyness and so we kept the relationship always on a very formal level, something that would be almost impossible between young people today. It was a psychologically interesting situation."[4]

She forgave him anything because she considered him completely lacking in any form of malice. To others he might appear esoteric and incomprehensible; to her he was, always, an extremely pellucid person. She felt completely unrestrained with him and he apparently felt at ease when communicating with her, for their relationship was without emotional obligation on either side. One of his qualities that Eileen found refreshing was his innocent surprise at discovering the existence of what for others might have been commonplace. Once in great seriousness he asked her: "What is this thing called jazz?" and he was really interested in being enlightened.

One afternoon Aubrey invited Eileen to his rooms on Corn Exchange Street for coffee and cakes. She found his bare, grimy quarters rather depressing, "Even Gershon had a print of Vermeer's *View of Delft* on one wall of *his* flat." But she said nothing, aware that he had no interest whatsoever in anything personal; that he had no possessive instincts; that his surroundings were of no importance to him.

Eileen introduced Aubrey to Joyce Nathan, tall, dark and slim, with sparkling brown eyes, a good sense of humor and a vivacious personality. She was charmingly beautiful. Her friends described her as "high-spirited." She was the daughter of a Labour Member of Parliament who later became a member of the House of Lords.[5] Her mother at that time was a member of the London County Council and immediately after the end of World War II would become the first woman in history ever to be elected chairman of the London County Council. Joyce was five years Aubrey's junior and had just entered one of the women's colleges of Cambridge as an undergraduate, but she had always associated with older people and was extremely sophisticated for her age. She and Aubrey with Eileen and Gershon made a foursome for dinners, theater parties and outings on the Cam. Although she was a Jewess, Joyce was as non-observant as the other three and so on Friday nights they would skip the religious service and go to the synagogue simply for the Shabbat supper.

In Joyce's presence Aubrey was always lively and entertaining. "He was never tongue-tied. He always seemed to say what he wanted to say by saying something else. He had a habit of talking about generalized things. He could talk either amusingly, informatively or entertainingly about all manner of things."[6]

Soon after Aubrey began his first year at Pembroke, Neville Chamberlain went to Munich, where on September 30 he joined with Hitler, Mussolini and Daladier in signing the Munich Agreement, giving Germany one fifth of Czechoslovakia's land and nearly four million of her people. When Chamberlain returned to London clutching his umbrella and talking about "peace in our time" cartoonists began using a black umbrella as the symbol of appeasement. In a public address in Cambridge in October Aubrey denounced the Chamberlain Government, calling it "this brollygarchy," a bon mot that only an Englishman could appreciate, "brolly" being British slang for an umbrella. That same autumn he addressed the Rotary Club of Cambridge on "The Refugee Problem," caustically saying of Paul Joseph Goebbels, Hitler's Minister of Popular Enlightenment and Propaganda:

"Every time he opens his mouth he subtracts from the sum of human knowledge."

A Cambridge reporter thought the remark clever enough to include in his account of the talk, but that was all the notice it received. A quarter of a century later Eban would revive it in castigating a quite different enemy and the remark would get worldwide publicity.

A few weeks later the Union debated the subject: "That the defense of Britain is safe in the hands of Chamberlain." Young Eban, future diplomat, argued for the opposition that the effective defense of the country depended on *diplomacy* diverting the potential enemy elsewhere and building up against it an overwhelming system of alliances. He warned that western Europe was faced with a reversal of Versailles, the encirclement of France and the isolation of Britain. No amount of possible rearmament, he said, could begin to make up for Chamberlain's "strategic disarmament." The vote was 107 for the motion, 233 against. The *Varsity Weekly* said of Eban's brief remarks: "He cast his pearls freely."

Just before Cambridge closed for the Christmas holidays Aubrey helped arrange for the introduction of a resolution at a Union meeting condemning the German persecution of Jews. It was adopted by a standing vote without effective opposition.

Early in 1939 Jewish and Arab representatives were brought together in London by the Chamberlain Government in the hope that after protracted discussion they could produce a settlement of the entire Middle East problem. The conference was called the St. James's Palace Round Table. Aubrey wrote an article for the *Zionist Review* which the editors of the *New Palestine* considered so cogent that they reprinted it. It began:

"A stately procession of Arab potentates is now assembled in London for Palestine discussions and British public opinion is naturally intrigued by the atmosphere of desert romanticism which they have infused into the drab winter scene. . . . Nevertheless the presence of so many Arab rulers illustrates very painfully the contrast between the landlessness of the Jewish people and the wide territorial potentialities at the disposal of the Arabs."

At the start of 1939, with World War II just eight months off, the majority of Cambridge students were still talking, thinking, writing and behaving as if it could never happen. Myrna Loy was the current favorite of the flick-goers. Margot Fonteyn came to Cambridge to dance. One of the university papers advised everyone to stop what he was doing and read "the great book of the century, *Grapes of Wrath*." In a poll by one of the university papers, only 22 percent of the students interviewed said they would be willing to fight if war broke out and 72 percent declared themselves in favor of the Chamberlain policy of appeasement.⁷ Aubrey, therefore, faced a somewhat hostile audience when in January he spoke for the affirmative in a debate on the proposition: "Resolved, that this house has no confidence in His Majesty's Government's policy of appeasement." Yet, as midnight approached and the vote of the tellers was announced, a substantial majority had supported the resolution.

That summer, as everyone wondered whether Europe was heading into an actual war or just another Munich Crisis, the Middle East question was being debated in the British Parliament and the Jewish Agency invited Aubrey to join a small group lobbying among members of the House of Commons. After his first day of work as a professional lobbyist he returned to his rooms and wrote Eileen the first almost serious letter he had ever sent her, telling his reaction to hours of trying to influence the parliamentarians:

"I was closeted with harassed legislators in the tomblike lobbies until past three, when I felt a sudden urge to issue a piercing scream. I fought this urge with manful success until I issued from the sacred precincts; and on the whole I am glad. I am not a pedant when it comes to the conventions, but I do feel that Westminster is not the best place for primitive self-expression. . . . On rare occasions—very rare—I attain a negative view of the universe in comparison with which Schopenhauer is simply a frivolous young thing."

The Commons debate resulted in no change whatsoever in the Government's position on Palestine, despite a speech by Winston Churchill that many called the greatest he had ever delivered. Perhaps Aubrey's depression had been justified.

During his Cambridge days Aubrey displayed to those who knew him intimately an intense love of gossip. "There was nothing petty about it," Eileen explained, "nor was it in any way malicious. It was just his ritualistic way of expressing his passionate interest in people, an interest of which many may not have been aware. It was proof that underneath he really was a man of deep feeling."[8]

Aubrey's letters were sprinkled with such gossip and with tidbits of reporting on inconsequential events. He told of encountering on a street in Cambridge a certain Mrs. G., whose ambition in life, as Aubrey put it, was to marry off her only daughter to any and all male undergraduates. "I have no experience of such things, of course, but she exactly fits my conception of a proprietress of a Parisian *maison de rendezvous,* as portrayed at least in most novels. She infuses an air of grossness into the most innocuous transactions. She asked me for your address, which I reluctantly yielded up."

In another letter he told how his life had suddenly been revolutionized:

"Walking with Gershon from the Blue Barn back to Kings it occurred to me that he ought to have more exercise as a relief from his tutorial cares, so I suggested a game of tennis for the following day. He said if he played it would have to be before 8 A.M. . . . The cold horror of the position paralyzed my wits. I did not believe that 8 A.M. really existed. I am not a cynic in these things, but merely an agnostic. What I never see or experience has no reality for me and in that category I include the Holy Ghost, spiritualism, the Niagara Falls and 8 A.M. On the other hand his assumption that I was incapable of arising at 8 A.M. irritated me beyond measure. I preserved a stolid gravity and said courteously, 'Eight o'clock will suit me very well.' . . .

"To make a short story as long as possible, I awoke at 6 this morning and eked out the remaining ninety minutes. A half hour later I issued forth into the street clad in tho whito shects of penitence. It is only in a rigidly technical sense that I can be said to be alive before breakfast. Yet here I was, bent on an hour of unrestrained violence beneath the eyelids of the dawn. . . . We played a set with unnecessary violence and to my triumph, whereupon the episode ended. On the way back Gershon suggested we should do this each morning. I muttered assent and staggered home to eggs, hot tea and the *Times*. Full recuperation occurred at about 7 o'clock in the evening. And so my mornings stretch before me, barren of repose, and all because of a casual word and a stubborn pride."

Apologizing one day for writing a letter and then forgetting to mail it, Aubrey commented on what he characteristically called his "absence of mind," instead of using the more common term. Even though it was confined to small things it worried him, although, he wrote, "tactful people assure me that it is no more than a presage of future professorship"—an indication he had almost made up his mind to follow an academic career. He said he anticipated he would go on forgetting small things and this would be all right. "As long as I don't forget the forty-two ways of forming the Arabic plural I feel that the world will have a niche for me."

In another letter he labeled as "a monstrous thought" the possibility that someday he might "become respectable" and move in "respectable circles" and say "all the respectable things."

Once he wrote:

"I was going to say that patience brings its own reward, but that is exactly the sort of maddening platitude which, in a well-ordered society, would be a capital offense."

Eban's hatred of hackneyed expressions began in his preparatory school days and would grow more intense year by year during the rest of his life.

He described his own life in Cambridge that summer:

"I spend long hours and have little to show, as when the mountain begat a mouse. . . . On the eleventh of August I intend 'to render myself in Swiss to pass there the vacations.' I shall be away a month."

It was typical that he did not tell Eileen the chief purpose of his trip to Switzerland was to attend the twenty-first Zionist Congress in Geneva. Having now passed his twenty-fourth birthday, he was finally eligible to be a delegate, so he combined his Swiss vacation with attendance at what would turn out to be the last Zionist Congress for the next seven years.

Aubrey's relationship with Eileen illustrated the way he departmentalized his life. With no single person did he seem to have a complete relationship. He was involved with each of his friends or acquaintances in some limited intellectual, political or emotional area and each contributed to some special need. To his many young Jewish friends in London he seemed to have a one-track Zionist mind. With Eileen he never discussed his parents. As she put it, "It was difficult to imagine Aubrey as ever having been subjected to the normal indignities of infancy."

Mrs. Eban and Carmel decided to accompany him to Geneva. They had great trouble getting transportation because there was a general feeling that catastrophic events were about to take place and so hundreds of thousands of tourists were all suddenly trying to get home at the same time.

It was not by accident or coincidence that Aubrey picked the Hotel Oxford and Cambridge on the Rue St. Honoré when they arrived in Paris. After getting his family settled there, he found a sidewalk café on a sunny boulevard and wrote a long letter while drinking what he described as "the Parisian equivalent of tea; like the quality of mercy it is unstrained; unlike it, it blesses only him that gives." Along with most other tourists who have ever visited Paris in August, he was surprised at how deserted the city was.

"Truth to tell the Gay City is not making a special effort at present to live up to its name. A newspaper vendor explained the matter to me in a long conversation in the style of stichomythia; he was a subtle fellow and enjoyed a good oratorical antithesis. There is apparently a fête on August 15 and the fascinating thing is that nobody knows what it is for, but it is quite momentous. Rather like Einstein's theory. In any case shopkeepers display curt 'clôture annuelle' signs and go off to fish in Brittany, leaving the city to a few jaded agents of police and some disgruntled waiters to feed the insatiable foreigners. . . . But it is a relief to be where London duties cease from worrying and telephones are at rest."

The next day the Eban family left for Geneva, where they stayed at the posh Richemond Hotel, just off the waterfront. While the representatives of world Jewry were meeting in Geneva, the Soviet-Nazi Pact was signed, the Russians promising to remain neutral if Germany went to war. Aubrey heard the news by radio in his hotel room—with disbelief.

For a Socialist, for one who had been part of the Popular Front and had defended the Soviet Union in public debates, it was incredible. Thirty years later his sister still remembered how shocked he seemed as he listened to the news repeated again and again by the Geneva announcers. Typically, however, he showed his reaction principally by deep silence.[9]

Now the war clouds were coming rapidly together to form a great thunderhead. Most of the Zionist delegates knew it might be a long time before they would be able to assemble again. The principal piece of business was to vote on the white paper which had been submitted by the Colonial Secretary, Malcolm MacDonald, after the failure of the St. James's Palace Round Table and which declared the British intention of setting up after ten years an independent Palestinian state in which Jews and Arabs would participate in the government in proportion to their numbers; Jewish immigration would be dependent on Arab approval and the sale of land to Jews would be restricted or in some cases absolutely forbidden. Aubrey voted for rejection of the plan.

But the high point of the twenty-first Congress for Aubrey, already an orator himself, was Weizmann's farewell address late on the evening of August 24. Everyone was in a hurry to get home, for there was now no question but that the unspeakable was about to happen. The final session was held in an atmosphere of impending destiny. To Aubrey, Weizmann seemed to be standing taller than ever as he began:

"There is darkness all around us and we cannot see through the clouds. . . . It is with a heavy heart that I take my leave. . . . If, as I hope, we are spared in life and our work continues, who knows, perhaps a new light will shine upon us from the thick black gloom. . . . There are some things which cannot fail to come to pass, things without which the world cannot be imagined. The remnant shall work on, fight on, live on until the dawn of better days. Toward that dawn I greet you. May we meet again in peace."[10]

Deep emotion gripped everyone within hearing, Aubrey among them. As Weizmann left the hall hundreds of hands stretched out toward him. Many sensed that the Jewish agony was about to commence. Aubrey stood on the sidewalk watching as Weizmann stepped into his car and sped out of Geneva toward the French frontier.

The Ebans had great difficulty getting back to Paris. They traveled across Alpine France in what amounted to a troop train, for most of the hundreds of passengers were French reservists. Aubrey observed that many spent their time laconically polishing bayonets. He talked with a bearded general who seemed to embody the combined aggressiveness of Napoleon and Foch and who predicted that Hitler's forces would meet instant defeat as soon as they came to grips with the French Army.

The Ebans found the French capital a different city than the Paris they had left only ten days earlier. Already it was in a war mood and was rife with wild rumors. Explaining later what trouble he had in Paris trying to find porters to carry their luggage, Aubrey said:

"French porters are all in Class T of reservists and are called up whenever M. Daladier has indigestion."

From London they drove across south England to the village of Felcourt near East Grinstead in Sussex. Even in these peaceful surroundings "all were accoutred in the habiliments of war."

On September 1 over a radio in the cottage in Sussex Aubrey and his family heard the news that Stuka dive bombers had attacked Polish troops, thus commencing the war that everyone had been fearing. Aubrey immediately volunteered to serve in several capacities. A week later he wrote that "the Empire has so far turned a deaf ear to my ardent advances and my self-immolation must wait upon the slow unwinding of red tape." Meanwhile, he was working temporarily at a first-aid post in the Sussex village "going through the routine of handling hosts of imaginary casualties. My function is to drive a car from one shadow hospital to another shadow hospital with an imaginary surgeon to patch up imaginary bodies. My father has organized the whole scheme and is merely waiting for the shattered bodies. Until then he will not be happy."

The censor's office approached him and put him on their list for French, Arabic and modern Hebrew. "But since I have not heard from them," he wrote to Joyce, "I presume they looked for aged and infirm Arabists first, and then for women and other immobilisable elements."[11]

One agency that thought it might use Aubrey's services was the Ministry of Information. He wrote Eileen that it would involve war work of "deep and sinister secrecy." "If you see me soon slinking down Whitehall in a large-brimmed hat, dark glasses and a conspiratorial guise, do not suspect The Worst. It will be all for King and Country. [From Eileen he had acquired the habit of capitalizing, which he indulged, however, only when writing to her.] In brief The Future is very vague and I loathe Vagueness."

Describing how he felt now that World War II had actually begun, he wrote:

"I have preferred not to write with much seriousness this time, as it would sound either melodramatic or trite, for nothing has happened yet to convince me that there really is a war. The worst thing so far is the sheer irrelevance of all one's past life, the complete hiatus between yesterday and tomorrow. I suppose we knew it was coming, but we subconsciously shunned the idea as primly as any Victorian heroine shunning the fate which was commonly but I should think erroneously regarded as worse than death. But here it is."

He told of his unsuccessful efforts to get into some branch of service.

"I have yielded up all my secrets to the penetrating glare of White-hall. They know all about me except my abnormal hatred of spinach and cinema organs. My grandfather's birthplace was a genuine surprise to the Ministry of Information, who had never heard of Yanishki. I am not really expecting officialdom to show any haste to utilize me or anyone else. Dash it, war or no war, decencies must be preserved, what? and a fellow must take his time.

"Meanwhile, our first aid post is still impossibly handicapped by a lack of corpses and other raw materials necessary for its full efficiency. I am also doing a few translations from Arabic papers for an official department, chiefly the pronouncements of obscure desert potentates loudly asserting their loyalty."

A few days later Aubrey left the rural quiet of Sussex and went back to his Corn Exchange Street rooms. He wrote: "I am alone in this familiar haunt, enveloped in statutory darkness and in a room almost bookless, except for a Shakespeare, an Arabic Koran and a Hebrew novel of quite startling impropriety sent to me by an astute Tel Aviv publisher for review. . . .

"Cambridge is in a very frigid mood and unless you are a soldier or an expectant mother you feel like an intruder. [Hundreds of expectant mothers had been evacuated to Cambridge.] Think how noisy the place will be when the expectations of all the expectant mothers are fulfilled. They are expecting babies and that, no doubt, is what they will get."

He then reported on blacked-out London.

"Leicester Square is now a shambles of colliding pedestrians and only the fittest survive. I kept knocking outraged women off the pavement and I fear that as my honest countenance could not be seen, the wrong construction was put upon my bucolic familiarity."

Discussing his work for the Jewish Agency while in London:

"I was kept busy in one of my more esoteric capacities—as a pillar of Zionism or whatever the baby version of a pillar is. Everybody was creeping along corridors with a furtive gaze, clutching wads of documents with desperate secrecy. The conspiratorial air reminded me of the Congress at Geneva when letters would be pushed under my door by an Unseen Hand in the still watches of the night. I don't know why Jews always become so portentous and mysterious in emergencies. I found myself asking the time in a hushed whisper like Mata Hari probing an armaments secret. . . .

"I saw Weizmann. The Presidential Pate positively gleamed with conspiracy. It's all very sad. It appears that he is offering the War Office large hordes of Jewish Brains and Brawn and the Secretary of State calmly dismisses the offer with a casual wave of an unnecessarily expensive silk handkerchief and talks meaningly of acetone."

Often he accompanied Weizmann when the Chief went to call on British ministers and other government officials.

"I was always astonished at the way he behaved—as though he had all the power instead of them. He epitomized Jewish dignity at a time when there wasn't any real embodiment of it. For me he was immensely moving and consoling."[12]

To Joyce he wrote:

"Do you ever pick up the English broadcasts from Germany delivered in a nauseous accent, composed of Oxford and adenoids in equal parts? It is well worth it, if only to hear the descriptions of Winston Churchill boring holes in the hull of the *Athenia* as he did in the *Lusitania* in 1915."[13]

Aubrey always wrote to Joyce in a more serious vein than to Eileen. Twenty-five days after the start of the war he wrote to Joyce:

"I think it is best to regard the war as a siege of Germany rather than as a direct assault. In that case sea power is the decisive factor and given time the French may well get through or else Winston can go on murdering Balkan statesmen and blaming it onto the Germans until they all get exasperated and leap into the war. Everybody can then rush into the Dardanelles and we can have some historic battles, all over Hungary. I should like to see the Indian Army, a Jewish Legion and some Arab tribes along the Danube. Do you think I ought to communicate this strategy to the War Department? They may not have thought of it."[14]

In his continuing attempt to get into some branch of national service Aubrey filled out more applications, forms, questionnaires, guarantees, commitments, undertakings, pledges and references, always in triplicate.

One questionnaire asked if he had ever passed an examination of any kind, "a question that merits what the late Ethel M. Dell used to call 'a mirthless laugh.' Just as a matter of perfunctory interest they would also be pleased to learn whether I suffer from epileptic fits and would I specify the exact number of prison sentences I have served. They remain my 'obedient servants,' which is comforting."

Writing to friends he told how he had finally at Cambridge been "ushered into the APRB—the Awful Presence of the Recruiting Board—and made to converse experimentally in various languages. After much ado and a clandestine lunch with the chairman of the board, I was told to apply for a commission in the Intelligence Corps."

Toward the end of September Aubrey became a member of His Majesty's Emergency Officers Reserve, Intelligence, 13K/6297, spec. No. 43,700.

"It appears that when the country is fully mobilized, which should be in the neighborhood of 1941, there will be a little niche for me."

His acceptance had been preceded by a physical examination "of quite humiliating thoroughness, involving unheard-of indignities." He was required to fill in three forms in triplicate "and then I went around interviewing officers of ascending eminence, culminating in a fire-eating colonel with a bristly mustache and a suitable florid countenance. He seemed to think there must be something fishy about a man who claimed to have endured three tripos instead of the two which are the usual mortal span. So he went off looking very shy and worldly to look up the Cambridge *Reporter*, came back confused and contrite, filled in five more forms in duplicate, stamped them, tied them with red tape and went his way. Last scene of all, the Recruiting Board turned out to be three genial dons, one a close friend of mine. They spoke to me experimentally in French and German, but did not attempt Arabic or Hebrew. They then wrote a fulsome letter to the War Office (in triplicate) and asked me to lunch. We swept along a corridor full of expiring candidates filling in forms; many had been waiting for three weeks and were overlain with cobwebs."

What Aubrey in later years remembered best about his attempt to get into service was "the moment when a decrepit doctor with creaking joints asked me to take off my spectacles and read the letters on the board."

"'What board?' I asked, innocently staring straight at it."

This quickly disqualified him from a commission in the Observers' Corps.

"Some capacity to distinguish an ally from an enemy is apparently regarded as an indispensable asset in war."

Young Eban had many Arab friends in those days. On a student-deserted street in Cambridge he had an interesting farewell chat with one of them, Hussein Omar, "who was stranded from his motherland and was enjoying it in his nice primitive way."

Some of Aubrey's leisure these days was spent trying to decipher the handwriting of Eileen's letters. Seldom if ever did anyone write with such a fine pen, in such painstakingly small script, with so many words crowded into any given amount of space. In his tolerance Aubrey commented:

"It is no use complaining of the leaning tower of Pisa or the Rhone Glacier. You accept them as part of the cosmic variety and just ask yourself—why? So with your handwriting. My own solution is that it is a reflex economy devised by your subconscious mind to compensate for other extravagances—e.g. cigarettes."

Like Eileen, Aubrey wrote with a fine pen, precisely, punctiliously, neatly and economically, rarely crossing out a word, never making an error in spelling or punctuation, always seeming to know exactly what he wanted to say and how he wanted to express the thought before beginning. Only occasionally would words be underlined.

While he was waiting to be called up he filled his time studying a new language, Persian or Farsi, and enjoying "the delicate profanities of Omar Khayyam." He philosophized that "the scourge of our generation is boredom; people are being stifled by their own yawns, as the tedious farce of war drags on. Getting married is an obvious way out, but even Gershon is not quite as bored as that. His intrigue with the college nurse derives all interest from being furtive and illicit. Make it respectable and it becomes just sordid."

In addition to studying Persian, Eban that autumn became an author— or at least an editor—with the publication of a new edition of a Zionist classic. In Berlin in 1882 Jacob Loeb Pinsker, a Russian Jew then sixty-one years old, who had been converted from assimilationism to Zionism by the Russian pogroms, had published a pamphlet entitled *Auto-Emancipation*. Written in German, it was subtitled: *An Admonition to His Brethren by a Russian Jew*. Although it consisted of only several dozen pages, it soon became one of the canonical writings of Zionism. It was an almost ruthless dissection of the Jewish problem and offered just one solution: the establishment of a Jewish state in either Palestine or North America.[15]

In 1939 Eban decided that the antics of Hitler and his Nazis gave *Auto-Emancipation* a new pertinence and so under his direction the Federation of Zionist Youth on Passover in 1939 published a new sixpenny edition of eighty-four pages, with a lengthy foreword by Eban on the conditions under which the Jews of Europe were living at the time the pamphlet was written and an even more lengthy afterword, also by Eban.

Of current anti-Semitism he wrote:

"Having proved the existence of a fire and the likelihood that oil will increase it, we must ask why anybody should desire to pour oil on the fire, which might otherwise die down. . . . The idea that patriotism and trust in human tolerance are any safeguard against anti-Semitic outbreaks has received the derisive verdict of history."

Although Eban had never been to the United States, he showed an astute knowledge of the country in his comments on Pinsker's idea that North America might be a desirable site for the Jewish homeland. The United States, Eban wrote, was one of the few places in the entire world in 1939 not blighted by persecution of Jews, and yet, "despite the eclipse of the virulent anti-Semitism of Henry Ford and the Ku Klux Klan, anti-Jewish feeling has deep social roots." But then he added that "on the whole the multiplicity of races in the United States is some guarantee against the more blatant forms of minority persecution."

And so at the age of twenty-four Aubrey Solomon Eban, author, had his first book placed in the archives of the British Museum in London and the Library of Congress in Washington, as well as on the shelves of bookshops throughout the English-reading world.

True to the spirit of English essayists, Aubrey in those days found no subject too picayune, no thought too minuscule to serve as the subject of his writings. He could even take time out from his intellectual pursuits to pen lines about the common cold. ("It is chastening to reflect how much the human character owes to a clear nasal passage.") In another letter he wrote: "The petrol rationing is paralyzing. I have a sudden passion to visit remote places which I have never thought of approaching when the oil flowed freely."

Although he was aware of his own brilliance and often made reference to his achievement of obtaining three firsts at Cambridge, he sometimes accused himself of dimwittedness, as in a letter about his trouble in attempting to learn Persian in three months—a self-imposed goal—in order to enhance his value to his country:

"You must not be hasty in acquitting me of stupidity; it descends upon me as a thick blanket and I am full of dullness at this moment." Then he blamed some of his current trouble on the Persian textbooks he was using. "The manual is somewhat laconic. 'The Queen gave the unripe apples to the servant girl' is the kind of profound thought which is presented to me. After this example of royal parsimony there comes a more cynical note: 'The asses in this country are mostly white'— an oblique reference, I fear, to the British Consulate in Teheran. The final sentence in the exercise gravely announced that 'A certain man saw a turban on the head of every horse in the lanes of that city.' I am by no means a connoisseur of equine habits, but I have a feeling that the Persian Grammar is trying to make a fool of me."

Late in October, still not having been called up for officer training, Aubrey was back in Cambridge and there on October 31 in the Union hall he and Gershon took opposite sides in a debate. Warsaw had fallen. Poland had collapsed. Germany and Russia had divided between themselves the territory of the conquered land. The French had dug in behind their Maginot Line and the Germans sat behind their own Siegfried Line waiting for orders to continue their aggression. But the subject of the debate that night in Cambridge was: "That a marriagē of love is more likely to be convenient than a marriage of convenience loving." Perhaps the Union committee thought this was a good way to take people's minds off the war.

Gershon spoke on behalf of marriages of love. As he took the floor he solemnly opened his gas mask container and pulled from it a false beard, which he slowly fastened to his chin before beginning to speak. He declared himself an incurable romanticist, praised the institution of marriage and said that "no family should be without one."

Aubrey then rose to ask the house to put aside all thought of morality and to discount the convention which supports the marriage of love. "Neither convenience nor love by itself is enough to make a marriage successful and it is absurd to expect a couple to remain bewitched by a passionate affection all their lives. There are many problems such as buns or gutter which may break an ill-considered union and convenience must be there to act as a bridle on love's rapture."

A headline in one of the newspapers the next day read:

UNION VOTES FOR LOVE:
CAMBRIDGE GOES MORAL

The paper said it was highly significant that an overwhelming majority of the audience voted in favor of a marriage of love. Of Aubrey:

"The suave Eban twists himself around a sentence in a way that no one else can. Words simply poured forth from him, but unlike others we might mention he does not make them splash and overflow all meaning."

In December Aubrey was in London working again for the Jewish Agency and in a long letter described his activities:

"Eight or nine hours of concentrated political intrigue has a very different physical effect from the same number of hours of academic work. The latter ordeal induces a restful mental glow which suffuses the entire personality and demands an outlet in some cultivated entertainment or company. The former simply paralyzes the limbs, oppresses the eyes and makes the victim a burden to himself and his fellow men, fit only to renew his faculties in sleep. I go off each morning at 9:30 and remain at the Jewish Agency for Palestine until about seven, with a couple of hours at the Colonial Office in between. And I trudge back through the thick darkness in a helpless flabby trance. This is not to say that the work is not interesting. It is a fascinating glimpse into the ethics and conduct of High Places. And occasionally, as when we deal with immigration problems, I can feel the virtue of having helped people to escape a living hell, and the certificate extorted from a cynical Colonial Office is sped on its devious route to some wretch in Dachau, and the American Consulate do their stuff. All this makes me very naively romantic, though any veteran of political practise never stops to consider the human element at all, any more than most doctors give a damn for the happiness of the living masses of protoplasm on which they work. But I once promised myself not to become 'hardboiled' or cynical before my fortieth year, which, though you may not think it, is many months ahead." (Eban was actually twenty-four and a half years old at the time.)

In another letter he said: "You will find that I am very tolerant and broadminded as long as other people share all my views."

Late in December Aubrey was spending most of his time on behalf of the Jewish Agency to get increased dependents' allowances for the wives of twenty thousand Jews serving in the British Army in Palestine.

"I am fighting this good fight single-handed, but fortified by the implied support of twenty thousand wives across the seas. The War Office asks us if we mean 'married wives'! This led me to investigate and I discovered with a shock that under Leslie's regime[16] the 'unmarried wives' of soldiers also receive his avuncular bounty."

About this time Dr. Eban decided to give up being a general practitioner and specialize in radiology. That meant he no longer had to live in the Elephant and Castle area, so he, Alida and Carmel moved to Crag-side, Mount Park, Harrow, into a much smaller house but with an extensive garden dominated by four hundred rosebushes. He moved his office to No. 81 on that street of famous doctors in London called Harley. From the new home Aubrey, homesick for Cambridge as long as no one connected with the war seemed to want his services, compared himself to "a goldfish which has fallen out of its little bowl."[17]

While continuing to wait, he concentrated his energies on helping at 77 Great Russell Street. In mid-January he wrote to Joyce: "Went with Brodetsky to interview Malcolm MacDonald and his chief minion and I've only just finished writing the official report. He has a way of sitting on his hands while talking that I find disconcerting and which goes a long way toward explaining recent disorders in Palestine, Trinidad and other outposts of Empire."[18]

6

Useful for General Purposes

"DARLING, I DON'T UNDERSTAND why you were in such a hurry to join up!" Mrs. Eban said to her son one day when he looked up from the morning mail, disappointed there was no communication from the War Office.

Patiently Aubrey tried to explain, "Everything I am now doing seems so irrelevant. Even my work for the twenty thousand married wives."

His mother smiled at his little joke. With some show of emotion he continued: "When I was a student I thought the most wonderful thing in the world would be to spend the rest of my life working at Cambridge, but nothing on earth would induce me to go back to a peaceful academic life now. Maybe someday when this whole mess is over. But not now."[1]

On January 18, 1940, a letter finally did come, on official War Office stationery.

"We propose to send you to an officer cadet training unit. . . . The training will last three or four months and then, subject to a satisfactory report, you will be commissioned. You would then be employed, if possible, in a part of the world in which your special knowledge would be useful."

The next month, on his twenty-fifth birthday, he wrote:

"It does not please me to contemplate the future year or to think of going through it thus uprooted, sundered and transformed, but it is only a minor dislocation of the times and perhaps a time will come when a man's normal avocation can be pursued without the reproach of escapism, which I feel now attaches to the academic life. Next week I become a Number; a mere mass of Potential Officer Material realizing its potentialities. *Tempora mutantur.*

"I am now in bed with rather thick but, I feel, transient flu, nibbling grapes and receiving medical visits [from his father], which I am happy to think would cost other people a tidy sum. This reflection is hastening my convalescence, for my twenty thousand wives Need Me Still."

Eight days later he wrote:

"Today I am more in favor with my stars. My voice returned this morning after an unexplained departure and I used it to phone the War Office and Tell Them All. My desertion was received with cheerful sympathy. ('Don't hurry to Aldershot. Barracks there are bloody cold, old man. The war will last a bloody long time. A couple of days won't matter. Get fit. Flu is quite bloody, isn't it?') After this incarnadined conversation, I became more settled in mind."

"Incarnadined" was an example of Aubrey's meticulous choice of uncommon words to express precise meaning. An average man could go through a whole lifetime and never have occasion to use a word meaning "to make blood-red," and unless he remembered *Macbeth* he might not even know its meaning, but Aubrey was a devotee of Shakespeare and enjoyed sprinkling his conversation and letters with Shakespeareanisms.

His father decreed he should remain a few more days at home, which he spent reading a Persian novel, Shakespeare's sonnets and the *Oxford Book of Greek Verse*. "At least," he commented, "I shall be one of the more educated corpses in the local cemetery."

Before leaving for his basic training he went to Bath to visit his sister, Ruth, who had recently given birth to a second child, a girl. Aubrey had never had intimate contact with an infant and his reaction was slightly less than enthusiastic.

"I have just endured what must be that ultimate purgatory of all uncles. I have watched The Baby Being Washed. The gurgling infant (looking less like a poached egg than most two-month-olds) was immersed in what looked comparatively like an ocean, and subjected to all the customary indignities, which she endured with a look of stolid resentment. All this time I was expected by the proud and aggressive parents to produce new superlatives to describe the occasion. A dinner gong, more sweet than symphonies, released me just in time to avoid having to Hold the Young Lady and mutter the conventional gibberish.

"Frankly I love this place [Bath] with its air of faded gentility, for it is no light thing to be able to spend a weekend in the eighteenth century. You meet people in the Pump Room who quite obviously fought with Marlborough and drove up the Crescent in a coach and pair."

Before leaving London Aubrey presided over a meeting addressed by Professor Norman de Mattos Bentwich, who for twelve years had been Attorney-General in Palestine under the Mandate and then, because of his strong Zionist feelings, resigned and became professor of international relations at Hebrew University, Jerusalem, of which he had been one of the founders. He was a popular figure in London Zionist circles, especially with the young members. A scholar himself, he had great respect for Aubrey's scholarship and boasted that he, too, had been a Cambridge man.[2]

The day after the Bentwich meeting a London friend received a letter which began:

"I have never written under more exotic circumstances. I am taking the chair at a large meeting being addressed by Prof. Norman Bentwich. I have heard this lecture four times before, so my conscience in that respect is clear. Norman thinks I am taking notes, so he spares me an occasional glance of quite exceptional benignity. . . . Norman has just said, 'In conclusion, Mr. President,' for the fifth time in half an hour."

In mid-February of 1940 Aubrey finally began his basic training, writing from Mytchett Barracks in Ash Vale, Surrey:

"I have arrived at my barracks and am writing this in active service conditions, sitting on an improvised bed, surrounded by twenty recently-inoculated privates and recuperating from a copious but not exceptionally tasty meal consisting mainly of spinach. . . . You will appreciate the difficulty of conducting private correspondence amidst community singing of 'Kiss Me Good Night, Sergeant-Major.'"

To friend Bernard Lewis he wrote:

"They have sent us to a camp for a short time to be democratized."[3]

From the temporary barracks he was transferred a few days later to the 168th Officers' Cadet Training Unit, Ramillies Barracks, Aldershot, the largest and most complete military training center in the United Kingdom.

"So I now have become a cog in a machine. Wedged in this morning between a fluent Finnish scholar and a Fellow of All Souls, I endured the ignominy of squad drill, shot at moving targets, marched six miles to Aldershot and listened to a lecture on the grim and mysterious functions of Military Intelligence officers. Thus from day to day a routine of soul-killing tedium and extreme physical activity lies ahead; the contrast after Cambridge is disconcerting."

Since childhood, words had been an obsession with Aubrey: printed words, written words, spoken words. As a reader he consumed words. As a writer and speaker he created words. One reason he relished appearing in debates and delivering lectures was that this combined writing the words and then uttering them—a double pleasure. In his Cambridge days it was not enough that he was the most articulate member of the university's most important debating society, that he was popular as a Young Zionist speaker, that his vocal services were used by the Jewish Agency and that he was a contributor to many papers and magazines as well as the editor of one of them. With all that word activity he still needed to express on paper private thoughts for which there was no other outlet. And so he wrote innumerable letters to friends. Describing his new life to Joyce, he wrote:

"We are fifteen in a small barracks room, unheated and unlighted, and reveille, which is at 6:30, initiates a very dull and bleary day. The other nuisance is that there is nowhere, except in the selfsame barracks, room in which to spend the endless hours between one phase of duty and another. Thus the mind lies fallow from day to day without stimulus of thought or the comfort of privacy and a huge unnatural gulf appears between 'here' and civilization. . . . The only thing is that hardened veterans say this way of life grows on one in time and it is the inseparable condition of becoming an officer and a gentleman."[4]

About the officer-breeding process, he reported that it was not easy in its mental impacts. "This morning, for instance, after being drilled in endless formations like chorus girls, we resumed bayonet practise. The exercise was to attack some sacks stuffed with straw and to see who could extract the maximum amount of intestines. 'Go for 'em!' yelled the sergeant. 'Imagine that 'e went out last night with yer best girl.' This was a contingency which I might well resent but which would scarcely induce me to disembowel the culprit *pour encourager les autres. . . .*"

He also commented on the "character-killing influence of uniforms." He called the impact of military life on the academic temperament "little short of a cataclysmic convulsion." Reveille at 6:30 was not easy for a man who had only recently complained about an 8 A.M. tennis game. "The atmosphere is very pukka and the general outlook and routine not unlike a public school, with a tranquil consciousness of superiority."

Gershon had not yet managed to get into the armed forces and Aubrey sent him this advice:

"If you do join up, for God's sake have some arrangement for leaving the ranks as early as possible. Few of us were nurtured to live in an environment of refuse, physical or spiritual, and such, from the little I saw of it, really is the Tommy's lot. There is no exaggeration in this. It is just that human society rarely generates an institution as absurd as the British Army and its worst rigors are worth avoiding."

One day the members of Aubrey's unit were told that for "light relief" they were to think up slogans to encourage "our hypothetical troops." His contribution was: "Private soldiers are like the braces [suspenders] of the High Command; not noticeable but quite indispensable."

This was what came to be called the Phony War period. Since the fall of Poland in late September there had been no important military activity except Russia's invasion of Finland. It was now March, six months later. Aubrey expressed the feelings of many when, coming back from "a fiendish spell of manoeuvres in a violent rain," he told in a letter how he had been speculating fiercely "on the relative atrocity of Hitlerism and the English climate and I asked myself for what are we fighting. As always when I ask myself questions I get a damned silly answer. . . ."

Writing about his relationship with the opposite sex, he said:

"My greatest sorrow is the shattering effect I have on middle-aged married women who succumb long before any offensive is contemplated, whereas those with fewer attachments and less experience regard me with the same platonic affection as one has for the Encyclopaedia Britannica—and ostensibly for the same reasons."

In another letter he wrote:

"Cambridge friends who encounter me here express wonderment at seeing me spending my days crawling through gorse and ditches at midnight in pouring rain amidst the glare of exploding dummy shells. What matters is that I share their wonderment and often imagine myself that it is all a frightful dream and I shall wake up one morning and find myself in 6 Corn Exchange Street. . . .

"I am invited to dine with the officer commanding, so I must stop. He has a young French wife whom he married after a stiff drinking bout before the Battle of the Marne, to his own and everyone else's surprise. He speaks no French and she little English. Rumour has it that they have spoken to each other only twice. They have two children."

One morning the men of Platoon 3, A Company, 168th Officers' Cadet Training Unit, Ramillies Barracks, Aldershot, were awakened when reveille was sounded at 4 A.M. instead of the usual 6:30. Later that day Aubrey described his reaction:

"I began to ask myself for what are we supposed to be fighting. Magna Carta, Habeas Corpus, the Bill of Rights and the Surbiton Drainage Act are vital bulwarks of our democratic life, but they have no meaning to a citizen who had to arise at 4, begin heavy duties, breakfast at 6:45 and march for maneuvers across half a county and back laden with impossible equipment. . . . I am now going out to a spot of parachute shooting."

One day King George VI came to Aldershot "and gazed upon our serried ranks with ill-disguised nausea. Tomorrow the Press will announce that we are a Fine Body of Men, but even more disconcerting is the fact that I left my fountain pen at home while on a weekend leave," which necessitated writing with a canteen pen, making the letter almost illegible, British canteen pens being somewhat like American post office pens.

"Tomorrow, when I recover my fountain pen I shall be able to create"— an indication that he considered these letters as something more than mere communications to friends; they were literary exercises—practice writing—an attempt to keep sharp his ability to put trenchant words on paper in an unhackneyed manner, even while undergoing what to him were the indignities of military service.

When the Germans attacked western Europe in April of 1940 and the Phony War suddenly ended, the prospect of a Nazi victory became a stark possibility. Aubrey was acutely aware of the situation's solemnity and potential tragedy, yet he took refuge in his correspondence with a few intimate friends, whom he tried to cheer by writing humorously of developments the outcome of which might affect the future of Western civilization. This was characteristic. Often in the future he would use similar devices to escape the tendency toward gloomy introspection.

"There is much excitement about events in Norway whither some of our people have departed to fight for God's frozen people."

One afternoon Aubrey's unit was sent out on a tactical maneuver, the object to ambush an enemy patrol. Instead, by accident, they "annihilated" a colonel's garden party. This reminded Aubrey of a *Punch* cartoon of Lancelot standing beside a moat overlooking turreted battlements, with hosts of knights in the rear and a messenger arriving and breathlessly announcing: "I regret to inform you, Sir, that owing to a departmental error you are besieging the wrong city."

That same month throughout England, already beginning to worry about invasion, a campaign was inaugurated to persuade the populace of the danger of even whispering bits of military intelligence, such as where sons' or husbands' regiments were stationed. At Aldershot a prize was offered for the best idea for a poster to be used in the secrecy campaign. Aubrey's suggestion was a picture of two stout and almost naked British major-generals at a Turkish bath, lying on adjacent slabs, with one saying to the other: "Strictly between ourselves, General . . ." while one of them was being massaged and slapped by Hitler and the other by Göring. An artist friend turned the idea into a poster which won the prize and was hung in battalion HQ.

Late in May of 1940 Aubrey's unit was given orders to embark for France to join the British Expeditionary Force fighting a hopeless rearguard action against the German Army, which had swept across Europe almost to the English Channel. However, just as they were to board their transport ships, the evacuation of British and Allied forces at Dunkirk began and, as Eban later put it, "there was nowhere for us to go because before we actually set out they were coming back."[5]

In June of 1940 Aubrey went to London to ask Dr. Weizmann to help him get an assignment to the Middle East. He returned to Aldershot in gloom because Weizmann told him it was hopeless; his own son was in similar difficulties "and not all the broadsides of Cabinet Ministers have availed." That same day in London he also saw Joyce, whose father was about to be made a baron, which would require that Joyce herself henceforth be addressed as "the Honorable Joyce Nathan."

From Aldershot Aubrey was transferred to the 14th Battalion, South Staffordshire Regiment, stationed at a race track in Hereford. His job would be to help train raw recruits, "a pathetic rabble in trilbies and cloth caps."

On June 20, 1940, he was commissioned as a second lieutenant. He later said, wryly:

"It is only a coincidence that this was the same week the British High Command expected an invasion of England by the German Army camped on the other side of the English Channel."[6]

After a long silence Aubrey late in July wrote to Gershon that he had been "torn away from my recruits and posted (as an Intelligence officer) to Headquarters, where in a haze of red tabs and a plethora of white clipped mustaches I make the maps before which the senior officers strike impressive poses. Now and again I leap into the camouflaged car attached to me by a hard-pressed nation, elbow the suicidal lance-corporal away from the wheel and drive around the beautiful countryside to have tea by the Wye. This is known in my reports as Detailed Reconnaissance. Now and again I take my Sergeant with me, but this makes the tea more expensive and the Reconnaissance no more Detailed. So you see, it is all becoming more magnificent and more like war."

As part of his Intelligence training Aubrey was given instructions on how to deal with German prisoners. "It is pleasant to be lecturing imaginary prisoners in German with sonorous ferocity. It inflates the ego. 'Are you Gunner Blotz von Stumpfkin?' 'Yes.' 'Then damn well stand at attention.' Nod of approval from the instructor. 'More ferocity, Lieutenant Eban, *please!*'"

One day in July (1940) he wrote:

"On Thursday I received a wooden box which looked as if it contained a lot of oranges, a present, no doubt, from some distant admirer, but which actually turned out to harbor a pigeon and an ounce of bread crumbs. This weird package came from the police, who thought that the animal (sic!) might be carrying a message of military interest. I made the Intelligence Sergeant hold the sleek and petrified bird while I tensely unrolled a piece of red paper from its leg. All it said was 'Pigeon Fanciers Club, No. 10' and in the resultant disappointment it evaded the sergeant's arrest and escaped in the general direction of Trafalgar Square. So you see, things are not dull whatever else they are."[7]

In August, still at the Hereford racecourse, Aubrey reported he had become "the butt of brigadiers, the scapegoat of Colonels and the terror of the Troops." He was spending "restless days and fevered nights tormented by phantom Colonels with outstretched hands saying: 'That looks like a good position; get Eban to appreciate the situation for us.' Or, 'Let's have a demonstration of air cooperation. Tell Eban to get an aeroplane. Don't understand these new fangled things meself.'"

Later that month he reported that his company commander, "an elderly commercial traveler with a nauseous accent, no knowledge of war, but an expert grasp of crossbow tactics . . . periodically goes to bed with gout, leaving me to command the company. Every such morning I sit in judgment while trembling privates are marched in with hats off and I dispense the awful rigours of King's Regulations, more in sorrow than in anger. Then there are maneuvers, a holy terror, for the colonel regards me as the Bright Lad of his flock and, pointing vaguely into a field of turnips, says: 'Does anything occur to you, Lieutenant Eban?' This is always an Ugly Moment as I consider whether I can pass it off with a remark about the weather or the disintegration of our Social System. Our leisure is spent in violent cricket matches between officers and sergeants, when the C.O. issues a confidential order of the day to the effect that in the interests of discipline Officers Will Win."

Reporting that his batman or orderly was one Private Nightingale, Aubrey wrote:

"When I asked him if he ever sang in Berkeley Square he merely replied:

"'No sir. I live in the Wolverhampton area. Will there be anything else?'

"He then marched off to join his batman colleagues in a discussion of officers' eccentricities. He had good material and must have been the lion of the party. Anyway, the asperities of camp life are mitigated if you have morning tea and hot water brought to you with the first gleam of dawn so I don't care a damn where he lives."

In early August Aubrey went to Oxford to attend a farewell party for his brother Raphael, now fifteen, who was about to go to the United States as part of a plan to send hundreds of thousands of British children abroad to escape the terrors of aerial bombardment and possible invasion by the Nazis.[8]

Aubrey was glad to be back in an academic atmosphere and wandered through college buildings now filled with government bureaucrats, drank chartreuse at the Randolph and had a punctured tire going home so that he arrived back at his race track camp at 4 A.M. "to the consternation of the guard, who scarcely had time to change his vilification into statutory deference." At 6 A.M. he was up again inspecting a roadblock.

Late in August Gershon was enrolled in the Royal Air Force at Blackpool and Aubrey went out on maneuvers for a week, which was an ordeal "because brigadiers never will learn to be accurate about maps and the most portentous orders go all awry. I had the function of informing one colonel all his tanks had been put out of action by his own infantry during an epic engagement. With a discretion more priceless than any valour, I . . . sent my Intelligence Sergeant to the colonel with the message, while I went forward to question hypothetical prisoners. The sergeant has a wife and children, so perhaps it was not a human thing to do. But he has a sound insurance policy and he has met brigadiers before.

"One of our officers has just got married at the third attempt. I am going into town now to help Make the Night Hideous. My batman, Private Nightingale (who, by the way, took a few days unnecessary leave last week and whom I confined to barracks for a week so that I had to do all my errands and shopping myself while he played tennis in the camp grounds) gets very sentimental about weddings and has just arrived with a glistening Sam Browne [belt] and my revolver gleaming brightly. I haven't looked but he has evidently spat upon every bullet and lavished unstinting Brasso on it."

In October, as Italian troops swept through Greece, Aubrey was sent to the most eastern point on the British Isles, Great Yarmouth. "There is nothing between me and the enemy but a narrow beach, a storm-swept sea and the vigilance of Private X, a member of my Intelligence section ensconced on a cliff in what was once a gay and lascivious holiday camp—a Solemn Thought Not To Be Contemplated Without Deep Emotion."

Discussing the possibility of a Nazi invasion, he said that if the Germans did make a landing it would undoubtedly be on the day that Private Nightingale "will have taken my gun out of its holster to clean it. But, as Private Nightingale says: 'It 'tain't no use fretting nohow, zirr. That's what I always say.' It is this serene philosophy of Britain's countless Nightingales which Helps Build Empires. (It has built only one so far, but it is a damned big one.)

"The Intelligence Sergeant has just brought me a bomb fragment. This involves a tedious ceremony for me. I stare at it solemnly for a while, wrap it up, label it and send it to Higher Quarters with the profound remark: 'The enclosed appears to be a bomb fragment.'"

During almost all of 1941 Lieutenant Eban remained at Great Yarmouth as an Intelligence officer, his days and nights concerned with "maps, summaries, appreciations, reconnaissances, sketches, charts, pillboxes, minefields, codes, ciphers, security and liaison with Navy, R.A.F., Home Guard, Merchant Navy, Observer Corps, Civil Police, Royal Engineers, Artillery and the Coast Guard." In addition he had to serve as interrogation officer whenever German airmen were shot down in the area, because the other Intelligence officers at Yarmouth knew no German, "and so all our involuntary aerial guests come home to roost on my doorstep." Among his other "exotic functions" was serving as the prosecuting officer in court-martials, a duty he said he performed "with relentless ferocity."

"I am having a fairly interesting time plotting and mapping our little Maginot Line, hurling insults at captured seamen and airmen and scouring the countryside in a staff car on dark purposes bent."[9]

One day in January of 1941 he was awarded his M.A. degree at Cambridge in a Congregation of the Senate, the proceedings entirely in Latin. In celebration he dined lavishly with friends.

Back in Yarmouth "I found a German plane in my scooter and its occupants patiently awaiting disposal. A Yarmouth skipper had shot them down last Sunday and my sergeant had rescued them from the ferocity of the Home Guard. I stopped them playing poker with our guard, relieved them of documents which were so informative they must have been planted, and went to the pictures to see *The Great Dictator*. I wrote an account of the Enemy Action but scarce was the ink dry when more Enemy Action took place."

Each letter to friends told of more raids on Aubrey's particular part of the East Anglia coast. "It is all very tedious for us to have to count the craters and the fragments, the wounded, the homeless, the direction of the plane and the wind. I only keep sane by imagining that it is all a piece of academic research, where one collates information only in order to swell the footnotes and throw dust into the eyes of the reviewer."

In March he took a camouflage course at an army school in Woking. He remembered only one quotation from the lectures: "Camouflage, gentlemen, is not so much a science; it is an attitude of mind."

He returned to Yarmouth just in time to be injured "by an unfriendly land mine which flung a door, a window and the contents of a chimney onto my recumbent form." This was followed by an attack by German planes dropping incendiaries.

In May he was sent to Bedfordshire to take two special courses entitled: "German Prisoners, Interrogation of" and "German Prisoners, Disposal of."

Describing a certain Saturday night when the British forces guarding the coast were informed the German invasion was actually going to take place within a few hours, Aubrey said:

"With his usual subtlety Hitler timed it on a day when I was Orderly Officer and Acting Adjutant. I had a hectic time at the telephone, drawing company commanders from their respective pubs and shooting them into the night. Bristling Generals then rang up to demand Intelligence reports, logs, diaries and dispatches, which I poured into the gaping hands of dispatch riders. The rest of the night was spent speaking into four telephones, drawing sketch maps by candle light and ordering Alka Seltzer for the more pickled officers. At six in the morning I was interrogating a suspected fifth columnist who turned out to be merely a drunken tramp. Then an hour's sleep, a vast breakfast and a frenzied mapping tour of road blocks.

"Life is now hard, real and earnest, an endless succession of motorcycle jaunts and much burning of midnight kerosene. As far as motorcycles are concerned, I retain an irrational prejudice in favor of those with brakes—a prejudice not shared by the battalion mechanics. . . ."

In July (1941) Aubrey's brigade departed for some distant front, but he was left behind, in the brigadier's words "for purposes of Intelligence, liaison and any general purposes for which the officer may be deemed useful." Aubrey commented:

"I am not vain but it pleases me to be deemed 'useful for General Purposes.'"[10]

He was an extremely unhappy man by now, admitting:

"I meet nobody, read only military manuals and the *New Statesman and Nation* and think practically nothing. . . . I remember no period in my life of equivalent monotony and frustration. I expect it will break out into some stupendous climax and we shall sigh for the old stagnation once again."

Writing to "Pop" Goldenberg in the summer of 1941 he said:

"The last time I saw Weizmann he promised me a generalship in a Jewish army—a distant prospect now! I still can't get GHQ to recognize me as an orientalist!" (Aubrey rarely used exclamation marks.)[11]

With the war almost two years old, he felt his services had been wasted long enough, so he went again to London to see Chaim Weizmann, who in turn went to see the Secretary of Colonies, Lord Lloyd, and said in effect:

"It's ridiculous. Here's a man who speaks Arabic, Hebrew and other oriental languages. Surely he should be of use in the Middle East."

"But the war isn't going to happen in the Middle East," Lord Lloyd replied.

Nevertheless, Dr. Weizmann's intervention was finally fruitful and late in 1941 Second Lieutenant Aubrey Solomon Eban was told that in a few days he was being shipped to Cairo, Egypt. When he was given a brief embarkation leave he met his family in Oxford, where they attended a musical play that took their minds off submarines, bombs and the fearful war that was now raging on the eastern front. Before the play, between acts and after the play, Mother Eban repeated "a hundred times, I think it must have been" how lucky he was that he was going "to a place where there is peace—to Cairo." She also remembered the way he said good-bye.

"Excuse me, darling, I want to fetch a handkerchief," he said to her, and then he walked out and was gone.[12]

On December 16, 1941, aboard a ship in convoy somewhere in the South Atlantic, Aubrey found a quiet spot on the top deck, propped up a large writing pad on his knees, took out his favorite fountain pen and began long letters to friends. He had already been at sea for several days and was finding it even more boring than being an Intelligence officer at Yarmouth, except he finally knew the British Army was going to make some use of his knowledge of oriental languages and his special talents. Yet he was restless.

"It is comfortable beyond decency, very pleasant as to weather, superb as to food, abundant even in Craven A [a British cigarette]; and I am bored to tears. I spent my first amusing day by censoring troops' letters and thus gained a glimpse of the violent and colourful intrigues which are found in such unexpected places as Bury St. Edmunds, Taunton, Hartlepool and even Winchester. Usually I subsist on the ship's library, rich enough in political biography and Wodehousiana, and on a sufficient ration of one news bulletin a day. Otherwise, not even the frenzied enthusiasms of a whist drive (officers vs nurses) have done much to derange my pleasant apathy."

Four days later, still at sea, he was promoted from second to first lieutenant, an occasion he celebrated by ordering wine for all the men at his table in the officers' dining room.

Almost five weeks later, still on the same ship, still at sea, he wrote:

"The Moslem year 1361 begins today, which must be in some way significant; in any case it gave me an excuse to order sauterne (very frappé) for our table at dinner and to invoke picturesque blessings of Allah on behalf of the astonished wine steward. You see, if you want excitements on board you have to conjure them up, for otherwise all is monotony and since January 10 anti-climax. That was the date when we left our last port where we had gone ashore for four days and I renewed strange native memories and attachments in a riot of lavish hospitality, being received in some places with incredulous hysteria, in all others with violent welcome. Welcoming convoys has become a sort of profession amongst the folk of these parts—especially the womenfolk who offered the troops all entertainment (as one of them wrote home, 'in the Fullest Sense of the Word') in unwearing succession. All was light in the evening and everything from peaches to Craven A flowed with profusion. So we put to sea again with heavy hearts. I recalled James FitzPatrick of travelogue fame whose ship is always 'reluctantly saying farewell' and for the first time I appreciated his adverb."

He was on his honor as an officer and censor not to communicate any "information of value to the enemy," which included where, precisely, he had been, where, precisely, he was and where, precisely, he was going, but he gave plenty of hints in that short paragraph. The "last port," of course, had been Cape Town, South Africa.

Just a few days before his twenty-seventh birthday he came to the land of his birth for the first time since leaving it at the age of six months. For the first time he met some of his South African relatives, among them a cousin Matthew Pamm, a Hebrew teacher who had also served as a critic on the staff of the *Cape Times*. For the first time he saw the house of his birth on Hofmyer Street in the Gardens. On a visit to the Jewish Community Center he saw hanging on the wall an enlargement of a photograph taken of his mother and father at the time of their wedding and in Jewish archives he found a record of his father's intense Zionist activity.

Walking through the business district of Cape Town, crowded with men in uniform, he suddenly saw a face he recognized. Several years ago at 77 Great Russell Street he had met the ebullient Teddy Kollek, who would one day become mayor of Jerusalem. Now he was here, looking into a shop window. After friendly greetings they discovered that although they had not been on the same ship, at least they had been in the same convoy of thirty or forty ships these past many weeks.[13]

The high point of his Cape Town experience, oddly enough, centered around a bottle of champagne—oddly because, despite his references to wine in letters to friends, he has no taste—then or later—for alcohol in any form. As his cousin told the story, at his bris one bottle of champagne had been left over and it was agreed by all present that Matthew Pamm would keep it until the celebration of Aubrey's barmitzvah, at which time the family would drink a toast to him. When news reached Cape Town that Aubrey had had his barmitzvah in London, Mr. Pamm announced he would keep the champagne "until Aubrey either visits South Africa or gets married, whichever takes place first." And so, on his first night ashore in Cape Town, the champagne, now well aged, was produced and a toast was drunk to First Lieutenant Aubrey Solomon Eban.[14]

Almost thirty years earlier, just before the start of the First World War, Aubrey's mother had come here to Cape Town by ship and the voyage had taken three dreary weeks. Now, in the middle of the Second World War, her son had come by another ship and his voyage had taken even longer—five weeks. For several years he and the other men in the convoy had been living in blacked-out places. No wonder Aubrey wrote, almost in wonderment, "all was light in the evenings." No wonder he and the thousands of other soldiers in the convoy were reluctant to put to sea again.

As they steamed up the east coast of Africa heading for the Middle East, Aubrey wrote he was looking forward to the end of the long voyage, "for despite our astonishing amenities here, I remain, at heart, a land-lubber and for those that go down to the sea in ships I maintain a distant respect. . . .

"The last time I did an honest day's work was October 13, when I explained the layout of coastal defenses to a rum-sodden naval staff officer and his solace-bearing Wren. I contemplate the vista of leisure which I have since enjoyed, ask myself what use I have made of it and feel like bursting into contrite tears. But at heart I do not regret the period of freedom and shall not soon look upon its like again"—a precisely correct prediction.

7

Where Snow Falls on Banana Trees

EVEN IN NORMAL TIMES no one ever forgets the first time he sees Cairo, although he may be just an ordinary tourist. Cairo is traversed by a river like no other in the world. It is a city with extremes of squalor and splendor that astound the sensitive. It is a place of slums, mansions, filth, vice, poverty, disease and luxury. Everywhere there is evidence of Egypt's panoramic past.

But Lieutenant Aubrey Solomon Eban was no ordinary tourist when he saw Cairo the first time. He was already an orientalist of certain distinctions, able to speak and write at least three languages used in this part of the world. Also, he was a Jew, meaning that this place to which Britain had sent him was the land from which his ancestors had fled into the desert more than three thousand years ago.

Also, these were not ordinary times. Despite catastrophic things that had been happening elsewhere in the world to the British, they still held the Middle East and Cairo was their GHQ for this entire crucial area. In the desert General Rommel's Panzer divisions were more a threat than ever. In Cairo few shared Lord Lloyd's conviction that "war isn't going to happen in the Middle East." As soon as Aubrey came ashore he learned that there was no logical reason to think the Middle East would remain, as his mother had described it, "a place where there is peace."

The war had brought great numbers of troops to the Cairo area from Britain and other Allied countries, so the city had lost its provincial Arab quality and taken on an unusually cosmopolitan character. It was a violently active, effervescent place. Because the war was never far away, there was tension and a peculiar sharpness to life.

While Cairo was the center of the Arab and Moslem world, many other cultures were represented—British, French, Italian, Greek and

Spanish. The life of the city had an extraordinary kaleidoscopic character—the multiplicity of colors, the extreme range of sounds, the interplay of ideas, the human pathos of people trying to pursue normality and enjoyment during a war, with its volcanic atmosphere. No one who lived in Cairo between 1940 and 1945 would be likely to forget it or regard the experience as humdrum or banal.

Aubrey felt himself fortunate to be in a place where he could put to use his years of oriental studies and penetrate the outer surface of a world so much different than he and most of his military colleagues had ever known. Also, Palestine was not far away and because Cairo was an open society Jews like Weizmann, Shertok and Ben-Gurion could come to Cairo without difficulty, and often did.

Before he could get used to being on land again, before he could do much touring, before he had even seen his first pyramid, Lieutenant Eban was put to work as a censor handling letters in Arabic and deciding what certain Arabic newspapers could and could not publish. It was a routine job which became boring after a few days. The air letters soldiers and officers were permitted to send abroad provided a space only $3\frac{1}{2} \times 3\frac{1}{2}$ inches for the message. Aubrey found that even if he used an unusually fine pen and crowded his words very closely together he could get a maximum of only a hundred and sixty-six words into the allotted space, which provided little scope for his literary talents.

But being in Cairo enabled him to become acquainted with many figures in Egypt's literary and political world, so his months in the capital city were not wasted. Using his knowledge of written Arabic during the day on behalf of His Majesty's Government, he exercised his spoken Arabic evenings by accepting invitations to address various gatherings of Arabs. One such meeting was of scholars studying at the world-famous Al-Azhar, both a mosque and a university and at this time close to a thousand years old. In the chair was Dr. Taha Hussein, a blind novelist regarded by Egyptians as one of the greatest Arabic writers of the day. After the young British officer had delivered a lengthy address in the native language of his auditors, Dr. Hussein congratulated him, first on his polished Arabic, then on the brilliance of the thoughts he had expressed.[1]

(Egyptians who introduced him glowingly to local audiences were probably kept busy years later—after the creation of Israel and after the Egyptian revolution—explaining to Nasser that they didn't really mean it.)

About the time of Aubrey's arrival in Cairo the British were forced to surrender their great naval base at Singapore to the Japanese. Three weeks later Rangoon was abandoned. By this time the Japanese were masters of all Southeast Asia except Upper Burma. In the hope that Orde Wingate could help stabilize the Burma front, the British Army ordered him to go with all possible haste to the Far East and organize a guerrilla force to harass the enemy. On the way, for some reason never explained, he was held up in Cairo for two weeks.[2] He was staying at Shepheard's Hotel and one day in the lobby he and Aubrey literally bumped into each other. Aubrey reminded "the Friend," as Wingate was called by Zionists, that they had met in London through Weizmann and then asked:

"Can I come around and see you sometime?"

First Wingate looked at his watch, but said nothing. Then he whipped out a small datebook, flipped a few pages and asked:

"What about two o'clock tomorrow morning?"

Whereupon Lieutenant Eban whipped out an almost identical pocket diary, flipped a few pages and replied:

"Yes, I just happen to be free at that time."

Promptly at 2 A.M. (contrary to a reputation of never being punctual) Eban knocked on the door of Wingate's suite at Shepheard's. The man who had recently played such a vital role in the defeat of the Italians in Ethiopia shouted:

"Enter!"

He was lying on his back, completely naked, brushing his stomach with a large, long-handled, stiff-bristled brush.

"Do you know why I do this?" he asked. Without waiting for a reply he delivered a long monologue on how it benefits a man to curry his own hide.

"Did you ever stop to realize why horses have such fine skins? Of course you didn't. It's because they are brushed so frequently with stiff brushes. Just like this one."

Then he reached for a book on his bedside table and began reading to Lieutenant Eban the Prophecies, arguing that the curse would eventually descend on British officials in Palestine as punishment for what they had done to the Jews. Next, he gave his guest some advice about how the Middle East problem should be handled militarily.

"He was just too militant to be realistic," Eban later said, in recounting the visit.

Before Aubrey left, Wingate gave him a lecture on how to avoid dysentery and loaned him a bottle of pills which he said would solve the problem when it arose, asking that he return "those for which you have no need."

Also, in a discussion of other matters, he disclosed that he never did up certain vital buttons (this being before the age of the zipper) "because of the time it wastes during a busy day."[3]

Several times during the early months of 1942 Aubrey used the expression "so near and yet so far" in letters and conversations to describe how he felt about being a Zionist, getting as far as the Middle East and still not seeing the Promised Land. In the time of Moses the Egyptian Pharaoh had given the Israelites permission to leave the country. Now, although it was little more than an hour from Cairo to Jerusalem, even by slow military plane, Aubrey for weeks was unable to get "orders" or even permission to make the trip. The frustration depressed him. Finally he wrote a moving letter to his friend Shertok saying "like our illustrious forefather, Moses, I am within sight of the Promised Land yet am unable to get there; can't you do something about it?"[4]

In reply he received a visit from Reuven S. Zaslani,[5] who often had visited the Eban home in London with Shertok and was an intimate friend of the family. Now he was the Jewish Agency official in charge of relations with the Intelligence services of the Allied powers.

Zaslani recounted the current Middle Eastern military situation. For months the British had been fighting a seesaw campaign against the Germans and Italians in North Africa, taking and losing ground. But now the Afrika Korps of General Rommel, nicknamed the "Desert Fox," had mounted a powerful offensive. They had captured Tobruk in Libya and were moving toward Egypt.[6] Unless they were stopped, anything could happen. Egypt might be occupied and then the Nazis would probably turn northward. In this eventuality nothing could stop the combined Nazi and Italian divisions from sweeping through Palestine on their way toward Syria and Turkey. But perhaps, with the help of the inhabitants of Palestine, the enemy advance could be at least slowed down. Or, if the drive succeeded, the invaders could be harassed during their occupation by guerrilla-like activity, and if the day ever came when the British could mount a counterattack, the enemy might be obstructed in their retreat.

As Zaslani talked, Eban, listening intently, wondered what this could possibly have to do with him, a mere lieutenant, a censor. Apparently seeing this perplexity Zaslani finally came to the point. Under the regulations established by Britain, as the mandatory power, Palestinians were not supposed to be armed. Yet in the early 1920s the Jewish settlers had organized a secret underground army called Haganah (Defense), motivated by the inadequacy of the protection given them by the British administration and out of a determination to entrust their security to their own volunteer organization.[7]

After the 1929 riots and in reply to the British policy of appeasing the Arabs, intensive efforts were made to strengthen Haganah, and again during the 1936–39 Arab disturbances. Wingate had been responsible for encouraging self-defense by helping the Jews of Palestine establish what were called night squads.[8] The policy of Britain was to treat all such activity as illegal and determined efforts were made to destroy Haganah. Whenever possible its caches of arms were ferreted out and seized and any Palestinian Jew found in possession of weapons was arrested and jailed. But now Britain had potent reasons for wishing the Palestinians to be armed. Rather than have the mandatory power reverse its entire policy, the British decided to operate not only independently of the mandatory officials but actually behind their backs. And that was the purpose of Zaslani's visit.

"What does this have to do with me?" Eban asked.

Zaslani smiled. "I am speaking for Moshe Shertok and the Jewish Agency as well as British Intelligence. We are about to open secret headquarters in Jerusalem from which a select group of British officers will assist young Palestinian Jews in the organization of an underground striking force. It will be part of Haganah. Its members will undergo special training in sabotage and other commandolike activity behind enemy lines. Of course it will be illegal vis-à-vis the British mandatory government. It will be directed from GHQ here in Cairo. The man in charge is a certain Wing Commander D. I have already spoken with him and recommended you as the liaison officer between the British Army and the Jewish settlers whom we will be training. I am sure you are the perfect man for the job, because you have the complete confidence of the Jewish Agency, which is important. Does it interest you?"

Eban, thinking of his routine task of censoring Arab mail and newspapers, replied quickly in the affirmative. Zaslani jumped to his feet and put a hand on the younger man's shoulder.

"Marvelous! Wonderful! This is the business!"

The next morning at ten o'clock Zaslani took Eban to headquarters to see Wing Commander D and make specific arrangements, but the Wing Commander—even though it was only ten o'clock—was already in such a euphoric, alcohol-induced state that he seemed hardly aware there was a war on, so they left with their mission unaccomplished.

"This was symptomatic of Cairo at that time," Eban said later, recalling the incident. "Whiskey flowed like water and it took clever planning to arrange to see certain people during their brief daily periods of total sobriety."

It reminded Eban of one of his favorite stories—how Winston Churchill once said to Lady Astor, "Madam, you are very ugly," to which she replied in anger, "Mr. Churchill, you are very drunk!" To which he replied, "Ah yes, madam, but tomorrow I shall be *sober!*"

The next day Wing Commander D did happen to be sober when Zaslani and Eban appeared at his office at an early hour, and arrangements were made for Eban's immediate transfer to Jerusalem.[9]

And so in February of 1940 Abba Solomon Eban came to the Promised Land. Since he first learned to read he had been studying about it. Since he had been able to talk he had been talking about it. Since he had been able to write he had been writing about it. As a Zionist he had been working from the time he was a boy in short trousers for the eventual re-creation of Israel as a sovereign state. Now he was here as an officer in the army of the country that lately had been making so many difficulties for Zionists, and his job was going to be to help arm Jews, secretly, against that even greater enemy, the Third Reich.

One of the first Jewish towns Eban saw from the train was Rehovoth, where Weizmann had stood in 1917 during another war and had declared to General Allenby that someday he would make his home there, in what was then a sandy wasteland. The young lieutenant was unaware that in just a few years Rehovoth would become his own home place. Staring from the train window he saw for the first time Jewish farmers working in the fields. The road through the Rehovoth orange groves was lined with trees he knew had been planted by Jews. The perfume of the orange blossoms was heavy and heady. War was not many hundreds of miles away, but Eban was impressed with this idyllic Judean scene. The western approach to the Holy City was not yet scarred by ugly housing developments. The few buildings, all of Jerusalem stone, seemed as if they belonged to the landscape.

There were dozens of people in Palestine Eban was eager to see. He even had a relative by marriage here. But the first name that flashed across his mind was that of Berl Katznelson, "because," as he later explained, "he had that sort of hold on people, so it seemed the natural thing for me to try to find him immediately." After reporting to British

Army Headquarters he took a car to Tel Aviv and found his old friend in his small, rather cluttered office at the *Davar* newspaper plant on Allenby Road, almost inundated by books and papers. Katznelson greeted him cordially and suggested they go together to see Ben-Gurion.

Aubrey, as long-legged as he was, had difficulty keeping up with Katznelson as they strode down Allenby Road to Keren Keyemeth Street, where Ben-Gurion lived. As chairman of the Zionist Executive and the Jewish Agency Executive, Ben-Gurion was the No. 1 man of the Jewish community of Palestine, a demanding task in those days of war and crisis. But he pushed the books on his desk aside and sat for a long time talking with his two guests. That night Aubrey wrote his mother about his first meeting with Ben-Gurion. She replied by telling him the story of why he had not met Ben-Gurion in London, adding:

"I hope he was impressed!"[10]

In Jerusalem the first person Aubrey went to see was Annie Landau, the grande dame of the Jewish community, a sister of Dr. Elsie Sacks, wife of Aubrey's Uncle Sam. In 1897, although she was then only twenty-two years old, she had been offered a post as headmistress of a school in Jerusalem endowed by the French branch of the Rothschild family, the Evelyna de Rothschild School for Girls, a position she had held for more than forty years. She was almost violent in her religious orthodoxy, but was extremely anti-Zionist, contending that Zionists were modernist intruders; too secular; too political. For years Annie Landau had had as her faithful servant and bodyguard an Arab who had made the pilgrimage to Mecca and therefore was entitled to be called *Hagi*, which everyone at the school used as a nickname for him. He always referred to his mistress as the "Queen of Sheba." Miss Landau not only had made her school one of the best in the Middle East, but had become known as Jerusalem's most delightful hostess. Entertaining became her avocation and during the war she gave larger and more frequent social gatherings than ever because there were now so many young Jews from abroad in the British forces in Palestine. Her door was always open for Aubrey and he especially remembered the Seder nights at her table, but she never got over being disappointed by his strong Zionist emotions and connections.[11]

The secret organization to which Lieutenant Eban was now attached was officially known as Subversive Operations Two and was under MI. Its headquarters were in a nondescript house in the Tabiyeh section of Jerusalem, not far from where, a quarter of a century later, Eban would live as Minister of Foreign Affairs. The house was called Bet Malluf, after the name of its owner. The British officer in charge was Major Antony Webb, who later became Chief Justice in one of Britain's African colonies. The camp in which the young Jews would be trained for their commando-type work was in a wooded area in the Valley of Jezreel, close to the kibbutz Mishmar Ha-Emek, which had suffered heavy attacks by Arab bands in the disturbances of 1929 and 1936 and therefore was acutely defense-conscious.[12]

There were no ranks among these underground soldiers, but the commanding officer was Yitshak Sadeh, a white-haired, white-bearded man of fifty-two with a personality that made him loved by everyone. He had fought with the Bolsheviks during the Russian Revolution and had helped Trumpeldor found the Russian He-Halutz movement. The young people had strong feelings for "the Old Man," as they called him, respecting him as a father and teacher. He interspersed military instruction with talk of literature, the theater, the humanities and Socialism, and he taught that war is not an end in itself; that after the fighting it would be necessary to build a new society in which there would be no place for such barbarity.[13]

Palmach is an abbreviation of the Hebrew words *peluggpt machatz*, meaning "shock companies." This was the name by which the secret force came to be known. The British Army agreed that Palmach could consist of five hundred men and it is true that at any given moment there were no more than five hundred undergoing training at Mishmar Ha-Emek, but what the British High Command did not know was that Haganah kept rotating the men; those who were there today might not be at all the same five hundred men who had been in training two weeks ago. Some sympathetic British officers knew what was happening, but there was only one man who had the exact figures—Lieutenant Aubrey Eban—for in his capacity as the chief British staff officer he had the only list of names, which he never let out of his possession. Before it was over approximately seven thousand Jews had received training in sniping, parachuting, the use of explosives, sabotage and general guerrilla tactics, all at the expense of the British taxpayer. It was only a few years later that these same men were using this training in the struggle against the British, trying to persuade them to give up their Mandate and leave Palestine to its indigenous people, the Arabs and the Jews.[14] Everyone was playing tricks on everyone else. But the strangest of all was the relationship between the British Army and the British mandatory power.

Officially Eban's assignment was to serve as liaison between the Jews of Palestine, as represented by the Jewish Agency, and the British Army.

In actual practice he had a thousand strange jobs in connection with the training of parachutists and saboteurs. Whether anyone connected with the mandatory government knew what was going on, it was a dour fact that almost every day members of Palmach would be picked up by officers of the mandatory government, thrown into jail and charged with illegal possession of explosives or firearms. As soon as this happened word was flashed to Bet Malluf and Eban would go into action.

"I spent a lot of my time running around the country in a white Plymouth convertible supplied to me by my generous employers, which looked like an appendage of some slick Robert Taylor. My principal task was getting people out of jail. It was not always easy, even though the jailors were British and I was British, and even though I was always armed with masses of official papers with red seals and very official looking signatures."[15]

Another problem, from the British point of view, was that the Palmach trainees became so enthusiastic they wanted to put their learning into practice without waiting for the arrival of the Nazis. Eban invented two words to describe the process.

"They all became Wingated or Wingate-ized, and then they infected others with it. It is a process that people go through in this part of the world. I found then—and I have found since—that Israel arouses every possible emotion except apathy."[16]

The training was varied, intensive and extensive. Under British direction the trainees actually drilled holes in the bases of most of the country's bridges so that when and if the Nazis approached, explosives could be quickly inserted and the bridges blown. They were taught how to get to and from various parts of the country without using highways or roads. Groups of German-speaking Jews learned how to penetrate German prisoner-of-war camps and Italian-speaking Jews to get into Italian camps. (There were already some such camps in various parts of North Africa.) As the training became more sophisticated, Palmach established a line of secret radio sending and receiving stations in various kibbutzim.

The longer the training went on the greater the problems for young Eban. Palmach needed an automobile, but Palmach couldn't buy one without a license issued by the mandatory government and Palmach couldn't possibly apply to the mandatory government for a license because the mandatory government wasn't supposed to know that Palmach existed. Palmach needed petrol, but Palmach couldn't buy petrol without a license issued by . . . etc., etc. Permits. Licenses. Whatever anyone needed they expected Staff Officer Eban to produce. He was the liaison. He was the one trusted by both sides.[17]

One of Eban's associates in the secret project was Captain Grant Taylor, an expert in sniping, whose task was to teach marksmanship to the trainees. He was a man of no modesty and what he liked to boast about best was his skill with firearms. One night he and Eban were sitting in a sidewalk café in Haifa when suddenly he said:

"Do you think I could put out the candle on that table over there?" and he pointed to a table twenty feet away.

Eban, suspecting what was about to happen, tried to assure Captain Taylor that such a demonstration of skill was quite unnecessary, but Captain Taylor whipped his service revolver from its holster, took casual aim and suddenly the candle went out.

"He never missed anything! It gave me a strange feeling of insecurity."[18]

One of the young Palmachniks who received secret training and whom Eban often saw on his visits to Mishmar Ha-Emek was Yigal Paikovitch, whose grandparents had been among the founders of Rosh Pinna, the first Jewish settlement in Upper Galilee, and who himself just a few years earlier had helped found Kibbutz Genessar. After the creation of the State of Israel Paikovitch changed his name to Yigal Allon and in the War of 1948–49 as commander of the Palmach liberated the Negev and became an almost legendary figure.[19]

In Jerusalem Eban's path crossed that of his friend Teddy Kollek, whom he had seen a short time ago by chance in Cape Town. Kollek was also involved in arming and training the underground army, but from the Jewish side. Kollek and his Palestinian associates were extremely jealous of the unlimited funds and supplies—including various forms of alcohol—available to the Subversive Operations people.

"Once we saw two great army lorries from Egypt roll up outside the house in Tobiyeh," Kollek reminisced, "and of course we presumed it was secret documents of some kind. Actually the lorries were loaded with nothing but regimental whiskey and gin."[20]

Writing about his travels around Palestine, Aubrey said in a letter:

"We have seen farm settlements and heard a sturdy Jewish yeoman proclaim simply, 'We breed day and night,' a reference to the efficiently collectivized cows with Hebrew names who produce endless milk under the auspices of the Labor Federation Group B."[21]

Quite unexpectedly—as are most happenings during a war—Aubrey received a visit from his cousin, Neville Halper, who as a boy had often conspired with Ruth to disrupt his weekend studies with Grandfather Sacks. Neville was also a lieutenant in the British Army, in an armored brigade stationed in Iran, and had come to Jerusalem on leave.

"All I ever remembered about our visit," he later said, "was that Cousin Aubrey was spending his spare time studying Turkish, because he said he had a hunch the Turks would be in the war before it was over and it might be helpful if he knew their language."[22]

In July (1942) the British finally stopped the Germans in the Battle of El Alamein and the threat to Palestine seemed a little less imminent, but there was no letup in the secret training during the rest of the summer and early fall, and so those connected with Subversive Operations were still not able to relax.

In the fall of 1942 Eban's letters to friends were headed:

CAPTAIN A. S. EBAN
G.S.I. (J)
Palestine Base

To one he wrote:

"Here I am belatedly but retrospectively (and as yet unsubstantively and provisionally) exalted. I believe that it was done in deference to my conveyance which always carried me with an aggrieved air, as though I was beneath its station. Now the proprieties are appeased."

Almost anyone else would have written:

"I have just been promoted to captain. I am sure my white convertible is happy."

In Jerusalem he made a new friend. Nelson Glueck[23] was fifteen years his senior, a rabbi, an archeologist and an American. Because he was also an intellectual Jew, a Zionist and a scholar and had a keen sense of humor he and Eban had much in common. His wife, Helen, was a medical doctor who later became a professor of internal medicine at the University of Cincinnati, the fourth generation of medical doctors.

Nelson Glueck had come to Palestine first in 1932 as director of the American School of Oriental Research to survey archeological sites in Trans-Jordan and other parts of ancient Palestine.[24] From 1936 until 1940 he was back again digging, exploring, writing. Now he was here for a third tour of archeological duty. He and his wife lived at the American School of Oriental Research, which was in a closed compound just outside Herod's Gate, near the St. George Cathedral, on the east side of the Dominican church. Aubrey often went there for an evening of talk with the Gluecks. Sometimes Nelson would be off on an archeological trip across the Jordan River and when he came back would recount to his wife and Aubrey his adventures. One tale he told them Aubrey never forgot.

"My Arab servant and I were getting ready to pitch camp one night on the desert when he reminded me I had not yet paid my respects to the chief of the Bedouin tribe in that area. I knew this was the custom—that it would be a serious breach of desert etiquette not to do so—but we had had a rough day and I was tired so I continued putting up our tents. When my servant persisted in his argument I pointed out that if we went now to the chief he would insist we spend the night in his tent and that would be more than I could bear, because there was no longer on my body room for a single additional fleabite. So we went to sleep in our own tents, but before long my servant awakened me. Without uttering a word, he raised the flap of the tent and pointed. Out there in the moonlight, completely surrounding us, were at least a hundred Bedouin tribesmen. There was nothing to do but try to go back to sleep. As soon as it was dawn they took us to their chief. It required a great deal of time, the drinking of a great many cups of black coffee and a great deal of apologizing before we were forgiven and permitted to go our way."

Tennis was another mutual bond. There was a good court in the school compound on which Eban and Glueck played together several times a week. They made it almost a ceremony. Two or three sets, then they would go to the Glueck house, where Helen would serve them a large pitcher of fresh orange juice, followed by tea and cakes.

"I played atrocious tennis," Glueck later explained, "but I always managed to beat Aubrey."

"I go further than that," Helen Glueck said. "My husband was the second worst tennis player in the Middle East. The worst was Aubrey Eban. Maybe it was because in those days he was quite clumsy—not just on the tennis court but anywhere, everywhere. I have never forgotten the day in our home when he broke one of my best teacups. But Nelson and I were both fond of him and we encouraged him to come and see us as often as he could."

The two men also had in common the language of the Arabs. Aubrey by now was a master of classical Arabic, whereas Glueck was fluent in the current jargon of the desert, so they had many conversations about grammar, vocabulary and the idioms of the tribesmen. They would often exchange stories about their travels around the country. To all appearances Glueck was carrying on his archeological researches as if there were no war. He spent much time with the desert people, who were well aware he was an American, but it apparently never occurred to them that he was also a Jew.

Close friends as they became, the two men never discussed their real work. After Glueck's death in 1970 newspapers published for the first time the fact that from 1942 until 1945 he was a field agent for the Office of Strategic Services of the United States Government (OSS), the secret intelligence agency of the country during World War II, headed by William J. Donovan and entrusted with gathering and analyzing information and conducting psychological and guerrilla warfare until succeeded by the CIA in 1947. Using his archeological explorations as a cover, Glueck established links with the Arabs of many Middle Eastern countries, who liked him as a person, respected his courage and endurance and supplied him with information of wartime value.

Aubrey knew all this intuitively, but during their long and intimate relationship he never asked Glueck an embarrassing question. Contrawise, the archeologist was aware of what Aubrey was doing, but he, too, kept out of that pigeonhole. Instead they would discuss Middle Eastern history, oriental languages and how foolish the West had been in this part of the world—for example, trying to teach the Arabs Shakespeare, a subject as remote from their consciousness and their interests as lunar exploration.

Glueck several times went to gatherings at which Eban spoke and, a professional speaker himself, acquired admiration of the younger man's platform ability.

"In later years I felt he was even above Churchill in cadence and perfection of delivery."[25]

On several occasions Glueck took Eban with him on his travels into Trans-Jordan. Late in October (1942) they went together to Jerash in the north of Trans-Jordan and ate sheep in a Circassian village, in the shadow of what Aubrey called "the most perfect Roman theater ever conceived and preserved."

One afternoon at a tea party in Talpiot at the home of a medical doctor named Kleeberg, Aubrey met an Egyptain Jew from Ismailia, Simcha Ambache, to whom he took a liking. Ambache had been born in Palestine, had gone to an engineering school in France and immediately upon graduation had been appointed manager of a power plant on the Suez Canal at Ismailia. Dr. Kleeberg had been the family physician and was credited with saving the life of Mrs. Ambache during a critical illness. The husband and the doctor thus became good friends and after Dr. Kleeberg moved to Jerusalem Mr. Ambache visited him frequently.

During their brief conversation Mr. Ambache mentioned to Aubrey that he had sent his wife and three daughters to South Africa when it seemed possible that Rommel's army would sweep across all of Egypt. He told wistfully how much he missed them, but he added: "C'est la guerre! I hope it will soon be over." While his family was away he was living in a house in Cairo belonging to an uncle of Aubrey's university friend Eileen Alexander. Also, Aubrey had known Mr. Ambache's son, Nachum, at Cambridge.[26]

Aubrey's friends and relatives abroad were being kept totally in the dark about what he was doing in his travels through Palestine. In one enigmatic letter he wrote:

"I go around in feverish quests of conciliation up and down the country and try to infuse sweet and lightness where it is lacking, which is practically everywhere." Which could have meant anything.

The British Council was a semi-official government body organized to spread British ideas and culture throughout the world. (Britain's enemies looked upon it as a cover for an international network of spies and propagandists. The truth was somewhere halfway between.) In the fall of 1942 the British Council in Jerusalem asked Captain Eban to deliver three lectures during its winter series. It was a compliment, since the other speakers were much older men, with more important titles, ranks and positions. Aubrey accepted.

The talks were delivered in the auditorium of the YMCA, across the street from the King David Hotel. The first, entitled "British Foreign Policy and the War," was delivered on the evening of November 19 (1942) before a large audience of British military men and civilians, and many Palestinians, a majority Jews.

Aubrey began by confessing he had been apprehensive about accepting the invitation to deliver three lectures in rapid sequence "lest the stoicism and endurance of Jerusalem's citizens might be tempted too far." When he found himself wedged in, on the lecture series, between an Oxford don and British Attorney-General, he suddenly felt like "the humble and inadequate interior of an otherwise illustrious sandwich." As for trying to be objective about British foreign policy, he said it reminded him "of an absent-minded judge, summing up a case between prosecution and defense, who said: 'I have tried to be scrupulously fair, avoiding partiality on the one hand and impartiality on the other.'"

Speaking of Hitler, he said he had once heard him described as a self-made man. "If we accept this estimate we can only ponder mournfully on the melancholy results of unskilled labor."

Then he became serious as he discussed the controversy in England over "whether Naziism is an ingrained and ineradicable mood in German life." He told how the Vansittart camp in England considered that Hitlerism "is but the latest manifestation of a deep-rooted trait in the German character; that German history is a long series of aggressions . . . that Germans, whatever their other qualities, have this in common—that they have continually and copiously killed their neighbors. . . . A single lineage of violence joins Charlemagne to Barbarossa to Frederick the Great to Bismarck to Wilhelm II to Hitler and unless we make ruthlessly certain that the power is taken from her hands, Germany will generate another Fuehrer in the same grim and grisly line. . . . You cannot allow freedom to German industry, German opinion, German institutions; for her industry will generate a wartime apparatus, her opinion will breed a hideous spawn of fanatical self-assertion, her institutions will merge into a Brown House."

A few minutes later he was giving the arguments of the opposition: that you cannot indict a whole country; that every nation, including Germany, is liable to aggressive as well as peaceful impulses; that if the violent theme has predominated in German life its predominance can be traced to specific political and economical factors; and that "if these factors are eliminated, as they can easily be, the aggressive mood which is their consequence will pass away."

Then he presented his own opinion.

"When your symphonies or lyrics, your South German *Gemütlichkeit*, your science, your art, your letters, your technical genius begin to prevent Germans from killing their neighbors—then and only then can you begin to reckon them as political factors and count them as political influences. Until then not."

It was an address in which he perfectly balanced erudition and serious discussion of current and future issues with frequent light touches. For example:

"I remember the day when we were not allowed to define this as a war against Germany at all. A distinction was made between Naziism, the author of the war, and the German people, its unwitting victims. Our inadequate flotillas sallied forth over German cities expounding this theme in leaflets of turgid prose. The story was told of a pilot returning from one of these raids who was asked how he had delivered his cargo. He replied that he had made up one great bundle and thrown it overboard. His commander winced and said: 'You fool, you might have hurt somebody!' The gulf between that spirit and the spirit of the thousand-bomber raids is a gulf of outlook as well as of strategy."

His own solution of what to do with Germany after her defeat was: "Either go all out to make the Germans friendly; then if they are strong their strength will be no threat; or go all out to make them powerless; then if they are hostile their hostility can have no practical effect. One or the other. Do not fall between the two stools."[27]

As soon as the meeting was adjourned he was surrounded by congratulatory fans, some even asking for his autograph. A few days later he wrote his reactions to a friend:

"I have been doing propaganda as a sideline and had a successful show last week when the Chief Secretary, the Attorney-General, the Chief Justice, the Mayor and Counselors attended a lecture I gave to six hundred people in the town. You get such a mixed and at the same time selective sort of audience here that the psychological kick of holding forth is vastly greater than usual."

Several days later he drove his white convertible to the north of the country on official business. Coming back late at night he ran into a torrential rainstorm while traversing a ravine between Janin and Nablus. His windshield wipers were broken so he pulled to the side of the road and spent the night stretched out on the back seat, shivering, as he listened to the howling of jackals and wondered if the silent Arabs who slithered past through the rain were smugglers or spies for the enemy. Telling about it later he said:

"I had a better opportunity that night than ever before to contemplate the Eternal Verities."

Despite the war and his manifold duties, Aubrey found time during the winter of 1942–43 for a busy social and cultural life. He went to most of the symphony concerts and the theatrical performances of Habimah in Tel Aviv. He also attended dedication ceremonies on Mount Scopus for a new Hebrew University building and became friendly with the president, Dr. Judah Leon Magnes, former Reform rabbi from Brooklyn and advocate of a bi-national Jewish and Arab commonwealth in Palestine. He spent what he called "a memorable weekend" at Rehovoth, where he saw for the first time the Daniel Sieff Research Institute, founded eight years earlier by Baron Israel Moses Sieff, British Zionist, which after the war would grow into the Weizmann Institute and of which Eban himself would someday be president. He was deeply impressed by Rehovoth, describing it as "surely the world's greenest place, surrounded by orange groves and eucalyptus trees and now white buildings."

Summing up his experiences during his first year in the Middle East, he said:

"It was an absolute stroke of luck getting to the only really civilized portion of the Middle East, though it was not entirely fortuitous or without direction on my part."

Having the rank of captain in the British Army carried with it certain social obligations, which meant that Aubrey began to develop a new side of his personality.

"Since I have become a political officer I have learned what a perfunctory social world really is. The first time you cut an engagement it becomes significant."

On December 17 (1942) he did his second British Council lecture, with Lord Oxford and Asquith as the chairman of the meeting. His subject was "British Home Policy and the War." There were many smiles when he declared that the *Times* (of London) is so cautious in its judgment of events that "if the *Times* were published the day after the creation of the world, that event would be recorded under a small heading reading: A HOPEFUL EVENT, and the first sentence would begin: 'While it would be as yet premature to foresee the full consequences of this event . . .'" He used one word unknown to his audience and to Webster when he said:

"It is no mean society which, in the grapply of war, can maintain its essential liberties intact and even extend them into new fields of human activity."

On February 18 (1943) the audience of his third lecture, on "Controversies on Post-War Reconstruction," was larger than on the two previous occasions but what made him more nervous than heretofore was noticing that the British High Commissioner was in one of the front rows, a fact he tried to ignore as he began:

"In the task that now confronts me I am sustained by the example of the acrobat who introduced the most violent and perilous of his contortions with the poignant words. 'My next trick is impossible.'

"To foretell the future with an air of certainty you must have one of two qualifications: either you must be clairvoyant or you must be Mr. H. G. Wells. Those of us who have long ago despaired of ever attaining either of these two felicities must resign ourselves to mere conjecture and confess our limitations in advance."

He reviewed how, over the past four hundred years, every time

Europe had been plagued by war there was always thereafter a great surge of aspiration toward a stable international order and he predicted that the end of World War II would see the most ambitious scheme so far to create a world government. Another prediction that eventually came true:

"The Nazi collapse will leave a vacuum, abhorrent to nature, and there will be no alternative to many years of Allied occupation."

Speaking of the inherent British desire of detachment—to exist economically without Europe—he said:

"One of the very few points of resemblance between the British Foreign Office and Miss Greta Garbo has been their profound desire to be alone; and the manner in which that desire has been frustrated by constant intrusion."

He declared that English businessmen were already beginning to worry about Britain's export trade after the war and added:

"Businessmen are usually realists, if only because they tend to go out of business the day after they lose touch with reality."

What the newspapers the next day quoted from his address, however, was his peroration:

"People interested in having gardens buy themselves packets of seed with the picture of the green flower emblazoned on the label. To the logic Gallic or Teutonic mind this can convey only one thing—the prospect that, all things equal, the seed will burgeon into a flower somewhat resembling the picture on the label. Otherwise the whole thing is insane. According to English humor, however, no such possibility whatsoever exists. There are only two possibilities. Either, as is most probable, nothing will grow at all and the sweat of toiling brows will peter out in mockery and disillusion; or something will grow, completely different and hopelessly inferior to that which was designed and planned. I commend that skepticism to you with which to temper any exaggerated hopes that I may have fostered here [about postwar reconstruction and international cooperation]."[28]

The United States Consul-General in Jerusalem apparently was in Eban's audience that night and was so impressed that when Goldberg's Press, Jerusalem, turned out a limited number of printed copies of the full text he procured one and dispatched it to Washington with a request that it be placed in the archives of the Library of Congress.[29]

The three British Council addresses were an indication of the maturity and political wisdom Eban had acquired since leaving Cambridge. They disclosed a sound grasp of subjects far removed from the area of his chief interest: orientalism and Zionism. In them he dealt with economic matters like an economist; with British internal problems like a member of the British Parliament; with Europe's past mistakes like a profound historian; with foreign policy like a diplomat. The British High Commissioner was not the only one impressed. Also, for the first time in his life he received a considerable amount of fan mail. One letter amused him. It was from what he called "a Teutonic interrogator" and asked, apropos his reference to Greta Garbo, "What means please the Garbo politic and is it perhaps to do with Machiavelli?"

February was full of minor disasters. One dark night in a blinding rainstorm he ran out of gasoline far from any town and finally reached, on foot, a settlement where he borrowed a horse to get to the nearest filling station—miles away. Several days later he was evicted from his living quarters. Miss Landau came to his rescue and gave him a pied-à-terre at the Rothschild School. That same week a thief stole his beautiful white convertible. It was found abandoned the next day, all four tires missing. But February was also the month of a skiing trip into the mountains of Lebanon, which reminded Aubrey of Switzerland, except for lack of decent accommodations. There was even snow in Jerusalem that month, which led him to observe that snow on a banana tree is a sight worth a trip all the way to the Mid-East.

By the spring of 1943 the Allied troops under Lieutenant General Dwight D. Eisenhower, which had landed on the coast of Algeria and Morocco, as well as the British Eighth Army, were doing so well against the Nazis in North Africa that Palestine no longer had anything to fear, so Subversive Operations Two was terminated and the British went back to their uncomplicated single-mindedness of trying to disarm the Jews of Palestine. Thus the men whom Captain Eban and his colleagues had been helping to train in guerrilla warfare no longer had anyone to get them out of prison if they were caught in possession of guns which Subversive Operations Two had given them and taught them to use.

On March 20 (1943) Aubrey wrote to a friend:

"I am going down in a couple of weeks to Cairo to search for employment, my mission here having terminated."

Spiking a rumor that had reached England, he wrote:

"I have no intention of deserting Cambridge. If I influence this place at all [he still, technically, was not permitted to tell exactly where he was] it had better be by remote control for the time being. . . . I am beginning to find the Levant a bit much. I could do with a period of

Occidentalism again, or, alternatively, with a holiday in Algiers or Casablanca or some such unlikely place. In point of fact, all I shall get is a week in Nathania making sand castles and drinking chocolate. There is a morbid concentration here on things of the stomach."

8

He Can't Even Open His Mouth

EARLY IN APRIL of 1943 Captain A. S. Eban flew from Jerusalem to Cairo in a Misr military plane "ingeniously kept together in precarious cohesion by copious use of string and chewing gum." All the other passengers were airsick. "I felt it might be considered standoffish if I did not join in, but I was saved from this fate when the inconsequential pilot had a whim to land in Port Said to give a message to his brother-in-law, so I refuelled with ersatz brandy and reached Cairo with honor preserved and face kept."[1]

Commenting on his military career, he said:

"My own future is on the knees of the gods and is being dangled there, I think too light-heartedly. I was not sorry to leave that particular job in Palestine, where I lived as you can well imagine in a constant state of conflict and stress. There are efforts to send me back there in the name of duty . . . but I yearn for a little peace and routine, which I should have thought the army would be well able to provide. . . ."

He also reported that his sister Ruth had had another child and so "I am defiantly and astonishingly an uncle again, such a rare and momentous departure from routine that the air here in Cairo has a new zest. To crown this great process of eruption into new capacities, it only remains for me to become a father, but for this I have not the Necessary Facilities here in Egypt, although in Palestine the desire to escape Minority Status is leading to all sorts of what my duet of landladies (in Cambridge) used to describe as Goings On."

While he was waiting for his new assignment Aubrey joined Gershon in the apartment of Eileen's father, who had a reputation of being incontinently hospitable. The Alexanders often entertained thirty guests at luncheon or dinner. Many of their house guests took advantage of their extreme hospitality, coming for several days and staying weeks, or coming for several weeks and staying months, and so Mr. Alexander built a bungalow guesthouse at the far end of the garden of his extensive Cairo estate, thus giving guests and host alike a measure of independence. When the American military arrived in Cairo the Alexander house was commandeered by the U. S. General Staff, but Mr. Alexander and his servants were permitted to move into the guesthouse. After a few months, however, some of the high-ranking American officers decided it was a violation of their tight security rules to have people not connected with the American military operation living on the grounds, so they rented a luxury apartment in the Zamalek section of Cairo and gave it, rent-free, to Mr. Alexander in return for his bungalow.

The Alexander staff consisted of a male servant named Said, who spoke only Arabic, and a female servant named Adele of indeterminate age, having been born so long ago there was no one left to help her remember, but who Gershon figured must have been between eighty and ninety—and she lived another twenty years. Aubrey and Adele conversed in French, although he soon discovered that she spoke a sexless language, with utter disregard for gender. Adele was small, compact and scrawny, and every visible part of her leathery skin was crisscrossed with wrinkles. Neither Aubrey, Gershon nor any member of the Alexander family ever saw her eat anything during the day, but sometimes late at night, encased from head to foot in long woolen combinations, she would be surprised in the kitchen wolfing a bowl of rice and washing it down with coffee. She resented being caught and would aggressively insist she had not had a bite all day. It seemed a point of honor with her that she needed less food than anyone else.

Aubrey soon discovered Adele had a ferocious temper which she frequently vented in high-pitched tones in several ill-digested languages. About twice a year, in one of her various tongues, or in all of them, Adele would denounce the Alexanders as slave drivers, deliver her notice with horrible imprecations and floods of tears, then pack her spare aprons, combinations and a small picture of the crucifixion into an old Gladstone bag, place on her finger a magnificent diamond and emerald ring she had won in a raffle and leave. She always came back, however, in time to cook dinner. Once in a rage she hurled a vegetable knife the length of the immensely long kitchen at Said, piercing his shoulder. Nevertheless, after his recovery he continued to remain her devoted slave.

Adele called everyone she liked "ma coquette," including Leslie Hore-

Belisha, who had once been a house guest and for whom Eileen was now working in London. Just as she had acquired an instant liking for Hore-Belisha, she took an immediate dislike to Aubrey. Perhaps it was because Gershon maliciously told her Monsieur Eban was a general, knowing Adele had an unexplainable loathing of generals. Thinking him to be a general she purposely addressed him as "Monsieur le Colonel," thus unknowingly elevating him a few ranks while intending to demean him. Perhaps her contempt was because she felt Monsieur le Colonel did not treat Porly with proper respect. Porly was Adele's hideous-looking, ill-tempered, mouse-colored parrot. One explanation why she was so attached to the unlovable bird was because it was the only living creature who ever succeeded in shouting her down.

Aubrey and Gershon were joined in the Alexander flat by a young RAF flight lieutenant, who looked eighteen, although he was the father of four children. Aubrey described him as "a vivacious youth who appears to be collecting material for an exhaustive thesis on Houses of Ill Fame, and his research is commendably thorough and of first-hand authenticity." Adele took the young flier to heart and nicknamed him "Le Petit." For the next eighteen months the household consisted of Adele, Said, Porly, Le Petit, Ma Coquette (Gershon) and Le Colonel.

Said each day found new ways of expressing to Aubrey in Arabic his esteem, respect and prostration, which he often displayed in strange ways. Whenever Aubrey put an article of clothing down on a chair, Said would grab it and commit it to the laundry. After a few days Aubrey complained to Gershon:

"I am practically naked. Look at that clothesline outside! Almost every garment I own is hanging there."

Describing his Cairo life Aubrey wrote:

"I am still at Ellenbogen Towers, exposed to the shrill indignation of a loathsome parrot whose distaste of my character and qualities are not concealed by any veneer of courtesy. I resent this, for I am a Harmless Citizen in most ways, and a living creature, even a parrot, which literally vomits at my mere approach deflates my ego in no inconsiderable measure. I must either see a doctor or kill the parrot, though respect for the conventions of hospitality will probably deter me from the latter and more logical course."

During his hiatus between jobs, Eban was concerned with personal problems, especially what path to follow after the war's end. He wrote:

"Shertok is due here tomorrow . . . wild horses will not drag me from my chosen craft, which, incidentally, has been much illuminated during my sojourn here. What is your view of the relative merit of an academic or political interest, assuming an almost equal stress of predilection and experience in each direction? Academic seclusion may be a form of egotism, but the hustings have a corrupting effect. . . . I went round to the home of X yesterday and prayed in their private synagogue and was filled with a surge of anti-clericalism and anti-orthodoxy which surprised me in its intensity. . . ."

In the same letter he commented on a Seder celebration he had attended. "The Haggadah was read by one of the guests as if he were announcing a small dividend to a meeting of disgruntled directors. After drinking the four ceremonial cups of wine I got a bit stupefied and stupefaction always increases honesty, so when Mrs. X [the hostess] said: 'You really shouldn't have sent those lovely flowers!' I replied absently, 'Yes, I suppose it *was* unnecessary, really, but it was The Thing To Do.' Her prospects of ever being the same again do not seem, on the most sanguine view, to be strong, for that household, hospitable though it is, is not built to withstand unexpected or unconventional impulses."

Reacting as many another visitor to Cairo, Aubrey was filled with both sympathy and disgust for the beggars and urchins who swarmed the city streets.

"I sally forth shining in every button and with toecaps gleaming brightly, but a ragged boy pointing to my feet accusingly offers his own services in a rigid formula, 'Klin shoes Gabidam? Very, very feelthy!' All the parasitism of this place is fiendishly reflected in these wizened brats who are a mockery of the very soul of childhood and fill anybody with blank despair who has the smallest sensitivity."

In Cairo he found plenty of opportunity to use his Arabic, for he had frequent social engagements with Arab intellectuals. Reporting on one dinner with Arab professors at the University of Cairo he said:

"We spent the evening in an involved discussion in Arabic of the meaning of 'meaning.' We still don't know what it means."

In late June (1943) he wrote he was "completely in the toils of the Egyptian literati," and added:

"I write articles about their cultural movements and laud their renaissance. I find their better minds turning away from politics toward education and literature. There is a backwash of self-dissatisfaction about the war; not that they could have done more than they have . . . but they could have *thought* more bravely than they did, been less equivocal, less inclined to have a pied à terre in each camp; been, in fact, allies in moral as well as in juridical terms. This they were not, and the lack is not fully compensated by the fact that all clauses of the covenanted treaty were in the letter carried out sometimes with the assistance of friendly pressure."

Among the Egyptian literati, Aubrey met Twefik el Hakin, considered by many critics one of Egypt's most talented authors. He had recently published a novel, *The Maze of Justice,* the diary of a legal officer in an Egyptian provincial town assigned to investigate a murder. Through conversations over endless cups of coffee with magistrates, clerks and sheiks, the author reveals not only the background of the crime but the life of the Egyptian countryside, its customs and its problems. Aubrey arranged with Twefik el Hakin and his publisher to translate the book. The introduction was done by Hafiz Affifi Pasha, a former Egyptian ambassador to London, who praised both the original work and the translation. When the novel came out as a hardcover book at seven shillings sixpence, the publisher, Harvill Press of London, said of it:

"This translation from the Arabic has three assets: it is a good story, an important social document and the first work of one of Egypt's leading authors to be published in English."

A. S. Eban now had two entries in the British Museum catalog.

(In 1971 an Egyptian weekly carried an article analyzing the reason Eban in the 1940s had chosen a book of social criticism to translate, finally concluding that it was a diabolical plot to expose the weakness of Egyptian society. Eban's own explanation was, to the contrary, that he wanted to show Egyptian writing at its best; that *The Maze of Justice* had the virtue of containing some commendable self-criticism.)

About this time, discussing one of his emotional-intellectual problems, Aubrey wrote:

"You can't achieve anything without getting in somebody's way. You can't be detached and also effective. That is the problem of those with a social conscience. I see no solution."

Cairo's flies bothered him, as they do most visitors. He was also annoyed one day upon receiving a letter from someone in London for whom he bore great animosity and so he exploded:

"Whenever I think of X some primeval, murderous urge comes out in me and I rush around slaughtering flies with frenzied zeal, though otherwise I try to bear their existence with oriental passivity. . . . I shudder when I contemplate the vista of sticky fly-infested days and remember the health-drenched air of Palestine."

June in Cairo was almost more than he could bear.

"That heat is thick and wet and oppressive. There's nothing to be said for Cairo now. It is the realm of the flies and all that crawls upon the earth and the most reasonable office routine seems an intolerable burden.

"We had a United Nations parade today. Jumbo Wilson stood steaming and melting beneath the morning sun, surrounded by Balkan worthies, and Embassy and Ministry of State people, scrutinizing each other with cold antagonism, as if Montague and Capulet had been inadvertently asked to the same cocktail party. My suggestion that Intelligence should furnish a contingent dressed in black cloaks and pointed hats with banners inscribed in invisible ink was coldly received, so we had to watch from our window, while flies assembled unmolested in our dossiers.

"The parade was a good sight and seems to mark a turn in our business here, but a gloomy officer slammed our window afterwards and said: 'Now our troubles really begin!' meaning that the Near East is now a tedious political problem again and we go back to where 1939 left us. So we swatted flies and plunged into archives on Pan Islam Federation, and Caliphate and Levantine Unity, and Partitions and Minority Rights and other things which seemed trivial when the Eighth Army was on the move but become insistent now that peace has become imminent in these parts."

As the letter indicated, Aubrey had been doing Political Intelligence work in headquarters since his return to Cairo, a job which bored him exceedingly, but now, thanks to the activity of a man he had known in Cambridge, Robin Maugham, a scheme was being developed to set up a bureau to train potential officials of British embassies in the Middle East, British consuls, attachés, oilmen and others, so Britain would not repeat after the war some of the gross errors she had previously made in the Middle East, largely out of ignorance of the people, their ways, their language, their mentality and their uniquely oriental attitude toward life. The prospects excited Aubrey and revitalized him, despite the weather.

While he waited for the scheme to materialize, he did considerable socializing. Edwin Samuel came for a visit, as precise and interrogative as ever. "He shot nineteen personal questions at Gershon, inspected the flat like a conscientious subaltern taking over a platoon, borrowed a bathing costume and was off. But there was some good talk in between."

Wingate came through again. He had by now been forgiven everything, even by his bitterest British critics, because of the success of Wingate's Raiders, or the Chindits, as Wingate himself nicknamed them, after the dragon statues in front of Burmese temples. The first Chindit campaign had ended brilliantly. His well-trained commandos had sliced behind Japanese lines in Burma, cut rail routes, blown up bridges and

highways, exploded ammunition dumps and destroyed military installations. Wingate was a hero. Now he was on his way back from attending a
meeting with Churchill, Roosevelt and their chiefs of staff in Quebec,
Canada. When Aubrey saw him on the veranda of Shepheard's he was
in high spirits. ("I observed his exaltation over his being made a General
and the continued disintegration of his sartorial habits.") This was the
last time Aubrey would ever have a chance to talk with him. During
their brief conversation Wingate revealed himself to be as fanatical a
Zionist as ever. He disclosed, for example, that at Quebec he had pressed
on both Churchill and Roosevelt the urgent need of a Jewish army and
both had replied in an encouraging tone.[2]

Shertok came often to Cairo and Aubrey had long sessions with him.
Once Charles de Gaulle came through the lobby of Shepheard's within
Aubrey's sight. No one introduced them, but the young British captain
was instantly impressed.

"I remember it so well. He was tall, slim, angular and very sombre
as he strode past. Already I had admiration for anything French. I had
had a command of the language since my youth and I also had the feeling many people get that if something is said in French it must be
correct. And so, because of the fall of France and the sudden eruption of
De Gaulle, I developed a really romantic vision of him. After seeing
him that day it became a romantic adulation."[3]

Norman Bentwich, on his way from Jerusalem to Ethiopia, not only
came to dinner but moved into the Alexander apartment and remained
for many days. One night the sixty-one-year-old guest amused his twenty-
eight-year-old host with the story of how, when he went to Jerusalem to
take over the newly created chair of International Relations in the Hebrew University in 1932, his first public lecture was entitled "Jerusalem
City of Peace."

"The hall was crowded. Everyone was there, including the British
High Commissioner. I was able to get out only one sentence before a
crowd of students began a demonstration. I think it was as much against
Dr. Magnes, the university president, as it was against me. He had been a
pacifist in World War I and was head of a group called the Covenant of
Peace, which was very unpopular with the students. The leader of the
rebellious students was Avraham Stern, a very good student, but a confirmed and convinced terrorist, who later became head of the group
called the Lohame Herut Israel, or Stern Gang. They threw stink bombs
and created a great hullabaloo. British gendarmes came and formed
a circle around me with fixed bayonets and thus protected me while I

finally delivered my lecture on 'Jerusalem City of Peace.' But the students boycotted my lectures the rest of the year, not more than one or two ever attending."

It was a story Aubrey never forgot. What Bentwich himself remembered, from sharing the apartment with Aubrey, was how conscientious he was about his army work.

"He used to bring masses of Intelligence documents home and spend half the night poring over them. Sometimes he seemed very worried about something, but I never questioned him."[4]

Aubrey's true feelings about Army Intelligence were exposed when, hearing that Eileen was trying to pull strings in London to get Gershon into Intelligence, he wrote distressedly to her:

"Cease! No happiness awaits Gershon there, I assure you with the certainty of a man that hath seen affliction. Those who love to welter in swamps of intrigue may bed down happily there. Those who, like Gershon, are unarmed against such barbs had better abstain. I know this. It isn't a question of opinion. I have endured a wretched few months for no other reason. In fact, the most restless places are where the war impinges upon politics and those of us who are confined to such areas look with wistful envy on those who toil and spin according to a fixed routine."

One hot summer day Aubrey was assigned to explain Egyptian politics to an American Intelligence officer. After being briefed for a full hour the American officer thanked Eban and then, as he was about to take off for Algiers, in a burst of honesty said:

"Well, Cap, I may be stupid. I may be dumb. But all you've told me has meant absolutely nothing to me!"

Aubrey repeated the story himself, concluding:

"I like Americans."

Absent-mindedness and an uncanny ability to lose things plagued him in Cairo as it had in Cambridge. In a single day he lost a letter he was about to post to a friend, a tube of shaving cream, a tobacco pouch and a textbook of Sudanese dialects, not easy to replace.

In June of 1943 he remembered the Egyptian engineer he had met at a tea in Jerusalem many months earlier and wrote him a letter:

"Dear Mr. Ambache: May I have the pleasure of calling upon you? I was lecturer in Arabic literature at Cambridge where I knew your son Nachum well. I also recall meeting you in Palestine at the home of my friend Dr. Kleeberg. Flying Officer Ellenbogen, who is the fiancé of

Eileen Alexander and is staying with me, is also anxious to make your acquaintance. Yours sincerely, Aubrey S. Eban."

While waiting for a reply Aubrey told Gershon:

"I understand that he has a lot of daughters and a piano in every room."

The next day he told Gershon:

"I think I made a mistake yesterday. What he has a lot of is pianos and a daughter in every room."

Mr. Ambache replied promptly to Aubrey's letter and invited him and his friend to pay a call. Of the visit Aubrey recounted:

"We were well received and vouchsafed a glimpse of *one* daughter and *one* piano."

About this time Captain Eban received a new assignment to serve as one of the two principal aides to Brigadier Iltyd (Ivan) Clayton, chief of British Military Intelligence in the Middle East.[6] Aubrey was not at first aware of it but he soon learned the brigadier was a great deal more than a mere military officer. He and two die-hard British ambassadors, Lord Killearn (formerly Sir Miles Lampson) and Sir Walter Smart, were the real molders of British policy in that entire area of the world. Clayton already had as an aide a well-known young Arab, Albert Hourani. He and two brothers, George and Cecil, were Lebanese Christians. Albert had gone to Oxford, where he studied under Richard Crossman, later to become one of Britain's foremost parliamentarians, authors, editors and political commentators but then a don at Oxford in the field of classical philosophy. Instead of becoming politically and intellectually an Englishman, Hourani turned into an intense Arab nationalist. Now Eban was to join him on Clayton's staff. Those who were privy to Intelligence's own secrets half facetiously said Clayton had appointed Hourani, the Arab, to investigate political feelings and developments in the Jewish world and Eban, the Jew, to investigate political feelings and developments in the Arab world. It was sometimes put even more baldly:

"Hourani, the Arab, is supposed to keep his eye on the Jews, while Eban, the Jew, is supposed to keep his eye on the Arabs. All for the benefit of Clayton and the Empire."

The two young men had much in common: three languages (for Hourani knew some Hebrew), their Oxford-Cambridge education, an inherent intellectualism, a common enemy (the Nazis), great facility with words (Hourani was also a brilliant public speaker) and a deep-rooted suspicion of each other. With a neat display of humor the brigadier ordcred them to share the same office, the same secretary, the same wash-room. And so, on opposite sides of the room, Hourani studied the writings of Herzl, Ahad Ha'am, Borochov, Eban and other Zionists, while Eban studied the complicated pattern of Arab politics and personalities, including Hourani.[6]

During August of 1943 Captain Eban was granted a two-week leave and went to Palestine, then to Amman where he had a long conversation with the Prime Minister of Trans-Jordan, who furtively offered to show him the night life of Amman. At a cocktail party at the American Consulate Aubrey drank four glasses of what he thought was pineapple juice, "but which was actually a cunningly contrived snare for teeto-talers." From the Consulate he went on somewhere else to dinner. There his sibilants were erratic and he was the center of all attention as he did an imitation of both Winston Churchill and the chief rabbi. Despite his respect for Churchill as both a writer and a speaker, Aubrey delighted in satirizing him. He never missed a chance to poke fun at the Prime Minister in his drawing room imitations and in letters to friends. When Churchill began signing his name Winston Spencer Churchill, Aubrey insisted it was because, when he signed "W.C." to memoranda, "zealous secretaries took it not as an intimation of assent but as a suggestion for disposal."

He returned from Amman to Jerusalem in a railroad coach deserted except for four Palestinian Waafs (Women's Air Force volunteers) who, assuming the very proper-looking British officer reading a book was monolingual, began talking about him in Hebrew. They discussed such intimate matters as his possible attributes and potentialities, while Aubrey listened in silent amusement, pretending to be deeply engrossed in his book. As the conversation continued it became clear that none of them expected to see "a white man" for another six months. Then the girl with the loudest voice gave the others her opinion that officers are less "susceptible" than sergeants. ("This I nearly denied, at the risk of my alibi.") Another said the British captain with the book looked like an anti-Semite. ("This sent me to the mirror as soon as I got back to the Alexander apartment; I still think that any resemblance between me and Julius Streicher is coincidental.")

Upon his return to Cairo Aubrey found in his mail news that his brother Raphael, having followed him to St. Olave's, would in the fall enter his old college, Pembroke. There was also an annual check ("a pittance") from Pembroke. Receipt of this retainer fee led Aubrey to debate again whether he wanted to follow an academic career after the war, and prompted thoughts about what the new world order would be like, with its "scientific obsessions and its scorn for humanism." Would there be room in the post-war world for scholars? There was also a letter from Norman Bentwich saying he would be back in Cairo "on the eve of Five Thousand Nine Hundred and Four." This use of the Hebrew calendar rather than the Gregorian gave Aubrey an excuse to use a rare word out of his eclectic vocabulary. He wrote:

"There is a pleasing ovolimity about the Jewish date. Just imagine, I was up at Cambridge in Five Thousand Eight Hundred and Ninety-Seven!"[7] (Both Bentwich and Eban had their dates wrong.)

Also, there were rumors that Chaim Weizmann would soon come to the Middle East again ("which I hope is true, for there are some awful fusses here which nobody else in his camp is remotely fit to cope with and which left alone will presage no good").

Late in 1945 the British Council, pleased with the reaction to the three YMCA lectures he had already delivered, asked him to prepare a series of three more. The first was entitled "The Liberal Tradition." This time Eban became a one-man road show, giving his lecture in Haifa, Tel Aviv and finally Jerusalem. His preamble:

"It is the prudent custom of theatrical producers in England, whenever they have reason to doubt the popularity or quality of a play, to precede its performance in the capital city by a rehearsal in a provincial center, renowned for its industrious, critical and hard-headed outlook."

The British Council, he said, in its cunning, was doing the same thing by having him open in Haifa before his appearance in Jerusalem.

Of the British liberal tradition, he said it "makes the welfare of the individual the criterion of social activity; it postulates that what serves the ends and ideas of the individual will promote the welfare of society, which is merely an aggregate of individuals banded together for protection."

Admitting that many even intelligent people cannot define liberalism, he compared them to the schoolboy who, when asked to define an elephant, confessed he was unable to do so but insisted he could recognize an elephant when he saw one. "Anyone brought up in the liberal tradition . . . will be able to judge whether a scheme or procedure conforms to it or not."

He received applause when he told his Haifa audience that "the habit of the liberal mind is to turn a critical eye on whoever exercises power and to ask if that power is being exercised with all necessary respect for liberty of criticism and conscience. This judgement must be applied even to an elected majority exercising power by right of suffrage. Not even a majority has carte blanche."

The big problem of the post-war world, he thought, would be to "reconcile the necessity for planned economy with the habits of liberalism."[8]

In early 1943 the RAF decided to transfer Gershon to London, so he began packing suitcases and trunks, his future settled, but Aubrey's was more uncertain than ever. It had been officially decided that the school set up by the British Army would be called the Middle East Center of Arab Studies. In early February, in anticipation of the important role he would play in the enterprise, Eban was promoted from captain to major.

For some months Gershon and Aubrey had had a British insurance man named Bryant living with them. Looking back over this period Aubrey wrote:

"I am sorry that we shared [sic] so few wild oats with Mr. Bryant, who is an advocate of the Good Life in its epicurean forms. He is by profession so morbidly linked with imminent catastrophe that he is entitled to a philosophy of carpe diem."

On March 7, 8 and 9 (1944) Aubrey delivered the second of his lectures, this one on "The Diplomatic Tradition." It was well received in Haifa, Tel Aviv and Jerusalem by large audiences of distinguished Palestinians and Britons.

Early in March he wrote to Gershon, who by now was in England preparing for his wedding, that he had been busy socially, having entertained in succession several British professors, Nelson Glueck, just returned from the United States, and Norman Bentwich, who waited several hours in one of Groppi's several tea shops for Aubrey, while Aubrey was waiting several hours in another of Groppi's tea shops for Bentwich, one of the two professorial minds having forgotten or erred.

Somehow Adele heard about Aubrey's promotion and was confused, because she already addressed him as "le Colonel." Why had he been demoted? She also heard rumors of Aubrey's possible departure for Jerusalem and insisted he tell his superior officers he would not leave Cairo under any circumstances, even if commanded so to do.

Late in March (1944) Orde Wingate, sitting in the copilot's seat of a Mitchell bomber, went to his death not far from the Burma-Indian frontier in a plane accident never fully explained. Aubrey wrote to friends that he was "terribly depressed."

During the spring of 1944 Aubrey frequently called at the Ambache home to see not the father but the eldest of the three daughters. Her name in Hebrew was Shoshana, the translation of which is Susan or Susanna. From childhood she had always been Susie, only she spelled it Suzy. She was twenty-two years old, five feet five inches tall, with light auburn hair, a gentle personality and a sweet disposition, yet with a sharp mind and a variety of intellectual interests. In future years when she would be interviewed by male and female reporters, the greatest disagreement in their printed descriptions would concern the color of her eyes. Some would call them "pale amber," or "hazel," or "gray." Perhaps they actually did change color according to her moods or the quality of the light, but in Egyptian Passport 64350 she herself put the color down as "green."[9]

All three Ambache girls were unusual, "so different from any other girls you'd meet," as one friend put it.[10] Suzy had just graduated from the American University in Cairo in social sciences, but had also majored in English literature. Her most ambitious collegiate project had been a paper on Charles Langbridge Morgan, the British novelist, playwright and critic. She was a collector of his books and on the three-week voyage to South Africa early in the war she had taken Morgan "for a traveling companion," which had made the trip not only tolerable but pleasant. Her favorite was *Sparkenbroke,* the novel he wrote several years before the start of World War II. She told Aubrey she had written to Morgan and showed him the reply she had received, which was more than just polite. He told her he liked many things about her long letter and about her style of writing, although "obviously your first language is not English."[11]

There was a great deal of telephoning back and forth between the Alexander flat and the Ambache house and almost all the calls were "monitored" by Adele, who had a great ear for romance and who would conspiratorially report the progress of the courtship to Gershon, until he left for London, and then to whoever else would listen.

One of the family jokes among the Ebans is the story of how, early in the courtship, Mrs. Ambache greeted her husband when he came home one day by saying:

"Simcha, have you noticed that that young British officer, Eban, seems to be quite interested in our Suzela?"

To which the husband retorted:

"What can she possibly see in him? He can't even open his mouth."[12]

Gershon and Eileen were married in London. Aubrey had been invited to be best man but he was unable to fly to England for the ceremony.

In April (1944) just before he was to deliver the third of his British

Council lectures, on "The Academic Tradition," it was discovered the date conflicted with Purim, so the Council issued the text as a pamphlet. In it he defined the difference between Oxford and Cambridge:

"The Oxford man walks down the street as if he owns it; the Cambridge man walks down the street as though he doesn't care in the least who owns it."

Much of the pamphlet was about the drastic changes that would have to take place in educational methods in the Middle East after the war. How preposterous it would have seemed to Eban, then twenty-nine, if someone had told him that when he was forty-five he would be Minister of Education of a reconstituted Jewish state and that he would propose drastic changes in the state's educational system.

While awaiting a final decision on the location of the British Army school Aubrey received a call from Michael Comay, a South African Jewish captain in the Eighth Army, inviting him to come sixty miles across the desert to where Comay's troops were bivouacked and deliver a lecture to them, giving an analysis of the Middle Eastern situation. Comay explained that all the talks during the four-day program would be delivered by top-level men. Aubrey's presentation was so brilliant that Comay invited him to come back again and do the same talk to another Eighth Army group, which he did. During conversations with the South African officer Aubrey said:

"I myself was born in South Africa, although at the age of six months I decided to leave."

In June it was finally decided that the Middle East Center of Arab Studies would be set up in Australian House in the Old City of Jerusalem, with Colonel Bertram Thomas in charge and with Major Aubrey S. Eban as second-in-command. Thomas, who for five years had been Vizier or Prime Minister of Muscat and Oman, had come to the world's attention in 1930–31, when he crossed the Rub' al Khali in Saudi Arabia, which he himself called "the last unexplored desert in the world," in fifty-eight days by camel, traveling from Zufar in the south to Qatar on the Persian Gulf. Then he wrote a book, *Arabia Felix*, that became popular in both Britain and America. He never actually disguised himself, but for years he dressed exclusively in Arab garments.[13] He was an accomplished Arabist, but his British friends said that while he was willing to have his name used as head of the school in Jerusalem, he was little interested in its operation. In those days beer was one of his chief obsessions, which meant that Major Eban was the one who actually ran the school.[14]

Reporting to Gershon, Aubrey wrote that the initial class consisted of three RAF wing commanders, three squadron leaders and fifteen army officers and civilians "of all types, ranks, shapes and sizes." As soon as the classes began Major Eban lectured each day from 8:15 A.M. until 1 P.M. on everything from monuments and excavations in the Arabian peninsula, game birds of the Middle East and Palestinian flora and food production, to the holy cities of Arabia—anything whatsoever to do with the Middle East. But principally he drilled his students in the Arabic language. Nelson Glueck, who several times paid visits to the school, said:

"Eban could make the conjugation of a verb seem as romantic as a Persian love poem."[15]

Aubrey had much social and intellectual exchange with Moshe Shertok. At the Shertoks' home in Jerusalem he met Gideon Rufer, liaison officer between the Jewish Agency and the British Army, and David Hacohen, who had been in charge of the plan to drop Jewish parachutists behind Nazi lines in Europe. Of Eban Rufer said: "He was as shy then as he still is, speaking beautiful Hebrew, which startled us. We attributed it to the efficiency of British Intelligence and not to his Jewish background, which was not the case, of course."[16]

Aubrey's forensic talents had been getting plenty of practice while in the Middle East, but he had done little writing. Now that he was settled in the routine of his teaching position he made a secret arrangement which gave him a chance to have some influence on public opinion. He became the anonymous author of editorials for the *Palestine Post*, the English-language daily published in Jerusalem and circulated throughout the country. What pleased Eban's sardonic sense was sitting in officers' mess listening to his fellow British majors, captains and colonels fuming over one of his *Post* editorials and saying, as they often did:

"If I could just get my hands on the bloody bastard who wrote this claptrap I'd wring his dirty bloody neck!"

After listening to such denunciations, Eban would often head directly for the *Post* to write another blast at the mandatory government.

In the Rehovia section of Jerusalem a *chug* or circle of friends met informally in each other's homes to discuss current affairs. One of the group was the son of Ahad Ha'am, the great Hebrew essayist and philosopher, who believed the revival of the Jewish state must involve a revival of Judaism.[17] Another was the son of Menahem Ussishkin, pioneer Zionist and chairman of the Jewish National Fund until his death in 1941.[18] Proceedings were always in Hebrew. One evening Aubrey was invited as a guest. The *Zionist News* reported:

"All were curious to learn how this young English orator would deliver a Hebrew speech. When Eban started there was a hush. The hush remained for over an hour. He spoke of ancient Arabic influences on Hebrew. His analysis was brilliant. His command of classical Hebrew was amazing. He had to run back to the barracks as soon as he finished his address. He was due to talk the next morning before some Arabic literary society. In the hub of conversation that arose when he left I heard the son of Ahad Ha'am say: 'It's a long time since I've heard such classical Hebrew.'"

For months Mr. and Mrs. Ambache had treated Aubrey as they did the many other young men who came to call on their daughters, but when Mrs. Ambache finally convinced Mr. Ambache that this young British major had really serious intentions, he decided to do a little investigating, or, as Suzy herself once put it, "He said to himself: 'Oh my God, it's all very nice but who *is* this fellow?'" For many years the Ambaches had been good friends of Shertok, who several times had been their house guest and who at least telephoned them every time he came to Cairo. So they asked Shertok about Eban and received a wholly favorable report. But how about his parents? Shertok said he could also vouch for Dr. and Mrs. Eban.

Late in 1944 Aubrey went on leave to Cairo and on New Year's Eve he and Suzy became engaged.

9

Honeymoon at Luxor

CAIRO HAD SOME excellent bookstores and one of Aubrey's delights in the Egyptian capital was to browse through the shelves looking for esoteric volumes in either Arabic or English. That was what he was doing one Friday late in March (1945) when, glancing at the shoulders of a British officer with captain's pips, he had a strange feeling he knew the man, so he went over to him and said:

"Excuse me, but . . ."

The officer who turned around was Captain Neville Halper, M.D., son of Lina Halper and first cousin to Major Aubrey S. Eban.

"Weeks ago I wrote to your mother," Aubrey said, "to tell her I'm getting married and wanted you for my best man if you were in this part of the world and where could I find you? She wrote back: 'Darling, how can I tell you? He's in the Army. Who knows where he is?' So here you are! It's perfect because the wedding is Sunday. . . ."

Neville interrrupted to explain he had been stationed in Bagdad; he was now on his way through the Suez Canal headed for India; he was due back on board ship the next day, Saturday. Aubrey suggested that maybe Neville could communicate with his commander and arrange a twenty-four-hour extension of his leave, in view of "the emergency."[1]

The wedding was in the Ambache home in Cairo in the presence of almost a hundred and fifty guests, including Paula and David Ben-Gurion, who happened to be in Cairo for a conference; Bertha Gaster, British journalist; Aubrey's commanding officer, Brigadier Clayton, and Teddy Kollek. The Orthodox marriage rites were performed by Rabbi Nahum Effendi, chief rabbi of Egypt. The best description of the wedding was written by the bridegroom himself, who, in a personal letter to friends, said:

"I enjoyed it far more than any other wedding I have ever attended. It was the first time I was close enough to hear what was going on. Suzy looked very radiant. (I looked pretty good myself, but Suzy's white tulle quite overshadowed my khaki barathea and she looked far better, really.)"[2]

Two incidents were never forgotten by either Suzy or Aubrey. When the outspoken Paula Ben-Gurion passed down the receiving line she said in English to the bride, as they shook hands:

"Congratulations!"

"*Todah rabah* (Thank you)," Suzy replied in Hebrew.

Instead of moving along, Mrs. Ben-Gurion, whom Suzy had never seen before, stood there and said back in Hebrew:

"So you know a little Hebrew?"

"Yes, a little," Suzy replied, modestly. (Hebrew and French were her mother tongues, Hebrew the language of the home, French the language used in the schools she had attended.)

"Where did you learn it?" Mrs. Ben-Gurion persisted. Finally she moved on.[3]

During the reception the British journalist, Miss Gaster, standing next to Aubrey's commanding officer, remarked to him:

"General, I'm sure you are aware that the Book of Deuteronomy prescribes a full year's leave of absence for all officers and other ranks in the Mosaic Army Group who contract matrimonial commitments during their period of service."

Brigadier Clayton's evasive reply was lost in the hubbub of voices, but Aubrey, commenting on the incident later, said:

"The Brigadier, for all his piety, is governed more closely by army regulations than by the Deuteronomic Code, so I will not get a year's leave, but I feel I could certainly use it, for it is no easy matter resuming contact with ordinary life so soon after The Great Change."

On their honeymoon the Ebans went to Upper Egypt. Suzy agreed with her husband that Luxor was "too perfect for any prose description." At Aswan they enjoyed the glories of pre-Arab Egyptian architecture, never dreaming how important a role this place would play in the political history of a Jewish state not yet re-created. They stopped briefly in Cairo, where Aubrey introduced Suzy to Adele. The wrinkled old servant looked over the young woman carefully through narrowed eyes and then, turning to Aubrey, said:

"*Je suis d'accord!*"

From Cairo they went by train to Palestine. The hills and valleys were

verdant and even the desert in many places was splashed with spring
flowers. ("It is an ideal background for our Blessed State.") But Suzy was
suffering from severe pains behind the ears and at Hadassah Hospital in
Jerusalem she was told she had mumps. So she spent the rest of the honeymoon—a week or ten days—in a hospital bed.

Before the marriage Nelson Glueck had told Aubrey that if he didn't
have a better idea there was a vacant apartment at the American School
of Oriental Research in which he and Suzy could live. They would have
a good view of Mount Scopus; they could take their meals in a communal
dining room; and there would not be many people bothering them
because, due to the war, the hostel, which had been built for Americans
coming out to do archeological work, was almost deserted. After moving
in, Aubrey wrote:

"We are in a delightful part of Jerusalem and are fortunate that our
arrangements save us from the worst aspects of domestic tyranny. We
cook not, neither do we wash up; we just consume and enjoy. We hope
to travel as much as my work in Jerusalem allows and to utilize the
interests and amenities of Jerusalem to the full."

Among the other inhabitants of the hostel were an American engineer
and his wife, a couple recently arrived from Bagdad, and Lady Petrie,
widow of Sir Flinders Petrie, celebrated British archeologist. Nelson
Glueck was still filling his dual role as archeologist and American
Intelligence agent. When he returned from a trip he would recount to
the Ebans stories that were both entertaining and informative. Years
later Suzy would look back on the months at the American School with
nostalgia.[4]

Already Aubrey had decided married life "is really another and a
better world." As he described it to his friends: "Things have run such a
smooth and felicitous course for me recently that I fear lest a note of
complacency may invade my letters."

In May (1945) Germany surrendered and the war in Europe came to
a quick end, but Aubrey was told there was no intention of closing
the Middle East Center; Britain's problems in that part of the world
had now only begun. There were even suggestions that the British
Foreign Office might take over the operation of the school from the
Army. Eban was urgently requested to continue with the center for at
least another year. He accepted, "partly for official, partly for academic
reasons, as I am writing a few things for publication." Actually he was
still torn over which of several possible careers he wanted to follow.
While he worked at his desk Suzy, sparked by his literary ambition,

began rewriting her college critique of Charles Morgan into a magazine article. Not long after their marriage they began discussing their joint future.

"When I first met him," Suzy explained later, "there was this very academic person, a professor of oriental studies. When I married him I thought I had married a professor. I thought someday he would have a chair of Arabic studies in some great university and would devote his life to lecturing, writing and research. Then, gradually, I began to realize he had a passion for politics. He was still a professor, of course, but I began to understand he would use his academic interests for political purposes. I never guessed the day would come when politics would be everything."[5]

One night in July (1945) most Englishmen in Palestine and every Jew who could get near a radio listened to the election returns the BBC was broadcasting from London. It was the first election Britain had held in years—Labour vs. the Conservatives; Attlee vs. Churchill. Despite the feelings Aubrey had for Churchill as a writer, orator and friend of the Jews, he and Suzy, along with most others in the Yishuv (the Jewish community of Palestine), were hoping for a Labour victory, because Labour was firmly committed to a pro-Zionist program and also to repudiation of the Tories' white paper. Labour's spokesman had just recently proposed not only that Palestine become a Jewish national home but that there be an exchange of populations, with the Arabs encouraged to "move out as the Jews moved in."[6] They went to bed that night elated that Labour had won and certain the gates of Palestine would now be opened to the Jewish remnant in Europe and the Balfour Declaration would finally be taken seriously.

During that same summer (1945) Aubrey was deeply affected for the fourth time in his life by a death. One of his British Army students was shot and killed by Jewish terrorists, presumably members of Menahem Beigin's Irgun Tzevai Leumi. Because the total enrollment of the school was so small, there was intimate contact between members of the staff and students. For Aubrey the victim of the shooting had not been a symbol of British imperialism, as he had been for the Irgun, but an intelligent human being into whose face he had looked each day since the course began. It was a shock that this man was now dead, not because of anything he personally had either said or done. ("I fully understood the need for resistance, but I also understood the human innocence of many of its victims, such as this young man without the slightest political interests, who was simply trying to learn something about Arabic and Hebrew culture."[7])

In August (1945), apologizing to friends for weeks of silence, Aubrey wrote:

"I was brought up on illusions and never realized that being married is a full-time job. I now understand the case of valued friends who after years of intimacy vanished into a cloud of confetti and were never seen again. I like to linger on this theme because I intend to use it for at least a year as a correspondence-alibi and a retort to my creditors.

"We are a happy lot and busy in Jerusalem; our chief delight is to meet people from Cairo who describe how much hotter it is there. A limp and sodden envelope, wilting at the corners, arrived from your father, Eileen, who writes that it is hot. He is refreshed only by nostalgic evocations of Swiss Cottage [the area of London in which the Ellenbogens were now living] and its healthful breezes. We are left alone more now, as Jerusalem has a pleasant habit of estivation, which makes August a tranquil month.

"I have given a few more lectures on aspects of world order, with Suzy sitting in terrified devotion bang in the center of the front row."

Among Jerusalem visitors was Arthur Koestler, who was gathering material for a new novel, *Thieves in the Night*. Aubrey met him and was not enchanted.

"He has a certain morbidity and feels that you are not very 'realistic' unless you are thinking about bad drains, constipation or the Oedipus Complex all the time. He has engaging drawing room conversations— e.g., 'Have you met Miss So-and-So? She was my mistress for several years.'"

Late in 1945 the Ebans decided they had lived the communal life long enough and now wanted to be entirely on their own. Suzy explained their decision to move to North Talpiot:

"It was typical of Aubrey that although he was a British Army officer he wanted to be in a completely Jewish neighborhood; not side by side with British colonial administrators. [Eban never in his life had any doubt about where his first loyalty lay.] That's how we came to settle on a furnished house in North Talpiot, on the way to Government House. Not Talpiot, but *North* Talpiot."

During its second year the Middle East Center had a slightly larger enrollment but Aubrey was beginning to feel he had had enough.

"The recent frenzy of work has left me limp. The ambitious yearnings of twenty-five men converging upon me have a tiring effect; and then the abnormal, neurotic intensity of the atmosphere here makes one long for a little of that distance that lends enchantment. It's all very silly, too, because nothing of any importance to the political future of this country is transacted here, a fact which local politicians refuse to face."

As 1945 drew to a close something happened in London that depressed Zionists everywhere. Ernest Bevin, whom Attlee had chosen as Foreign Minister over Dalton, publicly repudiated his party's official position on Palestine, refused to cancel the British white paper that had drastically limited Jewish immigration into Palestine and announced appointment of an Anglo-American Commission of Inquiry to consider the position of Jews in Europe. His subsequent speeches indicated to many he was being motivated by personal anti-Semitism, quite apart from political considerations.

Aubrey, who had been a supporter of Labour since his schoolboy days, was shocked—politically and emotionally. He felt as if someone had stabbed him in the back.

When the Anglo-American Commission arrived in Jerusalem in February (1946) to hold its hearings in the same YMCA hall in which Aubrey had delivered his British Council lectures he became acquainted with some of the members, especially Crossman, teacher of his Cairo associate, Hourani. Aubrey admired Crossman's sharp wit, biting sarcasm and lack of respect for the gods of the market place. This was the first visit to Palestine by Crossman, a non-Jew, although he subsequently came often.[8]

Aubrey labeled the other three British members "responsive to the ideas of the Palestine Administration and the British Government." On the American side he felt that Professor Frank Aydelotte and Ambassador William Phillips "maintained the detachment usual to the academic and diplomatic disposition," but he sensed that Bartley Crum and James McDonald, former High Commissioner for Refugees, were obviously "in strong sympathy with the Jewish cause." To Aubrey's amusement, a colorful southern judge, Joseph ("Texas Joe") Hutcheson, "enlivened the deliberations with a carefully contrived informality of ideas and expression."[9]

The surprise of the hearings, for Eban, was that Hourani appeared as a witness representing the Arab Office in Jerusalem. With considerable eloquence the young Lebanese put into the record Arab opposition to any Partition scheme and warned that any solution whatever would provoke conflict. To Eban he seemed moderate in both delivery and argument, at least in comparison with Ahmed Shukairi, who followed him and professed loyalty to the former Mufti of Jerusalem, even though there was testimony that the Mufti had supported the Nazis.[10]

Several times during the hearings Eban saw Weizmann briefly. It depressed him that his mentor looked so weary, so ill, yet on March 2 he stood before the full commission and for two hours spoke with such intensity and logic that everyone was impressed, Crossman writing in his diary: ". . . a magnificent mixture of passion and scientific detachment. . . . He is the first witness who has frankly and openly admitted that the issue is not between right and wrong, but between the greater and lesser injustice."

The sight of Weizmann pleading so eloquently for what he knew was right also had a deep effect on Aubrey's decision-making.

10

The Quixotic Decision

FOUR ROADS, each one quite challenging in a different way, stretched out before him.[1]

In Britain, as a result of the war, there was more interest than ever in the Middle East. Chairs in Arabic literature were being established in British universities that had never had such departments. There was a limited number of scholars in this particular field and few who, at such a young age, had become as distinguished as Major Aubrey S. Eban. He had a First Class in both parts of the oriental language tripos at Cambridge and had won most of the prizes offered in that field at the university. His translation of the Egyptian novel was receiving acclaim. And he had not lost touch with teaching while in the Army due to his position with the Middle East Center of Arab Studies. Already several universities had approached him. Following this road he could return to his position as tutor and research student at Cambridge and in the place for which he had such great affection gradually work his way toward one of the chairs of oriental studies. He knew he was emotionally and temperamentally fitted for the academic life. There would be tranquillity, which he enjoyed, and time for deep research and intensive writing. His associations would be exclusively with his peers and there would be opportunity for brilliant conversation and a constant exchange of ideas.

The second road was politics. He had never forgotten Laski's remark the night they were on the same side in the Socialism debate at the Cambridge Union. At that time Laski was merely a member of the executive of the Labour party. Now he was chairman. When the lists were being drawn for the 1945 election, Aubrey had been invited to present himself as a possible candidate on the Labour ticket from Aldershot, the small city in the south where he had received his first army training. Aldershot was inhabited largely by elderly colonels who wrote blimpish letters to the *Times* condemning change and denouncing anything progressive. His chances of being elected from Aldershot would have been one in a million. Or so he thought before the election. But in the 1945 landslide of the Labour party many men running from "impossible" constituencies were swept in, among them Francis Noel-Baker, son of Philip Noel-Baker, who had gone back home from the Middle East to run. Labour was in the saddle now and there was every indication it would command the support of the British public for a long time. It was not too late to choose politics. Since his boyhood he had been a Socialist. He had had good grounding in Socialist doctrine; his emotional attachment for the objectives of Socialism was deep. At Cambridge he had been prominently connected with Socialist organizations and in the Union debates he had argued the Socialist position doggedly and consistently. He had good connections in the party. It would take only a few years to win a seat in Parliament and from there . . . After all, Benjamin Disraeli, Earl of Beaconsfield, twice Prime Minister, had been a Jew. So, also, Léon Blum, twice Premier of France. The life of a politician would be quite unlike that of an academician. But there would be opportunities for writing and always a platform for the expression of ideas. As he tossed this possibility around in his head he imagined himself making brilliant speeches in the House of Commons. More importantly, as a political leader he could work effectively for the ideals in which he so stubbornly believed. The Socialist Foreign Minister, Ernest Bevin, had been guilty of outright treachery to the Jews. He and those like him needed to be opposed within the party. Surely, here was an opportunity for service and a career.

A third path was to remain in the Middle East Center. Both General Clayton and Bertram Thomas had asked him to stay. There were reports that it was to be moved to Beirut[2] and would be taken over by the British Foreign Office. The Center was a good show window. There would continue to be a constant parade of British leaders coming through the Middle East. If he wanted a career in diplomacy, in foreign affairs, here was his opportunity. He had already had indications that Whitehall was eying him with interest. Once in the Foreign Office, he knew progress would be rapid. There was no reason he could not someday help shape British foreign policy—at least as long as Labour remained in power. In diplomacy, as in politics, he would have the chance to serve his principles.

The fourth path was an offer to go with the Jewish Agency the minute he was discharged from the Army—to use all his talents to help bring the Zionist dream to fruition.

For months Aubrey struggled, silently, with his problem, weighing the possibilities, assessing the advantages and disadvantages. At first he talked to no one. Then just to Suzy. Finally to other people whose advice he respected.

As he saw it the choice was between full participation in the life of a liberal, democratic British society, and a voluntary removal from the milieu of his early life—a withdrawal—an adoption of something in a way remote and precarious. It was a duality which many Jews in Western countries no doubt also felt. But with Aubrey it was especially intense because of the unusual balance between his relationships in the two worlds. There were probably few Jews living in the West who had such total immersion in Jewish and Hebrew life, language, culture, traditions. Men like Herzl, Nordau and many of the German Zionist leaders had been remote from all Jewish loyalties until some event, some shock, some spiritual or physical experience, some humiliation had brought them back to their roots. In a sense they had gone out of the Jewish fold and then returned. But in Aubrey's case there had been no going out. Since the first weekend he spent with Grandfather Sacks at the age of seven he had lived part of his life in the normal British or Anglo-Jewish world and the other part, beyond any geographical context, in a world of historic pride and cultural fascination. This was the effect of his grandfather's training. Since childhood he had been bilingual, having learned the Latin and Hebrew alphabets at about the same time. As a result he was equally at home in two separate cultures. He mulled to himself: destiny would decide to which he would give his life. No, not destiny. He himself must make the choice.

He knew the roadblocks on each of the four paths. Although his natural predilection was to be academic, one of his teachers, Nackdemon Doniach, had once warned him that if he chose an academic career he would find his Jewishness a handicap.

"In England," Doniach had said, "in the apportionment of academic posts in Arabic studies there has always been a certain element of higher anti-Semitism. Jews do not always get the posts for which they are eminently qualified. You are outstandingly the best Arabic scholar of your generation, but for some reason there may not be a vacancy when you are ready."[3]

As for going back to Cambridge and trying to work his way to the top, he pointed out to Suzy that the head of the department of oriental studies was a relatively young man and even if he became his likely successor it might involve an interminable wait.

As for a political career, Professor Bernard Lewis,[4] passing through Jerusalem on his way to Iran, told him:

"I think your style is much more suitable to the House of Lords than the House of Commons."[5]

As for remaining with the Center, Aubrey felt an inherent contradiction working in the Middle East as an Arabist, while being a Jew and a Zionist. In the present political situation it would be difficult to utilize his specialized talent in this part of the world without a feeling of dichotomy.

That left the Jewish Agency. Here were the most disadvantages. The Agency was under siege by the British Government. Its members were being harassed and the possibility of its continued existence within Palestine was compromised by the attitude of the administration. It might even have to go underground like Haganah, its military arm. To be an official of the Jewish Agency—even a high official—carried no particular social status or public eminence compared with any of the other possible roles and seemed less likely to offer a career either glittering or glamorous. It also promised considerably less financial security.

In addition Aubrey was apprehensive, at first, about his family. What would be the reactions of Suzy and her parents, with their rather affluent concepts, if, so soon after his marriage, he turned his back on the several attractive opportunities for a perhaps impecunious lifetime of struggle within a very dubious framework? Then there was his own mother, whose opinion he always respected. She dreamed of a career for him in British politics.

When he told his Cambridge friends and people he knew in the British Foreign Office that he was seriously considering going with the Jewish Agency they almost unanimously expressed astonishment at what they considered a foolhardy choice.

But there were counteracting influences. Reuven Zaslani (Shiloah), who had recruited him for the Palmach job, was one of those who urged him to join the Agency, wildly quixotic though it might seem to some of his other friends.[6] Teddy Kollek added his similar arguments.[7]

Lord Edwin Samuel, son of Herbert Louis Samuel, the first British High Commissioner, was living at this time in Talpiot not far from the Ebans and each Saturday he and Aubrey would go walking to the outskirts of Jerusalem, discussing the state of the world and Eban's problems. One day, when Aubrey was pondering aloud the predicament of the four paths, Lord Samuel smiled and said:

"Whatever you do don't take the Jewish Agency!"

"Why not?"

"Because there's no future in it. If you don't take my advice, remember I warned you that there's no future in it."

Instead of helping his young friend decide which of the paths to choose, Lord Samuel suggested a fifth. He said Aubrey should become part of the mandatory government.

"Who knows, someday you may fill the chair my father sat in. You could end up running this whole Jewish land!"

Although Aubrey expressed no enthusiasm for this fifth idea, Lord Samuel persuaded the mandatory government to offer him an assistant secretaryship, which he promptly refused to consider.[8]

About this time Michael Comay came to Jerusalem to help present the Jewish case before the Anglo-American Commission of Inquiry which had been appointed by Bevin and after listening to Aubrey's problem told him he would never regret joining the Agency.[9]

Then, somewhat to Aubrey's astonishment, not only Suzy but her parents gave their full endorsement to what they sensed was his true desire. Mr. Ambache went further. Knowing that Aubrey was worried about the financial hazards of joining the Agency, he promised that if, as a result of the decision, he and Suzy fell into financial difficulties he would help them out for a year or two "while you find your way to other things." It was an indication to Aubrey of the depth of the Ambaches' Zionist roots, which pleased him even more than the assurance offered.

The wife of Lord Samuel, not at all in agreement with her husband about Aubrey's future, while on a trip to London made a special call at 77 Great Russell Street, cornered Dr. Weizmann and Shertok, and told them:

"In Palestine there is a very brilliant young man named Eban, whom you of course know. He is at the crossroads right now. He's so talented that he could possibly become a Cabinet minister if he were to choose British politics. Or he may end up as a don in one of our great universities. But I think you ought to draw him into Zionist activities."

Both men replied that they were in full agreement with her and were doing everything possible to encourage him to choose a Zionist career.

As Lady Samuel later recalled, someone at 77 Great Russell Street suggested that Eban could be named one of the editors of *Davar*, the Histadrut daily newspaper in Tel Aviv, to which she angrily retorted:

"Ridiculous! He is much too big a man for such a post. You must make full use of all his talents."[10]

In March (1946) when Dr. Weizmann was in Palestine to make an appearance before the Anglo-American Commission of Inquiry he one day asked Aubrey to call on him at Rehovoth. With him when Aubrey arrived was Joseph Linton, political secretary of the World Jewish Congress who, apparently at Dr. Weizmann's request, took Mrs. Weizmann to a concert that evening so her husband and the young British officer could be absolutely alone.[11] In the quiet of his study Dr. Weizmann for several hours discussed with his guest the current political situation, the stubbornness of Bevin, the power of the opposition and, after so many centuries of waiting, the chance of getting international approval for a return to some sort of re-created Israel. In this struggle, he said, the talents of every good Zionist were desperately needed. He dismissed Aubrey's other career possibilities and urged him to join the staff of the Jewish Agency in London the moment he could get out of the Army. He told how at 77 Great Russell Street they needed a Middle Eastern expert with a British background who could meet with members of Parliament, university professors and the people at Chatham House on their own intellectual and academic level, and that the obvious man for the post was Aubrey Solomon Eban.

The evening ended with Aubrey's agreement. As he later put it: "When Weizmann asked you to do something you did it."

But the relationship between these two men was not as simple as that. One mutual friend described it in these words:

"Eban often spoke of Weizmann as his mentor. I had the impression that this was the strongest intellectual influence in his life. He not only respected Weizmann but there was great mutual affection. It was a unique relationship. Weizmann was the master. It was almost a rabbinical, Hasidic relationship."[12]

But Eban felt he also must talk with Shertok, with whom he had much more in common than with Weizmann. He and Shertok were both Arabists; both were intellectuals of a similar genre, and they had many of the same personal problems. The relationship here was like pupil and teacher. They had profound respect for each other's intellect, cemented by affection of a reserved nature. Aubrey admired Shertok for his "relentless logic" and for his "immovable reliance on common justice."[13]

Circumstances—sometimes called fate or luck—often affect decisions, no matter how logically they seem to be made.

On June 29 (1946), which was the Jewish Sabbath, Shertok was to have had lunch with the Ebans in their Talpiot home. Aubrey did not pretend that it was merely a social affair. He had already several times discussed the future with his friend; this was to have been a final conference. He had told Shertok that he would be getting out of the Army in a few weeks and the die had to be cast. The appointed hour was 1 P.M. When 1 P.M. came and went and there was no sign of Shertok—not even a message from him—Aubrey and Suzy knew something was wrong, for Shertok was fanatically punctual. They waited until 2 P.M. and then, just before sitting down to lunch without him, turned on the radio. In Arabic, Hebrew and English it was being announced that the British High Commissioner had begun "military operations" against the Jewish Agency and Haganah, on the ground that they were responsible for the "lawlessness" which had broken out since the Anglo-American Commission had issued its report recommending that a hundred thousand Jewish refugees be admitted at once to Palestine but rejecting the idea of a Jewish state. (Bevin had immediately announced that European refugees would be admitted only after Haganah and other underground armies were disbanded and after the Jewish Agency suppressed what he called "terrorism.") The radio said British troops had occupied Jewish Agency headquarters, had dynamited their way into the offices of other Jewish organizations which were locked because it was Shabbat, and had begun a roundup of thousands of men and women, leaders in various walks of Jewish life. Dr. Weizmann, who was about to go to London for a serious eye operation, had not been taken and the active head of Haganah, who was to have been a star prisoner, had slipped through the British net and gone into hiding. Ben-Gurion, his political secretary and the treasurer of the Jewish Agency were in Paris. But all other members of the shadow government had been seized and placed in internment at Latrun, among them Shertok.[14]

Aubrey reacted like a Jew, not like a British Army officer. His realization that he *had* reacted this way had something to do with the final decision.

Later that same afternoon a messenger arrived with a note from Shertok. Although the Jewish leaders were political prisoners they had managed, thanks to the cooperation of Jewish sympathizers within the police force, to set up a courier service that enabled them to send messages from Latrun to their followers all over Palestine. As incongruous as it seemed, here was a letter from a man who was supposed to be incommunicado. It consisted of just one word, just two letters—"*Nu*"— the Yiddish word meaning "So?" Suzy looked puzzled but Aubrey smiled knowingly.

"He's asking us 'Nu? So what are you going to do? Are you going to join or not? Nu?'"

"And what's your answer, Aubrey?"

"I think you know the answer already. How can I go back and study the Mamelukes and Arab literature in the fourteenth century after what has happened in Europe, and what's happening here in the Middle East right now, and what's going to be happening during the next few years? I *must* become part of this thing. For better or worse."

And so the Ebans began getting ready, emotionally and practically, to leave Jerusalem, happy the choice had finally been made. As Aubrey later explained it:

"The other possibilities had been more tranquil and serene. The road we chose involved the greatest element of adventure and uncertainty. It was in a sense a *halutz* decision, like the decision others took who had come to Palestine even when greater opportunities were open to them elsewhere. It was a poetic rather than a prosaic decision, romantic rather than pragmatic. It was a decision I knew I would never regret."

Here was the turning point in Eban's life. His choice of careers showed little concern for personal aggrandizement. He had no way of knowing, then, that the Jewish Agency would someday become the government of a state, that the state would have embassies, that the government would have ministries and that he would achieve eminence first as a spokesman, then as a policy maker for a nation that would play a role in world affairs quite out of proportion to its population and area. Had he decided otherwise he might have become one of the six hundred and thirty members of the British House of Commons or one of the hundreds of British university professors, making his contribution to the Zionist cause in an ancillary manner. Fortunately for Israel and his own career he made the quixotic decision.

11

Eighteen-Hour-per-Day Propagandist

LONDON WAS NOT THE IDEAL PLACE and September 1946 was not the ideal time for a young man to begin his career as a professional Zionist working for the Jewish Agency. In Palestine British soldiers were being killed by Jewish underground organizations and the British commander had issued an order bidding his troops act "with hatred and contempt" toward all members of the Jewish race and especially "to hit them in the pocket where it hurts."[1] Illegal immigrants were pouring into Palestine in defiance of the British Navy—and to its humiliation. The Agency itself was being blamed by one segment of the British press for the turmoil in the Middle East. World War II was over in the Pacific as well as in Europe and what most Britons wanted more than anything else was to get back to the ante-bellum state as quickly as possible, but the trouble in the Middle East threatened the peace won so recently at such terrible cost and there was open hostility toward those considered in any way responsible. On the official level the representatives of Palestine's Jews were treated as if they were enemies of the British Government and on the part of the public at large there was not a great deal of friendship toward the Zionist cause. British policy in the Middle East seemed to be dictated by a small group of reactionary generals and ambassadors, among them Aubrey's old commander, Brigadier Clayton. They had no understanding of the progressive spirit of Zionism; they seemed to be thinking, still, in terms of British imperialism. They wanted to retain Arab support because of what it would mean in relation to the rest of the Empire. Also, with World War II over they were thinking of the possibility of World War III. That was the atmosphere in which Eban began his new work.

And London was not a happy place in which to live. The city was gray, dreary and dirty, the people enervated and dejected. They had to continue to queue for almost everything. The war had left its mark on them and their city; there were still large empty places in the landscape where buildings had once stood. Surely it would take years for a return to even a semblance of normality.

For the first three months Aubrey and Suzy lived with his parents at Harrow, one of the thirty-two boroughs of Greater London. The Eban house was twelve traffic-congested miles from the heart of the city, so as soon as they could they moved into a flat of their own in Highgate.

Aubrey's office was in the much-publicized Jewish Agency building at 77 Great Russell Street, "remarkable for its dinginess, discomfort and lack of hygienic provision—but in these respects it did not differ greatly from the more aristocratic ministries in Whitehall."[2] His starting salary was £900 a year ($3,631),[3] less than he would have received in any of the other fields he had been considering.

He was assigned to the information department of the Agency, then headed by Morris Rosetti, whom he had met years ago on a visit to Oxford. He wrote pamphlets and booklets, watched the press closely and made contact with editors, reporters and leader (editorial) writers. He cultivated a wide circle of friends in the Foreign Office and kept them informed of the Agency's attitude toward Middle Eastern developments. He haunted Whitehall, the street in Westminster lined with government offices, and got to know many members of Parliament well enough so they welcomed his visits and listened to his arguments. In short, he became a professional lobbyist for the cause of Israel. He also worked at the highest political level for both Shertok and Weizmann.[4]

Describing the almost instantaneous impression Eban made on his Agency associates, Rosetti said:

"Whenever I was in contact with an M.P. who required convincing and his intellectual level was above that of the average M.P.—which, God knows, is low enough, with certain notable exceptions—I would take care to arrange a meeting for him with Eban, because I knew Eban would be able to communicate with him. His presentations were always brilliant and remarkably analytical."[5]

Eban contended with the Arabs whenever and wherever there was an opportunity—on paper, on public platforms and in the halls of government. For example, one night in the fall of 1945 he went to Oxford and debated the Palestine issue with an official from the Arab Information Office, Haig Mgioniades, who told the Taylor Institution audience that "Palestine simply will not hold all the Jews who want to go there," and "America, England and the Dominions want to continue pushing the displaced Jews into this one country, while refusing to admit a single Jew into their own countries." His solution was to send all homeless Jews to Venezuela or Brazil. Eban countered by declaring that the Jewish community of Palestine could easily and immediately absorb the one hundred thousand Jews for whom entrance permits were then being sought, and that it was beclouding the issue to talk about "room" in a land of such vast open spaces.

While in Oxford he called on Professor Reginald Coupland, who had been a member of the Palestine Royal Commission appointed by the British Government in 1936, after the outbreak of Arab violence in Palestine, to investigate "the causes of unrest and the alleged grievances of Arabs or of Jews." At a commission hearing in 1937 in Jerusalem Coupland had startled everyone, including Dr. Weizmann, by saying:

"If there were no other way out to peace, might it not be a final and peaceful settlement to terminate the Mandate by agreement and split Palestine into two halves, the plain being an independent Jewish state . . . and the rest of Palestine plus Trans-Jordan being an independent Arab state. . . ."[6]

It was now ten years and a world war later and Eban was eager to know whether Coupland's feelings had changed. The professor told him he was still "very firm in his support of Partition," which still seemed to him "the only solution compatible with justice and logic—the lesser injustice."

Coupland told Eban of a subsequent meeting he had had with Weizmann in a hut on the grounds of a girls' school at Nahalal during which he told Weizmann:

"There needs to be an operation; no honest doctor will recommend aspirin and a hot-water bottle."

Eban's theory was that that all-day conversation with the Oxford professor at Nahalal created in Weizmann's mind the germ of what some years later was to become the State of Israel. Weizmann, after leaving the shabby Palestinian hut late in the day, told a group of farmers:

"Hevra, comrades, today we laid the basis for the Jewish State!"[7]

As Eban dashed from newspaper offices in Fleet Street, to government offices in Whitehall, to briefings of Parliament members, to lecture engagements all over the British Isles and then back to 77 to consult with Shertok or Weizmann, he realized that once again it was a matter of "too little, too late."

"I had a feeling that if information work like this had been done much earlier a climate of opinion might have been created in Britain in which it would not have been so easy for His Majesty's Government to carry out such a repressive Palestinian policy."[8]

Eban's old Cairo associate, Albert Hourani, and his two brothers were now in London, active in all manner of anti-Zionist activities. The principal arena in which Eban met Hourani was Chatham House, the popular designation of the Royal Institute of International Affairs, named for the building in London which housed its offices. Organized during the war as a learned society to inform and assist the Foreign Office, it was headed by Sir Harold Beeley, sometimes called "the moving spirit of British anti-Zionism,"[9] and by Arnold Toynbee, the British historian whose anti-Zionism was not then as evident as it would be a few years later. The Institute carried on its work through publication of surveys and reports which had a consequential influence on British foreign policy. Sometimes these papers were made public; sometimes they were leaked to press and public; often they were "top secret." One of Chatham House's publications was a quarterly journal, *International Affairs,* and it was therein that the two protagonists crossed swords: Hourani, the Arab, Eban, the Jew; Hourani, Oxford, Eban, Cambridge; Hourani, able propagandist, Eban, learning to be.

Irked by a Hourani article in the journal, Eban early in 1947 wrote an article for *International Affairs* in which he argued that merely because some people in some Middle Eastern countries had begun to wear Western clothes, drive automobiles and go to American films it did not mean that they had understood or adopted the culture and spirit of the West, contrary to the claims of Hourani. He told of an average life expectancy of twenty-seven years in Iraq, of Lebanese villagers subsisting on four piasters per head per day and of the disease-ridden population of Egypt with a per capita average income of £5 a year.

"To lick the jam off the Western pill will bestow some of the sweetness but no cure."

Then he wrote:

"Arab society starts off with an Eastern environment to which it endeavors to adapt Western ideas. Jewish society starts off with Western ideas which it must contrive to adapt to an Eastern environment. . . .

Men do not part easily with their traditions, either in the East or for that matter in the West."[10]

In October (1946) Dr. Weizmann had a second serious eye operation, but after recuperating in Lugano, Switzerland, was well enough in December to go to Basle for the twenty-second World Zionist Congress. There was much about this Congress that was momentous. It was the first in seven years—the first since that tragic gathering Aubrey had attended in Geneva on the eve of World War II. It was held in the city in which, forty-nine years earlier, the World Zionist Organization had been created, the Basle Program formulated and Herzl elected to lead the dreamers. As Eban and many others realized, even before the banging gavel called the opening session to order, this Congress would go down in Jewish annals as the Congress that drove Weizmann from office.

Many leaders of the American and Palestinian delegation were coming to Basle with the fixed idea of replacing the man who for thirty years had been the leading star in the Zionist sky. "There were ambitions, envies, causes, lobbies, jostlings and shovings—as well as the overriding conflicts of ideology and policy which gave legitimacy to all of these."[11]

Weizmann was aware that his opening address to the Congress would be one of the most important public pronouncements of his life. Pleading that he needed help because of the condition of his eyes and his general health, he asked Eban to work on the speech with him. Instead, his young protégé wrote the entire address and then read it aloud to Weizmann, who liked it so much he decided to deliver it word for word as written. On the day he addressed the Congress he spoke the words with as much conviction as if he had written them himself, but anyone studying the text could see Eban in almost every sentence— his ideas, his phraseology.

"Jews came to Palestine to build, not to destroy. [Eban would often use that sentence again, addressing world bodies.] . . . Masada, for all its heroism, was a disaster in our history. Zionism was to mark the end of our glorious deaths and the beginning of a new path whose watchword is—Life!"

Weizmann denounced the white paper, saying: "Few documents in history have worse consequences for which to answer." He castigated the British for broken promises. "It seemed incredible that anybody could be playing fast and loose with us when we were so battered and exhausted." He explained the anti-British feeling on the part of world Jewry: "If their antagonism is directed against the British Government its sole origin is indignation at Britain's desertion of her trust." He said he understood why many young Palestinian Jews had turned to violence: "It is difficult in such circumstances to retain a belief in the victory of peaceful ideals." Weizmann's American and Palestinian opponents could not possibly disagree with these thoughts.

Eban has always held that if Weizmann had kept to his line of argument in this opening speech he might have weathered the storm and kept his leadership. Instead, on December 16 (1946) he gave his personal enemies a spontaneous, extemporaneous tongue-lashing. Eban compared him on this occasion to the blinded Samson. Having reached a decision, "he would grip the pillars of the Temple and bring it down upon his head. With delicate scorn he lashed out at those who recoiled from the necessity of patient toil, both in diplomacy and in development. . . . An American Zionist leader had urged Palestinian Jewry to revolt against Britain, while American Jews 'would give full political and moral support.' Weizmann was enraged by this formulation. He would have none of this division between the battlefield and the sidelines. He now uttered the rebuke which may have cost him the presidency: 'Moral and political support is very little when you send other people to the barricades to face tanks and guns. The eleven new settlements just established in the Negev have, in my deepest conviction, a far greater weight than a hundred speeches about resistance —especially when the speeches are made in New York, while the proposed resistance is to be made in Tel Aviv and Jerusalem.'"[12]

One of the delegates shouted "Demagogy!" All eyes were on Weizmann.

"He stopped his discourse, took off his glasses and stood in stunned silence. Never had this happened to him. His age, infirmity, patient toil and sacrifice had been violated in a moment of dreadful rancour. The Assembly sat in horrified tension as he pondered his reply. . . .

"'Somebody has called me a demagogue. I do not know who. I hope that I never learn the man's name. I—a demagogue! I who have borne all the ill and travail of this movement (loud applause). The person who flung that word in my face ought to know that in every house and stable in Nahalal, in every little workshop in Tel Aviv or Haifa there is a drop of my blood. (Tempestuous applause. The delegates all rise to their feet except the Revisionists and Mizrachi.) You know that I am telling you the truth. Some people don't like to hear it—but you *will* hear me. I warn you against bogus palliatives, against short cuts, against false prophets, against facile generalizations, against distortion of historic facts. . . .'

"No dramatist could have conceived a more overpowering climax. He left the hall never again to make a controversial address to a Jewish audience. Between the rows of applauding delegates standing in awe and contrition he made his way painfully, gropingly, into the street."

Winding up his story of the Congress, Eban told how a few days later Weizmann made a short farewell, saying:

"If I have said harsh things to anyone, I did not intend to hurt. The Jewish people, especially those waiting in the camps, look to you to open the gates. I thank you all."[13]

Weizmann had made his presidency dependent on freedom for the Zionist Executive, if it so decided, to conduct discussions in London with the British Government. The motion made by Golda Meyerson was voted down and thus Weizmann's leadership was rejected. What was ironic to Eban was that one month later the newly elected Executive attended talks in London with the British Government. The Zionist movement had dismissed Weizmann—and then had followed his advice.

Weizmann's resignation created a great personal crisis for Eban. He felt if Weizmann had been repudiated, so had he been; if Weizmann was not wanted, he, too, must not be wanted. He had been writing occasional editorials for the London *Jewish Chronicle* and when David Kessler, the publisher, suggested he take over the editorship he gave the offer serious consideration.

Shertok was one of those with whom Eban discussed his future. (Weizmann felt Shertok had abandoned him at Basle and for several years refused even to speak to him.)

"You can't make the beginning of your career dependent on the end of his," Shertok advised Eban.

Then Eban went to see Weizmann in his suite at London's Dorchester Hotel. The older man told his protégé he was convinced that his policies would eventually triumph; he felt he still had contributions to make to the concept of a Jewish state. (A prophetic remark, for in less than a year and a half the entire Zionist world would be turning back to him for help in not just one but several crises.) With some reluctance Eban finally promised Weizmann he would remain with the Agency.

In June (1946) Weizmann had laid the foundation stone for the Weizmann Institute of Science. In February (1947), still bitter over his defeat at Basle, he moved to Rehovoth to take an active part in running the Institute, and left Zionist leadership to others.

Behind in London Eban became one of a small group of experts—among them Arthur Lourie, Michael Comay, Moshe Tov and Dr. Jacob

Robinson—who were technically called "staff advisers" of the Jewish Agency. They were more commonly known as "the back room boys," because they operated well behind the scenes. But when a final attempt was made to negotiate with the British Government, Eban became a member of a sizable body of Jewish representatives who met with an equally sizable body of British representatives from the Foreign Office and the Colonial Office. On the British side of the table were Foreign Minister Bevin and Colonial Secretary Arthur Creech Jones, buttressed by a formidable array of titles and pomposity. On the Jewish side were Ben-Gurion, Shertok, Joseph Linton, David Horowitz, Shabbtai Rosenne, Izhak Gruenbaum, Professor Selig Brodetsky, Nahum Goldmann, Emanuel Neumann, Berl Locker and Eban. Now he was, indeed, in high company—surrounded by many of the top leaders of world Zionism. But both groups were overpopulated and unwieldy for any good purpose.

Although the war was over it was a cold and gloomy time for the British, literally. Coal was scarce. Many elevators were not functioning. Even government offices were inadequately heated, especially the private office of Creech Jones in which the meetings were held. It was a spacious room, more like a salon than an office, with a thick carpet on the floor and a long table around which several dozen people could sit comfortably and on which were several tall candelabra, in case the electricity failed, a likely happening.

Bevin waited until all the others were seated and were impatient for the proceedings to commence before he finally appeared—a thickset man, bulky, broad-shouldered, with eyes that seemed to look through people. Eban found his personality as unattractive as his politics; he was impulsive rather than contemplative, aggressive rather than cordial; an obvious egocentric.

The room was also cold temperaturally, especially for a man who had spent the last four years in Cairo and Jerusalem. The electric lights began to flicker and then finally went out. The unmistakable voice of Bevin said:

"Well, the Israelites have gone out."

Some of his British colleagues snickered, but Eban found it "very heavy stuff" and said so in a whisper to the man beside him.

As the conferring began again Eban was annoyed that Sir Harold Beeley of Chatham House, now Bevin's personal adviser on Palestine affairs and no friend of the Yishuv, persisted in whispering almost constantly into the Foreign Secretary's ear. Eban was especially nettled because he observed that not for a single moment did Bevin permit a conciliatory mood to take root. Whenever they tried to discuss Partition as a solution of the Palestine problem Bevin would arrogantly announce that he was not entitled to impose or even suggest such a thing. Whenever a federated plan was discussed Bevin would amend it in what Eban considered a "ferocious" manner. Frequently he insisted that it would be wrong to place three hundred thousand Arabs under Jewish domination, but he had no answer when Eban asked why, then, would it be all right, under his proposals, to subject seven hundred thousand Jews to the domination of the Arabs?

To the logical mind of the young man so recently out of military uniform it seemed incredible that the same Cabinet which had carried out the partition of India, with what he called "audacity and sweep," could stand paralyzed before the Palestine issue. British policy, he felt, was at its lowest level of representation, having neither its old imperial dignity nor the liberalism of the post-war age. Britain was showing herself to be a tired nation, weary of responsibility. Each day Eban felt more certain she was going to pull out of Palestine, and in the not distant future. This was an unpopular thought for a Zionist at that particular time, because most Jewish leaders in Palestine were convinced that Whitehall was using the threat as a diplomatic weapon. Eban agreed that with shortages of food and fuel, with rationing, with all the post-war problems Britain was having, it made no sense to keep a hundred thousand British troops in Palestine "for a strategic advantage which does not seem very great."[14]

The first time Eban's name ever appeared in New York newspapers was early in 1947 when he accused Bevin of having "skipped a page of his notes" during his last speech to Commons, and thus "the Foreign Secretary omitted to tell the M.P.s that Britain, in the absence of a reasonable settlement, should revert to the terms of the League mandate as they existed before the 1939 White Paper set the immigration quota and limited land sales. The Jews are prepared to accept such a minimum condition for an indefinite period."[15]

As the talks in London dragged on, Bevin began to threaten the Zionists with washing his hands of the whole affair and dropping it into the lap of the United Nations. Many on the Zionist side reacted with skepticism. They were dubious as to how the Jewish case would fare in what Eban called "the arena of multilateral diplomacy." But how they felt was of no importance to Bevin, for in February (1947) this announcement startled the world, including almost everyone at 77 Great Russell Street:

"His Majesty's Government have of themselves no power under the terms of the Mandate to award the country either to the Arabs or to the Jews, or even to partition it between them. . . . We have therefore reached the conclusion that the only course open to us is to submit the problem to the judgment of the United Nations."

Expressing his own reaction and that of his colleagues, Eban said:

"The first sensation was of solitude rather than exhilaration."

He thought of the slight role the League of Nations had played in the administration of the Mandate, of how little attention the British had paid to Geneva. A robust new international organization had been built on the ruins of the League. But there was a danger "that the special ethos and pathos of Zionism would be submerged in the torrent of global politics." Then his natural optimism took hold.

"But there was also an opportunity. The Jewish people's claim would now be weighed on the scale of international justice, remote, to some degree, from the strategic interests of any single power."[16]

If the United Nations was to decide the future of the Jewish people, then it was imperative that instead of worrying about what Fleet Street and Whitehall thought, 77 Great Russell Street had better quickly cultivate the leaders of those countries that might soon be voting on what should be done with Palestine.

Eban was made responsible for France, Belgium, the Netherlands and Luxembourg. He was to see the highest government officials in each of those countries and explain the case for Partition—to plead for the right of the Jews of Palestine to create their own state. It was a difficult and important assignment. He had been to France and Belgium several times in his youth and spoke French fluently, but he had never made an official visit to a foreign government before and he was nervous.

First he went to Paris, where he succeeded in obtaining an audience with the Premier, Paul Ramadier. Eban had recently celebrated his thirty-second birthday; Ramadier was almost sixty. But they had in common that both were Socialists. After shaking hands the Premier offered his guest a cigarette, then pulled a lighter from his pocket and snapped it several times. Nothing happened. As Eban took a package of matches from his own pocket, Ramadier laughed and said:

"*Voici la France. Rien ne marche. Mais c'est charmant, n'est-ce pas?* (This is France. Nothing works. Charming, isn't it?)"

Eban smiled but decided it would be diplomatic to make no comment. Still looking at the non-functioning lighter, Ramadier said:

"This Cabinet of which I am a member was formed two weeks ago.

Therefore, it is a Cabinet of very long standing. Here in France ministers never hold office long enough to find out what's in the drawers of their desks before they get moved over to something else."

As soon as Eban began talking about Palestine Ramadier listened attentively and as they parted indicated that the Jews would have the support of France.[17]

From Paris Eban went to Brussels and again had the good fortune of getting to the top at once. Paul-Henri Spaak, then forty-eight, was his country's Foreign Minister and Prime Minister as well, and had also been elected the first president of the United Nations General Assembly. Here again was a fellow Socialist. Eban found him eloquent, ebullient and rhetorical. ("He spoke to you personally as though you were an audience in Madison Square Garden.") An immediate rapport developed between them. ("As I listened to him I realized I was in the presence of a very deep, very sharp intellect."[18])

When Eban began making his bid for Belgian support for Partition, Spaak interrupted, saying:

"Partition is certainly the logical solution. If we see any possibility of supporting you we will."

So far Eban had scored 100 percent. Now he had only Luxembourg and the Netherlands to win. He was in Amsterdam on his way to The Hague when he received a cable from Shertok in New York reading:

> PLEASE WIND UP AS SOON AS POSSIBLE
> AND COME TO NEW YORK.

What Eban did not learn until later was that Shertok in New York had enlisted the assistance of a number of people to write the general brief that would be used in presenting the Jewish case before the United Nations, among them Judge Samuel Irving Rosenman, onetime member of the New York State Legislature, Justice of the Supreme Court of New York for fifteen years and for three years special counsel for Presidents Roosevelt and Truman.[19] Also enlisted was attorney Murray Gurfein, who had been assistant to the chief U.S. counsel at the Nuremberg trials.[20] The original idea had been to employ or consult only legal experts. But Shertok soon discovered that while they might know their international law and all be Jews, they lacked what he called "the authentic Zionist passion and the authentic Zionist knowledge." As a result, what had emerged so far was formalistic, cold, intensely juridical but not very moving. Therefore Shertok had thrown most of their work into a wastebasket. He knew that what he needed was someone who could do more than write grammatical English. He needed, urgently, someone who burned with an intense inner flame. It was then that he thought of Eban and without a second's reconsideration sent the cable.

When Eban reached London he excitedly told Suzy the news.

"What does it mean?"

"A great opportunity, I'm sure," he replied. "It may be the big break of my life."

"How long will you be gone?"

He looked at her affectionately and replied:

"If you think I am going without you, you are wrong."

"Will they pay my way, too?"

"No, I'm afraid not, because you are not included in the invitation."

"But can we afford it?"

"Somehow we will."

So they began liquidating their flat in Highgate, their fourth place of residence in less than three years, packing for the first trip either of them had ever made to America.

"How long do you think we'll be staying in New York?" Suzy asked.

Her husband smiled. "Days, months, years, who knows?"[21]

Carmel, the young sister for whom Aubrey had so much affection, had preceded him by a few months to take a position in the legal department of the United Nations, but Eban was aware that for weeks there would probably be little time for family or friends—for anything but work. After he and Suzy were settled in a downright dingy hotel on upper Broadway, the Empire, he warned her that she would have to get accustomed to seeing him infrequently, now that he had an eighteen-hour-a-day job.

One night he brought a letter to Suzy from her younger sister telling about her marriage to Chaim (Vivian) Herzog, now a lawyer in Jerusalem and liaison officer between the Jewish Agency and British authorities. They had had no desire for a big wedding so the ceremony was performed in the village of Gedera. Because of a road curfew their car had been stopped by some especially cantankerous British soldiers who pointed to a cardboard box on the back seat and asked:

"What's in the package?"

"The cake . . . our wedding cake," Herzog replied.

Instead of opening the box, the British soldiers took turns jabbing it with their bayonets to be sure, they said, that it didn't contain a bomb or grenades. The bridal couple was then permitted to proceed and the wedding was held without further incident, the punctured cake serving as the conversation piece of the afternoon.

The United Kingdom had requested a special session of the UN General Assembly to prepare for a substantive discussion of the Middle East at the autumn session and so on April 29 (1947), just a few days after the Ebans' arrival in New York, the General Assembly convened at Flushing Meadow with the Palestine question inscribed on its agenda—where it remained for many long years.

The UN's answer to the question of what to do about Palestine at first looked not much different from the tired old solution the British had so often advanced: Appoint another commission. Investigate. Submit a report. Argue. Debate. The new investigative body voted into existence by the General Assembly on May 15 (1947) was to be called the United Nations Special Committee on Palestine, but it became better known simply as UNSCOP. On the committee would be representatives of eleven nations: Australia, Canada, Czechoslovakia, Guatemala, Holland, India, Iran, Peru, Sweden, Uruguay and Yugoslavia.

The Arabs and the Jews were each given the right to appoint two liaison officers to the committee. The Arab Higher Committee, committing what would be the first in a long series of self-defeating Arab blunders—the end of which is still not in sight, at this writing—decided to boycott the committee and appointed no liaison officers. (Commenting on this blunder, Eban said: "We live on the mistakes of the Arabs."[22]) The Jewish Agency promptly announced that its liaison officers would be David Horowitz, once a kibbutznik,[23] now economic adviser to the Jewish Agency, who would handle economic matters, and Aubrey Eban, who would deal with all political aspects of the case, as head of the Jewish Agency's Middle East department in London.

This was another turning point in the career of Aubrey Solomon Eban. Suddenly New York became the important stage. Had he remained in London he might have played a very inconsequential role in this most important drama in 1,877 years of Jewish history.[24] The cable from Shertok summoning him to New York and his subsequent appointment as one of the UNSCOP liaison officers presented the opportunity for a full play of his talents as scholar, linguist, writer and public speaker.

12

Death of the Mandate

THEY ALL KNEW—Weizmann, Shertok, Ben-Gurion, Eban and everyone else involved—that the recommendations of UNSCOP were going to be cardinal. If UNSCOP did not recommend Partition and the establishment of a Jewish state, there was no chance whatsoever that the General Assembly would approve such a plan. If UNSCOP *did* recommend it, this did not necessarily guarantee passage of a favorable UN resolution, but at least it would mean there was a chance. As had so often happened in the past—as would happen so often in the future—in military affairs and in diplomatic contests, the opposition could lose a battle or even a war and go on. But not the Jews.

The mere appointment of UNSCOP was important, for it was the first recognition by the United Nations that the Jewish Agency was entitled to a special status on the world scene. The appointment of Jewish Agency liaison officers was semi-recognition that the Jewish population of Palestine constituted a political unit on its way to independence. For Eban the appointment was personally significant—another turning point in his career—for he now had a definite international status.

Whether UNSCOP recommended Partition would depend on whether the committee members decided that two sovereign units could be carved out of Palestine and could live in any sort of stability. To make such a judgment they required a knowledge of the socioeconomic situation. That would be Horowitz's responsibility. The other problem was political and international. What would be the effect on the Arab world of the establishment of a Jewish state? Would it advance or retard the prospects for peace? How would it affect the power balance? It was in those fields that Eban was considered an authority. It would be his task to help UNSCOP find the answers.

Looking over the list of the eleven men appointed to the committee, Eban decided that as a whole they were not especially eminent, yet these eleven men of diverse backgrounds, from scattered parts of the world, would make the all-important life-or-death decision.

The committee had been set up on a territorial basis. Western Europe was represented by an elderly Swedish judge, Emil Sandstroem, chairman, and by Dr. Nicholas Blum of the Netherlands, former lieutenant-governor of the Dutch East Indies; the British Commonwealth by Supreme Court Justice Ivan Rand of Canada and John D. L. Hood of Australia's Department of External Affairs; Latin America by Dr. Jorge García-Granados, Guatemalan Ambassador to the United States, Professor Enrique Rodriguez Fabregat, former Minister of Education of Uruguay, and Dr. Arturo García Salazar, Peruvian Ambassador to the Vatican; Eastern Europe by Dr. Karel Lisicky of Czechoslovakia, Social Democrat and friend of Dr. Jan Masaryk, and Vladimir Simitch, president of the Yugoslav Senate; Asia by Nasrollah Entezan, former Foreign Minister of Iran, and Sir Abdur Rahman, a judge from Lahore, India.

These were the men the two liaison officers would have to try to impress as they flew the Atlantic with them, shared the same hotels with them, ate with them and guided them around Palestine.

The Jewish Agency Executive, in briefing Eban and Horowitz—and Shertok as well—gave them clear instructions to work for the creation of a Jewish state in a "suitable area" of Palestine. Nothing less.

In an old York aircraft they flew the Atlantic and then to Malta, where the British Government was so hostile that it housed the committee members, the aides and the liaison officers in barracks and tents.

"Imagine putting distinguished diplomats in Nissen huts, with no regard for their age or diplomatic status!" Eban said, in recounting the trip.[1]

Then to Palestine, where the work of the liaison officers really began. UNSCOP had appointed a three-man secretariat. One was a Chinese, Dr. Victor Hoo, Assistant Secretary-General of the UN, who spoke Chinese, French, English, Russian and German, all fluently. Before he left Palestine he had also been exposed to Hebrew. Another member of the secretariat, Dr. Ralph Bunche, American Negro, turned out to be the driving force that kept the committee functioning in high gear. He and the two Jewish liaison officers were soon good friends, with admiration flowing both ways.

Because the Arabs were still boycotting the committee, Eban, Horowitz and a British liaison officer, Donald C. MacCillivray, a pleasant young Scot free of the usual British colonial prejudices, did all the planning and guiding.[2] Most of the committee members wanted to be fair to both sides, so they insisted on seeing Arab factories as well as Jewish factories, even when told that Arab factories in most of Palestine were almost non-existent, Arab farms as well as Jewish farms, and one of them even wondered why they couldn't see an Arab kibbutz. Eban and Horowitz took them to Haifa, the Dead Sea, the Arab town of Ramallah, Mount Carmel, Tel Aviv, down into the Negev, up to Safed, to factories, canneries, orange groves, harbor installations. The enlightening, the pointing out, the persuading went on at breakfast, lunch and dinner; as they drove from place to place; sometimes in French, sometimes in English or German; unceasingly but subtly.

Chairman Sandstroem was reticent and usually stern. The Dutchman, with his colonial background, seemed sympathetic to the British. The Canadian judge was a liberal humanitarian with a desire to serve his conscience rather than to obey directives. The Australian was as ebullient as most of his countrymen are. The Czech behaved like the diplomat that he was by profession. The Yugoslav from the start favored a bi-national state. The Peruvian had close ties with the Vatican and indicated that his sole interest was what would be best for Rome. The Iranian, who would one day become General Assembly President at a critical moment in history, was fluent in French, German, English and Persian, and was greatly impressed when Eban disclosed he could converse with him in any of the four languages. The Indian, a Moslem, was openly and stubbornly pro-Arab from the start. Eban's favorites on the committee were the Guatemalan and the Uruguayan. Both had served time in prison for their revolutionary beliefs. Dr. Gracía-Granados[3] at first favored the cantonization idea and had to be convinced that dividing the populace in this manner would lead to congested Jewish islands resembling ghettos. Dr. Fabregat was won to the Jewish side by his sympathy for the sufferings of Jewish children in Europe.

Some committee members were disgusted when the Arab owners of a tobacco factory in Haifa refused to permit the liaison officers to accompany the committee members on a tour of the installation "because they are Jews."

There were other incidents that may have swayed them, but most indelible was what two committee members saw one day in the harbor of Haifa. When Eban and Horowitz heard that the Haganah ship

Exodus 1947 had arrived off the coast of Palestine with forty-five hundred Jews from the D.P. camps of Germany and was being boarded by British sailors, they suggested that this might be something that UNSCOP should see. Chairman Sandstroem and the Yugoslav member expressed interest. By the time they reached Haifa the actual fighting was over—one of the most peculiar battles in naval history, with the British boarding party using rifles and tear gas, the refugees trying to fight them off with cans of food and broomsticks. (Three of the refugees were killed.) But they did arrive in time to watch—for as long as they could endure—the transfer of the forty-five hundred men, women and children (minus three) from the *Exodus 1947* to three British prison ships, there to be locked in cages below decks. The British soldiers guarding the area refused to permit Eban to accompany the committee members onto the dock, so he was forced to sit in the café of the Zion Hotel drinking innumerable small cups of black coffee until they returned.

"They looked very tired, very poor!" Sandstroem told Eban.[4]

That night two American newspapermen appeared at the apartment of Dr. García-Granados in company with a tall, blond-haired, blue-eyed man about thirty who was introduced as the Reverend John Grauel of Worcester, Massachusetts, a Christian who had been in the *Exodus 1947* crew as a volunteer cook—the only non-Jew aboard. He stayed for an hour detailing an experience which, he said, had made him feel "honored and humbled."

Telling of the trip to the Haifa dock, Eban later said: "I had a feeling that the British Mandate died that day. A regime that could maintain itself only by such incongruous and squalid acts was clearly on its way out. What they were doing was against the whole temperament and structure of the British character. It was both cruel and ridiculous. Of course I didn't know, then, the worst—that the forty-five hundred would end up in German camps again. But I was sure that seeing with their own eyes this British behavior, the committee members would realize that the British simply had to go."

But a recommendation that the Mandate ought to be ended would not be enough. At least a majority of the committee had to be won over to the idea of a Jewish state, and so Eban and Horowitz took the committee in two groups—on two separate evenings—to Rehovoth for dinner and a long conversation with Dr. Weizmann. Eban's mentor was in his usual superb form the first night. He started his story on a personal level in Pinsk, talking casually of his boyhood, weaving his own life story into the larger tapestry of Jewish history in the nineteenth and twentieth centuries. He made convincing propaganda while seeming to be casually telling a story. Everyone was impressed.

News pictures taken the day Weizmann made his formal appearance before the committee showed young Eban sitting nearby, his brow furrowed with anxiety. He was worrying over the trouble Weizmann was having, because of his bad eyesight, reading the report he had prepared for the committee. He was also worrying about Suzy, who that morning had been taken to Hadassah Hospital on Mount Scopus with acute appendicitis. As soon as the session was adjourned he rushed to the hospital to find that a celebrated New Zealand surgeon had performed a successful appendectomy.

One evening Eban addressed the *chug* or study group before which he had appeared some years earlier. The meeting was held in the home of a Jewish journalist, Moshe Medzini, and Eban spoke on *The Arab Novel*—a subject about as remote from the affairs of the moment in Palestine as possible.

As the committee members were getting ready to leave Jerusalem for Geneva, where they would write their report in a peaceful Swiss atmosphere, Dr. Sandstroem invited Eban and Horowitz to join them there.

In Cairo, en route, they read an article in a local monthly magazine written by a high-ranking Egyptian Army officer in which he said the Egyptian Army was incapable of fighting outside the country. But they were depressed when by radio they heard the news of what had happened as soon as UNSCOP left Palestine. On July 29 the British hanged three members of Irgun and two days later Irgun hanged two British sergeants being held as hostages.

Shertok was already in Geneva when Eban and Horowitz finally arrived there—worried and nervous. From Washington, London and Paris had come word that unless the UNSCOP report called for repeal of the British Mandate and unless it also recommended the creation of a Jewish state, not a single country represented in the UN would be ready to support such an idea.

Some indication of how the eleven members might line up came when they debated whether to take a side trip to the D.P. camps of Europe. The question involved was whether there was any connection between the general Jewish problem, represented by the Jews in camps, and the Palestine question. India, Iran, Yugoslavia and Peru were against such a trip. Czechoslovakia abstained from taking sides. The other six voted in favor of visiting the camps and so the deputy members of the committee went, but a six-to-five victory was too close to be comfortable.

Eban and Horowitz had a long discussion at the Palais des Nations in Geneva with Dr. Sandstroem about the latest developments in the *Exodus 1947* case. Hitherto all illegal immigrants had been sent to Cyprus, where they took their places in the queue awaiting legal British permits to enter Palestine. But the *Exodus 1947* people had been sent to France. This meant the British intended that they never should be admitted to Palestine.[5] The three British prison ships had put in to a small French port, but the forty-five hundred miserable refugees refused to go ashore, despite their hunger, thirst and suffering. The British threatened that unless they disembarked immediately they might be taken to Germany, whence they had come. The UNSCOP chairman expressed what seemed to Eban sincere regret that he had no power to intervene.

Worried about the Yugoslav member's advocacy of a bi-national state, Shertok went to Belgrade to see the Foreign Minister. While he was gone the deputy members came back from their tour of D.P. camps, all apparently deeply affected. They had found not a single camp inmate who was not eager—almost insanely eager—to get to Palestine. Hood of Australia, the leader of the tour, was so impressed that Eban credited the visit to the D.P. camp with Australia's support of the Jewish cause.

As the UNSCOP members conferred, debated, wrote preliminary reports and tried to reconcile their differences, Eban and Horowitz had long discussions about the enigma of Britain's policy. The one question neither could answer was why Britain was willing to evacuate Egypt, India and Greece, yet seemed so reluctant to get out of Palestine, even though it was an almost intolerable burden. Was it all because of the stubbornness of one man? Was Bevin alone responsible?

In the hope of getting some clarification of British policy, Eban decided to make a fast trip to London. His chief purpose was to find out whether, even if the UN passed a Partition resolution, Britain would accept it. The answer would greatly influence Jewish tactics. Among the leaders he saw were Harold Beeley of Chatham House, Harold Laski and Richard Crossman. Beeley told him flatly:

"There is no likelihood of mobilizing a two-thirds majority for an anti-British solution, because of the split between the great powers, and any such motion is doomed to failure."[6]

The fashionable British view, he discovered, was that an imperial power never moves out of anywhere voluntarily and even if the UN adopted a Partition resolution Britain would cling to Palestine "by its nails and its teeth." But an important British minority felt that the economic crisis made the Palestine burden unpopular and if in addition there were to be international opposition to maintaining the Mandate it ought to be given up. He met with the editorial boards of several important London newspapers and at the *Times* was told of a statement Attlee had made privately:

"England will carry out any reasonable decision reached by the United Nations to the best of its ability."

Eban saw this as a not very favorable promise. The trap was the word "reasonable." It was typically British diplomatic language, with an ostensibly positive look, yet Attlee himself would decide whether the decision was reasonable and therefore whether England would carry it out.

He also brought back to Geneva an expression of the British military position: experts estimated it would require considerably fewer battalions of British soldiers to cope with any Jewish opposition to an imposed solution favorable to the Arabs than it would require to cope with the fury of the Arabs if the solution failed to please them.

As a result of Eban's London trip the Agency paid little attention thereafter to direct relations with the British, for it was obvious that their attitude would be governed not by what Agency representatives told them but by whether the Agency was able to get international support for its case against the Mandate and for Partition.

Back at the Palais des Nations Eban learned that the committee members had reached unanimity on only one point: that they must propose a definite and unequivocal solution. Finally a meeting was held at which the chairman bluntly asked:

"Does anyone favor an Arab state in all of Palestine?"

No reply.

"Does anyone favor a Jewish state in all of Palestine?"

No reply.

But then the trouble began, as once more they debated cantonization, a bi-national state and separate Arab and Jewish states.

The committee had been given a deadline—September 1 (1947)—when its recommendations were to be submitted to the UN. At times in August it seemed unlikely the deadline could possibly be met. Meanwhile both Eban and Horowitz were working on the vacillating members. At one point they had to try to prevent an agreement on "a democratic bi-national state, run by the majority," which would have meant the

Arabs. They also had to work to keep the committee from dividing into several irreconcilable groups, unwilling to compromise. Most important, they had to see that the committee did not submit a report in which no positive solution of any kind was recommended. The task called for diplomacy of the most cautious yet effective sort. It was a tremendous test for a young man so new to the subterfuges of high-level dealing. A single false step might lead to resentment, anger and antagonism to the Jewish cause, and even to an end to the Zionist dream.

One day while the deliberations were still in progress a cable came from London announcing that the British had finally decided to make good on their threat to transport the *Exodus 1947* refugees back to Germany. Perhaps *this* would sway some of the undecided members.

One of the vacillators was the Czech delegate, who, in chats with Eban and Horowitz, always talked as if he favored Partition, but in committee meetings never voted that way. Jan Masaryk came through Geneva in August, tired, ill and looking for a place to rest, incognito. Shertok saw him and Masaryk agreed to put pressure on the Czech member.[7]

Aware of their great responsibility, Eban and Horowitz decided to confer with Dr. Weizmann, who was vacationing in a Swiss village near the Austro-Italian frontier. While they were briefing him on the status of the committee deliberations, Shertok called from Geneva to report a conversation with a French political adviser to the committee, who had just told him, bluntly:

"You must choose between complete independence in a limited area or limited autonomy in a larger area."

As August waned the eleven men agreed unanimously to recommend an end to the British Mandate. A bare majority also favored Partition, but from day to day, as the final report was being written, there were rumors that this one or that one had changed his mind, turning the majority into a minority. As a result, although this was Switzerland's perfect time of the year and the liaison men needed relaxation as much as the committee members, there could be no lessening of tension until the eleven signatures were finally on the document.

On August 31, with the deadline hours away, Eban and Horowitz were unofficially informed there would be two reports: the representatives of Canada, Czechoslovakia, Guatemala, Uruguay, Peru, the Netherlands and Sweden would sign a report favoring an independent Arab state, an independent Jewish state and a *corpus separatum* of the city of Jerusalem under the UN, all of which should come into being after a transitional period of two years from September 1, 1947. During this transitional period Great Britain, as Mandatory, would carry on the administration under the UN.[8]

The minority report, which Yugoslavia, India and Iran would support, favored a form of cantonization, with Jewish immigration ultimately up to the Arab majority of the new Palestinian state. Australia would abstain.

It was much better than anyone had expected. The small group that celebrated the victory included, besides Shertok, Horowitz and Eban, Moshe Tov, whose contacts with the South Americans had been of great help, and Mordecai Kahane, Gideon Rufer, Eliahu Sassoon and Leo Kohn, all connected with the Agency and all involved in the effort to win statehood. Everyone was tired from the plethora of last-minute rumors, false reports and fears, and from the constant danger that something would go wrong. But now they could relax. Or could they?

Someone said:

"Let's open a bottle of champagne . . . after we know the thing is signed."

The signatures were to be affixed at 9 P.M. Eban and Horowitz had been told to be at the Palais at that hour to receive copies of the report for the Agency. The mandatory government's liaison officer was there, too, but when nine o'clock came there were no reports. The three men looked impatiently at the locked door of the committee room.

Ten o'clock. Eleven. There was reason aplenty for the tension Horowitz and Eban felt. How it turned out would determine whether they and their Jewish Agency colleagues would continue the battle with a hopeful victory behind them or would go back to a revolutionary situation of conflict with the Arabs and the mandatory power as well. If the UNSCOP vote went against Partition many of the Jews of Palestine, with some reason, would say it would have been better not to have brought up the possibility at all.

Knowing all this, Eban paced the hallways of the Palais like a lion in a cage. Some of the time Horowitz paced with him and they debated their chances of victory. Once, alone, Eban wandered into the assembly hall in which Haile Selassie had pleaded before the League of Nations for help in the face of the Italian invasion, and thought of how the international community had failed Abyssinia. Several times he walked the long corridors up to the library and down to the cafeteria, doing what had become a habit with him when in tension: walking very quickly as if he had a destination; as if he were late for an appointment.

At a few minutes after eleven the door was flung open and a committee member dashed out, saw the three liaison men and said, wryly:

"Oh, here are the expectant fathers!"

At midnight the door opened again and the eleven members and their deputies filed out. Several had tears in their eyes. Minutes later, at 12:05 A.M. on September 1 (1947), the report was officially handed to Eban and Horowitz. The recommendations were as they had been reported in the afternoon—unchanged.

Aubrey Solomon Eban had played a paramount role in obtaining for a state yet unborn its first great diplomatic victory.

When Eban and Horowitz took the UNSCOP report to Ben-Gurion he happened to be deeply involved in an internal problem—how to curb the independent activities of the two extreme Jewish armies, the Irgun Tzevai Leumi (Etzel) and the Lohame Herut Israel (the Stern Gang). After greeting his visitors he gave them a long explanation of why he felt the Yishuv could make no progress unless the two underground forces were liquidated. Finally Eban interrupted:

"We have come to tell you that UNSCOP has recommended a Jewish state."

Ignoring the remark, Ben-Gurion went on, with typical single-mindedness:

"We will definitely have to liquidate the Etzel."

"And they have included the Negev," Eban reported.

"We'll also have to finish off the Stern Gang," Ben-Gurion said.

Finally Eban and Horowitz, despairing of getting Ben-Gurion's attention off his own concern, started out the door. Ben-Gurion came rushing after them.

"What was that you said? They recommended a Jewish state in the Negev? Why didn't you tell me that before?"

13

How Partition Was Won

ZURICH WAS THE NEXT STOP, for there the Zionist General Council was in session. On the train Eban settled back and read the long report fully for the first time. Then he wrote in his diary this comment: "A splendid gleam of friendship has lit up the Jewish solitude."

The Council was in a state of elation and the two liaison officers received public and private congratulations on a job well done. But then they met with the Jewish Agency Political Committee and the talk was all of the future—of the struggle ahead and what the chances were likely to be in the General Assembly. They went down the list of United Nations members, country by country—fifty-seven in all. In Jerusalem and Geneva there had been only eleven to worry about. In New York it would be much more difficult.

The Political Committee assigned Eban and Horowitz to go immediately to London and put their fingers on the British political pulse and then join the others on Long Island, where the General Assembly would soon be meeting.

The atmosphere in London was worse, if anything, than when Eban had so recently been there. The UNSCOP report pleased almost no one in the Government. Fleet Street was more hostile than ever, judging by the newspaper editorials. In some usually well-informed Jewish circles there was wild talk that Palestine would have to be evacuated, for the UNSCOP report, they said, would set the whole Middle East on fire. Dr. Weizmann told Eban he had an appointment with Winston Churchill and some people in the Colonial Office, but that Bevin had bluntly, curtly, almost insultingly refused to see him.

Horowitz saw Jon Kimche, Jewish editor, Harold Beeley and others whose opinions were worth something. Eban held endless meetings with newspaper editors, correspondents for Canadian, American and South American papers, diplomats, Intelligence officers and anyone else who could give him information or who wanted a briefing.

One of Eban's most valuable contacts was Lieutenant-Colonel the Hon. Martin Charteris, former head of Military Intelligence at Force Headquarters, who was blamed by many for the campaign of suppression and terrorization of the Jews in Palestine in 1946, but who had a great gift for personal friendships with such people as Weizmann, Eban and Kollek. (He was later in charge of the Palestine desk at the War Office.) Eban invited him to lunch at Prunier's in St. James's Street. Eban's advance information was that Charteris had a plan to smash the Jewish Agency and Haganah. He was represented as feeling that if this could be done, it would then be a simple matter to take care of the Irgun and the Stern Gang. He thought "it could be arranged" for more moderate Jewish leaders to take over after elimination of the Agency.

At the luncheon Charteris was nonchalant and easygoing, making light conversation in a bantering manner. Horowitz, greatly impressed, characterized him as "sophisticated, clever and civilized."[1] Charteris talked almost exclusively about the military aspect of the Palestinian struggle and surprised the two men facing him by predicting that war between Arabs and Jews would inevitably end in a Jewish victory— an opinion few of his British colleagues then shared. After indicating that Britain would not remain much longer in Palestine, he told a story to illustrate how he felt about the probable evacuation:

"A man threw himself off the top of the Empire State Building in New York and as he plunged past the fortieth floor someone shouted at him: 'How do you feel?' to which he shouted back, 'Everything's all right so far.'"

It was a pleasant luncheon, for the English officer was affable and quick-witted, and the three-cornered conversation sparkled. As Eban was making one of his own acidulous remarks, Charteris interrupted, saying:

"That's an important point that I'll use in the report I'll be making of our talk."

Everyone laughed, for Charteris was aware that Eban and Horowitz were trying to pry information from him, while they knew that he was trying to get all he could from them.

(In 1971, when Eban paid the first official visit of any Israeli Foreign

Minister to London, he was wafted into Buckingham Palace by Charteris, by then private secretary to Queen Elizabeth.)

Eban took Horowitz to Oxford to meet his friend Sir Reginald Coupland. After being introduced Horowitz commended the professor for having written "the most objective, profound and thorough-going document ever produced on the Palestine question."[2] The professor reciprocated by congratulating Eban and Horowitz on the UNSCOP report, which he said revived the proposals his Royal Commission had made in 1937, "although adjusting them to the altered conditions of the times." He bemoaned the increase in worldwide anti-Semitism and expressed a hope that if guarantees against aggression and expansion were added to the UNSCOP report it would prove a definitive solution to the entire problem.

Most important was a meeting arranged by Kimche with the leading Arab diplomat, Abdul Rahman Azzam Pasha, Secretary-General of the Arab League, which represented the last attempt by the Jews to get an arbitrated political settlement. It took place late one afternoon in the Savoy Hotel, where the Arab leader was staying. He received his three guests—Eban, Horowitz and Kimche—courteously, but he was adamant in his attitude. When they told him the Jews were a *fait accompli* in the Middle East and suggested working out a plan so Jews and Arabs could live together in peace and cooperation, he bluntly replied:

"The Arab world is not in a compromising mood."

Several moments later he made this amazing statement:

"You won't get anything by peaceful means or compromise. You can, perhaps, get something, but only by force of arms."

Eban replied:

"The UNSCOP report established the possibility of a satisfactory compromise. Why shouldn't we at least make an effort to reach agreement along these lines? At all events, our proposal is a first draft only and we shall welcome any counterproposal from your side."

The answer was:

"The Arab world regards you as invaders and is ready to fight you."

At another point he said:

"War is inevitable. If you win the war you'll get your state. If you get your state you have a chance of the Arabs having to accept you. But please don't imagine that you'll ever have a chance of getting them to accept you in advance, voluntarily. This is an historic conflict which must reach a decision and the decision will have to be by force."

The conversation went on for a long time, but the Arab leader's obvious admiration of force and violence did not change and Eban left depressed. The welcome had been cordial, the encounter dramatic, the significance historic, but they had seen the collapse of the final effort to bridge the great gulf. As Horowitz put it:

"We saw looming up before us latent, powerful forces, pushing us irresistibly and inescapably toward the brink of a sanguinary war, the outcome of which none could prophesy."[3]

From London Eban and his wife went back to New York. Soon after they arrived an incident occurred about which the Ebans were never informed. One of the most popular radio talk shows of the time, "Town Hall of the Air," had arranged a debate on the Palestine question, with Shertok and Senator Warren G. Magnuson of Seattle opposed by Albert Hourani and Congressman Lawrence Smith of Wisconsin. At the last minute Shertok tried to beg off on the ground he was tired and would not be able to make a good impression.

"Whom do you suggest to replace you?" asked I. L. Kenen, the Jewish Agency director of information.

"I know the perfect man," Shertok replied, brightly. "Aubrey Eban has just arrived from Palestine by way of Geneva, Zurich and London. He'll do better than I would, even if I were well."

"This isn't a little Palestine station," Kenen said angrily. "This is millions and millions of people. This is going out over the entire network, across forty-eight states and the District of Columbia. Thumbs down on Eban! That young Englishman doesn't even know how to open his mouth."

Shertok shrugged his shoulders and finally agreed that he would do it himself. Telling the story years later Kenen said:

"Shertok was a terrible flop that night. I guess he was really tired —and he showed it. Worse than that, Hourani provoked him and Shertok lost his temper on the air and—well, he was just awful! Of course I had never heard Eban speak. When I finally did, I realized what a fool I had been!"[4]

When Eban arrived in New York he went immediately to a five-story brownstone building at 16 East Sixty-sixth Street that had become general staff headquarters for the battle. Here the Jewish Agency had its offices. Here documents were prepared, speeches written, press releases issued, conferences held over tactics, strategy mapped. The summer was lingering on and it was still hot but there was neither air conditioning nor even electric fans. Eban worked far into every night. As one associate put it:

"Speeches, pamphlets and memoranda poured from his speeding pen."[5]

The secretary assigned to him was a tall, stately and extremely intelligent woman, Regina Medzini, who had already worked for Arlosoroff, Shertok, Ben-Gurion and Golda Meir, and in whose home in Jerusalem Eban had delivered one of his most recent speeches—to the *chug*. He was not aware then that for the next twelve years she would remain his confidential secretary and she was not aware that twenty-five years later she would be tempted to write a book entitled *Under Five Dictators*, describing her experience in working for Eban and four Israeli Prime Ministers.[6]

The General Assembly was convened on September 22 (1947) and three days later an ad hoc Palestine Committee, comprising the entire General Assembly membership, went into session. In those days the UN offices were at Lake Success in an abandoned gyroscope factory, while the General Assembly met in a large auditorium at Flushing Meadow (sometimes incorrectly called Flushing Meadows). It took thirty minutes by car from the Sixty-sixth Street GHQ to Flushing Meadow and at least another half hour to Lake Success, and so Eban and his associates spent a great deal of their time commuting, but there were no wasted minutes, for they planned it so that no one ever traveled alone and even if there were only two in the car it was an opportunity for a strategy conference.

In order to obtain passage of a Partition resolution a two-thirds vote was essential. This was not possible without the support of the Soviet Union and her associates, as well as the United States and those who followed her lead. Since the creation of the UN, the USSR and the USA had never voted together on any important issue, so the question that was asked again and again at the Agency was whether the Russian desire to get the British out of the Middle East was great enough for them to forget, at least temporarily, their Cold War conflict with America.

For two months and four days the struggle went on: speeches in public and diplomatic maneuvering behind the scenes; depression in Sixty-sixth Street when some friendly nation wavered and threatened to vote with the opposition, rejoicing when someone claimed he could see a pinpoint of light at the end of the tunnel.

The first piece of good news was that at a caucus the Slav bloc had decided not to support the minority report Iran, India and Yugoslavia had drawn up. Maybe this was some indication of what Russia would do.

A bad piece of news was that Paul-Henri Spaak, still Prime Minister of Belgium, who had assured Eban when he saw him in Brussels that his country would surely support Partition, now was working doggedly against the idea of a Jewish state.

"I learned some political facts of life from the case," Eban said later. "We tried to find out the reason for the switch and he said: "'Well, when you came to see me I thought the British were for it.'

"It was pure opportunism—because the Belgian Socialists were then so closely linked with the British Socialists."[7]

Early in the session the Arab opposition produced two extremely effective speakers: Camille Chamoun, a Maronite from Lebanon,[8] and Sir Zafrullah Khan of Pakistan, both cultured and intelligent. They were to be countered by Dr. Weizmann, Shertok and Dr. Abba Hillel Silver, Reform rabbi from Cleveland.[9]

Ordinarily Weizmann would have needed little help with his address, but when he arrived in New York in early October to lend his support to the struggle for statehood Eban and associates told him bluntly that it was up to him to counteract the effect of Chamoun and Sir Zafrullah Khan; that if he made enough impact on the wavering or uncommitted delegates it might be possible to get the two-thirds vote that was needed. Weizmann's reply was that he wished his address to be very carefully formulated, because this might be his last appearance at the bar of the nations. His eyesight was so bad and the work of preparation was so "agonizing" for him that Eban would have to be relieved of all other duties to work with him.

On October 16 (1947) Eban made this entry in his diary:

"Saw Chief after he lunched with Henry [Morgenthau]. Worked on draft for four steady hours. After each sentence was written in huge letters and agreed on, he would go to the lampstand and bring the text right to his glasses, endeavoring to learn it by heart. By the end of the session his eyes were watering as if in tears. Finally he said: 'We'll make this do, but how about a *posuk* [biblical verse] for the ending?' We looked for a Bible and eventually found one supplied by the hotel in the bedside table. Spent a half-hour on Isaiah, looking for 'Return to Zion' passages. Finally his mind was caught by the prophecy of 'an ensign for the nations.' As I left he said, 'Well, this is it. Over the top for the last time.'"

As Eban listened to Weizmann delivering the speech he had helped write he experienced a feeling of pride and self-satisfaction.

"The delegates of fifty-seven nations listened to him in suspense," he later wrote.[10]

Some days earlier Faris el-Khouri of Syria had claimed that Jews are not descendants of ancient Hebrews at all, but came "from the Khazar tribes of Southern Russia who embraced Judaism."

Eban suggested that Weizmann use his power of sarcasm in reply. And he did. Pushing his glasses up onto his forehead with superb irony he said:

"It is strange, very strange, but all my life I have been a Jew. I have felt like a Jew. I have suffered like a Jew. So now it is fascinating to learn that I am a Khazar!"

The ridicule brought the house down. Then the speech wound up with the quotation Eban had found in the hotel Bible:

"The Lord shall set his hand the second time to recover the remnants of his people. And he shall set up an ensign for the nations, and shall assemble the outcast of Israel and gather together the dispersed of Judah from the four corners of the earth."

When a nine-nation subcommittee was appointed to hold hearings on the Partition plan, the Jewish Agency representatives were given permission not only to attend the sessions but to make comments on each point discussed. Shertok generally served as the Jewish spokesman. After one of his brilliant rebuttals General John Hilldring, adviser to the American delegation, said:

"Shertok could sell ice to the Eskimos."[11]

What Hilldring did not know was that Shertok had such a thorough grasp of the situation under discussion—that he was able to be so convincing—because he was being fed a constant stream of memoranda, statistics and answers to opposition arguments by his young British colleague, Eban, who before long would be the one receiving such compliments himself.

In addition to providing the others with documentation, Eban helped write their speeches and took an active part in the continuous lobbying. The membership of the UN was divided among the back-room boys, each being responsible for trying to influence the final vote of a certain bloc of countries. Eban's allotment was France, Belgium, Holland, Luxembourg, Norway, Denmark, Sweden and Iceland. It was an especially difficult assignment because this was the area in which Bevin and his colleagues had the greatest influence.

Eban's argument to the delegates of these countries was that if the Partition resolution was passed and a Jewish state established peace would be a possibility; otherwise peace was inconceivable.

The most serious crisis came when the opponents of Jewish statehood, realizing that the Partition plan might be approved by the General Assembly, began working to truncate the Jewish area. Early in November the United States delegation, acceding to such pressure, hinted to the Jewish Agency representatives that unless they agreed to give up the southern Negev to the Arabs the United States might oppose Partition and thus defeat Jewish statehood.

Again it was an emergency needing Dr. Weizmann's help. Ill though he was, on November 19 (1947) he left his bed and went to Washington, obtained an audience with President Truman and plunged immediately into an explanation of why it would be a political and economic disaster if Israel failed to get all the Negev. Eban had prepared the memorandum Weizmann used in the talk and had cautioned him not to let Truman sidetrack the conversation into any other aspect of the situation; whatever Truman said, Weizmann in his reply was to get back to the Negev. As Eban reported the outcome:

"The President became fascinated by the unexpected excursion into a phase of remote political geography. Grasping the simplicity and force of the argument, he gave his assent."

At three o'clock the next afternoon the American delegate, Herschel Johnson, summoned Shertok and Horowitz to the UN lounge to hear the State Department's decision that there would be no compromising about the Negev—the Jews must reconcile themselves to a state without the great desert. Ambassador Johnson faced Shertok and began to pronounce what amounted to a judgment of execution.

Just then Johnson received a telephone call which he told General Hilldring to take in an adjoining room. In a moment the general returned and said the President was on the Washington end of the line.

"Johnson leaped to the telephone booth like a startled and portly reindeer. Twenty minutes later he returned. Seating himself opposite Shertok and Horowitz he blushed out an embarrassed retraction. 'What I really wanted to say, Mr. Shertok, was that we have no changes to suggest.'"[12]

Dr. Weizmann's talk with Truman had produced results.

1. Alida Sacks Solomon Eban. Twinkling brown eyes. A delightful sense of humor. And one simple rule for bringing up children.

2. Abraham Meir Solomon, Aubrey's Zionist father, who sent Alida Sacks "the most beautiful love letters a man ever wrote to a woman."

3. Isaac S. Eban, Scottish doctor, who gave Aubrey Solomon his name as well as greater affection than most sons get from their natural fathers.

4. Eliahu Wolf Sacks, the "dear and learned grandfather," who inculcated in Aubrey a passion for knowledge for its own sake and whose fanatical ambition was to make of his grandson one of the world's most exceptional Hebrew scholars.

5. Aubrey Solomon as a five-year-old hoop-roller looked as serious as he would fifty years later pleading Israel's cause before the United Nations.

6. His days as a pipe-smoking Cambridge student were the most carefree of his life.

7. As a British Army officer he served in Intelligence, helped train Jewish underground fighters, became the head of an Arabic school.

"Suzy looked very radiant. I looked pretty good myself, but Suzy's white tulle quite overshadowed my khaki barathea. . . ."

Every large American city inaugurated an Ambassador's Ball and the ambassadorial couple they honored was the Ebans.

10. After the Sinai Campaign of 1956 there was chance for occasional days of relaxation at Martha's Vineyard with Suzy, Eli and Gila.

11. There were many bonds between Eban and Eleanor Roosevelt, who once told him: "It is wonderful to be young today . . . and to have your ability. . . ."

12. President Truman to Ambassador Eban: "Look, we don't have to have any of this official crap. Let's just sit down and have a good talk."

13. Eban on Dag Hammarskjöld: "In him I detected a personal humiliation behind his official pride. He believed the world was destined to be drawn together in a covenant of law and order." (The center figure, Ambassador to the UN Josef Tekoah.)

14. A cordial, amiable relationship existed between Eban and UN Secretary-General U Thant when this photograph was taken in 1966. After 1967 things were different.

15. Addressing the General Assembly in 1952.

16. An historic moment: 7:58 P.M., May 11, 1949, as members of the
Israeli delegation take their seats, after Israel's admittance to the UN.
Foreign Minister Sharett is being congratulated by the Haitian delegate.
Eban is on Sharett's right.

France was a special problem for Eban, because of its large Catholic population, the Moslem character of many of its colonies and its susceptibility to British influence. Belgium was doubtful because her Socialists were committed to coordinate their policies with those of the British Labour Government. Also, the Belgian Catholics were expressing great concern about Jerusalem. The Swedish delegates were aware of the shortcomings of Partition but considered it perhaps the lesser of two evils.

Even getting access to the delegates of his eight countries was difficult. After all, he was not the representative of a state or any other politicogeographic entity and the delegates had no obligation to see him. Although there were many others on the Jewish Agency team in New York, Eban and Horowitz continued to work in unison. Together they would haunt drugstores in the hotels inhabited by those delegates they wished to influence. They ate innumerable sandwiches and drank gallons of tea and coffee as they waited for a "chance" meeting with key delegates. When they ran into them—so casually and so inadvertently—they would ply them with propaganda.

Eban's private life during this period was not idyllic. He and Suzy had moved from the Empire to the Barbizon-Plaza Hotel, but they had a daily living allowance of only twenty dollars and so both had to devise devious ways to get free meals. Entertaining—even of UN delegates —was out of the question, a great handicap to a lobbyist.

Another of Eban's assignments was to maintain the closest possible relations with Trygve Lie, whose influence as Secretary-General was great. Fortunately, while maintaining a strict organizational impartiality, Lie took a pro-Partition attitude on the ground that once UNSCOP had reported, he had to support and protect the committee's findings. He felt that the UN, being in a fragile condition, could vastly benefit if it performed some historic act, such as bringing the Jewish people, the main victims of Naziism, back into the international community. On many occasions the Jewish battle for Partition might have sunk into a slough of procedural complications if it had not been for Trygve Lie.

On November 25 (1947) the penultimate act in the Partition drama took place when the Palestine Committee voted in favor of UNSCOP's proposal 24 to 13, with 10 abstentions. This was short of the required two-thirds majority. Eban was especially disconcerted, because while four of his assigned states (Denmark, Norway, Sweden and Iceland) had voted "yes," Belgium, France, Luxembourg and the Netherlands had abstained. There was still much work to be done.

As a delaying action, a committee of three rapporteurs was appointed to present to the General Assembly a report on the Palestine Committee's findings. There was a grave danger that they might report to the General Assembly their belief that an agreed solution between Arabs and Jews (obviating Partition) might result if a final vote was delayed.

The head of the rapporteur committee was Thor Thors of Iceland, the smallest country in the UN, population 175,000. On November 29—the fateful day—Eban arose much earlier than usual and went to the Barclay Hotel to call on Thors. His objective was to get the Icelander to report to the General Assembly that nothing would be gained by postponement; that there was no chance for an Arab-Jewish agreement before Partition. He argued with Thors that if the General Assembly adopted the UNSCOP resolution, there was a chance the Arab world would come to terms with a new Jewish state, but it was unrealistic to imagine the Arabs would be willing to live in peace with a Jewish community that had no statehood.

"History is strange in its manifestations," he told Thors. "Here is Iceland, the smallest nation in the international community, able to have a decisive effect on whether the Jewish people achieve their independence. By some slip of the pen or the tongue you could banish the Jewish people and end, perhaps forever, their hopes and dreams."

The Icelander, profoundly religious, like most of his countrymen, was moved by Eban's words and kept repeating:

"How did it ever come to this that our little island should have such an influence on the history of such a great people?"

A few hours later the General Assembly opened in an atmosphere of tension and excitement. The eyes of the Jewish world were on Flushing Meadow. Several million New Yorkers whose business or domestic affairs made it possible had their radios tuned to stations carrying the UN proceedings, live and in full. The UN building seethed with excited crowds: delegates, correspondents, photographers, Jewish Agency people, UN officials, lobbyists of various types, officials of national Jewish organizations and ordinary citizens eager to be eyewitnesses to what the newspapers said was about to occur. The enormous General Assembly hall was filled to overflowing. Thousands of people were lined up outside, refusing to leave even when told no more places were available.

When Eban reached the building he heard of many last-minute developments. General Romulo, who had spoken so brilliantly against Partition in the Political Committee, had left New York and there was a chance the Philippine delegation might vote "yes." Because of a revolution in Siam, the Thai prince, who had voted against Partition in the Palestine Committee, but whose authority was now in question, had quietly left the country on the excuse that he had reservations on the *Queen Mary* and if he stayed over how would he ever get home. American oilmen and their lobbyists were making desperate last-minute efforts to corral anti-Partition votes. There were indications Liberia and Haiti might favor Partition.

The session opened with Dr. Oswaldo Aranha of Brazil, president of the Assembly, standing at the podium beside Trygve Lie. Thor Thors made his report, which was favorable to Partition and gave momentum to the day's action. Making a last frantic effort to postpone the voting, Camille Chamoun of Lebanon proposed a compromise full of pitfalls for the Jews. Herschel Johnson for the United States and Andrei Gromyko for the USSR exposed the suggestion as a trick. Dr. Aranha kept the meeting in a state of urgency by the way he handled the equivocators and by his insistence that a vote be completed by nightfall.

Finally the dramatic moment arrived. There was a hush as the representative of each country responded with a "yes," "no," or "abstention." France the previous day had succeeded in postponing the vote for twenty-four hours, in the hope of a last-minute compromise. Now, as her name was called, a clear "yes" rang out. Further balloting was interrupted by a storm of cheering. After the last country had been heard from, President Aranha rapped his gavel and announced:

"Thirty-three in favor, thirteen against, ten abstentions, one absence."

A few moments later Eban and his Jewish Agency colleagues were in the corridor, surrounded by correspondents, well-wishing friends and a host of almost hysterical Jews shouting Hebrew, Yiddish and English words of joy.

The tally of votes was proof of how well the young man from Cambridge had played his role. All eight of his countries had voted "yes." He was still relatively unknown to most of the Palestine Jewish community and to the Jewish world in general. The work he had done in Jerusalem and Geneva with UNSCOP and in New York with the delegations had been crucial yet completely unpublicized. However, the favorable UNSCOP report and the November 29 victory would assure him political recognition. He was now definitely on his way up.

14

Midwife at a Birth

WHILE INTENSIVE DIPLOMATIC MANEUVERING went on at Lake Success, the British, preparing for what they must have realized was inevitable, began Operation Chaos. Gangs of Arab irregulars were infiltrating Palestine from three sides. Seventy-five thousand British troops were still stationed in the country, yet Jewish settlements were being attacked indiscriminately and in cities with a mixed population it was dangerous for Jews to appear on the streets. British soldiers did everything in their power—which was considerable—to obstruct the Yishuv in its attempt to defend itself. Operation Chaos was also designed to make self-government for the Jews as difficult as possible. If a Jewish state was ever set up, the entire mandatory machinery of administration would already have been utterly dismantled, in the hope that the postal service, the railroad, power plants and all other public services would collapse, resulting in wild confusion.

The British, Arabs and other opponents of Partition, however, were still continuing their fight on the diplomatic front, in the hope, slim at first, of being able to reverse the November 29 vote. They were abetted by some who had been the Jews' most powerful friends. Using UN Delegate Warren Austin as its handmaiden, the State Department decided to ignore both the White House and American public opinion and do a volte-face. Instead of permitting the creation of a Jewish state, the State Department now wished to put the Yishuv under another mandate, which this time would be called a "transitory trusteeship."

There were many explanations of the State Department switch. Because of the fighting that had already broken out in Palestine, some were skeptical about whether the Jews would be able to hold out. There was also fear that the Arab-Jewish conflict might assume such proportions that the Great Powers would become involved. Then there were officials in the State Department, including Dean Rusk, who expressed the opinion that the Jewish immigrants who had already arrived from Eastern Europe and those who would follow might introduce Communism into the Middle East. This was an insidious argument, for the Jews who had come from such Eastern European countries as Romania were running away from Communism and would become the greatest enemies of Communism in the Middle East, yet the anti-Communist obsession of the State Department was so great that this was used as an excuse for the attempted reversal of policy. Also, there was oil, a word that was said in Washington only in a whisper. Like an iceberg, it was a larger, more frightening threat to Jewish independence than might appear. The argument was that if a Jewish state was declared American oil companies might lose their Middle East holdings, a fear that later events would prove to be groundless.

In December (1947) Palestine was put on the agenda of the Security Council for the first time. Eban and Horowitz were permitted to attend open meetings as observers but could not make a statement, reply to false charges or even ask questions. Day after day they sat in frustrated silence as speeches were made rich in eloquence but generally devoid of serious content. Two of the five permanent Security Council members had voted against Partition and now a third, the United States, was threatening to switch. While the Arabs in the Middle East were girding themselves for outright war, the Arabs at Lake Success were preparing for a decisive diplomatic battle.

In mid-December it was decided that Shertok, Eban and Horowitz would leave New York for London and Palestine. After reservations had been made on the *Queen Mary* Eban wrote a memorandum to Shertok expressing his fear that despite the General Assembly resolution "the whole thing will come apart" if the Security Council took an opposing view, which it had the juridical right to do. "If we abandon the front and leave the Security Council members to themselves, we will face the disintegration of all we have accomplished."[1]

It is true that there were American members of the Jewish Agency on hand, but they had already been nicknamed "weekend statesmen." Rabbi Silver, for example, had to spend some time each week at his temple in Cleveland. None of them was able to give his full attention to the cause and none was a professional diplomat.

Suzy and her husband had their valises packed and their steamship tickets in hand when word came from Shertok that Eban should remain behind so there would be some Jewish political representation in New York.

"Looking back, it is astonishing to think that in a fit of inexperience we nearly left New York unattended professionally," Eban later said.[9]

It was a great responsibility, at such a critical time in Jewish history, for a man not yet thirty-three and with a limited amount of diplomatic experience. Just two years before he had been teaching Arabic culture in a school in Jerusalem.

Symbolic of the unprecedented diplomatic situation was "the Case of the Five Lonely Pilgrims." They were members of what was technically called the Palestine Committee of the UN, its purpose to see that the Partition plan was put into operation as effectively as possible. But now the British refused to permit this committee to enter Palestine until the last mandatory official had left the country. (Another Operation Chaos trick.) And so they sat in New York, frustrated, useless, snarled in procedural nonsense, while Palestine was being bled. One of the committee members, off the record, said:

"The British want to create a vacuum in Palestine, but they're refusing to hand over even the vacuum."[3]

As Eban himself summarized the situation:

"The vastest anticlimax in Jewish history was being prepared. Having been placed on the threshold of statehood, the Jews were going to be urged back into the vacuum of tutelage."[4]

At this time strenuous efforts were being made to get the Security Council to adopt an anti-Partition resolution. Eban feared that the Five Lonely Pilgrims in their frustration might abet the opposition by sitting in New York and writing an anti-Partition report of their own. With diplomatic and historical astuteness, he realized the importance of getting into the record some UN statement that in the fighting which had broken out in Palestine the Arabs had been the aggressors, and so he worked on members of the Palestine Committee, especially the Bolivian delegate. In April the committee finally did submit a report stating that powerful Arab interests, both inside and outside Palestine, were defying the General Assembly resolution and attempting to alter it by force.

Eban was rightfully proud of having obtained this verdict, for while no one was going to give the Jews a state just because they were victims of Arab aggression, that quotation would resound across the years and in the history books as an authoritative judgment by a competent international authority as to who the Middle East aggressor had been.

Unable to get the Security Council to endorse the General Assembly resolution, because of British influence and the wobbly American position, Eban by his work in New York early in 1948 at least prevented any erosion of the November 29 victory.

Although the Palestine Committee never left New York, the British finally agreed to a compromise. What was euphemistically called an "advance guard" was permitted to go to Palestine. It consisted of five men who actually were much more sympathetic than the committee members themselves. The group was headed by Dr. Pablo Azcarate, who had been the Spanish Republican Ambassador to the Court of St. James, and included Colonel Roscher Lund of Norway, close friend of the UN Secretary-General. While they were on their way to Jerusalem the Agency appointed as liaison officers with this advance guard two prominent young Palestinian Jews.

Several weeks after the advance guard's departure, Dr. Azcarate returned to New York on official business and called on Eban with a strange request:

"Will you please have your wife prepare a package for me to take back to her sister?"

Then he explained. The two liaison officers were Walter Eytan, philology lecturer from Oxford, and Vivian Herzog, Eban's brother-in-law, who had suggested that Azcarate might be willing to bring back a package. Eban immediately passed the request on to his wife by telephone and then questioned his guest about conditions in Jerusalem. The reply was that the advance guard had been received by neither the British nor the Arabs. No one would help them even find housing, so the five men had taken up residence in a "hole in the wall"—the cellar of a building under construction in Security Zone B not far from the King David Hotel and just across the street from the YMCA's tennis courts.

"I guess we are getting food and other essentials only by virtue of the fact that we have two quite attractive girl secretaries, one Australian, one British. They seem to have established good personal relations with the British police."

After Mrs. Eban made up the package and had it delivered to Azcarate's hotel she received a call from him.

"I am sorry, Mrs. Eban, but I opened the package to see what was in it. You have sent your sister stockings and underwear and such things. I am afraid you do not realize what the situation is in Jerusalem today. Your sister and the others are almost starving. They're under siege. I'm sure you know that your sister was wounded. They need food, not things like . . . like this."[5]

On January 23 Eban was so worried about the diplomatic outlook that he sent Dr. Weizmann a cable to the Dorchester Hotel, London, where the Chief was making his headquarters:

IN VIEW WORSENING SITUATION ADVISE YOU IF POSSIBLE RECONSIDER
DECISION TO GO PALESTINE JANUARY. . . . EVERYTHING DEPENDS
UPON OUTCOME NEGOTIATIONS HERE LAKE SUCCESS AND WASHINGTON
STOP MOST CRUCIAL PHASE OF ALL NOW APPROACHES HERE IN
WHICH WE SURELY MISS YOUR PRESENCE ADVICE ACTIVITY
INFLUENCE AFFECTIONATELY EBAN

Eban's cable was buttressed by similar messages from Shertok and Arthur Lourie.

Exactly six days later Dr. Weizmann, accompanied by his wife, sailed from England on the *Queen Mary*, arriving in New York on February 4 (1948). That night Eban dined with them at the Waldorf. The Chief began the conversation belligerently:

"Why in heaven's name did you drag me to this frozen waste when I might have been in Rehovoth?"

Eban replied by explaining there was a serious danger the General Assembly might reverse itself. Also, the situation in Washington was worse than ever. President Truman was the only person alive who could stop Warren Austin and the State Department from their planned sabotage of Partition, but for more than a month Truman had been "furious" with American Zionist leaders, even refusing to see them. Truman said they were "wanting in moderation and in respect for his person and office." The only hope was for the Chief to talk to the President.[6]

During the six weeks between Weizmann's arrival in America and the meeting with Truman, Eban was in constant communication with him, sometimes visiting him in his hotel room, sometimes sitting for hours beside his bed, reporting developments and receiving lessons in top-level diplomacy from the veteran of so many diplomatic struggles over so long a period of years.

(The Eban-Weizmann relationship was psychologically interesting. Perhaps because of Eban's intimate intellectual relationship with his grandfather, he had had from childhood the ability to get onto close and confident terms with people not only twice his age but, as in Weizmann's case, forty years older than he was.)

The story has been often told of how Truman's stone wall was finally breached by his former partner in a clothing store, Eddie Jacobson of Kansas City, who went to Washington, ignored the advice of White House aides that he should not mention the Middle East and finally persuaded Truman to see Weizmann by likening his hero, Weizmann, to Truman's hero, Andrew Jackson. Weizmann saw Truman on March 18 (1948), getting out of a sickbed and traveling by train to Washington for the interview.

As Truman himself summarized the conference:

"When he left my office I felt that he had reached a full understanding of my policy and that I knew what he wanted."[7]

However, the very next day, March 19 (1948), which became known in Jewish circles as "Black Friday," Austin demanded that the Security Council halt all attempts to implement Partition and that the General Assembly be convened in special session to pass on a plan for temporary trusteeship.

At 7:30 A.M. on March 20 (1948), which was a Saturday, President Truman, according to one of his biographers, called in his administrative assistant, pointed to a report of Austin's Security Council speech and demanded:

"How could this have happened? I assured Chaim Weizmann that we were for Partition and would stick to it. He must think I'm a plain liar. Find out how this could have happened!"[8]

Weizmann was the only one who took the development calmly. He told Eban he had telephoned Jacobson to express his belief, irrational though it might seem, that Truman would still fulfill the promise he had made on the eighteenth. Several days later, with Eban's assistance, he drafted a letter to Truman giving devastating arguments against trusteeship and declaring that the choice of the Jewish people was between "statehood and extermination."

Eban left the hotel with the letter ready to be sent to Washington, but when he reached his own hotel he received a call from the Chief. Dave Ginsberg, prominent Washington attorney, had just telephoned from the capital to say that the State Department was thinking of asking the British to carry on with their administration of Palestine despite British plans to quit the country.

"This would be the worst possibility of all," Weizmann told Eban.

"You'd better come back quickly and let's see if we can add a paragraph to the Truman letter."

They worked for several hours to get the wording just right and finally the letter was sent off with this Eban-Weizmann addition:

"I would sound a note of solemn warning against the prolongation of British rule in Palestine. As you may know, I have cherished the British-Jewish relationship all my life. I have upheld it in difficult times. I have been grievously disappointed by its recent decline. . . . I tremble to think of the wave of violence and repression which would sweep Palestine if the conditions and auspices of the recent unhappy years were to be continued under British, or indeed any foreign, rule. I also know how passionately the British people desire the end of this troubled chapter. Should your administration, despite all this, press for any prolongation of British tenure, it would mean a responsibility for terrible events. . . ."[9]

(The Eban touch is apparent in almost every sentence in that paragraph.)

After Horowitz returned from Palestine, he, Eban and Hayyim Greenberg, Labor Zionist journalist and one of the American members of the Jewish Agency Executive,[10] paid a call on the Chinese delegation in the hope of ameliorating its hostility. They were received in the delegation's Fifth Avenue skyscraper offices by Dr. T. F. Tsiang, China's representative on the Security Council, who had shown his personal enmity for Palestine Jews by abstaining on November 29. (It was thought that only the intervention of Dr. Wellington Koo, China's ambassador in Washington, prevented Dr. Tsiang from voting "no.") The three visitors took turns explaining the need to implement the UN decision and to oppose Arab aggression. Eban reminded Dr. Tsiang of Japanese aggression in Manchuria and its effect on the League of Nations, warning that the fate of the UN, as well as the Jewish people, hung in the balance. The Chinese delegate's answer was to ask why the Jews did not assimilate and thus end all their problems forever. Then Dr. Tsiang, explaining that he was a historian, went off on a long and remote historio-philosophical tangent and finally bid his guests good-bye, saying:

"I shall await instructions from my government."[11]

Eban never forgot the smiling mask which had concealed all the inner thoughts and feelings of their host throughout the long interview.

One day Dr. Weizmann and Eban had lunch with Alexandre Parodi, head of the French delegation, who was full of doubts about Partition, even though France had voted for it.

"If the Jewish state is proclaimed, I fear that your people will be massacred by superior Arab forces. How can a few hundred thousand stand up against millions?"

"Numbers are not decisive," Weizmann replied. "The trouble with the Egyptian Army is that its soldiers are too lean and its officers too fat."

Eban chuckled. This was exactly the sort of colorful phrase he liked creating himself.[12] Just then Josef Cohen, one of Weizmann's close associates, rushed in with a copy of that afternoon's New York *Post* in which there was a dispatch about a spectacular Jewish victory at Mishmar Ha-Emek, a kibbutz in the Valley of Jezreel—the first major victory in a war which had not yet even begun, officially, against a state which had not yet been proclaimed.[13]

The relationship between Dr. Weizmann and his protégé was warm and affectionate, like that of a young man and his grandfather. Each respected the other's intelligence and abilities. Weizmann, like many another world figure, welcomed constructive help on his public statements, especially from Eban. It was always true collaboration; never ghost writing. Shertok was different. He had once been a newspaperman, so that writing was at least part of his business. Also, he had been responsible for his own speeches since succeeding Arlosoroff as head of the Agency's political department in the days when every man had to be on his own because there were so few to do so much. But in this frenzied period (1948) Shertok was so pressed that he turned to Eban for assistance. One address he delivered before the Security Council early in 1948 was written entirely by his young assistant. Eban was proudest of the passage:

"What is it the Security Council is looking for—a just solution or a solution against which the Arabs will kindly condescend not to use force? That is the issue!"

Shertok had delivered it with exactly the right touch of cynicism. To his acute embarrassment he received more cables, telegrams and letters of praise for this particular speech than for any he had ever made.

April (1948) was a febrile month. Syrian and Iraqi Army units used artillery for the first time against Jewish settlements. Jerusalem also was shelled. There were furious battles in Jaffa, Safed, Tiberias, Haifa. Jews in great numbers were being killed. Arabs by the tens of thousands were fleeing from Palestine into neighboring countries. In London the House of Commons enacted a law setting May 15 as the termination date of the Mandate. The General Assembly convened at Flushing Meadow in a special Palestine session, the announced aim of the American delegation being to reverse the Partition vote and adopt some sort of trusteeship arrangement. Because there was fighting—a threat to world peace—the Security Council was in session. It was like a movie film being run at fast speed. Every hour or two there was another crisis, another emergency, another sensation. Those involved—in New York as well as in Tel Aviv and Jerusalem—got little sleep.

Shertok was like an actor trying to play two roles in three different theaters at the same time. And the theaters—New York, Lake Success and Flushing Meadow—were miles apart. Eban was giving him all the help possible. Often they both read, wrote and researched until almost dawn.

Suzy and her husband had moved from the Barbizon-Plaza Hotel into the Riverside Drive apartment of Meyer Weisgal, a close associate of Dr. Weizmann, who was leaving the country for some weeks. There late on the night of April 30 (1948) Eban was working on a speech opposing trusteeship, which Shertok was to deliver in the General Assembly the next morning, when the telephone rang. It was Shertok calling from his hotel room, where he, also, was working late. His voice was weary as he said:

"Look, Aubrey, I've just decided something. Since you're writing it, why shouldn't you also deliver it? We don't have this tradition of . . . anyway, you deliver it tomorrow."

As Shertok hung up Eban slowly put down his own receiver, then went back to work on his script. Even after the first draft was finished he spent hours changing words, revising, polishing. Finally he went to bed, but after only a few hours' sleep he was at his desk again making changes he had thought of while horizontal.

There were few people in the Sixty-sixth Street headquarters when he arrived there with his bulging briefcase, long before the start of New York's working day. One of them was Regina Medzini; she knew that it was going to be a busy day for everyone. As fast as a sheet of script came from her typewriter Eban took it and started making corrections, amplifications and improvements. Someone went into the street to hail a taxi and keep it waiting for him. When he reached the General Assembly building Shertok was already there, to give him moral support.

"I didn't have much time to reflect on the solemnity of the occasion and its importance for me, personally, as I sat waiting to be recognized. I do remember feeling much younger than anyone else in sight. I remember the apparent curiosity of many delegates when I finally rose to speak. The only Jewish spokesmen they knew were Rabbi Abba Hillel Silver and Moshe Shertok. I was a stranger to them. I had done a lot of speaking in public before this, of course, but never on a world stage—never to an audience that represented most of mankind. I wasn't any more nervous than any speaker is during the first few minutes he's on his feet. It was just that I wanted so intensely to succeed. There was no use pretending that this was the Cambridge Union or a Young Zionist meeting in London. I tried to remember that I had been given the opportunity to plead for justice for my people—for their right to live like others, without benefit of trustees or guardians. I suppose the reason the words flowed easily was because I was pleading a cause in which I believed so deeply."[14]

As he got into his stride there was not a whisper in the large hall. Every eye was on him. Secretary-General Trygve Lie, who had come in just when he began, studied the speaker intently.

There had already been several crises in the life of this young man. Here was another. Had his performance that day in the General Assembly been humdrum and officialese—had he spoken without a touch of passion, without any special distinctive quality—the opportunity would have been lost and he would have remained one of the back-room boys. But, first, he had written a devastating critique of the American trusteeship proposal, convincing in its logic, demolishing in its fire. And he delivered it in such a manner that seasoned diplomats serving on UN delegations, as well as attachés and reporters, were awed by a presentation that was "symmetrical in grace and withering in polemic," as one correspondent later put it.[15]

He called the trusteeship plan "an attempt to appease Arab violence . . . an ill-fated digression." He said the current suffering and grief could be avoided only by quickly "seeking the way back to the highway of the Partition resolution."

As soon as he finished and sat down Shertok clapped him on the back—an unusual gesture, because Shertok was not a demonstrative man—and said words of congratulation in Hebrew. Then Shertok slipped from the room. It was many days before Eban knew where he had gone and why. There was a telegraph office in a far corner of the building from which Shertok sent a cable written in longhand to Dr. and Mrs. Eban in London:

HAPPY BE ABLE CONGRATULATE ON AUBREY'S STRIKING MAIDEN SPEECH IN APPEARING AS OFFICIAL SPOKESMAN JEWISH PEOPLE IN

INTERNATIONAL COUNCIL STOP HIS EXTRAORDINARY BRILLIANCE IN
THOUGHT AND EXPRESSION POWERFUL COGENCY OF REASONING
DIGNITY OF PRESENTATION DID OUTSTANDING CREDIT TO OUR CAUSE
AND MADE US ALL IMMEASURABLY PROUD STOP SPEECH MADE
PROFOUND IMPRESSION ON ALL STOP FRIEND AND FOE LISTENED
WITH RAPT ATTENTION MANY CHARACTERIZING IT AS ONE OF THE
HIGHEST WATER MARKS OF ENTIRE SESSION STOP WARMEST
REGARDS.[16]

That night there was a diplomatic dinner at the home of Trygve Lie in
Forest Hills, Long Island. For the occasion Suzy Eban had a new party
dress and not only her husband but many others thought she looked
more radiant than ever. But he was glowing, too, especially after the
chief Soviet delegate to the UN, Andrei Andreyevich Gromyko, not
famous for his effusiveness, came rushing over with extended hand to
congratulate him, saying:

"Good! Good! You have killed trusteeship!"

Before the next twenty-four hours had passed it was obvious from the
reaction of American and Palestinian Jews, as well as the people at the
UN, that Eban had scored a triumph. For days he and Suzy reveled in
the newspaper clippings, telephone calls and cables.

Although the press in Palestine was concerned with matters of imminent life or death, several papers in effect asked: "Who is this new
spokesman we have in New York? Where does he come from? How is it
that he articulates some of our deepest historic emotions with such
precision and passion?"

At a Jewish meeting in New York not long after the UN speech,
Rabbi Silver, who preceded Eban on the program, in a florid tribute
likened Eban to a meteor. When Eban himself rose to speak he began
by saying:

"I hoped that Rabbi Silver would not carry his simile too far, because,
as everyone is aware, a meteor flashes suddenly in the sky and then just
as suddenly disappears. I therefore trust his metaphor will have only
half its normal application."

The story of two UN correspondents sitting at their typewriters trying
to think up leads for their stories of Eban's maiden speech was one that
Eban himself probably never heard, although it became a minor UN
classic:

"He makes three words do the work of one," said the first correspondent.

"You mean a thousand," his colleague corrected.

As the prospect of military invasion and "political solitude" (Eban's own expression) grew greater, Dr. Weizmann and Eban shared the fear that some Jewish leaders would be intimidated into renouncing the idea of immediate statehood. Even among the Jewish Agency team in New York there was much tormented anguish as the fighting between Arabs and Jews intensified. Reports from Palestine said many people there questioned whether the Yishuv could stand up in a war, outnumbered as they were.

It was significant that Weizmann and Eban, both of whom would later be labeled by their political opponents as doves, were adamant that the state should be proclaimed. At an important meeting of Jewish Agency representatives in New York there was heated discussion of whether a truce should be sought. Eban took a firm position of hostility to anything that would postpone statehood, which, he said, might not end the Jews' troubles "but will enable us to face them in a better and more logical posture." He told his colleagues that in his opinion an Arab invasion was inevitable on the day the British evacuated Palestine, "whether we proclaim a state or not." The only question, he said, was "whether they'll invade us in our capacity as a state or as a people who has recoiled from its own statehood." Morally, juridically and in every other way he felt they had a better chance against invasion if they proclaimed their statehood and then tried to get it recognized. "The worst thing would be to fight the Arabs from a situation of not only numerical but also constitutional inferiority."[17]

About this time Weisgal telephoned from Europe at the request of Ben-Gurion to ask Weizmann's views. The Chief made this reply, which was almost a command:

"Proclaim the state, no matter what ensues!"

Then he urged Shertok to fly home and make certain that there was no backsliding. His parting words to him were:

"Don't let them weaken, Moshe!" He added: "Remember it is now or never."

With Shertok gone, Eban was once more in a position of full responsibility—and the forces working for annulment of Partition were growing ever stronger. Now it was a race against time.

On May 13 (1948), with less than forty-eight hours until the British were due to leave Palestine, Dr. Weizmann began to grow nervous. Eban was in the UN delegates' lounge that afternoon when he received an urgent phone call. The Chief was on the line. Please, would Aubrey come to his hotel immediately? Eban pleaded that he was engaged in vital lobbying.

"With Moshe away we are very thin on the ground here."

On the phone the Chief explained he had heard a rumor that the UN was going to adopt the trusteeship proposal and appoint a High Commissioner after all.

"If this happens we're wrecked. What do you think? Is it possible?"

Eban told him of Gromyko's remark at the Trygve Lie dinner. That was eight days ago. He felt that since then support for trusteeship had begun to dwindle. He saw no cause for alarm.

"I am sure we have blocked it. At the worst the Assembly may appoint a Mediator, not a High Commissioner, and this would create no juridical fact incompatible with the proclamation and recognition of a Jewish state."

Having given the Chief these reassurances, Eban begged for permission to hang up and return to his work. Later that day Weizmann wrote a letter to Truman asking him to recognize the Jewish state as soon as it was created, which he sent by messenger to Washington. But it was still not time to relax, diplomatically. The next day, May 14 (1948), the United States, abandoning its attempt to put all Palestine under a trusteeship, decided to force a vote on a resolution to appoint a temporary trustee for Jerusalem. The Arabs promptly staged a filibuster. Meanwhile a flash was received over press association wires that a state to be called Israel had been proclaimed by Ben-Gurion in a semi-secret ceremony before about two hundred carefully selected guests in a museum on Rothschild Boulevard in Tel Aviv. The news was brought into the Assembly first by Rabbi Silver and spread like a forest fire through the whole building.

As the chair called for a vote on the Jerusalem trusteeship resolution most delegates were watching the clock. The British Mandate was due to end at midnight Palestine time. That meant 6 P.M. New York time. It was close to that hour now. As the minute hand reached sixty and started ticking off a new hour the Iraqi delegate rushed to the tribunal and exultantly proclaimed that the Mandate had ended—it was too late for the UN to act. The vote was announced, however. The American-supported resolution had passed, 20 to 13, short of the necessary two thirds. Thus the State Department lost its final effort to vitiate or nullify the November 29 action.

Just a few minutes later—at 6:11 P.M.—the Assembly got the stunning news that President Truman had authorized the recognition of Israel by the United States. There was even greater joy on the part of Israel's friends, even greater consternation among her enemies. Ambassador Jessup of the American delegation rushed out to a telephone to get confirmation or denial. When he returned he read the Truman announcement to the Assembly, which, as Eban described it, "was now plunged into a pandemonium of surprise."[18] In all five New York boroughs there was dancing in the streets and wild celebrating.

Aubrey, emotionally and physically exhausted, went with Suzy to Weizmann's hotel suite for a brief visit, then to a quiet dinner à deux, then to bed.

That all happened just at the start of the Jewish Sabbath. On Monday night, May 17 (1948), there was a mass celebration of the diplomatic victory at Madison Square Garden, attended by all the Jewish leadership except Weizmann, who was too exhausted from the fatigue of the preceding weeks to leave his bed. During the evening someone at the hall, listening to a radio, heard a bulletin from Tel Aviv that Weizmann had just been elected President of Israel. The news was announced to the crowd, already worked up to an emotional frenzy. Slipping away from the Garden as soon as it was diplomatically possible, Eban took a cab to Weizmann's hotel, the Waldorf-Astoria. There he found that the Chief had first heard of his appointment from some news agency which called on the phone for a statement. Then he had snapped on his radio and listened to a broadcast about it.

Within a few minutes the room began to fill with top Jewish Agency people, arriving to offer congratulations. Dr. Weizmann produced a bottle of champagne and they all raised their glasses and said:

"*Lechayim!*"[19]

Three days later, on May 20 (1948), Aubrey Solomon Eban was appointed by the Provisional Government of the State of Israel as its representative to the UN—the spokesman for a state not even a week old, which was not yet a member of the UN and might not be for some time to come. Until then Gromyko, age thirty-eight, had been the baby of the diplomats accredited to the UN. Eban, who three months ago had had his thirty-third birthday, now took that honor from the Russian.

The previous year, through his brilliant work on behalf of the Partition resolution, he had helped create Israel. More recently he had been largely responsible for frustrating a diabolical attempt to kill Israel in its gestation. Now, in a key diplomatic role, he would have to fight for years to see that she was not murdered in infancy.

15

Prevention of Infanticide

THE CABLE to Secretary-General Trygve Lie announcing the appointment of Aubrey S. Eban as head of the delegation representing Israel in the UN and listing the other members as Arthur Lourie, Gideon Rufer (Rafael), Michael Comay and I. L. Kenen created some embarrassments.

In pre-independence days the Jewish Agency, set up in accordance with Article IV of the British Mandate, had been spokesman for the Jewish population of Palestine and was so recognized by the British. It eventually became a shadow government. The Jewish Agency had an American section. Its chairman for years had been Rabbi Abba Hillel Silver, one of the most vocal of American Zionists. During the UN hearings on Palestine in 1947 and 1948 he had been a witness and became known, in America at least, as one of the principal champions of the Jewish state then in process of formation. But as soon as the state was proclaimed, a citizen of the United States could hardly appear as spokesman for a foreign country and so Rabbi Silver was forced to leave the center of the stage. As one member of the Israeli delegation put it:

"When the cable came we had to break the news to Silver. Suddenly the back-room boys were out front. Those who had been in the spotlight now became advisers, as we in the back room were appointed to the official positions."

Most of the men in the delegation lived in New York City at Hotel Fourteen, next door to the Copacabana. Their working headquarters was the five-story brownstone front at 16 East Sixty-sixth Street, which now became the nerve center of the new state. Here they began issuing passports (the first were printed in Hebrew and French), granting visas, whipping out speeches, releasing statements for the press and selling the first Israeli stamps (with biblical designs). An ancient country was getting reorganized after almost two thousand years of non-feasance. There were weapons to be procured for an army that was underground no longer, but because an arms embargo had been imposed this activity was sub rosa.

There was an air of camaraderie at 16 East Sixty-sixth Street. If the mimeograph machine broke down it would be fixed by Lourie or Comay. If the office workers, whom Eban nicknamed "the stokers of the furnace of Israel," were too busy to go out for lunch Eban would bring them sandwiches from a delicatessen around the corner. Each Wednesday night most of the staff stayed after work to study Hebrew, which they practiced on each other the rest of the week, adding to the general confusion.

Reporters came to get their first glimpse of what an Israeli military uniform looked like. Refugees from abroad came to savor these first visible signs of Jewish freedom. Crackpots came with wild ideas, such as the man who had a scheme to blow up the British Isles in one great blast. A sculptor said he had a commission to do a giant bust of Eban immediately—it would take only ten or fifteen hours of posing—this week, please. Several painters wanted to do his portrait. Reporters came for feature story interviews. Also photographers. Until now Eban had had the reputation of being camera-shy, but he soon lost this sort of modesty. The newspapermen found him easy to interview. He seemed to be more relaxed with them than with other people and his raillery made good copy. For example, he enjoyed telling how Warren Austin, in one of his extemporaneous addresses to the UN, had said:

"We call upon the Arabs and the Jews to settle their differences in a true Christian spirit."

(There was a perhaps apocryphal story going the UN rounds that in private Austin had expressed it a little more strongly: "The way to settle this whole Middle Eastern mess is to get those damn Arabs and those damn Jews into a room and pound their heads together until they agree to settle it all in a spirit of good Christian brotherhood.")

The reporters also liked to interview Eban because he had an endless collection of human interest stories about himself. Whenever the fact came up that he had been born in South Africa he would hastily explain:

"But when I was six months old I decided to emigrate to England."

The newspapers made much of his youth. One reporter wrote that his appointment had served notice to the representatives of other nations in the UN that the younger generation "would provide names as thunderous as those of Weizmann, Ben-Gurion and Shertok. . . . Here is a young man with a future. In all the excitement he remains cheerful, calm and competent."

The paper quoted him as saying:

"I shall be a citizen of Israel and go where they send me. I shall serve . . . I am a perfectionist. I am also a sentimentalist and I am the only one in the civil service without ulcers."[1]

The reporters discovered him to be a man of sober habits, both in dress and living. At the delegates' bar in the UN he ordered only orange juice or soft drinks, which he explained was "a matter of taste, not principle." Often he put in a seventeen-hour workday, which began at 8 A.M. and ended sometimes at late as 1 A.M., permitting little time for his favorite diversion, sitting in an armchair with a pipe and a book. The reporters also discovered some of his weaknesses. One quoted an anonymous friend as saying:

"If you ever can't find him, just look for somebody who's forgotten his briefcase. That will be Eban."

Another, mentioning the good work he had done as liaison officer between the Jewish Agency and UNSCOP, said:

"But he is often so disorganized himself that what he needs most is liaison between Aubrey and Eban."

The New York *Post* reporter described him as having a "friendly but abrupt manner, a somewhat breathless voice, a walk reminiscent of a happy bear cub. But there is nothing vague about his mind. It has whip-lash swiftness and precision, and he can analyze the contents of an enormously complicated document in seconds. He often completes a response during a translation."

A UN delegate from Latin America was quoted as saying:

"He makes most members of the Security Council seem illiterate."[2]

Although until now he had delivered only two or three prepared addresses at the UN, the newspapermen were already commenting on his forensic ability. Wrote one:

"His speech is smooth, brilliant, richly ironic and marks him as a rare stylist in an organization marked chiefly by its boundless capacity for talk."[3]

Eban found the publicity he was now getting quite ego-satisfying. He was beginning to acquire a public image, which was essential if he was to have a successful public career. But there was one sentence of praise that pleased him more than all the rest:

"Aubrey Eban, then one of the youngest aides in the United Nations and at this time of writing the brilliant representative of Israel before that body, and, I might add, one of its most distinguished members . . ."

Those words came from the pen of Dr. Chaim Weizmann as he sat in a hotel in Glion, Switzerland, in the summer of 1948, putting the finishing touches to his autobiography.[4] It was the only reference he made in the long book to his protégé, but from Weizmann, generally sparing in his praise of individuals, this was a magnificent tribute.

Eban knew the best way he could repay Weizmann for the faith he had always shown in him, and for what Weizmann had done to place him in this important spot on the world stage, was by proving the faith had not been misplaced. This he could do by fighting with every ability at his command for Israel's right to live—without a diverting interest, except, of course, his love of Suzy.

After Weizmann left for Switzerland and later, during the four years of his presidency, Eban had little direct personal contact with him—they were generally separated by an ocean and a continent—but in public speeches, in printed words and in private correspondence he was constantly paying tribute to the man whom he once described as "moving in regal confidence through the victories and agonies of his times."[5]

On May 22 (1948), two days after Eban's official appointment, the Security Council voted for an unconditional cease-fire. Four days later, as their armies advanced deep into Israel, the Arab governments rejected the cease-fire and delivered an ultimatum: Israel's statehood must be abrogated and Israel armed forces immediately disarmed. On that same day Eban appeared before the Security Council and made this thunderous and epigrammatic reply:

"The sovereignty regained by an ancient people, after its long march through the dark night of exile, is to be surrendered at pistol point. It becomes my duty to make our attitude clear beyond ambiguity or doubt. If the Arab states want peace with Israel they can have it. If they want war they can have that, too. But whether they want peace or war, they can have it only with the State of Israel."

As long as the Arabs were making reasonable headway militarily they had no desire for a cease-fire. Then Eban began to get urgent cables from Prime Minister Ben-Gurion and Foreign Minister Shertok telling him that Jerusalem was being besieged, that the Israelis were drastically short of arms and that they passionately needed a few weeks of respite to regroup and rearm. The cables said this need for an immediate cease-fire, acceptable also to the Arabs, was just as vital as the November 29 Partition resolution had been. Unless it was obtained quickly, all might be lost. (Israeli military leaders in their postwar writings agreed on the transcendental importance of this first armistice.)

Eban's reply to Ben-Gurion's first cable was that he would try to get the Security Council convened "tomorrow morning."

Back came an irascible cable:

"What do you mean 'tomorrow'? Try to get them to meet during the night, because every hour counts and water is running out in Jerusalem."

One of Eban's major contributions to the life-and-death struggle of the infant state was his success in getting the Security Council to call again on "all Governments and authorities" to "order a cessation of all acts of armed force for a period of four weeks."[6] This time the Arabs agreed and the cease-fire went into effect on June 11. As the end of the four weeks of relative peace approached, UN Mediator Bernadotte appealed to all governments for a prolongation of the truce. The Arabs, however, insisted on another attempt to destroy Israel by force and rejected the appeal.

On July 13 (1948) Eban delivered the best of his Security Council addresses. The opening sentence, especially, was memorable:

"There is not a single person in this room or outside who does not know in the depths of his heart that the Arab states, by resuming their attacks upon Israel, have committed an act of aggression."

Spurred by events that might be catastrophic for Israel, he was beginning to develop the polemic style for which he would someday become so famous. In closing he told the Security Council:

"Israel is the product of the most sustained historic tenacity which the ages recall. . . . The Jewish people has not striven toward this goal for twenty centuries in order that, having once achieved it with the full endorsement of an international opinion, it will now surrender it in response to an illegitimate and unsuccessful aggression."

Those who heard him were deeply impressed. His voice was sonorous, his bearing majestic and there was conviction in his delivery. Few of his listeners questioned that here was a statesman of stature; an articulate voice with the power of persuasion or chastisement; a colorful personality with both a heart and a mind.

On July 15 (1948) the Security Council resolved that the Arabs had committed a breach of the peace and ordered a permanent cease-fire under penalty of sanctions. Finally, after having lost vital ground, the Arabs on July 21 agreed to put down their arms. Israel could now draw a deep breath. The first great crisis of its young life was over. Soldiers and civilians in Jerusalem, Galilee, the Negev, in dozens of frontier kibbutzim, on land, sea and in the air had performed magnificently. On the diplomatic front young Eban had done just as well.

Besides these primary occupations involving the life and death of a nation, Eban, as Israel's chief diplomatic representative in New York, had been concerned with many minor matters. Just nine days after his appointment he faced a delicate situation. *The Churchman,* fortnightly magazine of the Protestant Episcopal Church, each year gave an award to a person who had made some outstanding contribution to the promotion of good will and understanding among the peoples of the world. The 1948 award was to go to Secretary of State George Marshall. However, a Red-baiting magazine, *Counter-Attack,* published an article denouncing *The Churchman* for its political leanings and urged readers to pressure Marshall into rejecting the invitation, which he did. *The Churchman,* long a supporter of the right of Jews to a state of their own, then announced that instead of the award to Marshall it would present a citation to Israel "for offering a refuge to the persecuted Jews of Europe and a home for displaced persons, and for championing the dignity of man," and Eban was invited to be the evening's guest of honor. A week before the banquet Eban issued a statement that his government would not participate in the proceedings "to avoid any involvement of the State of Israel in domestic controversial matters." Several days later Rabbi Israel Goldstein, a prominent New York liberal, agreed to speak at the dinner and receive the citation on behalf of Israel. Thus everyone was made happy. The Secretary of State and the Truman administration were pleased with Eban's rejection of the invitation. *The Churchman* and its liberal supporters were happy that a distinguished Zionist leader did appear. And Israel received the citation—its first from a Christian source.

Shortly after his appointment Eban had his first forensic feud in the Security Council with Sir Alexander Cadogan, British delegate. It was the start of what would be a long series of bitter exchanges. Sir Alexander made a proposal that Israel be forced to limit immigration. In reply Eban coldly said:

"I should like to remind the delegates that this is not a subject that can be discussed. Immigration to Israel belongs to the domestic jurisdiction of Israel and under the Charter of the United Nations no other state has a right to intervene."

There was a gasp around the room at what some considered Eban's audacity. If Israel's representative to the UN had looked and talked like the usual caricature of a Jew—if he had spoken with a Polish-Russian accent—if he had been embarrassed in the presence of Great Power diplomats—it would have been easier to accept, but here was a spokesman for Israel whose accent was pure Cambridge and whose vocabulary was at least the equal of Cadogan's and who had never learned to cringe. This was apparently what annoyed the Englishman, and others. They could never forgive Eban that he was not a stereotype Jew.

Cadogan was a small, rather wizened man, with a little mustache, placid and phlegmatic, and (in the words of Eban himself) "so crushed by tradition as not to have any vital juices left at all."[7] He was the antithesis in many ways of Bevin, with whom Eban had already tangled. Bevin had vehemence and heat; Eban doubted whether Cadogan had any views of his own whatsoever.

"I think that if he had been told by his superiors to say that Israel should have a state on both sides of the Jordan he would have said it with exactly the same face as that with which he opposed the idea."

But early in 1948 his instructions apparently had been to be an obstructionist to the Israelis in every way possible. And he was. Because Britain still had not recognized Israel diplomatically, Cadogan refused ever to use the word "Israel." His favorite circumlocution was to refer to the new state as "the Jewish Authorities in Palestine."

When the 1948 spring session of the UN terminated, Eban and Cadogan happened to sail for England on the same ship, the *Queen Elizabeth*. On Sunday morning, as Eban was promenading the deck, he saw Cadogan coming out of the ship's chapel and was unable to resist the temptation to say:

"Good morning. I expect that you have been praying to the gods of Abraham, Isaac and the Jewish Authorities."[8]

The problem of nomenclature was not with Cadogan alone. At his table in the Security Council Eban sat behind a sign or plaque which read: "Jewish Agency for Palestine." Israel had already been diplomatically recognized by the United States, the Soviet Union and more than a dozen other countries, but that did not seem to impress the UN secretariat. What was worse, whenever representatives of any Arab nations made public statements in which they found it necessary to refer to Israel, they would say, "the Zionist Terrorist Group" or "the Tel Aviv gangsters."

"Our problem," Eban explained, "was to get the word 'Israel' into the international consciousness and the place to begin, of course, was with that little plaque behind which I had to sit."[9]

That year (1948) the Security Council consisted of the five permanent members, plus Argentina, Belgium, Canada, Colombia, Syria and the Ukraine, eleven in all. The Security Council rule was that it took seven votes to pass any procedural measure, but looking over the eleven Eban realized it would be impossible to get any seven of them to vote to change that annoying sign on his desk, for Israel had five implacable opponents on the Council. On the other hand, if it could somehow become a fait accompli and the motion was to force Israel to go back to being the "Jewish Agency for Palestine" the five opposition members would be in the same fix—they might be unable to get two other countries to make it seven. The chairmanship of the Council rotated and so Eban waited until Dmitri Manuilsky, the Ukranian delegate, took the chair. Now was his opportunity, for this was during Israel's honeymoon with the Soviet Union—Russia and her allies were still passionately supporting the Jewish state they had helped bring into existence. The plot Eban concocted was that as soon as President Manuilsky opened the first Council meeting of the session he would say:

"I call the representative of the Provisional Government of Israel to the table."

Thereupon Eban would take his place at the table and a sign reading "the Provisional Government of Israel" would be clamped down in front of him. Then, if his opponents wanted to make a motion of objection to the President's ruling, they would have to muster seven votes to pass it. Eban realized it was a great risk, for if anything went wrong and the President was overruled, it would be a damaging setback, not only for him personally but for Israel's juridical and political situation, so he consulted with Philip C. Jessup, the international lawyer who headed the American delegation, and several others, especially the delegates from Argentina and Cuba. What they told him was that they would not take the initiative themselves, but if it became an accomplished fact they would not oppose it. Eban reported all this to Foreign Minister Shertok, who, being a cautious diplomat, was disturbed over whether Eban could "get away with it." He admitted it all depended on an astute knowledge of parliamentary procedure, which Eban had, and so he would leave the decision to him.

The ploy was carried out in an atmosphere of tension early in July

(1948). Manuilsky opened the proceedings by saying in a clear, firm voice:

"I call the representative of the Provisional Government of Israel to the table."

There was consternation among the Arabs as Eban walked slowly to the table and put down in front of him a lovely plaque reading:

ISRAEL

Then, as Eban himself later described it, "all hell broke loose." Quite a few delegates wished to take part in the debate. The President of the Council was accused of "forcing the issue." The Arabs vehemently declared they would not sit in the same room with Eban as long as that plaque was on the table. The British, not unexpectedly, were opposed to what had been done, but the support Cadogan gave the Arabs was considerably greater than had been anticipated. The arguing went on for two hours, while all-important world business was shoved aside. Then the voting began. Eban turned pale as Argentina, assuming that Israel had more votes than were needed, decided to win some Arab good will by challenging the President's ruling. That gave the other side six votes, uncomfortably close to the number needed, but still not enough. And so, by a piece of clever parliamentary maneuvering Eban succeeded in getting Israel "into the international consciousness."

(Postscript: After the vote was announced Jamal el-Husseini, vice-chairman of the Palestine Arab Higher Committee, stalked from the room, vowing not to return unless Eban was "demoted." The Syrian delegate, however, did not follow him.)

The next month, when Russian delegate Malik succeeded to the presidency, the same drama was played out all over again, with Mahmoud Bey Fawzi of Egypt doing most of the protesting. The headline in the next day's New York *Times* read:

EBAN WILL SIT AGAIN
AS ISRAELI DELEGATE

Late in June (1948) Count Folke Bernadotte, head of the Swedish Red Cross, who had been named UN Mediator for Palestine, came up with a plan for the solution of the entire Palestine problem. It involved taking from Israel: her only seaport, Haifa; her airport at Lydda, northern Galilee, the entire Negev desert and Jerusalem. One critic promptly said that "the hand might be the hand of Bernadotte, but the voice was the voice of Bevin." Another commented:

"When the Mediator's proposals reached Lake Success they were received much as the news was received in heaven that a myopic saint had baptized the penguins—there was neither joy nor sorrow, only surprise."[10]

Eban made the best comment of all:

"A bizarre operation in which the surgeon walks away with vital parts of the patient's anatomy."[11]

A fight against this plan became one of Eban's major occupations. On June 27 (1948) he appeared on the same program with former Secretary of the Treasury Henry J. Morgenthau, Jr., and former Governor Herbert H. Lehman at a meeting of the Council of Organization of the United Jewish Appeal. Twenty-five policemen guarded entrances of the hotel because of a demonstration two days earlier at the Israeli Consulate by members of the American League for a Free Palestine, supporters of the Irgun Zvai Leumi. Eban, departing from his prepared text, denounced the American League for a Free Palestine and two of its leaders, the authors Ben Hecht and Louis Bromfield.

"They are not partners in Israel's destiny. They have not thrown in their lot with Israel. Yet they have incited rebellious elements to mutiny against Israel. Their august feet have not trodden the soil of Israel. They do not intend to leave the fleshpots behind and become citizens of the new republic. By what right, therefore, do they pour forth this hatred and abuse at Israel's lawful government and hold it up to criticism in the press of a great and friendly country?"[12]

Eban was generously applauded and before the meeting adjourned those present had pledged a quarter of a million in gifts to Israel.

In July (1948) Eban and *The Economist*, conservative London weekly, engaged in a duel. The conflict had actually begun six months earlier when *The Economist* in an editorial stated that 270,000 Jews had entered Palestine since the white paper quota had been exhausted. Writing to the paper as "Director, Political Information Department, Jewish Agency," Eban said it was a grossly exaggerated figure and demanded a printed correction. The paper blushingly admitted that the figure should have been 37,000. Now, in July, *The Economist* came out editorially in support of the Bernadotte plan. This prompted Eban to write from New York:

"It is to live in a real wonderland to imagine the Jews giving up the entire Galilee and the entire Negev. . . . Speaking as one of those most anxious for compromise and for an Arab-Jewish settlement, I must tell you that I personally would not remain in a room in which your line from Samakh to Majdal was even discussed. Yours faithfully, A. S. Eban."[13]

The following week in an editorial *The Economist* said:

"They [the Israelis] have a fatal gift for irking even their well-wishers. The tones in which their representative at Lake Success—Mr. Aubrey Eban, who is as fully a British subject as Brigadier Glubb[14]—has been addressing the Security Council do not promise well for their future entry into the council of the nations."

This infuriated Eban and he promptly wrote an excoriating letter to *The Economist,* which was never published. Unfortunately a copy was not kept, but a British friend, David Carrington, then with the Jewish Agency's London headquarters, guarded carefully the original of a cable he received that same week from Eban:

HAVE WRITTEN ECONOMIST MYSELF AM NOT IN THE SLIGHTEST DISTURBED BY ATTACKS BY ORGAN WHOSE WHOLE CONTRIBUTION IRRESPONSIBLE FRIVOLOUS TENDENTIOUS VENOMOUS STOP FOR YOUR BACKGROUND USE HAVE RENOUNCED BRITISH APPLIED ISRAELI CITIZENSHIP ONLY TECHNICAL MATTERS DELAYED CHANGE AM ALSO JEW THEREFORE NO ALIBI FOR GLUBB NOR DO I SHOWER SHELLS ON JERUSALEM.

It was typical that though he said he was "not in the slightest disturbed," he took the time to write to *The Economist* and to send a long cable to the Jewish Agency in London not just mildly protesting but denouncing as "irresponsible, frivolous, tendentious and venomous" —rather strong words—a publication which, by linking him with Glubb Pasha and accusing him of being "a British subject," he felt had slandered him.

Criticism, especially in cold print, had always bothered him. Sometimes, when he thought it was unfair, it stirred him to great anger. No matter how important the task with which he was then occupied, he would take time out to reply. If his reply was not published it raised his ire to a still greater intensity. It was also typical that while he was moderate, always, in speech, when he put indignant words to paper he often went vehemently superlative.

The Economist's flat assertion that Eban was "as fully a British subject as Brigadier Glubb" was fallacious. Although Glubb commanded the Arab Legion of Trans-Jordan, he did so as a British officer and there was never any question of his citizenship. He was British and nothing else. British law permits British citizens to have dual nationality —to carry a British passport as well as the passport of another country. However, in Eban's case he became a citizen of Israel by applying for citizenship under the nationality law passed soon after Independence Day and at the same time he gave up his British citizenship by formal renunciation, as stated in his cable.

After the end of the spring session of the UN, Eban and his wife went home by way of London. When they left it had been Palestine; now it was Israel. When they left, the British had been in control; now Jews were the masters in their own land. There were shortages, food was rationed, all necessities were scarce, luxuries were non-existent. Yet it was home—the state Eban had had so much to do with bringing into existence.

It was a triumphal homecoming in many ways. His firm and defiant addresses in the Security Council had stimulated the country during its brief but cataclysmic war. By short-wave radio the people of Jerusalem had listened to him under siege. Few Israelis knew what he looked like, but they knew the sound of his voice. His welcome at the airport and in Jerusalem was warm. In Tel Aviv, still officially the capital of the country, he was formally presented by Foreign Minister Shertok for the first time to the people whom he had been representing. Unaware of his background and education, many were astonished at his eloquence in Hebrew. Newspaper stories and editorials with few exceptions were complimentary.

From Israel the Ebans went to Geneva on their way to Paris. There, on September 17 (1948) Aubrey had a long and pleasant lunch with Weizmann in a restaurant overlooking Lake Leman. One of the matters they discussed was a cable from Shertok that Eban had found waiting for him on his arrival:

> PLEASE APPLY FOR MEMBERSHIP
> IN UNITED NATIONS

Views about the UN might differ. Especially about its importance. But membership in the UN was of value. It was like a badge of citizenship. It gave stability to Israel's international personality. So long as Israel was not a member, the Arabs could say her statehood was in doubt and there might still be some hope of replacing Israel with Palestine again. Moreover, membership in the UN automatically got a member into all the so-called specialized agencies such as FAO, WHO, UNESCO, UNICEF, the International Monetary Fund, ILO and many other bodies, participation in which helped create the fabric of international community life. As for Switzerland not being a UN member, Eban was always quick to point out that nobody questioned Switzerland's statehood. Besides, Switzerland had the privilege of being a member of any international body she pleased to join. Japan and Italy were not members, but that was because the Soviet Union was keeping them out in order to bargain for her own clients, Romania, Hungary and Bulgaria.[15] But for Israel to be outside the UN was very dangerous because it caused a question mark to hover over her very statehood. There were, however, those who opposed it. Menahem Beigin and many of his Irgun followers were against Israel even applying for membership. So was Nahum Goldmann, perhaps, as one of the critics said, "because maybe he isn't ready yet to be named Ambassador to the UN."

But Eban's assignment was not an easy one. Israel must circumvent the Security Council veto that had blocked from UN membership longer-established states such as Ireland, Japan, Finland, Austria, Romania and Hungary. Then he must repeat his 1947 performance of winning two thirds of the General Assembly against what would of course be violent Arab opposition.

It was such matters that Eban and Weizmann discussed that day at luncheon. When the Chief retired for his afternoon nap Eban returned to his own hotel, where he found another cable from Shertok telling of the assassination of Count Bernadotte, presumably by Israeli terrorists. Geneva had seemed so peaceful, Switzerland so serene. He stuffed this cable into his pocket with the other. There would be many repercussions to this latest piece of foolishness. It would make his diplomatic task infinitely more difficult. It might even make it impossible for Israel to gain admittance to the UN for a long time. He wondered what the assassins thought they would gain by such terrorism. How could it possibly compensate for the ammunition it would give Israel's enemies?

"I was left with the contradiction of one cable saying, 'Get us into the UN' and the next saying, 'Oh, by the way, the UN representative has been killed here.' "[16]

That night, reluctant to cut short his holiday, yet pulled by duty back to his responsibilities, Eban accompanied by Suzy left by train for Paris, where the next afternoon the Security Council was to convene. During the all-night trip he was depressed and sleepless, wondering what kind of atmosphere he would find awaiting him.

The next day his gravest fears were fulfilled. At the opening session of the General Assembly in the massive Palais de Chaillot—normally a scene of Parisian splendor—the entire Swedish delegation appeared in somber black, for on that day Count Bernadotte's body arrived in his home country for burial. The whole UN was mourning the late Mediator. Among the Jewish Agency people the general feeling was that fate had stacked the cards against Israel. How could she possibly defeat the repercussions of an assassination? It seemed impossible, now, that Israel could ever get into the UN. And in a burst of emotionalism the UN might approve the so-called Bernadotte plan, simply out of respect for its slain author.

Eban had a brief meeting with Secretary-General Lie, who was eager to convert the current truce into a permanent peace; crossed swords briefly in the delegates' lounge with his old adversary Albert Hourani and received the news that little El Salvador, which Israel would soon outstrip in population, had become the seventeenth country to accord diplomatic recognition.

Regina Medzini was in Paris for the session. One night when she was in Eban's room at the Hotel Raphael typing a speech, as he stood over her shoulder dictating, there was a frightful pounding on the wall. They looked at their watches. Though it was after 1 A.M. Eban insisted the script be finished before they stopped work for the night. They tried again, Eban lowering his voice almost to a whisper. Again the occupant of the adjoining room complained by thumping the wall vigorously with the heel of a shoe. Finally they compromised with him by going into the bathroom, where Regina set up her typewriter on a small make-up table and the chief Israeli delegate to the UN sat on the toilet seat, as he resumed dictating. Her memories of that session are eighteen-hour days, of working Saturdays, Sundays and holidays, and of the debates between Eban and Cadogan, who, at the end of one exchange, told the Security Council:

"Mr. Eban knows English as well as I do. (Pause.) Perhaps better." No one rose to disagree.[17]

One of the British journalists covering the Palais de Chaillot sessions, John Shaftsley of the *Jewish Chronicle,* recalled the day a reporter for Cairo's *Al Ahram,* one of the most important Arab papers in the Middle East, asked Eban for an interview. Although the interviewer and the interviewee had two other languages in common—English and French— Eban insisted that the questions and answers all be in Arabic.

"Of course!" the reporter stammered in surprise.

Later he told his colleagues that he had never heard such fluent classical Arabic in his life.[18]

Eban and Shertok now turned their attention to the Bernadotte plan, which called for diplomatic activity of the most intensive sort, for if Israel were to lose the Negev, as the plan proposed, it would cut the size of the state in half and leave no room for future economic development. Eban's task was to see that the UN did not approve the plan but at the same time did not pass a resolution refixing the limits of the state as defined by the November 1947 Partition plan. Israel wanted to be free to delineate her frontiers in agreement with her Arab neighbors.

Eban's problem was more formidable than many Israelis realized. First, he had to fight the plan of a man who, as a result of his assassination, had become a martyr. Also, Secretary of State George C. Marshall had already committed the United States to support of the plan. The only hope was in trying to cut the ground from under Marshall's feet. First, President Truman must be persuaded to oppose the plan. Then, an attempt must be made to create a split in the American delegation.

At this critical moment Eban had a stroke of luck. Marshall was called home from Paris because of the Berlin crisis, leaving John Foster Dulles, the deputy head of the U.S. delegation, in charge. Shertok and Eban went to see him at the hotel. The meeting was amiable, for all three men had certain intellectual qualities in common. This may have had something to do with the frankness with which Dulles explained his predicament: he was in the ambivalent position of having been appointed by Truman to the UN delegation and also being foreign policy adviser to Thomas E. Dewey, who was running against Truman for the presidency. But he was not ambivalent about the Bernadotte plan. He was dead set against it, because he thought Israel's military victory had proved something about the character of the Jewish people and therefore had strong moral and spiritual implications. He disagreed with Marshall so vehemently that he had stopped attending delegation meetings over which Marshall presided. Eban learned from Dulles that he was supported in his opposition to the Bernadotte plan by Eleanor Roosevelt and attorney Ben Cohen, while Marshall had as his allies Assistant Secretary Rusk and most of the service officers in the delegation.

In Paris at that time there was a strong feeling among many Americans that Dewey would win and that Dulles would soon become Secretary of State, so there was a constant round of dinners and other social events at which the political future was discussed. Dulles himself invited members of UN delegations to private parties at which he would outline what the Dewey-Dulles policies were going to be. Eban's invitation was for November 4, two days after the election. Had Dewey won it would have been a gala party. Instead, Eban later described it as "an occasion that had all the melancholy of a funeral."[19]

Eban won a notable diplomatic victory in helping defeat the Bernadotte plan, thanks to a strange coalition of allies. The Arabs and their friends were against the plan because they thought it would confirm the right of Israel to exist, even if with less territory. The Soviet Union was against it because they thought it was designed to give the British a base in the Negev by awarding the desert to Britain's friend, Trans-Jordan. Thus Israelis, Arabs and Communist countries for once were all on the same side.

Having made this first friendly contact with Dulles, Eban began seeing him frequently and from these contacts came a UN resolution on December 11 (1948) favorable to Israel, which provided an obscure formula for the return of the refugees and said nothing about frontiers except that they should be negotiated by the Israelis and the Arabs.

Eban gave Dulles major credit for the defeat of the Bernadotte plan and adoption of this friendly resolution. History should also record the role Eban played—with little publicity or credit—in preventing the truncation of Israel at that critical moment in her history.

Eban and Shertok celebrated November 29, 1948—the anniversary of the passage of the UN Partition plan—by presenting to Secretary-General Lie formal application for Israel's membership in the UN, along with a declaration that Israel would accept all obligations stipulated in the Charter. A few days later the American and Russian delegates moved for the admission of Israel "as a matter of urgency." Eban was not surprised that Cadogan objected, calling it "premature and doubtful" and insisting on "indefinite postponement." The French delegate moved for a one-month postponement. Both motions were defeated. Then the question was put. The United States and the Soviet Union both voted in favor of Israel's admission, as did the Ukraine, Argentina and Colombia. Syria voted "no." Belgium, Canada, Great Britain, China and France abstained. Because she had failed to get the required number of votes Israel's application was rejected. Eban, privately disappointed, publicly cheerful, reported to his government that there would be some changes in the Security Council next year, so he would try again in the spring, with hope of a better result.[20]

During the autumn and early winter of 1948 there was severe fighting in the Negev. On January 7, 1949, Israeli fighters shot down five British planes—four Spitfires and one Mosquito—that had been carrying out reconnaissance of Israeli positions. Apparently Britain had entered the war on the side of the Egyptians in compliance with her treaty commitments. As Eban privately explained the diplomatic problem:

"It was a rather dangerous situation. We seemed to be taking on not only the Arab world but what was then the major military power in the Middle East, with a Foreign Secretary of extraordinary malevolence toward us."[21]

Eban, who was in Jerusalem when it happened, flew back immediately to the UN and found that Sir Alexander Cadogan had called on the deputy Israeli representative, Arthur Lourie, with a protest, but because it was addressed to "the Jewish Authorities in Palestine" and because Eban had instructed Lourie to accept diplomatic representations only if they were properly addressed—that is, to Israel—Sir Alexander's protest was rejected, unopened.

Bevin thought he could now turn the wrath of the world against Israel, but he miscalculated. After a stormy debate in which Winston Churchill gave Bevin a verbal trouncing, the chagrined Foreign Minister was forced to accord Israel de facto recognition, which Eban and Shertok considered a sign of the bankruptcy of British policy in Palestine.[22]

After Israel and Egypt formally signed an armistice agreement on February 24, 1949, Eban decided the atmosphere was so euphoric that it would be a good time to renew his bid for Israeli membership in the UN, and so in the spring (1949) session of the Security Council he brought the question up again.

Colombia, which had voted for admission last time, was no longer on the Council. Neither was Belgium, which had abstained. Syria had been replaced by Egypt. What made Eban's task difficult was that any one of the Great Powers could bar Israel by using its power of veto. This meant that he would have to win China and France to his side, while hoping that his old adversary, Cadogan, would have the grace to abstain again. Also, he had to swing Canada in a hundred-and-eighty-degree arc from the "no" to the "yes" column and try to get the votes of two new members, Cuba and Norway.[23]

As he began his campaign, Eban made friends with an amiable pre-Castro Cuban delegate, who seemed amenable to persuasion. He found the Chinese more difficult.

"I even went to the extreme length of eating unpalatable Chinese meals with them in various New York City Chinese restaurants in order to win their good will."

But all this missionary work was not futile, for when, on March 11 (1949), the vote was taken nine out of the eleven countries voted "yes."

The only "no" was Egypt's. Cadogan abstained, so there was no veto. Eban had won one more great diplomatic victory.

The best comment on Britain's decision to abstain that came to Eban's attention was in an article by Gershon Agron, editor of the *Palestine Post:*[24] "If the British sit on the fence long enough, iron will enter their souls." He liked the remark so well that he had his secretary paste the clipping in his scrapbook.[25]

However, the fight was not over. Admittance had to be ratified by the General Assembly. There were now fifty-eight nations in the UN and every one of them had been admitted without debate or even discussion. Except for the original members, the others had mostly been ex-colonies, whose applications were sponsored by the colonial powers. Israel's case was different, as might have been expected. Early in April (1949) the Assembly's steering committee insisted that the case go not to a plenary session of the General Assembly for a vote but to the Political Committee for discussion and debate.

Foreign Minister Shertok had been at Lake Success for the opening of the spring session, but had permitted Eban to handle the application for UN membership in the Security Council and when that battle was won to plan the General Assembly strategy. Naturally he was delighted with the results so far. But the procedural setback caused him great pessimism. He had anticipated that Israel might get the necessary two-thirds vote in the Assembly without having to compromise her principles, but he was afraid the Political Committee would never permit the case to get to the floor of the Assembly. He felt that if he, as the ranking member of the Israeli Cabinet, were to present the case to the committee and then lose, it would be not only a serious personal humiliation but a dangerous setback for the State of Israel. Whereas, if Eban continued to handle the matter and if he were defeated before the Political Committee it would not be so bad. After all, Eban did not even hold the rank of Ambassador to the UN, for Israel was not a member. He was only a young freshman diplomat and if he failed to pull off the coup, people would say: "Too bad! But after all, he's young."

So Shertok went home to Israel and left Eban alone, to try to get the necessary two-thirds majority in the Political Committee. Eban knew he was in a difficult position. The entire Arab world was against him. Plus the British. Plus many others. For example, the Catholic powers were not very friendly to Israel at this time because of the Jerusalem problem.

When General Carlos Romulo of the Philippines, as chairman of the Political Committee, invited Israel to answer the Arabs' long list of reasons why the application for membership should be rejected, Eban delivered (on May 5, 1949) a three-hour address, with only an occasional pause to put a glass of water to his lips. Coincidentally, it was one year and one day (by the Hebrew calendar) since Israel's proclamation of independence. The committee had asked him to state his government's attitude to the question of Jerusalem. Eban suggested two possible solutions: limit the internationally controlled area so it covered only that part of Jerusalem containing the greatest concentration of religious and historic shrines, or, establish an international regime for the entire city that would be concerned only with holy places and not with any secular or political aspects of life and government. His final words, as the three hours drew to a close, were:

"A great wheel of history comes full circle today as Israel, renewed and established, offers itself, with all its imperfections but perhaps with some virtues, to the defense of the invincible human spirit against the perils of nihilism, conflict and despair."

When he sat down he might have thought his task had been completed, but he was immediately subjected to a barrage of questions he had to answer off the cuff.[26]

"It was a cross-examination rather like that which a prisoner in the dock must undergo," he said later.

"What will be Israel's attitude, if accepted into the UN, toward UN resolutions?" demanded Charles Habib Malik, chairman of the Lebanese delegation.

"I am not going to commit myself in advance to any particular resolution," Eban replied sharply, "but our attitude will not be the same as that of Lebanon and six other Arab states who fell upon a UN resolution in November of 1947 and tried to tear us to bits by violence."

At another point in the questioning he made this barbed comment:

"It's very strange for me to be appearing before a bench of judges when I see that six of the judges have recently attempted to murder me. It hardly gives them title to judge my case objectively."

This, of course, was the essence of the UN paradox in its relationship to Israel, and it would remain so indefinitely. At least some of the delegates were grateful to Eban for pointing it out.

Eban's exhausting appearance before the Political Committee on that spring day in 1949 demonstrated what a consummate diplomat he was— he knew when to be scintillating and emotional, when to be coldly logical and factually convincing. His address was a masterpiece of organization; his reasonings mostly unanswerable. He sandwiched in just enough sentimental appeal and when the bombardment of questions began, although he had already done an exhausting day's work, he handled them with the skill of a man who knows every facet of his subject—never embarrassed, never insulting, never ingratiating, replying even to malicious questions with such dignity that he was always in control of the situation.

Several days later, just before the voting on Israel's admission was due to take place, Asst. Secr. of State Dean Rusk telephoned Israel's ambassador in Washington, Eliahu Elath, and complained that Eban had not gone far enough in his address on what concessions Israel was willing to make about refugees and frontiers. It was a not very subtle attempt at political blackmail, for Rusk said the vote on Israel's admission to the UN might go against her unless Eban complied with the State Department's wishes on these two matters. When Elath communicated this information to Eban, he replied:

"That's strange because I have taken soundings in the UN and my address seemed to satisfy most of them. In fact, I have taken a head count and we are way ahead of the support we had last time. I have no worry. This is a war of nerves, but if we stand firm I am sure we will get our membership without any unnecessary concessions."

Several days later, when the Political Committee voted, Eban's prediction was borne out. Israel obtained a few more than the two thirds she needed and the committee's recommendation was put on the agenda of the Plenary Session for the next day, May 11 (1949).

As he relaxed for a moment from the strain of the ordeal, Eban began thinking of the acceptance speech he would make in the Plenary Session. It would be a big moment. He would relish appearing before the statesmen of the world in the role of a young David—a freshman diplomat who had scored a giant victory. Suddenly he thought of Shertok; not of Moshe Shertok, Foreign Minister, but of Moshe Shertok, friend. He remembered what Shertok had often done for him in decisive moments. Although he had fought this battle alone and was eager to be in the center of the spotlight to enjoy the acclaim, he sent an urgent cable to the Foreign Minister:

YOU MUST COME YOU MUST MAKE THE SPEECH WE WILL HOLD UP
THE VOTING IF NECESSARY

Back came a quick reply:

WHAT HAPPENS IF I SET OUT FROM TEL AVIV TO COME TO GENERAL
ASSEMBLY AND PLENARY SESSION DOES NOT GIVE US REQUIRED
TWO-THIRDS WON'T I LOOK FOOLISH

Eban's reply was that he could almost guarantee a favorable vote, but if Shertok wanted to be that cautious he could have a plane ready and as soon as the actual voting started—as soon as they could be positive of the outcome—he could start for New York. Then Eban would try to delay the speechmaking.

Back in Tel Aviv Shertok permitted himself to be convinced and boarded a plane at once. If Eban's optimism were not justified it would be a disastrous situation—embarrassing for everyone. When Eban heard of the decision he started pacing. During the next eighteen hours he covered almost as many miles as Shertok. The voting had already started when word was flashed from New York International Airport at Idle-wild[27] that Shertok's plane had landed and he was on his way to Flushing Meadow by police-escorted car.

One of Eban's most unforgettable moments—and probably also one of Shertok's—was when, after the favorable vote was announced, the Foreign Minister and the man most responsible for Israel's admission walked to the table on which the word "Israel" was planted and formally and officially joined the world community as the fifty-ninth member—as an equal partner with the lesser powers and the great powers, too.

The vast assembly hall was in a state of excitement. Stephen Alexis, representative of Haiti, was the first of many delegates to rush forward and shake the hands of Eban, Shertok and other members of the delegation. Spectators in the crowded balcony applauded vociferously. Professional and amateur photographers vied with each other in taking innumerable flashbulb pictures. After it was over Eban paid high tribute to Dr. Herbert V. Evatt, who served in the early part of 1949 as President of the Security Council, for his help.

"Nobody could describe him as an engaging personality," Eban said. "He was egotistical, brilliant, curt and entirely tolerant of all those who blindly accepted his own views. But what was important for us, he had decided to help Israel get into the United Nations. He thought historic destiny was at work here. There was some sense of historical romance behind this somewhat brusque Australian lawyer's temperament."[28]

The next day during a moving ceremony the blue and white Israeli flag bearing the Star of David was hoisted in front of the UN building and in Rockefeller Plaza.

In 1947 Eban had been just one of the architects of the accomplishment. In this 1949 victory he was the leading figure. Shertok had been skeptical. Israel's Herut party had even opposed applying for UN membership, in order to avoid the indignity if rejected. But Eban had persisted and won. In many ways it was more important than the victory of November 1947.

Regardless of whether the General Assembly or the Security Council passed resolutions for or against Israel at some time in the future, membership of the Jewish state in the UN would always be a symbol of the country's international dignity and equality, and was something to be cherished. It was an outward and visible sign of Israel's return to full sovereignty, after so many centuries in the political wilderness. Now it was no longer possible for anyone to say Israel did not exist. Now she was equal in status with all other members of the organized world community. Henceforth Arab statements about her non-existence or illegitimacy would sound absurd.

The day after Israel's admittance to the UN she began having her headaches as a member of the international community. The matter under discussion was the rehabilitation of Spain. Because Franco had been an ally of Hitler and Mussolini and because he was still the dictator of Spain, Israel joined with the social-democratic countries of Europe in voting "no," thus putting principles above practicality. Eban was aware that for years Spain might use this against Israel, which is what happened, even though Spain found excuses for forgiving the other forty states that voted likewise.

At the Flushing Meadow assembly hall the delegates sat around U-shaped tables in alphabetical order. Until Israel's admittance the delegates of two Arab countries, Iraq and Lebanon, had been side by side. But now Israel was put between them. The day after the admission, when the dark-haired young man with the heavy horn-rimmed glasses strode into the room and took his place, the Iraqi and the Lebanese delegates were leaning across the empty space, chatting, but as soon as they saw the newcomer they straightened up. Eban sat down nonchalantly, drew his pipe from his pocket, slowly filled it, then lit up. There was no ash tray in front of him, so he reached over and put the dead match in the Iraqi's. The Iraqi delegate promptly called an attendant and asked for another ash tray. Several times during the morning, when there was a pause in the proceedings, the Lebanese and the Iraqi delegates would lean toward each other, behind Eban's back, and engage in whispered conversations, sometimes of a very confidential nature. This went on for days, to Eban's delight, until someone warned the two Arabs that Eban was an orientalist and undoubtedly understood every word they said. Immediately the whispering stopped and was superseded by the passing of notes back and forth—behind the Israeli's back.

Eban, age thirty-four, now had the title of Ambassador to the UN. He also had a world stage on which to perform and an opportunity few men his age ever had to make an international reputation. It would mean hard work and the sacrifice of a normal life. He and Suzy had moved to the Sulgrave Hotel on Park Avenue. Although they had been married five years, they still had nothing remotely resembling a home.

What kept their life from being calm and conventional was the situation in the Middle East. Defeated militarily on every one of Israel's frontiers, the Arabs licked their wounds and nursed thoughts of revenge. Soon Israel was being plagued by border incidents, by fedayeen raids and by an Arab economic blockade. The battle became more diplomatic than military. Eban had to be constantly on the alert for surprise maneuvers. Some of his opponents were men with decades of experience in international politics, far more talented in their field than the Arab generals were in theirs. In the Security Council, the General Assembly and the Political Committee Eban used every weapon in his formidable arsenal: disarming dialectics, searing sarcasm, an occasional appeal to emotions, frequent historical references, the exposure of Arab falsification and error, and the repeated, insistent defense of a people's right to existence. Often he went back to his hotel late at night bone-tired and mind-weary, but at eight o'clock the next morning he would always be in action again, vigorous and alert.

President Weizmann had promised that he would come to the United States in January (1949) for a fund-raising dinner for the Weizmann Institute. His reluctance to leave the infant country and the reluctance of Ben-Gurion and others to permit him to leave, combined with ill health, delayed his visit, but he finally came in early April. It was planned as the most elegant, high-level banquet ever held by the Jewish community in the United States. Invitations went to Secretary-General Trygve Lie, all the delegates to the UN (Arabs excepted), senators, congressmen, members of the Washington diplomatic corps and to hundreds of wealthy and prominent American Jews. Because she knew that she and her husband would be very much in the spotlight that night, Suzy Eban, typically feminine, worried about what she would wear, especially since she was some months pregnant.[20] Her mother and father, who now lived in Israel, solved the problem by ordering a Parisian couturier to make a stunning evening gown for her. The next dilemma was to get it to New York without risking postal delays. By good fortune Mr. and Mrs. Ambache had met in Tel Aviv Mr. and Mrs. Harry Levine of Wellesley Hills, Massachusetts, who were in Israel on a visit. With them were Mr. and Mrs. Dewey Stone of Brockton, Massachusetts. Both men, founding governors of the Weizmann Institute, were on their way to New York and were going to be stopping en route in Paris. That was how Suzy Eban got her French creation in time.

The night of the banquet the Waldorf-Astoria ballroom was packed. As Mr. and Mrs. Stone moved along the receiving line and were introduced to the Ebans, Mrs. Stone said in a whisper:

"I was with Leona Levine when she picked up your dress in Paris. It looks wonderful!"

Suzy laughed and replied:

"It is pretty, isn't it? And I like *yours* very much, too."

Years later Mrs. Eban said:

"I remember the night so well. It was Chaim Weizmann's first appearance in the country as President. Mr. Lie was there and no end of other important people. Of course there's always a certain amount of tension when hundreds of women are dressed to the teeth, wearing all their jewelry and their fresh hairdos and they all look at each other and make critical judgments and sometimes say things that sound so very sweet but aren't meant that way at all. Well, here was this stranger, old enough to be my mother, and she spoke to me with such warmth and she seemed so happy that I looked nice. And so I thought of her as being totally different. I knew that with a woman like that I could always feel secure. No competition. I think we intuitively liked each other from the start."[30]

Mrs. Stone said:

"Even though it was twenty-two years ago, I remember so well her dress that I can describe it down to the smallest detail. And just last year Suzy described the dress I wore that night down to the smallest detail. Apparently from the very start there was something between us."[31]

That was the beginning of an unusual relationship between the Brockton-born Anne Stone and the Egyptian-born Suzy Eban, and later between their husbands, one an affluent Massachusetts businessman, the other a Cambridge-educated orientalist scholar who had been hurtled into the field of diplomacy. On the surface they seemed to have nothing in common except their pride in being Jews and their interest in the survival of Israel.

The Weizmann dinner was notable because the unprecedented sum of $38,000,000 was raised that night for Israel—mostly in checks dropped into a basket on the speakers' table—and because the ailing President delivered an exceptional address in which he endorsed an Israeli foreign policy of non-identification, or as he put it, "a policy of friendship to all the nations, whether or not they diverge amongst themselves in other respects of their policy."

In June (1949) Eban shared an honor with a man he had admired since the day they met in Palestine, when both were attached to UNSCOP. He and Ralph Bunche, who replaced Bernadotte as acting Mediator after the assassination, were given honorary degrees as Doctors of Hebrew Letters by Hebrew Union College.

That summer (1949) the Ebans went to Israel, where among the many other gatherings held in their honor was a party on Jabotinsky Street in Tel Aviv, with Chaim Herzog as host. Suzy's brother-in-law, now director of Military Intelligence, invited as guests the key figures of the victorious Israeli Army—tough young men, mostly Haganah, some Irgun, many of them sabras.[32] These were the men who had led several underground armies against the military might of five Arab nations. They represented a new breed of Jew. Herzog thought they and Eban should know each other. Most of them found the shy yet very articulate diplomat an enigma. Eban, because of his role in arming and training the Palmach during World War II, had met a few of Herzog's guests before, but never socially like this. Before the long evening was over a number of substantial bridges had been built between some of Israel's most important young military leaders, who seldom before had met such an Anglo-Jew as Eban, and one of her most indelible diplomatic leaders.[33]

When the General Assembly opened its fall session (in September, 1949) Eban delivered a speech that had been churning in his head all summer. This was the first address by a representative of Israel to the General Assembly since the state's admission to the UN. Taking a global view of the current situation, he told his fellow delegates:

"Anxious people all over the world are asking whether governments with different and opposing interests could achieve a point of mutual tolerance, above their differences and above their opposition. They are asking whether divergent and contrasting political doctrines can live together in peace, side by side. The main issue is the coexistence of different ways of life and within a common allegiance to an international code."

He said there was hope for mankind in the fact that such a "savage and inveterate conflict as the Middle Eastern war" had been ended through the good auspices of the UN. He was even so optimistic as to suggest that perhaps such principles of conciliation "under neutral and mutually accepted auspices might be applied anew to acute problems of such other parts of the world as the Balkans, and to atomic energy."

He talked long and convincingly about Jerusalem—how the Jewish population had been subjected to "siege and famine, while the international community had remained supine for months." Flatly he declared that Israel aspired to "full international recognition of the political status of the Government of Israel in Jerusalem."

The next day Shertok sent him a cable of "heartiest congratulations on a highly dignified, skillful, incisive presentation." The Israeli press was also complimentary.

In October (1949) Eban faced a peculiar diplomatic situation. In the Political and Security Committee of the General Assembly the Soviet Union had submitted a proposal for immediate independence for the former Italian colony of Libya and the withdrawal of all foreign troops within three months. Both Great Britain and the United States had opposed immediate independence, for reasons of their own. What should Israel's position be? Last year the Arab bloc had tried to smother Israel at her birth.

Eban was aware of the criticism he would face, yet on October 4 (1949), in a forceful statement to the General Assembly, the representative of the youngest state in the UN explained why Israel was voting with the seven Arab states that had sought her destruction in favor of the creation of still another Arab nation. It was Israel's steadfast desire, he said, to see that all the countries in the Middle East not only achieved their individual independence but also their "collective harmony."

Noting that some of his UN colleagues had expressed their surprise "to see Israel supporting the emergence of an eighth Arab state after deriving so little enjoyment from its relations with the seven already existing," he said Israel regarded "the prospect of eventual harmony as immeasurably more important and significant than the reality of the present discord."

Israel's vote was not needed to obtain passage of the resolution, yet the situation gave Eban an opportunity to put unselfish principles ahead of Israel's own narrow interests. If any Arabs welcomed this gesture of good will they kept that appreciation well hidden. Not only did no one make a move to take the outstretched hand of friendship; before many years Libya, for no good reason, would be one of the Arab nations shouting most vociferously for Israel's obliteration.

16

Can You Do Both?

ISRAEL'S FIRST PRIME MINISTER changed his name from Gruen or Green to Ben-Gurion on arrival as a young man in Palestine. After the establishment of the Jewish state in 1948 he urged all Israelis to drop their diaspora nomenclature and take pure Hebrew names. Many did, voluntarily. The only compulsion was that those going to diplomatic posts abroad must have Hebrew names in their passports. In some cases it meant changing first names, in some cases family names, in a few cases both names. Thus it was that Moshe Shertok became Sharett,[1] Gideon Rufer became Gideon Rafael, Eliahu Epstein became Eliahu Elath.[2]

For Eban there was no problem. His last name in Hebrew would be Even, the Hebrew word for stone. (In Hebrew *b* and *v* are the same letter.) For a first name he would simply use the Hebrew name he had been given at his bris. And so, starting in 1949, his calling cards, his signature on letters and his name as it appeared on government documents became Abba Eban, although for the rest of his life his pre-1949 friends and associates, as well as members of his family, would continue to call him Aubrey. (Halfway through 1950 the New York *Times* began referring to him as "Abba (Aubrey S.) Eban," and in 1951 finally dropped the parenthetical material.)

Years later, after her son had moved permanently to Israel, Alida Eban said:

"Whenever I get a letter from Jerusalem signed 'Abba' I know it's not his real signature but that of a secretary."[3]

A columnist for the *Evening News* of London, writing about the change in names, said he preferred Aubrey because it is of Teutonic origin, because it literally means "self-ruler" and because "according to my book of reference it fits someone who is disciplined, impartial, scrupulous, with a good sense of humor and alert in judgment."

While Abba Eban was a perfect name for a writer, actor, artist, politician or other public figure, being short, almost musical in its rhythm and easy to remember, it caused certain embarrassments for him among those whose native tongue was Hebrew. "Abba" is the word Hebrew-speaking children use for "father," "daddy," "papa." A political colleague who was some years older than Eban said:

"I had always called him Aubrey. After he changed his name I tried to call him Abba, but . . . I just couldn't. That was what I had always called my father."[4]

After Egypt, Jordan, Lebanon and Syria finally signed armistice agreements with Israel during the winter, spring and summer of 1949, Eban delivered an address in which he declared that "a new stability has now come upon our region." As the head of the UN delegation, he felt this new stability would mean that there would be, for him, a period of intense activity starting with the opening of the General Assembly in September and lasting through December. He anticipated that during the rest of the year life would be considerably less hectic. Occasionally, now, he and Suzy could go to concerts, dance recitals and plays. Their favorite musical that year (1949) was *South Pacific*, which Suzy said "I could see a dozen times." Both of them liked New York.

"It was so dynamic, so interesting, so invigorating," Suzy expostulated. "New York was lovely then! I found it—I guess 'liberating' is the word. I loved it!"[5]

If Aubrey worked long into the evening at delegation headquarters or at the UN building they often had a late dinner in the Oak Room of the Plaza Hotel, where, it was said, most people go either to see or be seen. The Broadway columnist Leonard Lyons normally dropped into the Oak Room between 10 and 11 P.M. on his round of night clubs and restaurants, which was just when the Ebans would generally be there, and they became friends. This occasional contact was fruitful for both men—Lyons could always count on Eban for a fresh anecdote, a glittering phrase or a pungent comment for his column, and Eban could always count on Lyons to write favorably of him personally, and/or of Israel. Lyons became the first of many American newspapermen to discover the inexhaustibility of Eban's store of verbal pyrotechnics.

In these post-armistice days, when the frontiers of Israel were quieter than they had been in several years—and quieter than they might be again for a long time—Eban was engaged in a sporadic, entirely unpublicized correspondence with one of the principal Arab spokesmen, Dr. Charles Habib Malik, chief of the Lebanese delegation to the UN since the formation of the world body, who, like Eban, would later be named his country's ambassador to Washington. Malik had studied in the Middle East, Europe and America, and had begun to gather honorary degrees from universities around the world. He was nine years Eban's senior. Like Eban he was an intellectual, a philosopher and a scholar. Other UN delegates often compared the two men as speakers. Although their style was quite different, they both had the ability to hold the attention of an audience for hours. Politics aside they exchanged discreet respect for each other. Their letters were written either on personal stationery or UN paper and were always in longhand. Malik, like Eban, wrote with a fine pen and his calligraphy was similar—careful, precise. His letters always began "Dear Mr. Eban" or "Dear Ambassador Eban" and were signed simply "Charles Malik." They were never dated. In one letter he wrote about the "absolutes of Spinoza and Schelling," quoting Hegel on "the night in which all cows appear to be black," then added: "I, also, do not believe in such absolutes." Another letter ended:

"One day, when the final conciliation between Christ and Israel is consummated, which was craved for by St. Paul, then you can speak for me and I can speak for you."

Once, as they sat side by side in the General Assembly, Malik passed over to Eban a torn piece of envelope on which he had scribbled:

"Mr. Eban: I am sorry I was unable to hear you yesterday, but of course I read your statement afterwards. Charles Malik."[6]

One of the best show windows Eban had in 1949 was a conference arranged by the American Academy of Political and Social Science in Philadelphia on the theme: "World Government: How? Why? When? How?" Seventeen distinguished men of various nationalities were on the program. Eban followed Kermit Roosevelt, who had served in the Middle East in the early 1940s with the State Department and the U. S. Army and had written a book, *Arabs, Oil and History*. Ignoring the theme of the conference, he let loose a violent attack on the United States and the UN for "assisting this foreign element [sic!] to establish itself" in the Middle East. He called the re-creation of Israel "a racist, imperialistic venture which is bound to promote hatred, violence and confusion and to make more difficult than ever the tasks of peace and unification in the world." Eban, ignoring Roosevelt, pleaded for worldwide cooperation rather than unity.

"Cooperation accepts the existence of independent units of life and thought and government but aspires to harmonize the activity of those units in a general stream of universal peace. Unity would abolish those horizons. . . . Let us no more think in terms of ramshackle confederations in which peoples surrender their separate capacity for organizing their national life and let us think rather in terms of harmonizing differences that we acknowledge as they are. . . ."[7]

Late in 1949 Suzy Eban, expecting a child in several weeks, said to her husband:

"Look, Aubrey, I just can't have a baby in a hotel room!"

He agreed and one month before the child was due they moved into a building at 241 Central Park West. From the large nineteenth-story windows they had a view of Manhattan that never ceased to excite them.

On January 27 (1950) Abba Eban had to leave for two and a half months in Europe and Israel. His plane tickets were purchased, his reservations made, his itinerary carefully mapped. If the medical prognostications were correct the timing would be perfect, for the baby was scheduled to arrive about the middle of January.

Eli Eban was born on January 18 at the Harkness Pavilion of the Columbia Presbyterian Medical Center, New York. Aubrey was busy that evening making a UJA fund-raising talk, but he rushed from the meeting to the hospital, arriving just before the birth took place. Suzy commented:

"My sense of timing was good, wasn't it?"[8]

The boy was named after his grandfather, Eliahu, and also after Eli, one of the last of the Judges, who succeeded to the high priesthood at the age of fifty-eight and died at the age of ninety-eight as a result of falling from his chair on hearing of the Philistine capture of the Ark.[9]

The mother and child were brought home to the Central Park apartment on the afternoon of January 27, and a few hours later the father rushed off to catch his plane. It was the only lengthy separation since their marriage and neither was happy about it.

In her first letter to Aubrey in Israel Suzy wrote:

"I don't know if you are a subject of public interest, but your son Eli is. I never thought a baby could arouse so much curiosity and excitement in strangers." She was spending all her time acknowledging gifts and congratulatory messages. "The apartment seems dead without you." She wrote of how much better the apartment looked after the arrival of a new armchair. "Our living room now has an air of quiet elegance and invites one to relax and take a peaceful view of the world."

In another letter she warned him that the apartment was "a chaotic mess." There were piles of unanswered letters and other piles of envelopes not even opened. "Every drawer in the desk is full of papers. My next acquisition is going to be a filing cabinet—a big, office-size one. In a way I am glad you are not here to see the chaos. It reflects the last few months of a disorganized life. . . ."[10]

Eban went from Israel to Geneva to address the Trusteeship Council. When he arrived there he found a letter from Suzy that began:

"There is a soft radiant world that is like a fairy tale written under a soft light. Your world and mine. Just ours, with its deep emotions, its laughter, its charm, its gaiety."

On February 2 (1950) she wrote reminding him that this was the first birthday of his on which they had been apart.

"Eli is like Abba, because he is so gentle and well disposed. He has alertness and poise and a real will to progress."

On February 11 she sent him the manuscript of an article she had written, asking him to correct and revise it, if necessary. After reporting on Eli's health, his length and his weight, she added:

"I am sure you will make as wonderful a father as you make a husband. Sometimes I feel like standing on a roof and telling the world how wonderful you are. And I don't mean just your mind. When you return you will find me very changed. Having a baby is a great lesson in humility. It brings you nearer to every being and to the elementary things of life. It makes you mature without aging, because the whole thing makes you happy and gives you a big lift."

A few days later she wrote:

"I presume that you will spend the weekend preparing your speech—marching up and down your room looking very thoughtful and very offensive and very single-minded and very detached from the world. Monday night I shall be glued to the radio and will try to be satisfied with one of those frustrating UN broadcasts from Geneva, so brief they are. But I know it will surely be nothing but another wonderful presentation of our point of view on Israel."

Eban entitled his Trusteeship Council address "If I Forget Thee, Oh Jerusalem." It was a carefully reasoned, exceedingly cogent, well-organized and beautifully presented argument for political freedom for Jerusalem, with international supervision only of the holy places. Step by step he reviewed what had happened to Jerusalem and its people from the November (1947) approval of the Partition plan up to the cease-fire; the destruction of Jewish holy places; how close the Jewish population came to annihilation. Then he made his plea:

"The spiritual ideals conceived in Jerusalem are the moral basis on which modern democracy rests. Would it not be incongruous if the United Nations were to advance the course of democratic liberty everywhere, and yet prevent self-government from taking root in the very city where the democratic ideal was born? . . .

"Our vision is of a Jerusalem wherein free people develop their reviving institutions, while a United Nations representative, in all tranquillity and dignity, fulfills the universal responsibility for the safety and accessibility of the holy places. . . . This is a vision worthy of the United Nations. . . . Perhaps in this, as in other critical periods of history, a free Jerusalem may proclaim redemption to mankind."

In Tel Aviv a meeting of Ben-Gurion's Cabinet instructed Foreign Minister Sharett to send Eban a cable of appreciation of his "magnificent effort on behalf of Jerusalem."

Suzy in her message of congratulations told him the UN announcer had called the address "eloquent."

"Mail these days," she reported, "is made up of Hadassah notices, bills, advertisements and nudnicks."[11]

On their fifth wedding anniversary, after thanking him for the flowers he had sent and a telephone call, she wrote:

"I don't know how this separation has worked out for you, but for me it is one big dreadful bang in my emotional life. I shall never forget the lonely days and nights—alone, just watching tenderly and sadly over little Eli. When I lecture myself and tell myself that this will probably have to happen again and again in my life, my courage fails me at the mere thought."

In another letter, describing her inability to live on her budget while he was gone, she wrote:

"I hope you won't be upset at my financial inefficiency. . . . I know that I was supposed to be the financial minister of our household, but unlike Kaplan [Eliezer Kaplan, first Finance Minister of Israel] I can never say no in a very drastic and emphatic way."

Reporting on a short speech she had made she wrote:

"People said I was calm, but inside I was trembling. Darling, are you, too, calm only on the surface?"[12]

Eban returned to New York in time to attend the annual Nation Forum at the Waldorf-Astoria, sharing the platform with Lord John Boyd-Orr, winner of the Nobel Peace Prize for that year, and a galaxy of distinguished foreign and domestic scientists, educators and journalists. The theme was "The Atomic Era, Can It Bring Peace and Abundance?"

The address contained only a few witticisms, but great profundity, mixed with rapier-like raillery. Speaking of Israel's new international role he said:

"Having anxiously watched other governments sedulously intervene in our affairs, we suddenly became endowed with a modest capacity of interference in theirs. We are fully persuaded that inexperience and recent arrival do not diminish the international responsibilities of newly emancipated states. Indeed, as we survey some of our more established colleagues we sometimes find it hard to discover a precise relationship between length of experience and infallibility of wisdom."

The sophisticated audience, many in evening dress, were delighted with him. A little later in his talk he said:

"Any state desiring a quiet life would have done well not to be born in the twentieth century. . . . We have shown a deep ardor in the pursuit of material power and little or no ingenuity in the art of controlling and harnessing that power."

Because atomic power has the ability "to enliven or destroy, to fructify or cause to perish," he saw the world "poised on an extraordinary frontier between Utopia and Armageddon," and he appealed for world-wide conciliation.

Late in 1949, after the Communists took control of China, Chou En-lai was named both Premier and Foreign Minister. Israel was one of the first countries to give mainland China diplomatic recognition. Some months later Eban put his thoughts about China on paper in an article he wrote for *The Nation* in which he said:

"Despite our clear and categorical reservation from the form of government practised in China today, it appeared evident to Israel and to many democratic governments that the association of China with the United Nations by the links of permanent contact, common responsibility and mutual obligation was the essential foundation of an understanding. . . . The first premise of the UN charter was that diverse ideologies could live in one united world. If this premise be denied then let the UN be disbanded."[13]

Great Britain finally gave Israel de facto recognition early in 1949 and de jure recognition on April 27, 1950. Thereafter Eban found proof of what he called Ambassador Cadogan's "uncanny professionalism." Now that it was the policy of Her Majesty's Government to permit Israel to live, the Cadogans invited the Ebans to their home at Oyster Bay, Long Island, and all was sweetness and light.[14]

Eban had long been an admirer of Mrs. Eleanor Roosevelt and on

May 12 of that year (1950) joined in a tribute to her as one of four speakers at a ceremony during which Mrs. Roosevelt received the Four Freedoms award.

In late June Eli, although still not six months old, went on a trip of more than ten thousand miles when his parents took him to Israel for his first stay. After their return to the United States Eban made several speaking tours. In Atlanta, Georgia, one night in August (1950) he received a cable from Foreign Minister Sharett:

CAN YOU DO BOTH?

"He didn't say both of what. It was very enigmatic. But I knew what he meant: could I hold down the UN post in New York and at the same time accept appointment as Israeli ambassador to Washington."[15]

Eban consulted with only one person before dispatching a reply. He telephoned Suzy, told her of the offer and asked what she thought of it. Her excitement was instantaneous, so that night he sent an uncoded cable from Atlanta accepting the appointment.

There had already been rumors that the Washington post was going to be vacant. The Israeli Minister to the Court of St. James, Mordechi Eliash, had died very suddenly. To fill that vacancy Ben-Gurion and Sharett decided to move to London Eliahu Elath, then ambassador in Washington.[16] To fill the No. 1 post in the entire Israeli diplomatic corps a man was now needed who would make a positive impression, not only on Washington but on the United States as a whole. As one Israeli explained it:

"Washington was growing in importance to us and we realized we must have as ambassador a man who could attain a public position, so that when he came into the State Department they would not look at him in relation to a few hundred thousand Jews in Israel but as somebody whose word carried weight in the world, and especially throughout the United States."[17]

Sharett persuaded Ben-Gurion that Eban was already making an impact on the American public through his UN speeches and that if he were also given the Washington post he could not only articulate Israel's policies but would be in a position to help make those policies.

One day Eban and an Israeli colleague took a cab from delegation headquarters in Manhattan out to Lake Success. Eban left the cab first and rushed into the building. As the other Israeli was paying the bill the cabbie, obviously Irish from the name on his hack permit and from his accent, said:

"I don't know who that man is, but I listened to everything he said to you and I tell you he could easily be mayor of New York if he wanted to be."

He paused, then added:

"Or governor!"

As the Israeli smiled and turned toward the building he heard the Irishman add:

"Or even President—if he wanted to be."

As Eban prepared to move his headquarters from New York to Washington, he thought of the warning he had been given years ago by Lord Edwin Samuel when he was debating which of the four roads to follow: "Whatever you do don't take the Jewish Agency. . . . There's no future in it." Even if he progressed no further than this, he would now be at the very top of the diplomatic ladder. And it had all happened so quickly. It was only four years ago that Sharett, then Shertok, had sent him the enigmatic message: "Nu?"

Felix Frankfurter, even after joining the U. S. Supreme Court, continued to take a keen interest in Zionist affairs and when he learned that a new Israeli ambassador to Washington was about to be appointed, he is reported to have sent this cable to either Prime Minister Ben-Gurion or Foreign Minister Sharett:

PLEASE DON'T SEND US A CLEVER JEW

(The authority for this story is a close aide of Ben-Gurion, although Ben-Gurion himself, interviewed at Sde Boker in 1970, said he could not definitely recall having seen such a cable and Sharett's former aides said they had never heard Sharett mention it.)

Eban's comment:

"What would the antithesis have been? What did he want, a stupid goy? I knew Frankfurter very well. I had considerable correspondence with him. He had a lot of froth about him. He reminded me of what Churchill once said about somebody: 'He is profoundly superficial.'"[18]

In September (1950) Eban, in striped trousers, morning coat and Homburg, appeared by appointment at the White House to present his credentials to the President of the United States. Having seen photographs of other ambassadors presenting their credentials to other Presidents, he was aware that this, normally, is one of the most pompous ceremonies in American democratic procedure, having almost as much formality as the changing of the guard at Buckingham Palace.

A White House aide escorted him down a broad hallway and then opened the door of the President's office. Eban had difficulty concealing his astonishment, for there sat President Truman at his desk with his coat off, his suspenders showing, wearing brown and white sport shoes—very informal attire for a President.

Pulling an official-looking document from his pocket, the new Israeli ambassador in an oratorical voice began reading his credentials. The President quickly interrupted.

"Look, we don't have to have any of this official crap. Let's just sit down and have a good talk."

The conversation they then had was frank, unrestrained and enlightening—for both men. As he left the White House half an hour later Eban suddenly realized that here was something that minuscule Israel and the gigantic United States had in common—informality in high places, even though President Truman did put on his coat when the customary, formal photograph of the ceremony was taken. The prepared statement issued by the President's office for the occasion said:

"You take up your post at a critical time. In some areas of the world there is actual fighting, as free people struggle against aggression. In other areas there is mistrust and tension which will require much good will and patient effort to overcome. . . ."

Eban decided that until the autumn term of the General Assembly was over he would continue to make his home in the subleased Manhattan apartment and shuttle back and forth between New York and Washington. It was the start of a strange commuting life. Occasionally he even made two round trips—New York–Washington, Washington–New York, New York–Washington, Washington–New York—in a single day. Fortunately it was not far from La Guardia Airport, New York, to Lake Success or Flushing Meadow, nor was it far from National Airport, Washington, to the Embassy. Also, there was no wasted time en route, for Eban has the faculty of being able to concentrate on the reading of ponderous diplomatic documents, or on speechwriting and speech correcting, while flying at twenty thousand feet.

"I never would have been able to succeed in both jobs," Eban said, "had I not had an able alternate to sit in for me at the UN when I was in Washington: first Arthur Lourie, then Reggie Kidron and finally Yosef Tekoah."[19]

David Zysman, Chicago director of the Development Corporation for Israel, tells a story of a conversation with Eban about this time. The ambassador went to Chicago to deliver a talk at a Bonds for Israel meeting. En route from the plane to the hall he was discussing languages with

Zysman, who had been born in Russia and in 1935 had fled east instead of west, spending the war years in China, before finally emigrating to the United States. In discussing their polylingualism (Zysman is fluent in seven languages) the Bonds executive discovered that he knew one language not on Eban's list: Spanish.

"I think I'll start learning Spanish one of these days," Eban remarked. "I'd like to hear how they translate my UN speeches into that language."

As Zysman tells the rest of the story:

"It was not more than three or four months later that Eban came to do another Bonds talk, which happened to be in one of the remote North Shore suburbs. As we were making the long drive up the lake front Eban insisted on talking exclusively in Spanish."

Zysman, who speaks Spanish almost as well as he does English, gave Eban a better-than-passing grade. It turned out that Eban had done most of his studying of the new language on plane trips between New York and Washington, and had perfected his accent by listening to the Spanish-language simultaneous translators at the UN over his earphones.

In October (1950) Eban was called home to Israel for consultations. On the morning of October 5 he was conferring with Sharett in his Tel Aviv office[20] when an attendant noticed a stranger in dark clothes behaving suspiciously. The man was carrying a bundle which was ticking distinctly. The package was seized and plunged into a bucket of water just in time. It contained six and a half pounds of explosive and a clock mechanism timed to destroy the building in just a few minutes. It was Eban's first experience with an assassination attempt. (No one was ever certain whether the intended victim was Sharett, Eban or some lesser Foreign Office functionary.)

On the third anniversary of the UN approval of the Palestine Partition plan a $500-per-plate dinner was held at the Waldorf-Astoria to help raise five and a half million dollars for the Weizmann Institute, Hebrew University and Technion. Fifteen hundred people came in their best regalia, the dinner was special, there were talented entertainers, Albert Einstein sent a message and Secretary of State George C. Marshall was the keynote speaker, but many of the guests were principally impressed by the address of Ambassador Eban, who said that until the establishment of the state "we were supplicants and mendicants before the civilized conscience of mankind, but the UN decision of November 29, 1947, marked the emergence of the Jewish people from anonymity and its entry and full acceptance into the world family of nations."

Israel's first ambassador to the United States had lived in a hotel, but shortly before Eban's appointment the State of Israel received as a gift from one of Washington's prominent Jewish families a three-story residence at 1673 Myrtle Street—a tree-shaded avenue only a block long, overlooking Rock Creek Park and almost on the edge of the suburb of Silver Spring. It is an area of Dutch colonial and English Tudor homes, well planted with myrtle, Japanese yew and various sorts of pine. The house, which became the Ebans' first real home, stood on the crest of a hill. The chancellery was several miles away, on Massachusetts Avenue, the wide boulevard lined with the embassies of the most important countries having diplomatic relations with the United States.

The staff Eban inherited was small, for a full embassy. At the start he had no minister. There was a counselor of embassy, two first secretaries, a second secretary, a press attaché, an agricultural attaché and an economic counselor. More by coincidence than plan his first military attaché was Suzy's brother-in-law, Vivian Herzog, who had graduated to this job from his post as head of Intelligence for the Israeli Army. He, too, had a son, just three months older than Eli. He became the only Israeli to meet regularly with Arab representatives, under the United Nations Military Committee's agreement. Another addition to Eban's staff was Pinchas Eliav, the first personal assistant he had ever had, whose duties were to keep an hour-by-hour summary for him of Middle Eastern developments, prepare drafts, arrange meetings and make minor diplomatic decisions.

Eban had been performing on the world stage for almost two years, but he now discovered how vast a difference there was between the life in New York and the life he would live in Washington. Until now there had been few social obligations, but in the capital much of the business of diplomacy seemed to be conducted at cocktail parties, receptions, dinners and balls. The formalities might be concluded the next day in somebody's office, but multi-million-dollar loans were arranged, promises of military equipment were exacted, diplomatic deals of all sorts were made with cocktail glasses in hand, or between the fish and meat courses, or while waiting for the ladies who were upstairs comparing fashions.

At that time there were fifty-eight other countries in the United Nations, but many more than that had embassies or legations in Washington. Whenever an ambassador retired and got ready to leave Washington for home there would be a round of parties given by his own Embassy, by ambassadors of allied countries and also by personal friends he had made during his years in Washington. Then when his replacement arrived it would be the same thing all over again. Invitations for such parties might go to the entire diplomatic corps and it was important not to snub the retiring or arriving ambassador by not appearing. It was especially important for Israel, in her infancy as a modern state, to make as many friends as possible by doing the correct thing socially and to make no enemies by committing any diplomatic faux pas. Smaller dinners at which there might be only twenty or thirty guests were being given continually. To "regret" an invitation to such an affair might be taken as a diplomatic insult and could even lead to strained relations between the two countries involved. Still more intimate dinners, with perhaps only ten at the table, presented an even better opportunity for strengthening political ties. To such gatherings the Ebans were now being invited. Even so small a country as Israel was also expected to reciprocate. There were senators, congressmen, key government officials and other diplomats to be entertained. Washington was full of people who could be helpful in one way or another. The list of potential guests ran into the hundreds.

Suzy Eban was an ideal hostess, beautiful, well groomed, an interesting conversationalist and a good listener. But in social gatherings her husband was considerably less at ease. At a dinner for some political or diplomatic personage, the guest of honor would, by protocol, be seated at Mrs. Eban's right, with the next-ranking guest on her left. The wives of these two men would be on the host's right and left. But unfortunately, while the men might hold important positions and perhaps be good conversationalists, this did not guarantee that their wives would scintillate. And so, during a long, six-course dinner, Abba Eban, who had never really cultivated the art (or is it a science?) of small talk, might be surrounded by two women who wanted to discuss the weather, the problems of raising teen-age children, gardening or what to do when one has to preside at a P.T.A. meeting and the car won't start and the taxi company won't answer its phone.

Eban gave his aides and social advisers as much trouble as Ben-Gurion gave his, for the same reason: neither liked to waste time engaging in idle chatter. But the problem with the ambassador was more serious than with the Prime Minister, because Ben-Gurion, being much older, would be excused for his eccentricity more readily; also, he was on home territory and not in the goldfish bowl called Washington; also, he was not constantly dealing with diplomats, as was Eban. If Ben-Gurion, cajoled into attending a reception in Tel Aviv, quickly looked over the crowd, then picked one man from whom he thought he could learn something, took him into a corner and talked only with him until it was time to leave, critics would say nothing worse than that "the Old Man is a little eccentric." But Eban, brought in to represent a new country that was still struggling for full recognition, had to guard against giving critics cause to carp. He could not afford eccentricity. Plenty of people would probably be critical of Israel's politics—for one reason or another—but it was essential not to offend anyone unnecessarily.

"It was difficult in the beginning," Suzy Eban said. "I remember very well. I am sure some people thought Aubrey was quite hopeless because he couldn't do small chat. But he's changed so much. Now he's simply marvelous with people. He has no problems anymore. But at first . . ."[21]

Eban's predecessor in the past two years had made many friends for Israel at the diplomatic level and Eban had to try to keep them. He also had to make a host of new ones. Israel needed friends, desperately. On many occasions the vote in the UN had been so close that one or two extra "friends" might have swung the decision in the opposite direction. Now that military activities seemed to be over, the diplomatic front was where the battles had to be fought and won.

In 1949 the story was told of the governor of an eastern state who, presiding at a banquet celebrating Israel's first birthday, saw Eban's name on the program and turned to an aide, asking:

"But does he speak any English?"

It was not long before most of the country was aware that Eban not only spoke some English, but spoke the language with a brilliance that would make almost any governor, senator or President envious.

In the years before he succeeded to the ambassadorial post in Washington he had delivered relatively few public addresses, but now everybody wanted him—Hadassah, Histadrut, ZOA, Bonds, UJA, Misrachi, the National Conference of Christians and Jews, theological seminaries, Jewish conferences. He also had invitations from the Council on Foreign Relations, the UN Correspondents' Association, the Library of Congress, the War College, city clubs, the Export Managers Club of New York, the Commonwealth Club of California and the Economic Club of Detroit, as well as from innumerable colleges and universities, many of which wanted to trade an honorary degree for a speech.

Now editors began badgering him for manuscripts. Publishers sent him galley proofs of forthcoming works and asked him to write introductions. Authors with books on subjects sometimes only remotely connected with Israel thought he ought to say a few words in praise—for use in advertisements, of course.

Considering that Ambassador Eban was only thirty-five years old at the time of his appointment—

Considering that he had never held any diplomatic post before except in the UN—

Considering that there were in the Washington diplomatic corps gray-haired men who had spent a lifetime in career diplomacy working up to the Washington post—

Considering that Eban was at that time the only ambassador Israel had (even in London and Paris the head of Israel's diplomatic mission had the rank of only minister plenipotentiary)—

Considering that he represented only a million and a half people, fewer than the population of relatively obscure countries like Sierra Leone, Paraguay or the Ivory Coast—

Considering that the competition for the center of the stage in Washington is often ruthless and sometimes unscrupulous—

Considering all the handicaps, as well as the intensity of the rivalry, it was a miracle almost like Israel's military victories that Eban made such an electric impact on the American capital.

Often he was invited to social gatherings at which his fellow guests were all representatives of the great nations. He was given prominence on committees, was offered many more speaking engagements than he could possibly fill and was in constant demand for television appearances.

His popularity was not confined to Washington and New York. Every time he made a public address, especially if it was carried by radio, he extended the circle of his venerators. One of his colleagues in the Embassy had this explanation:

"Of course he was admired for his innate dignity and his facility of language. His great knowledge of how to handle the public media helped. But the key to American society is public posture, as in no other country in the world. He mastered that. Then too, Americans suffer from a certain feeling of inferiority toward British culture. It's a strange thing—you threw off the Royal House in 1776, yet you didn't throw off your sense of obligation to the source—to the British people—to British institutions. Whenever queens or kings come to Washington, senators on the Appropriations Committee, who could buy and sell them ten times over, show them extreme deference. And so everyone was impressed by Eban's Cambridge tones and his Churchillian vagueness and his endless use of language. They loved it!

"This also applies to the Jewish community. Not all of them understood what he was saying, but they sat there entranced. He had a

British stance when he was talking to the American people and he had a non-Jewish stance when he was talking to his fellow Jews. Every Jew in America has a double touch of inferiority. He wants to be accepted, somehow. And here he had a spokesman—a representative of the Jewish state speaking English better than American diplomats, better than most Americans whoever they are. So they sat at their big dinners at the Waldorf or in the Catskills or at the Fontainebleau in Miami Beach and as they listened to him they felt they were making it in American society. I don't understand the first ABC about music, but when I hear a great orchestra playing Beethoven or Brahms—especially a classic piece I recognize—I sit there entranced. That's how it was with the Jewish audience in America and Eban."

There were also enemies. Eban's relationship with Secretary of State Dean Acheson was good, but the Arab bloc in the State Department had never recovered from its failure to reverse the vote on the 1947 Partition plan. Now that Israel had become a state, over the bloc's violent protest and despite its subtle conniving, it intended to do everything possible to frustrate Israel's existence. Many men in the group seemed to Eban to be above and beyond party politics. Presidents could change. Republicans might succeed Democrats. These men remained. On the surface—at receptions and dinner parties—they were punctiliously correct to him and to any other Israeli diplomat, yet their opposition was no secret.

President Truman might not have admitted it then, but in his memoirs, published after he left office, he said:

"The Department of State's specialists on the Near East were, almost without exception, unfriendly to the idea of a Jewish state."[22]

There were also the Arabs themselves. Clever Washington hostesses had to make sure that the Ebans were never invited to parties at which Arab ambassadors were also guests, otherwise the Arabs would stage a boycott. They had already learned to hate Eban for his eloquence in the UN; now their hate took on a new dimension because of his instantaneous success along Diplomats' Row. Ambassador Malik was probably the only one who had undisguised respect for him. The others found his logic annoying, his erudition frightening, his popularity a cause for bitter envy.

There were also some diplomatic and government quarters in which latent anti-Semitism, while never being permitted to show, colored the attitude toward Eban, who would be maliciously criticized for such peccadilloes as the ultra-conservative cut of his clothes, not wearing the right tie, arriving late or leaving early—for everything and anything he did or neglected to do. They called him too sophisticated. Or too naïve. The more popular and influential he became the more they attacked him. This was one strange measure of his success.

17

An Israeli Abigail

SUZY EBAN is a much less complicated person than her husband, has a much greater social sense, makes friends more easily and her egoism is not as pronounced as his, yet she is almost as much an individualist.

When the Ebans moved to Washington Suzy was twenty-eight, a bride of only a few years, with a warm, genteel manner, an engaging continental accent, the ability to put people quickly at ease, a modest simplicity, a disarming smile and a girlish sort of beauty. She had the freshness of youth, a translucent complexion that would have delighted any cosmetologist and delicate Dresden-china features enhanced by a slightly turned-up nose. Her figure was as slim as a model's, her hair silver blond and her eyes nearly always sparkled. She generally appeared to be happy being exactly where she was, doing exactly what she was doing.

She dressed with elegant simplicity, often in black. Sometimes she wore a single strand of pearls, sometimes two or three.

Once she flew from Washington to San Francisco for a meeting, preceded by a press conference at which all the female reporters remarked —to her and then in print—how sitting up all night in a plane had done nothing to dim her fresh beauty.

Despite her youth she was in some ways better equipped than her husband for the Washington social life. In pre-World War II Egypt, before elimination of the large British, French, Italian and Jewish colonies, there was considerable sophistication in the international circle of Cairo. Everyone had servants. Entertaining was on an elaborate scale. French wines were served, as well as Russian caviar and Dover sole. Most people were bilingual or trilingual. Conversation was witty and cosmopolitan. It was in this milieu that she was born and brought up. She played the game and knew the rules. But she had never been the hostess of an ambassador. For anyone her age, regardless of background, it was a difficult position.[1]

Protocol demanded that she pay a formal, official call on the wives of all the other ambassadors and ministers plenipotentiary. Nearly a hundred countries had diplomatic relations with the United States. Even if she did one a day it would take months. Then all those ambassadorial wives, speaking English or French in a polyglot way, would repay her calls. That meant staying home and pouring tea and listening to proper conversation for more weeks and months. When other new ambassadors arrived their wives would also call—and have to be called on. There was almost no end to it.

Back in Israel they expected her—as well as her husband—to spread as much good will for Israel as possible. This meant traveling from coast to coast, making public appearances, speaking to women's groups large and small, appearing on radio and television, giving newspaper interviews, posing for photographs. She would have to open bazaars, attend fashion shows, sponsor art exhibitions, accompany her husband to all the dinners he addressed, listen to the same repetitious jokes, hear the same monotonous introductions, pretend to enjoy classical music played or sung by amateur musicians and appear to be interested in the painful platitudes of long-winded amateur orators. (One thing she could be grateful for—her husband never gave the same address twice.)

The young State of Israel had limited funds for the salaries of the Embassy staff, so Suzy Eban took upon herself the task of serving as the Eban archivist. She began the A.E. file with the barmitzvah speech Aubrey had written with the help of his grandfather, given to her by Alida. Next, a collection of his speeches from Cambridge days. Then newspaper clippings that had begun to pour in from such remote places as South Africa, Australia and far corners of Europe. Then photographs. If she was present when Aubrey was being "shot" she would ask the cameraman to be sure to send her a copy "for the archives."

Suzy organized her life intelligently so that it was all "fairly rhythmic." Mornings were reserved for domestic planning, telephoning, mail and such personal matters as hairdressing appointments, shopping for clothes, dressmaker's fittings, problems with the staff and seeing that her husband's clothes were always in condition for a sudden trip to Israel or the West Coast. At noon the round of appearances began: luncheons, appointments with press, radio and television interviews, social calls. There was often just enough time left to dress for the evening, the most important time in any diplomatic family's day.

Suzy inherited her social secretary from the Elaths. Ethel Ginberg had become a member of the staff soon after the Embassy opened and a quarter of a century later would be the only one of the veterans still there. She was an unmarried, native-born Washingtonian with a law degree and already had had a varied career in Central Intelligence, the Washington public school system and the quartermaster general's office. In addition to being protocol officer and social secretary to the ambassador's wife, she handled the Embassy's tax problems, social security matters and innumerable other technicalities. At the same hour each morning she appeared at the Embassy residence and sat down with Suzy Eban, first to go over mail. One letter they laughed over was from a woman in Harrisburg, Pennsylvania, who wrote:

"I would appreciate it very much if you would settle an argument we had recently. I think I read an article concerning you saying you came from royalty. They all said I was wrong and that I must have dreamed it. Please answer at once, even if it is only a yes or no."

In the mail there would always be invitations to be accepted or rejected. Then plans would have to be made for the next Eban party. Ethel Ginberg always had a list ready. It might include several diplomats, some high-ranking government officials, one or two members of Congress, a famous author, a well-read columnist, a political writer, plus their wives or prospective wives or, now and then, a mistress.

From Ethel Ginberg, Suzy Eban learned about protocol.

"It's a word that frightens the uninitiated," she said, "because it sounds so ominous, mysterious and also, perhaps, a little outmoded. But the truth is it's a wonderful thing, the standby of every official hostess. Protocol determines not only the seating arrangement, but when a party should break up and even the order of leaving. It regulates the precedence among diplomats, Cabinet members, judges and justices, members of Congress and lesser lights."

After they had agreed on the guest list Miss Ginberg would send out the invitations. The big party was always the Independence Day reception, for which two thousand invitations were generally sent out. On the afternoon of a dinner Miss Ginberg would arrange the place cards. One night when the appointed dinner hour was 8 P.M. she got a telephone call at her Arlington apartment about 7:30 P.M. from Suzy, who distressedly said:

"Ethel, the wife of the ranking guest has just telephoned that she can't come. Will you hurry over and redo the seating arrangement before the guests begin to arrive?"

As a result of that near-catastrophe, Miss Ginberg revised her procedure and henceforth never arranged the place cards until the last guest had come.

Another problem arose one night at an Eban dinner party when it was discovered at the last minute that the guest of honor, the Israeli Foreign Minister, was outranked by another guest, the Vice-President of the United States.

On many occasions the Ebans gave informal dinner parties with the guests sitting at three or four round tables, obviating protocol problems and making possible much more intimate conversation.

The general rule in selecting guests is to be sure that there are no "conflicting interests" around the table, except that Suzy Eban, after discovering how dull parties can be if there are no sparks flying, often intentionally invited "conflicting interests." One night her guests included the conservative Republican Senator William F. Knowland of California and the fiery labor leader George Meany. There were sparks but no pyrotechnics, leading another guest to say to the ambassador as he left:

"Sir, if the Meanys and the Knowlands can get along together in your home for a whole evening, I don't see why Arabs and Jews can't get along in the Middle East."

Suzy Eban and Ethel Ginberg worked in complete harmony because each discovered that the other was a perfectionist, believing in the old adage that if a thing is worth doing at all it is worth doing well. For this reason the Eban social functions soon became the talk of Washington's diplomatic circle at a time when Israel still had a population of only about a million. This was especially true from 1952 on, because that year the General Assembly met in Paris and the Ebans brought back with them a French cook whom Aubrey called "one of the best results of the 1952 Assembly." One of his specialties was a "crepes surprise": very thin crepes wrapped around an egg, then covered with cheese and tomato sauce. The surprise was cutting the crepes and suddenly finding the egg.

Some countries represented in Washington had only one building, but because Israel had its offices in a chancellery separate from the residence, it was possible for Suzy to have a luncheon at the chancellery followed a few hours later by a formal dinner at the residence.

Having the color sensitivity of a good artist, she always tried to make her dinners pleasing to the eye as well as to the palate, never permitting either blandness or monotony of color. A mild diplomatic crisis occurred the Ebans' first year in Washington when some columnist published a report that ham was served at an Embassy dinner. It was not true and the columnist was compelled to print a formal denial. With the French influence in her life, Suzy was always careful about wines, although she never served any but Israeli products. Believing that most men prefer beef, and having a good butcher in Washington who gave her the best cuts, she generally had the chef build his main course around some form of beef.

She learned that even after assembling a perfectly congenial group of guests for a dinner, seating them perfectly, planning an exciting menu, making sure that the white wine was properly chilled—even after all that, the hostess must both stimulate and regulate the conversation so that no egoist delivers a long monologue and no timid soul is left ignored.

The year after Eban was named ambassador (1951) Mr. and Mrs. Joseph Cherner, prominent members of the Washington Jewish community, offered the Government of Israel a handsome gift—a four-story Tudor mansion of fourteen rooms at 1630 Juniper Street, only a few blocks from the Myrtle Street house, but larger and on more extensive grounds. The news was brought to Suzy by Teddy Kollek, who had recently arrived in Washington to become minister at the Embassy. At first Suzy protested. She was content where she was.

"But it's a gift; you have to take it!" Kollek insisted.

After seeing the Juniper Street house Suzy knew it was going to be a difficult place in which to entertain because of the layout of the rooms, but she immediately began working with carpenters, bricklayers, masons and interior decorators, transforming it into what eventually became the subject of considerable Washington talk. The Washington *Evening Star* in a full-page article and the New York *Times Magazine* in a three-page spread called it a "House of Light" because it was flooded by sunlight daytimes and at night was lighted to simulate sunset time. Suzy called the house "trad-mod," the exterior being traditional, the interior modern. The walls were oyster white, the furniture and carpets of muted colors, the general impression of uncluttered spaciousness. There were many modern paintings by Israeli artists, handwoven homespuns for furniture coverings and in the spacious library a possession Suzy liked to talk about —a set of large black books.

"They belonged to Aubrey's grandfather. They were his Talmud. I remember once when we were short of money and Aubrey said: 'That's no problem; we'll sell the Talmud.' I said: 'Are you mad? We'll get along somehow but we'll keep the Talmud.' And we always have. It never leaves us."

Suzy had to learn to adjust herself to Aubrey's unorthodox schedule. She had to relieve him of as many of the small details of life as possible. She had to be willing to travel herself, sometimes when all she wanted was to stay quietly at home with her family. She had to talk when she would rather have listened. Although she had never been interested in politics, it was now necessary to keep abreast of political developments in Washington, Jerusalem and around the world. She found that the public expected her to be able to answer almost any question about Israel— whether it dealt with biblical history, events during the Mandate or the price of tomatoes in Jerusalem. American guests expected her to know as much as they did about the United States. The senator from Wyoming would be insulted if she thought the capital of his state was Phoenix and sports fans expected her to know that the Dodgers didn't play basketball. When she entertained guests from foreign countries she must also know something about their part of the world. One needed to be encyclopedic-minded. It was intellectually exhausting.

Once Suzy Eban had wanted to be a writer. Also she had thought that given the chance to study and develop she might have become a passably good artist. As a child she was given lessons in dancing, art and music, "the finishing process for all nice little girls, a little bit of this and a little bit of that." Later she became an accomplished drawing room pianist, but her favorite diversion was painting. She called art "my great passion." She haunted American art centers. In the early days of her marriage she sometimes found time to paint. She did little scenes in the manner of Raoul Dufy—in gay, happy colors.

The Ebans went deep-sea fishing for the first time off the coast of Florida aboard a boat called the *Jerry Mar III.*

"Maybe it was luck, maybe not, but I caught a sailfish that measured seven feet four inches and weighed fifty-eight pounds. Aubrey didn't catch anything. We had a photograph taken with one of us on each side of the fish. The next day the newspapers printed the picture, but gave Aubrey full credit for the catch. He said to me: 'See what an asset you are to me!' "

A few days before Aubrey's birthday that year, wondering what would be a suitable present, Suzy went to her little studio and quickly did an oil for him—himself holding aloft the fish he had *not* caught. It was whimsical, and he liked it so much that later she redid it as a needlepoint pillow. The painting was hung in the Embassy's gallery where Martin Agronsky, the Washington commentator, saw it one evening and admired it so much that Suzy did a copy for him, adding polka dots to the fish, because Agronsky had worn a daring polka dot shirt that night.

Before long it was impossible for Suzy to indulge any of her diversionary loves. Washington life was too demanding. Yet, despite the social whirl, it was in many ways lonely. Would anyone else understand this? Aubrey's endless coming and going between Washington and New York had destroyed any semblance of family life. Often the only time she would be alone with him during a twenty-four-hour day would be during the fifteen minutes in the Embassy limousine on the way to a dinner party and the fifteen minutes on the way home again. Whenever they *were* alone he tried to tell her of political developments of special interest, while she would report, as succinctly as possible, on what she had seen, heard and done, then on strictly family matters.

Sharing their recreations was a problem with the Ebans from the start. He enjoyed golf. She would go with him on the understanding that there would never be any discussion of "my unmentionable score." Her favorite golf story was of the day they were playing on a Washington course and his ball landed just in front of a tree and he didn't know what to do except stand there and say: "Isn't that terrible!"

"When I walked up and saw his predicament, I said: 'Well, Aubrey, you're going to need a committee to get you out of this one!' And he really did burst out laughing."

Suzy was never able to get Aubrey enthused about or even much interested in art. One of her favorite stories is of a trip they took to Belgium, where, at an official dinner, they met Baron Lambert, a man of culture and exceptional taste, who had one of the finest private art collections in Europe. After the dinner he invited the Ebans to his penthouse for a drink and a brief tour of his galleries. As Suzy tells it:

"So we entered the place with its breathtaking art and what do you imagine Aubrey did? After a hurried look, he turned his back on us and the art and went right to the library and started examining the books. Our host looked at me and I looked at him. Finally I said: 'Just leave him be. He's happy!' So we did."

In her early days in Washington she smoked cigarettes constantly, even while posing for a portrait by Ruth Levine, an artist friend, who got so annoyed with the smoke that she finally gave Suzy a twig from a tree to hold in her right hand as if it were a cigarette—and she painted the twig into the picture. Smoking of any kind stopped when she became interested in the work of the Israel Cancer Society and made this her principal philanthropic work.

"How could I work for cancer control and smoke myself?"

Suzy from the start was popular with newspaper people; with photographers especially if they were male, because she didn't have to be told which was her best profile and when to smile, and with reporters, especially if female, because she fed them tidbits of fashion, cookery and feminine intimacies. She had quick, quotable answers to all their questions:

Ambition? "To return someday to America as a plain tourist so I can visit every art museum in the country and then meet all the artists."

Ever get tired of listening to your husband's speeches? "I don't, but if I did I wouldn't tell you."

Most unforgettable experience? "Just before one of the crucial votes in the UN, when the future of Israel hung in the balance, a delegation of Jewish gangsters called on my husband at our apartment in New York one night and said: 'We are Jews and we want Israel to live. We can rub out a few UN delegates who may be going to vote the wrong way. Just give us their names.' My husband eventually persuaded them to give up any such plan."

Your opinion of the chemise look? "I would like to see a line drawn between the bedroom and the living room."

How many American cities have you visited? "I've seen the inside of the grand ballroom of every Hilton and Statler in the country."

How difficult is the life of a diplomat's wife? "It's as hard as the job of a clergyman's wife."

What about American women? "Middle-aged American women are the most active in the world. I marvel at their freedom from domestic duties and what they do with their freedom. Even young women with growing families have hobbies and special interests."

What about Washington? "It's terribly steeped in politics and diplomacy. Sometimes they forget there's an outside world. Everyone is here by selection. Everyone is a specialist of some sort."

Is there a big turnover in Washington? "During my first year I saw thirty new ambassadors come and thirty old ones go."

She was clever enough never to give the same story to more than one reporter, except when she entertained them in a group. If an Ambassador's Ball was going to be held in some other city, such as Boston, one female reporter from each daily newspaper would be invited to come to Washington for the day, have lunch at the Embassy, see Mrs. Eban model the gown she had had made for the ball and get answers to any questions she wanted to ask.

If to reporters, guests at her parties and the general public Suzy Eban appeared master of every situation, happy with her lot and completely adjusted to the new life she suddenly had to lead, it was because she was also a good actress. Occasionally she confessed to close friends she thought might understand that she was constantly under tension, resented the enforced separation she and Aubrey had to suffer and most of all disliked the complete lack of privacy. Every facet of her life was now considered public property. Women guests at receptions, often on the pretense of "powdering their noses," would snoop through the house, even opening closet doors and desk drawers. But worse, there was no longer time for anything except official business.

Whenever reporters or new friends or anyone else interested in her background had time to listen Suzy Eban liked to tell the story of her early connections with the Promised Land.

"When you drive now from Jerusalem to Tel Aviv you see on the left-hand side of the road at a place called Motsa a brick and tile factory. That belonged to my grandfather, on my mother's side. He was one of the very early settlers of Motsa. Quite often I used to come up from Ismailia, Egypt, where I was born, to visit my grandfather. He had many Arab workers and I remember they had to keep the kilns working night and day, and there was an Arab watchman who played on the flute through the night and I was entranced listening to him. That music in the loneliness of the night was absolutely marvelous. My grandfather had his own house near the factory. He owned quite a bit of land—all those groves you see now in the valley—about forty dunams.

"In the Arab trouble of 1929 the factory was burned down. And again some years later, I can't remember the year but I was a small girl. My grandfather was with us in Ismailia and I remember that we got a call giving us the news and it was Shabbat so they waited until sunset to tell him—after Shabbat was over. He was about seventy then. My own mother said:

"'Well, never mind, you'll come and live with us.'

"'Never,' my grandfather replied. 'I won't give up or give in. I'm going to rebuild.'

"And he did. He lived to be eighty-five. I visited him shortly after the State was proclaimed. He was ill. It was almost the end for him, but he cried with happiness and said:

"'Just to think that my granddaughter is married to someone who works for the State of Israel!'

"A few days later he called his brother in to read with him the prayer for the dying and then put his head back and died. But he went happy, because he had lived to see it—a wonderful thing!"

Stories about Suzy appeared often in newspapers and magazines, and she was frequently on radio and television. She also received a few awards of her own. On one occasion she, Eleanor Roosevelt, the wife of Mayor Wagner of New York, Mrs. Averell Harriman and Dorothy Schiff, publisher of the New York *Post,* all received medals as "first ladies in their own fields."

While Suzy Eban never had anything to do with the preparation of her husband's addresses, she did perform an important role.

"When he has a thought he doesn't say to me, 'I think I'm going to say so and so in my next address.' He just starts discussing the thought with me. Then I understand that he is discussing it because this is what he wants to say in public. Sometimes he lets me see the first draft of a speech. Or he comes from his study and reads passages to me. Then I must stop being a wife and assume the public role. I may say to him, 'Look, this is too complicated for me.' Sometimes it's amazing; it registers immediately on him. At other times he ends up by convincing me and the next day I find myself expounding his ideas."

Suzy divides public figures into three groups: politicos, politicians and statesmen.

"I put Aubrey between a politician and a statesman. Maybe it's too early to tell. The future will prove it. But he's certainly not a politico. He's not one of those who shuffles and trades; not one who says, 'You rub my back and I'll rub yours.' I see him principally as a statesman. I know from what he says to me when we discuss things that he is a statesman. I remember once he wanted to say something to the people and I said, 'For God's sake don't say it! People won't understand it. They won't be with you.' He got very angry and said to me, 'What do you think statesmanship is? It's not to give the people what they want but what one thinks is right, what one thinks is good for them in the long run.' He said it very vehemently because he felt it so strongly."

In the early Washington years Suzy often gave the impression of being reticent. She never pushed herself into the foreground, although she was often put there by those in charge. She knew how to maintain a discreet silence when to have said anything would have been a blunder. She caused many a seasoned diplomat to say to his own wife on the way home from a reception:

"That's the way *you* should look and behave, my dear!"

She soon discovered that in Washington's social and diplomatic life the safest procedure is to "follow the rules." For example, she once said that "everyone in Washington has been weighed in, to an infinitesimal fraction, delicately and ruthlessly, as on a jeweler's scale. You accept that weight as valid and don't argue about it."

Sometimes her sense of humor and her patience with stupidity were strained. The first year in Washington at a diplomatic reception the wife of an important official, trying to make conversation, said:

"How is your king, my dear?"

"But we don't have a king in Israel," Suzy replied, as graciously as possible. "We have a President and a Prime Minister."

"Don't tell me," came back the retort, "that you've had another one of those horrible Middle Eastern revolutions where the king escapes and the republican regime takes over. First Egypt. Then Iraq murders its king. And now Israel, you say, has become a republic!"

"But Israel has always been a republic," Suzy responded.

"Please, Madame Eban, who do you take me for? I know all about your King Solomon and King David."

Suzy Eban never enjoyed public speaking, yet she was often called on for speeches and accepted it as part of her duties. Her success may have grown out of a rule she set for herself: never talk more than ten or fifteen minutes. She also was careful never to say anything controversial. She was embarrassed only once. It was at an important Bonds for Israel dinner in New York at which her husband delivered a long and brilliant address. When he finished there was the usual thunderous applause. Then the chairman, with not an instant's advance warning, announced:

"We are now going to call on the brilliant wife of our brilliant ambassador to say something."

There was more applause and then Suzy Eban in her sweetest voice said:

"Ladies and gentlemen: Having written every word of that address you just heard, I have nothing more to say."

In a Boston talk she told how the first time she appeared in the Massachusetts capital she felt very self-confident, "because I felt I was fairly elegantly dressed, until I happened to look down at my feet and to my horror noticed that I had on two different shoes."

The Dewey Stones came often to Washington, now that the Ebans were there, and the casual friendship developed into intimacy. It is no secret that Eban used the older man as a sounding board. He considered him in many ways Mr. Typical American. Or at least Mr. Typical American Jew. It was not necessary to submit an idea to a Gallup poll. Instead,

Eban's method of putting his finger on the pulse of American Jewry was to talk the matter over with Dewey Stone, for his reactions were nearly always representative. He was a hardheaded, unemotional businessman whose advice was generally sound.

Mrs. Stone gave Suzy a copy of Irving Stone's *Those Who Love*, the biographical novel about John and Abigail Adams. For her Suzy was Abigail. She considered the Eban marriage "made in heaven."

"However," Mrs. Stone said, "being the wife of a political figure is not easy, and especially of a political figure who is away from home so much. It's a hell of a life! But this beautiful, intelligent, cultured and most of all brave girl became the perfect wife. She is the modern Abigail, taking care of the shop while the husband is sent all over the world."

One of the trips the Dewey Stones made to Washington was to attend a Bonds for Israel dinner at which Ambassador Eban was the principal speaker. They sat at the same table with Mr. and Mrs. Ambache who also happened to be in Washington.

"As Aubrey began to talk," Mrs. Stone said, "Mr. Ambache was so moved that I leaned over and put a hand on his arm and with a smile said:

"'Mr. Ambache, remember—"He can't even open his mouth."'

"He smiled back at me through his tears."

In July and August Washington slumbers in sweltering heat, and politicians and diplomats try to escape to somewhere, anywhere, to replenish the life juices. The Dewey Stones had a summer home at East Brewster on Cape Cod and introduced the Ebans to that part of the world. At first they rented a house on Martha's Vineyard.

"We enjoyed getting back to the simple life, after ten months in Washington," Suzy Eban said. "We loved the informality. We walked around in blue jeans, without shoes. We listened to frivolous music like the score of *My Fair Lady* and *The King and I*."

Often a crisis in the Middle East interfered with this tranquillity, forcing the ambassador to make a fast trip back to Washington. But the fogs that sometimes creep in from the sea and keep planes from leaving the Martha's Vineyard airport are not respecters of diplomatic necessity and so the next year the Stones helped the Ebans find a house on Cape Cod from which Aubrey could leave by ground transportation if there was a fog. The summer home they finally rented was on one of three hundred and sixty-five lakes, so that a man could fish a different lake each day of the year. There, during subsequent summers, they refreshed their spirits and stored up physical energy for the next ten months in Washington.

Over the years, Suzy Eban cultivated her innate talents to become the diplomat's wife par excellence and to achieve a measure of personal fulfillment. She developed great organizing ability, had naturally wide cultural interests and intellectual curiosity, keen perception in human relations, concern with the social, medical, educational and economic problems of the underprivileged in her own country and an understanding of the need, at times, to blend her husband's intensely cerebral personality with the more mundane and even trivial aspects of her own life.

18

Ambassador on the Double

DURING THE NEXT SIX YEARS—until the Suez-Sinai military operation created a major world crisis—Ambassador Abba Eban was one of the busiest men in either Washington or New York. In that period he delivered one hundred and eighty-three major addresses before the Security Council and General Assembly, to university convocations, Jewish fund-raising meetings, gatherings of rabbis, Christian conventions and testimonial dinners, and into radio and television microphones. He made more round trips between Washington and New York than anyone bothered to count, crossed the Atlantic twelve times, had one near-fainting spell, got on friendly terms with one President of the United States and four future Presidents (as well as several who wanted to be), fathered another child, debated before millions with an Arab he was not permitted to see, listened to so many third-rate after-dinner speeches that he finally exploded, publicly, and made millions of friends for Israel—and himself —as well as a few enemies (very few).

Although being Israel's chief delegate to the UN as well as ambassador to the United States imposed on him a heavy work load and forced him to spend much time commuting between the capital and New York, it gave him tremendous advantages in Washington, where few ambassadors are in the public eye or get much national recognition. Because his addresses to the Security Council and the General Assembly usually made the front pages of the nation's public prints and because he appeared so frequently on radio and television, he gained prestige in Washington all out of proportion to the size of the country he represented, and so when a Washingtonian received an invitation to the Israeli Embassy residence, even though it was one of the most inaccessible and least splendid in the city, it was regarded as an honor not to be slighted. Eban's dual role also gave him greater weight in his discussions with government officials.

He used all these advantages in pursuance of a definite diplomatic strategy. He was trying to build a special relationship between his small country and the United States—a structure that would be resilient enough to absorb the divergencies and occasional conflicts that were bound to occur. He sought to make Israel so popular with the American public that any administration would think twice about violating the friendship. He set out to make himself such an important national figure that when he appeared at the State Department or the White House it would be known that he had general as well as Jewish support and he would be treated not at all as if he were the ambassador from Liberia, Luxembourg or some other small country. That was the reason he rushed from college campus to Jewish meeting to statehouse appearance to television studio to press conference.

Also, he realized that in the 1950s Israel's greatest danger would probably be economic and not military. Unprecedented immigration had brought with it the threat of national bankruptcy. It was necessary to obtain immense American aid—tens of millions of dollars—so that during most of his years in Washington he was constantly negotiating for economic assistance. (In those days the question of whether Israel would get a grant or loan was as full of tension for the Israelis as would be the question of Skyhawks and Phantom jets at a later date.)

A third objective was to get a defense treaty with the United States. Although Dulles at one point told Eban he would like to work toward such a goal, there was a serious roadblock: the State Department argued that the United States could guarantee only permanent boundaries and not armistice lines, to which Eban replied that if Israel and her Arab neighbors ever agreed on permanent boundaries there would be no need of an American guarantee. Because of this conceptual conflict, Eban, while successful in developing ever more friendly relations with the United States government, was unable to obtain the desired defense treaty.

A final objective was somehow to obtain the sympathetic support not only of American Zionists but of Jews of all the diverse political and religious communities. In this he was so successful that by the time his Washington mission ended all but an infinitesimal percentage of American Jews were committed to the ideological and financial support of Israel.

In his UN mission Eban's aim was to be defensive: to try to bring about the defeat of Arab and Soviet resolutions; to try to consolidate the economic, political, demographic and international gains already made; to see that the armistice rights were not corroded; to defend Israel's military reaction now and then; and by active participation in general international questions to eradicate from the Arab consciousness the idea that Israel was something peculiar and fragile, something not equal to others. As Eban himself once put it:

"Every time an Arab comes in and sees us there the concept of our illegitimacy or of our non-existence is affronted and that is why our participation in international bodies is of such importance."[1]

The year 1951 began for Eban with an opportunity to play an important role on the world stage. On January 4, after a massive retreat in Korea, the Communists occupied the city of Seoul. Nine days later, although he represented one of the smallest countries in the UN and the youngest member of the international body, Eban introduced a compromise truce plan. When the Arab nations let it be known they had no objections to the text but would vote against it because it bore Israel's name, Eban was taken to a Long Island restaurant for lunch by Canadian Foreign Minister Pearson and Hans Engen, the chief Norwegian delegate, who pleaded with him to permit Norway to sponsor the resolution in order to win the Arabs' votes.

"This is petty nonsense!" Eban expostulated, and his hosts agreed, but they argued that getting the resolution passed was more important than prestige, so Eban finally consented.

The incident made a deep imprint on Eban because he thought it symbolic: Israel could contribute advice and counsel just as long as she made no attempt to take credit for it. Several Tel Aviv newspapers took the editorial position that it was presumptuous of Israel to try to contribute to a solution of problems beyond her own area of interest; to interfere in the affairs of the *goyim*. Eban called this the "Diaspora Complex" and said that if Israel could build some credit in statesmanship through her membership in the international community this might be helpful in the future.

It was almost two and a half years before a Korean truce agreement was signed and hostilities finally ceased, but to Eban's credit he played an important role in the first faltering steps toward peace.

During the first week of April (1951) a border raid by Syrians in which seven Israeli policemen were killed touched off a diplomatic explosion that gave Eban weeks of labor. The next day Israeli planes bombed Syrian military positions in retaliation. The day after that, while

Eban was at the State Department protesting what he called "unwarranted Syrian aggression," Israeli forces demolished two small Syrian villages. When the United States finally went into action, diplomatically, it merely denounced Israel for the bombing. Again Eban went to the State Department and complained. The day after that Syrian and Israeli planes had a dogfight and the next day the Security Council, fearing a threat to world peace, convened. In a wild speech Syrian delegate Faiz el Khouri charged the Israelis with using "atomic weapons." Eban chided him for his reckless words, forcing him to recant, publicly, the next day. What he meant to say, he explained, was "automatic," not "atomic"—a slight difference.

The next day Eban made a formal statement to the Security Council on Israel's position and included an apology for the bombing. After a few days of military and diplomatic peace, during which Eban was able to get a little much needed rest, Syrian forces on May 2 (1951) attacked across the demilitarized zone. Israel repelled them, but with the loss of four Israeli lives. On May 3 Eban vigorously protested to the UN. On May 5 Syrian-Israeli fighting was resumed. On May 9 the Security Council called for a cease-fire. At the center of the controversy was the Huleh reclamation project. Since biblical times this ten-thousand-acre area in Galilee had been a malaria-infested swampland. Now the Israelis were trying to stamp out the malaria, reclaim rich farmland and release water for irrigation by an ambitious reclamation project. But the Syrian frontier was close and the issue was whether the Israelis had a right to do such work in an area that had been declared a demilitarized zone. Israel's answer was that demilitarized meant what it said; it did not mean the area had to remain a swamp or become a desert.

On May 17 Great Britain, France, Turkey and the United States joined in sponsoring a resolution which condemned Israel and called upon her to suspend all work on the Huleh project immediately. It was presented by U.S. delegate Warren R. Austin. Eban was infuriated and had more difficulty than usual remaining calm. In a statement he called the resolution "rash and one-sided." He said his apology for the bombing had been "churlishly and unappreciatively" received. He said the resolution "whitewashes, ignores and appeases Syrian aggression and attempts to strike a blow at Israel's most vital and legitimate interests."

On the evening of Thursday, May 17 (1951), in his room at the Sherry-Netherland Hotel he began working on the address he was scheduled to deliver the next afternoon before the Security Council. He labored diligently, doggedly and determinedly, pushing aside the food his aides brought him. At midnight he had a rough first draft finished, but then began polishing, eliminating, substituting, adding, editing, correcting. The morning light was just beginning to shine through the hotel room windows when he stopped and went to bed.

He looked tired not many hours later when he stood before the Security Council and began orating against the proposed resolution. He accused the four sponsoring nations of a double cross. He said they had assured him before the introduction of the resolution that it would contain no reprimand of Israel for the bombing of the Syrian position in view of his apology, but there the reprimand was, in cold print. He used strong words in telling the delegates that he had been instructed to express to them "the profound resentment of the Israeli people and their government" to this "insult to our gallant dead, killed by Syrian bullets" and he said "Israel can attach no moral value or credence to such an unjust presentation of the case" as contained in the resolution.

He had been talking for about one hour when he suddenly felt faint and had to leave the hall. A physician from a nearby hospital found he was suffering from nervous exhaustion. Late that afternoon, with Eban absent, the Security Council unanimously approved the four-nation resolution, with only the Soviet Union abstaining. After remaining quietly in his hotel suite over the weekend, Eban on Monday was back in action, as vigorous as ever, but he was annoyed by the manner in which *Time* reported his indisposition under a headline:

DIPLOMACY BY SWOON

The article said he "keeled over" and compared him to Iran's new Premier, Mohammed Mossadegh, "who swoons whenever he gets really worked up during a political speech." Eban pointed out there is a difference between feeling faint and fainting. As a matter of fact, he had never in his life fainted.

Prime Minister David Ben-Gurion came to the United States in May (1951) in the middle of the diplomatic crisis. To pay him tribute and celebrate Israel's third anniversary, nineteen thousand men, women and children jammed Madison Square Garden. Other thousands were turned away. It was Eban's task to introduce the man who the previous day had been cheered by one and a half million people as he drove up Broadway in an open car during a ticker-tape welcome.

"Their own deeds are the memorial of great men," he told the enthusiastic crowd. Then he explained Ben-Gurion's greatness, concluding his introduction:

"If you link yourself with such a cause as this at such a time as this, you link yourself with immortality."

That same month in one of a series of UN broadcasts entitled "The Price of Peace" Eban said:

"The price of peace can never reach such dimensions as to equal the smallest fraction of war's deadly cost."

Dean Gooderham Acheson was Secretary of State during Eban's first three years in Washington. It was no secret that Acheson had urged Truman not to support the Partition of Palestine and creation of a Jewish state. Eban put his own opinion of Acheson in these words:

"He had an aristocratic bearing and great intellectual power. There was no sentimentality about him. Only once did I witness him emotionally moved."

In the summer of 1951 the Government of Israel decided to try to get Germany to pay reparations. The plan was to have the initiative come from the four occupying powers in Germany: the United States, Great Britain, France and Russia. Eban was given the responsibility of discussing the situation with Washington. He considered it "the most burdensome task ever assigned to me" because he had to try to impress Acheson with the horror and enormity of the crime perpetrated by the Nazis against the Jews. In his presentation he spared no details as he discussed gas chambers, crematoria and the sufferings of the Nazis' six million victims. When he finally finished, Acheson sat staring into space, silent.

"I was afraid that this man who held his feelings in leash so completely would terminate our conversation with a cold official remark," Eban later said. "But I suddenly realized he was silent because of how profoundly moved he was. After that he became one of the firm backers of Israel's claim for reparations. He gave instructions to John J. McCloy, American High Commissioner in Germany, to support our claim and as a result of McCloy's intervention with the German Government he became one of our good friends. Since then no Independence Day has passed without a personal message of warm greeting from McCloy to the Government of Israel."[2]

John F. Kennedy was two years younger than Eban, but the ambassador often referred to him as "an exact contemporary." Perhaps one of the reasons he felt such empathy for him was that Kennedy, too, was originally going to be either a writer or teacher. The year Eban was discharged from the British Army and went into politics by joining the Jewish Agency, Kennedy entered politics by running for Congress. He was elected for a third term soon after the Ebans arrived in Washington. One day he appeared at the Israeli Embassy, said he was going to Israel with Franklin D. Roosevelt, Jr., and asked if someone could arrange for him to have an interview with Prime Minister Ben-Gurion. A routine request was forwarded to Jerusalem. When the two young Americans reached Israel they called at the Foreign Ministry. The person in charge of the American desk thought Kennedy wasn't important enough to take up the Prime Minister's time and told him it was impossible for Ben-Gurion to see him. Several days later Franklin D. Roosevelt, Jr., applied for an interview with Ben-Gurion and his request was granted immediately "because his name sounded so important." When he said he had a friend with him he would like to take along, he was told to take whomsoever he pleased. Thus did John F. Kennedy get to see David Ben-Gurion.

Relating the incident, Eban said:

"It's a good thing it came out that way, because otherwise Kennedy might have left Israel feeling affronted."[3]

Speaking at a plenary session of the General Assembly in 1951 Eban, after listening to hours of empty talk by representatives of various Arab nations, told the other delegates:

"In a previous chapter of Israel's history the walls of Jericho fell to the mere sound of trumpets, but I've never heard of an edifice being built up by vocal exercise alone."[4]

The year 1952 began for Eban with a walkout. On Monday, January 21, in a public square in Bagdad two Iraqi Jews were hanged on some vague bombing charge. On Tuesday Israel staged a one-day strike at the UN, its delegates walking out of all meetings. Ambassador Eban led the move by arising in the Special Ad Hoc Political Committee and declaring that what had happened the previous day in Bagdad was "a public degradation of human dignity" and he was leaving the meeting "as a point of grief and a matter of conscience."

In February (1952) the General Assembly held a meeting in Paris, attended by both Foreign Minister Sharett and Ambassador Eban. Ten months earlier General Dwight D. Eisenhower had taken up his duties as Supreme Commander in Europe for the North Atlantic Treaty Organization at Supreme Headquarters Allied Powers Europe (SHAPE) near Paris. There was already talk of nominating him for President, so Eban suggested to Sharett it might be a good idea to seek an audience and try to win his friendship "just in case."

"I remember that he spoke the whole time we were in his office with the utmost fluency," Eban recalled later, "and when we came away we couldn't remember a single thing he had said. He had the gift of being extremely articulate without being coherent. It was a very strange experience. His thoughts were always ahead of his capacity of expression. It was an occasion I have never forgotten. I can even remember the date—it was February 6—because while we were there a general came in and handed Eisenhower a note and after he finished reading it he looked up and said, 'I've got to go to London. King George the Sixth has just now died.' So that fixes the date as February 6, 1952."[5]

But Eban did not put all Israel's eggs in that one basket. He was already an admirer of the wit, speaking ability and literary style of Adlai Stevenson. Once Stevenson had been Eban's introducer at a mass meeting in the Chicago Stadium at which they became well enough acquainted so that for years they conducted a sporadic correspondence. In one letter to Eban Stevenson wrote:

"If I could only speak like you I might get on in the world."

"That was typical of him," Eban said. "It was typical of his diffidence. He often wrote to me when he felt really frustrated. I liked him very much. He was a pure man. But I think he was not a good politician."[6]

Suzy Eban said of Stevenson and her husband:

"On human grounds they were so different. Aubrey has never shirked any responsibility. He is ambitious, but Stevenson was the other way around. He didn't really seek office. Aubrey does seek office. He's more dynamic from that point of view. If you think of them as both being erudite there was a similarity. Few politicians are erudite. The statesman must be. I think the real similarity was in their code of ethics—their behavior. Neither was an opportunist. They were both willing to place human considerations above opportunism—to the detriment of their careers, of course. But there was nothing really decisive about Stevenson. He wavered. Aubrey, to the contrary, leaps into things."

Mrs. Eban likes to tell the story of how a hatcheck girl at the conclusion of a UJA banquet in New York gave Eban Stevenson's hat and Stevenson Eban's. A glance at the initials inside the two hats explained how the girl made the error—ASE and AES. When Eban tried to put on the Stevenson hat and found it several sizes too small he turned to his wife and said:

"I'm afraid my head has got too big for my hat."[7]

There were other ways in which Eban and Stevenson were alike that Suzy Eban did not mention. Senator J. William Fulbright, commenting on the way Stevenson wrote his speeches, once said:

"The Governor ran everybody crazy, including me, over what we called his perfectionism. We thought he did as well impromptu, particularly on those short speeches about anything, but he insisted on having something prepared and he would work—well, he would work until three or four o'clock in the morning changing a word. And he was always late. The texts were never available. And the reason they weren't is he wanted to go over them and change a word. He rewrote or reworked no matter what it was."[8]

During Stevenson's campaign for the presidency a letter was received by Abba Eban from a fan in the United States which said:

"The trouble with Stevenson is that he is too much of an intellectual. No one in the United States understands his speeches excepting Eban and he hasn't got a vote here."[9]

In a brilliant discussion of "Nationalism and Internationalism in the Middle East" at the Jewish Theological Seminary early in 1952 Eban declared that the "historic debate which has portrayed nationalism and internationalism as opposite concepts is one of the most sterile of all ages. . . . National differences and linguistic varieties are just as much a part of the cultural landscape of the world as mountains and valleys are part of the geographical fabric. To aspire to any elimination of these differences and varieties is no more intelligent than to wish that the earth would lose all its contours, all its heights, all its depths and all its oceans."

Striking out at empty nationalism, he said:

"Not everybody who assassinates a Prime Minister, not every student in Cairo who throws stones through the window of a foreign establishment is necessarily the spiritual descendant of Thomas Jefferson or Robespierre. . . . The imagination falters at the magnitude of the opportunity which has, almost overnight, been presented to the liberated Arab peoples . . . less as a result of their own sacrifices and effort than as a consequence of international influence in two world wars. . . ."

In May (1952), addressing nearly a thousand supporters of the Jewish National Fund at a gathering in Washington honoring President Truman, Eban declared:

"It is a good test of friendship for men or nations to recall the moment of their greatest loneliness and ask themselves who then stood at their side. By this crucial test President Truman must be surely accounted Israel's most authentic friend. . . . We should be less than human if we did not have a special place in our hearts for those who supported us in our days of solitude and adversity, when our prospect of survival was dim and the forces arrayed against us appeared insurmountable."

Then, turning to face the President, he said:

"We do not have orders or decorations. Our material strength is small and greatly strained. We have no tradition of formality or chivalry. One thing, however, is within the power of the people of Israel to confer. It is the gift of immortality. Those whose names are bound up with Israel's history never become forgotten. . . . We are, therefore, writing the name of President Truman upon the map of the country. It is the most illustrious living name to be thus recorded upon the contemporary map of the Holy Land. In this village of farmers, near the airport of Lydda, at the gateway to Israel, we establish a monument not of dead stones but of living homes. Thus for all eternity when the eyes of men alight on Truman Village in Israel they will pause in their successive generations to recall the strong chain which, at the middle of the twentieth century, drew the strongest and the smallest democracies together with imperishable links."

The next day President Truman wrote Eban a letter in which he said:

"The only thing is it made me feel that I was dead, because nobody ever speaks like that about people when they are still alive."

One October (1952) day in the General Assembly Dr. Fadhil Jamali, Iraq's Foreign Minister, noted for his intemperate language, compared Israel's treatment of the Arab refugees, then in camps in neighboring Arab countries, to Hitler's treatment of the Jews. After his own anger had subsided Eban made this temperate and effective response:

"Would to God our six million martyrs were now alive as the Arab refugees are alive; were amidst their brethren and kinsmen in Israel as the Arab refugees are among their own brethren and kinsmen in Arab lands; were receiving lavish assistance through relief and rehabilitation from the nations of the world, as the Arab refugees are now receiving."

In another UN speech that year he accused the Arabs of saying, in effect, to the Israelis, through their boycott tactics:

"We tried to murder you. Having failed to kill you in one blow, we shall now continue to attempt your slow strangulation."

During the 1952 election campaign Eban may have had his own idea whether Stevenson or Eisenhower would have made a better President, from the Israeli point of view, but with diplomatic caution he was careful never to give anyone except his closest associates a hint of his feelings. The night following the election, after it was certain that the Eisenhower-Nixon ticket had won, he delivered an address to the Zionist Organization of America in which he voiced confidence that "traditional U.S. sympathy for Israel will be continued by the new administration." His personal tie with Eisenhower was slim, but he had been cultivating Nixon from the time he switched from the House of Representatives to the Senate.

"His committee assignments when he was in the House and later in the Senate had nothing to do with foreign affairs," Eban said.[10] "But somehow we often seemed to come in contact with each other."[11]

Much more important, during the last four Truman years Eban had been keeping in periodic touch with John Foster Dulles, who, having served one year of an unexpired term in the U. S. Senate, by appointment, had been defeated the next year (1950) and had gone back into relative oblivion as a member of the New York law firm of Dean, Sullivan and Cromwell. Every month or two Eban would invest the time to go down to Wall Street and call on Dulles, who always appeared touched by the fact that a busy ambassador considered him worthy of attention. Eban was operating on the assumption that Dulles's role in American politics had not ended and that whatever happened in the future it would be to his advantage (and Israel's) if Dulles was kept fully informed of developments in the Middle East. Dulles, being a lawyer, was impressed with the logic of Eban's thinking and with his eloquence. He enjoyed listening to the Israeli present his case, as if he were trying to convince a jury.

Just before the Republican Convention in 1952 Dulles had sought Eban's advice about formulation of the Middle Eastern plank in the Republican platform. After their conference Dulles himself wrote the plank, which committed the Republican party to support the independence and sovereignty of Israel. As Eban later put it:

"It was obviously written by somebody who was not thinking just of the election but of having to cash the checks after the election."[12]

Now that Eisenhower had been elected, Eban hoped his investment in Dulles might begin to pay off.

November 9 (1952) was a Sunday and so the Ebans were at home in Washington when they received the news that Chaim Weizmann had died in Rehovoth, Israel. It was not a shock because the illness had been long and death had been momentarily expected. Still, it gave Aubrey Eban an empty feeling that the man who had done so much for him was no longer part of the world.

Two days later (November 11, 1952) at the precise hour of the funeral, dressed in somber black, he rose in the General Assembly to thank the other delegates for having paid silent homage to Israel's deceased President.

"He led Israel for forty years through a wilderness of martyrdom and anguish, of savage oppression and frustrated hope, across the sharpest agony which has ever beset the life of any people; and at the end of his days he entered in triumph upon his due inheritance of honor as the first President of Israel, the embodiment in modern times of that kingly and prophetic tradition which once flourished in Israel and became an abiding source of light and redemption for succeeding generations of men. His presidency symbolized the swift journey of the Jewish people, in this its most awesome decade, from the horror and degradation of European slaughterhouses to the shelter and freedom of a sovereign state securely established in the international family."

For once the Arab delegates sat mute, having the good grace neither to protest, denounce nor contradict.

Some days later Eban received a coded message from Prime Minister Ben-Gurion instructing him to talk with Professor Albert Einstein and find out what his reaction would be if he were offered the presidency of Israel. Eban put through an immediate phone call to the seventy-three-year-old mathematician, already recognized as one of the greatest scientists of all time.

With Einstein was a young Romanian political scientist who had become one of his few genuine confidants, Professor David Mitrany, who later said Einstein's "main and urgent thought was how to spare Ambassador Eban the embarrassment of his inevitable refusal."[13]

Eban later said that Einstein was "obviously moved by the splendor and audacity of the thought, but his rejection was firm and vehement."[14]

As both Eban and Mitrany remembered the exact words, Einstein said:

"I know a little about nature and hardly anything about men."[15]

After stating that his rejection of the offer was final, Einstein implored Eban to do everything possible "to divert and banish the press, whose representatives were laying siege to his house in Princeton."[16]

Eban told Einstein it would be improper to reject such a proposition on the telephone and so the following day he sent the scientist a formal telegram asking him to receive a spokesman who would "seek his reaction on a matter of the utmost urgency and importance." In reply Einstein telephoned Eban again declining the offer. But Eban still persisted. The following day he sent Israeli minister David Golten to Princeton with a formal letter. In it Einstein was told that acceptance of the presidency would entail moving to Israel and taking Israeli citizenship, then:

"The Prime Minister assures me that in such circumstances complete facility and freedom to pursue your great scientific work would be afforded by the Government and people, who are fully conscious of the supreme significance of your labors."[17]

Einstein's reply:

"I am deeply moved by the offer from our state of Israel and at once saddened and ashamed that I cannot accept it. All my life I have dealt with objective matters. Hence I lack both the natural aptitude and the experience to deal properly with people and to exercise official functions. For these reasons alone I should be unsuited to fulfill the duties of that high office even if advancing age was not making increasing inroads on my strength. I am the more distressed over these circumstances because my relationship to the Jewish people has become my strongest human bond since I became fully aware of our precarious situation among the nations of the world."[18]

The more frequent the crises in the Middle East and the greater the pressure under which Eban had to operate, the more epigrammatic he appeared to become. In December (1952) he brought nostalgic smiles to the faces of many when, in an Ad Hoc Committee meeting at the UN, discussing the parliamentary tactics of the Arabs, he said:

"They remind me of the practice in which some of us indulged in our early youth of ringing doorbells and then running away when there was the least chance of the door being opened."

In the same speech he called the Middle East "a proud and venerable area where the arts of civilization were born and whence the call for universal brotherhood came down to successive generations of men."

In the general debate of the General Assembly that same month, speaking of the reparations treaty between Germany and Israel, "which marked the ultimate victory of justice over brute force," he said:

"For the first time in its bloodstained martyrdom, the Jewish people was able, as a result of Israel's renewed sovereignty, to receive the public penitence of its most savage foe, acting under the dictates of a tormented conscience."

Toward the end of 1952 Eban was elated over his own success in getting the General Assembly Political Committee to accept a pro-Israel resolution providing for direct negotiations between Arab and Israelis over boundaries and refugee problems. Had this resolution been passed by the plenary body Israel's entire political future might have changed for the better, but before a vote was taken Prime Minister Ben-Gurion gave an interview to Cyrus Sulzberger of the New York *Times* about Jerusalem, which so antagonized representatives of predominantly Catholic countries that they voted almost solidly against the pro-Israeli resolution when it came up in the plenary session. At the same time the Soviet Union did a turnabout and sided with the Arabs—the first indication that the Israeli-Soviet honeymoon was coming to an end.[19]

In December (1952) Suzy Eban gave birth to a daughter they named Maira. Three weeks later Aubrey, in New York for a meeting with Secretary-General Trygve Lie, received an urgent telephone call from Washington. In broken sentences his wife told him the tragic news that Maira had been found dead in her crib, "one of those mysterious cradle strangulations." It was a shock from which neither of the young parents ever fully recovered. As soon as possible they left together for Florida, where they spent several weeks trying to forget.

Dwight D. Eisenhower was sworn in as President on January 20, 1953. Because Israel's emergence had been linked more with the Democratic than the Republican party, there was a hypochondriacal fear among many Israeli leaders of how the Jewish state would fare under a Republican administration. At first some of the fears were justified, but Eban had been preparing for such a contingency. Soon after Dulles was named Secretary of State he had a long talk with his old Wall Street friend, during which "we went over our common memories and the principles which we had [previously] discussed together, and I had no feeling whatever that there had been any kind of marked change in his [Dulles's] position."[20]

However, the new Secretary of State told the Israeli ambassador that he intended to begin his mission by making a foreign tour which would include the Middle East. Then and only then would he start to formulate a policy on Israel. When the timetable was announced the Egyptians were elated; Dulles would spend eight days in Arab capitals, three of them in Cairo, and only two days in Israel. Israelis and their friends the world over were incensed when Dulles, on reaching Cairo, presented Prime Minister Mohammed Naguib with a silver-plated .32-caliber automatic revolver inscribed "To General Mohammed Naguib from his friend Eisenhower." When Dulles got to Israel and it was discovered he bore no gift from the American President to Israel's Prime Minister, Ben-Gurion presented him with a Bible and suggested he read it. The British were particularly enraged. Winston Churchill told the House of

Commons Britain could defend herself in the Middle East without the help of America or anyone else.

When Dulles got back to Washington he saw Eban and told him his principal impression had been that Israel was "taking on too much—trying to solve all the problems of history in too short a time." He had developed a theory, he said, that America could have relations with Israel and the Arab states which would not be mutually contradictory.[21]

Eban was disturbed as the State Department began to develop what was called the "New Look," an expression taken from the French haute couture, which could and did make sudden and drastic changes in women's fashion. Eban argued that a foreign policy must evolve out of everything that has gone before and cannot be changed the way fashions are, from year to year. Most distressing was that under the New Look, Arab interests were going to be upgraded, Israeli interests downgraded. This gave the Israeli public the impression that with the passing of Truman from the American political scene, the United States was no longer a friend of Israel. Eban felt this was not necessarily true, even though Dulles did take the attitude that Israel's existence was responsible for the rift between the Arabs and America, and that the Arabs had to be compensated for the existence of the Jewish state.

In the spring (1953) Dag Hammarskjöld succeeded Trygve Lie as Secretary-General of the UN. Eban had had an amiable relationship with the first Secretary, but in his successor he found a friend. Often he would go to Hammarskjöld's thirty-eighth floor office overlooking the East River for intellectual communion. He liked to listen to the sensitive, mild-mannered young Swede "carving out his subtly complex sentences in tolerant and affectionate comment on the human situation." Eban discovered that logic was the only path to Hammarskjöld's mind—that "the warmer passions were rigidly barred." They agreed with each other that men would finally, someday, achieve peace if not by moral insight then by the sheer necessity of self-preservation. In the meantime, the important thing was to prevent a "premature and irreparable explosion." Eban came to know Hammarskjöld well enough to discover how firmly he believed in an international personality, "stripped of all national predilection so as to embody the common interest and aspiration of the human family as a whole." As Hammarskjöld became, at times, the central figure in simultaneous crises on three continents, Eban saw him as a symbol of man's yearning for universal peace. Although they were to have many major conflicts during the eight years Hammarskjöld served as Secretary-General, Eban felt his attitude toward Israel was "never lacking in basic good will."[22]

One of Eban's major concerns during 1952–53 was Israel's relationship with the Soviet Union. There were many issues—some of major importance—on which Israel voted in the UN with the Soviet Union and against the United States, but the Korean war presented a more difficult diplomatic problem. Early in 1952 Eban had a long conversation with Jacob Malik, who assured him that the Soviet Union's attitude toward Israel was unchanged.[23] Malik even spoke with contempt of certain Arab delegations and said Israel had nothing to fear from his country's support of anti-Western Arab movements. All this Eban reported to Jerusalem, but he had his personal doubts.

During 1952 and 1953 Eban continued to play an active role in trying to work out a compromise Korean peace plan. On one occasion when he presented Andrei Gromyko with details of such a plan, the chief Soviet UN delegate objected that some points were too pro-American, but he graciously thanked Eban for his efforts.

Then in January of 1953 the Soviet press announced discovery of a conspiracy of doctors, seven of them Jews, to liquidate many Soviet military and political leaders by medical means. Israel's Knesset passed a resolution of denunciation. In retaliation the Soviet press fired a violent barrage at Israel, including an article accusing Eban of being an employee of British Intelligence and with acting on behalf of Britain and America in the UN in order to defeat Soviet peace efforts. Three days later a bomb exploded in the garden of the Soviet Embassy in Tel Aviv and the Soviet Union promptly broke off diplomatic relations with Israel. That same day, briefing the Israeli delegation to the UN, Eban said the Soviet decision was "the result of a planned line which had been marked out for a long time."[24]

During this period Eban had many contacts with Vice-President Nixon, who "lived right around the corner from us in Chevy Chase." Often they were guests at the same dinner party. Once when Foreign Minister Sharett came to Washington for a short visit the Ebans gave a dinner party for him at which the ranking guest was the Vice-President. Nixon was a member of the National Security Council, the interdepartmental defense cabinet of the country which met at least once a week on matters of foreign policy and military matters. He often telephoned Eban and told him he would like to discuss with him something that had come up at one of these meetings.

"I frequently went in and had a half-hour talk with him. Most ambassadors concern themselves only with Presidents and Secretaries of State and neglect whosoever may be Vice-President. My strategy was to be in touch with everyone who might ever become President or Secretary of State. That was why I cultivated Johnson, Nixon, Stevenson and Kennedy during the 1950s. I wanted whoever might become President to be a man who had once dined in my house during his humbler days and who would be able to recall that I had not sought his aid only when he became eminent."

Eban found Nixon "a very cautious man in those days. He didn't talk much about foreign affairs. Of course he wasn't able to express himself very freely."

Nixon repaid the Eban friendship by attending every Israeli Independence Day celebration and with his wife Pat joined with Eban in opening an Israeli exhibit, "From the Land of the Bible," at the Smithsonian Institution.

Eban had especially good relations with Secretary of Agriculture Ezra Benson, a devout Mormon who believed literally in the inevitability of Bible prophecy. Every month or two Eban would call on Secretary of Defense Charles E. Wilson, former General Electric president, "but it was not easy for me to get on the same intellectual plane with Wilson; he once asked me whether Turkey was 'one of those A'-rab states you ain't in good relations with.' "[25]

On the night of Monday, October 11 (1953), Jordanian terrorists crossed the frontier, invaded the Israeli village of Yahud and murdered a Jewish woman and her small child. Two nights later, in retaliation for this and similar raids in which a total of one hundred and seven Israelis had been killed, an Israeli force, half a battalion in strength, crossed the frontier, attacked the Jordanian village of Kibia[26] and left forty-one houses and a school in ruins, several police cars damaged, forty-two men, woman and children dead and sixteen so seriously wounded that many died later.

Ambassador Eban got the news by diplomatic cable Tuesday morning, a short time before newspaper offices began calling him for comment. Tuesday evening the foreign ministers of France, Great Britain and the United States agreed to take the incident before the Security Council. On Wednesday Eban flew to New York to take charge of the diplomatic struggle his country faced. To assist him the Government sent from Jerusalem Gideon Rafael, counselor for the Foreign Ministry on UN and Middle Eastern Affairs; Yosef Tekoah, deputy legal adviser to the Foreign Ministry and Brigadier General Moshe Dayan.

When Rafael received his order he said to Foreign Minister Sharett: "We have already sent Aubrey everything. How can we help him by going to New York?"

"It is not important," Sharett replied, "whether you take any new material to him. I just want you to be with him to give him moral support. I know he is going through a very, very tough time emotionally and you can certainly prop him up a bit."[27]

What Sharett had sensed from Eban's cables was his personal disapproval of the Kibia raid. As Eban himself later explained it:

"I was not against all retaliation. There were some actions I thought good. But there were others in which I felt there had not been any weighing up of the advantages and the disadvantages. Sometimes we set up political and public relations currents against ourselves that defeated our purpose. I also thought that some of the raids were provocative. Our army under Dayan was ordered to march under the very eyes of the people on the other side of the boundary. There were three or four very expensive examples of overreaction without prior explanation or due provocation."[28]

Sharett was aware how Eban felt as he prepared to do his ambassadorial duty by defending the Kibia raid with all his diplomatic and forensic skill, so he sent the three stalwarts as a gesture of his understanding.

One of those who worked closely with Eban in the weeks that followed said of him:

"He performed brilliantly—with a scar on his heart."[29]

In his final statement to the Security Council, after more than a month of debate, Eban referred to it as "the regrettable incident at Kibia" but said Israel most severely objected to "what comes close to being an acceptance and a condonation of existing Jordanian policies in respect to infiltrations, which are the source of the present security problem."

The resolution of condemnation was passed unanimously, except for the abstention of the Soviet Union and Lebanon.

One day in 1954 Ambassador Eban sent a memorandum to Ethel Ginberg:

"I keep meeting the Kennedys. Isn't it time we had them to dinner? It's becoming embarrassing."

Although John F. Kennedy was now a United States senator, the Embassy's social secretary sent back this note to her ambassador:

"You can if you like, but you have only fourteen places at the table.

Shouldn't you have someone important like Senator Symington [Missouri] or Senator George [Georgia] or someone like that?"

To which Ambassador Eban replied:

"Nevertheless, in spite of what you say, please put him on the next list."[30]

Recalling his social relationship with the Kennedys, Eban has said:

"It was very difficult to get him and her together, because she really hated Washington social affairs at this time. She couldn't stand them. As for him, you always knew he would come late, because of his work in the Senate.

"Once he said they would like to come alone—with no other guests —so the Senator and Mrs. Kennedy came and we had a family evening, sitting around watching television. It was the time of the McCarthy hearings when McCarthy was being deflated by the interrogation of Welch and others. I tried that night to get Kennedy to talk about McCarthy, but he was very reticent, so I finally changed the subject. I later realized why—the whole McCarthy issue was dynamite in his state."[31]

Four months after this dinner Kennedy underwent surgery for his wartime back injury, but on June 5, 1955, he, Eban and Charles Munch, the famous conductor, were awarded honorary degrees by Boston University. By custom one of the honorees makes an address for all. Eban was chosen over Kennedy for the honor.

"Senator Kennedy (who had resumed his Senate duties only ten days ago) was still on crutches and was obviously in great pain. He seemed sad and forlorn. I had the impression he felt history was passing him by."[32]

Eban had in common with Nixon and Kennedy that much was made of their youth, Nixon and Kennedy having been chosen by the United States Junior Chamber of Commerce for its "Ten Most Outstanding Young Men of America" award. Nixon was two years older than Eban, Kennedy two years younger.

One day on the "Tex and Jinx" NBC radio show this colloquy took place:

Tex: Pardon the personal question, Mr. Ambassador, but how old are you?

Eban: (Pause) I'm thirty-nine. I hesitated because I spoke at a meeting in the Bronx just now and I had to wait an hour and a half before they called on me and when I arose I said that when I came into this room I was a relatively young man.

Later in the same program Eban defined a UN representative as "a man who can approach any question with an open mouth."

Discussing the austerity program in Israel he said "about the only thing not rationed in our country is trouble; we have plenty of that."

Writing in the *Jewish Post* in 1954, a Chicago rabbi suggested the organization of a Society for the Prevention of Cruelty to Distinguished Speakers, after having attended a dinner scheduled to begin at 6:30. Because the principal speaker was to be Ambassador Eban, most of the guests had arrived by 6:00, "so the dinner was well and speedily served and by 7:45 the proceedings begun. The main address was to be delivered by one of the most gifted speakers of the English language in the world at that time. He was, of course, last on the program. Preceding him was an interminable number of minor greetings, presentations, salutations, invocations and then the appeal. The audience was so worn out by the time of the appeal that some people left the hall; others sat on their generosity. The truly distinguished guest, who had torn himself away from essential and consuming tasks in Washington, was presented to a somewhat worn-out and hostile audience at 10:45. He began: 'I came here as a comparatively young man and I have grown old with the evening.'"

It became one of his stock openings. Unfortunately, subsequent sponsoring committees saw to it that the story was almost always appropriate. But sometimes it happened in reverse. On the first anniversary of Israel's independence the celebration was held in New York's Carnegie Hall. Every one of the thousands of seats was filled. Eban was the principal speaker but he was preceded by Rabbi Silver, Senator Lodge, Paul Douglas and a considerable number of minor luminaries. To hold the crowd until the speaking was over, Eban was to be followed by a performance of Israeli folk dancing.

Even though the proceedings commenced half an hour late, there would have been no tragedy if everyone had kept to his allotted time. But this speaker took an extra fifteen minutes, the next one an extra twenty, until it was finally 11:45 before the introducer stepped to the podium to present the ambassador. Naturally he couldn't permit Eban to begin talking until he had told what few people were still in the hall how great, how distinguished and especially how eloquent the next speaker was. Then Eban came forward.

Under similar circumstances decades earlier Chauncey Mitchell Depew, president of the New York Central Railroad but more celebrated as one of the world's wittiest after-dinner speakers, was given a lengthy introduction at 11:30 P.M. which finally concluded with:

"And now ladies and gentlemen, the great Chauncey Depew will give you his address."

Depew arose, cleared his throat, pulled out his notes and said: "My address is 247 Park Avenue. Good night."

But on May 4, 1949, in Carnegie Hall, New York, at 11:45 Ambassador Eban drew from his pocket the text of his well-prepared half-hour talk and delivered every word of it—to a great many empty seats.

P.S.: No one saw the Israeli dancers. Their act was canceled.[33]

Eban's own remembrance of the evening was that "Cabot Lodge's speech consisted almost entirely of quotations I had intended to use that evening. When he saw me he said with embarrassment, 'As Ambassador Eban has said . . .' and then went on quoting me for ten minutes, so that by the end he had stolen all my speech."

Two chief delegates to the UN, who sat side by side in the General Assembly, fathered children during 1954. They were archenemies politically, yet intellectually they admired each other and often exchanged letters. One day in January the post brought to the Ebans an engraved announcement of the birth of a son, Michael, to Dr. and Mrs. Charles Malik of Lebanon. Back went an immediate note of congratulations, which Dr. Malik answered in his delicate handwriting:

"Dear Ambassador Eban: It was most kind of you to have sent us your personal congratulatory note, for which we sincerely thank you. We, too, wish you and Mrs. Eban the true and abiding happiness that can in truth come only from God."[34]

Thirteen days before the end of the year Suzy Eban gave birth to a girl with brown curls and her mother's turned-up nose. They named her Gila, Hebrew for "joy," because "she was consolation for the child we had lost," but she came to be called Gigee. Eli had been nicknamed "our UN baby." Gila was called "our Embassy baby." As on the day of the boy's arrival, the father was away from home addressing a UJA meeting and he arrived at the hospital just before the moment of birth. And again Suzy laughed about it and repeated:

"My sense of timing is good, isn't it?"

Also in 1954 a mutual Texas friend brought Lyndon B. Johnson, then minority leader of the Senate, to the Embassy to meet Eban and the two such disparate men struck up a lasting friendship. On the evening of July 1, 1955, the Ebans gave a dinner party for the Johnsons.

"I remember that we cooked up a pretty good meal for him," Eban later recalled, "but he didn't eat a bite of it. He spent the whole evening asking questions—all through the meal and afterwards, too. He seemed to have a ruthless determination to suck a person dry of information. He probed me like a dentist—and with the same amount of clinical gentility."

The next day, listening to the radio, the Ebans learned that Johnson had been taken to the Naval Medical Center at Bethesda.

"We were afraid maybe it was our cooking, except that he had eaten hardly anything," Eban said. "Then we heard he had had a heart attack."

After Johnson recuperated and resumed his duties as majority leader, Eban called on him at the Senate Office Building every month or two to brief him on the Middle East situation.

"An ambassador is a very low form of life to members of the Senate and so one had to expect to be kept waiting for three quarters of an hour or even longer and there would never even be an apology about it. But then we would have a good talk. The main thing I remember from these sessions was that he exposed to me the most colorful vocabulary I had ever heard."[35]

In January of 1955 the Jews of Vermont dedicated a forest in Israel planted to honor Warren R. Austin, former senator from Vermont and for six years the chief U.S. delegate to the UN, with Ambassador Eban as the principal speaker. Austin, seventy-five and retired, was present as the guest of honor. With great diplomacy Eban gave the Vermonter credit for being the one who proposed Israel's admission to the United Nations, but he skipped over the historic fact that after passage of the November 29, 1947, UN Partition resolution, it had been Austin, apparently inspired by Middle East oil companies, the British Foreign Office and the Arab bloc in the State Department, who attempted to have the UN rescind the Partition plan and impose a trusteeship upon all of Palestine, a maneuver which, if successful, would probably have ended for years, perhaps centuries, the hope of re-creating a Jewish state—a maneuver which was foiled only when President Truman stepped in and took hold of the situation again.[36]

By 1955 Arnold Joseph Toynbee, British historian, had published eight volumes of his twelve-volume outline of the civilizations of the world. His treatment of Jewish history and the reestablishment of Israel had so shocked Jews of all political and religious colorations that rabbis, professors and scholars throughout the English-speaking world preached sermons, delivered lectures and wrote denunciations of him.

Abba Eban and Arnold Toynbee were homologous in many ways. Both were cultured Englishmen, one Oxford, one Cambridge. Both were scholars and both were intellectuals. But Eban had supreme contempt for Toynbee as a writer.

"It is my conviction that Toynbee writes the worst English that ever gets published. It is Latinized and almost incomprehensible. A professor of English ought to put up his sentences as examples of what to avoid."[37]

January of 1955 was an extremely busy month for Ambassador Eban, with a long list of platform commitments, in addition to his ambassadorial and UN duties, but after studious preparation he took on the great British historian. He chose as the place for the attack Yeshiva University in New York. There, on the night of January 18, before a scholarly audience, he spent one hour slashing into small ribbons this man he labeled a "heretic." No rabbi, professor or scholar had ever done it half so well. The address would go down in Eban annals as one of his masterpieces.

Again and again in his eight volumes Toynbee had called the Jews "fossils" or "a fossil remnant." He had said: "A number of fossils in Diaspora have preserved their identity through devotion to religious rights and a proficiency in commerce and finance." This sort of non-thinking Eban labeled "timeworn platitudes," akin to anti-Semitism. He said that unfortunately for some people the fossil whose lack of animation Toynbee had diagnosed "revolted against its petrified nature" and "keeps biting him [Toynbee] in the ankle."

He said Toynbee's aim was to "say something about everything but not to know everything about anything." Toynbee, he said, apparently aspired to be "the Attorney-General of the Almighty on Judgment Day." Bit by bit he dismembered his victim until by the end of an hour the pieces lay on display before the audience—not very attractive; no longer a reputable historian; no longer a man; just a lifeless charlatan, frightening no more; not even slightly believable.

Late in February (1955) Suzy Eban, looking over her husband's schedule for the rest of the year, realized that not only would he continue to commute between Washington and New York, but his speaking commitments were going to take him back and forth across the country many times; that he would rarely be at home for long. Immediately after Eli's birth he had gone abroad for weeks. Now that Gila was three months old and doing well she decided to turn the tables and go abroad herself. She was gone six weeks—to London and then to Israel. It was actually an exchange of Mrs. Ebans, for Alida Sacks Eban came to stay with her son and watch over her two grandchildren. The correspondence between husband and wife was the converse of the epistolary exchange during their last long separation. This time it was Aubrey who, like any other devoted husband, sent her an almost daily letter, often enclosing snapshots he had taken with the camera she had given him on his fortieth birthday. His photographs were not exceptional, but his letters gave a vivid, beautifully phrased picture of the life she had temporarily deserted. He called her by the pet names he had devised for her and interspersed his reporting with the phraseology of the young lover as he told her how much he missed her.

He had taken his mother to a cocktail party at the Iranian Embassy. "She is greatly enjoying herself." In New York for a Security Council meeting he had acquired "a stiff cold" and had stayed in his hotel room for three days doctoring himself. He had seen Allen Dulles, who asked about Suzy. "So does everybody. You are very popular." He took Eli (age five) for his first train ride—to Baltimore. "His excitement was intense." Gila (age three months) "was full of joy today, gurgling, smiling and waving her arms in sheer joy and exultation." Eli went to his first circus. "Have you seen the New York *Times?* I have been twice on Page One with General Burns." (Apparently General Burns was on his way back to the Middle East, because Aubrey told Suzy that if she saw him to "greet him kindly, for he is a man of good will and sympathy, as most Canadians have been toward us.") He went to a Japanese movie, *Gate of Hell,* which he thought "fascinating." Spring arrived in Washington early in April and he played his first game of golf. "At lunch today Eli broke the wishbone of the chicken and said he wished *Ima* [Hebrew for mother] to come back yesterday, or this afternoon, or not in three weeks, so you can work out the psychology." He hoped to see John Foster Dulles next week. Had lunch with James Rosenberg, "who asked about my pretty wife." Eli was in good spirits "and very devoted to Mother, despite his threat to 'put her in the garbage can and burn her.' This for telling him to go down to supper." To deliver a fund-raising talk he went to Miami and "it was fun but very nostalgic. I stayed in the new marble palace, the Fontainebleau, and visited old haunts, the Bay Shore Golf Course, the Sterling, Pumpernicks, Wolfie's, Lincoln Road and remembered how we used to get up at dawn and play golf and avoid the nudnicks. . . . I got back to New York for my honorary degree [at N.Y.U.], a very impressive ceremony, with purple hoods and gowns.[38] I spoke for fifteen minutes and it was one of the *very* successful ones, all the audience on its feet for many minutes on end."[39]

Early in April (1955) Eban's Embassy sent a letter to Albert Einstein asking if he would be willing to make an Independence Day television broadcast dealing with Israel's scientific and cultural progress, and stressing the peaceful uses of atomic energy. The scientist replied that he would be willing but would like to discuss the matter with Eban. Several days later, accompanied by Reuven Dafni, Israeli consul, Eban paid a call on the famous scientist in his home at 112 Mercer Street, Princeton, New Jersey, a simple, two-story frame house, where Einstein received them dressed informally in loose-fitting trousers, a turtleneck sweater and sport shoes. They talked briefly about general intellectual matters, then about Israel.

"Professor Einstein told me he saw the rebirth of Israel as one of the few political acts in his lifetime which had an essentially moral quality," Eban later said. "He believed the conscience of the world should therefore be involved in Israel's preservation. He had always refused requests of radio and television networks to project his views to public opinion. This issue, however, seemed to him to be of such importance that he was actually taking the initiative through me of seeking the opportunity to address the American people and the world. He showed me the draft which he had begun to prepare. He had reached the end of a long preamble on the cold war and wished to hear my views before discussing the political aspects of the Middle Eastern situation."[40]

During the conference it was agreed that Einstein would write the address entirely himself, that it would be televised in his Princeton study and that it would go over a coast-to-coast network on April 27 as part of the seventh anniversary celebration. Einstein was enthusiastic about the idea but insisted he would make it a political talk. He told his guests that in his opinion the American public would pay little attention if he spoke about Israel's cultural, intellectual and scientific achievements, but if he boldly criticized the world powers for their attitude toward Israel it might make an impression. "I must challenge the conscience of the world." He said it would be easier for *him* to talk this way than for someone like Eban, who had to consider his official capacity.

At one point Einstein asked his guests if they would like a cup of coffee. Telling about it later Eban said:

"When I said yes I assumed he would ring for a servant. Instead, to my surprise, he went out to the kitchen and made the coffee himself."

As Eban and Dafni left 112 Mercer Street they asked Einstein: "How about a visit to Israel someday?"

He smiled wanly and replied:

"I'm afraid the time for travel is over."

After he got back to his Manhattan hotel Eban could not resist the temptation to put in a telephone call for his wife in Israel and when she asked if anything interesting had happened that day, he replied as casually as possible:

"Well, I went out to Princeton and Einstein made coffee for me."

After the brief phone conversation he wrote Suzy a detailed description of the meeting in which he said he had found Einstein "enchanting." While he was certain the broadcast would be of great help to Israel, "he [Einstein] is very strong-willed and I fear he will say things I would prefer remain unsaid. However, the overall value of his pronouncements is morally enormous."

Four days later Einstein was taken to Princeton Hospital. He carried with him many pages of notes he had already completed for the broadcast. During the next three days, as he lay in his hospital bed, he continued to work on the script. Early on the morning of April 18 (1955) he died in his sleep of a rupture of the main artery. Only the night nurse was at his bedside.

After the cremation a search was conducted for the broadcast notes. The plan was for Ambassador Eban to take Einstein's place before the television cameras on April 27, reading the Einstein script. But only one page could be found. Dr. Otto Nathan, professor of economics at New York University and executor of Einstein's estate, was especially concerned when he learned that on the back of the second page of the script was a mathematical formula that Einstein had been working on during his last days. But the lost pages were never found. Instead of doing the telecast, Eban wrote his own script, which he broadcast over a radio network.[41]

Four weeks after Einstein's death (on May 15, 1955) a memorial meeting was held in Town Hall, New York, with Ambassador Eban sharing the platform with Associate Supreme Court Justice Hugo L. Black, Dr. Norbert Wiener, M.I.T. professor of mathematics, and Nahum Goldmann, president of the World Zionist Congress. Entitling his address "A Titan Passes," Eban told of his last visit with the great scientist and repeated one of Einstein's final remarks to him:

"Israel's establishment in the aftermath of the hideous persecution was a victory for the conscience of this generation and was one of the few political events in my lifetime which was of an essentially moral character."

Then Eban paid Einstein this magnificent tribute:

"He lived in solitude and grandeur, in a realm of transcendent thought. . . . It is difficult to think of any single man since antiquity who so sharply transformed the thought of mankind by the influence and impression of his life. . . . Because of the modesty of his bearing we were not always aware that we had in our midst a giant of history, the chief pride and ornament of his generation."

Linking Einstein and his background, Eban said that for four thousand years the Jewish mind "has been dominated by one single theme . . . that the universe is not a chaos of wild, uncontrollable, arbitrary, mysterious forces, but that it is a pattern of order and progress, guided by an articulate intelligence and law."

Finally, he revealed that Einstein three years earlier had written to him:

"My connection with the Jewish people is the deepest human emotion of my life."[42]

Just after Suzy left on her trip Eban was awakened one morning (March 1, 1955) by a Foreign Office cable from Jerusalem giving him the news that late the previous evening an Israeli force had penetrated two miles into Egyptian-held territory in the Gaza Strip and had blown up the Egyptian Army's administration headquarters and the well and pumping station which provided one third of the water supply to the hundred thousand residents of Gaza and refugees billeted there. Thirty-seven Egyptians had been killed, including fourteen soldiers, and twenty-nine wounded. The attacking force had lost eight men. It was in retaliation for months of harassment of Israeli frontier villages resulting in four Jewish deaths.

This was one more military operation about which Eban had had no advance warning. He well knew there would be worldwide resentment, yet, like a lawyer defending a presumably guilty client, he would have to put all his wits to work organizing and presenting a defense that would make some impression on the jury. The jury in this case would be the Security Council, which, on the occasion of the "regrettable incident at Kibia," had voted unanimously (except for two abstentions) against Israel.

For one month the debating went on and then—to no one's surprise—the eleven members of the Security Council in what the newspapers called "a rare instance of complete unanimity" voted 11 to 0 to condemn

Israel for what had been termed a "premeditated and murderous attack" not justified by Israel's argument that it had been preceded by months of harassment by Egyptian infiltrators. Three days after the vote Eban sent a cable to his own Foreign Office which he himself described, privately, as "letting off steam." In writing to a friend he summarized the feelings he had expressed in the cable:

"I conveyed how absurdly the Gaza episode had worked out. The international and Jewish disappointment is extreme where no advantage of a local military character has been secured. It's just 100 percent loss. We must draw the conclusion that to send armies across a frontier losing eight boys to avenge the four killed in five months is just ridiculous. Retaliation is just finished [Eban's underlining] as a policy and our people should get used to obeying the same rules, even under provocation, as other governments when provoked."[43]

The cable to the Foreign Office was not his only protest. Later he engaged in a lengthy correspondence with Prime Minister Ben-Gurion about retaliatory raids.

Commenting years later on the Gaza episode Eban said:

"There is some foundation for saying that the Gaza raid was one of the elements that made Nasser decide in favor of the Soviet arms deal. I don't believe it was the only reason but at least the excuse was there."[44]

For a short time in 1955 the United States cut off all economic aid to Israel in protest against her refusal to obey UN resolutions. Eban was under intensive diplomatic pressure and yet he had what his Yiddish- and Hebrew-speaking friends called the *chutzpah* (gall) to put his own name down as a candidate for vice-president of the General Assembly. His election to the post indicated to some that he obviously had a special position among UN delegates apart from whatever his country's standing might be.

Five months after diplomatic relations between Israel and the Soviet Union were broken off in 1953 they were recemented, but the mortar never really hardened and during 1954 and 1955 questions involving the Israel-Arab conflict were brought before the Security Council six times, with the Soviet Union always taking the Arab side. Again and again Eban attacked the non-objectivity of the USSR, which always brought a bitter retort from its delegates.[45]

Finally on September 7, 1955, Gamal Abdel Nasser announced the conclusion of an agreement with Czechoslovakia to supply Egypt with the latest and most deadly sort of military equipment. In Washington

Eban learned some of the details, which he cabled to Jerusalem, giving his own opinion of the "enormity of the danger." Emergency Cabinet meetings were held. Gideon Rafael, now serving under Eban on the UN delegation, was assured by the Soviet delegation that the Czech deal was not directed at Israel, but this was a foolish disclaimer, for it was obvious the Russians were exploiting Arab hostility toward Israel. In many speeches Eban rejected the idea that any nation that gives arms to another nation has a right to earmark them and say against whom they shall be used.

That was the status of the relationship when on November 7 (1955) the Soviet Embassy celebrated the thirty-eighth anniversary of the Bolshevik Revolution. The Washington party was superlative in many respects, with more than a thousand guests jamming every square inch in the Embassy, formerly the old Pullman mansion, on Sixteenth Street, only a few blocks from the White House. After an hour the waiters ran out of food and many of the thousand guests got nothing at all to eat. Ambassador and Mrs. Eban had their picture taken with Soviet Ambassador and Mrs. Georgi N. Zaroubin directly under an immense portrait, four times life size, of Josef Stalin, who had been dead for two years but had not as yet been destalinized. The Soviet ambassador was wearing a military uniform emblazoned with four large medals. Although it was a diplomatic rule of all the Arab countries not to attend functions of any kind at which any official Israelis were present, the Egyptian ambassador, Dr. Ahmed Hussein, came to the Soviet party. One newspaper[46] reported: "Hussein and Eban stayed until the vodka was poured, obviously trying to outstay each other. It was not considered odd, since Egypt has just bought arms from Russia and Israel is a willing prospect." (The article obviously was written by the society reporter and not by the paper's political, military or diplomatic expert.)

In the general debate at the fall (1955) session of the General Assembly Ambassador Eban concentrated his fire on the Soviet Union for aiding and abetting in the arming of Egypt, but he worded his denunciation in such a way that it could apply, also, to the United States.

"Countries which manufacture armaments bear a heavy political and moral responsibility. This responsibility cannot be discharged by supplying armaments on purely commercial criteria, without reference to their political context, or by using them as currency for purchasing political influence. . . . It is hard to comprehend how any government which values its moral position can give or sell arms to governments whose primary international objective is to harass, besiege, intimidate and if possible destroy a neighboring state with which they refuse to establish peace."

At one of the last sessions of the UN in 1955, Italy and Ireland were admitted to membership. This meant a reshuffling, for one of the UN rules is that all delegations must be seated in strictly alphabetical order—by the Latin alphabet. When Israel was admitted she was wedged in between two of her Arab rivals, Iraq and Lebanon, but now she would have Ireland on her left and Italy on her right. Eban seemed loath to be separated from his off-the-record friend, Dr. Charles Malik, but as the delegates of Ireland and Italy took their places on either side of him he said to them:

"I believe the three of us together account for the whole of New York City and most of Massachusetts."[47]

19

Not Backward to Belligerency

ABBA EBAN became an important international figure in 1956, when, for a brief but frightening moment in history, the Suez crisis appeared to be the spark that might set off World War III.

When the Czech-Egyptian arms deal was announced in 1955 it became obvious that the balance of power in the Middle East was going to be changed. The commission Eban received from Jerusalem was to try to get the United States to do two things: (a) to use its influence in deterring the USSR in the Middle East and (b) to see that Israel got the military equipment she needed to defend herself against the massive buildup of Communist armament in Egypt. They especially wanted jet fighters, because at that time Israel had not a single jet plane.[1]

Despite the close personal bond Eban had cemented with John Foster Dulles, many political conflicts broke out between Israel and the United States. Under Eisenhower's guidance the State Department had developed, with the assistance of Eric Johnston, a plan for the unified development of the Jordan waters, but Israel was going ahead with her own Jordan water plan. The United States, in anger, withdrew economic aid from Israel and in the United Nations voted to force Israel to stop work on her Jordan project. (There was such an outcry in Israel and the United States that in little more than a week Washington restored the aid.)

During this period Dulles was motivated by the belief that through diplomatic action he could succeed in improving relations between the United States and Arab countries. He and his associates insisted to Eban that this policy was not directed against Israel. They argued that any improvement in the rapport between the United States and the Arabs would enable Washington to use its influence to create a more peaceful climate in the Middle East.

Eban told Dulles that this policy overlooked the continuously occurring frontier tragedies. Hardly a day passed without some skirmish in which Israeli men, women and children were killed or wounded. Every two or three months the Israelis would organize a counterattack. Dulles took the attitude that Israel should expect and tolerate a certain amount of bloodletting. He suggested that the Israelis refrain from counterattacking and be satisfied with the sympathy that the rest of the world would feel for the harassed victim. However, there was more public indignation over the few intensive Israeli retaliations than over the daily attacks by the Arabs. Once the ambassador of a leading European power, discussing this situation with Eban, said:

"Consider how much more impact is made by a single airplane accident in which seventy people are killed than one hundred separate automobile accidents in which one hundred people are killed. C'est la vie!"

In 1954–55 Eban began working for a treaty under which the United States would agree to guarantee Israel's existing frontiers against any change by force of arms. Dulles was sympathetic to the extent that in correspondence and conversation with Eban he referred to Israel's "sense of isolation" and one memorable day even said he thought Israel and the United States should try to move toward a treaty relationship. But then in an address in August, 1955, to the Council of Foreign Relations, Dulles made such a treaty dependent on prior agreement on frontiers between Israel and her neighbors. Eban pointed out once more that if Israel and Egypt were ever to agree on frontiers there would no longer be need of a U.S. guarantee or treaty.

During his contact with Dulles Eban discovered that the Secretary of State had not only amazing mobility, but expected others to have it, too. Once during a talk in Washington Dulles said to Eban:

"Look, we haven't really finished this, but I've got to go to London. If you can be in London on Tuesday we can continue the matter."

In the summer of 1955, while Sharett and Eban were having a discussion with the American Secretary of State in Paris, Dulles suddenly said:

"Look, I have to go to Geneva now for the Summit Conference. Let's meet there and continue this."

Which they did.

As for arms, Eban had specifically asked the United States for twenty-four F-86 jets—a modest order. Later he said that the Sinai war of 1956 could well have been called the War of the Twenty-four Aircraft, "because if the United States had responded to our requests when we first made them a totally different situation would have developed. There would have been confidence in our ability to stand the increase in Egyptian strength as a result of the Soviet armament and internal pressure in Israel for action would not have developed."[2]

Just as Dulles and the State Department did not seem ready to support Israel by treaty, so the Pentagon did not seem ready in 1955 to supply Israel with jets. There was a difference of opinion between Eban on the one hand and the Pentagon and State Department on the other, in that the Israeli ambassador interpreted the Czech arms deal literally, while those making American policy thought, to use Eban's words, "that there was more promise than fulfillment." It turned out that Eban was right and they were wrong.

There were other government forces—both British and American—which took the attitude that if Israel actually were as weak militarily as she pretended, then she should make an accommodation with the Arabs to save her skin. Eban immediately rejected this attitude, referring to it as "a Munich-like atmosphere."

As ambassador to Washington and to the UN, Eban had never contented himself with merely executing the directives of his government; he also strove continually to help shape Israel's foreign policy. He was in constant touch with Sharett, who at this time was both Prime Minister and Foreign Minister, and with Ben-Gurion, who had come out of retirement to resume one of his old posts as Defense Minister. Whenever he went back to Jerusalem, which was frequently, he was admitted to the Cabinet table, sat through all important policy discussions, gave press conferences, appeared on radio and television, and delivered public addresses on Israeli foreign policy.

Late in 1955 he sent Sharett a cable stating that "we should give ourselves a period of six months or so to see if we can get arms support from the United States, but if we are not able to achieve this breakthrough then it might become necessary for Israel to take military action against Egypt while the balance is still not hopelessly tipped against us."

This cable, which is in the archives of the Foreign Ministry, is a denial of the assumption sometimes made that Eban was a complete pacifist and that he never initiated a proposal for military action. Nearly a year before the Sinai operation he had not only predicted but actually advised Israel to be prepared for military pressure against Egypt, "although I would have much preferred to get the arms and therefore be in a position to hold the balance without military action."

This cable was badly received by Sharett, who was not willing to think in terms of military initiative by Israel. However, when Ben-Gurion a few months later resumed his old position as Prime Minister and found the Eban cable he read it "with some surprise and gratification."

Late in 1955 word finally came from the office of Secretary Dulles that he and his advisers felt that when the first Russian MIG-15s arrived in Egypt the balance of power would be seriously disturbed. Therefore, a specific date in December (1955) was set when Israel would get a reply to her request for jet planes. Moshe Sharett, who by now was simply Foreign Minister again, came to Washington to be on hand at that time. But the day after his arrival there was a military development that not only overshadowed the diplomatic progress but brought it to at least a temporary halt.

The 1947 Partition plan, in dividing Palestine between Arabs and Jews, decided that Lake Tiberias[3] would be entirely Israeli territory. Early in 1955 the Mixed Armistice Commission, on which sat both Israeli and Syrian members, established the lake as Israeli territory and rejected any claim of Syria to interfere with Israeli activities on the lake.

On December 10 (1955) Syrian artillery fired on Israeli boats on the lake in an effort to deny the Israelis use of both the lake and a ten-meter strip on the northeast shore, which the armistice agreement had also put under Israeli control. The next night Israeli forces crossed over into Syria and engaged Syrian troops. By the time the battle was over fifty-six Syrians and six Israelis lay dead, with many others either wounded or missing. (The Syrian death toll was later placed at seventy-three.)

When Sharett and Eban got the news by diplomatic cable in Washington they were "appalled," to use Eban's own word. Privately at the time and publicly much later Eban described the Israeli incursion as "retaliation for an Arab attack on our fishing vessels which had scraped paint off the vessels and had not caused any fatal casualties. This was, of course, a distressing situation, because the gulf between the effects of the retaliation and the thing which had brought it about was greater than any engagement that had happened before or since."[4]

Although both Sharett and Eban disagreed with the military action, it was their duty as Foreign Minister and ambassador to the UN to defend it.

The Security Council held eight emergency meetings at which the Syrian delegates made eight addresses or statements, and Eban five. There was no indication in any of his public utterances that Eban personally disapproved of what Israel had done. Powerfully, vigorously and at times convincingly he defended the Israeli right of retaliation. Charges and countercharges flew back and forth. Eban demanded that Syria be condemned and ordered to keep her artillery shells out of Israeli territory. Syria wanted Israel condemned, expelled from the UN and punished by the imposition of an economic boycott of all UN members. Dr. Victor Belaunde of Peru, that month's president of the Security Council, took a grave view of the situation, stating that the fate of humanity might be decided in the Middle East.

After weeks of debate, the Security Council in January (1956) passed a resolution sponsored jointly by the United States, France and Great Britain condemning Israel. The vote was unanimous.

When Sharett got back to Israel he protested bitterly to Ben-Gurion about the Kinneret action. He was supported by Eban, who wrote the Prime Minister a long letter asking what possible reason or excuse there could be for this action, which he called "extraordinary" for two reasons: "the dimensions of it and the timing." He asked why an action of this sort should not have been delayed "until we saw whether we were going to get the arms we had requested." He contended that Israel's representatives in Washington had been put in a "ridiculous position."

Back came an immediate reply, by cable. Eban's remembrance of the wording was:

IF YOU READ YOUR SPEECH TO THE SECURITY COUNCIL YOU WILL
FIND A BRILLIANT AND TO MY MIND CONVINCING EXPLANATION I
FIND NOTHING FURTHER TO ADD.[5]

Ben-Gurion, years later, recalled the cable with a twinkle in his eye. The exact wording as he remembered it was:

I MYSELF HAD SOME DOUBTS ABOUT THE OPERATION UNTIL I READ
YOUR BRILLIANT EXPLANATION TO THE SECURITY COUNCIL WHICH
HAS CONVINCED ME THAT WE WERE RIGHT AFTER ALL I HAVE
NOTHING FURTHER TO ADD.[6]

Ben-Gurion said that by coincidence he had received the full text of Eban's Security Council address and Eban's letter of protest in the same diplomatic pouch. He often repeated the story, publicly and privately.

For Eban the Kinneret action and the diplomatic aftermath constituted a traumatic experience, for once again he had to play the role of a lawyer pleading in court for a defendant who, this time, he felt in his heart, was guilty. The seriousness of the attack diplomatically was that it put a sudden stop to American consideration of Israel's plea for jet fighters. This was why Eban saw a conflict not only between Israel's military and diplomatic operations, but between the military's desire for retaliation and the military's desire for defensive arms.

Several weeks later James Reston, chief Washington correspondent of the New York *Times*, told Eban he had good reason to believe that if the Israeli attack on Syria had not been launched the United States would have released to Israel some of the jets it had on order in France and Canada.

Eban was grim. In a fund-raising talk in New York honoring Herbert Lehman toward the end of January (1956) he warned that "our peril is progressively mounting."[7]

February brought another diplomatic crisis. It began on a Wednesday (February 15, 1956) when several dozen members of a Zionist youth organization learned that there were eighteen M-41 Walker Bulldog tanks on lighters tied up at a Brooklyn dock alongside a freighter, the SS *James Monroe*, which was to take them to Saudi Arabia as the first installment of a considerably larger tank order. When they began picketing the dock the story broke in New York newspapers. On Thursday Ambassador Eban quickly lodged a protest with the State Department. From here on the story moved at double or triple normal speed. At midnight Thursday President Eisenhower from his vacation headquarters in Pennsylvania issued an executive order imposing a ban on all arms shipments to the Middle East. Eban was delighted by this quick action; the Arabs were distraught. But forty-eight hours later, under pressure from certain forces within the State Department, the ban was just as suddenly lifted and the SS *James Monroe* was told it could take on the tanks after all. As a sop, Eban was advised that Israel would get $100,000 worth of spare parts for trucks, jeeps and planes she had long ago asked for. Three hundred pickets paraded up and down in front of the dock until 2 A.M. Sunday.

Sunday night Eban was the interviewee on the CBS television program "Face the Nation." When the engineer asked him for a voice check, he said into the microphone:

"Fourteen . . . sixteen . . . eighteen tanks for Saudi Arabia."

The program was mainly concerned with arms for the Middle East. Caustically Eban stated:

"British tanks to Egypt; American tanks to Saudi Arabia, Egypt's ally; British planes and tanks to Iraq; British planes and tanks to Jordan; American arms to Iraq; Soviet bombers, fighters, tanks and submarines to Egypt, and no arms for Israel. Bombers to Egypt to terrorize our cities? Yes. Fighters to Israel to help ward off these perils? No!"

As for the $100,000 worth of spare parts, he said:

"You might as well call it cans of beef or lemonade."

With about fifteen seconds of air time left the moderator announced:

"Mr. Ambassador, I have just been handed a piece of wire copy that indicates that those eighteen tanks are being loaded at this very moment and that the loading is expected to be completed by midnight tonight. I am sure that this is a pretty serious moment for you. I wonder if you would give us a final comment."

Eban replied that the news only reinforced how desperately urgent it was "to rescue Israel from this unseemly and unnecessary vulnerability by giving her weapons with which to defend herself against the supreme and ultimate perils which confront her."

A few hours later—at dawn on Monday—the SS *James Monroe* sailed for Saudi Arabia with the tanks aboard.

One of the most popular broadcast programs in those days was "The American Forum of the Air," originating in Washington and broadcast between 1 P.M. and 1:30 each Sunday over the NBC radio and television network. There were usually two guests defending opposing positions on some topic of current interest. Guest A would be questioned by two interlocutors sympathetic to Guest B, then Guest B would be questioned by two interlocutors sympathetic to Guest A, after which each guest would be asked a few objective questions by the moderator.

For the afternoon of March 11 (1956) NBC invited Abba Eban and Dr. Farid Zeineddine, ambassador of Syria, to be the guests. Dr. Zeineddine said it was impossible, because he and his fellow Arab diplomats had an agreement they would never appear in the same room with any ——. (The producer of "The American Forum" was not sure at a later date exactly what word the Syrian used, but he was certain that it was a less precise and more emotive word than "Israeli.") Still, Dr. Zeineddine was obviously eager to be on a program to be heard and seen by millions of people, so finally he and NBC worked out a compromise: Dr. Zeineddine and Abba Eban would sit on the same platform in the same studio but between them would be a partition so that both could be seen by the studio audience, by the questioners and by the viewing public, but neither would be able to see the other.

Dr. Zeineddine was the first to be questioned—by two young Israeli students, Amos Melamede and Meron (Ronnie) Medzini, son of Eban's UN secretary.[8] The show opened with the following exchange:

Melamede: Mr. Ambassador, I am most delighted to have the privilege of facing you directly. I only wonder if you could explain why you insisted on putting up an artificial wall so as to deprive yourself from facing my ambassador?

Dr. Z: This wall is not artificial. There is a wall between us because Israel is an act of aggression upon Arab land. . . .

A moment later, in answer to another question, Dr. Z said that Zionism "is very similar to Naziism." Medzini asked him to explain "the act of aggression committed by Syria in which four Israeli policemen were killed just three days ago." Although the killings took place on the shore of Lake Tiberias, recognized by the armistice agreement as Israeli territory, Dr. Z said:

"To begin with those Israeli policemen had no reason to be there."

The two Syrian students who interviewed Ambassador Eban were so much more interested in making speeches than asking questions that the moderator several times reprimanded them and finally Eban said to one of them:

"Mr. Sa'ad, I suggest that one day you get yourself interviewed by 'The American Forum of the Air.'"

In his closing remarks Eban said that Israel was prepared to establish a peace settlement on the basis of mutual recognition, "but the whole trouble has been illustrated here today. Here I sit, a few yards away from Ambassador Zeineddine, with a ludicrous partition between us to give the impression of separation. It is their refusal to recognize our sovereignty, our statehood, the integrity of our membership in the United Nations that is the cause of the trouble."

Newspapers all over the country the next day carried photographs of the "partitioned ambassadors," which, in Eban's view, was good publicity for Israel.

Yankee Stadium was the scene in April (1956) of a Salute to Israel Rally celebrating Israel's eighth birthday. John F. Kennedy and Abba Eban sat side by side in the distinguished guests' box and during a lull in the proceedings the young senator turned to the young ambassador and said:

"For one with the style of Macaulay, this is not exactly the perfect place to speak, is it?"

It was a remark that would have endeared Kennedy to Eban even if there had not already been intense admiration. Recalling the Yankee Stadium event years later Eban said:

"For several reasons I haven't been able to remember, I recall that there was also in the box with us the actress Marilyn Monroe."

He and Kennedy were driven in an open jeep around the stadium to the applause of the crowd.

"As I recollect, we were greeted no less rapturously than Miss Monroe, although our visible assets were far less impressive."[9]

At the start of his short address Eban said:

"I look forward to the football contest we are about to witness. I am quite impartial. I don't care who wins so long as it's the Israel Olympic soccer team."

Solemnly he predicted "the possibility of Arab aggression this summer." The crowd thundered its approval when he added:

"If we are attacked we shall defend ourselves with tenacity and the result will be no different from what it was eight years ago. But our ambition is properly in peace not war."

(The Israeli team beat the American League All-Stars 2–1.)

In April (1956) the ice that separated Israel and Washington began to melt. Dulles sent for Eban and notified him that the United States was ready to do something to correct the military imbalance in the Middle East, starting with planes. But, he explained, he was in a corner. If F-86 planes were given directly to Israel there would be an outcry from the Arabs who would insist on equal treatment if the United States wished to retain their friendship.

"What suggestions do you have?" he asked.

Eban replied that the French Mystère was equivalent to the F-86 but Mystère production for the next two years was committed to NATO. The F-86 was also manufactured in Canada. Dulles brightened up immediately.

"I am seeing Mike Pearson [Lester B. Pearson, Canada's Secretary of State for External Affairs starting in 1948 and Prime Minister from 1963 to 1969] tonight and I'll see what he can do."

He would also see whether the United States could release some of the Mystères that France was making for NATO.

At first both France and Canada took the attitude that if the United States wanted Israel to have planes she should supply them herself instead of using this devious device. If there was going to be Arab hostility why should it be directed at Canada or France and not at the United States? Also, Canada was not inclined to take orders from Washington, and French Foreign Minister Pineau wanted a letter from Dulles authorizing the release of the planes to Israel before he would even make a commitment. In reply Dulles said he was prepared to say only that the shipment of jets was with the "acquiescence" of the United States. Nothing more.

All the time this arguing was going on, the Egyptians were furiously arming. Fedayeen attacks were becoming more frequent. The Israeli public was nervous; Ben-Gurion and Golda Meir were growing impatient. Eban remained confident that if he persevered, something would come of it, but the cables he received from Jerusalem often raised a doubt as to whether it was worth following these tortuous paths. Eban then (and later) felt that if Washington had given him an earlier, clearer, more decisive reply to the arms request the history of the Middle East might have been different. However, starting in April (1956) he was confident Dulles was actively and unquestionably trying to see that Israel got the weaponry she needed. Every few days Dulles was on the phone with the Canadian and French ambassadors in Washington talking about "planes for Israel."

The French finally agreed to supply Mystères—many more than the thirty-four Eban had originally asked for. The Canadian-American approval came in September, too late, because the deal had already been made with France. What the French agreement involved was Israel going along with the policy of the Quai d'Orsay, which was interested in Israel making war on Egypt in order to relieve Egyptian pressure on French positions in Algeria.

Sharett resigned as Foreign Minister in June (1956). In his public announcement he did not give his fundamental reason for quitting the government of Ben-Gurion, but it was no secret to Eban and to many others that he was in serious disagreement with Ben-Gurion's policy of massive retaliation. Discussing the resignation years later Eban said:

"The differences Sharett had with Ben-Gurion were as much of temperament as of opinion, but there was also a basic tension. Sharett still thought that patient diplomacy would enable Israel to hold her ground without military efforts, but Ben-Gurion was proceeding through various contacts in Paris via Shimon Peres and others to create something like an alliance on the basis of common French and Israeli interest in putting pressure on Egypt. Ben-Gurion thought that Sharett would not be a compliant Foreign Minister for such a course, namely for a somewhat conspiratorial agreement with France leading to a preemptive war against Egypt."[10]

Eban shared Sharett's feeling about some of the retaliatory raids, but he did not follow his friend's example and resign, feeling that he still had a role to play within the government framework. Yet he knew he was going to miss working with Sharett.

"His resignation was a very grave blow to me. He had been my mentor and my guide, and I had had an intimate personal relationship with him."

Sharett was succeeded by Golda Meir, former Minister of Labor, who was known to be in agreement with Ben-Gurion's get-tough policy and was expected to leave the direction of foreign policy and security in Ben-Gurion's hands.

Although Eban had no intimation from Jerusalem at this time about future military plans, one of his first tasks after Sharett's resignation was to reassure Dulles, who was worried that Sharett's disappearance from the Cabinet meant that Ben-Gurion would resume reprisals in force.

A few days after Golda Meir took office Eban flew back to Jerusalem because Ben-Gurion suddenly suggested that he give up his ambassadorship, move to Jerusalem and work closely with the new Foreign Minister in an advisory capacity. When Eban saw Golda Meir she indicated she was not entranced with the idea, suspecting that Ben-Gurion was trying to use her as a figurehead, while Eban did the actual behind-the-scenes work. It was therefore agreed he would continue as ambassador in Washington and chief UN delegate in New York, where he could be more effective than by duplicating her work in Jerusalem. Unless history reversed itself, there would continue to be Middle Eastern crises which would call for adroit diplomacy at the American end.

Early in July (1956) the United States and Britain withdrew their offers to finance construction of the Aswan High Dam across the Nile River. On July 26 Nasser, in retaliation, seized the Suez Canal. Meanwhile, Egyptian fedayeen raids were growing in number and intensity, and in Paris secret discussions between France and Britain were continuing.

It was a volcanic summer for the young Israeli ambassador. Hoping to get some rest before the normally hectic autumn set in, he, Suzy and the children went to Martha's Vineyard, but between urgent cables from Jerusalem, frontier incidents, the discussion of arms deliveries with American officials and the necessity of appearing before emergency meetings of the Security Council, he spent a goodly part of the summer on planes.

The matter of the Aswan Dam and the seizure of the canal technically lay outside the Arab-Israeli question, but Israel obviously was involved. Eban had to understand the complexity in Washington. Southern senators were opposed to Nasser and everything he did because of the competition of Egyptian cotton with the cotton of the South. Those Americans who were virulently anti-Communist were antagonized by Egypt's new friendship with Communist China. Dulles made it clear to Eban that he was alarmed and angered by Nasser's threat that if America wouldn't build the dam for him, he would appeal to Russia. Dulles called it "blackmail."

Feelings were mixed among Israelis. Some thought it was to Israel's interest to have America build the dam and involve Egypt in "economic preoccupation." Eban and most of his colleagues disagreed. They felt that if Nasser got arms from Russia and the dam from the United States his prestige in the Arab world would be "completely invincible" —that he would then easily dominate Jordan, Lebanon "and everybody else."

"I felt he would become insufferable through the sheer extremity of arrogance," Eban said.[11]

Meanwhile, Israel was neither getting arms from the United States nor making progress with her water plan. Politically Eban felt that Israel's influence should be thrown against American support of the dam. Whenever his opinion was requested he gave it and whenever possible he used his influence against the building of the dam by the United States. There were many in the Senate and the House who opposed American financing for that reason. When the cancellation came he applauded it.

On the Suez question he succeeded in persuading Dulles that the Egyptians had no legal right to close the canal to Israeli ships. But Dulles wanted Israel's complaint to be kept separate from the Anglo-French-Egyptian conflict. However, there was pressure from another direction. The British and French wanted to use the ban on Israeli shipping as proof that Egypt could not be permitted to be the guardian of the canal. Eban finally reached an agreement with Dulles that while he would not intervene at the Security Council in the dispute between the French and British and the Egyptians, he would reserve his legal position.

Following closely the behavior of the British and French delegates in the Security Council, Eban became convinced that they were "getting ready for the idea of military action." It was also obvious to him that the United States would oppose such action, even by its closest allies.

Just at this time, without prior announcement, Yososhavat Harkavi, head of Israel's Military Intelligence, arrived in New York and asked Eban to arrange a meeting for him with French Foreign Minister Christian Pineau and a French general, who were in this country. Although Eban was not being told the details, he began to have suspicions about what the conspirators were up to.

Israeli ambassadors in all other major capitals were recalled to Jerusalem for consultations with the Prime Minister and the Foreign Minister on October 16 (1956). Before leaving Washington Eban had a long talk with Dulles, who said he was sending a personal message to Ben-Gurion pleading for moderation on Israel's part. There was no indication during the conversation that Dulles had any inkling of the British-French plans.

Eban went by way of London, as usual, and as his plane was taxiing to its gate he saw British Prime Minister Anthony Eden, British Foreign Minister Selwyn Lloyd and a group of advisers waiting at the bottom of steps leading up to a British plane. As he watched they boarded the plane and flew off to Paris, where, it later turned out, they reached the decision to take the fateful action in the Middle East.

The Israeli ambassadors were not made privy to any military secrets in Jerusalem. The discussion was all about the possibility of war between Israel and Jordan, for there had been many recent incidents on that frontier. (The aggravation there was being used by Ben-Gurion as an excuse for a clever feint.)

But as Eban prepared to fly back to Washington he knew that "something rather volcanic was going on." This was confirmed on Sunday (October 21), the day he was supposed to leave. He was packing his bag in his Tel Aviv hotel when a messenger appeared with a note from Ben-Gurion saying he would like to have an immediate talk with Eban.

When they were alone in the Ben-Gurion study the Prime Minister disclosed that in a few hours he was leaving for France to have a secret meeting with French Premier Guy Mollet during which it was possible the French would try to obtain his agreement to undertake a coordinated military action against Egypt. He wanted his Washington ambassador to know that "things are developing between France and Israel" of a sort that would affect his mission in America. Thus Eban became one of the few people to be given what he has since called "some authoritative premonition" of the action in Sinai. Yet Ben-Gurion behaved at that time in an extremely skeptical manner. He said that at the last moment Britain would certainly decide not to take part in such an expedition and he doubted whether France alone could maintain her resolve.

Eban returned to the United States sufficiently alerted. It was certain to be a busy autumn for everyone. During the next week he was occupied in the Security Council with discussions of the Israeli-Jordanian situation. It later seemed ironic to him, in view of the joint military action then being secretly plotted, that his most bitter exchanges during the week preceding the Suez-Sinai blowup were with Sir Gladwyn Jebb, the British delegate, who warned Israel to keep her hands off Jordan, to which Eban replied that if Britain had such solicitude for Jordan she should help Jordan stay out of trouble by advising Hussein to restrain his fedayeen.

"There we were, just one week ahead of the alliance in the Sinai campaign, exchanging malevolent observations with each other across the Security Council table!"[12]

At one point during a Security Council address on Thursday, October 25, Eban said:

"If we are not attacked we shall not strike."

Then he added:

"If we are attacked we fully reserve the inherent right of self-defense."[13]

(In the debates which followed the invasion of Sinai by the Israeli Army four days later, this statement—"If we are not attacked we shall not strike"—was thrown back at Eban. His reply: "There was nothing at all embarrassing about what I said to the Security Council. That meeting was entirely about Israel and Jordan. The idea of an Israeli-Egyptian confrontation had not entered anyone's head."[14])

During this period (October 21 to October 27) the State Department pestered Eban with questions about what was happening or was about to happen in the Middle East and during a conversation with Allen W. Dulles, the director of the Central Intelligence Agency and brother of the Secretary of State, Dulles asked Eban what he thought the British and French were "likely to be up to in the Middle East." Eban replied that if he heard anything from Jerusalem he would let Allen Dulles know. Actually all Eban was receiving these days were what later turned out to have been "decoy messages."

On Saturday, October 27, Eban was playing golf at the Woodmont Country Club in Washington with Martin Agronsky, radio commentator, and Congressman Sidney R. Yates of Illinois, when a caddy came rushing across one of the fairways to tell the ambassador that he should come quickly to a telephone because the Secretary of State wished to speak to him.

"I was reluctant to give up the golf game," Eban said later, "because I was hitting the ball better that day than ever before."[15]

After some running around, a telephone was located at the first tee, and Eban was put through to a very agitated Mr. Dulles, who said that strong suspicions had been aroused by recent troop mobilization in Israel and he had heard that everyone in the country had been called up and this was creating grave uncertainty. At the same time there was a blackout in communications between Washington and both London and Paris. Almost in the same breath Dulles added that President Eisenhower very much wanted an explanation from Israel. Then he added a postscript: a message would be going out from President Eisenhower to Prime Minister Ben-Gurion. Dulles was impatient. He wanted some immediate answers.

Eban's reply was respectful but sardonic. He said he didn't think he could "develop these solemn themes with full efficiency" from the first tee of a golf course—that he would leave the country club immediately and be at the Secretary of State's office as quickly as motor transportation could convey him there.

Eban's golf game was a subject of intense speculation at the State Department after the Sinai campaign began and for months thereafter. Had he arranged it deliberately to draw a veil of complacency over the explosive events then being prepared? They never found out for certain.

When Eban arrived at the State Department and was ushered into Dulles's office he found the Secretary and a number of deputies and assistants bent over an immense map—not of the Israeli-Egyptian front but of Israel and Jordan. Their intelligence had all been to the effect that Israel's concentration of troops was against Hussein. (The ploy was working.)

Dulles expostulated that American ambassador Lawson had sent word that the mobilization was "enormous" and that there was "tremendous activity" in Israel . . . tanks on the road . . . an electric air. What was going on?

Eban reacted inconclusively to Dulles. He explained that mobilization in Israel was a measure of security. He described the pressure under which nearly all Israelis were living, with assaults from Egypt, the Egyptian blockade, the terrorist attacks from Jordan.

"I could see that my explanations did not satisfy them."[16]

When Eban discovered for himself that there was a complete lack of telephonic and telegraphic communication between Washington and Jerusalem he became more certain that a major military operation was in the wind: that the Israeli-French cooperation Ben-Gurion had mentioned was actually coming off. One ironic twist: knowing that there would be no other way to get word to Ambassador Eban, Foreign Minister Meir had written him a letter and had given it to an American Jewish industrialist whom she knew and trusted completely, asking him to hand it personally to Eban. Because the man had no way of knowing how urgent the letter was, he stopped off in Paris for a few days on his way from Tel Aviv to New York. In the meantime "the event" had occurred.

Eban was at the Embassy until long after midnight on Saturday (October 27) and most of Sunday. He kept a stream of cables going to Jerusalem, but received nothing back. Long-distance operators kept reporting that the blackout of telephonic communication was still in force.

On Monday, October 29 (1956), at about 2 P.M. Eban and his Israeli colleague Reuven Shiloah, now Minister of Embassy, were in the office of William M. Rountree, Assistant Secretary of State for Near Eastern, South Asian and African Affairs, discussing the situation on the Israeli-Jordanian frontier in which the State Department still seemed to be especially interested. Present also was Fraser Wilkins, the State Department's director for Near East Affairs. Their discussion had been going on for about an hour when suddenly the door was flung open and an agitated messenger rushed in with a sheet of paper which he handed to Rountree, who read it first to himself and then aloud:

"Israeli forces have crossed the frontier and are striking deep into Egypt toward the Suez Canal. It is a full-scale invasion."

Rountree turned to Eban with the simple question:

"Well?"

"I know nothing about it," Eban said calmly. "I can probably learn more by going back to my Embassy where I can read the messages as fast as they come in."

He and Shiloah hastily departed. By the time they reached the chancellery cables from Jerusalem told that Israeli forces were already far into the Egyptian desert and were advancing with little sign of opposition. Almost immediately word was received that an emergency meeting of the Security Council had been called. This meant that Eban had to rush up to New York.

On Tuesday (October 30) Eban's address to the Security Council was a two-thousand-word explanation that the Israeli Army had moved into Sinai in the exercise of her "inherent right of self-defense" in order to wipe out the fedayeen bases from which armed Egyptian units had staged raids that had left more than a hundred Israelis dead and nearly four hundred wounded.

The resolution up for debate in the Security Council called for Israel's immediate withdrawal to the previous armistice lines. Eban was aware the Soviet Union and the United States would support it. Because he had still not been made privy to the terms of the deal with France and Britain, he anticipated that they, too, would probably vote against Israel. When the Security Council president called for a show of hands of those against the resolution he was astounded to see Britain's Sir Pierson Dixon and France's Bernard Cornut-Gentille raise their hands. In effect they were vetoing the resolution which the other nine members had supported.

"I felt at this moment for the first time that Israel was rescued from its solitude and was part of a struggle greater than its own dimensions," Eban later said.[17]

The next development in this fast-moving military drama came when Britain and France ordered Egypt and Israel to retire their troops to positions ten miles back from the canal. Israel accepted but Egypt refused. Thereupon British and French planes began bombing Egyptian military bases. As Eban put it:

"That was when all hell broke loose between the United States on the one hand and Britain and France on the other."

Eban tried to telephone Elath, the Israeli ambassador in London, but he was still in Israel, not having been told about plans for the forthcoming Anglo-French assault. Eban did confer that day with British Minister of State Selwyn Lloyd, who had had a brief talk with Dulles. Lloyd told Eban that although the Secretary of State was "opposed to the whole thing and of course was very angry, especially with the British for the deceit and concealment, he had expressed himself rather comfortably about the blows that Nasser was taking and thought the chastisement might be salutary."[18]

When Eban sounded out Hammarskjöld he found that the Secretary-General was taking "an extremely formalistic line that nobody must get any gain out of the Sinai campaign—that one must restore the status quo."[19]

Eban's reaction was that this would only build another bonfire and even put a match to it.

In Eban's first conversation with Dulles after the launching of the Israeli attack, he told the Secretary of State he had just received an important telephone call from Foreign Minister Meir in Jerusalem.

"Mr. Secretary, I am told we have won a complete victory."

At this time Nasser over Cairo Radio was still claiming the Israeli Army and Air Force had been annihilated. Apparently Dulles had taken little stock in such reports. His eyes lit up with what Eban described later as "a sort of glint" and he said:

"Now what does all this mean? We have been talking—you and I —for over a year. You have been telling me how vulnerable you are —that you can hardly stand up—that you are so very weak while the Egyptians are formidable and invincible. *We* have been telling *you* that you underestimate yourselves and that you are overestimating them. Well, here it is. I was right and you were wrong."

It was a strange first reaction. It seemed to Eban that Dulles was principally interested in scoring debating points—an indication of the forensic character of his mind. Who was right in a discussion was extremely important to him, quite apart from the substance of the matter. As a lawyer he wanted to have it on the record which side had proved its case.[20]

Eban got the impression that Dulles "was not exactly unhappy" over the news that the Egyptian Army had been routed. But then he turned to the Israeli ambassador and with a worried look asked:

"Are your forces planning to remain in Sinai?"

Before Eban could reply he added:

"If they do it will certainly affect the relations between our two countries. We could hardly continue economic aid and the other assistance we give you."

"Israel has no ambitions in Sinai beyond self-defense," Eban replied. "Our objective was not the conquest of the desert but the achievement of peace and maritime freedom."

Dulles seemed unimpressed, so Eban tried a new tack that was a masterpiece of diplomacy.

"Mr. Secretary, a very fundamental event has occurred as a result of this total victory. This is the first time an aggressive dictatorship has been resisted. As a result of what Israel has done, Nasser is going to lose prestige. It is possible that a more moderate government will replace his regime. Then it may be possible for Israel to make peace with Egypt."

Dulles seemed impressed.

"Another thing. Russia's influence in Egypt will be reduced by our victory, which may cause a complete change in the map of political power."

By this time Dulles was striding up and down the room, his hands thrust deep in his pockets, his face wrinkled in thought. Apparently Eban's concepts appealed to him. Finally he stopped and said:

"Look, I'm terribly torn. No one could be happier than I am that Nasser has been beaten. Since spring I have had plenty of cause to detest him. I am torn, yet can we accept this good end when it has been achieved by bad means—by means which violate the Charter? I am forced . . . I am forced to support international law and the Charter. I have to work on the basis that the long-term interests of the United States and the world are superior to the consideration of self-benefit. . . ."

He began pacing again. When he stopped he said:

"If the invaders don't evacuate and go back to the old armistice line, Secretary-General Hammarskjöld will resign."[21]

Just before leaving the State Department Eban learned that as a result of the deadlock in the Security Council, a meeting of the General Assembly had been called, under the United for Peace Resolution. This was a parliamentary device conceived in order to get around the Soviet veto by taking an urgent world problem to the General Assembly, in which the power of veto did not exist. It was paradoxical that it had been conceived in 1950 by Dulles and that Eban had played a prominent part in its formulation, having proposed decreasing the time necessary for applying to the General Assembly. It was Dulles who had recognized Eban's role by suggesting he be placed on the committee to put the resolution into effect. (The suggestion was adopted.) Now Britain, France and Israel were victims of the device which had been designed to outwit the Soviet Union.

Dulles and Eban both rushed to Washington's National Airport and caught a plane to New York, but fog set in over Long Island and for a time it appeared that the Israeli ambassador and the Secretary of State might be landed at some "alternate airport" like Buffalo or Chicago, but finally they reached Manhattan.

During the talk at the State Department Eban had noticed that Dulles spoke rather slowly and in a labored way, as though he were in pain, and that he kept putting his hand to his midriff. A few days later he learned why, when Dulles was taken to the hospital for his first cancer operation.

Eban went directly from the airport to the General Assembly. The taxi driver had his radio on full blast. Some Arab delegate was talking in difficult-to-understand English.

"What do you think of the war?" the driver asked over his shoulder.

"I don't know much about it," Eban replied.

The rest of the way to the UN building the cabbie enlightened the ambassador.

The papers on the newsstand in front of the UN building bore immense headlines. Eban sensed an air of tense excitement as he walked across the ground-floor lobby to the elevators.

At the Israeli delegation office they told him that violent speeches had already been made by Arab and Soviet bloc delegates.

The first question he discussed with his colleagues was when and how he should speak. They agreed that this was not a situation which called for one of his formal, carefully prepared, well-polished speeches; also there was no time for such preparation. The opposition was already making flamboyant charges of unwarranted aggression, unprovoked invasion, premeditated violation of the Charter, slaughter of the innocent. The world would be solidly against the three nations on trial unless the defense was dramatic and convincing. It was important to try to reach the greatest possible number of people and, therefore, timing must be the first consideration. Eban held a quick consultation with General David Sarnoff of R.C.A., who told him that after 11 P.M. the networks would all stop normal programing and carry the UN proceedings live and so if he spoke after 11 P.M. he would be heard by literally tens of millions of people. It was therefore decided that "some of our Latin American friends" would make their presentations between 9 and 11 P.M., then Eban would go on.

From the General Assembly building he went quickly to the Westbury Restaurant near the Israeli delegation office at 11 East Seventieth Street, for he had had nothing to eat all day. He took with him

Dr. Jacob Robinson, the delegation's legal advisor. Over a hurried supper they discussed the legal aspects of the case and decided Israel's act should be explained in terms of Article 51 of the Charter relating to the use of force in self-defense.

Then Eban went to the delegation office and began making notes on small sheets of paper. He was back at the UN building by 10:30 P.M., ready to speak.

He began prosaically, yet his entire defense was in that first sentence:

"On Monday, 29 October, the Israel Defense Forces took security measures in the Sinai Peninsula in the exercise of our country's inherent right of self-defense."

Then he began to weave his spell of words, pleading for Israel's right to defend herself in this manner.

". . . the unique and somber story of a small people subjected throughout all the years of its national existence to a furious, implacable, comprehensive campaign of hatred and siege for which there is no parallel or precedent in the modern history of nations. Not for one single moment throughout the entire period of its modern national existence has Israel enjoyed that minimal physical security which the United Nations Charter confers on all member states, and which all other member states have been able to command."

His voice was clear, his words distinct, his earnestness compelling. There was not a diverting sound in the large Assembly chamber. Even the Arab and Soviet delegates were leaning forward, listening intently.

"What we confront tonight is a point of explosion after eight years of illicit belligerency."

"Belligerency . . . belligerency . . . belligerency . . . belligerency . . . belligerency!" He kept repeating the word. "Egypt has practiced *belligerency* against Israel by land. Egypt has practiced *belligerency* against Israel by sea." Belligerency! Belligerency! Belligerency! It was a brilliant device of political oratory.

"Our men, women and children fell by the thousands while this wave of aggression threatened to convulse us."

Next he was talking about "rights."

". . . every citizen of Israel is entitled to till every inch of Israel's soil and to navigate every yard of Israel's waters without let or hindrance . . ."

He was uttering words that would not soon be forgotten.

". . . an inferno of insecurity and danger . . ."

". . . embattled, blockaded, besieged, Israel alone amongst the nations faces a battle for its security anew with every approaching nightfall and every rising dawn. . . ."

"We know that Israel is most popular when she does not hit back [was John Foster Dulles listening?] and world opinion is profoundly important to us. So, on one occasion after another, we have buried our dead, tended our wounded, clenched our teeth in suppressed resentment and hoped that this very moderation would deter a repetition of the offense. . . ."

But instead, "we have witnessed a constant sequence of aggravation."

Then he struck a powerfully rationalistic note as he asked his intent listeners whether Israel was not acting "legitimately within our inherent right of self-defense when, having found no other remedy for over two years, we cross the frontiers against those who have no scruples in crossing the frontier against us?"

The next moment, in a sudden burst of sarcasm, he said Nasser's system of commando raids against Israel "is one of his contributions to the international life and morality of our times."

As he worked toward his peroration he said that Israel had been not the author of the belligerency in the Middle East but the victim, at the hands of "the dictatorship which has bullied and blustered and blackmailed its way across the international life of our times."

Finally:

"Our signpost is not backward to belligerency, but forward to peace. . . . Egypt and Israel are two people whose encounters in history have been rich and fruitful for mankind. Surely they must take their journey from this solemn moment towards the horizons of peace."

As he sat down and wiped the perspiration from his forehead there was an enormous burst of applause, which was unusual in the General Assembly. There was no doubt but that it had been a historic address—resonant, reasoned, reverberating.

Someone who had been sitting near Secretary of State Dulles later reported that when Eban sat down Dulles turned to Henry Cabot Lodge, Jr., whom Eisenhower had appointed Ambassador to the UN, and said:

"It's a pity we can't have him instead of you as our delegate here."

Unfortunately for Eban and for Israel, Lodge did not take Dulles's comment in very good grace.

Eban did not leave the UN building until almost 4 A.M. As he was going through the lobby to get a taxicab he saw Dulles waiting for his car, so they had a brief discussion during which Eban said that "this is not only a time of great disappointment for the United States; it could also be an hour of opportunity." Years later Eban remembered clearly that during the discussion he used the phrase (which was rather ironical, in view of what next happened) that "sometimes surgical treatment is necessary" and another phrase that "there is something in science known as fusion at high temperature when things reach a tremendous height and then come together. Perhaps we can get peace and security out of this very crisis!"

At that point Dulles's car came and Eban took a taxi to his hotel. On the way the cabbie said:

"Were you in there when that guy from Israel made the speech? Jeez, he sure knows how to talk, doesn't he?"

Later that day the general reaction. First telephone calls. Then eulogistic newspaper reports. Then cables, telegrams and special-delivery letters. A call came from a recording company that wanted the right to make a disc of the talk. During the next few days thousands of letters poured in. They would eventually fill many large scrapbooks. A majority came from people who identified themselves as non-Jews. Almost all expressed sympathy for Israel's position, including a short note from a man serving time in an Illinois prison:

"Sitting here listening to you I feel sorrier for you than I do for myself. I don't want you to think I am in prison for doing something bad. I am only a bigamist."

(Eban's reply to the man in prison: "I am sorry you are in prison for bigamy, because I thought bigamy was its own punishment.")

It was significant that public opinion in the United States and elsewhere in the world had not been very pro-Israeli during the brief Sinai operation. The situation in 1956 was quite unlike what it would be in 1967. Yet Eban's eloquence had had a transforming effect. A climate had been created in which Israel at least would be able to bargain for security in return for withdrawal.

The radio and television services estimated that thirty million people in the United States had listened to the speech. Millions more abroad heard it by short wave. Additional millions read it. It would go down as a classic of extemporaneous speaking—the foundation on which Eban's fame as a twentieth-century Demosthenes would be established.

20

Diplomacy Fashions a Compromise

"The Sinai campaign was politically the most unplanned war in history. It was based on a complete lack of political appraisal. Exaggerated importance was attached to France and Britain. We appeared before the whole world as tools of the imperialists. We should have avoided the Franco-British collusion and been satisfied with their political support. If we were going to break through and free ourselves of the fedayeen and clear the Gulf of Aqaba, it should have been a completely Israeli operation and we should have done it after the American election. It was an absurd idea that a few days before the election we would get a better American reaction. In fact, it was the fear that we had entered the American campaign that made Eisenhower much more irascible than he would have been otherwise. We should have spent some time trying to get at least part of American public opinion used to the idea that Israel was being so harried and hard pressed that she would have a right to break out against the fedayeen and the blockade. It was not necessary to get the violent UN and American reaction we did get."[1]

That was Abba Eban's well-considered opinion of the Sinai venture, as expressed fourteen years after the event in the quiet of his own study. He had held this same opinion at the time, but it was not his function then to say so. He was not consulted when the military operation was being planned, he was given only a vague hint by Ben-Gurion that there was going to be a major troop movement against Egypt in cooperation with Britain and France and after the start of hostilities no opinion—his or anyone else's—would have made any difference.

On October 29 (1956) the task dumped into his lap was to defend what Israel was doing in the face of almost worldwide hostility. And when the world's highest international authority, the United Nations, demanded that Israel withdraw its troops immediately, his duty was to argue, plead, point out, entreat and resist, while Ben-Gurion, who had taken supreme command of the situation, decided whether or not to accede to the demand. For weeks he had to stall for time—and all the while everyone knew that that was just what he was trying to do. Seldom in the history of world diplomacy had any one man so difficult an assignment. Surely no diplomat ever had the odds so greatly against him. For several days England and France were Israel's allies, equally condemned and equally defiant. But then, acceding to UN pressure, they agreed to retire, leaving Israel alone in the prisoner's dock, the only culprit before the court of world opinion. On several occasions the vote in the General Assembly was something-or-other to zero, or to one (Israel).

It was exactly one hundred seventeen and a half days from the October evening when Israeli troops crossed the armistice line and plunged into the Sinai desert until March 5, when Israel announced to the United Nations through Ambassador Eban her decision for full and prompt withdrawal of her troops from Sharm el-Sheikh and the Gaza areas. These were days of intense, high-level diplomatic maneuvering, some of it verging on the frantic. Eban had to be constantly open-eyed, for he was opposed by some of the shrewdest diplomatic poker players in the world. At one point it seemed inevitable that the other UN members would impose sanctions on Israel, which would have almost snuffed her out of existence. President Eisenhower at certain moments behaved as though the whole tripartite operation had been undertaken with the intention of insulting him personally. Dulles was bitter, feeling he had been double-crossed. (He used the words "deceit" and "concealment.") The Soviet Union and the United States, partners in bringing Israel into existence in 1948, now were partners in insisting that Israel was a criminal. The Arab countries were taking full advantage of this situation. Egypt had been caught off guard and humiliatingly defeated. Now she was determined to inflict on Israel a crushing rebuff in the diplomatic field.

Eban had a good team of colleagues and assistants,[2] but the burden was his. He had to map the strategy, deliver the speeches, give the interviews, make the radio and television appearances.

While there was no one nation in the world behaving as a true and loyal friend in late 1956 and early 1957, there were individuals who were. When there was talk of sanctions in the UN, Senator Lyndon B.

Johnson got very excited. Almost every morning he called Eban and on the open phone asked:

"Are those fellows dealing properly with you?"

Eban would try to assure him that everything was going to work out all right. But whatever he said Johnson would reply:

"Well, they're not going to get a goddamn thing here [from Congress] until they do."

He was referring to the Administration's desire to get congressional support of the so-called Eisenhower Doctrine, pledging U.S. military aid to any nation that felt itself threatened by Communist aggression. The Democrats again controlled both houses of Congress (after the 1956 elections) and Johnson was still Senate majority leader. Eban also was encouraged by the threat of Senators Knowland and Humphrey to resign from the UN delegation if it voted for the imposition of sanctions.

Among minor handicaps that made Eban's task difficult, Eisenhower had a slight illness that kept him out of Washington, Dulles was recovering from his first cancer operation, while in Israel Ben-Gurion was ill in bed the day he ordered his troops into Sinai and did not completely recover for a long time.

The United Nations passed six resolutions calling on Israel to withdraw from occupied territory. President Eisenhower personally wrote six strong letters. Once he cut short a holiday to rush back to Washington and make a broadcast warning Israel of what might happen if she failed to cooperate.

Foreign Minister Meir came twice to the United States. Ambassador Eban was twice called home for consultations. They were shuttling continually back and forth between Jerusalem, Tel Aviv, New York and Washington. Sometimes they were in the same city, sometimes not.

Eban's New York hotel suite became a twenty-four-hour-per-day office in which no one did much sleeping, partly because of the difference in time between Jerusalem and Washington, which meant that diplomatic cables were generally pouring in between midnight and dawn. Every hour or two messengers would bring in more newspapers, which Eban would scan whenever he had a spare minute or two. Twice a day a maid would be called in to take away the pile of read and unread papers. For relaxation late at night Eban would often stroll down Fifth Avenue to a bookshop that remained open until midnight. He always returned with an armload of books, mostly on political science.

On several occasions Washington reporters, searching for the elusive Israeli ambassador and being assured he had not gone to the UN or to

Israel, played a hunch and went to the suburban home of Dulles. Each time that's where he was. The newspapers began describing the length of his visits with Dulles in terms of minutes: "twenty minutes" or "thirty-five minutes" or "fifty minutes." Soon they were saying "two hours," or "three hours" and once a conference lasted three hours and thirteen minutes. At one critical period (in February, 1957) Eban had three long meetings with Dulles within a period of forty-eight hours.

The tabloid headline writers liked the Eban conferences much better than meetings between leaders with long names, like Eisenhower and Khrushchev. One night the entire front page of a New York tabloid contained just five words:

DAG
EBAN
IN KEY
TALKS

The United Nations debates often got acrimonious. In February (1957) Eban tabled photostatic copies of Egyptian documents captured by Israeli soldiers in Sinai which, he said, proved that the Arabs had planned to attack Israel. In rebuttal Egyptian Foreign Minister Mahmoud Fawzi claimed that they were fakes, because, he said, they contained many errors in Arabic. Eban was immediately on his feet:

"I am not responsible for the grammar of the Egyptian High Command."

Another day the Iraqi delegate got so angry at the Foreign Minister of Israel that he exploded:

"She should go back to Milwaukee where she came from!"

Then, turning to face Eban, he said that the Israeli ambassador could "go back to either South Africa or England, whichever he prefers."

When international pressure began to be applied on Israel to retire to the 1948 armistice lines, Ben-Gurion felt that the longer he could draw out the war of nerves the better the chance might be of convincing the world that Israel, the only nation denied the use of the Suez Canal, at least should have the right to send her ships in and out of the Red Sea port of Elath and that she should be permitted to keep the Egyptians from using Gaza as a launching site for more deadly fedayeen raids. It was Eban's job to do the "convincing."

Gradually, as the sledge-hammer blows of Eban's logic began to make an impression, the press, at first generally critical, began to take a more tolerant attitude, with many important papers saying that the reluctance of Israel to pull back her forces from Gaza and Sinai without adequate assurance of security from fedayeen raids and the right of free and innocent passage for its shipping was thoroughly understandable.

In the intricate diplomatic game Eban was being forced to play he had personal friends in many quarters, despite the almost unanimous UN votes. From British Minister of State Lloyd he heard an amazing story. After the Anglo-French withdrawal from Suez, Dulles had asked Lloyd why the British collapsed so quickly under Eisenhower's phone calls. When Lloyd replied, "But you put pressure on us!" Dulles said, "Yes, but the decision to yield to pressure is your sovereign decision."[3]

This was what gave Eban the idea that it ought to be much easier dealing with the Secretary of State than with the President, but Dulles seemed to be torn between Hammarskjöld's attitude—that Israel must withdraw unconditionally and just hope the future would be all right— and the opposing view that Israel's withdrawal should be conditioned on her demands being met.

The compromise formula Dulles and Eban finally worked out was that there would be parallel actions: unconditional withdrawal and simultaneously an attempt to satisfy Israel's demands. Actually there was no difference between what Eban had been demanding and the compromise Dulles now offered, except that Dulles had a strangely legalistic mind and to him it was important to pretend that there *was* a difference. It was all a matter of subtle semantics—something very difficult to try to explain to the man in the street in Tel Aviv or the man in the street in Omaha, Honolulu or Seattle.

One of Eban's greatest difficulties with Dulles, in addition to his legalistic punctiliousness, was his almost ecclesiastical appeal to morality. He argued that a country which has the traditions and democratic in- stincts of Israel and which itself was the creation of the UN should have "a decent respect for such an overwhelming verdict of the UN" as expressed in the unanimous or almost unanimous votes calling upon Israel to retire.

Eban's answer, put bluntly in private, a little more delicately in public, was that Dulles and the forces of morality he represented had never heretofore exerted themselves to help Israel and if Israel had had to depend on them alone it would have long ago been put on the list of victims of the crimes of which Dulles so often accused the Soviet Union.

Early in February (1957) Robert Murphy, Assistant Secretary of State, who lived four doors from the Ebans, made an early morning call and invited himself for breakfast. Over toast and coffee he said

he thought "something can be worked out." Then he explained the
State Department's position. They felt it was imperative to get Israel
out of Aqaba and Gaza. Eisenhower had promised King Saud that this
would be done. If Israel did not go back to the 1948 lines the President
feared that general warfare would sweep the Middle East. If Egypt
tried, militarily, to expel the Israelis from Egyptian territory, the United
States, under normal circumstances, would have to help Egypt.

Then they talked about Israel's proposal for an international force in
the Gulf of Aqaba to maintain free passage and in Gaza to keep the
Strip neutral. Again Murphy said:

"I think something can be worked out."

On February 11 (1957) Eban was called to the State Department
and was handed what came to be known as "the Dulles-Eban memorandum," setting out the doctrine of free passage and the arrangement
for the evacuation of Gaza.

A few days later Eban had a long and grave conversation with Dulles,
who was more impatient than ever. He thought the Israelis would have
jumped at this latest proposal, he said, but instead they seemed to be
haggling and bargaining, and all the while the situation was deteriorating.
He was seriously afraid of a world conflagration. If the Egyptians
attacked he was worried that the Russians would help them. In that
case, he warned Eban, Israel could not count on assistance from the
United States.

"If you and I can't work this thing out," he solemnly said, "then
we are of no use at all. Can't you get your people to see that this is the
turning point?"

Eban replied that he believed the February 11 memorandum carried
the seeds of a possible solution and so he was prepared to try to get his
government to agree, but he could not do it from a distance; he would
have to get himself recalled, but this would mean the United States
would have to hold up proceedings in the UN for three or four days.

On February 20 (1957) Eban arrived in Israel. One of his first
questions to the Prime Minister was what he considered of chief importance in the situation. Ben-Gurion's reply:

"Free passage through Aqaba, which is our link with Asia and Africa."

Finally Eban got Ben-Gurion's agreement to the Dulles-Eban memorandum, on condition that Eban would get from the United States a
firm formulation of the doctrine of free passage; that is, that the United
States would put an oil tanker through the gulf, would encourage other

maritime powers to act and would see that the Egyptians did not return to Gaza.

On February 24 (1957) Eban returned to Washington and went immediately to see Dulles at his home. All the top State Department officials were there. At one point in the consultation Bedell Smith, now an Eisenhower adviser, telephoned Ben-Gurion in Jerusalem and said:

"Give him [Eban] some flexibility so he can work things out."

At the end of several hours Dulles suddenly said:

"I think we have settled it!"

Eban's greatest difficulty had been that his own people in Israel wanted to take their time discussing and debating, while Dulles was pressing him for a definite commitment. He had also been handicapped by the attitude of Hammarskjöld, who, Eban felt, was extremely unhappy that something was being worked out between Israel and the United States, outside the UN. But Eban had already decided it would be hopeless to try to solve the problem through the UN because of the Arab-Afro-Asian majority and what he called Hammarskjöld's "formalism." Even Ralph Bunche had told him:

"If you want to work something out do it in Washington and then bring it back here [to the UN]."

During the next week the formula was finally completed—that Israel would withdraw providing a UN force came in to Sharm el-Sheikh and Gaza, and remained there until there was peace. When Eban went to the home of the Secretary of State to tell him of Israel's agreement, Dulles said:

"You will not regret this."

Then with a smile he added:

"We must celebrate this turn of events," and went to a cabinet and brought out a bottle of French cognac.

"I assure you this is excellent. I received it just a few days ago from Mollet."

Then he poured two generous libations and they raised their glasses to the Israel-American honeymoon they were inaugurating.

"Dulles was very restrained in his social relations," Eban later explained, "but on this occasion he was unusually convivial."

Almost immediately Israel began benefiting from her decision. American economic help was renewed. A delegate from the Import-Export Bank went to Israel. An American tanker anchored in Elath. The U. S.

Government sent notices to shipping companies informing them that the United States maintained the principle of free navigation in Aqaba.

But diplomatic maneuverings of this sort were only part of the ambassador's duty. He had to keep the store open. All the while it was necessary to fulfill the normal social obligations, help with fund raising, be seen at the right places with the right people, accept any important invitation from the communications media and otherwise maintain the public image.

So it was that one evening when his mind surely was on developments at the UN, the White House and the State Department, he had to attend a concert by a fourteen-year-old Israeli virtuoso passing through town. While Suzy appreciated the music he enjoyed an exchange, during intermission, between John Simmons, who had been chief of protocol for the State Department for many years, and his wife, Caroline. Said the husband, after the Israeli boy had played an especially difficult Chopin scherzo:

"One can't play Chopin until one has lived."

To which his wife replied:

"Well, you have lived and you still can't play Chopin!"

At one of the most brilliant social gatherings of the season—a dinner party given by the dean of the diplomatic corps, Norwegian Ambassador and Mrs. Morgenstierne—when someone expressed surprise that Eban wasn't in New York at the UN, he said:

"The more you stay away from there the more you solve problems."

While the situation in the Middle East was still Page One, Horizon Press published *Voice of Israel*, a collection of Eban's public addresses. It was one more device that helped increase his popularity in the English-speaking world.[4] One Israeli newspaper, commenting on the title, called it a little presumptuous for Eban to imply that he was the one and only voice of Israel. But in the United States there was not a discordant note as the daily press, as well as the Jewish weeklies, sang the praises of the author from whom, as one paper put it, "words gushed forth effortlessly, with the power and rhythm of a waterfall."[5] Although books of speeches do not normally sell well—not even those by Winston Churchill—*Voice of Israel* sold thirty thousand copies in the United States alone, plus British and Spanish editions. Eban's favorite review was by Hal Lehrman, who wrote in the New York *Times* that the book of speeches showed the ambassador's "equal facility with the majestic phrase, the mild word and the blunt rejoinder" and that whereas Churchill, with whom he was often compared, was eloquent in one language, Eban was eloquent in at least four. For Eban the only distressing thing about the American reviews was that almost every critic somewhere in his article used the word he was coming to detest: "eloquent."

At the height of the diplomatic crisis the New York *Times* ran a two-column profile entitled "Tough in Six Languages." It was typical of Eban that with all that was occupying his mind at the moment, he went through the one thousand words or more and discovered not an error in fact or figures until he reached the final paragraph. Then he sat down immediately and in longhand addressed the editor of the *Times:*

"May I clarify one point relating to the last paragraph. My daughter, Gila, aged two, is not sensitive about publicity. She feels, however, that her name belongs to a complete description of the Eban family." (The *Times* writer had given the Ebans a son but no daughter.)

Early in March Ambassador Eban left for Florida on his third attempt at a winter vacation. Reporters eagerly asked if this indicated any easing of tension in the Middle East.

"No," he replied, "it only indicates that I am tired and may collapse unless I have a vacation."

While Suzy Eban was waiting for him at the Palm Beach airport she told reporters:

"In four months I have hardly set eyes on him!"

But it was no use. Several days later he had to rush back to Washington to deliver to the Secretary of State a personal message from Ben-Gurion urging the United States to do something to prevent Egypt from moving back into the Gaza Strip. One week later he made his fourth attempt at a vacation and finally did have a few days in tweed jacket, Bermuda shorts, knee socks and walking shoes.

Eban was now known by taxi drivers, waiters, doormen, stenographers and the American public at large much better, oddly, than he was known by his own people, for he had received in the United States weeks of intensive publicity on radio and television, and in newspapers, news-weeklies and magazines. During this same period Israel had been concerned first with mobilization, then with the actual military operations and finally with what was happening in Gaza and down in the Sinai desert. Eban's now famous speech of November 1 had not been carried live and in full by Kol Israel, the government radio network, and Israel had no television. Not more than a few dozen copies of the New York *Times* with its two-column profile ever reached Israel. Eban was still someone thousands of miles away who had never lived in the

State of Israel and who was, as he had so aptly termed himself, merely the "Voice of Israel."

But in the United States reporters were writing about what he ate for breakfast, how many hours of sleep he usually took, where and how he wrote his speeches, who designed his wife's clothes and how he liked to relax. Marguerite Higgins, who was closer to the State Department than any other Washington reporter, wrote that despite the strains of his many-faceted life "one does not recall his ever having lost his temper or being guilty of an indiscretion in his speeches." Editors of Jewish weeklies called on their readers to pray for Eban's health. One pointed out that he had "two tough jobs," to "interpret Israel to cynical nations and translate the cynical nations to Israel."[6]

The months of crisis had a strange effect on Eban's health. Except for golf, which he considered a luxury, the only exercise he normally got was walking, but after his face became so well known to New York television audiences he found he was stopped about six times in every block by people who wanted to say something or ask something, so it was difficult for him to walk any more. Accordingly he gained considerable weight.

In April (1957) Ambassador Eban faced one of the most alert and inquisitive audiences he had ever encountered when he was the guest on the television show "Youth Wants to Know." The first young questioner asked him about a report in a column by Joseph Alsop that the Sixth Fleet was in the eastern Mediterranean because Israel feared an invasion by Jordan. Eban replied he had "great respect and affection for Mr. Joe Alsop but here I say he has fallen on his face," because there were three grave errors in his report.

Another young man wanted to know why, in border clashes, five Arabs were always killed to each dead Israeli. "I am afraid the answer is that we are rather more competent militarily than they are."

Eban called his questioners by their first names and by the end of the program had made a number of youthful friends in the studio and also, perhaps, among the viewers.

At the Biltmore Hotel in New York in May (1957) Eban was scheduled to address the founding assembly of the Independent Zionists of America, organized by the American Jewish League of America. At 12:57 P.M., three minutes before his scheduled arrival, the hotel manager received a phone call. A male voice speaking with a foreign accent said in a low tone:

"Abba Eban . . . you hotel . . . speak . . . Room 108. . . . Get him out or we put bomb in your place."

The nearest police station was called. Three detectives, a captain and eight uniformed patrolmen arrived promptly, followed a few minutes later by Eban, who was taken to an eleventh-floor room while Room 108 was searched. Nothing was found, so the meeting was called to order, with policemen guarding all the doors. So many attended that tables had to be set up in the hallway. While being introduced the ambassador puffed unconcernedly on a large Havana cigar. Policemen remained in the room during his address. Although no bombing materialized, Eban the next day was the target for attacks by certain Zionist groups and individuals, who criticized him for speaking at a meeting of maverick Zionists who had broken away from ZOA.

That summer one of Washington's Jewish country clubs, Woodmont, where Eban played golf whenever diplomacy gave him a chance, added another nine holes to its existing eighteen and as part of the opening ceremonies Eban and Vice-President Nixon played a match. As they started on the eighteenth, the score was even.

"I remember trying not to win that last hole," Eban later recalled, "because after all we had fifty million dollars tied up in the Senate Appropriations Committee and he was Vice-President, but in golf, as in many other things, when you don't strain, everything goes all right. Well, I gave an easy swing and the ball went two hundred and fifty yards right down the middle, landing on the green. On the putt I closed my eyes and when I opened them I saw the ball rolling right into the cup. I had beaten the Vice-President of the United States, 89 to 90."

As they were comparing scores Eban said quietly to Nixon:

"If you and I are ever going to achieve the fullness of world fame, it will have to be for something other than golf."[7]

Some months later Eban was in hot water. He was invited to be a guest, along with his wife and children, on Edward R. Murrow's television program "Person to Person," which would be shot live at the Embassy residence on September 20 (1957). Weeks in advance the rabbi of Ohev Sholom Talmud Torah Congregation gave CBS permission to erect its one-hundred-and-ten-foot tower for microwave relay on the synagogue's property not far from the Eban residence, but almost at the last minute the rabbi withdrew the permission, explaining he now realized that September 20 would be a Friday and his was an Orthodox congregation and religious law forbids work on the Sabbath, which commences at sundown on Friday. Finally a diplomatic compromise was arranged: the equipment would be set up before sundown Friday and no one would touch it until after sundown Saturday.

But the trouble had only begun. An Orthodox Jew in Cincinnati, reading the program listing in his newspaper, wrote condemning Eban for planning to violate the Sabbath by appearing on Friday evening. He saw that his letter received considerable publicity. Eban replied that many rabbis, Orthodox and Conservative, had advised him he would be offending no religious principle. From Cincinnati came the rebuttal that "what you need, sir, is a public relations department that has a little knowledge of the Jewish religion." The complainer said the fact that radio is used in Israel on the Sabbath is "a sin committed in private, but when you come here and do this in front of non-Jewish Jews, this is a sin committed in public and if you know Talmudic law you know the difference." Misrachi-Hapoel Hamisrachi (the Religious Zionists of America) wrote protesting. So did the president of the Union of Orthodox Congregations of America. The Union of Orthodox Rabbis of the United States and Canada sent a telegram of protest. Eban's answer to all of them was:

"Few Jews anywhere can have had an opportunity to spend the Sabbath eve in a manner more appropriate to a reverent dissemination of central Jewish ideals."

On Friday, September 20, the program was seen and heard by many more millions than would have tuned it in except for all the advance publicity. On the air Murrow asked Eli, age seven, if he was lonesome when his father was in Israel or at the UN in New York, to which Eli replied:

"I miss Abba's cigar smoke."

On the air Suzy was asked what she disliked most about the life of a diplomat's wife, and she said:

"You never know what tomorrow will bring."

In the autumn Eban did a series of lectures at the New School in New York. The question period after the first lecture was so lively that a record crowd turned out for the second, during which he made these statements:

About Toynbee: "If a man writes fourteen volumes on history he must be right some of the time."

Advice to would-be diplomats: "Learn many languages, for only thus can men of all nations learn to conceal thoughts. Achieve a passion for mobility. In this age, diplomatic eminence is measured by aeronautic mileage. Approach every international question with an open mind unless you aspire to service in the UN, in which case approach every international question with an open mouth."

About Israel's Arab neighbors: "Their standards do not exactly meet the standards of Jeffersonian democracy."

About Israel's friends: "It is not very encouraging to know that the further people are away from us the more they like us. The first country to recognize Israel was the United States, six thousand miles away. Then Uruguay, eight thousand miles away. Then the Soviet Union and South Africa. Then the orbit narrowed down until the only exceptions to the rule of recognition now are our immediate neighbors."

About patriotism: "There are certain things men call patriotism if they are doing it and chauvinism if they see it in others."

Late in the year (1957) another son of the chief Ashkenazi rabbi of Israel joined Eban's staff when Yacov Herzog, brother of Suzy's brother-in-law, came as Minister of Embassy, after having been head of the American desk in the Foreign Office in Jerusalem for three years.

For the Ebans the first social event of 1958 was a reception following a concert by Isaac Stern, who went directly from Constitution Hall, after enthralling a standing-room-only audience, to the Israeli Embassy, where Stern expounded to Eban, his host, and to Edward G. Robinson, Attorney Ben Cohen, Max Friedman of the Manchester *Guardian*, David Brinkley, Martin Agronsky and half a dozen senators and congressmen who gathered around him a scheme to better Russian-American relations by sending a symphony orchestra of young Americans —all under thirty—on a one-year tour of the Soviet Union. Several members of Congress agreed to support the idea.

In February (1958) with his friend Eliahu Elath, his Washington predecessor and now Israeli Ambassador to the Court of St. James, in the chair, Eban spoke in the Friends' House in London to fifteen hundred admirers who had assembled to celebrate—a little prematurely —Israel's tenth anniversary. After an especially eulogistic introduction he began his address:

"Such praise is like perfume; it's all right if you don't swallow it."

It amused the audience so much that he would repeat it on many future occasions—whenever an introducer used too many superlatives, which would be often.

The passage from the London address that made the most impression:

"Israel has marched across history for three thousand years bearing the message of order and progress in the universal design. Her road rises and falls through deep valleys of grief and high peaks of exaltation but nothing since her first redemption from bondage can compare in the life of this people with the sudden ascent of the past decade."

In an address in the United States several weeks later he said, commenting on how a recession might affect the amount of aid Israel would receive:

"The fact is that when America coughs Israel gets pneumonia."

Tenth-anniversary celebrations began in the United States on November 29 (1957) when those communities which wanted to get the jump on others decided to observe not Independence Day but the tenth anniversary of the passage of the UN Partition plan. In April, 1958, the birthday parties began in earnest. No matter where the idea of an ambassador's ball may have originated, Eban's popularity was such that cities all over the country wanted to have ambassador's balls, and they wanted a live Israeli ambassador as the guest of honor. Suzy went along to many of them and wore out several gowns, one designed by Pauline Trigère and made of hand-woven Israeli fabric. The most important Washington party had as guests Cabinet members, ambassadors, newspaper owners, senators, congressmen, labor leaders, television commentators and others with headline or society-page names.

As part of the tenth-anniversary celebrations the Ebans gave a party at the Embassy for a small group of top-level people, among them Mr. and Mrs. John Foster Dulles. As the dessert was being served the Secretary of State turned to his host and said:

"As I am now on sovereign Israeli territory, I would like to get your permission, Mr. Ambassador, to say a few words."

What he then said remained strictly off the record, but it indicated his friendship—at least that night—for the Ebans and Israel, despite what had been and what might be.

In New York five thousand people streamed into the Polo Grounds to hear Eban, Eleanor Roosevelt, Moshe Dayan, Herbert Lehman and Henry Fonda, to see Melvyn Douglas and Ralph Bellamy and to enjoy the music of Mischa Elman. B'nai B'rith celebrated by giving Eban its President's Medal. At Boston eleven thousand turned out to hear the Israeli ambassador. At Constitution Hall, Washington, Senator John F. Kennedy was on the anniversary program with Eban. Justice Frankfurter shared the platform with him at a dinner in the Waldorf-Astoria, New York. In Philadelphia he had his picture taken with Harry S. Truman and Chief Justice Earl Warren ringing the Liberty Bell ten times. New Orleans had a tenth-anniversary ball, with Moshe W. Denery sharing honors with Eban. At Indian Head Country Club,

Washington, as Eban danced with the film star Carroll Baker some of the thousand people present heard her counting for him, "one, two, one, two, three," as he tried to cha-cha with her.

In Miami Beach he shared the platform with Shelley Winters. Atlanta and several dozen other cities had celebrations at which he was the chief attraction. He crisscrossed the United States innumerable times. He tried to make a different speech on each occasion, this way getting national and even international publicity each time he spoke. Until midsummer the Arabs cooperated nicely, creating no crisis that would keep him in Washington or New York. In June some communities that had not been able to schedule him earlier were still celebrating. Finally, with the trousers of his tuxedo getting shiny, his speeches being repeated and the perfume story now a little overused, he made this confession:

"It is much less strenuous to survive a decade than it is to survive the celebration of it."

There were many anniversary broadcasts. One of the best was an interview on the CBS television network with Mike Wallace, who had recently returned from the Middle East. Early in the quarter hour Wallace waved a red flag in the ambassador's face by quoting a statement of Toynbee, which Eban quickly characterized as "a monstrous blasphemy." About a statement made by Dr. Feid Sayegh, Arab spokesman, that Israel should relinquish 40 percent of her territory Eban said:

"There is nothing more grotesque or eccentric in the international life of our times than the doctrine that little Israel, eight thousand square miles, should become even smaller in order that the vast Arab empire should still further expand." (Later he added a few more adjectives: "sated, fat, huge, lavish.")

During a discussion of whether a man could be a good Jew and be opposed to Zionism and Israel, this exchange took place:

Wallace: But isn't Jewry a religion, sir?

Eban: It is a religion, and it is a peoplehood, and it is a civilization, and it is a faith, and it is a memory. It is a world of thought and of spirit and of action, and it cannot be restrictively defined.

The Washington *Star* of August 3 (1958) carried a small advertisement urging readers not to miss Ambassador Eban on the CBS program "Face the Nation" at 5:30 P.M. that day. The ad was signed "Contributed by an Admirer." After the conclusion of the show the CBS producer accused Eban of having placed the ad himself, to which the ambassador replied:

"Oh no, if I had placed the ad it would have read, 'Contributed by an *Ardent* Admirer.'"

The Ebans expected to have a quiet summer vacationing in Israel, but Gamal Abdel Nasser interfered. Due to his various machinations it appeared that before the year was over he might control the entire Middle East except for the eight thousand square miles called Israel. He had already swallowed Syria by incorporating it into his United Arab Republic. (As Eban put it, "Syria is united with Egypt rather in the manner that our Prophet Jonah was united with the whale . . . an uncomfortable gastronomic confinement. . . ."[8]) Jordan tried to maintain its independence from Nasser by joining with Iraq in another loose federation, but rebellious army officers in Bagdad overthrew the monarchy, killed the king and cut away from Jordan. Hussein promptly appealed to the British for military assistance. Nasser supporters in Lebanon rebelled against their pro-Washington government and President Chamoun asked the United States for help. Five thousand American troops were expressed to Lebanon, two thousand British paratroopers to Jordan. Then the diplomatic fidoodlings began, first in the Security Council, then in the General Assembly. It was a hot summer, temperately and diplomatically.

Ten Arab states sponsored a resolution calling on the world to respect the political and territorial integrity of all states in the area. Eban cabled for instructions as to how his government wanted him to vote. After all it was an Arab resolution and in a way was aimed against Britain and America. When no reply came he tried to put through a telephone call to Jerusalem, but there were unexplained delays, so he went to the president of the General Assembly, New Zealand's Sir Leslie Munro, and asked to have his name put last on the list of speakers. Sir Leslie said there would probably be a recess and then a night session, giving Eban a few more hours in which to receive his call. At 6 P.M., as the Israeli delegation members were in the delegates' lounge still waiting to hear from Jerusalem, a messenger from Sir Leslie appeared and whispered in Eban's ear:

"All who wish to speak have already spoken and unless you take the floor immediately there will be no opportunity for you to be heard, because some of the Assembly members are impatiently pressing for a vote."

Eban was forced to make a quick decision. As he walked through the doors of the Assembly hall Sir Leslie announced that Israel would now be recognized. He thereupon made one of the shortest speeches of his life, announcing that Israel would support the resolution because it guaranteed the political and territorial integrity of *all* the states of the Middle East.

The vote was unanimous. Unwittingly, the Arabs had bound the UN to a course guaranteeing the integrity of Israel as well as the Arab countries.

During this summer crisis Eban kept in close touch with Dulles, who informed him at the start there was a serious conflict in the State Department between the interventionists and "the more careful guys," and he asked Eban to urge his friends in the Senate to let President Eisenhower know that they supported intervention.

Late in August (1958) Dulles sent Eban a letter in which he finally agreed with the Israeli ambassador on the nature and character of Nasserism as a subversive force seeking to set aside the sovereignty of other states and not just a legitimate nationalism confining its activities to its own territory. He also sent Eban a memorandum for Ben-Gurion which suggested that Israel should view what the United States had done for Lebanon as an example of what she would do for Israel if Israel were attacked and asked for help under Article 51 of the Charter. Eban, aware of the intricacies of American politics, suggested to Dulles that presidential power being what it is, it would be well to get something from Eisenhower in writing. Dulles agreed and he was able to get the President to write that what he had done for Lebanon was what the United States would do for Israel if she were threatened and asked for help.

When Dulles went to the hospital again, early in 1959—it was now no secret that his illness was terminal—Eban felt that despite all the vicissitudes, his relationship with the Secretary of State had ended on a harmonious note. During the six years Dulles had been Secretary, Eban had made a practice of having almost monthly meetings with him and a personal relationship had developed that became decisive. The drastic changes that some Israelis had expected in relations between Jerusalem and a Republican administration in Washington had not occurred. Instead, a bipartisan tradition had been established. There was agreement—at least for this brief moment in history—between little Israel and the powerful United States on a broad political and economic level. It was what Eban called "both an intellectual and almost sentimental harmony."[9]

After the death of Dulles Eban gave this analysis:

"His talks with me were always personally sympathetic and intellectually rewarding. As you look back now, it is obvious that his mind was moving in our direction, but always a little behind the current of events and that he reached favorable decisions at a time when history had passed them by."[10]

Meyer W. Weisgal had various titles at various times with the Weizmann Institute, but more than any one man, even more than Dr. Weizmann himself, he was the one who had been responsible for the growth of the Institute into one of the world's great scientific centers. He and Eban had known each other for years. Their Jewishness was about all they had in common, yet they were good friends. Weisgal was twenty-one years older, born in Poland, son of a cantor, brought up in the Bronx, unpolished, with a vocabulary akin to that of a sailor. His principal task was acquiring money to enable the Institute to function and to expand. In doing so he had raised begging to a fine art—the fine art of Schnorrology.[11] He once said: "I don't raise money. I sell immortality. Every man wants to leave part of himself here on earth. I merely make it possible for him to do so." Since the death of Dr. Weizmann the presidency of the Institute had remained vacant, putting much additional work on Weisgal's shoulders.

Weisgal was among the guests at a dinner in New York late in 1957 at which Eban was the principal speaker and Henry Cabot Lodge, Jr., U. S. Ambassador to the UN, the guest of honor. Eban's address was masterly, for he praised Ambassador Lodge, yet between the lines, subtly, managed to let the entire large audience—Lodge included—know what he thought of the policies of Lodge's Government.

Suzy had come up from Washington with her husband and they had a suite at the Plaza. There, after the dinner, they were relaxing when the door burst open and Weisgal came crashing in.

"Aubrey, you're a genius! I want to make you president of Weizmann Institute."

Aubrey and Suzy stared at him, wondering whether they had heard correctly. Weisgal then pulled Eban down on the couch and began his campaign to convince him he should accept. It would not be necessary for him to devote his full time to the job; he, Weisgal, would handle the executive work. The Institute presidency would not stand in the way of Eban's political career. He could become Foreign Minister, Prime Minister, anything he chose, but like Weizmann had done he would lend his name to the Institute. He would be like the chancellor of a British university, who is a public figure without any administrative duties.

Before Weisgal left they worked out a code. There would be an important affair at Rehovoth on November 2 of 1958, a memorial for Dr. Weizmann. He hereby extended Eban an invitation to be the speaker. If and when Eban sent a cable agreeing to speak, that would also signify his acceptance of the presidency.

Suzy and Aubrey got little sleep that night. At first she was against it. Their debate went something like this, as they later remembered it:

Suzy: I think the president of a scientific institution ought to be a scientist.

Eban: But wouldn't it be a good idea to remind the world the Institute has a political mission, too, by having a political figure as president?

Suzy: But would you be happy running such an institution?

Eban: Meyer would do the running. Besides, there's also a scientific director.[12]

The last few months of 1958 were busy for Eban.

Foreign Minister Golda Meir came to America. The list of guests at the formal dinner party given for her at the Embassy was indicative of the standing her small country had in the capital of America: Chief Justice Earl Warren, Associate Justice Felix Frankfurter, Attorney General William P. Rogers, Undersecretary of State Christian A. Herter, who before long would succeed Dulles, and a bevy of important senators and congressmen.

Shortly after Eban sent a cable to Rehovoth accepting the invitation to speak at the Weizmann memorial in November it was announced that he had been elected the Institute's president. (The code had worked.) By mutual agreement he would receive no salary.

Late in October Eban flew to London, where he delivered two addresses before going on to Israel. One, entitled "Tide of Nationalism," later published as a small book, was the third Herbert Louis Samuel memorial lecture. He began:

"Twenty-two years ago it was my duty to confront Lord Samuel in a debate at the Cambridge Union. . . . I felt much like Daniel in the lions' den, except that my renowned ancestor was not alone and he could rely in his ordeal on divine salvation, which I invoked vainly in my cause." (Modestly, Eban did not mention that his own side won the debate.)

Speaking of Lord Samuel's qualifications as "the ideal philosopher-statesman," Eban said:

"Plato laid down rigid standards of scholarship and integrity as qualifications for political leadership. If these standards were rigorously applied today many governments, alas, might become seriously depleted."

The quotation was significant in view of the decision Eban himself was soon to make about his own political future.

In two addresses late in the year, the forthcoming Weizmann president discussed science. To the General Assembly he declared:

"The present nuclear peril is not the result of scientific success but of diplomatic failure."

At the Weizmann memorial he concluded a brilliant address:

"The harmony between statesmanship and science is destined to be the ladder by which Israel can ascend to its full potential stature."

The year (1958) ended as it began—with crisis.

Starting on the night of December 3, Syrian artillery began an intermittent but nerve-racking bombardment of Israeli agricultural villages in the Lake Huleh region. After five days and nights of it, Eban went before the Security Council and declared that his country considered the bombardment "an act of war" and warned that if it did not stop it would lead to "drastic and exhaustive retaliation."

It finally did stop.

21

End of a Journey

AFTER MONTHS OF RUMOR, denials and vigorous speculation, it was finally announced officially on the night of February 22 (1959) that Abba Eban was resigning as both ambassador to Washington and head of the Israeli delegation to the United Nations and would return home to run for the Knesset in the fall election.

During the eleven years he had been in the United States helping to mold global history, the Eban diplomatic career had developed a personality distinction all its own.

Since the Second World War the foreign service of most countries had become a bloodless bureaucratic institution, staffed largely by nameless men. Colorless envoys, appointed as a reward for political or financial kindnesses, were content to rest on any laurels they may have previously won. Those appointed from the ranks served as dutiful errand boys. There had been a drastic decline in ambassadorial status. An ambassador plenipotentiary was no longer very plenipotential.

There was now almost instant communication between capitals on opposite sides of the globe. A Prime Minister or Foreign Minister could fly from Bagdad, Damascus, Jerusalem or Dar es Salaam to Washington in less time than it once took to exchange messages back and forth. Work decisions were now being made by heads of government, leaving their diplomats scattered around the world little to do except serve as obedient mouthpieces.

Although there were hundreds of ambassadors in Washington and in New York attached to the UN, the average well-read citizen of Denver, Des Moines or Dubuque probably could not have named or identified even two or three of them if his soul's fate had depended upon it. Yet Eban was as well known across the country as a Hollywood actor, a baseball star or a fugitive gangster. Millions of Americans were aware of his name, recognized his voice and knew about Israel because of him. In the UN he had a special place in the spotlight because he was involved in a polemic that was constant, spectacular and fascinating. If Israel's affairs had been as complacent and her international problems as simple as Norway's, for example, it would not have been easy for him or any other permanent representative of Israel in the UN to have made himself a national figure in the United States and an international personality in the eyes of the world. Circumstances created the opportunity. But history is made only when such an opportunity is seized by an ambitious and able man. Eban was both. The delegates of all the Arab countries had the same opportunity, for the spotlight was focused on them, too; they were involved in all the same controversies. Yet in those eleven years not a single Arab had established a reputation comparable to Eban's.

In reviewing *Voice of Israel* a critic of the London *Times* put Eban in the category with Venizelos of Greece, Masaryk and Benes of Czechoslovakia and Titulescu of Romania—representatives of small countries whose international resonance reached far beyond what their own countries' weight would seem to command.[1]

Eban's achievement in New York was more impressive because the UN in the 1950s was smaller in size but of much higher human quality than in the 1960s and 1970s. In the General Assembly masterful speeches were made in the 1950s by Schuman of France, Bevin of England, Spaak of Belgium, Pearson of Canada, Lange of Norway, Unden of Sweden and Acheson of the United States. Their successors seldom equaled them. For Eban to stand out against such a competitive background was a notable accomplishment.

It is the custom in the general debate which commences each General Assembly session for a Foreign Minister or even a Prime Minister to speak for his country. While Sharett was Foreign Minister he often let Eban deliver the general debate address and would go to New York only for some crisis. When he was Prime Minister he never went to New York at all, although he was also serving as Foreign Minister.

Because the fate of Israel often rested in UN hands, the country's representative to the international organization played a greater role in her destiny than any one of her other forty or fifty ambassadors. Many Israelis were aware of this, especially those connected with the government, and so whenever Eban returned home he was met at the airport by a large contingent of the press, was invited to address public meetings and was consulted about policy, and this was not entirely displeasing to him because he had good political instincts, which was fortunate, for although he was a career diplomat his peculiar position required him to be also a political figure.

When he was given the Washington post at the age of thirty-five his own prestige as well as that of Israel increased considerably. In the dual capacity Eban advanced his country's cause with wisdom and dignity, and also enhanced the standing of the diplomatic profession in general. Knowing that colorfulness can be overdone—especially under prompting by press, radio and television—he showed just the correct amount of reserve. He ignited the imagination, raised the sights and gave expression to the spiritual and aesthetic longings of the multitudes of Americans who listened to him, for he had the grand concept of man's destiny and a passionate belief in the nobler aspirations of the human race, which he knew how to express.

He challenged the often malicious portrait of the Jew as a prayerful but cringing creature of the Eastern European ghetto. His own language, demeanor and diplomatic adroitness served notice on the world that here was a new and different Jew, capable of asserting with vitality, devastating logic and oratorical splendor the rights of his own people to the same life, liberty and pursuit of happiness enjoyed by others.

In these eleven years he had established an amazing rapport with the American Jewish community—amazing because he was so different from any of them. He was not a good mixer. He learned none of the techniques of the American politician: back-slapping, first-name-calling, hail-fellow-well-metishness. He remained shy, diffident, even aloof. He spoke, wrote and understood many languages well, but not Yiddish, the second language of most American Jews. They had come from Eastern Europe; he was a Western Jew. He had the accent and many of the characteristics of a snobbish Englishman, which Americans do not especially like. Yet they were delighted with him, proud of him and heaped upon him honors, invitations, gifts, mementos. He fitted the image they had of a gentleman of distinction—competent, impeccable, dignified, cultured, commanding, articulate. Here was a Jew who spoke English like Winston Churchill and French like Charles de Gaulle, who could stand up to any American Secretary of State in debate, was at ease with Einstein and apparently didn't know what it was to be humiliated. No wonder American Jewry had taken to him as to no other Jew who ever came from abroad, not even Ben-Gurion or Weizmann.

But it was not only the Jews of America who respected and honored him. The intellectual community in the United States found him stimulating, provocative and challenging. Here was a man who was attempting to elevate politics, dared speak with a vocabulary of more than six hundred words and was not ashamed he had been to Cambridge. It was no wonder he was given more than a dozen honorary degrees by American colleges and universities, and had repute among men of letters, as well as men of high principle.

His political and diplomatic accomplishments had been great. Defensively, he had stood off the Arabs, the Communists and their sporadic allies. Despite belligerency, boycotts, blockades and a certain amount of blatant bamboozling, Israel still survived, relatively secure within her armistice frontiers. No one had forced her to cede any land, take in any refugees or give up Jerusalem as her capital city—all objectives of the opposition. Much economic aid had been obtained, while support in the United States had been put on a permanent bipartisan basis. There had been a few tempests but the tree had not been blown down.

The official announcement of his retirement was made by the first U.S. ambassador to Israel, James G. McDonald, at a dinner in Washington's Mayflower Hotel celebrating Eban's forty-fourth birthday. The ambassador himself had several explanations. He said he felt he needed "new contact with both the spirit and the realities of his own people."[2] Although he denied it at the time the truth was that Ben-Gurion had summoned him home. His party, Mapai, was in trouble. To retain its hold on the country it needed an injection of new blood. Fortunately Ben-Gurion could turn to Moshe Dayan, who was as close to a military hero as Israel had yet produced, and Abba Eban, the first and only really distinguished diplomat to come out of modern Israel. Both were "invited" by Ben-Gurion to run on the Mapai ticket, but it was really a command, for Ben-Gurion was not just the Prime Minister but also the undisputed leader of the country and the political boss of the Socialist Labor party. The plum that Ben-Gurion dangled before Eban's eyes was the post of Foreign Minister. When Golda Meir retired Eban would be the logical successor. Ben-Gurion asked both Dayan and Eban to take part in the coming political campaign and help Mapai roll up a sizable vote.

Abba Eban by now was politically ambitious. He had been the "voice" for eleven years, most of the time carrying out policies formulated by others, even though he often considered those policies ill-conceived.

Now he felt he had the experience and political wisdom to do some of the decision making himself.

The first non-Jewish reaction in the United States was one of surprise. Why would a man of his stature, who had achieved such distinction, even consider descending into the muck of the political arena? In the United States the process is generally the reverse: when the politician becomes successful enough and has achieved all the elective goals possible, he then wants to become an ambassador. One Washington correspondent figured the decision resulted from Eban having lived so long in the American capital, where politics are contagious. Some soothsayers deplored the move, pointing out that Eban was a diplomatic sophisticate but a political novice, well experienced in the niceties of the international game, but unaccustomed to the rough-and-tumble of domestic vote getting, and so they feared for him. His great handicap would be that he had never had time to build up a political following at home. This was to his credit, for what had been important to him during these last eleven years had been fighting Israel's diplomatic battles in Washington and New York, not in spending time, energy and thought on his personal future.

Ben-Gurion launched Eban on his political career with a six-hundred-word letter accepting his resignation from the diplomatic corps. It was a eulogy such as few men get while still alive, especially from a man like Ben-Gurion, who was not known for hyperbole.

"As the representative of a young and a small country you were sent to the capital of the greatest power in the new world. You immediately evoked a rare degree of attention and respect from the leaders, representatives and thinkers of that great country. With remarkable skill and a unique grace of exposition you won the hearts of your listeners in all regions and amongst all groups in America. You succeeded in explaining to American public opinion the intricate and controversial problems surrounding our ancient people as it restores its national life in its original home. . . . Your appearances in the General Assembly and Security Council brought honor to your country and pride to all your people. . . .

"Our international situation continues to improve and you have no small part in this achievement. . . . I am, however, confident that the destiny of Israel with which the historic mission of the Jewish people is intimately intertwined will be determined primarily by what is done in Israel. It is in that spirit that I welcome you home. . . ."

It was exactly three months from the resignation announcement until the Ebans sailed away. They were months crowded with activity. Every major city in the United States wanted to have a farewell party for him. Just as during the early days of the state everything that happened was for "the first time in two thousand years," so this Eban departure was unique. Never had a Jew in the history of the United States received such nationwide acclaim, a testimonial not only to Eban's personal prowess but to the uniqueness of his role in American life.

It was to be expected that the editors of papers like the New York *Times* and the Washington *Post,* having watched him at close range for so long, would write of the impact he had made on the national scene. But the outpouring of tributes came from such unexpected sources as the *Daily Tribune* of Royal Oak, Michigan, the *Mining Journal* of Marquette, Michigan, the *American* of Austin, Texas, the *Press* of Middletown, Connecticut, the *Call* of Allentown, Pennsylvania, the *Press* of Sheboygan, Wisconsin—papers in communities with relatively few Jewish residents. Would even the mayor of San Antonio, Texas, know the name of the British ambassador in Washington? And yet the *Light* of San Antonio (where only 1 percent of the population is Jewish) published an editorial bidding farewell to the Ebans.

The final Eban trip back and forth across America was like the farewell tour of an opera star. There were lunches, banquets, balls, mass meetings. In Detroit he told the farewell audience:

"Peacemakers are not needed in the troubled Middle East. Peace grows out of long periods of tranquillity instead of negotiations between nations or public debate."

In Denver he said it would be "the Arabs' most spectacular achievement if they were to maintain their hostility toward Israel for another ten years." (Unfortunately ten years later the hostility was not only still there but greatly intensified.)

He went back to Chicago many times during the three months. On one occasion Maurice Chevalier was on the program with him and they became good friends—in French. On his next visit Senator Paul Douglas told an audience of six thousand that Eban was the most powerful and moving orator in modern public life. After the meeting he was interviewed on an open-end television program which continued as long as incoming calls proved the man being interviewed still had an audience. Eban set a record. He stayed at the microphone until 3 A.M. and even then there were still calls coming in. Later that morning Adlai Stevenson called on him, first to express surprise that anyone would resign as an ambassador to become a politician, and then to discuss Middle Eastern affairs.

When Eban was in Chicago again in April he and King Hussein came close to meeting face to face. They landed at Midway Airport thirty minutes apart. Their hotels—the Drake and Ambassador East—were not far apart. On the way back to the airport Hussein's cavalcade and Eban's limousine met at a traffic light. Hussein was surrounded by policemen; Eban by friends.

Speaking in Louisville he revealed a little-known fact—that two years earlier he had been made a Kentucky colonel by Governor Chandler. This time the governor told Eban what he most needed was "a key to the voting machine, to help remove from your election democracy's only disadvantage—doubt."

In Philadelphia he was made an honorary citizen and was told that since William Penn founded the city only four foreign personalities had ever received this honor.

In Rochester, New York, commenting on the fact that Nasser had "opened the Middle East to Communism and now was screaming at his own Communists," Eban said it reminded him "of the man who cries 'Thief! Thief!' while the missing watch is in his own pocket."

In St. Louis he was given a gold volume of honor. In Miami there were sixty-five people at the speakers' table and all were introduced.

In Tucson the ambassador was slightly annoyed when the local press referred to his "*Oxford* accent." In Hollywood both Ebans had an interesting time talking to Peter Ustinov, Laurence Olivier, Charles Laughton and Kirk Douglas on the set of *Spartacus,* in which they were all appearing. Jesse Lurie, writing in the Jerusalem *Post* from New York, said:

"He has an Ambassador's Ball in Miami Beach Saturday night, a UJA farewell dinner in Atlanta Sunday, followed by a press conference and lunch with the mayor and other civic dignitaries at Atlanta's most exclusive club and is then going to Albany, where Nelson Rockefeller has invited him to address the Council for Foreign Relations and if that sentence leaves you a bit breathless imagine how Eban feels!"

The most interesting of the many New York farewells was a United Nations dinner, with U Thant as one of the speakers. One nation which had helped bring about the creation of Israel and had helped get her admitted to the UN—the Soviet Union—stayed away. Another nation which had fought Israel all along the line—Britain—was represented by its ambassador, who paid Eban one of the most uninhibited compliments of the evening. Present were the ambassadors of fifty nations, as well as university presidents, editors and other distinguished persons. It was the first kosher dinner ever served in the UN dining room. Eleanor Roosevelt in her tribute said:

"It is wonderful to be young today . . . and to have your ability and already so much experience and now to have a new opportunity to go to a country which, although small, has had such an impact on so many nations."

Former Governor Thomas Dewey said:

"During your service here there have been crises when only greatness could stand up among the swirling currents. You stood up."

When Eban himself finally got to his feet he said with a smile that in the coming election campaign in Israel "my qualities will probably be discussed with less balance and judicial objectivity than they have been discussed here this evening."

At a Festival of Freedom in Madison Square Garden eighteen thousand people bade him farewell. General Yigael Yadin read Ben-Gurion's moving eulogy. Eban began his own address:

"I have come to the end of a journey which began eleven years ago when I first came to Washington bearing letters of credence from President Weizmann to the President of the United States, empowering me to work for the development of friendly relations between the greatest and the smallest of the world's democracies."

The next day in Washington the National Testimonial Committee for Ambassador Eban, headed by the Vice-President, the Chief Justice, two ex-Presidents and assorted governors, senators, congressmen and judges, held an Independence Day dinner. At a farewell dinner given by Lyndon B. Johnson, the Senate majority leader made such a eulogistic speech that Eban responded:

"As a pure-minded diplomat, I used to disassociate myself from such praise, but now as a political aspirant I cannot afford to regard such praise of myself as excessive."

It was nothing new for him, when eulogized, to combine blushing diffidence and modest disassociation with not-always-hidden flashes of self-satisfaction and agreement. He often spoke of the "ordeal of eulogy" and complained to one reporter that "I am now being wafted wearily across the continent on a torrent of praise," but he secretly relished it, thrived on it and would have been sorely disappointed had there been any less of it.

At one of the Washington farewells Eartha Kitt, who sings in nine languages, included in her program some of Eban's favorite songs, several of which she sang in what the ambassador declared to be faultless Hebrew. Because of doctor's orders she reserved her pear-shaped tones for on-stage use, keeping her conversation to a whisper, which was so contagious that the Ebans and everyone else at the head table were soon whispering, too.

The only embarrassment of the entire three months was when two identical and very expensive evening gowns met under the weeping cherry blossom trees surrounding the swimming pool at the Nicaraguan Embassy—white faille strapless dresses with flared skirts, topped with a broad band of beige and brown pansies and tied with an obi bow. One was being worn by the wife of a prominent Washington attorney, Harold Baker, the other by Suzy Eban. Instead of going home in tears the two women graciously consented to being photographed back to back, then explained they had purchased their gowns in two different shops in New York. The photographs got wide national circulation in papers and magazines—more publicity for Israel, albeit of an unusual sort.

The last week the State Department gave an official farewell luncheon at Blair House, where visiting kings and presidents are housed, with William Rountree, Assistant Secretary of State for the Middle East, as host. That night Justice Frankfurter entertained for the Ebans.

At the final party—cocktails in the Embassy garden—Herter planted a kiss on Suzy Eban's cheek, Justice Warren dropped in for a few minutes to say good-bye, congressmen and senators came by the score. Also judges, State Department people, a baroness or two, columnists, commentators and other ambassadors.

Then there was a "Meet the Press" appearance on television and a last talk at the Overseas Press Club. In the longest appearance he ever made on television, he discussed the Middle East with David Susskind. It was a compliment that Susskind, who normally had two, three or even four guests, invited no one else this evening but Eban. It was good judgment, for the ambassador kept the dialogue lively and brilliant for more than an hour. Some of the exchanges:

Susskind: How much of an irreconcilable conflict exists between the Arabs and Israel?

Eban: I don't believe in the existence of irreconcilable conflicts. . . .

Susskind: Would you like to don the toga of prophet and predict . . .

Eban: I come from a people which has had many prophets in its history. Nearly all of them got into serious trouble.

Susskind: Do I tread on tender diplomatic feet if I ask you . . .

Eban: You need not worry, Mr. Susskind. There's no such thing as an indiscreet question. There are only indiscreet answers.

Susskind: In your personal life . . . are you able to salvage hours for your own reading, for your family?

Eban: I do not know what I would have done in that respect but for those long airplane journeys which enable me to read and conduct my private correspondence.

Susskind: What about English as a language of communication compared to the other languages that you've mastered?

Eban: In Hebrew and English I feel myself in command of the inner sources of language. . . . I don't feel that I have thoughts which go beyond my capacity of expressing them and they are two languages which are not as far apart as you would think . . . because the great masters of English literature were people nurtured on the Hebrew Bible in its English translation and if you take a writer such as Milton or the prose orators and writers all the way up to Edmund Burke and beyond, you find the biblical rhythms very strong in their style.

Susskind: Is individual forensics availing? Is it persuasive?

Eban: There are possibilities of impact.

Susskind: What would be some of the frustrations inherent in the UN?

Eban: There is the length of the speeches . . . there is the acrimony in discussion, there is the constant discussion of issues which never seem to be solved by discussion, the repetitiveness. You sometimes have the feeling that certain speeches make tensions more tense than they were . . . all that is overwhelmingly counterbalanced by the sheer indispensability of this bridge upon which all nations meet in sovereign equality to explain their views to each other. . . .

Susskind: Are there aspects of the American scene that give you pause, that give you concern? Does that strain diplomatic discretion?

Eban: Well, if there were I wouldn't mention them here because I understand that we're not alone.

Susskind: You have been inflicted with the scourge of rock and roll in Jerusalem?

Eban: I must say I've come into too little contact with it myself to express an opinion.

Susskind: You are an extremely fortunate man.

Eban: In the diplomatic corps there's very little rocking and rolling.[3]

One other little task he performed during the final breathless weeks was to make a number of recordings for Spoken Arts, an organization pro-

17. The Israeli-USSR honeymoon was still on. Stalin had not yet been de-stalinized. A thousand guests at the Soviet Embassy were celebrating the anniversary of the Bolshevik Revolution. Vodka and good will flowed freely. The Soviet Ambassador was friendly. The UAR Ambassador and his wife tried to outstay the Ebans.

18. Three weeks before the start of the Six-Day war, Eban and his wife tour the northern frontier with Colonel Dan Laner.

19. After Eban sliced a 150-yard drive into the rough ("I was below my usual form!") and Sam Snead won the inaugural tournament, the two golfers discussed the opening of Israel's first course (given by the Rothschild family) with Mrs. James de Rothschild.

20. The seven-foot sailfish Suzy caught—and for which her husband got all the newspaper credit. ("See what an asset I am to you!")

21. "He [Eisenhower] had the gift of being extremely articulate without being coherent. . . . His thoughts were ahead of his capacity of expression." (At right, Foreign Minister Moshe Sharett.)

22. Senator Lyndon B. Johnson, then Majority Leader, to Abba Eban, then Ambassador to the United States: "Are those fellows dealing properly with you? . . . they're not going to get a goddamn thing here [in Congress] until they do."

23. Foreign Minster Eban, former Prime Minister Ben-Gurion and Ben Nathan, Israeli Ambassador to Bonn, attend the funeral of Konrad Adenauer, April, 1967.

24. Pope Paul VI and Foreign Minister Eban discuss Jerusalem and the Holy Land—the first private audience His Holiness had ever granted an Israeli cabinet member.

25. Different in race, religion, nationality and sometimes points of view, Eban and Ralph Bunche, first Negro to win the Nobel Peace Prize, were always good friends.

26. Secretary of State Dean Acheson and Ambassador Eban sign a treaty of Friendship and Navigation, Washington, 1951.

27. Mother Alida and daughter-in-law Suzy, in the Eban home in Rehovoth, Israel. The photograph on the bookcase is of Adlai Stevenson, with whom Abba Eban had a close intellectual relationship.

28. As Israel's Foreign Minister, Abba Eban (accompanied by Ambassador to Poland Dov Satat) tours the desolate grounds at Auschwitz.

29. Dr. Gunnar Jarring, United Nations peacemaker, listens as Eban explains Israel's intense desire for peace—but not at any price.

30. The start of a new era. The Foreign Minister of the Jewish state calmly discusses the political future with Willy Brandt, leader of a country which less than a third of a century ago had sought the extermination of the Jewish people.

ducing records of famous people speaking famous words. Eban recorded Psalms 8, 19, 23, 24, 31, 90 and 148 and Chapters 1, 3, 6 and 8 of Ecclesiastes, all proceeds to go for the establishment of a chair of American drama and literature at Hebrew University, Jerusalem.

During Eban's few remaining days he helped pack souvenirs and mementos. Also his grandfather's precious black Talmud. As he did he figured out that in this momentous decade he had visited thirty-nine of the fifty states, traveled two million miles (including numerous trips to and from Israel) and had fulfilled more than a thousand engagements at radio and television stations, banquets, luncheons and rallies.

Someone else figured that his longevity had been unusual. He was the only Middle Eastern ambassador left who had been in Washington a year ago. In this past year thirty-four ambassadors had been replaced. Few who had come to say good-bye had been in Washington nine years ago to say hello.

Halfway through this farewell tour he had been shocked when he saw himself on television, so he stopped eating bread, butter and desserts and managed to drop from 210 to 193. His announced objective of the tour had been "sheer survival."

As the Ebans were packing, the United States Government decided to reverse its earlier decision and restore direct grant aid to Israel. This year Israel would get seven and a half million dollars, the same amount she had received the previous year. It was a great political windfall for a man about to run for public office.

On Friday, May 22 (1959), Abba, Suzy, Eli and Gila Eban, along with one thousand six hundred and ninety-one other passengers, left Pier 86 on the Hudson River, New York, aboard the SS *United States*, for a brief visit with the London Ebans before going on to Switzerland for a month's recuperation and then to Israel.

When a ship reporter asked the ambassador if he was going to miss his barnstorming around America he replied:

"One thing about Israel. It's so small a country that I will always be able to get home at night."

During the Ebans' visit in London Alida Eban asked her son about a head that had been done of him by an Israeli sculptor, Hebroni, a German Jew who had emigrated to the Palestinian city of Hebron, from which he took his name. He happened to be in Paris in 1951 when the General Assembly met there and had persuaded Eban to sit for him. Aubrey admitted he had left the piece of sculpture behind in the Embassy in Washington.

Some months later Alida Eban went to America to visit her daughter Carmel and made a trip to Washington for one express purpose. As she told the story:

"I found out that the Israeli Embassy did not have a museum for the heads of ex-ambassadors. I asked them, 'Have you got my son's head?' So they brought it up from some place or other and I said, 'Surely the new ambassador won't want the head of his predecessor around, so I'll just take it with me.' I thought I would put it in my pocket, but it turned out to be quite large, so they had to have it crated. When I got to London the customs man said, 'What's in that box?' I answered, 'The head of my son.' He got very angry because they thought I was lying, so they opened the box and when they did . . . of course they found the head of my son."

22

Statesman Turns Politician

IN LONDON on the way home Abba Eban had a slight taste of what it was going to be like, now that he was a politician instead of a diplomat.[1]

After he had appeared on a BBC program called "Israel Rises," the radio-television critic of the London *Jewish Chronicle* wrote this caustic comment:

"Mr. Abba Eban in particular was guilty of speaking over the heads of his viewers. Outstanding as an orator, he was equally at home before the television cameras, but here he was not speaking to the world's diplomats and his fluency, precision and logic could have little impact on an audience nurtured on 'Cheyenne' and 'Wagon Train.'"[2]

In the same issue the *Chronicle* ran a letter from a reader who took Eban to task for his praise of Dulles. The letter writer said Dulles had directed American foreign policy for years during which the United States gave "much aid and encouragement to Nasser."

While in New York and Washington Eban had grown accustomed to adulation. Rarely had he been subjected to criticism. But now that he was embarking on a political career he would have to get inured to attack or suffer excruciatingly. Still, it was consoling that there would continue to be occasions like a dinner given for him by the Weizmann Institute Foundation of Britain at the Dorchester Hotel, at which he was loudly applauded by a large and distinguished audience when, in a brilliant address, he said "statesmen must be rescued from their scientific illiteracy and must seek to understand the forces that shape their world," just as "scientists must seek to shake off their political antagonism and accept responsibility for a world whose destiny is determined in their laboratories." Although he did not say so, it was clear that he was explaining what he saw his task to be as president of the Institute.

It was 1 A.M. on a hot July night when the Ebans reached Lod Airport in Israel, yet they were given a welcome such as they had never before experienced. The entire leadership of Mapai was there and a large contingent of reporters, photographers and broadcasters, who bombarded them with questions, personal and political. On the way back to their Tel Aviv newsrooms, this conversation took place between two of the journalists:

First Journalist: The politicians have a bull on their hands now.

Second Journalist: He's going to disturb a lot of complacencies.

First Journalist: The question is: Will Israel welcome modern ideas from the outside world? If so, Eban can be an exciting influence.

Second Journalist: He'll be a great asset to Mapai, if they'll only listen to him.[3]

From the airport they went to Rehovoth, fifteen miles south of Tel Aviv. The house that had been made ready for them was on the handsomely landscaped grounds of the Institute, in a setting of date palms, purple flowering jacaranda, flame trees and garden walks perfumed by roses and carnations. Most of the two dozen buildings on the two-hundred-acre campus were garlanded with crimson and scarlet bougainvillaea.

"And to think that only twenty years ago this was all sand dunes!" Suzy exclaimed.

As Weisgal took them around he gave them a few statistics: The Institute had a staff of twelve hundred, of whom two hundred were scientists working on four hundred projects. Their salaries averaged seventy-five hundred dollars a year. Many had turned down offers of three or four times that amount from scientific institutions in other countries. The Institute library already contained seventy thousand volumes.

Eli and Gila had been left behind in London. They would come with a British nursemaid after their parents were well settled. Writing to Alida, Suzy said:

"At last we are in our own country and our own home. The house is beautiful beyond all expectations. Especially will the children love their charming and very comfortable room. I can hardly wait to hear their voices and see them in the delightful garden and all the little neighbors waiting for them. We are happy and excited. . . . It all seems so logical. We had a terrific welcome at the airport with speeches and cameras and flowers. The Institute and Meyer [Weisgal] have put themselves out most warmly and generously. . . . I feel for the first time that we can really live like a family and it moves me very deeply."[4]

Early in July (1959), just a few days after their arrival in Rehovoth, the inauguration of Abba Eban as president of Weizmann Institute took place before two thousand members of the Government and diplomatic corps, representatives of national and public institutions and the general public. Ben-Gurion (the only one on the platform without a necktie) congratulated the Institute on "its wise choice" and called Eban "the most distinguished emissary of the Jewish people in our generation." Mrs. Weizmann sent greetings from France, saying she knew Eban would be "a worthy heir to my husband's spiritual, moral and intellectual values."

In his inaugural address President Eban discussed the role of science in the future of Israel, but the headlines the next day were based on his announcement that much of his energy during the year would be devoted to planning the first international conference, late in 1960, to which leading scientists, economists and political thinkers from every part of the world would be invited to "explore the capacity of science, to advance the life of nations which have not yet reached the full momentum of their development."[5]

The Institute's Board of Governors had rewritten the duties, obligations and prerogatives of the president to fit Eban's peculiar situation. For him it would not be a full-time job, because in just a few days he would begin to devote much of his time to politics. He would live on campus, always be available for advice and consultation and entertain important visitors who came to the Institute, but would not be encumbered with any administrative duties.

Eban went into the 1959 campaign with a thousand more handicaps than any other politician ever had. He had no personal following, never having lived in the country. He had no group of devotees, no well-organized political machine. While abroad he had had no chance to build up the web of loyalties which the politician normally creates.

Then he had personal handicaps. He seemed as cold and aloof as a god on Mount Olympus in the typical Israeli atmosphere of the open shirt, the pioneer spirit, the lack of formality. His friends feared that his polished rhetoric might be rejected by people as emotionally charged as most Israelis are.

Back in America he had several times discussed his future with Dewey Stone, who questioned him about whether he thought he could take the rough-and-tumble of politics, because of his cultural background and his extreme sense of honesty. Eban's answer was that he wanted to try.

He was often compared to Adlai Stevenson, yet when Stevenson ran for the presidency he was no neophyte, having won the governorship of Illinois by the largest plurality in the state's history.

One of Eban's great problems was that he was entering a struggle for political power with the ruling clique of Mapai composed largely of men who were not distinguished by either intellectual prowess or academic distinction. Many were actually anti-intellectuals. In the early days they had dug ditches, worked in the vineyards and wine cellars, plowed the earth, spread manure, drained swamps, pioneered. Later they had helped establish kibbutzim and moshavim. They formed a closely knit group. Almost all were from Central or Eastern Europe. They were roughhewn, blunt-speaking, short on formality, suspicious of rhetoric, given more to emotionalism than intellectuality and defiant of propriety and conventionality, especially in matters of dress and social niceties. Those who had done only a few years of manual labor in their youth, like Ben-Gurion, never stopped using it as their credential for leadership. The main asset of these men was their political shrewdness and the sort of ruthlessness that goes with political infighting. Eban the scholar, who retained his high position by force of his intellectual brilliance, seemed strangely out of place among them.

Even his close friend Sharett was not an intellectual in the same sense he was. Sharett was from Russia and began his advanced education in a now famous high school in Tel Aviv, which made him almost as good as a kibbutznik. As for Weizmann, although he had been a British Jew by passport, his roots, too, were in Russia, he spoke English with a foreign accent and was always looked upon by the British as an Anglicized Jew —an outsider. Born in Pinsk, he had had more in common with his sometime political rival, Ben-Gurion, who had been born two hundred miles away in Plonsk, than with his British protégé.

All these party stalwarts acknowledged Eban's great contributions to Israel, respected his superior talents, recognized his vote-getting potentiality and gave him provisional approval, yet at the same time he did not fit their pattern and they made no secret of their feeling that "he is not really one of us."

The nominating in Mapai was done by a group called the Gush, composed of the party's leaders in Tel Aviv. Its members were not favorable to either Eban or Dayan at first. As one of them put it, the objections were "biological and conceptional."[6] The Gush argued that both men were newcomers to politics and should be required to "queue up." It was the first serious confrontation in Israel between youth and the establishment.

The answer to all this, of course, was that Israel, like America, was a melting pot of many cultures and there was no reason, now that the country was growing up, for the kibbutzniks of Central and Eastern Europe to have a political monopoly. A good dash of something as piquant and potent as Ebanism would surely improve the quality of the mixture.

One of Ben-Gurion's aides likened the attitude of the Gush toward Eban to that of the Tammany Hall political machine in New York toward Woodrow Wilson. In both cases the organization never really comprehended the man, yet after he became a candidate the professional politicians were impressed by his ability to get out the crowd. In the case of Mapai and Eban, it was obvious they had acquired a campaign asset. He was once compared to a parachutist who had landed with a certain amount of apprehension in a wilderness, only to discover that the animals were not nearly as ferocious as he had expected; that he could get along with them and even tame them. The parachutist had landed on soft ground, surrounded by acclamation, which reinforced his self-confidence.

It was proper that during his diplomatic career Eban had been a neutral in domestic political affairs, not affiliated with any one party, for he represented the whole country, but one of his first acts after his resignation was to affiliate with Mapai. It was the obvious party for him, since he had been an active socialist from his early university days. Mapai was one of twenty-six parties entering the contest for the one hundred and twenty seats in the Knesset. Under the Israeli electoral system each party puts up a list of candidates and the voters signify their preference for one list or another. The number of seats each party gets is determined by the percentage of the total vote it polls. Each party determines the order of the candidates on its list. The higher on the list, the better the chance of election. Ben-Gurion headed the Mapai list, with Eban in twelfth position and Dayan thirteenth.

The need for an election at this particular time had grown out of West Germany's order for more than three million dollars' worth of grenade launchers from Israel's infant munitions industry. Parties on the left accused the Government of "selling arms to the devil." When the vote was taken the Government won, 57 to 45, but because Ben-Gurion felt the two leftist parties had broken an agreement, he submitted his resignation and forced the first general election since 1955.

Two days after the Weizmann inauguration Eban made his second public appearance in Israel when he told an overflow audience in the Orion Cinema in Jerusalem that science must be harnessed to the needs of the nation, the ideological conflict with world Jewry must be brought to an end and in the field of economics Israel must place emphasis on industrial development.

From Jerusalem he went cross-country and that same evening made his first official contact with Mapai at a meeting of campaign workers. Introduced by Finance Minister Levi Eshkol, he said there were historical reasons for his joining Mapai: Katznelson had been one of those who first introduced him to Zionism. Later Sharett and Ben-Gurion had drawn him into the political life of the Jewish Agency. Also, he firmly believed Israel needed a workers' society. These remarks pleased his audience, but after the meeting there was a buzz of talk about this new political meteor. Some thought his Hebrew the most sparkling they had ever heard; others complained that much of what he said had gone over the heads of the hard-boiled, down-to-earth crowd. There was criticism that he had appeared in a business suit and a necktie, whereas everyone else had come in the casual costume of Israeli Jews: slacks and open-neck shirt, symbols of the austere pioneer life.

During his talk, in making the point that this workers' rally was the preliminary to an arduous campaign, Eban had likened it to a "cocktail before dinner," a simile that was completely alien to the tea-drinking men in the audience, most of whom had never in their lives had a cocktail before dinner.

The next issue of the *London Jewish Observer and Middle East Review* carried this report of the meeting:

"Eban quoted liberally from the works of a well-known American expert, Professor Weiner, to prove that constituency elections are the only true form of democratic selection and much fairer than proportional representation. After half a dozen references to the famous Weiner (a name which his audience has been hearing for the first time) a shout went up from the back benches: 'Weiner for Prime Minister!' Eban saw the point."

When copies of the paper reached Rehovoth Eban immediately dispatched a letter to the editor:

"Your correspondent may inadvertently have left your readers with a wrong impression of the degree of knowledge prevailing at the Mapai rally which your correspondent evidently did not attend. No. 1, the authority on constitutional and electoral power problems whom I invoked was not 'an American authority called Weiner' but Professor Herman Finer of the University of Chicago, author of the great standard work *The Theory and Practice of Modern Government*. Since the Israeli people is now engaged in a great constitutional debate it will be hearing much of the authorities who have analyzed this problem. . . . No. 2, the views of Dr. Finer were respectfully and silently received. The 'shout from the back benches' is a fiction of the imagination. I am sorry that this is so, because our meetings could do with a little animation and gentle humor."

Even before the campaign actually got under way the opposition indicated the line its attack on Eban would take. A routine check of the voters' register for the forthcoming election had revealed that Eban was not a registered voter. Then it was contended that he was not even a citizen of the country he had been representing with such distinction these past eleven years. He had not been in the category of those who automatically gained citizenship with the founding of the state and as a holder of a diplomatic passport he apparently had never thought it necessary to make formal application for citizenship. The Minister of the Interior hastily signed the papers necessary to legalize Eban's status, but the opposition used the incident to stress that here was a man who, if Mapai was successful in the election, would probably become a member of the Cabinet and yet he had never lived in Israel. The answer was obvious—he could hardly have worked on a kibbutz while fighting Israel's diplomatic battles in Washington and New York.

From the start in Israel he was called "Abba Even," with the last name pronounced as if spelled Eh-vehn. Oddly it is the Hebrew word for "stone," and so now he bore the same name as his Massachusetts friend.

During the campaign Suzy Eban served as her husband's public relations manager, librarian and correspondence clerk. Also she shared intimately with him the joys and occasional bitternesses of his initiation into politics.

The campaign opened officially on August 19 when Eban and Golda Meir appeared together on the platform at a Mapai rally in Tel Aviv.

"After eleven years in Washington and New York," he told the audience, "I thought that nothing in the realm of politics or diplomacy would ever surprise me, but now I see that Washington and New York are kindergartens in this respect compared with Tel Aviv and Jerusalem."

Eban drew a crowd of twelve thousand in Tel Aviv, ten thousand in Ramat Gan, fifteen thousand in Haifa, twenty thousand the next time in Tel Aviv, almost seven thousand in Bet Yam, fifteen thousand in Rehovoth, five thousand in Bene Beraq. In the Aichron-Josef quarter of

Jerusalem, populated principally by Jews from Kurdistan, Yemen and Iran, a stronghold of Menahem Beigin and his Herut party, six thousand turned out on a chilly autumn night to listen to him. In the squalid Tel Aviv quarter called Hatikvah he drew twelve thousand. Of this last experience Eban said:

"I looked down into that mass of Moroccan faces and then threw away my speech about electoral reforms and talked to them from the heart." (He was, indeed, learning to be a politician.)

The reason for Eban's popularity with Sephardic Jews apparently had something to do with their respect for words—their dedication to the oral tradition. In Nazareth, talking Arabic to an audience of a thousand, he said:

"I wait for the day when I shall again represent my country at the UN with an Arab colleague at my side."

In a nation like Israel that takes its politics so seriously, this bright new luminary on the political scene was naturally the object of bitter attack, which was a compliment, for it proved how important a figure he was in Mapai's struggle for continued supremacy. Ephraim Kishon, the popular humorist on the staff of the newspaper *Ma'ariv*, whose column also appeared in translation in the Jerusalem *Post*, hit Eban in his most vulnerable spot when he wrote of a visit he had made to the UN in New York:

"Attendants distributed the text of Eban's speech among the delegates, who immediately started marking the words that called for further study at home. . . . Abba kicked off in splendid form. . . . 'Thummed periapts orgulous of their gules, forbid renyons and bona-robas affied to their cheveril-fitchens, dearn gally-maufries and obidicuts, to you all I say: "Avaun nothooks, stop pheezing and sneck-up." . . .'

"The interpreters were sweating profusely in their booths with the expression of hunted deer in their eyes. And American Jewry in the gallery sighed raptly and breathed with difficulty, in the throes of ecstatic pleasure: 'Where on earth does he find such words?' As Abba sensed his audience warming up, his sentences became more flowery and he switched to classical Gaelic. The Belgian delegate had not yet discovered that by mistake he had been listening to the Chinese translation all the time. Hammarskjöld gave up, snapped the Webster's shut and went out for a breather. The British delegation demonstrated its superiority by listening to Abba's words without benefit of earphones and dictionaries; everyone knew that they were simply showing off and that they would later receive the speech translated into everyday English. . . .

"The speech ended . . . the gallery broke into spontaneous cheers.

"'Whole sentences,' one of them shouted, 'whole sentences I didn't understand! There's nobody like our Abba!'"

This was typical of the opposition attacks. Most of the stories they told about him were apocryphal or grossly exaggerated. There was little ground on which to criticize him for acts of commission or omission, so they manufactured stories, like the one about how at the end of a thirty-minute talk in Hebrew to immigrants at a camp at Tiberias someone in the audience arose and asked:

"Please, can we now have a translation into Hebrew."

Once, one of his political colleagues, who was also one of his most ardent admirers, urged him to simplify his complex and literary Hebrew style to suit an audience made up of immigrants, many of whom had just learned the language, and of young people, who had evolved a very informal way of speaking.

"I said to him, 'If you would eliminate just five of your most frequent Hebrew expressions you would speak Hebrew more like the ordinary Israeli.' That was the only time I ever brought up the matter. First, he is very touchy. Also, he is perhaps rightfully conceited about language matters. His attitude seems to be, 'Who are you to tell me how to use the language?' But even more important, I doubt whether he could change his manner of speaking if he wished."

Also, Eban feels that the style is the man; to distort the style would be to distort the man. There was still another reason for his resistance to change. He knew that Stevenson, after his defeat in 1952, tried when he ran again four years later to be folksy, with fatal results.

Despite the exceptionally large percentage of intellectuals in Israel, he became the victim of the same sort of anti-intellectualism that Stevenson had suffered in both his campaigns. Many Israelis looked with suspicion on this urbane, Cambridge-educated Demosthenes who had a larger vocabulary in any language than they had, yet had never helped drain a swamp; who made Hebrew sound even more beautiful than Italian or Spanish or French, yet had never broken rock on the road.

Then there was his conflict with the military. He and Dayan were running on the same ticket, but the intense rivalry between them became one of the campaign's conversation pieces. In July Egypt put on a display of its military power during a three-hour parade in Cairo and Egyptian Field Marshal Amer made a threatening speech against Israel.

Dayan countered by urging Israel to adopt a policy of returning hostility for hostility with Egypt. Three days later Eban took issue, declaring that an outbreak of fighting between Egypt and Israel could lead to World War III and estimating that since the Sinai campaign fewer Israelis believed in an exclusively military solution of the country's problems. One paper commented that the more Eban's arguments were weighed against those of Dayan the more the scales seemed to be tipped against Dayan.[7]

The Eban-Dayan conflict helped widen the schism between those who wished to rely exclusively on military strength for Israel's preservation and those who still hoped there might be other solutions. The Dayan followers were responsible for the circulation of the slogan:

"We can afford a Foreign Office only because we have an army."

Yet Eban often shared the same platform with Dayan, as when they both appeared before forty thousand spectators at a football match between Israel and Yugoslavia.

Another criticism made during the campaign was that "he sees events through rose-colored glasses and sometimes led his government to believe that things were better than they really were because of his incurable optimism."[8] They also accused him of being an intellectual snob. One of his opponents was quoted as saying:

"If Eban considered a man a fool, it wouldn't matter to him if that man was the representative of a hundred thousand workers, all with votes; he would still have contempt for the man and take no pains to hide it."

Golda Zimmerman, an Israeli journalist, wrote of his campaign that while he seemed at the start to have "all the attributes of a triumphant politician," nevertheless, many people were surprised at the size of the crowds he drew, especially in districts inhabited by Oriental Jews and new immigrants.[9]

Men are often victims of their own successes. This was true of Eban in 1959. As ambassador to Washington and more especially as chief of the Israeli delegation to the UN he had been Israel's voice to the outside world. So impressive, so effective, so convincing was this voice that he became a world figure. But now that he was contending for public office his opponents started using the word "only." One night at a Mapai rally in the Tel Aviv theater of Habimah, Eban and Ben-Gurion were on the program. The Prime Minister in his address referred to the former ambassador as "the greatest spokesman of our nation's cause since Weizmann." The audience applauded what everyone considered an unreserved compliment. Everyone but Eban. Silently he suffered, for he understood Ben-Gurion well enough to know that often when he said something positive he meant something negative. "Spokesman" to Ben-Gurion meant someone who expressed a policy but had nothing to do with making it. As for his reference to Weizmann, Israel's first President had been much more than a spokesman; he had been an extremely active leader. And so in that one sentence Ben-Gurion had also belittled Weizmann, with whom he had often quarreled. As others took up this "only a spokesman" theme, Eban regretted that he had called his book of speeches *Voice of Israel*—now that he aspired to *make* policy, not just voice it.

During the campaign Suzy helped form a League of Women Voters of Israel, patterned on the American organization of the same name. While she did not attend many of her husband's meetings, she was present with him on the platform at a rally of Egyptian Jews and when it was announced that she was of Egyptian-Jewish origin the chairman coaxed her to make the first political campaign speech of her life—not long but delightfully effective.

The campaign lasted two and a half months, during which Eban spent his days as president of the Weizmann Institute, surrounded by scientists, and his evenings as a candidate, surrounded by politicians and voters. As he put it at the time: "I therefore see objective truth by day and subjective truth by night."

On the stump he vigorously articulated Mapai's arguments for changing to a political system similar to that of the United States and many other Western countries, in which each representative to the legislative body is elected by and represents the voters of a given geographical area.

For seventy-five days he trekked up and down and back and forth across Israel, until he knew intimately every corner of the country. He was aware that in his audiences were natives of Palestine who had never been abroad in their lives. Others, living for years in what was virtually a fortress surrounded by enemies, had developed a fortress mentality. For these people he tried to open doors and let in breezes from the outside world. He also tried to get them to see their country in a global context and from a historical perspective. He told them that although Israel was small it was the focus of a worldwide pilgrimage. Men from distant lands came here to seek and find a contagion of spirit which they found nowhere else. "They look here for the secret of spiritual resilience. They see the mysterious impulse which has given this land and this nation an unbelievable power of recuperation. The fabric of

Israel's history has a single unifying thread, a constant, gallant belief, sometimes against all apparent evidence, in the positive direction of human history, in the capacity of man to solve his problems and find a cure for his ills."

This sort of talk may have been beyond the comprehension of some, but to others it was refreshingly different from the usual campaign speech of the politician. Many of his listeners liked the way he vocalized their hopes and their fears, even though some of the phraseology may have been a little obtuse for them.

He told them it was doubtful that Israel had ever known a time when her national life had been so effervescent and flowering as during the past thirty months. This was not an accident but the outcome of a calculated policy composed of bold initiative outside the Middle East, combined with deliberate restraint inside the area. Nasser's violent language was not a good reason for abandoning a perfectly good policy which had brought Israel to the peak of her position.

He talked robustly and with hope for Israel's bright future. He seemed to have inexhaustible energy. His training on the UJA-Bonds-Hadassah circuit in the United States was now standing him in good stead. In the size of the crowds that came out to hear him he saw denial of the theory that the people want to hear "nonsense discussed in bad Hebrew."[10]

Wherever he went there was tremendous curiosity about him. People wanted to see him, hear him, listen to his oratory, find out what manner of man he was. He inspired awe among kibbutzniks, Jews from Africa and the Orient and all the other diverse Israeli elements, just as he had among more sophisticated people whenever he spoke in world bodies or to American audiences. Even his harshest critics realized that "Eban is something special" as they often put it.

His audiences were encouraged and uplifted by the breadth of his vision. He made them aware that Israel was not merely a small country covering a few thousand square miles at the farthest end of the Mediterranean but a significant factor in world affairs.

Although nearly all Israeli newspapers are owned by political parties or have close political ties, Eban was well treated by the press during the 1959 campaign, the notable exception being the Herut paper, whose editor assigned a reporter to dig into his private life. The findings were then served up in an article malodorous with tittle-tattle and innuendo.

In America, especially after his 1956 speech to the General Assembly, Eban had little chance for privacy. Now in Israel it was even worse. In restaurants, at the theater, even walking down the street he was besieged by autograph hunters and people who wanted to shake his hand or just stare at him, for until now he had been almost a mythical figure for them. In addition there were visitors from abroad, who first wanted to see Ben-Gurion, then Eban.

As the campaign drew to a close he summarized the first political experience of his life:

"I carry in my heart the image of tens of thousands of Israeli citizens in towns and villages, factories and farms, whom I have addressed in massive assemblies throughout the land and the seriousness, the maturity of their approach to public issues in their poignant search for an idealistic backdrop to material concerns. These crowds bring to mind the qualities of public character which must have characterized the Athenian city-state and which much later adorned the town meetings of New England."

It was estimated that in large meetings and small Eban talked to a total of almost a quarter of a million people—this in a country of fewer than half a million families. Next to Beigin he had drawn the largest crowds of any candidate of any party. He had spoken to Israeli Arabs and members of the Druze minority in Arabic, to immigrants from Iran in Farsi, to settlers from Egypt in French and to onetime American and British Jews in English. In between public appearances he wrote to his mother:

"The house is palatial and modern. The garden is full of joy. The children have friends all over the place." Parenthetically he mentioned that "the wave of public adulation exceeds anything I have ever known before, anywhere. Great throngs storm my meetings and the press is uniformly ecstatic."[11]

His last campaign rally was in the Zafon Cinema in Tel Aviv. Every seat was taken long before the announced hour of the meeting and hundreds were turned away, but some were so eager to hear him that they broke the glass in the doors and swarmed down the aisles.

The election was held on Tuesday, November 3 (1959), a stiflingly hot day, with the temperature in some localities reaching 95 degrees. Most political experts had predicted that Mapai would lose at least five seats. Mapai leaders themselves would have been happy if they had been able to preserve the status quo. Instead, the dominant Labor Socialist party received the greatest vote in its history, gaining seven seats.

In his post-election statement Abba Eban said the results would be greeted with joy by Israel's friends throughout the world as a demonstration of the country's democratic stability and the Israeli public's clear thinking. More than that, however, it was a great personal triumph for this man who now, at forty-four, had embarked on still another new career—as politician-statesman.

23

Endless Jockeying for Position

WHEN EBAN'S DECISION to return home and run for the Knesset was announced in the spring of 1959, dispatches from Tel Aviv and Jerusalem said Golda Meir had hinted she did not wish to remain in the Cabinet after the fall election. The conclusion in Israel, as well as in the United States, was that she would be replaced by Eban. The New York *Times* went further and wrote of Eban as Ben-Gurion's most likely successor whenever the veteran Prime Minister decided to go into retirement. From a distance it looked like clear political sailing for this young man who had now made such a substantial contribution to the Mapai victory.

Eban also had Ben-Gurion's word, given in a face-to-face meeting in November of 1958 when the Prime Minister first broached the idea of his Washington ambassador entering politics. At that time Ben-Gurion had said "Golda wants to retire" and stated that as soon as the post was vacated it would go to Eban.

But the moment the 1959 election was over the infighting began. To get a majority of the Knesset votes and form a government Ben-Gurion needed to make an alliance with at least two minor parties, to whom certain Cabinet posts would have to be given. Then, to complicate matters further, Golda Meir suddenly changed her mind about resigning. It was in the now accepted Israeli tradition. During the eleven years the state had been in existence Ben-Gurion himself had frequently resigned or threatened to resign in order to get his way. So had others. One of his Cabinet members, Rabbi Fishman, had resigned so many times he was nicknamed "the Minister of Resignation."

Now, among Ben-Gurion's many other party problems was what to do with Eban—how to reward him—how to satisfy him?

Eban's reaction to the twenty-seven days of silence between the election and the Cabinet announcement was a feeling that he had been used. He blamed Ben-Gurion for misleading him and for not fulfilling his promise.

Finally a formula was worked out. Eban would be named Minister Without Portfolio. His rich experience abroad would be used by making his particular province international affairs. He would work closely with the Foreign Minister, relieving her of many duties, undertaking special missions, supervising certain operations, helping direct the diplomatic struggle on its many fronts. In effect he would be her deputy.

On November 31 (1959) Eban and the other newly elected legislators took their seats in the Knesset and were sworn in. Although Ben-Gurion was not yet ready to name the rest of his Cabinet, that day he let it be known the post he had in mind for Eban and the general feeling was that the talents of the former ambassador would not be wasted.

Two weeks later Ben-Gurion made the formal announcement of his Cabinet. He himself would continue as Defense Minister and Golda Meir as Foreign Minister. Dayan would become Minister of Agriculture and Eban Minister Without Portfolio. The story in the New York *Times* stated Eban would be "working closely with Mrs. Meir."

Despite his disappointment over not getting the post he had expected, Eban paid a call on Mrs. Meir, congratulating her on her decision to remain in the Government and offering his full cooperation in the field of foreign affairs. Mrs. Meir's response was disconcerting, although natural. While expressing the opinion that Eban might someday be a successful Foreign Minister, she thought that any sustained activity now on his part in foreign affairs would be likely to interfere with her responsibilities. In her opinion he was far too competent to be a deputy minister and therefore it would be better for him to deal with "other matters."

Eban told her he would avoid friction but that he intended writing to Ben-Gurion for clarification of the situation. As he left Mrs. Meir's office he felt for the first time in his life that things had gone wrong for him. Since his university days he had been concentrating on international affairs. He had had thirteen years of nonpareil experience and had gained a special eminence as a world figure. Now he was being asked to deal with "other matters."

In his letter to Ben-Gurion he said he did not know what he was going to do in the Cabinet if his cooperation in the international field was not wanted. He received no reply.

His resentment was never against Golda Meir, whose attitude he fully understood; it was against Ben-Gurion. He felt both he and Mrs. Meir had been victims of the Prime Minister's creation of an illusion—the possibility that more than one minister could work on foreign affairs.

For Eban the paradox of the situation was intense. To his chagrin he had found that his Cabinet post was nebulous and frustrating. Minister Without Portfolio now meant exactly what it sounded like—a post without duties. Explaining the situation to James Feron of the New York *Times*, he said:

"In some countries this [position] has meaning. The British, for instance, have two or three who take on extraministerial duties. In Israel, however, all portfolios were so jealously guarded that everything was covered."[1]

After years of intense activity in Washington and New York, with every waking minute occupied, Eban found he now had little to do, except his Institute work and some activity as a member of several ministerial committees. Perhaps rationalizing a little, in a letter to a friend in London he wrote:

"Freedom from departmental duties has some advantages. One is the capacity to read, think, compose, draft, plan, without the crushing burden of the 'in' and 'out' trays. I rarely had this opportunity in Washington. . . .

"The ability to be concerned with policy rather than detail is one of the advantages which I have in prospect. The complications are, of course, self-evident, especially in the climate of the sensitivities you have noticed here."[2]

Not long after Eban's appointment as Minister Without Portfolio, Paula Ben-Gurion called Suzy Eban and said she wanted to see her. As soon as the younger woman arrived the Prime Minister's wife—famous all her life for her brutal outspokenness—asked:

"Tell me, is Eban happy?" (She always referred to him by his last name.)

Without hesitation Suzy replied:

"I can tell you one thing, Paula; we have learned that politics is the art not only of what you give but also of what you are denied."

Mrs. Ben-Gurion showed no reaction, but Suzy surmised by the way she suddenly changed the subject that the arrow had hit the target.[3]

One of the best friends Eban had in these days in Jerusalem was Gideon Rafael, with whom he had been associated in Palestine in wartime and later in New York and Washington. Now Rafael was in the Foreign Office.

"For a time he was almost in a state of shock over what seemed to be happening to his career," Rafael later said. "It took him a long time to rally and get over it."[4]

Although he had no formal responsibilities in the foreign field Eban was placed on the Cabinet committee for foreign affairs, as well as on several other committees entrusted with the formation of policy. The rhythm of life he established that winter was to spend Monday, Tuesday and Wednesday as a Cabinet minister in Jerusalem, where he had a small flat; then from Thursday through Sunday in Rehovoth. Whatever entertaining the Ebans did—which seemed slight, remembering Washington—was now done at Rehovoth.

One Thursday Eban brought home to Rehovoth from his Jerusalem office a letter from Mayor Wagner of New York congratulating him on his Cabinet position:

"New York is proud of you. Do not forget that you are one of the six men ever to have been awarded the freedom of the city." (The only others still alive were former Presidents Truman and Hoover and Secretary-General Hammarskjöld.) It was a reminder of a more triumphal era.[5]

For Suzy Eban these were dichotomous days. She was happy to be free from the pressures of diplomatic life in Washington; now there was some semblance of a normal family relationship; they even spent occasional evenings à deux in front of the wood-burning fireplace in their Rehovoth living room. But she knew that behind the mask her husband now wore, even when they were alone, there was suffering.

"I think Aubrey must be going through a deep and silent inner crisis," she wrote to a friend. "After commanding for eleven years on two such broad scenes as Washington and the United Nations by himself, and so successfully, it must be hard to be tied down the way he has been and there are times when I almost fear he may not stick it out. But he is courageous and he will overcome his great intellectual loneliness. I wish I could do more for him."[6]

No one could possibly know as much about Abba Eban's dreams, hopes, personal ambitions and motivation as Suzy. In another letter she analyzed him with great objectivity:

"I so little want for us a position of more power than we have, but I do want for him what he wants, and of course pomp and glory mean nothing unless they are the thrills of a position whereby one determines things, one decides things, one opens new avenues—a whole world of original thinking, accompanied by facilities for execution. . . . When our diplomatic work started the substance was there—historical background, the intellectual disciplines, but there was no structure. Now our life is just the reverse. . . .

"We have to live in the present reality. . . . We help each other a lot in moments like this, but we are determined to get through and I hope we shall, because it is not only *us* getting through; it is our vision and our ideas and the way of life we want for our country . . . a greater dignity in human relationships . . . 'only to thine own self be true.' . . . We are like that. We believe like that.

"But it is obvious that Aubrey's talents need other horizons. We are marking time as gracefully as we can and waiting for his time and his proper place. So far the appearance of things is excellent, but the substance is lacking in completeness, sweep, authority and above all in a chance to do a creative job for the country and its people.

"We sometimes have gruelling days and since the jockeying for positions is an endless process until one finds one's proper place, the restlessness and deliberations come and go but are always latent in our present set of circumstances. However, it seasons us politically and challenges us!"[7]

Suzy was busy now with household matters and with her children, instead of cocktail parties, Hadassah speeches and ambassadorial entertaining. Eli was almost ten years old. "He is very concerned now with the duties and expectations put upon him by others on account of his name. Because of this he is not and never will be a fully free child. But I am trying my best to talk very freely with him about it and to make him carry his name with poise and comfort and hopes of having a good time anyway. I suppose all of us are a matter of great curiosity, some of it rather provincial, too."[8]

Late in January (1960) Eban made Page One in American papers in an oblique way. Following the publication of Anthony Eden's memoirs, *Full Circle*, President Eisenhower in a press conference made comment about the book and the events of 1956, including this statement:

"I think it was, well, sometime in early October. Mr. Eban was going back to Israel for a short time. He came in to see me and I told him I'd hoped that he would not allow any misrepresentation of sentiment in this country to sway him and particularly because of possible Jewish sympathy for what seemed to be an intention of building up around the mobilization of Israel at that time. I hoped he would not allow this to sway his judgment as to what this administration would do in doing its very best to prevent any outbreak of hostilities you might say the settlement of international issues by force. And I told him that if he thought that this would have any part, iota of influence on the election [of 1956] or that that would have any influence on me, he should disabuse his mind about it."[9]

Eban, who was in London, immediately communicated with Prime Minister Ben-Gurion by cable and a denial was issued in Jerusalem that any such meeting ever took place between the American President and the Israeli ambassador or that Eisenhower had ever spoken to Eban about the influence of American Jews on American foreign policy.

In opening his next press conference (on February 3, 1960) President Eisenhower said:

"I have one correction I want to make for a statement I made in my last press conference. I said that Ambassador Eban was actually in my office when I made a certain particular statement about my attitude toward the impending Suez crisis at that time [1956]. I have had the staff look up the records. Actually J. F. Dulles came to my office at 6 P.M. stating he was to see Mr. Eban in a few minutes and I made the same statement that I gave you last time but I made it to him and I had confused the particular—that incident from what I said then with other visits or at least another visit of Mr. Eban. So, again it shows that my memory at least is not perfect."[10]

Eisenhower's correction did not immediately quiet the editorial storm that had swept the country. Jewish papers from coast to coast exploded, many taking the President to task, first for the remarks he had allegedly made to Eban, which some critics said verged on anti-Semitism; then for reiterating them in a press conference years later; and finally for his "forgetfulness." Publicly Eban made no comment.

The next month (March, 1960) Eban got into the middle of an unfortunate controversy. After it was announced that Billy Graham, American evangelist, was going to Israel to hold several revival meetings, the extreme Jewish religious elements in Israel made such a stir that Graham was refused the use of Mann Auditorium in Tel Aviv. When he arrived he announced that he had not come to proselytize among Jews but to preach to Christians. In the YMCA at Jerusalem and St. Peter's Church in Jaffa he had capacity audiences, which included a sprinkling of religious Jews in their traditional yarmulkes or skullcaps. During his five-day stay he was received by President Ben-Zvi, had luncheon with Foreign Minister Golda Meir and was Eban's guest at Weizmann Institute, to the disgust of the protesters, who called all three officials traitors to their religion. It was many days after Graham's departure before the storm abated.

In an effort to find something for a Minister Without Portfolio to do that would not infringe on the privileges and prerogatives of the other ministers, the government assigned many rather innocuous tasks to Eban during the first half of 1960. In February he went to the British Isles, making addresses in London, Glasgow, Manchester, Leeds, Liverpool and Brighton. Commenting on this tour, Suzy Eban told a friend:

"He really is conscientious and he is now known personally by the entire Jewish community of Britain. But I know that he missed the adulation that the American Jewish community showed him throughout the years, although he never says so. The welcome in Britain was warm, but not the same."

One reason the welcome was warm was because he had become the first British Jew ever to be given an Israeli Cabinet post.

In May (1960) Ben-Gurion offered the Ministry of Posts and Telegraph to Eban, who turned it down not only quickly but with some indignation, convinced it was a ploy devised by some of his personal-political enemies who were trying to make him look ridiculous.

Early in May (1960) the Cabinet asked Eban to undertake a special mission to Argentina as part of the country's summitry attempts. The occasion was the official celebration of one hundred and fifty years of Argentinian independence. Eban would spend ten days in South America meeting various heads of state. Among the aides assigned to him were Brigadier General Meir Zorea of the Northern Command, his military aide for the trip; Samuel Yeshaia, governor of the Jerusalem District; and Yehuda Yarri, director of the cultural department. They would fly in an El Al Britannia, Flight No. 601, leaving Lod Airport on May 18. Several days before the scheduled departure ads appeared in Israeli papers announcing Flight No. 601—the first flight ever scheduled to Buenos Aires—and offering bargain rates to anyone wishing to make the trip.

In private conversation Eban and his wife speculated on why a special plane was being used when he could just as easily and at a fraction of the cost make the trip by commercial airline. One theory was that maybe the plane was going to be used to transport secret military equipment on the return.

The rest of the story is still slightly clouded in official mystery. Neither Eban, Ben-Gurion nor anyone else involved has ever given an official version of what happened. The facts that follow have been pieced together from information obtained from many sources.

The night before Flight 601 took off from Lod Airport Ben-Gurion sent for Eban. It is now known that six days earlier Eichmann had been captured in Buenos Aires and the problem was how to get him to Israel for questioning and trial. Eban has never denied that Ben-Gurion that evening told him of the capture and the plan to have the El Al plane bring the prisoner back, but he cautioned that the entire operation must be kept a closely guarded secret.

The plane left in normal manner on May 18 with nineteen persons aboard, including the crew. At Recife, Brazil, where a refueling stop was made, there was a prolonged delay for some technical reason and those aboard the plane who were privy to the secret became irritated and nervous. General Zorea tried to reassure them, saying:

"What's the hurry? Why so nervous? Even if we are a few hours late, what's the difference? Enjoy this nice Brazilian sunshine and relax!"

He obviously did not know.

The balconies of the airport building at Buenos Aires were crowded with some of the 420,000 Jewish residents of Argentina, there to welcome the Israelis. Scanning the faces, the people on the plane suddenly recognized the serious countenance of Isser Harel, head of Israel's Security Services, who, it later turned out, had had charge of the entire Eichmann operation.

The understanding was that there would be no announcement of the Eichmann arrest until he was in Israel and until the Eban delegation had left Argentina.

Flight No. 601, having arrived on Thursday, May 19 (1960), was due to take off for the return trip at 3 A.M. on Saturday. Instead it suddenly left at midnight Friday, with Eichmann aboard. It left without incident and without the Argentinians suspecting anything. Those who knew Eichmann was aboard did little sleeping that night while the plane was flying over the South Atlantic and Africa. The next day no news was good news. Flight No. 601 apparently had made it.

It was not until May 23—three days after Flight No. 601 left Buenos Aires—that Prime Minister Ben-Gurion made a formal announcement that Eichmann was under arrest in Israel, but nothing was said of where he had been caught. Two days later reporters were permitted to say in their dispatches that "a special El Al flight carrying Abba Eban and other Israeli notables to Buenos Aires for the anniversary of Argentina's independence had made an unscheduled stopover in Recife, Brazil, where it was held for three hours by the airport manager, who tried to prevent the plane from taking off again, but finally relented." That was all.

On Friday, May 27, Eban, still in Buenos Aires, was besieged by so many reporters and foreign correspondents that he held a press conference. Asked about the Eichmann affair he stated:

"I know nothing about it."

"Is the plane on which you came still in Argentina?" he was asked.

"I do not know."

One Israeli, justifying Eban's evasiveness, said:

"It was an intelligence thing. No one has to confess such things. If you confess them you commit the other party to take some action. It was like the U-2 thing with Eisenhower. There are certain fictions which you simply have to keep to."[11]

The U-2 reference was quite appropriate, for the Eisenhower Government had at first denied the United States was flying any planes over Russia, but finally was forced to admit that such flights had been going on for four years. At this particular time the U-2 story was all over the front pages of American newspapers, almost crowding out the Eichmann sensation.

24

In the Parent-Teacher Nutcracker

PEOPLE SPEAKING twenty-three African and Asian languages met at Bandung on the island of Java in 1955 in an atmosphere of bitterness and exultation to celebrate the end of colonialism. One of the dominant participants was Gamal Abdel Nasser. Israel was not invited. Little if anything constructive was accomplished. The atmosphere at Bandung was of acrimonious resentment against the white nations for their past oppressions.

People speaking for forty nations attended the Rehovoth Conference in the August heat of 1960 to discuss the role science could play in the advancement of what Abba Eban euphemistically called "countries which have not yet reached the full momentum of their development." The atmosphere at Rehovoth was of hope instead of hatred. The only enemies condemned were poverty, ignorance, mosquitoes and the tsetse fly.

August is always a bad month, anywhere, for intellectual endeavors and especially in a desert country. The conference lasted twelve sweltering days. Eban, whose dream child this was, shared the platform at the opening ceremonies with Ben-Gurion. The delegates included some of the world's greatest authorities on water, health, agriculture, energy and economics, as well as statesmen and educators. Until now Israel had been boycotted by most heads of state and foreign ministers out of fear of alienating the Arabs. U Nu of Burma had been the only exception. Now twenty or thirty presidents, prime ministers and foreign ministers were in attendance. Even if the conference were to have no other results, it was taking Israel out of her diplomatic isolation.

Eban made one of his most beautifully organized, epigrammatical addresses in welcoming the delegates. Nasser might be brandishing his Damascus steel scimitar in several directions at once, China and Russia might be eying each other suspiciously, large nations and small might be arming for slaughter, but against this background minuscule Israel was bringing politicians and scientists together, trying to point out that behind the bright new flags and other nationalistic panoply millions were languishing in squalor, illiteracy, exploitation and disease. Being free in the constitutional sense was not enough.

Always sensitive to the reaction of the press, Eban was delighted that Israeli papers, which generally see a domestic political angle in everything, were almost unanimous in their praise of the gathering, several of them calling it "The Conference of Hope." It ended rather unexpectedly. On the last day at 4:30 P.M. a Rehovoth policeman whispered to Eban that a tip had been received there was a bomb in the auditorium timed to go off at 5 P.M. Speech-weary delegates, dripping with perspiration, were not told why the final session was brought to such a sudden conclusion, but they asked no questions, happy to have time for a nap or a swim in the sea before the gala banquet and farewell oratory.

As enough clippings to fill three immense scrapbooks began to pour in from around the world, Eban was invited to explain the significance of what had happened at Rehovoth for a plethora of publications, from the *Reader's Digest* to the *Bulletin of Atomic Scientists*. In summation he said:

"The fabric of Israel's history has a single unifying thread—a constant belief, not always easy to sustain, in the positive direction of human history and in the responsiveness of men, when challenged by great issues and lofty ideas. Strong currents of passion still sweep across the awakening continents, threatening to submerge liberties hardly won and deeply cherished. It was a moving experience for us at such a time to set the stage for an international assembly consecrated to the pursuit of truth in the service of man's expanding welfare and enduring peace."

He had been most impressed by a remark he heard Dr. Solomon Caulker of Sierra Leone make in commenting on this first dazzling contact with the world of science:

"I came in darkness, but I leave in light."

Dr. Caulker's death in a plane accident at Dakar while on the way home a few hours later was the only sad repercussion of the conference for Eban.

From a purely selfish viewpoint, Eban felt Israel's position in the Western world was now fairly secure and everything might henceforth depend on developing a strong relationship with Africa, Asia and Latin

America. The Rehovoth Conference had pioneered in this direction. At least it had provided the first human contact between leaders of the emergent nations and scientists, who had never really known each other before.

On the personal level, Eban, denied the role in foreign affairs he wanted to play, had organized the largest international relations project Israel had ever known and had focused Israel's interest at least momentarily on something less provincial than her myopic concern with her own frontier problems.

August (1960) was a good month for the Ebans because it was also in August that Ben-Gurion asked Eban if he would like to take over the thorny job of Minister of Education and Culture, a major post in the Cabinet. As Suzy and her husband discussed the offer they had the fleeting thought that maybe it was made in the belief it would be destructive. They debated whether Ben-Gurion was that Machiavellian, without reaching a unanimous decision. As they talked Eban recalled that at Cambridge he had heard Lord Keynes give this definition:

"Education is the inculcation of the incomprehensible into the ignorant by the incompetent."

The State of Israel was only twelve years old but Jewish education had a history stretching back to the days of the Temple. During the period of the Ottoman Empire and the British Mandate no public education was provided for the children of Palestine Jews, who therefore had to organize and finance their own schools. As a result, when the state came into existence there was already a traditional body of Jews with experience in education—teachers, principals, supervisors, administrators. Yet in 1960 there were grave problems.

The public school teachers were organized into two strong but sometimes competing trade unions which used the threat of strike in their continuous fight for larger salaries and better working conditions. The problem facing any Minister of Education was that there were never funds available to satisfy the teachers' demands, no matter how legitimate they might be. Also, schools were overcrowded, facilities were inadequate and parents were dissatisfied. Any Minister, no matter how brilliant, was in the parent-teacher nutcracker. Also, there was the melting pot problem. Education in Israel bore the stamp of Eastern Europe, for most pupils and almost all the educators had been Ashkenazim. But very rapidly Jews from North Africa and Asia were becoming a majority of the population. Their children needed much different educational treatment than the offspring of European parents. Also, there was the problem of making secondary education free as quickly as possible for as many as possible.

Suzy Eban, knowing the frustration that had oppressed her husband while holding the anomalous position of Minister Without Portfolio, was delighted with Ben-Gurion's offer, whatever the motive. She argued it would give Aubrey scope for his imagination and originality.

"It will be like a beautiful tournament for all of us outsiders to watch," she said. "You can contribute so much by the new thinking and new methods you will introduce."

As soon as announcement of the appointment was made Eban began looking for a director-general, aware of what his own shortcomings would be after he took over the department. He relished formulating policy, devising plans, solving problems, but he dreaded the thought of having to keep a nine-to-five office routine and dealing with the million details of running the educational system of even so small a country. Fortunately, while ambassador in Washington he had given a reception for a group of visiting Israelis that included Chanock Rinnot, who had worked with Henrietta Szold, organizer of the women's Zionist organization Hadassah, and with her, as the Nazis came to power, had helped found Youth Aliyah, an organization that rescued thousands of young European Jews. Because Youth Aliyah developed many pioneering educational concepts, Eban decided Rinnot would be an ideal man to assist him in carrying out the ideas that were already beginning to germinate in his mind.

Outlining the general educational policies he wished to follow, Eban told the twenty-fifth Zionist Congress, meeting in Jerusalem, that education was the key to Israel's security.

"Only by means of a high qualitative superiority can two million confront fifty million. We should not be a small people dwelling along the Mediterranean coast in the current century but an eternal people marching ahead of the confines of time and space. Provincialism can apply to time as well as space and he who lives in the present is doomed to provincialism."

But he soon found that the job of Minister of Education required more of him than voicing lofty objectives. In his daily work he had to deal with many people who, even though connected with the field of education in some way, were his intellectual inferiors. Two minutes after someone began talking to him—no matter what about—he understood the situation and then became exceedingly bored with the details, anticipating everything the other person was about to say. He had never been good at hiding boredom. As one associate of those days described him, "he was a university man dealing with primary and secondary problems."

People by the hundreds came to see him. They came with books they had written. They came tugging by the hand children who had had problems with their teachers. They came complaining, suggesting, arguing, pleading. People by the thousands wrote letters to him demanding replies. Because Israel was so small a country everyone expected personal attention to his own problems.

In Washington as an ambassador he had made most decisions himself. In Jerusalem as Minister of Education he had to submit even minor matters to the Knesset for approval. The pettiness of the job soon began to annoy him.

One of the major problems was that children from oriental families now comprised 60 percent of primary pupils, 30 percent of those entering secondary school, 15 percent of those graduating from secondary schools and 5 percent of those entering universities. Only one of the fourteen Cabinet members was of oriental origin and no Supreme Court judge, no officer of the Army's High Command and no member of the Jewish Agency Executive. Eban was aware that this segment of the population—no longer a minority— needed special education attention.

He also had to try to change the anti-intellectual bias of Israel's pioneering society. The hero of the Zionist saga until now had been the Jewish farmer milking his cow and if he had previously been a mathematician or an economist, so much the better. But Israel's 1960 situation demanded a steady increase in academically trained people. Also, Eban was constantly pointing out to his associates that modern Jewish thinkers like Ahad Ha'am saw cultural vitality rather than physical refuge or national sovereignty as the Zionist aim.

On Purim in March of 1961 fifteen hundred secondary teachers went on strike, closing classrooms for thirty thousand pupils across the country. Unfortunately, Eban was scheduled to deliver two weeks of fund-raising talks in the United States just at this time. Finance Minister Levi Eshkol offered to handle the strike negotiations for him, so despite the crisis Eban left for America. Early in the tour, because of plane trouble, he arrived in Pikesville, Maryland, at a Jewish charity banquet too late to have dinner but just in time to deliver his address. After talking for forty minutes he announced he was unable to continue and was taken to a local hospital, where doctors called it "fatigue collapse." Later in the week he left the hospital and continued the tour saying:

"I had three full days of sleep, a cure I can recommend to my friends back home."

The strike lasted fifty-five days. The agreement with the teachers was finally signed after a four-hour session presided over by Eban himself.

While he was constantly being sniped at as Minister of Education, he found that the rest of his title—"and Culture"—also got him into trouble. Now that he was in such a vulnerable position he was the victim of constant picayune attacks.

For example, the Israel Philharmonic announced it would perform Beethoven's Ninth Symphony and Eban would attend to demonstrate his view that such performances of German works were permissible in Israel. In the face of wide criticism Eban announced he would or would not attend purely on the basis of taste, not principle.

For example, the Israel soccer team went to Italy and while there played a match on Saturday. Eban was criticized for countenancing this violation of the Jewish Sabbath. (He agreed the match should not have been played on the Sabbath but he also pointed out that as many as a quarter of a million Israelis often watched soccer matches at home on Saturday, with few people objecting.)

For example, an English rabbi expressed concern because Eban had said something favorable about "scientific humanism" and wasn't this a non-religious concept of ethics?

(Eban's reply: "In Israel's educational system ethics and moral behavior have always been taught in relation to the spiritual insights of Judaism. It is my resolve that they shall continue to be so taught.")

For example, in a Book Week speech Eban accused some sabras (native-born Israeli Jews) of speaking Hebrew carelessly and of having a limited vocabulary and a regrettable ignorance of grammar—a criticism probably justified yet offensive to a large segment of the population.

For example, ultrareligious Jews in the Knesset tried to pass a law to forbid Jewish parents sending their children to non-Jewish schools, especially to schools run by certain Christian denominations. Eban opposed the proposed law, stating that only about one thousand of the ten thousand children in such schools were Jews. Moral persuasion, he said, was a better solution than legal prohibition. He won this fight, but antagonized many of the ultrareligious.

For example, in the Knesset he was attacked by the extreme left and the extreme right (Communists and Herut) for permitting a German pastor to make a tour of Israeli schools. Eban explained that the visitor had been a noted and active anti-Nazi and he criticized those who "exploited the holocaust for political purposes." This remark further antagonized his opponents.

He was even blamed because at a dinner given by the Ministry of Education after a Philharmonic concert in Tel Aviv dessert and coffee were not served until 1:30 A.M. because of the length of the half-dozen scheduled and unscheduled speeches, and some of the guests had to be at their Jerusalem offices at 7:30 A.M.

He opened himself to more criticism when he publicly declared the need to do something to beautify the New City of Jerusalem, which he called "a rocky, dusty, barren place . . . more like some small provincial city than a great metropolis."

Early in 1961 Israel's first golf course, built by the Rothschild family, was formally opened at the ancient Roman city of Caesarea, north of Haifa. At the inauguration members of both the French and British branches of the Rothschild family were present, as well as the entire diplomatic corps and two thousand spectators, many of whom had never seen a golf match in their lives—maybe not even a golf ball. The first player to tee off was Lord Rothschild, followed by Eban, in a striped sport shirt, who sliced his hundred-and-fifty-yard drive into the rough.

"It was below my usual form," he commented, as he hunted the ball.

The opening tournament was won by Sam Snead, wearing a lemon-yellow sweater and one of his famous straw hats. Several weeks later Eban, chairman of the club's management committee, played a match with Danny Kaye. When asked who won, Kaye said:

"I decline to comment on the score. We do not want to cause a new government crisis!"

Asked by the New York *Times* to contribute to a column of golf quotations by such people as Will Rogers and Jack Benny, Eban said:

"Playing the game, I have learned the meaning of humility. It has given me an understanding of the futility of human effort."

All this publicity about golf boomeranged. Some newspaper critics pointed out that golf is a rich man's game (at least in Israel); that in becoming the only high government official to join the new club Eban was reinforcing the impression that he was "different" from most Israelis. Eban countered that he did not see any difference between golf, football or tennis; "all are sports and all ought to be encouraged."

During "The Affair," the most bitter domestic political controversy since the creation of the state, Eban had been critical of the actions of Pinchas Lavon when he was Minister of Defense. Now Lavon, using Eban's membership in the Caesarea Golf Club in counterattack, censoriously declared that a Socialist minister should make himself at home with workers and pioneers and not with "the small number of officials who are part public servants and part dominators of the public."

Even the British press joined in trying to embarrass him. Tom Pocock, defense correspondent of the London *Evening Standard,* wrote a story that appeared under the bold headline:

'ESPIONAGE SCHOOL LEAKED BRITAIN'S MILITARY SECRETS

The article said Mr. Pocock had discovered (rather belatedly) that during World War II Major Aubrey Eban, "a senior Haganah officer working in a British Intelligence organization" (there were three errors in that one phrase alone), was infiltrated by Haganah into the Middle East Center of Arab Studies and during the rest of the war "was able to provide the Jewish Agency with a constant flow of British military and political secrets."

Eban immediately cabled the paper that the only secrets the Middle East Center investigated in his time "were those of Arabic grammar and syntax. Sometimes, but not always, our pupils penetrated those mysteries. There were no others."

The *Evening Standard* printed his denial and apologized for any embarrassment the erroneous report may have caused.

On Remembrance Day (1961), a non-religious holiday when Israelis commemorate Jewish deaths in World War II, the trial of Adolf Eichmann was recessed and Eban, standing on a hilltop three miles from Eichmann's prison, looked down at the mausoleum containing the ashes of Nazi concentration camp victims, and declared:

"Memory is the father of conscience. Whoever flees from his memory liberates himself from the full dictates of his conscience. There was never a time when it was more crucial for men to let their minds dwell on the awesome drama of conscience—a conflict within the human heart between love and hate, cruelty and compassion."

Eban wrote about the trial, and later about the execution, for many publications in Israel, Europe, the United States and even South Africa. As always he took the long view, writing less about Eichmann himself than about the portent of the case. In *The Reporter* he wrote:

"The human conscience needs an alarm bell not a sleeping powder. . . . Man has probed deeply into the spectacle of nature, but stands baffled before the incalculabilities of his own character. . . ."

In these years Eban's pen was in constant use, as well as his voice, in furthering principles important to him. If a prominent Zionist died he would sit down and write a eulogistic obituary. He wrote articles for innumerable magazines. If an author asked for a foreword for his book or an appreciative comment Eban graciously obliged. He even found time to translate *Oedipus* by Sophocles into modern English, devoid of forsooths and thees and thous.[1]

He went frequently to the United States to make fund-raising addresses. ("You can't milk a cow in absentia.") On three occasions Mapai asked him to fly home in a hurry because his vote was needed in the Knesset to assure a majority.

Each time he arrived at Lod Airport he was met by his driver, Yonkale, known as "one of the Teheran boys," because he had been a member of a group of Polish orphans rescued during the Nazi occupation and transported to Palestine via Iran. He had been with Eban since Eban joined the government. (In Israel if a Cabinet member moves from one ministry to another he has the privilege of taking his driver with him.) Yonkale was short, always was smiling, wore civilian clothes, spoke only Hebrew and Yiddish and was an establishment in himself. As soon as Eban was settled in the car he would start his report on what had been going on behind the scenes during the minister's absence, who was now against whom, what Eban should do to offset this or that pressure and which side he ought to take in the newest political quarrel. Talking once about his relationship with his employer he said:

"He listens to me. Why shouldn't he? He finds out what's going on from me. Otherwise what would he know?"

Aware of Eban's carelessness about money Yonkale handled all financial matters, saw that Eban had the latest edition of every newspaper and managed many of his private affairs. Occasionally he would be taken on a trip abroad as a reward for faithful service. He is one government associate Eban trusts completely and listens to silently.

Taking part in the 1962 Dialogue, an annual event in which Israeli and American Jewish spokesmen debate the relationship of the two communities, Eban suggested that Israelis stop lecturing American Jews about their insecurity.

On the sixteenth anniversary of the founding of the UN, he wrote in the Jerusalem *Post:*

"The founders of the UN assumed that the whole human future was their responsibility . . . that their work would become a blueprint for a positive order of society. . . . The truth is the UN has outlived all the basic assumptions which attended its birth. . . . Indeed, the history of the UN is largely the story of collapse."[2]

Confused by the Minister of Education's various names, a newspaper columnist wrote:

"The time has come for an international conference or a conciliatory commission to settle the issue between Abba and Aubrey, and Eban and Even, because now the Jewish Agency in some of its publications is calling him Even."[3]

The headline over the story read:

IT'S ODD TO BE EVEN

(Eban's explanation of why he retained the British spelling of his family name was that "I wanted to do my stepfather the honor of not changing his name, because of the extraordinary love he had shown in bringing me up as one of his own children; all I could do in return was to try to bring kudos to the name he had given me.")

At the funeral in Stockholm of Dag Hammarskjöld, following his death in a plane crash, Eban represented the state of Israel. Recalling his long association with the UN Secretary-General he said:

"He was insatiable in conversation. In him I detected a personal humility behind his official pride. He believed the world was destined to be drawn together in a covenant of law and order. This vision, which the Hebrew mind had once seized in an ardent flash of revelation, presented itself to his view as an austerely rational necessity."

Lyndon B. Johnson was at the funeral representing the United States. Since Eban had last seen him he had been elected Vice-President, so after shaking hands Eban asked:

"Mr. Vice-President, how do you like your new job?"

"I don't like it!" snapped back Johnson. Then, indicating his cutaway coat and striped trousers, he added:

"Do you see these things I'm wearing? Never wore them before in my life. Now I even sleep in the damn things!"

Early in 1961 (March 2) Meyer Weisgal, aware of how unhappy Eban was in his aggravating ministerial position, wrote to him suggesting that he resign from the Government and become head of Weizmann Institute in fact as well as in name.

"You were the first to admit in our conversation that the experience of political and governmental life which you have had the past eighteen or twenty months has not been exactly exhilarating. Politics at best is a rough-and-tumble game and invariably deteriorates into a rat race. You have been running that race since you came back to Israel. Much as I regret saying this to you, your prestige in Israel has suffered considerably following your acceptance of government office. Were it not for the fact that you hold the title of President of Weizmann Institute and in that capacity convened the highly successful international conference . . . I honestly believe your prestige in Israel would have been even lower. It is a sad state of affairs but these are inescapable facts. . . ."[4]

Weisgal argued that if Eban would "bow out gracefully from all government and parliamentary offices and activities" and devote the next five years exclusively to the Weizmann Institute it would "electrify public opinion and draw attention to your own high moral stature without in the least damaging your prospects for a political career in the future."

Eban felt that some of what Weisgal said was inaccurate, some of it unfair, for the post of Minister of Education and Culture was one of the top five or six positions in the country. As the Ebans debated the Weisgal suggestions, a call went out for a new election. That meant the eventual formation of a new Cabinet, so Eban decided to work in the campaign for Mapai and then to demand, after the election, that his abilities be put to their proper use.

Tel Aviv newspapers agreed that next to Ben-Gurion, again, as in 1959, Eban was the chief drawing card of all the candidates, which seemed to prove that Israelis came out to hear what he had to say, not merely because of curiosity.

Carl Alpert, Haifa journalist, writing a syndicated column for American Jewish papers, found the 1961 Eban less stiff, less formal, a little less literary in his style, more down to the people's level, than the Eban of 1959 had been.

Suzy Eban made campaign addresses to several audiences of Egyptian Jews. At one meeting she had thirteen hundred people. ". . . they were so terribly nice to me and showed warmth and appreciation."[5]

Writing to her parents-in-law she said:

"The weeks after the election will be full of arm-twisting all around. We shall try to be wise—as wise as human beings can be—and the rest is destiny."[6]

Late in the year (1961), in London to deliver the Robert Waley Cohen Memorial Lecture before the Council of Christians and Jews, Eban began by saying that this was the first time the Council "has reached across the seas" to find a lecturer for the series, then added:

"I presume it does not reflect a counsel of despair or a confession that local sources of eloquence and learning have dried up."

The address was notable for a definition that Eban, seasoned diplomat, gave of his profession:

"Modern diplomacy is largely a holding action, designed to avoid a premature explosion until the unifying forces of history take all nations into their embrace."

(In just six years, as Foreign Minister, he would put this concept of diplomacy as a holding action into dramatic effect.)

While carrying out these extracurricular activities, Eban was conceiving and trying to execute many revolutionary ideas in the field of education. One was changing over from a regime of eight elementary years and four secondary to a six-six system. Another was the idea of wealthy Americans giving money for the construction of high schools in Israel. Another was sabbaticals for secondary school teachers.

In this field of his principal activity he had many frustrations, but some achievements. Due to rivalry between the union of secondary teachers and the union of elementary teachers he was never able to put into full effect his idea of a sabbatical every seven years for secondary teachers, during which they would become revitalized by a year of travel and study.

He had more success in closing the gulf between Ashkenazi and Sephardi children by the introduction of homework clubs to rescue pupils from squalid, crowded homes; a longer school day for children in development areas; reduction in the size of classes; free kindergartens; boarding schools for gifted children from oriental homes; and increased grants to enable needy children to have secondary education, which was not yet universally free. Yet his big worry continued to be that "the advance part of our population is becoming more advanced and the backward part therefore relatively more backward and the gap between them is increasing and broadening."

Regardless of progress there was much to keep a perfectionist from complete self-satisfaction. Eban found that one third of the Sephardi children who had completed eight years of elementary school still could not read a newspaper or a light book, nor could they write legibly or sensibly.

One night the Ebans were invited to dinner at the home of Finance Minister Eshkol. The guests of honor were two British millionaires. During the meal the talk turned to Israel's educational problems and Eban's description of the need for money to build high schools was so poignant that both men promised him substantial contributions. As they were leaving one of them turned to his host and said:

"I think tomorrow we'll dine in our hotel. The food there is much less expensive."[7]

One of his victories as Minister of Education and Culture was in the battle for educational television. His friend Lord Edwin Samuel, while serving as a British official in Palestine under the Mandate, had introduced educational radio. But in 1948 it had been dropped. It was reintroduced by Eban, who then appointed a committee to investigate the possibility of educational television, following the recommendation of a UNESCO survey mission. In a private comment on the virulence of the opposition (which even included his superior, Prime Minister Ben-Gurion) Eban said:

"Despite herself Israel is going to be pulled, kicking and screaming, into the twentieth century."[8]

Major opposition came from the religious parties. There were many nettlesome Knesset debates. During one Ben-Gurion waved a finger at Eban and predicted that if he (Eban) had his way and succeeded in introducing educational television, the day would come when his (Eban's) grandchildren would spend their time in their homes "watching the boom-boom machine."

During one of the debates Eban asked:

"Where is the logic of saying that because murder stories are televised in the United States we should not televise physics lectures in Israel?"

The discussion went on for several years. The fight in the Knesset was so bitter that "at one stage it looked as though we might lose, in which case either I would have had to resign, or the government would have had to resign—over television."[9] This was typical of Israel, where no Government has ever fallen over a major issue of security or foreign affairs, but over such matters as "Who is a Jew?" or the Kastner case, or religious education in immigration villages.

Eventually Eban persuaded the Cabinet and then the Knesset to accept an offer by the Rothschild family to finance establishment of an educational television network. The final vote was close, 55 to 43. (As the opposition had predicted, educational television led in a few years to general television.)

A New York editor, acknowledging receipt of a manuscript from Eban, wrote with an effusion not at all common to New York editors:

"To one at the mercy of relentless manuscripts, mountainous, though already screened, your lucid prose restored faith in the relationship of thought to expression."[10]

But his relationship with all editors was not as amicable. In 1962 he had a direct-by-mail feud with Norman Podhoretz, editor of *Commentary*, whom he accused of no longer having "a positive interest in the culture and destiny of the Jewish people." Eban therefore withdrew an endorsement he had given the magazine.[11]

To a group of prospective contributors to an Israeli scientific research program he said:

"Science is not a sacred cow. Science is a horse. Don't worship it; feed it!"

Political squabbles, crises in the field of education, the petty sniping of small-minded critics and Israel's concern with her security unfortunately overshadowed the progressive steps Eban took as Minister of Culture. He told Florence Berkman, art editor of the Hartford (Connecticut) *Times*, that Israel wanted to be an Athens not a Sparta, "standing for the arts, the intellect, culture and all refinements of the mind and the spirit, which was Athens, and not for military might, which was Sparta."

Soon after taking office he appointed an Arts Council and appropriated almost a third of a million dollars to aid the plastic arts, music, dancing and literature. Then he announced plans for an international conference of the creative arts, with writers, musicians and artists invited from all corners of the world.

Minister of Education Eban worried about Israelis not living up to their reputation as "people of the book," because libraries were almost non-existent, so his department took steps to encourage the establishment of libraries throughout the country.

When he learned that his ministry was also responsible for sports (sports being considered by the framers of the Israeli government structure a cultural enterprise) he remarked:

"It always seemed to me that rhetoric was the only sport in which Israel had a chance of acquiring the world championship."

In the spring of 1963, as the supreme sports authority in the Government, he took a stand against professional boxing. His position had the backing of a majority of the press, one paper reporting that the profession produces each year a pathetic assortment of human wrecks, "men reduced to a state of idiocy by damage to their brain tissue from head blows."

There was some opposition, however, when Eban announced in the Knesset a code of rules that would henceforth govern cultural relations with Germany. Forbidden were entertainment shows by Germans in Israel or by Israelis in Germany; use of foreign exchange for studying by Israelis in Germany; the opening of branches of German enterprises or institutions in Israel. Permitted were visits by certain Germans to Israel; participation by Israelis in international events in Germany; opening of an Israeli information office in Germany. As one summary put it, "Not everything is permitted; not everything is forbidden." Eban's explanation was that he was attempting to bring about "a breakdown of negation that won't affront too many people." Despite virulent opposition, especially by right-wing extremists, his code won approval.

Two items in the Eban scrapbook for 1962 tell the same story:

Al Rosenfeld, Israeli correspondent for the New York *Herald Tribune*, in a three-thousand-word dispatch devoted exclusively to Eban, wrote that in the three years he had been home he had succeeded in establishing himself as a political personality of significance.[12]

Suzy Eban, writing to friends, said:

"I don't feel anymore that we are looked upon as intruders, but as welcome participants."[13]

Late in 1962 Golda Meir went to New York in her capacity as Foreign Minister to speak in the General Assembly debate. Before leaving she told her fellow Cabinet members she wished Eban to serve as Foreign Minister in her absence, an announcement that caused much discussion in political circles. When she had gone to the General Assembly the previous year the Cabinet had passed over Eban, with his wealth of experience in international affairs, and had chosen Finance Minister Eshkol to assume Mrs. Meir's duties as well as his own. While she was away on that occasion a crisis had come up in the Cabinet over Israel's vote in the UN against seating Peking. Eshkol, brilliant in matters of finance but admittedly ignorant of foreign affairs, begged Eban to substitute for him in the Knesset debate. This time Mrs. Meir, despite the chill in her relations with Eban, which was a matter of common knowledge in Mapai circles, decided not to entrust the keys of her office to an amateur again. No vital crisis occurred while she was away this time, but Eban had the evanescent pleasure of filling for several weeks the Cabinet position to which he had so long aspired.

One day in Jerusalem Suzy met a friend on the street and mentioned how busy she was in her various activities, to which the friend replied:

"Sometimes you must wonder yourself in what capacity you are entertaining."

When Suzy relayed the remark to her husband that night he laughed and said:

"That's true. Look what's happening in our bed. Two presidents and two ministers sleeping with each other." (He was still president of

Weizmann Institute, she was president of the Cancer Society of Israel, and he was Minister of Education and Culture, as well as Minister of Foreign Affairs, temporarily.)

One night in 1962 Eban made an announcement to his wife and children.

"I have a revolutionary idea. We're going to live in a house of our own."

Eli and Gila shrieked with joy and the young son exclaimed:

"Abba deserves the Nobel Prize for this."

And so the Ebans built a house for their own eventual use on a lot in Herzlia, next to the home of the Ambaches. As Suzy explained to a friend:

"It's so essential, as we have jointly agreed, to have something always ready in the background amidst the tremors of political life."[14]

In New York they had lived in hotels and furnished apartments, in Washington in Embassy houses, in Rehovoth in an Institute building, and if he ever achieved his dream of becoming Foreign Minister they would have to live in a government house in Jerusalem. He always remembered how his friend Sharett, as well as a former Minister of Education, when they suddenly left office had no roof over their heads and people had to pass a hat to collect money to buy them apartments.

"I thought there was a terrible lack of dignity and independence in Israel's political life and since Suzy had means and since I was making some money on book royalties, we decided to be in a position where we could, if we wanted to, walk out of all these official residences and tell everyone to go to hell, and therefore we built our house on what was then a lonely piece of land but subsequently became a heavily built-up area."[15]

25

Facts Scarce, Opinions Free

ONE WARM DAY in 1963 the members of the Cabinet met as usual in Ben-Gurion's office to conduct routine business. After rapping for order and waiting for the usual chattering to cease, the Old Man (as most of them called him) made a simple announcement—he was resigning as both Prime Minister and Minister of Defense. It was his eighth resignation and so the initial reaction was that maybe this was just one more attempt to get his own way by threatening to retire to the desert. But when he added he also wanted to give up his seat in the Knesset, his colleagues realized he was serious.[1]

That evening Eban telephoned Suzy to tell her the news. There was little doubt in anyone's mind that Finance Minister Eshkol would be named by the President to head the government. Would he shake up the Cabinet? Whatever this resignation might mean for the country, Eban was certain it meant a turn in the road for him personally.

On June 21 (1963), after weeks of discussion with political leaders, Eshkol, as Premier-designate, announced the make-up of his Cabinet. The most important change was that Eban would be elevated from Minister of Education and Culture to Deputy Prime Minister. His main function would be to use his wealth of experience in advising the new head of government on matters of foreign policy, a field in which Eshkol had had little experience, and to serve as a coordinating link between the offices of the Foreign Minister and the Prime Minister.

The Jerusalem *Post* saw Eban's new position as another step "in the progress toward the Foreign Ministry." So did Eban. To his parents in London Suzy wrote:

"Life is so full of movement. . . . Unless one lives it from day to day one cannot know all the hidden intensities of political life and how much of it is plagued with human factors and not necessarily with ideas and ideals. . . . Things look promising for Aubrey now and it is so exciting to think that foreign affairs is open to him once again. It was a cruel denial, like tying the hands of a musician so he could never play the piano or the hands of an artist so he could never paint. The trouble is that in so many countries foreign affairs has been handled by people of such varied backgrounds and by so many nonentities that the true nature of diplomacy is rarely known these days. It seems so absurd, retrospectively, that Israel, having such talent available, should have chosen to remove it from the field. For us, however, it has been a useful school. It has tempered the metal. We have been closer to reality, both national and human."[2]

The Cairo correspondent of the *Jewish Observer and Middle East Review* reported that Egyptian politicians, from Nasser down, and "the more knowledgeable professors at the universities," were intensely interested in the Eban appointment.

"He is very much admired and sometimes envied by many of the more thoughtful people here; he is something 'different' and also something unmatched in the political life here. He is rated especially high because of his gifted pen and tongue and because of his inside understanding of the Egyptians in particular."

The first reaction of many Israelis was that Eban had been sidetracked into a meaningless position which had a name but no function, no authority. Within a short time, however, it was clear this was no protocol occupation. With Mrs. Meir's agreement Eban now had full access to all Foreign Ministry matters that might concern the Prime Minister, which meant anything of any importance or significance.

Being Deputy Prime Minister had two advantages for Eban. It saved him from further wrangling over teachers' salaries, a form of domestic debate not at all to his liking, and put him back in the international field. He would go to the UN again, attend international conferences and return to the world stage. Also, others' misfortunes would be his gain: both the Prime Minister and the Foreign Minister were in ill health so he would be called upon to sit in occasionally for both of them, giving him an opportunity to create an image.

Two weeks after the Cabinet was sworn in, Dayan, speaking for what the papers called "the young" in Mapai, made an attack on the Eshkol government which was immediately answered by Eban, who said:

"How odd that the only really discordant voices raised against the government should have come from within their own party. Surely the

Prime Minister and the government are entitled to a period of leniency before judgment is passed on them."

One month after Eshkol's assumption of power it was generally agreed —Dayan to the contrary—that the new Prime Minister had made himself "master of his own house" and that Eshkol and Eban had "established a state of communion that augurs well for this new combination."[3]

During his Ministry of Education days Eban had often been criticized journalistically, but as he began to fill the new role Eshkol had created for him the press was fair, complimentary, even eulogistic, this synopsis of his political career being typical:

"He has had to plough a difficult furrow since he abandoned diplomacy for politics, and he has often been written off by his colleagues. But Eban was made of tougher stuff than many of the hardened politicians. Behind his somewhat shy standoffishness, which many Israeli politicians misread, Eban stuck to his guns. He refused to be drawn into political intrigues or petty quarrels. He kept his sights high. He did not talk down to his audiences, and they appreciated it. Despite the rough-and-tumble of domestic politics, he has managed to maintain his former aloofness. His colleagues thought he was making a mistake. He knew better. For suddenly, out of the mist and fog of the political scene, his Mapai colleagues and the Israeli public now see Eban sitting on one of the commanding heights of the new Government. If, in the past, there was any doubt about his political future, there is little room left for it. Without intrigue, without 'a machine' for personal advancement, he has arrived."[4]

The Ebans continued to live in Rehovoth, for Aubrey was still president of the Weizmann Institute. His day in Jerusalem began with a conference with the Prime Minister during which they would go over incoming cables and frame replies. Then a discussion of overnight developments in the field of foreign affairs. Then conferences with Knesset committees. Next Eban would help Eshkol with the first draft of the next speech he had to deliver. Then he would meet with the ministerial security committee of which he was a member. Twice a week he and Eshkol would have lunch with Golda Meir. He also kept in close touch with members of the diplomatic corps and entertained visiting dignitaries. As head of the Weizmann Institute he was involved with an ever growing stream of leaders from underdeveloped countries coming to Israel for technological and scientific indoctrination. He played an important role in Israel's foreign aid and exchange program, which joined Israel intimately with forty small and large nations. He also represented the government at cornerstone layings, dedications, conferences, conventions and miscellaneous public affairs.

Early in 1963 Eban went to Geneva to take part in a conference that was superlative in many ways. It had the longest name of any international gathering in history: The United Nations Conference on the Application of Science and Technology for the Benefit of Less Developed Areas. Even the initials were a mouthful: TUNCOTAOSATFTBOLDA. It was in some ways an outgrowth of the Rehovoth Conference Eban had organized. (It took the UN three years to catch up with Israel.) There were 2,500 delegates, including thirty Nobel Prize winners. They submitted 1,873 papers. Just the titles made a 360-page book. Eban headed a 23-man Israeli delegation that submitted 36 papers. After two weeks of meetings, discussions, briefings, press conferences, cocktail parties, dinners and receptions even the toughest of the delegates was exhausted.

In addressing the concluding session Eban said:

"This is the first generation of mankind in which the elimination of poverty and disease has become objectively possible. . . . Scientists have the will and the capacity to transform the human situation. If we can only fertilize their will and organize their capacity we may yet inaugurate one of the great ages of history."

Not only was the address well reported by wire services and daily newspapers but excerpts were printed in papers and magazines all over Europe, Africa, Asia and North and South America.

Later that year Eban presided over his own conference at Rehovoth: eleven days, eighty delegates from twenty-nine countries, dealing principally with agricultural planning in what Eban this time called "emerging countries." In opening this conference he set the mood with the remark:

"There is nothing more universal than the cry of the hungry child."

Although now technically out of politics and living in the desert, Ben-Gurion continued to stir the political stew with his own personal paddle. He refused to permit the Lavon Affair to die a quiet death. He was loyally supported by Peres. Three months after taking office as Deputy Prime Minister, Eban delivered an address in which he attacked the Ben-Gurion-Peres military orientation and said it was the duty of a modern army to safeguard peace and not to depend on victory in battle.

Soon after becoming Prime Minister Eshkol went to France on an official visit and in his absence Eban served as Acting Prime Minister, with all the power and prerogatives of the office. In the twelve days Eshkol was away, however, the most serious matter that came Eban's way was a dispute between the Chief Rabbinate and some cattle dealers about an abattoir.

After the assassination of John F. Kennedy Eban delivered an address which stuck in the memory. He began: "Tragedy is the difference between what is and what might have been." He concluded: "There will, of course, be other eras of zest and vitality, when men feel that it is morning and it is good to be alive. This, however, belongs to the future. In the meantime let us be frank with each other. The world is darker than it was a week ago."

The Encyclopaedia Britannica some months later published a Kennedy book containing the most significant tributes to the late President and Eban's was included.

Several months after becoming Deputy Prime Minister Eban went to London and there gave an interview to the *Jewish Chronicle* in which he said Ben-Gurion's resignation had inevitably led to "a reexamination of our situation in many respects." At another point in the interview he said he believed an investigation ought to be made of the possibility of bringing about a thaw in Israeli-Arab relations. A British news agency put out a résumé which made it appear Eban was linking Ben-Gurion's resignation and reappraisal of Arab relations. The matter reached the Cabinet, before which Eban explained what he had originally said. The next day's Jerusalem *Post* carried a headline:

EBAN BACKTRACKS ON
CHRONICLE INTERVIEW

With his usual sensitivity to what the press said about him, Eban had his office complain to the *Post* that the headline was inaccurate. He had done no backtracking.

(Over the years Eban had brittle relations with more than one newspaper at home and abroad, but he was in a constant state of war with the Jerusalem *Post*, which he considered uncritical in its worship of Ben-Gurion and later of Dayan, and prejudiced, unrepresentative and hawkish in its editorial policies.)

Reviewing books was one of his favorite avocations. When the Jewish Publication Society of America put out a new translation of the Torah (the first five books of the Bible) and the Jerusalem *Post* asked him to review it, he had a perfect opportunity to answer, obliquely, those who criticized his way of speaking and writing. Commenting on the objection that the thees and thous of Elizabethan English and of the King James Version are as archaic to modern ears as the fancies of Gothic architecture to modern eyes, he asked whether matters would be improved by installing neon lights and elevators in a medieval cathedral. He said Dryden, Bunyan, Addison, Milton, Ruskin and Gibbon would not have been captivated by such innovations in the new translation as "an ornamental tunic" for "a coat of many colors" and changing "Joseph found grace in Pharaoh's eyes" to "Pharaoh took a liking to Joseph."

In a letter about this time Suzy Eban wrote:

"We have been gripped by the fervour of governmental and official life and are at times horrified by its power to devour human beings. Yet we are also quite spellbound by its mystery and fascination."[5]

Nineteen sixty-four was a year of travel for the Deputy Prime Minister. He journeyed to France, England, Mexico, Canada, Colombia and Venezuela, and four times to the United States. He crossed back and forth over the Atlantic almost as in the days when he was ambassador. He did so many fund-raising speeches that it reminded him of the fifties. He was flattered that American audiences greeted him just as enthusiastically as ever; that Leonard Lyons was still eager to listen to his quips and put him in the "Lyons Den"; that his prestige was even greater, now, at the United Nations.

In London he suffered a minor insult during a meeting with Quintin Hogg, Minister of Science and Education, who remarked that many of the world's important events had had their beginning in small countries. To prove it the Englishman quoted a passage from Thucydides, first in Greek and then translated into English. It was the only time anyone had dared assume that Eban did not understand ancient Greek and he let the minister know how pained he was.

A London reporter told him the news that the foreign ministers of thirteen Arab states were going to visit world capitals to present their reasons why other nations should also adopt an anti-Israel position, and was Israel going to do anything similar?

"We cannot compete in ministerial abundance," Eban replied. "If what they say is not convincing, then sheer numbers will not count. If you multiply zero by thirteen you don't get a very encouraging result. Thirteen states with a total population of ninety-nine million threatened by a nation of two million—it doesn't sound very convincing to me."

On his first visit to the British Foreign Office since the mid-forties, when he was a member of the mission that called on Ernest Bevin, Eban discussed Middle Eastern problems with Richard Butler, Secretary of State for Foreign Affairs.

In the United States he denied the charge of seven Conservative and Reform organizations that there was religious coercion in Israel, saying:

"If I cannot have butter with my meat at a restaurant in Israel this infinitesimal sacrifice we can make for unity in the country."

Talking to the United Nations Correspondents' Association he said:

"The great powers have reached a paralysis resulting from the enormity of their own might. The more strength the less power they seem to have."

Of the UN itself he said:

"It is suffering from institutional conservatism. The time has come for the UN to discuss the UN."

As he was riding a shuttle plane from Washington to New York a stewardess said:

"How are you, Mr. Vice-President?"

Looking up from his book he replied:

"But I'm not the Vice-President; I'm the Deputy Prime Minister."

Then he noticed that the man sitting next to him, whom the stewardess had been addressing, was his old golf partner, Richard Nixon. They had a good talk during the rest of the flight.

Having been appointed by U Thant, along with seventeen other world figures, to an Advisory Council on Science and Technology, he conferred for two weeks in New York on ways to help developing countries.

For twelve days in June, while Eshkol was on a tour of the United States, he served as Acting Prime Minister, with Minister of Commerce and Industry Pinhas Sapir taking over Eshkol's duties as Defense Minister. Eli was impressed and addressed his father each morning of the twelve days as "Father Prime Minister."

In his capacity as Acting Prime Minister Eban participated in a Knesset debate on whether there should be a non-kosher kitchen on the Israeli passenger ship the SS *Shalom,* and whether there should be a curtailment of Yiddish-language broadcasts on Israel's radio. When he displayed surprising familiarity with Yiddish, he was asked how he had become such an expert in the language, to which he replied:

"Spending a year with Eshkol is enough to learn perfect Yiddish!"

In July the entire Eban family went on the SS *Shalom* to Europe, the first *en famille* trip they had ever taken. In Paris they did the usual things: the children were shown the Eiffel Tower, the Louvre, Versailles, went boat riding on the Seine, all at a leisurely pace quite unusual for Aubrey. Writing from somewhere along the way Suzy said:

"Aubrey is simply marvellous. He orders the children's breakfast and tells them when to go to bed. I can't believe my eyes or ears it is so good. We shall always remember these precious moments. . . . We are so relaxed, so human and familial. It is amazing what tensions must do to us, because really we are quite nice when not under pressure. Aubrey right through has been in charge of all of us. He even took care of the tippings and little arrangements which I have done for him for years. It is delightful to be a woman and not in charge. The children have had it on a platinum platter and we have found them so much enjoyment and such fun."[6]

In October, in the footsteps of some of the thirteen Arab foreign ministers, Eban went to Mexico, Colombia and Venezuela for sixteen days.

"The difference between their trip and mine," he later said, "is that they invited themselves; I went on the invitation of the host governments."

Back in New York in December, he made the Israeli speech in the general debate in the General Assembly. Speaking of the UN's financial difficulties, he said:

"The paradox of our age is that more will be spent on armaments on this one single day than will be required for all the activities of the UN and its many agencies for a whole year."

While in New York this time he had a sixty-minute conference with Soviet Foreign Minister Andrei Gromyko, but then he was suddenly called back to Jerusalem to participate in a Cabinet meeting on The Affair, which Ben-Gurion had heated up again.

Although he had been Ben-Gurion's protégé and at one time had felt Ben-Gurion was basically right in his criticism of the man who had been Defense Minister at the time of the sabotage in Egypt which led to The Affair, he now sided with Eshkol and those critical of Ben-Gurion's tactics in trying to keep the old conflict alive. He felt Ben-Gurion was behaving in a manner ill befitting an elder statesman.

The SOS from Jerusalem gave Eban just three hours to pack, cancel important appointments with a number of foreign ministers and get to Idlewild Airport at the height of the rush hour. It was a frantic scramble. When he arrived in Israel Suzy greeted him by telling him it was wonderful because he would be present for Gila's birthday the next day— a very important birthday, for she was going to be ten years old. Also, he would be able to escort her to the musical *My Fair Lady,* which was being put on as a benefit for the Cancer Society (she was still president) and was going to be one of the big social events of the season. The birthday party was a happy occasion for the whole family, but then Eban was suddenly notified he must return immediately to New York, so Suzy had to attend *My Fair Lady* alone. ("Damn it! There is too much alone."[7])

More important than anything else that happened in Israel that year (1964) was the visit of Pope Paul VI, who in January became the first Pope ever to tour the Holy Land. Because Golda Meir was ill, Eban was assigned to take her place in greeting the pontiff and during the visit spent more time with the distinguished visitor than any other Israeli. He was one of those who welcomed him when he crossed the Israeli frontier. Then he hurried ahead to Nazareth and when Pope Paul arrived at the Church of the Annunciation conducted him along the line of diplomats and their wives who had been waiting in the frosty air for more than two hours. Eban made a report to the Cabinet on his assessment of the trip—that it had had a good effect on the uneasy relationship between Jews and Catholics over the past hundreds of years and that Pope Paul had "increased his perception of Israeli statehood."

Eban's greatest honor in 1964 was being unanimously elected a fellow of the World Academy of Art and Science, a body of only a hundred and fifty members, among them Bertrand Russell, Stephen Spender and Gunnar Myrdal. He was elected as "a statesman who has contributed to the world's intellectual life."

During 1964 Eban sided with Eshkol and Golda Meir in favoring a more pro-American orientation of Israel's foreign policy and against Dayan and Peres, who wished to rely on France and other Western European nations, yet he risked the wrath of American officialdom when, in an article in the *UNESCO Courier*, he called for "a more logical system of human priorities in the world" and asked:

"How is it possible to justify the expenditure of billions of dollars in prestige projects in outer space when there is hunger, disease and illiteracy on this planet. . . . Is it our business to invade the moon or save the earth for our common humanity?"

During 1965 Israel's external situation was so little troubled that she was able to afford months of the bitterest domestic political battling the young country had ever known and Eban was highly involved.

Ben-Gurion had been engaging in a running fight with Eshkol from his desert home, principally because he wanted to keep The Affair alive and Eshkol insisted there were more important matters to command men's energies. The Affair overshadowed all else at Mapai's 1965 convention. Eban and Golda Meir were in agreement. They, with

Sharett, Sapir and Eshkol, opposed Ben-Gurion, who was supported by Dayan and Peres, among others. The debate was acrimonious, with Mrs. Meir hitting hard at Ben-Gurion. Eban, although speaking out, was more temperate, trying to phrase his criticism of the Old Man in more gentle words. He had agreed with many of Ben-Gurion's external policies, but considered some of his domestic decisions "nonsense." He thought Ben-Gurion's general political outlook "quite mature," yet he had never been captivated or mesmerized by him; had never adulated him. He was aware of the Old Man's weaknesses and considered his monomania about The Affair the greatest of them.[8]

The climax to the internecine feud came when Ben-Gurion resigned from Mapai and formed his own party, Rafi. Mapai leaders—especially those who were protégés of Ben-Gurion—had a soul-searching decision to make. Peres, Teddy Kollek and even Suzy's brother-in-law, Vivian Herzog, threw their lot in with Ben-Gurion. Also Dayan, after many hesitations. Eban was under great emotional and political pressure.

About this time *Foreign Affairs,* quarterly of the Council on Foreign Relations, published a thirteen-page article by Eban, "Reality and Vision in the Middle East," in which he outlined his entire philosophy about this part of the world and gave his own peace plan for the area. He was looking through the copy of the magazine he had just received from New York when a messenger brought a letter from Ben-Gurion, which congratulated him and said:

"It is the best article I have read about the Middle East in all my life."

From Eshkol on down everyone wondered about the significance of the letter. Some said that while Ben-Gurion was fiercely against Eshkol, he obviously had no enmity for Eban. Others said that of course Ben-Gurion was trying to win Eban over to Rafi. Still others thought there was nothing Machiavellian about it—that the Old Man simply enjoyed the article and quite honestly had said so. Nevertheless, Eban remained loyal to Eshkol and as preparations for the election began was placed high on Mapai's list of candidates.

It was the most acrimonious campaign in Israel's political history. As Suzy described it in a letter to a friend, "a big rubble-bubble." Personalities overshadowed issues. There was much mudslinging. One candidate was laughed off the platforms by being called "the Trojan donkey." Eban, quoting a famous British editor, told an audience:

"Facts are scarce; opinions are free."

The Rafi candidates spoke confidently of destroying Mapai and capturing at least a quarter of the Knesset's one hundred and twenty seats. In a restaurant one day Eban, Jon Kimche, the London editor, and Arye Dissentshik, editor of *Ma'ariv*, during a political argument wrote their names on slips of paper with the number of seats each expected Rafi to poll. Kimche's guess was thirty, Eban's ten.

Mapai had lost the support of two of the three bright young men Ben-Gurion had brought into top-level politics, Dayan and Peres. Only Eban remained. Golda Meir, in ill health, had let it be known she would resign after the election and was not extremely active as a campaigner. This meant Eban and Eshkol had to carry most of the burden. Next to the Prime Minister, Eban drew the largest crowds —and most of Rafi's fire. Suzy, whenever she attended one of her husband's meetings, sensed "a new electricity in the air." She felt this campaign was making him a central figure in the party.

Despite the political bitterness the Herzogs and Ebans continued a custom begun in Washington of having a two-family party whenever any Eban or Herzog had a birthday. On such occasions the rule now was: no politics.

No election in Israel's short political history had such an element of intensity as this one. In many ways it was like a family quarrel. Instead of getting the thirty seats they expected, Rafi wound up with just ten, the exact number Eban had written on the slip of paper. As one veteran Mapai politician put it:

"We were stunned by our success against such heavy odds, including Ben-Gurion's charisma, which we thought would sweep the country. The nation, however, showed more skepticism and maturity than the demigods expected."

Nineteen sixty-five was also the year of the Pacem in Terris Conference held in New York under the auspices of the Center for the Study of Democratic Institutions and presided over by Robert Hutchins, former president of the University of Chicago. Two thousand delegates came from twenty countries to discuss how the world's problems could be solved in the ecumenical spirit of the celebrated encyclical of Pope John XXIII. Seldom, except for the funeral of some world figure, had so many brilliant and distinguished men come together in one place. Among them were the Chief Justice of the Supreme Court, the Vice-President, four senators, the Italian Deputy Prime Minister, the Belgian Foreign Minister, two justices of the World Court, the Secretary-General of the UN, numerous Nobel Prize winners, leading figures from Russia, Poland and Yugoslavia—the cream of the Eastern world, the Western world and in-between countries.

One of Eban's ecumenical memories of Pacem in Terris was of a group of Roman Catholic clergy in a corner of the hall in earnest yet pleasant conversation with some of the delegates of the Soviet Union.

In his address to the final session Eban suggested a kind of super-summit meeting at which the heads of all sovereign governments would devote an entire week to considering the problems "not of any nation but of the human nation." Then he listed seven problems they might start with: the prospects opened up by new technologies, overpopulation, malnutrition, illiteracy, disparity of income, pollution and peace keeping.

"The world was created, according to biblical reckoning, in six days," he said; "it will take longer to repair the damage that we have been doing ever since."

To indicate what they thought of him and his ideas, the vast audience jumped to its feet and gave him a thunderous ovation. *Life* magazine provided still further circulation for his ideas by quoting extensively from his speech.

Two deaths occurred in 1965 which disturbed Eban, emotionally and intellectually. On January 24 Winston Churchill passed away at the age of ninety. Since his university days Eban had been doing impersonations of him and telling stories about him, but he admired him as a writer, orator and statesman. In his obituary tribute he said:

"His name is enshrined in Jewish history as the first and foremost of the knights to give battle against the worst of Israel's persecutors. He demanded the British promise be honored and he poured out his righteous wrath upon the betrayers."

The death of Moshe Sharett was a more intimate sorrow. He had cancer and died slowly, before the eyes of his friends. When he was no longer strong enough to move about, meetings were held in his home. One day Eban, Golda Meir and several other leaders were consulting with him about bringing the Soviet Jewry issue before world opinion. As they concluded their business and set a date for a reunion, Sharett quietly said:

"I think I shall not be attending the next meeting."

A few days later he died. In many ways he had been all that Eban aspired to be. In his tribute to him Eban spoke of his "creative, fastidious, exacting temperament," calling him "a romantic at heart," and said he had taught his foreign service subordinates "to expand our logic with a conscious appeal to nobility."

Although no one said so, there was only one person who might eventually fill the void left by Sharett's passing. Eban knew who that person was.

Midway through 1965 Eban tangled with Nahum Goldmann, controversial president of the World Zionist Organization, who had suggested that Jewish communities around the world could mediate the Arab-Israeli conflict. Eban countered that peace would not come "via New York and Buenos Aires, but through Israeli and Arab leaders." Goldmann then said he had been misunderstood—that what he had said was that Jewish communities in countries with important Arab minorities that had some influence on their home countries could help prepare an atmosphere of good will and understanding that might lead to direct Arab-Israeli talks.

Welcoming participants in an international chess tournament, Eban said a few words in the language of each country represented and then took subtle cognizance of the fact that most were Jewish by saying:

"I suppose you would all understand if I spoke Yiddish."

Because of the absence of Eshkol and Mrs. Meir at the same time Eban served briefly during 1965 as Prime Minister and Foreign Minister simultaneously.

Opening the National Museum in Jerusalem he had harsh words for domestic ugliness:

"There is much in Israel that needlessly offends the sensitive eye. Our cities are marred by agglomerations of ugliness. . . . Do we not carry informality of dress and speech to a point in which untidiness of form yields untidiness of thought and discord of emotions? Must the most beautiful and sacred landscape on earth become strident with advertisements announcing toothpaste or the seductive qualities of the national beer? Can we not plan housing communities even of modest economic level in such a way as to avoid such a varied display of the nation's underwear? . . . If our youth can be immersed in the study of painting and sculpture they will develop a healthy intolerance of ugliness and disharmony."

When West Germany offered to establish full diplomatic relations with Israel, thirteen Arab states called an urgent meeting to try to decide what to do. Israel was split, an extremely vocal minority objecting to any dealing with "murderers." Some feared there might be a repetition of the scenes a few years earlier when bricks were thrown through Knesset windows during a debate on German reparations. Golda Meir, who normally would have presented in the Knesset the motion to accept the German initiative, became ill. (Whether by coincidence or for psychosomatic reasons Mrs. Meir was generally ill when the German issue came up for debate. Friends suggest she suffered enormous emotional tensions when dealing with anything involving Germany.) The task then fell to Eshkol, whose speech was written by Eban. Partway through delivering it Eshkol developed a bad case of bronchitis and concluded in a hoarse whisper, saying:

"I am afraid I must go home, but the Deputy Prime Minister will fill in for me during the rest of the debate."

Telling Suzy about it that night Eban said:

"I felt like a tennis player who had just served and then was asked to rush to the other side of the net and hit the ball back."[9]

Eban's most telling point in the debate was that "if you listened to Cairo and Amman every day, as I do, you would know how much the Arabs would like us to turn down this offer of diplomatic relations."

It was a stormy debate, but the opposition slowly melted and the final tally showed only twenty-two votes against establishing diplomatic relations with Germany.

While in New York again on government business Eban was once more the guest of David Susskind on "Open End." During their two-hour talk on camera this exchange took place:

Susskind: Can I ask you whether there is a snobbery of its own kind in Israel today? We hear that the sabra, the native-born Israeli, is the aristocrat of Israel and some of us were troubled when you left the UN and returned to Israel; there was talk that Abba Eban would not fare as he might if he were a sabra. Is the sabra status special and peculiar?

Eban: In the first place one has to take an attitude of resignation. One thing a man cannot change about himself is where he was born. Secondly, many of my friends bade farewell to me very much in the mood that the friends of Daniel must have seen him off into the lions' den, expecting him to be torn to pieces without a trace. Well, this hasn't happened. I am here, as you see, completely intact. I have been given a chance to work and to exercise responsibility. That brings me to the general question. It is much too early for Israel to develop a Mayflower Complex.

26

Prelude for War

THE FOLLOWERS of Moses were kept waiting forty years in the desert before being permitted to enter the Promised Land. Abba Eban was kept waiting seven years in the political desert before being permitted to enter his promised land.

Late in November (1965) Eshkol called the Deputy Prime Minister to his office and told him it was almost certain Mrs. Meir would retire and asked him to prepare to take over her post.

"And so the great opportunity arrives at last," Eban wrote to his parents in London. "It looks certain enough for us to make preparations accordingly."

Suzy Eban's elation was more introspective.

"We are both so relaxed now. Our burdens have fallen off with the end of the campaign and a new light seems to shine on the horizon. I think this promise of the work that Aubrey loves so much and the new possibility to mold things his way is returning new confidence to him. It will be so good for him to be back in his profession, for we all know that he loves that kind of work and has his undeniable talent for it. He is between jobs now, so there is less pressure and less tension. In the morning when one wakes up it is a bit like half working and half being on a holiday. . . . We have all become pingpong players and Aubrey has lost eight pounds and looks so much better."[1]

Suzy Eban had the problems of any wife whose husband gets a new job in a city some distance from where they have been living. Eli and Gila would have to be pulled out of the Rehovoth schools in which they were doing so well. And it was the middle of the school year. There would be the emotional difficulty of separating the children from the friends they had made. Then the house. The Government provides the

Foreign Minister with an eighteen-room house in Jerusalem a few blocks from the King David Hotel. Their Rehovoth dwelling was modest by comparison, but during these past few years it had been more of a home than the Foreign Ministry house could ever be.

One of Suzy's minor worries was the staff. She would inherit a cook and other servants who for ten years had been keeping house for a woman. How to break the news to them that henceforth they were going to have to care for a family of four headed by a *man*—a man who was difficult in some ways; for example, a man who usually required fourteen clean shirts a week.

Before Eshkol finally made the announcement of his Cabinet there were weeks of uncertainty—the usual business of coalition making; appointments and disappointments; rumors and threats. In the middle of it Eshkol got sick. Many things could still happen to keep the dream from being realized. Mrs. Meir could change her mind again. But Eban was so sure, this time, that he began having exciting visions and making ambitious plans. He even spent hours a day at the Foreign Ministry studying procedures.

Finally on December 24 Mrs. Meir announced to the Foreign Affairs and Security Committee of the Knesset that she was definitely giving up her post. This made it official. Now, at last, there could be no reversal.

The day after Eshkol made public the list of his new ministers a telegram came to Rehovoth addressed to Suzy Eban reading simply:

CONGRATULATIONS ON YOUR HUSBAND'S APPOINTMENT. PAULA.

With some excitement she showed it to Aubrey, saying:

"Surely there's some significance to this. It's probably Ben-Gurion himself congratulating you in a backhanded way."

"About time!" was her husband's only comment.

Suzy immediately wrote a warm letter of thanks to Mrs. Paula Ben-Gurion, planning to post it after keeping an appointment with her hairdresser. As she was leaving the salon, the hairdresser, with a touch of disappointment in her voice, said:

"Didn't you get the telegram I sent you?"

Then light dawned. The telegram had not been from Paula, the ex-Prime Minister's wife, but from Paula, the hairdresser.

In the flood of congratulatory messages there was a note in her own hand from Jacqueline Kennedy, urging the Ebans to call on her next time they were in New York.

While the Ebans were still at Rehovoth Eli had his barmitzvah. The boy had no psychological problems being the son of a man so much in the public eye, because he was already preparing for a career in quite a different field—music. He went to extremes not to trade on his father's name. For this reason he asked that his barmitzvah be kept a family affair.

"I always hated big . . . big fusses or whatever you call them. So I wanted a little thing. We did it in the synagogue at Rehovoth, but somehow the boys at school got wind of it and they put up posters and what made me mad was they got the name wrong because they wrote me down as Eliahu Even instead of Eli Eban. They did it without my permission, so the place was packed and I was in kind of shock and I remember shouting out all the words and getting it over as fast as I could and after I finished reading the Torah they threw candy from the women's section of the synagogue, the balcony, because that's the custom in Rehovoth and there's a big chandelier in the synagogue and they threw the candy at the chandelier and it made a terrible noise, a fantastic clatter. It was like being in a zoo."[2]

In January (1966) Abba Eban took office as Foreign Minister of a country not yet nineteen years old, which in so short a time had quadrupled her population, was producing most of her own food, had put at least one foot forward into the industrial age and was engaged in scientific research respected throughout the world. All this in spite of encirclement by enemies who, almost without surcease, threatened her with extinction.

Eban took office at one of the most sanguine moments in Israel's modern history. The domestic scene would certainly grow calmer, now that the Rafi-Mapai feud was over. Israel's exports were flowing by ship and plane to distant parts of the world, especially through the Gulf of Aqaba. The National Water Carrier had been completed and water from Galilee was irrigating the southern desert. United Nations troops, symbolic of the outside world's interest in peace in the Middle East, had discouraged fedayeen attacks from the Gaza Strip. Arab hostility had become increasingly isolated.

Israel's relationship with other nations, which is the substance of foreign affairs, was satisfactory. The Rehovoth conferences, Israeli championship of the developing states in international bodies, and Israeli aid programs benefiting sixty African and Asian countries had combined to make her recognized as a friend of those many areas just emerging from the long night of colonial domination.

France had become one of Israel's most devoted friends. During the eight-year Algerian war, when Egypt provided sanctuary and assistance for France's enemies, Franco-Israeli friendship had been based partly on the old Middle Eastern proverb that the enemy of my enemy is my friend. But even after Algerian independence President de Gaulle had assured Prime Minister Eshkol that France was deeply committed to Israel's health and welfare. He even suggested that Israel should not tempt the Arabs by growing weak militarily. To see that this did not happen, France was generously supplying Israel with military equipment—especially planes.

Relations were also good with the United States. Washington had made it clear to Jerusalem it was opposed to Nasser's ambitions to rule the Arab world. Although no one had ever been successful in persuading the United States to *give* military equipment to Israel, as she had done on so many occasions to the Arabs, still Israel was being permitted to *purchase* limited amounts of American armament.

With the Soviet Union Israel had diplomatic relations which, if not exactly warm, were at least of a nature that made intelligent discourse possible.

The failure of the Arabs' nineteen-year campaign to destroy Israel or at least to keep her from prospering could be seen in every new village built, in the integration of almost two million immigrants, in how green the hills were turning, in how rapidly the desert was being conquered.

The Arabs were as divided as ever. Nasser's United Arab Republic had never been a real republic or very united. With the withdrawal of Syria it had now become little more than another name for Egypt. No two countries in the Arab world were trusting friends of each other.

Nasser had called three summit meetings in twenty months to plan Israel's destruction, yet, despite all the talk by representatives of thirteen states covering four million square miles with a population of eighty million, midget Israel continued to flourish. By January (1966) she seemed to have lost her earlier vulnerability and to be more firmly fixed in the constellation of nations than ever before.

As Eban himself put it:

"Israel's flag flew in a hundred capitals and with special pride in those places where formal diplomacy was enhanced by a practical role in development. It was clear that the official Arab view of Israel as a dark conspiracy, a rapacious colonial adventure or a transient crusade had been rejected by the opinion and sentiment of mankind."[3]

When Eban took office he was in complete accord with Eshkol's policy of modernizing and strengthening the Israel defense force and, although there was no reason then to question France's friendship, he favored not putting all of Israel's eggs in one basket, which meant seeking to obtain a larger percentage of Israel's military needs in America.

It was significant, although slightly ironic, that Eban, often considered the man of peace in the Israeli political spectrum, was involved in a military deal within a month of stepping into his new office—his first important official act as Foreign Minister. In February (1966) he was on a visit to Canada and was actually engaged in conversation with Prime Minister Lester Pearson, whom he had known well at the UN, when a message came through from President Johnson summoning him to Washington immediately.[4]

Because the whole deal was clouded in secrecy and high security, Eban told Pearson he must leave at once for New York and the Canadian Prime Minister put an official plane at his disposal. After they were airborne Eban told the pilot his destination actually was Washington.

His instructions were to proceed directly to the Pentagon Building and go through the service entrance—"the way the laundry goes in"— so as not to be spotted by reporters, and there to meet Defense Secretary McNamara, "because he's got an order to cut all red tape and give you the forty-eight Skyhawks you've been asking for."

After signatures were finally put on the Skyhawk document at the White House, President Johnson turned to Foreign Minister Eban and in his slow Texas drawl said:

"Remember, I never want to see your face again talking about planes."

(He didn't know Eban and the Israelis, or have much prescience about the Middle East, for in two years Eban would be back talking about planes again.)

Soon after taking office Eban, with a twinge of foresight, wrote to the French Foreign Minister that he had observed some cooling off of official French friendship for Israel. In February (1966) he conferred in Paris with Couve de Murville and other ministers, who assured him of France's "uninterrupted support of Israel's defense." Their only criticism was of Israel's "excessive nervousness" about whether France would continue to give her support. The French Foreign Minister suggested that Israel should explore any possibility of Soviet cooperation in creating Middle Eastern stability.

Prime Minister Eshkol had been born in Russia and one of his hopes from the day he took high office was to improve relations with the Soviet Union. When Eban became Foreign Minister he decided the coolness of relations between Israel and Eastern Europe was a source of weakness that ought to be rectified; that Israel gained nothing in the West by this form of isolation. Checking the records, he discovered that no Israeli Cabinet member had ever been to Eastern Europe in an official capacity. Furthermore, it was unlikely he or any other important member of the Israeli Government would ever be invited officially. So he hit upon the idea of having the regional conference of all Israeli ambassadors to Eastern European countries convene in Warsaw, Poland being a good place to start trying to repair Israel's crumbling bridges to the East. (Previously the conferences of Eastern diplomats had been held in Vienna, Paris, or some other city in the West.) He began by instructing his ambassador in Warsaw to sound out the Polish Government. Only a year before this, Poland had discouraged Israel's Finance Minister from attending an international trade show in Warsaw. Yet Eban had hope.

Back came a reply that the Polish Government not only would permit such a conference but was flattered that Warsaw had been selected as the site.

"We presumed that they immediately proceeded to wire all the hotel rooms and the conference chamber in which we would meet," Eban said. "We knew we would not be able to talk freely all the time we were there, yet it would be a demonstration that ought to be of value."

At the meeting were the Israeli ambassadors from Bucharest, Budapest, Prague, Belgrade, Moscow and Warsaw. Eban was accompanied by his political secretary, Moshe Raviv. The Polish Government was stiffly correct and accorded the Israelis the normal diplomatic courtesies. While in Warsaw Eban was received by Foreign Minister Rapacki, who assured him that the Polish Government would continue to maintain steadfast links with Israel, based on "memories of a common struggle and a common agony."

Before leaving Israel Eban had arranged for a visit to Auschwitz. He, the six Israeli ministers and Raviv went to Krakow by plane and from there thirty miles by bus to the spot where two and a half million Jews had been executed by gas and cremation and another half million starved to death.[5]

As Eban himself later described it:

"It was an uncanny experience. We were there in a very special capacity. The sovereign State of Israel was coming to this place. The road ran through beautiful countryside, exactly parallel to the railroad which had transported so many millions of Jews. What had happened then was in macabre contrast to the tranquil, rather prosperous scene through which we were now moving.

"The Polish Government sent its representatives to serve as our guides. The buildings were preserved just as if the people had moved out yesterday. Nothing had been taken away, none of the apparatus. The cells, everything, was just as it was—as though a few days ago it was still fulfilling its original purpose. We saw the prison, the torture rooms, the furnaces, the gas chambers—all as if they were accouterments of a normal life.

"I noticed that there was a certain diffidence in letting it be known that nearly all the victims at Auschwitz had been Jews. The emphasis was that some of the deportees came from Norway, Belgium, Holland or from Poland itself. In only one place was it mentioned that two and a half million of the three million killed there were Jews.

"What was most impressive was the mountain of hair shaved from the heads of the victims. It spoke more eloquently than any of the written things. The most anguishing sight was a pile of children's shoes reaching almost to the ceiling.

"We stood by the mass grave and said Kaddish [the Jewish prayer for the dead]. We were oppressed by the enormous desolation and by a feeling that Israel had come too late; that it would have meant a lot for the people now dead here if Israel had come sooner.

"It was an experience we were fortunate to have, because after the 1967 war it would not have been possible for us to go there."

Of Warsaw itself Eban said:

"It was like being in a museum. Once there were two million Jews. Now some of their buildings remained, a Yiddish theater, a Jewish museum, preserved by the state, rather as in New Zealand they might preserve a Maori museum."

A few weeks after the Warsaw visit Eban initiated closer relations with Romania by appointing a new envoy to Bucharest, Eliezer Doran, with instructions to work to raise the ministry to an embassy and try to foster a more intimate relationship between Israel and Romania, which was showing some signs of independence in its foreign policy. (Later this initiative bore fruit in a series of Romanian-Israeli agreements and in Romania's continuing to maintain diplomatic relations with Israel even after other Communist countries recalled their missions from Jerusalem.)

Next, Eban looked at what Golda Meir had done to create development links with Africa and decided that much along this line could be done in such places as Latin America and Southeast Asia, so in March of 1967 he made an official trip to Burma, Singapore, Thailand, Cambodia, Australia, New Zealand and the Philippines, being received with great pomp and ceremony in each of the capital cities, where he conferred with kings, presidents and foreign ministers. Despite Moslem influence in many of these places, a rapport was established resulting in increased support for Israel on the part of some Southeast Asian countries while the others at least did Israel no harm.

There was only one slight complication on the Southeast Asian trip. The Prime Minister of Singapore had had a brilliant academic career, receiving a double first at Cambridge, and somehow the cognoscenti of Singapore had gained the impression that this was the highest academic honor possible. When Eban arrived and the press was given his biography, making mention of his triple first in Cambridge, there was a crisis over whether to reveal this, to the possible embarrassment of the Prime Minister. Such are the minor problems of diplomacy and journalism.

In Latin America development programs were begun in fifteen countries. Before long the African experiment had been extended so widely that it was playing a major role in Israel's foreign relations.

One theory behind Eban's innovations was his belief the UN had lost the importance it had had in the 1950s and the Arab preponderance against Israel had greatly increased so it was now almost impossible to avoid unbalanced decisions against Israel, but this was not catastrophic, because the real weight of international relations is not in parliamentary debate but in bilateral relationships in diplomacy, trade, economics and culture. Wedded to this theory, Eban decided to use the UN for what it is—a tribunal, a forum, a microphone, a means of affecting world opinion, then develop close bilateral links with as many countries as possible, and cement an Israeli association with regional organizations such as the European Common Market and the Organization of American States.

This was a strange policy, considering that Eban's reputation was built largely on his brilliant performance at the UN, yet his feeling now was that the UN was important not so much for debate as for the means it provided of meeting foreign ministers from some seventy countries and doing business with them behind the scenes. (He once said: "If you want to do important things behind the scenes you have to have the scenes.")

Eban also discovered that since the Sinai campaign there had been virtually no contact either officially, para-officially or unofficially with the Arabs. He therefore set out to build "a network of connections." Much secrecy shrouded these efforts. However, there did develop during this period in Jordan, Lebanon, Tunisia and Morocco a more moderate attitude toward Israel's existence.

Summing up the developments during the first year of his foreign ministry Eban said:

"Opportunities beckoned wherever we looked. Every seed of new effort seemed to bear some fruit."

Israelis in general supported this new diplomatic approach. The opposition was limited to domestic political rivals. There were a few who almost every month advocated Israel going to war. Herut wanted violent retaliation against every act of Arab provocation. Rafi wanted the government to get its planes from France exclusively and not to seek weaponry also from the United States. Peres was most critical of the Skyhawk deal. Both Herut and Rafi were skeptical of Eban's attempt to thaw relations with Eastern Europe. In reply to all such critics Eban explained that his foreign policy was based on a universal quest for friendship, commerce and understanding, wherever to be found.

"Our strategy was plain; instead of allowing Arab hostility to isolate Israel, we would try to isolate Arab hostility until it choked for lack of sympathetic air."

Meanwhile there was relative peace on three of Israel's frontiers. Lebanon, Jordan and Egypt were waging war against Israel with what Eban called "purely verbal heroism." But in Syria in February (1966) there was another revolution and the new leaders decided on terrorist infiltrations as the way to destroy Israel. In October General Dayan in a Knesset debate contended that the terrorist raids were no cause for alarm.

"A few dozen bandits of El Fatah cross the border," he said. "This should not make Israel lapse into panic-stricken reinforcement of its defenses. A few dozen terrorists operate from Syria and Jordan. Is this adequate reason for us to enlarge the border police?"

Eban took the position that the Syrian leaders had "uncovered Israel's most vulnerable nerve"; that "no country in the world was more nakedly exposed to a form of aggression so cheap in risk and requiring such scanty investment and technical skill."

Also, Syria was able to harass settlements in Galilee and the Jordan valley from her fortified artillery positions on the Golan Heights.

After Israeli planes had shot down several Migs engaged in aerial nonsense over Lake Tiberias, it became clear to Eban that sooner or later Syrian pressure would have to subside or be resisted, and he conferred on the matter with Eshkol, who agreed with him that "all other possible remedies should first be exhausted." This decision received unanimous Cabinet support.

In October (1966) Eban told the Security Council:

"We want nothing from Syria. . . . We make no claim against Syria's sovereignty or integrity. We do not covet an inch of Syrian territory. . . . We have no interest in the character of its regime, in its social philosophy or in the orientation of its international politics. . . . You may hear it said or see it written that Israel on its own account or in league with others is planning to overthrow the present Syrian regime. That is utterly false."

After many weeks the Security Council drafted a resolution expressing regret at "infiltration from Syria and loss of human life caused by incidents in October and November 1966." It was so mild as to be innocuous, yet was vetoed by the USSR.

On October 11 (1966) the Syrian Prime Minister said:

"We shall set the whole region on fire!"

Meanwhile the Soviet press was spreading the falsehood that Israel was massing troops to overthrow the Syrian regime.

Tension increased month by month and on April 6 (1967), after a series of terrorist raids on Israeli settlements, the conflict between Israel and Syria reached the stage of aerial combat during which six Syrian Migs were sent crashing to the ground. After it was learned that two had fallen on Jordanian soil Eban declared that "never have Jordanian and Israeli hearts beat in such unison." Egypt made no move to go to Syria's aid.

From his ambassadors scattered around the world Eban received messages that ranged from satisfaction to overt congratulations from Paris, which was understandably pleased by the victory of French-Israeli Mirages over Syrian-Soviet Migs.

But there was one exception to this universal attitude. Moscow was highly embarrassed and conveyed to Eban what amounted to a threat: Israel would eventually pay heavily for her success.

Late in the night of April 21 (1967) Israeli Ambassador Katriel Katz in Moscow was called to the Kremlin, where Deputy Foreign Minister Yacov Malik told him Israel was guilty of aggression "liable to endanger the vital interests of the Israeli State."

About this same time, attempting to rescue Syria from her self-inflicted humiliation, the Soviet Union induced Cairo to send her Prime Minister, Foreign Minister and Chief of Staff to Damascus, along with a plethora of diplomatic and military experts, to plan what Eban and his colleagues decided could be only one thing—war.

From the Israeli Foreign Ministry to the Israeli Embassy in Moscow went orders to try to persuade the Soviet Union to adopt a restraining role, but while the Soviet officials spoke about "hotheads in Damascus" they gave no promise of trying to cool them off.

Then the Soviet Union, in notes and conversations, suggested that maybe El Fatah infiltrators were really representatives of American oil interests or American Intelligence agencies. But Syria disapproved of this line, taking full Arab credit for every dead Israeli.

On May 11 (1967) Eban toured the Israeli-Syrian frontier with the commander of the Northern Sector and found the hills and valleys of Galilee "bathed in perfect calm." Nowhere did he see a tank or artillery piece. His only worry was over how vulnerable the Jordan valley settlements apparently were to attack.

The next day the Foreign Ministry invited the Soviet ambassador to go by his own car, accompanied by his own attachés, and search anywhere he pleased along the Syrian frontier for the alleged concentrations of Israeli troops. The reply was that the Soviet ambassador's job was to "transmit Soviet truths, not to test their veracity."

On May 13 *The Christian Science Monitor* published an interview with Eban in which, replying to a question as to whether Israel's destruction of six Soviet-built Migs might not have offended Moscow, he said:

"If the alternative is to gain Moscow's sympathy or survive I would prefer to survive, because if we survive we can go on to work for Moscow's sympathy, but if we do not survive then Moscow's sympathy ceases to have any but obituary interest."

That same week United Nations observers investigated the troop reports and after receiving their findings U Thant on May 18 (1967) publicly stated there were no Israeli troop concentrations, yet Nasser continued to believe the reports he got from Moscow that Israel had eleven to thirteen brigades on the Syrian frontier.

On May 13 (1967) Foreign Minister Eban, replying to a Soviet note, said:

"If it were made clear to the Syrians that the USSR opposes terrorist acts it is probable that these would be stopped."

Eshkol and General Yitsak Rabin, Chief of Staff, warned Syria that there were limits to Israel's willingness to go on enduring the murder of her citizens. Some thought Israeli warnings too frequent, too little coordinated and that they therefore lost force. For example, in mid-May three Israeli newspapers carried interviews with Rabin in which he warned Damascus of what might happen if terrorism did not cease. Eban's feeling was that while it was not correct to say that this gave Nasser a legitimate reason for action, it did give him a pretext for saying there was a real danger Israel might invade Syria. Eban also objected to a briefing of foreign military attachés stationed in Israel which led them to believe a major assault was about to take place.

Meanwhile, Moscow was intentionally misquoting both Eshkol and Rabin, making it appear that both men were threatening a march on Damascus.

Inside Israel the public temperature was rising rapidly, despite official efforts to keep it down. On May 15 (1967) Eban instructed Israel's permanent representative to the UN, Ambassador Gideon Rafael, to assure the Arab countries through U Thant that Israel had no thought of initiating hostilities on any frontier.

As Independence Day approached, the Cabinet unanimously voted to put on the customary parade in Jerusalem, but strictly in accordance with the armistice agreement with Jordan. Eban's argument was that with the trouble on the Syrian front, it would be reckless to do anything to provoke Jordan and give anyone an excuse to complain to the UN. Ben-Gurion took vigorous exception, contending that Jerusalem the Holy City should not thus be slighted.

As was so often the case, the Soviet Union gave the decision to hold a modest celebration the most sinister interpretation: if there were so few troops for a parade, they must all be on the Syrian frontier.

In Moscow an Egyptian delegation headed by Anwar el-Sadat, president of the National Council (who would one day succeed Nasser), was told to expect an Israeli invasion of Syria immediately after Independence Day.

Describing the situation at this critical stage, Eban said:

"United only by common rancor, Moscow, Damascus and Cairo had laid an explosive charge of falsehood at the foundations of Middle East peace. The wick was to be three weeks long."

When Eban got back to his office after watching the Independence Day parade on May 15 (1967) he found many disturbing messages. The Egyptians were moving large military convoys through the streets of Cairo on their way to the canal, with no attempt at secrecy. The Egyptian Chief of Staff had flown to Damascus. Sadat had brought back from Moscow wild stories of Israel's plans to conquer Syria. Every radio station in the Arab world was spewing hatred of Israel. A state of alert had been declared in Egypt, Lebanon, Iraq and Jordan.

In consultation with Eshkol and Rabin, Eban learned of plans to reinforce the single Israeli battalion in the Negev. From London and Washington came official assurance the Egyptian troop movements were "without military intent."

On May 17 (1967) Egyptian press and radio announced Egypt's Chief of Staff had requested the commander of the UN Emergency Force (UNEF) to withdraw his troops in order to permit Egyptian troops to "go into action against Israel."

Studying the text of the letter, Eban recalled that in 1958, when he had asked Hammarskjöld whether there was any danger of the UNEF ever being withdrawn overnight without giving Israel time to correct any military imbalance, the Secretary-General had "emphatically rejected this apprehension."

In May 17 (1967) Eban instructed Ambassador Rafael at the UN to remind U Thant of the commitment Hammarskjöld had given. But it was too late. U Thant had taken only seventy-five minutes to send a reply to Egypt: UN troops would be withdrawn as soon as a formal request was received from UAR authorities.

Eban had a special relationship with the UNEF withdrawal. It was to him that Eisenhower and Dulles had given the pledge that the peace-keeping force would remain in Gaza and Sharm el-Sheikh until such time as its removal would not bring about belligerency. The removal of UNEF in these circumstances was the augury that what Eban had helped build in 1957 was being shattered.[6]

On May 18 (1967) Ambassador Rafael conferred with Ralph Bunche and U Thant and emphasized that "an established international situation was being disrupted without an attempt to ensure alternative means of preventing belligerency." U Thant replied that he had seen no legal way of refusing Cairo's request.

At this point it was clear to Eban that he and his ambassador were arguing a lost cause. His hunch was correct. Late in the afternoon of May 18 (1967) U Thant, having received the formal demand from Cairo, convened the Advisory Committee of UNEF for the first time and although some members urged him to delay compliance with the request, he soon adjourned the meeting and at once liquidated UNEF. What for ten years had appeared to be a stable international reality turned out, within hours, to be "as unsubstantial as a spider's web."

Eban had surmised at the time that Nasser had not anticipated that

U Thant would act so precipitously. This was partially confirmed in May of 1970 when Nasser in a speech declared that he had neither expected nor desired UNEF to withdraw from Sharm el-Sheikh.

In the panic of the moment, some officials in friendly nations and some people in the UN Secretariat suggested the possibility of stationing UNEF on Israeli territory. Eban's comment was sharp and epigrammatic:

"It was like suggesting that the firemen turn their hose-pipes away from the fire and concentrate them on the anxious spectators, on the ground it is useful to have water somewhere instead of nowhere. Israel's peril would quite conclusively have been aggravated by the transfer of the UNEF to her soil. Egyptian troops would have concentrated in battle formations in Sinai, and terrorists would have assembled in Gaza, while Israel's capacity to resist or deter would have been hampered by the complicating presence of international contingents with no function and no power to act."

During the next few days tension mounted, yet there was nothing to show that Egypt planned an immediate attack or was fully prepared to meet an Israeli attack. Most Israeli military men felt Egypt was simply trying to demonstrate solidarity with her Syrian friends. Eban doubted this theory. Listening to some of the wild broadcasts from Arab stations throughout the Middle East, he felt thunder in the air and advised political correspondents who came to his office that Egypt's motives might not be merely demonstrative or psychological.

As the diplomatic leader of the country Eban sent this message to the military:

"What does the Army need most from the diplomatic arm?"

The answer came back fast, and in one word:

"Time."

For the next two and a half weeks Eban bent all his efforts to supplying that need. He was told that the time needed by the Army to develop a serious deterrent posture in the Negev against Egypt would not be measured "in a few days." Senior officers kept repeating their need for political action as a screen behind which military preparations could proceed. Some even suggested that Eban try to force a meeting of the Security Council. The Foreign Minister was vehemently opposed to this, for many reasons. The Soviet Union would use its veto. The resultant political rebuff for Israel would encourage Nasser and create a desperate mood in Israel. Most serious of all, once a Security Council debate started, Israel would be in no position to take other measures—meaning military action.

"I knew from long experience it was easier to turn on the tap of UN debate than to shut it off."

Eban countered with his own stalling-for-time idea. The whole timetable might be delayed for days if U Thant went to Cairo, so he made the suggestion to his UN ambassador, who planted the seed among Western delegations. Eventually U Thant decided to make the Cairo trip, even though the Egyptians told him not to start until they gave him the green light.

On May 19 (1967) Eban summoned the Soviet ambassador to his office to ask him to have Moscow urge the Egyptians to join with the Israelis in a mutual deescalation of troops in the south.

"His demeanor," said Eban after the meeting, "expressed an almost sadistic delight in Israel's predicament."

Eban wound up his presentation to him by saying:

"If Egypt wants peace there will be peace. The initiative is with her."

As the ambassador left the Foreign Ministry, Eban reflected that "I had done what was required by professional duty and diplomatic ritual, but it was indecently clear that what the Soviet Union had in mind was not how to reduce tension but how to bring it swiftly to a boil."

The decisive diplomatic question was whether Nasser would actually blockade the Strait of Tiran. Eban felt if a blockade were imposed it would never be canceled except under tremendous pressure or threat of physical force. If Israel took no stand on such a grave threat to her existence, nobody in the Arab world and not many others would ever again believe in "the certainty of Israel's survival."

Accordingly, between May 18 and May 20 (1967) he dispatched messages to all the maritime powers stating that if the Strait was closed Israel would stop short of nothing to nullify the blockade.

On May 19 (1967) U Thant in a speech to the Security Council said:

"The timing of the withdrawal of UNEF leaves much to be desired."

Commented Eban:

"Amidst all my worries I found time to admire this phlegmatic understatement."

That same day Eshkol cabled De Gaulle and Eban sent a personal note to French Foreign Minister Couve de Murville, both stating that Israel would take no action against Egypt *unless the Strait was closed*. Eban sent a long message to British Foreign Secretary George Brown containing the same thought. Similar messages were then sent to the foreign ministers of all states that had supported the principle of international navigation in the Strait. One purpose was to let Cairo know in this indirect way that if she imposed a blockade she would do it with her eyes open to the possibility of war.

Some years earlier General Dayan had publicly stated that Israel should actually work for removal of UNEF in the belief that it would be a better achievement to send Israeli ships through the Gulf with Egyptian troops agreeing to their passage than to rely on a temporary and symbolic international presence. Eban disagreed. He called it unrealistic, contending that the Egyptians would never wave Israeli ships on their way if they had the power to stop them.

The international background of the present situation was that Britain, France and the United States in 1950 had agreed to support any Middle East nation threatened with aggression and in 1957 had recognized Israel's right to free passage through the Strait. In 1960 De Gaulle had told Ben-Gurion that if Israel were threatened "we shall not let you be destroyed" and in 1964 had repeated the promise to Eshkol.

No replies were received from the French, the British response was evasive and from President Johnson came this message:

"I am sure you will understand that I cannot accept any responsibilities on behalf of the United States for situations which arise as the result of actions on which we are not consulted."

On May 21 (1967) Eban received from the State Department a message that "the present grave problem should be handled in a peaceful manner, preferably through the UN."

Eban's reaction was: "I could not conceive that an armed pirate would be stopped in a peaceful manner, especially not by an organization whose vote he controlled."

When Avraham Harman, who had succeeded Eban as ambassador in Washington, pressed the State Department, on Eban's insistence, for an assurance that the United States had warned Nasser unequivocally against closing the Strait, he was informed that it was deemed preferable to delay any further bilateral action until U Thant reached Cairo.

Eban was most disturbed by a statement put out in Washington on May 22 (1967) which spoke of "supporting suitable measures in and outside the UN." President Kennedy's declaration of May 1, 1963, had said that if Israel were threatened with aggression the United States would "*adopt* other courses of action of our own." Eban felt the difference between adopting and supporting was of great significance. His sardonic comment: "The approach of danger always lends precision and refinement to the diplomatic art."

He felt that the United States, "traumatically affected by its isolation in Vietnam, was making its policy dependent on a concerted interna tional enterprise; it was naturally reluctant to act alone."

On May 22 (1967) Eshkol made a firm yet unprovocative speech in the Knesset. Again, for the hundredth time, it seemed, he insisted there was not a shred of truth to talk of Israeli concentrations on the Syrian frontier. The speech was an attempt to give Nasser a chance to retreat from the temptation of blockade.

U Thant had rejected an invitation by Eban to visit Israel as well as Cairo and on May 22 started for Egypt. When he reached Paris he was informed that his trip was too little, too late. Nasser had just imposed a blockade of the Gulf of Aqaba. U Thant's first thought, it was later revealed, was to turn back. He surely would have been justified, for never before had a Secretary-General been treated in such an insulting manner. Eban's comment:

"All the Nasser attributes were here at work—the smiling furtiveness, the slick maneuverability, the innocent face put on mendacity. The UN was the victim of a confidence trick pursued with perfection on an international scale."

The objective of Eban's diplomacy at this stage was twofold: On the part of the most sanguine there was the expectation that even in a victorious war Israel would lose not thousands but probably tens of thousands. Eban was also aware that victory might turn out as bitter as it had for so many victorious countries. Therefore, the prime object of his diplomacy during late May was to try to achieve Israel's objectives without war. But, secondly, if war was inevitable, in view of Nasser's adventurism, Israel should do everything possible to secure political support, which meant making it clear to the outside world she had exhausted every possibility of maintaining her vital interests by political rather than military means. To these twin goals he now bent all his wits and energy.

27

Tale of Three Cities

BRIGHT DAYLIGHT was streaming through the Ebans' bedroom windows when the telephone rang at 5 A.M. on Tuesday, May 23, 1967. The voice at the other end was dry, matter-of-fact.

"President Nasser has just announced the closing of the Gulf of Aqaba to Israeli shipping and to all other vessels bound for Israel with strategic materials aboard."

It was no idle rumor; the message was from Army Headquarters, Tel Aviv. Aubrey Eban's first reaction, strangely, was of "serenity." At least the terrible uncertainty was over.

When his senior advisers assembled in the living room of the Foreign Ministry residence on Balfour Street, Jerusalem, at 6 A.M. they found Eban bent over his transistor radio listening to a recording of Nasser's speech to officers of the Egyptian air base at Bir Gafgafa in Sinai, less than a hundred miles from Israel's frontier:

"We are in confrontation with Israel. . . . Our armed forces have occupied Sharm el-Sheikh. . . . We shall not allow the Israel flag to pass through the Gulf of Aqaba. . . . We are ready for war. . . . This water is ours."

By 8 A.M. Eban was on the road to Tel Aviv to attend a meeting called by Prime Minister Eshkol. It was obvious that people in other cars, people along the roadside, people in towns through which they drove had heard the news; everywhere there seemed to be an air of anxiety. The word uppermost in Eban's mind—and probably in the minds of most Israelis—was "survival."

By 9 A.M. cars and helicopters were unloading Cabinet members and military at the Ministry of Defense building. Those who finally gathered around an immense table included the Chief of Staff, General Yitsak

Rabin; the Chief of Operations, General Ezer Weizmann; the Chief of Military Intelligence, General Aharon Yariv; all the ministers and certain key members of the Knesset, among them Moshe Dayan, Golda Meir, David Hacohen, Shimon Peres, Menahem Beigin, Chaim Landau, Yosef Almogi and Elimelech Rimal.[1]

"We have news on the political front," Eshkol announced, thereby setting the non-emotional tenor of the discussion.

Military reports were not especially disturbing. The Egyptian Army was not yet in full offensive position. There was no noticeable movement on Jordan's part. Syria was ominously quiet. Yet the entire Arab world was in a state of frenzy. Howling mobs in the streets of Cairo, Damascus and Bagdad were screaming for Israeli blood. Their lust came distinctly over transistor radios into the Defense building.

General Rabin expressed confidence in an ultimate Israeli military success, but he warned that it would be no "walkover." Victory would be costly. None of the military men proposed any immediate action. Rabin said there was no military possibility to fight for Sharm el-Sheikh; this would be the worst and most difficult place to start a war.

Eban told the meeting there was no possibility of adopting a doctrine of peace at any price. Israel must now behave and think like a nation already invaded. The question was not whether Israel must resist, but whether she must resist alone or with the support and understanding of others.

France had not answered the Foreign Ministry's cables. From Washington came news that President Johnson had sent messages to Cairo, Damascus and Moscow urging deescalation of troop movements and free navigation in the Gulf. Israel was urged to abstain from unilateral action for forty-eight hours and to take counsel with Washington. Eban said a determined effort must be made to secure a warmer American understanding, "otherwise we may win a war and lose a victory." The next few days should be spent in recalling to Washington its own past commitments. He felt that there was urgent need for political effort.

He pointed out that no one in the room had suggested immediate military action to open the Strait. Therefore, the blockade was a central political issue. The blockade of a coast was equivalent to a forcible territorial encroachment. Resistance was legitimate. He gave the meeting four reasons why he felt an intense political effort was necessary:

1. To ensure support, especially in arms, if war came.

2. To prevent the fruits of victory being wrested prematurely from Israel if victory was Israel's lot.

3. To give weight to the 1957 commitments from which Israel's friends were shying away.

4. To make the obstruction of Nasser an international as well as an Israeli objective.

There was deep debate over the proposals, yet most of those present agreed that the moment for military reaction had not come and that a political phase was in order. (There is no confirmation of often published reports that there was bitter conflict that day between those who favored immediate military attack and those who opposed it. There is also no evidence that a specific proposal for immediate action was made.)

Finance Minister Sapir thought the forty-eight hours would probably become seventy-two. Minister of the Interior Shapiro felt Eban should make contact in Paris, London and Washington with leaders of the three countries. Minister of Religious Affairs Warhaftig was sure time would be on Israel's side. Eban's Foreign Ministry associates felt he should go only to Washington. Some Mapai leaders were against such a trip on the ground it would give Washington a chance to put direct pressure on Israel to weaken or abandon resistance. Eban disagreed. Golda Meir felt Eban should try to solve the mystery of France's attitude. One suggestion was that Mrs. Meir be sent to Washington because, not being an official, she would be able to evade requests for commitment. Eban and Mrs. Meir both rejected this suggestion.

Eban introduced the first formal proposal of the day—a statement that Israel had decided to give effect to the policy announced March 1, 1957, to regard any interference with shipping as an aggressive act against which Israel was entitled to exercise self-defense.

Before the day was over domestic politics colored the situation. On the way to the Cabinet meeting Beigin of Herut and Peres of Rafi conferred about replacing Eshkol with Ben-Gurion, on the ground that the Israeli Army was not ready for action; that only Ben-Gurion would have enough authority to avoid reacting to Nasser's provocation and thus to prevent war; that a change in government was necessary as a prerequisite to any successful military action; and that the Chief of Staff was in ill health.

Eban's own feeling was that "we ought to be thinking not of driving Eshkol out of Jerusalem but about banishing Nasser from Sharm el-Sheikh."

The ministerial meeting ended with unanimous approval of a proposal by Eshkol (drafted in part by Eban):

1. The blockade is an act of aggression against Israel.

2. Any decision on action is postponed for forty-eight hours during which time the Foreign Minister will explore the position of the United States.

3. The Prime Minister and the Foreign Minister are empowered to decide, should they see fit, on a journey by the Foreign Minister to Washington to meet President Johnson.

(It was incorrectly rumored in Israel that the trip Eban later took abroad had not been fully discussed or decided upon by the Cabinet. In fact, it happened as a result of a formal ministerial decision.)

There was discussion about whether a formal state of war should be proclaimed. General Staff officers thought it would add nothing and actually handicap the military. Eban said Nasser, by the blockade, had virtually proclaimed a state of war; no Israeli declaration was juridically necessary.

Back at his office in Jerusalem Eban found a mound of cables. Ambassador Eytan in Paris reported that an important meeting of the French Council of Ministers would be held the next day. After conferring with Eshkol, Eban messaged Eytan that he would arrive in Paris early the next morning, hoping for a conference with General de Gaulle, then would go on to Washington.

As Eshkol and Eban were walking together that evening into an emergency meeting of the Knesset, spokesmen of the religious parties were praying at the rostrum for "the survival of Israel's remnant." The Prime Minister spoke briefly but bluntly. Egypt now had eighty thousand men in Sinai. Israel had mobilized for what might come.

At 2:30 the next morning, accompanied by his political secretary, Moshe Raviv, Eban flew from Lod Airport in an otherwise empty Boeing 707 chartered by the Government from El Al and landed at 7 A.M. at Orly, Paris, where he checked in at the airport motel to get several hours' rest before facing the gravest diplomatic task of his career.

As he tried unsuccessfully to sleep, many conflicting thoughts churned through his head. Before leaving Jerusalem he had received a cable from Paris that General de Gaulle would see him at noon. He well remembered how tall and erect the general had appeared the day he saw him cross the lobby of Shepheard's in Cairo. Since then he had had many occasions to admire the lofty prose of the French President and the qualities of leadership he had shown in directing the modern French renaissance.

But recently there had been cause for concern about French-Israeli relations. Soon after becoming Foreign Minister Eban had written a memorandum to the Paris Embassy about certain bothersome signs. No Israeli minister had ever been formally invited to Paris. No French minister had visited Israel while in office. In the UN there was little tangible manifestation of the French-Israeli rapport. Israelis in the Paris Embassy, as well as important members of the De Gaulle government, talked reassuringly of the close military, economic, technological and cultural cooperation. Eban had been advised not to rock the boat. Aircraft were more important than speeches of amity, they said.

Lately there had been specific causes of concern. The Secretary-General of the French Foreign Ministry had just this month visited Arab capitals, reiterating France's friendship. While in Egypt he had stressed the closeness of Cairo and Paris. And no official comment had come from Paris on the UNEF withdrawal.

Also, Eban recalled how a few hours before Nasser's speech at Bir Gafgafa both France and Britain had renounced their adherence to the Tripartite Declaration of 1950 in which they had agreed to take steps if violation of the 1949 armistice agreements was ever threatened.

Going through the airport he had bought a copy of each of the Paris daily papers. If they correctly reflected French public opinion, the people were more friendly than their government.

Accompanied by Ambassador Eytan, Eban reached the Elysée Palace a few minutes before noon. In the courtyard were twenty identical black Citroën cars, in almost military formation. The Council of Ministers obviously was still in session. Soon after Eban and Eytan entered the presidential quarters the Council meeting broke up. Several ministers whom Eban knew personally shook hands with him as solemnly and silently as if it were a funeral.

De Gaulle and Foreign Minister Couve de Murville received the two Israelis with cold courtesy. De Gaulle and Eban faced each other across a table devoid of file baskets, papers or even telephones. The French President began the conference with a blunt word of counsel, spoken quietly but earnestly:

"Israel must not make war unless she is attacked by others. It would be catastrophic if Israel were to shoot first. The Four Powers must be left to resolve the dispute. France will influence the Soviet Union toward an attitude favorable to peace."

Eban then spent twelve minutes summarizing in his faultless French Israel's views:

A turning point had been reached in Israel's history. Therefore, she wished to consult her greatest friend. He talked of Syrian-based terrorism, Egyptian troop concentrations in Sinai and the blockade, an aggressive act that must be rescinded. In 1957 France had given "the most lucid and energetic definition of Israel's rights in the Gulf," including her right to defend herself physically against the outrage of blockade. Israel without Elath would be "stunted and humiliated."

"What are you going to do?" De Gaulle interjected.

"If the choice lies between surrender and resistance," Eban replied, "Israel will resist. Our decision has been taken. We shall not act today or tomorrow, because we are exploring the attitude of those who have assumed commitments. We must know whether we are alone or whether we shall act within an international framework. If Israel fights alone —and she does not recoil from this—she will be victorious, although the price in blood may be heavy. If the Powers act in accordance with their engagements, Israel will harmonize her resistance with theirs. . . . If there is to be concerted international action, such as some of the Powers seem to be considering, Nasser will yield, especially if there is a naval force in the area."

De Gaulle listened with great attention but again he told Eban that Israel must not fire the first shot. (*"Ne tirez pas la première balle!"*)

"We could not open hostilities," Eban countered, "since these have already been opened by Nasser, for the blockade is an act of war. Whatever Israel does will be reaction, not an initiative. A state can be attacked by many methods apart from gunfire. Civil law recognizes no distinction between assault through strangulation and assault through shooting."

It was an apt and brilliant simile, but De Gaulle rejected it, declaring that opening hostilities meant, literally, firing the first shot. As for the 1957 commitment, he said 1967 was not 1957; today "there are no Western solutions." The Soviet Union would have to be included.

"The more Israel looks to the West," he said, "the less will be the readiness of the Soviet Union to cooperate."

About U Thant's removal of UNEF, he thought the Secretary-General had acted correctly, although it might have been wiser if he had waited for consultations with the Four Powers. Then, for the first time, his tone softened as he admitted that the blockade and troop concentrations "could not last" and that "Israel must reserve its position," but he insisted Israel should not act until France had time to concert the action of the Four Powers to enable ships to pass through the Strait.

Bluntly Eban protested that France had raised no voice against Nasser's blockade.

De Gaulle countered that he upheld "the freedom of the seas" and that an international agreement on the Strait should be sought, "as in the Dardanelles."

After Eban had said he was not sanguine about the USSR playing a positive role, De Gaulle expressed skepticism about Western naval demonstrations, then added that Israel's enemies were hoping she would open hostilities, which she must not do.

Eban repeated that Israel would not accept the new situation created by Nasser, then expressed gratitude for France's help and friendship.

De Gaulle replied that this very friendship now moved him to advise Israel that she was not "sufficiently established to solve all her problems herself"; she should not undertake never to act, but in the meantime she should give a respite for international consultation.

Eban pointed out that sometimes inaction is more dangerous than action.

De Gaulle once more said: "I advise you now not to be precipitate. Do not make war."

As the meeting broke up Eban, finding himself alone with De Gaulle and out of earshot of Couve de Murville and Eytan, conveyed Eshkol's personal respects, to which the French President replied:

"I remember what I said to him when he sat in that chair. I said that the essential thing is that Israel should exist and develop."

As he walked out of the palace Eban, pondering De Gaulle's renunciation of the 1957 commitment, recalled that it was French advice, more than anything else, that had induced Israel to withdraw from Gaza and Sharm el-Sheikh in 1957. Now De Gaulle had made it clear that France was quietly but firmly disengaging herself from any responsibility for helping Israel if Israel chose early resistance.

(Couve de Murville in his memoirs published in 1970 made it clear that Eban's talk with De Gaulle gave the French Government the understanding that Israel would not be persuaded to put up with the Aqaba blockade and that war was simply a matter of time.)

Eban felt the value of the talk was that France and Israel had each made its position clear to the other; now France would not be taken by surprise if war did break out. Moreover, the weakness of the French position made it more essential than ever to get President Johnson's moral and political understanding.

The press was waiting on the steps of the Elysée. In a whispered conversation with Eytan, Eban agreed he would be noncommittal. He talked only about what he had said to De Gaulle.

"Israel is in a posture of preparedness but not alarm. . . . The blockade is a piratical act. A world which resigned itself to such acts would be a jungle."

Upon leaving the Elysée Eban was given a message that Prime Minister Wilson would see him without fixed appointment as soon as he arrived in London. Because he felt it imperative that Eshkol and his government learn as quickly as possible about France's attitude, he summarized for Raviv the main parts of the conference and instructed Raviv to cable them to Jerusalem, while Eytan prepared a more lengthy cable from his verbatim notes.

Eban had a hunch that the decision on the Middle East had been reached by the French Council of Ministers before he even arrived and this was confirmed when he learned that while he and De Gaulle were meeting, the French Minister of Information was telling journalists of the conclusions reached in the morning session—a policy little different from that enunciated by the President.

En route to London Eban recollected that Israel's relationship with Britain had never had the rhapsodic quality of the Franco-Israeli love affair, yet when UNEF was removed British Foreign Secretary George Brown had used the expletive "Mockery!" Also, Eban recalled that Israel's Army had a goodly quantity of British equipment.

Israeli Ambassador Remez met him at the airport and together they went to Downing Street. As their car drove up to No. 10, Conservative leaders Edward Heath and Sir Alex Douglas-Home were walking away. There was a crowd in the street and many press photographers who took Eban's picture facing the black door of the Prime Minister's house.

No. 10 Downing Street was quite different from the Elysée. Wilson sat in the middle of the Cabinet table, drinking strong tea. Eban was asked to sit beside him, so close that he was often enveloped in a cloud of pungent smoke from the Prime Minister's pipe. There was no attempt on the part of either man to make a speech, read a formal statement or otherwise engage in rhetorical, stylized discourse, as in Paris.

"I seemed to have crossed the Channel into the twentieth century," Eban later said.

Wilson's demeanor was solid and assured. Unlike De Gaulle, he appeared to have unembarrassed sympathy for Israel and her representative. He asked Eban, first, to talk about his conversation with De Gaulle, whose proposal for a Four Power consultation had already reached No. 10 Downing. Wilson was skeptical. He feared that Brown's talks in Moscow and the Security Council proceedings would show the USSR was in no mood to join with the West to help either Israel or regional peace.

Eban expounded on his belief that Israel had three choices: surrender, fight along or join with others in international efforts to force Nasser to backtrack. Israel could not live without access to Elath or under threat of Egyptian encirclement.

Wilson bluntly replied the Cabinet had met that morning and agreed the policy of the blockade must not be allowed to triumph; Britain would join with others in an effort to open the Strait. He had sent the Minister of State to Washington to see if a plan could be worked out for common action. He said the Washington talk would be "nuts and bolts." He asked if Eban thought the action on the Strait should be limited to the UN, to which Eban replied that because of the Soviet veto the UN was a blind alley.

Wilson was eager to know the mood of Israel. Eban told him it was grave, "but we will win if we have to fight."

Recapitulating, the British Prime Minister said his country would work with others to open the Strait and was seeking agreement with the USA as to how to proceed. Then he saw Eban to the door, where there was more photography. Despite his lack of sleep and the strain under which he was working, Eban displayed his ubiquitous sense of humor by commenting that this second photographic ordeal "presumably was designed to see if I had grown visibly older within the past fifty minutes."

On the way to a hotel he told Raviv he had found Wilson's lack of exhortation realistic and mature; also prudent, "since those who are giving us specific advice are obviously assuming heavy moral responsibilities which they may not be able to discharge." He felt Wilson had shown "distinguished statesmanship; that he was prepared for the maximum degree of commitment compatible with his country's real strength and responsibility." He was moving with assurance and precision "within the bounds of possibility."

Raviv sent to Jerusalem a detailed cable on the Downing Street talk in which Eban warned his colleagues that although Wilson's views strengthened the chance of international action, their effectiveness would obviously depend on what was concerted in Washington.

It was too late to get air passage that night for the United States, so Eban had dinner with his father and mother and then, overcome with a desperate and sudden exhaustion, took a cab to his hotel in the hope of getting the first sleep in forty hours.

Outside the door of his room there was now a heavy security guard. As he undressed he turned on his radio and television. Over both he heard expressions of sympathy for Israel, "but they had a distinctly funereal air."

"I spent a totally sleepless night in a mood of deep national and personal solitude."

The next morning (Thursday, May 25, 1967) Eban and Raviv flew to New York. On the way the Foreign Minister reviewed the American position by going over a briefcase full of cables and other reports. It was still cautious. Just before leaving Jerusalem he had received a note from the American Embassy expressing concern over Syrian terrorism, criticism of the UNEF withdrawal as "precipitous" and a renewal of U.S. support of free access in the Gulf of Aqaba, for ships of all nations. But there was silence about any possible action.

At Kennedy Airport the plane was met by Ambassador Rafael and Minister Evron. Also by a mob of press people. During an interview Eban said Israel would not expect American soldiers to lose their lives for Israel, no matter what happened.

One hour later, driving from National Airport to the Mayflower Hotel in Washington, he was briefed by Ambassador Harman. That morning before going to Canada for the day, President Johnson had made a speech condemning Egypt's blockade. The New York *Times* reporter at the White House had been told Israel could be held back for "only a matter of days." Eighty-seven members of Congress had signed a statement denouncing Nasser and calling on Johnson to support Israel. Then Harman produced a distressing cable from Tel Aviv. Egyptian armor had crossed the Suez Canal. Egyptian troop concentrations in Sinai were "dense." Egyptian airfields were on alert. An Egyptian surprise attack was expected. Eban was asked to convey all this to the White House in the most drastic and urgent terms and to ask if the United States would regard an attack on Israel as an attack on itself.

Eban found it difficult to understand how such an extreme change had overtaken Israel's military situation in the forty-eight hours since he had sat in Tel Aviv military headquarters getting firsthand reports. He had always believed in the axiom that "it is the duty of soldiers to exaggerate their dangers; it is the duty of ministers not to take reports of such dangers too seriously." However, someone obviously had convinced the Cabinet of this worsening of the military situation, so it was his duty to carry out the cabled instructions, even if it meant exchanging an attitude of military self-confidence for one of apparent weakness. As he considered the predicament, another cable arrived painting an even blacker picture, so he requested that his talk with Secretary of State Dean Rusk scheduled for 5:30 P.M. be advanced by two hours.

On the way to the State Department more telegrams and Intelligence reports were thrust into his hands. One was of importance—an account from a friendly government of a meeting in Cairo on May 21 at which it had been decided to impose the blockade. Nasser then and there told his military and political leaders why he was sure Israel would not fight: because she had no allies, was afraid of the USSR, knew the United States was too deeply involved in Vietnam to help Israel and the majority of UN members favored the Arabs. Also because of domestic division, the reserved attitude of France and the fact that only 5 percent of Israel's trade went through Elath. Eban was struck by Nasser's ignorance of the Israeli mentality.

Abba Eban and Dean Rusk had known each other for twenty years "in varying circumstances of harmony and divergence." Eban commenced their talk by telling Rusk of the two cables just received from Jerusalem. The Secretary of State excused himself, presumably to communicate the military news to the President.

Before leaving Jerusalem Eban had stuffed a large briefcase with papers and memoranda from his own archives. Among them was a document which would turn out to be more effective than all his verbal arguments. It contained the minutes of a conversation he had had with Secretary Dulles in the Dulles home on February 24, 1957, in which the Secretary of State had spelled out the American commitment to Israel on freedom of passage in the Gulf. A few corrections had been made in Dulles's own handwriting. As soon as Eban arrived in Washington a photocopy of the document was made and sent to the State Department. Somehow no copy of the vitally important *aide-mémoire* could be found in either White House or State Department files. However, Douglas Dillon, who had served in the State Department under Eisenhower, confirmed its authenticity from memory.

Faced with the promise made by the Eisenhower Government, now confirmed by the document, the only question was if and how the United States would live up to it. This was the question Eban discussed with Rusk.

That evening a "working dinner" was held, attended by Eban, Harman, Evron and Raviv, faced by Eugene Rostow, adviser to the President; Foy Kohler, expert on Soviet affairs; Lucius Battle, in charge of Middle East affairs; Joseph Sisco, director of the UN department; Roy Atherton; Leonard Meeker, legal adviser; and Townsend Hoopes, representing the Pentagon. One of those present told Eban that he had seen Johnson just before he left for Canada; that the President understood the gravity of the situation; that "he doesn't need to be pushed."

Late in the evening Eban and his American-based diplomats went to their hotel to put onto paper all they had learned. It was 1:30 A.M. before a cable containing Eban's own impressions was dispatched personally to Prime Minister Eshkol.

There was little sleep that night, for early the next morning (Friday, May 26, 1967) Dean Rusk telephoned to ask if Eban would be in Washington Saturday morning when the report on U Thant's visit to Cairo would be available. Eban replied that he intended to leave Washington in a few hours because an important Israeli Cabinet meeting he must attend had been scheduled for Sunday—"perhaps the most crucial Cabinet meeting in our history."

"I tell you frankly," he then said to Rusk, "that I think we are in for hostilities next week. There is an act of blockade which must be resisted. I doubt if anything at this stage can change the outlook. The only thing that might have an effect would be an affirmation by your President that he has decided unreservedly to get the Strait open. A public statement of that kind and a letter to the Prime Minister of Israel on some of the details and logistics might create an international atmosphere that is now lacking. . . ."

"I get you!" Dean Rusk exclaimed, and hung up.

Eban, accompanied by Harman and the Israeli military attaché, Aluf Mishne Yosef Geva, then went to the Pentagon, where they met with Secretary of Defense Robert McNamara, General Earle Wheeler, chairman of the Joint Chiefs of Staff, and others. The Pentagon conversation had scarcely begun when Eban was handed a cable from Jerusalem reiterating in drastic terms the military appraisal of the previous night.

The American military people offered no objections to Eban's political presentation but they were in drastic disagreement with his military report. Their information was that Egypt's armed forces were not in a position indicating an early assault; that Nasser was obviously waiting for Israel to incur the onus of an armed attack, which he felt able to repel. Despite the unanimous feelings that this was the situation, the

Egyptian ambassador, Mustapha Kemal, had been called in by the State Department the previous evening and had been warned stringently against any reckless act. This had been done because of the urgent tone of the messages relayed to Eban from Jerusalem.

Hearing this, Eban felt he had lost the first round because of the Jerusalem cables. They had resulted in a purely diplomatic gesture which was probably superfluous anyway and now Israel was in a difficult political position in case she felt obliged to engage Egyptian troops without delay.

The American military men also told the Israeli minister their studies indicated Israel would win if there was a war, no matter who had the initiative in the air. Their reports from the Middle East indicated logistic confusion in the Egyptian camp. Israel's lines of supply and communications were short and efficient; Egypt's were a nightmare of distance and complexity. Israel's immediate security was in good shape; Egyptian difficulties would grow every hour. Israel's air superiority was beyond dispute. None of them thought Israel was being outmaneuvered in the military domain and therefore would have to act in a mood of now or never.

Eban felt strongly that Israel's political business was to win international understanding of her right to break the closing ring—not to portray the country as a trembling victim of an imminent coup de grâce. The crux of Israel's predicament seemed to him to be the divergence between Jerusalem's estimate and the Washington estimate of Israel's security position. If the Pentagon was right and Israel's military success in any confrontation with Egypt was probable, then thought should now be taken primarily about Israel's political prospects *after* victory.

Before Eban got back to the Embassy a call came from the White House that the President wanted his talk with Foreign Minister Eban to be serious and balanced; therefore, he would like to postpone it until later. Also, he was concerned with the enormous pressure of the information media in connection with the prospective meeting. Scores of reporters and photographers were swarming around the White House and there had even been requests to station television cameras in the President's office for the occasion. Mr. Johnson wanted the meeting to be a working session and was displeased with all the theatrical atmosphere that had been created and also with a stream of telegrams he had been receiving.

Minister Evron replied to the White House official that the enormous public interest was natural and spontaneous; that Eban had refused to

appear on any radio or television program until after the meeting; that
the Embassy understood the President's need for more hours to weigh
his attitude, but the Middle East situation required that Eban make
an immediate report about the attitude of the United States; that the
time had come for Israel to know the American position.

The Israelis waited nervously most of the day for some word from
the White House about when the meeting would take place. Meanwhile,
Johnson concerned himself with such urgent matters as accepting a season
pass to the Washington Whips games, greeting the new Iranian ambassador, saying good-bye to the departing Italian ambassador and consulting with the ambassadors of Peru, Venezuela and El Salvador on
miscellaneous Latin American matters.[2] He was playing for time while he
waited for a military appraisal from the Pentagon. He did not want
to meet Eban on such a grave matter without all the documentation
before him.

As he waited Eban was being inundated by cables from Jerusalem
telling him in one way or another that it was essential for domestic as
well as international reasons that he be back home by Saturday night.
(It was now almost Saturday morning, Israeli time.) Important conversations were under way concerning an enlargement of the government
coalition. Israeli military circles did not share the Pentagon belief that
time was in their favor. They felt events were rushing toward a climax.
Eban feared vital decisions would be taken in Jerusalem without his
presence.

Early in the afternoon Israeli Minister Evron called the White House
and finally learned what was troubling the President. The Prime Minister
of a certain Western country had repeated in his own Parliament certain
things Mr. Johnson had told him in private conversation, to the great
annoyance of the President, who now wanted a clear understanding
about what would and would not be said by Eban if and when he was
received at the White House. Evron assured the presidential aide Eban
had no interest in publicity and would agree to say nothing publicly
except that he had had serious discussions with the President and the
Secretaries of State and Defense. This must have satisfied Johnson
and a few minutes later Evron was asked to come to the White House
at once for a preliminary conference.

Half an hour later, out of respect for Johnson's feelings about publicity,
Eban and Harman arrived by what Eban called "a circuitous route,
ending up at an unexpected point of entry."

The President came down the steps of the White House living quarters to greet them and escorted them to the Oval Room. Already present around the conference table were Walt and Eugene Rostow, Secretary McNamara, General Wheeler and George Christian, the President's press secretary.

Eban felt acutely the sense of drama in the situation. Israel's success depended on what sort of understanding she could achieve with her greatest and most stalwart friend, just as much as it did on her own valor. He had in the past several days repeated a number of times: "It is quite possible we may win in war and lose in peace." It had happened before: in 1956.

This meeting with Johnson was not like the one with De Gaulle. He had known the man who was now President for a dozen years or more—as a senator, majority leader, then Vice-President. Johnson's manner now was as courteous as ever, but his demeanor seemed exceptionally grave. He sat with his eyes very close to Eban's, staring into the Israeli's face.

Eban opened by saying that Israel had never before had a moment like this. The country was in a state of anxious expectancy. He had come to discuss the question of the blockade, but meanwhile an even graver situation had arisen—the reports from Jerusalem—"a total assault on Israel's existence."

"I have never received documents from my Prime Minister as urgent as those that reached me since I arrived here yesterday."

Eban reminded Johnson that ten years ago a solemn pact had been made between the United States and Israel that the Strait would be open to all shipping, including that of Israel. Again and again during his presentation and the ensuing discussion Eban hammered home this point: America had made an explicit commitment; was she going to live up to it, and how?

Eban recalled that in 1957 Ben-Gurion had written to Eisenhower that in pulling out of Sinai he was relying on the good faith of the United States. Eisenhower had replied that "he would never have cause to regret" placing his reliance on American good faith. Now, ten years later, Eban was here to find out the meaning of America's word. Does the United States have the will and determination to open the Strait?

If the President would state that the Strait would be opened again, if he would make common cause with Israel on this matter, there was a remote possibility that Nasser would retreat and a victory could be won without war. There was no use relying on the UN, for the USSR with its veto was in no mood for harmonious international action. If

Israel had to fight, it might be a bloody business, but Israel would win. Then he used a telling simile: what would happen if a foreign power were to ensure by force that the United States could trade only in the Pacific; that the Atlantic would be closed to her?

All this time Johnson had been listening with total concentration. There was a moment of silence, then he replied firmly and distinctly. He could help only if his Cabinet, Congress and the people felt Israel had been wronged. The question was how best to help. The Senate was out of town for the Memorial Day weekend. Nothing could be done before the Israeli Cabinet meeting on Sunday. In what Eban later called "robust and earthy terms" he told what he thought of the UNEF withdrawal. But he added that Israel must first exhaust all possibilities in the UN, even though he doubted that anything much would come of it. Israel should use all her diplomatic efforts to influence countries interested in keeping the waterway open. Israel must not jump the gun. Prime Minister Pearson had been wrong in circulating the impression that he, Johnson, was in favor of a Four Power arrangement. The United States was not going to do any retreating or backtracking. He was aware of what it was costing Israel to be patient, but it was less costly than to precipitate the matter while the jury was still out, and to have the world against Israel. With great emphasis he added:

"Israel will not be alone unless it decides to go it alone."

He repeated the sentence three times for emphasis. Then he recalled his long personal association with Eban. He said he knew the Israeli Prime Minister and President. He could not imagine that Israel would make a precipitate decision. He was not a feeble mouse or a coward. He was going to do what was right. But if Israel wanted the help of the United States it was absolutely necessary for her not to initiate hostilities.

Johnson tried to brush aside the promises that Dulles and Eisenhower had made by saying:

"I am fully aware of what three past Presidents have said, but that is not worth five cents if the people and the Congress do not support the President."[3]

At one point in the conversation Johnson asked McNamara to give Eban a summary of the findings of three separate U. S. Intelligence groups that had investigated the Middle Eastern situation. Then Johnson himself added:

"All our Intelligence people are unanimous that if the UAR attacks you will whip the hell out of them."[4]

At another point in the dialogue Johnson asked how vital access to the Gulf really was to the Israelis; after all, Israel had been blocked from using the Suez Canal since 1956 and still had survived.

"Perhaps," added the President, "Israel could . . ."

"Mr. President," quickly interjected Eban, "this is like asking a man who is forced to live on one lung whether he can't also live without any lungs at all."

Johnson smiled at the logic of the retort. When the UN came up again, Eban said:

"The United Nations is an important and incomparable forum, but it has no relevance to security problems. It would be like asking for 'action' from the Chicago Council on Foreign Relations."

Frequently Eban stressed the time problem. Only if there was a real plan could Israel continue to be patient. Finally he asked bluntly:

"Mr. President, can I tell my Cabinet that you are going to use any and all measures in your power to get the Gulf of Aqaba open to all shipping, including that of Israel?"

"Yes," Johnson replied, with emphasis.

It had begun to get dark by the time the conference broke up. Eban was given a short, typed *aide-mémoire* containing the two points Johnson had so frequently repeated: that Israel must not start hostilities and that "Israel will not be alone unless it decides to go it alone."

On the way to the elevator Johnson asked:

"What do you reckon will be the results in Israel of what I have said?"

Eban avoided a direct answer. Instead he asked:

"Again, Mr. President, can I tell my Cabinet that you will use any and all measures in your power to ensure that the Gulf and Strait are open to Israel shipping?"

"Yes," was the reply. Then Johnson shook Eban's hand with such an overpowering grip that the Israeli Foreign Minister later said in the elevator to Harman:

"I doubt whether I'll ever be able to use that hand again!"

(The exact wording of the twice-repeated assurance that Johnson would use "any and all measures" is important, for after the Six-Day war Eban's political opponents charged he had misled the Cabinet; that Johnson had never made such a promise. In 1971 Johnson in his own memoirs confirmed Eban's version of what he had been told, writing: " 'You can assure the Israeli Cabinet,' I said, 'we will pursue

vigorously any and all possible measures to keep the Strait open.'"⁵)
Thus Johnson put an end to three years of vilification.

As they left the White House Eban summarized for Harman his
impressions, stressing that "a new potentiality is only now beginning to
grow in American-Israeli relations." He felt there was the clear recognition
on Johnson's part that Israel had been wronged; that the situation
created by Nasser must be reversed and not permitted to congeal; that
the United States recognized itself charged with a commitment which
could not be allowed to languish and die. None of these elements
had existed in American policy in 1956. He felt Israel's position could
only be improved by giving the American initiative "a minimal area in
which to breathe"; that if Israel wished to retain and develop American
support she must invest a little time to secure it. "The least Washington
could ask was for an opportunity to test the ground on which it was
set." If all this failed, "Israel's solitary action would meet a different
reaction than if we gave no room for the initiative to be tried."

On the personal level Eban had raised his own stature with Johnson,
for the President in his memoirs said:

"Abba Eban is an intelligent and sensitive man."⁶

From Washington, Harman, Raviv and Eban flew to New York and
took rooms at a Kennedy Airport motel, where the ambassador began
dictating the full minutes of the meeting. Meanwhile Eban drove in to the
city for a conversation with Ambassador Arthur Goldberg at his Waldorf
Towers quarters. ("He is a man whose calm rationality always shines
forth in moments of crisis and peril.")

Goldberg reported confidentially that the Security Council proceedings
were "petering out in futility." U Thant had brought back "virtually
nothing" from Cairo except Nasser's assurance that he did not plan an
attack on Israel. Eban told Goldberg that this seemed logical because
Nasser wanted victory without war. Having cut Israel off from maritime
contact with two thirds of the world, he was prepared to wait and see
Israel strangle to death. "He has never been fastidious about the precise
manner in which Israel's destruction should be achieved."

After listening to a report of the meeting with Johnson, Goldberg
said that at this moment "only presidential commitments matter." He
stressed Johnson's need of congressional backing. Many in Congress would
wonder whether a small and innocuous-looking effort in the Red Sea
might not escalate into a major American engagement. What he considered of crucial importance was whether Eban had convinced Johnson
of Egypt's culpability and Israel's innocence.

Back at Kennedy Eban found that Harman had already sent a short account of the White House talks to Jerusalem and had edited his more extensive notes.

At midnight Eban and his political secretary boarded an El Al plane and slept for seven and a half hours to Orly, Paris. There he gave a short and cautious interview to the press, saying that in Washington he had found support for his contention that Israel had been the victim of an illegal and irresponsible act. Reporters for Israeli papers told him that war was certain "in a few days."

Ambassadors Eytan and Remez met the plane in Paris and gave Eban enough reading matter to occupy his time on the rest of the journey home. Most interesting was the full text of Nasser's speech of May 26 (1967) in which he declared that Egypt's basic objective would be "to destroy Israel." Soon newspapers throughout the world would be using that statement as the basis for bold headlines:

NASSER THREATENS TO DESTROY ISRAEL!

Of even more interest to Eban was an article by Mohammed Heikal, Nasser's confidant, in which he clearly indicated that a tactical situation had been created in which the next move was up to Israel; if victory could be achieved without war, so much the better; if not, then Egypt would lose nothing by absorbing the first Israeli reaction and passing on to the second decisive blow.

Commenting on the plan, Eban said:

"It implied that Israel would cooperate in her own annihilation. . . . This showed a curious inability to read the Israeli character. Arab leaders here were beginning to believe the contemptuous picture they had painted of their adversary."

As the very weary Abba Eban left the plane at Lod Airport he felt his mission had not been in vain. He had won some international support; he had gained the precious time Israel's military said was indispensable to victory. As Randolph S. and Winston S. Churchill put it in a book published a few months later:

"The efforts of Israeli Foreign Minister Abba Eban, although the subject of derision and deprecation by many of his countrymen and even some of his colleagues in the Cabinet, had managed to secure for Israel in his two weeks [this was an error: it was four days] of peregrinations backwards and forwards to Washington, London and Paris a climate of opinion in which it was possible for Israel to take decisive action."[7]

28

The Coiled Spring

WHEN EBAN'S PLANE touched down at Lod Airport shortly after 10 P.M. on Saturday, May 27 (1967), he was greeted by the largest assemblage of television, radio and newspaper reporters and photographers he had ever seen in Israel. This was an ominous sign, an indication of their apprehension about the exploding crisis. The first person through police lines to greet him was Aviad Yafeh, the Prime Minister's secretary, with news that the Cabinet had been in session in Tel Aviv for many hours debating the next step. They were awaiting his arrival. There was no time to be lost.[1]

After Eban had said a few noncommittal words to the reporters and posed briefly for pictures they started for the coast. On the way Eban learned that there was now a feeling of alarm about what would happen if Egyptian concentrations in Sinai were permitted to become further consolidated. The question the ministers were discussing was whether political conditions had been created in which a military victory, if achieved, would be ratified by political success. Or should there be further diplomatic action? Eban was also told the public was suffering the agony of waiting, which had never before been part of the Israeli military experience. The national spirit greatly needed to be rallied by eloquent leadership. School children all over the country were digging air raid shelters. Airliners, cutting their turn-around time to the minimum, had already taken fourteen thousand tourists and other foreigners out of the country and had brought home several thousand Israelis who wanted to be with their families if there was to be a war.

On arrival in Tel Aviv Eban was briefed further by the Director-General of his ministry, Arieh Levavi, who told him the Cabinet was in a deadlock. The ministers were almost equally divided between those who favored military action the next day and those who wanted further political consolidation. Legend has it that the rest of the Cabinet was on the brink of a military decision when Eban pulled it back. This was not the case. There was no clear consensus for or against immediate action.

The first point Eban made as he addressed the Cabinet was that on Thursday night, despite his own doubts, he had informed Washington that Israel expected a surprise Egyptian-Syrian attack and on the strength of this information the United States had given Cairo a powerful warning. If there had been any idea of Israel taking military action on May 28, Israel should not have asked the United States on May 25 to restrain Egypt. Instead of winning American political support, such procedure would lead to the accusation that Israel had acted without candor or consideration. Even if there were no other reason for delay, Eban argued, this one was sufficient to require a minimal period between the request to Washington and military action by Israel, during which more political exchanges could be pursued.

He reported briefly on the London and Paris conversations and in more detail on his conferences in Washington. Then, instead of joining the group urging immediate action or the group arguing for indefinite waiting, Eban made a compromise proposal of a forty-eight-hour period of disengagement, after which a decision would be made. This was his first restraining proposal during the 1967 crisis and it would be his last.

Fallacious reports have been reproduced in articles and in books that a vote was taken that night. Judging by the speeches that had been made around the table it is possible, had a vote been taken, the Cabinet would have split nine to nine, but no actual vote was taken. Two other inaccuracies that found their way into print are that Eban brought back from Washington a proposal for a two-week delay or that he himself suggested a two-week delay.

The conjecture in some books that Eban pressed his views to the point of threatening resignation was likewise without foundation. At no point did he feel himself "swimming against the tide." There were no violent arguments between Eban and military leaders. There was much support for his view that Israel had limited the possibility for immediate action by its request to Washington to restrain Cairo.

Most of the Cabinet ministers appeared deeply impressed by Eban's report of Johnson's unambiguous words. Eshkol said "all doubts about the utility of Eban's missions should now be dissolved."

From the Cabinet room, at Eshkol's request, Eban went to the second floor of the same building to brief the Foreign Affairs and Security Committee of the Knesset. While he was gone Eshkol suggested to the other ministers that they were all tired and should get some sleep and assemble the next day.

Suzy Eban was waiting for her husband in the Dan Hotel, where he finally arrived at 4 A.M. For the next hour he gave her a synopsis of all that had happened since they separated . . . could it have been only ninety-some hours ago? At 5 A.M. he went to bed with the hope of being able to shut off the mental processes long enough to get a little sleep.

The Cabinet assembled the next afternoon, Sunday, May 28 (1967). Meanwhile Washington had been making intensive efforts to persuade Israel to extend its respite. The record of these messages refutes the myth that the United States at this stage secretly wanted Israel to take unilateral action. From President Johnson came a message to Prime Minister Eshkol: Moscow had told Washington of receiving information that Israel was preparing for military action; Moscow had asked the United States to take all measures possible to ensure there would be no military conflict.

"As your friend," Johnson told Eshkol, "I repeat even more strongly what I said yesterday to Mr. Eban: Israel just must not take preemptive military action and thereby make itself responsible for the initiation of hostilities."

From Rusk came a message that "the British and we are proceeding urgently to prepare the military aspects of the international naval escort plan and other nations are responding vigorously to the idea."

Eban read these communications to the Cabinet without comment. Eshkol apparently had been ready to ask for a drastic decision, despite the forty-eight-hour agreement, but the new Washington messages put a different aspect on the dilemma. He was now prepared to advise the Cabinet to give the United States and others a chance for two weeks to succeed in their efforts. It was not the Soviet warning but the U.S. show of resolution that won the delay. Of the eighteen ministers only one, Minister of Transport Moshe Carmel, was now prepared to vote for immediate military action. It was an almost unanimous vote and it was not taken in panic.

Eban that day heard stories of chaotic dislocation among Egyptian forces in Sinai and also learned that military equipment previously ordered from Europe was now reaching Israel. At the same time

Eshkol told senior Israeli military officers, when they warned him that every hour of delay was working against Israel, "You're exaggerating quite a lot!" Commented Eban:

"It is the primary ministerial function to be skeptical of expert advice, however sincere, just as it is the duty of military commanders to over-estimate and never to underestimate the adversary's potential."

When Eshkol told senior military officers of the decision, most of them accepted it with disciplined serenity, although some others created a tempestuous scene, arguing that military success depended on immediate resistance. Of them Eban said: "They relied frankly on their intuitions and emotions."

Next, someone had to tell the public and Eshkol decided to do it himself. All Israel was waiting for news of some decision. An adviser, whose identity is still unknown, counseled Eshkol to deliver the government communiqué as if it were a speech. The Prime Minister, who had never been a sensational public speaker, was suffering from great fatigue. The scene with the army officers had frazzled his nerves. He read the dry, legalistic words in a dull, stumbling manner. Instead of doing it on tape, which would have made possible some editing of errors in delivery, he made the broadcast live. A nervous public, which had expected a clarion call to heroic sacrifice, or at least a Churchillian promise of blood, sweat and tears, got, instead, a depressing announcement of the postponement of action, read in a most uninspiring manner.

The public despondency was exploited by Eshkol's political enemies. The morning paper *Ha'aretz* published an anonymous letter (possibly written by a staff member) calling for Eshkol's resignation because of the broadcast. Exaggerated accounts of the meeting between the Prime Minister and the generals were spread, causing understandable public disquiet. It had not been necessary for Eshkol to consult anyone about the decision, or to make an improvised public radio explanation. It was his excess of democratic zeal and the Israeli passion for detailed argument that put him and his government in hot water.

During the next week Israel suffered a staggering series of agonies and disappointments. First, the Security Council exhibited its utter impotence. Nasser had made two speeches which were virtual declarations of war. UNEF had been humiliatingly banished. U Thant had gone on a desperate mission to Cairo, which was marked by failure. In the streets of the Arab capitals frenzied masses were demonstrating for slaughter. Israel had ordered total mobilization to defend herself. Never since the Cuban crisis had the press, radio and television of the world reflected greater international tension. Editorial writers, religious leaders and perspicacious intellectuals everywhere were aware of a moral crisis. So the eyes of the world turned to the building on the East River in New York, home of the organization whose sole responsibility was to keep the peace.

But the Soviet ambassador told the Security Council he saw nothing in the international situation to require concern. The Bulgarian delegate questioned why the Security Council had been called into session at all. The Indian delegate said immediate discussion was unwarranted because "the situation is still not clear." The UAR representative with vehemence told the UN to keep out of the Middle East situation. So the UN members did nothing but engage in idle talk and a fierce mistrust of the Security Council was burned deep into Israel's heart.

Next, after keeping Israel waiting for nine days, De Gaulle finally sent a reply to Eshkol's letter, which added nothing to what he had told Eban in Paris. Now he was even opposed to the action being contemplated by the United States and Britain.

Then, on May 30, King Hussein, apparently propelled by the wave of euphoria sweeping the Arab world, flew to Cairo and signed a mutual defense pact with the man who had several times tried to engineer his assassination. Thus it was made almost certain that war would come and Israel would have to fight on three fronts.

Ahmed Shukairi, Palestinian terrorist leader, flew back to Amman with Hussein, vowing that Israelis not born in Palestine would be driven from the land and only those native to the area would be permitted to remain, "but I estimate that none of them will survive." There seemed to be no limit to Arab arrogance.

From Washington Ambassador Harman cabled that President Johnson's mood was now somber and that he could see no outcome from the crisis. In whatever direction Eban looked he saw signs of hesitancy. Britain and the United States were contacting the capitals of eighty countries in an attempt to get signatures on a declaration expressing the right of free navigation in the Gulf of Aqaba, but few of the maritime powers were showing any interest in a confrontation with Nasser and the Arab world.

On the morning of May 30 Eshkol asked Eban to hold a press conference and "give the impression of intensified emergency." War correspondents from all over the world had now converged on Israel. Eban faced hundreds of cameras and microphones, which impressed him as "a forest of gigantic eyes and ears, thirsty for precision and eager, if possible, to pick up a triumphant note."

He told the reporters, first in English, then in French, that Israel was like a coiled spring: that the period of waiting could be measured in "days or at most weeks, certainly not months." As one correspondent present reported:

"In one of the most brilliant press conferences I have ever seen anywhere, Eban completely transformed the mood of gloomy fear of a Munich-type betrayal which had descended on Israel as a result of the most unfortunate radio speech by Eshkol. . . . Eban was completely relaxed and exuded confidence which appeared too great and too sincere to be acting."[2]

That same day Eban helped Eshkol draft a letter to President Johnson in which he bluntly stated that "the continuation of this position [of waiting] for any considerable time is out of the question."

By the night of May 30 the possibility that Israel would undertake unilateral action—and soon—had been communicated to the United States and the world.

On May 31 Minister Evron was called to the White House for an informal talk with Walt Rostow, who said he was disturbed by certain passages in Eshkol's letter. Specifically Rostow questioned whether Johnson had said he would use "any and all measures" to keep the Strait open. On Eban's instructions Evron held his ground and told Rostow that that was exactly what Johnson had said—a contention finally confirmed four years later when Johnson in his memoirs said this was exactly what he had said. During the Rostow-Evron conversation it came out that only three or four of the eighty governments invited to sign the joint declaration had indicated they would.

In the meantime Israel had been going through her most serious domestic political crisis. For more than a year Rafi had been waging a relentless campaign against Eshkol, accusing him and his administration of both senility and incompetence. One Rafi leader had expressed the opinion that the Israeli Army would not be ready for war for six months or a year and the only man who could tell the Israeli people this painful truth was Ben-Gurion, who, himself, was reported to feel that Israel was not ready for hostilities. Following a conference with Peres, Begin called on Eshkol (while Eban was in Paris) and asked him if he would turn over the premiership and the post of Defense Minister to Ben-Gurion and take for himself the Deputy Prime Minister's title. It was no secret that Eshkol's faltering radio address of May 28 had convinced many people—among them several distinguished apolitical Weizmann Institute professors—that he should be replaced. But Eshkol refused to step down.

On May 30 in a meeting of the Labor party (his own party) one speaker after another implored Eshkol at least to give up the Defense post to Dayan. As the speeches continued the Prime Minister handed Eban a scrap of paper on which he had scribbled:

"I don't intend to answer all the personal references. I ask you not to. Let us both hear and see where and who our comrades are."

But Eshkol had few defenders at the meeting. At 11 A.M. the next day (Wednesday, May 31, 1967) the political committee of the Labor party met in Tel Aviv. It was now clear that some sort of change had to be made in the Government. The first suggestion was that Yigal Allon be appointed Defense Minister, with Dayan as Foreign Minister, although the man who made the motion accompanied it with a lengthy eulogy of Eban's recent diplomatic work. During a brief but dramatic silence Eban wrote a note to Eshkol saying he "would not accept any titular office or stay in the Government with an inexperienced Foreign Minister whose talents are widely remote from the international sphere and whose heart and mind lie elsewhere." Allon, Golda Meir and Eshkol all severely rejected the proposal for a change in the Foreign Ministry. The three independent parties—Mapam, the Independent Liberals and the National Religious party—also registered with Eshkol their protest of the suggestion. One hour after it had been submitted, the proposal to change the Foreign Ministry died, never to be resurrected.

The meeting ended with the decision that Eshkol should offer the deputy premiership to Dayan and Defense to Allon, which was done, but Dayan rejected the offer, saying if it were not Defense he would go back to military service and take the Southern Command, where the war would be won or lost.

That same day Eban sat with department heads of the Foreign Ministry and declared to them that the idea of a two-week respite must be revised and Israel's dialogue with the United States modified accordingly.

That same day Kuwait and Iraqi forces arrived in Egypt, and Jordan celebrated her reconciliation with Syria by resuming diplomatic relations, and Bagdad Radio carried a broadcast by President Aref in which he told his air force officers he would meet them in Haifa and Tel Aviv. Reports from Washington were gloomier than ever.

That same day Eban, who was in Tel Aviv to be close to the Prime Minister and the Defense Ministry, called all his senior Foreign Ministry officers to come to him from Jerusalem as quickly as possible. While waiting for them he was told of a message just received in Jerusalem from an American close to the Johnson administration which read:

"If Israel had acted alone without exhausting political efforts it would have made a catastrophic error. It would then have been almost impossible for the United States to help Israel and the ensuing relationship would have been tense. The war might be long and costly for Israel if it broke out. . . . Israelis should not criticize Eshkol and Eban. They should realize that their restraint and well-considered procedures would have a decisive influence when the United States came to consider the measure of its involvement."

It concluded with the statement that time was running out and that it now was "a matter of days or even hours."

The message was a strong hint that the time had come for Israel to move. (President Johnson in his autobiography published in 1971 gave the impression that in another week he might have solved the problem. Eban felt at the time—and later in retrospect—that there was no evidence of this; that with each passing day Israel's position was becoming more beleaguered.[3])

In the same hour a cable from Washington quoted Rusk as saying brusquely, in reply to a question about whether any efforts were being made to keep Israel from precipitate action:

"I don't think it is our business to restrain anyone."

When his senior officers arrived Eban went over with them all cables that had arrived in the past forty-eight hours. They showed that no important American leader had taken the responsibility of urging Israel to wait for any length of time. And none was quoted as placing excessive reliance on international action.

At this point Eban came to the conclusion that he must take an immediate and decisive step, based on his knowledge that the diplomatic and political activities of the past ten days had achieved their maximum result. The draft declaration of the maritime powers languished unhonored, unsigned. The naval task force was only a figment of someone's imagination. World opinion was now on Israel's side. The days of patient political labor had created a quite different atmosphere than Israel would have faced without them.

At a quick conference with his most intimate adviser, Arthur Lourie, Eban was strongly urged to take the step he was contemplating and so, accompanied by his director-general, he went to a meeting with Chief of Staff Rabin and Chief of Intelligence Yariv where he stated that he no longer had any political inhibitions to whatever military resistance was feasible and necessary; that if Israel was successful the political prospects would be good. This time Israel would not be opposed by a united and angry world, as in 1956–57.

It was a drastic step, for while in theory the vote of a Foreign Minister is no greater than that of any other Cabinet member, in practice if he gives his vote for military action it has the strength of many, his assigned task being to pursue every possible peaceful remedy of a situation.

Eban had lived for several weeks with the knowledge that his vote might be the decisive one; that if he withdrew his inhibiting hand, military resistance with all its perhaps terrible prospects would become inevitable. For this reason, being an acutely sensitive man, he had spent days and nights of solitary anguish, although telephone calls, cables and letters kept him from any really uninterrupted soul-searching. He had been badgered by military men shouting for action and by mothers who wrote to him of their prayers for an honorable peace.

To the two generals Eban stated why he believed the waiting period had achieved its political purpose; now there was nothing more for which to wait. When he left their presence his step seemed lighter.

As he walked toward his Tel Aviv office he found Eshkol standing silently on the lawn. When he told him what he had just done the Prime Minister's relief was obvious. Together they went to a meeting of the Labor party Secretariat, where Eshkol began a long and dignified speech to his party leaders. After putting on the record that Dayan had predicted there would be no general confrontation with Egypt until 1970, he dramatically proposed, in the interest of national unity, to offer the Defense post to the distinguished man from Rafi, coupled with the inclusion of Gahal in a government of national unity. By midnight, although the two new members had still not yet been sworn in, the Cabinet met with Dayan and Beigin in attendance.

The next morning (Friday, June 2, 1967) the General Staff gave the Cabinet a thorough briefing. One officer after another arose to urge the necessity of immediate resistance. They were talking to an already convinced audience. Meanwhile vast crowds in the streets of Cairo were chanting:

"We will slaughter them! We will destroy them! Slaughter! Slaughter!"

Egyptian General Mourtagi announced:

"In five days we shall liquidate the little State of Israel."

In Damascus a Syrian general, not to be outdone, shouted:

"Egypt and Syria will be able to destroy Israel in four days at the most."

As Eban summarized the situation:

"We looked around and saw the world divided between those who were seeking our destruction and those who would do nothing to prevent it."

A new and compelling voice now began to have an influence on public opinion. Brigadier Vivian Herzog, Suzy Eban's brother-in-law, had become the chief military commentator and over Kol Israel told the people it was doubtful whether Egyptian aircraft could penetrate Israel's air defenses and if he had a choice of being in an Egyptian aircraft on its way to bomb Tel Aviv or sitting in his house in Tel Aviv, "for the good of my health I would prefer to be sitting in Tel Aviv."

On Friday, June 2 (1967), Eban, meeting with his advisers, surveyed a continuing decline of international resolve, plus an official French statement that whoever fired the first shot would be guilty of aggression and would earn France's disapproval. In Washington the atmosphere was what Eban called "thick with caution." But as the West became increasingly timid, Soviet militancy grew hourly more intense. Eban told his colleagues that in his opinion "the shorter the clash the less likely Soviet intervention will be."

Nearly a thousand tanks were now massed on Israel's southern border. Egyptian aircraft were reconnoitering over the Negev. The Jordanian Army was moving into battle positions. Forty thousand Syrian troops were on the Golan Heights.

And yet on Saturday, June 3 (1967), the beaches and picnic grounds of Israel were crowded with families of soldiers home on short leave. That day Ambassador Harman arrived from Washington and Eban took him to the Prime Minister's home, where they were joined by Dayan, Allon, General Yigael Yadin and the army chiefs. There it was agreed if Israel broke out of the siege and blockade, the United States would probably not take a hostile position. Harman's report confirmed Eban's belief there was nothing more to be expected from the outside. Briefly the military people explained their general military plan. The Jordanian front would remain quiet unless Hussein attacked.

When he reached home that night Eban found that Suzy, Eli and Gila, like the members of so many other Israeli families, had pasted tape on all the windows of the eighteen-room house to avoid flying glass in case of a bombing.

"I had to ask my long-suffering family to spend more hours peeling the tape away, since television crews were going to record interviews with me and I thought visible evidence of defense preparations in the Foreign Minister's home would give too sharp a hint of impending war."

On Sunday, June 4 (1967), Eban and other ministers were in session for more than seven hours, first in a Cabinet meeting, then in various committee sessions. There was an air of strange tranquillity, although Eban was acutely aware that he and his colleagues were sharing heavy responsibilities and were making decisions such as they had never faced before in their lives—and might never have to face again. One hundred thousand Egyptian soldiers in seven divisions had entrenched themselves deeply in bunkers and foxholes in Sinai. They had a reserve of sixty thousand. The Syrians had another fifty thousand mobilized. Jordan, if she went into action, could put at least that many men into the field. Then there were all the figures about bombers, fighters, tanks. More important, Arab morale was better than it had ever been since the creation of Israel. The street mobs were in the same frenzy as in other historic moments of fanaticism.

After the military appraisal, it was Eban's duty to describe the political environment in which Israel now found herself. He gave the Cabinet his assessment from the mass of evidence that had been pouring in from his listening posts around the world: an extraordinary tide of solidarity with Israel was now sweeping through every free civilized community in the world. For several days the British Government had not spoken about restraint. He had good reason to believe that understanding, good will and approval in America would reach into the very highest places. In France there was a wide chasm between official policy and the attitude of the public. Fifty thousand wildly cheering Frenchmen had demonstrated outside the windows of Israel's Embassy in Paris, even though De Gaulle had told Ambassador Eytan, when he protested about a ban on the export of defense material to Israel, that the embargo would remain "as long as it is not clear if you will not go to war"—punishment by a double negative. So, Israel's main supply artery was now cut, while Soviet military matériel continued to pour into Egypt and Syria.

When Eban finished, the silence was deep and long. Eshkol called on each minister to give his general view. When Eban's turn came he said:

"Our decision should be that the Government authorizes the security authorities, together with the responsible ministers, to decide on any action necessary to break the enemy's stranglehold and that the time should be determined in accordance with military necessities alone."

He summed up his recommendation as "total response to the next encroachments."

After the other ministers had spoken, Eshkol asked for a show of hands on a proposal that the Defense Ministry, in consultation with the Prime Minister and others concerned, should be empowered to decide when and how to resist the aggression. Eighteen were entitled to vote. All hands went up except those of two Mapam ministers, who added their agreement later in the day. The Cabinet then agreed to remain in daily session and to meet next morning in Tel Aviv.

Certain American newspapers the next day reported that Eban and Dayan had engaged in bitter debate at the June 4 meeting and that this had led to a divided vote. The report was totally inaccurate.

Eban suggested that in order not to galvanize Cairo into action— "to defuse the atmosphere"—the Cabinet ought to transact a little ordinary business for public notice, so the communiqué that was handed out after the meeting said that an agreement for cooperation with the Peruvian Atomic Energy Commission and a cultural pact with Belgium had been approved by the Cabinet, as well as certain legislation concerning State of Israel Development bonds. Also, it had been agreed that the new ministers would be sworn in Monday.

This communiqué sent a few unperceptive foreign correspondents back to their home bases, in despair over covering a war. A technical agreement with Peru hardly looked like a call to battle.

But Eban and his fellow ministers were acutely aware—as if their nerve ends had been sandpapered raw—of the full horror of the situation that faced them and their people—a quarter of a million Arab soldiers crushing in from the north, the south, the east; fifteen thousand tanks in some cases only a few minutes away from Israeli settlements; the not-distant airfields, with their loads of death designed for precisely determined Israeli targets; the careful labor of eight decades about to be engulfed in a kind of Mongol massacre; the piratical blockade which had cut Israel off from half the world and had stopped the flow of fuel so vital for her planes, tanks and other defensive weapons; the exultant voices on the airwaves proclaiming imminent war; the cool, wicked voices coming from the south, calmly declaring that Israel's destruction was at hand.

But as beds were being prepared in Israeli hospitals for the expected casualties and as crude bomb shelters were being constructed throughout the country, the flow of cables to Eban's office gave a warm picture of world reaction:

In Stockholm some members of Parliament discussed resigning so they could make themselves available to fight in Israel.

Israeli consulates and embassies on all five continents were crowded with young men asking to be sent to Israel for immediate service.

An elderly Christian spinster in northern Scotland said she would not be much good as a fighter but no one could drive a truck better than she could.

A blind man in Brooklyn offered Eban the money he had saved for twenty years to buy a house, saying if Israel went under there would be no point to living anyway; if Israel survived he was sure she would return his money.

In Holland's churches prayers were being offered for Israel's survival. Israel and the diaspora seemed linked as never before.

29

Total Response

ABBA EBAN was almost the only occupant of the Dan Hotel in Tel Aviv the night of Sunday–Monday, June 4–5 (1967). He awoke early and looked out into the street. The heat was already so intense that it could be seen, rising from the pavement.[1]

At 7:50 A.M., as he was en route by car to the Ministry of Defense, air raid sirens set up an alarming wail. Most children on their way to school and men and women en route to work hurried on, assuming it was another test.

When he reached the Prime Minister's office he learned Egyptian planes headed for Israel had been sighted on radar screens. In accordance with the Cabinet's decision of the previous night Israeli planes had gone out to meet them. A short time later Egyptian ground forces in the Gaza Strip bombarded the Israeli settlements of Nahal Oz and Erez. Israeli armored units responded. But in both cases it was neither angry pursuit nor minor retaliation. It was what came to be known in ensuing diplomatic exchanges as "total response." The war the Egyptians and Syrians had been trying for three weeks to promote had finally begun. What Israel's Foreign Minister had so aptly called "the coiled spring" had now been released.

When he heard the news Eban felt overcome by vast relief. He knew he had taken every politico-diplomatic step possible to defend Israel's interest by methods short of war and he felt certain the righteousness of the action now under way would be recognized by most of the world.

Even before a single report came in about how the battle was going, he began backstopping the military by instructing his deputy director-general, Yosef Tekoah, to telephone Ambassador Gideon Rafael in New

York and ask for an urgent meeting of the Security Council, before which he could tell the story of Egypt's aggression, Israel's resistance.

By 11 A.M. reports were flowing in of an almost unbelievable victory in the air. By noon the number of Egyptian aircraft destroyed ran into the hundreds. But Eban was aware that such military success did not relieve him and his ministry of urgent political duty. There were two immediate diplomatic aims: to make certain the USSR did not intervene and to give Jordan every opportunity to avoid involvement. Simultaneous war with Syria and Egypt probably could not be avoided, but a three-front war had always been one of Israel's darkest nightmares.

In the late morning Eban summoned the British, French, American and Soviet ambassadors to come one after another to his Tel Aviv office and while he waited for them he helped Eshkol draft a letter to the heads of all friendly states. The first, to President Johnson, said it was hoped that "everything will be done by the United States to prevent the Soviet Union from exploiting and enlarging the conflict." Similar letters went to De Gaulle and Wilson. In the letter to the British Prime Minister, and also in Eban's conference with the British ambassador, stress was laid on Israel's desire "to avoid any engagement with Jordan, unless Jordan makes conflict inevitable."

However, at 10 A.M. Jordan began a heavy bombardment along the entire Jordanian-Israeli front. With the thought that this might be nothing more than a gesture of solidarity with Egypt on Hussein's part, Eshkol and Eban decided to give him another chance to stay out of the fight, so a message was drafted from Eshkol to the king and dispatched quickly via General Odd Bull, chief of the General Staff of the United Nations Truce Supervision Organization. There was no doubt that it was received, for Hussein in his own memoirs of the day told of receiving a telephone call from Jerusalem in which General Bull passed on the Israeli message, which read:

"We shall not initiate any action whatsoever against Jordan. However, should Jordan open hostilities we shall react with all our might and the King will have to bear the full responsibility of the consequences."

Hussein's response was an intensification of the shelling of the New City of Jerusalem and bombardment of the outskirts of Tel Aviv. The explanation he gave after the war was that he was compelled to act by "Arab solidarity" and by the fact the Egyptians had already taken over command of his Army. (This made it one of the few wars in history in which both sides agreed on who started it.)

Still no Israeli countermove was made until 1 P.M., after Jordanian forces captured Government House in southeast Jerusalem, headquarters of the UN Truce Organization, and Jordanian tanks began moving on northwest Jerusalem. Now Israel had a three-front war on her hands, which, in Eban's opinion, could have only two possible outcomes, total victory or total defeat.

Briefing senior officers of the Foreign Ministry that afternoon Eban declared it was urgent for them to move in unison against two possible dangers, in addition to the chance of USSR intervention: that a cease-fire resolution might be adopted in the UN calling for a return to previously held positions and that foreign governments and world opinion might blame Israel for the war, overlooking the background of today's development. It was urgent to start moving diplomatically against these dangers.

In telegraphic communication with Ambassador Rafael, Eban made preparations to leave for New York as soon as a definite military decision was reached in the field. Meanwhile, he would devote his full efforts to trying to influence world opinion. Just as if he were conducting a military operation, he sent cables to his ambassadors on all continents instructing them to make contact at the highest possible level and explain how and why war had broken out, stressing that Israeli survival had been at stake.

At 1 P.M. he met with representatives of the world press, radio and television. Arab sources at that hour were still screaming about their own triumphs. Harsh experience at the UN had taught Eban and his associates that whenever the Arab states appear to be in trouble there are loud demands for a cease-fire and a return to previous lines, whereas if Israel seems in danger, the United Nations can be counted on to be as dilatory as only an international agency can be. At the moment Israel appeared to have the upper hand, militarily, despite all the Arab claims. Therefore, the tactic Eban decided to follow was to let the Arabs have all the rope they needed to hang themselves, so he told the massive audience of communications people only that Israel was responding not to the limited attacks that the Arabs had made but to the whole aggressive design of blockade and encirclement. That was not very satisfactory to the reporters. What they wanted to know was: How was Israel doing?

"To the best of my knowledge the Israeli Air Force has not been wasting its time," Eban replied, rather enigmatically and surely very unsatisfactorily from the journalistic point of view. As he dodged giving specific answers he thought of how many of these men and women he was facing had predicted to their editors during the past two weeks that Israel's doom was at hand. He even felt a remorseful pang for those who, like Winston Churchill's grandson, were not present, having gone back home convinced nothing was going to happen.

At 3 P.M., having explained Israel's case to the world press and to ambassadors from Washington, London and Paris, and through Israeli embassies to all other friendly governments, Eban decided to return to his headquarters in Jerusalem.

The Israeli radio, which, of course, was being closely monitored by the Arabs, had broadcast an announcement to the Israeli public—and to the Jordanian artillery—that the Knesset would meet at 4 P.M. in Jerusalem, which thus made the seat of government an inviting target for enemy guns. At the valley called Bab-el-Wad, where the wreckage of trucks shot up by the Arabs in the 1948 war still stood, covered with rustproof paint as memorials, Eban found himself in a chaotic situation. Cars containing Knesset members answering the call to assemble in Jerusalem were in a grand traffic tangle with Israeli tanks and infantry engaging the Jordanian enemy. In the confusion suddenly the former Prime Minister, David Ben-Gurion, appeared, as if out of nowhere. He, too, was trying to get to the capital. Finally civilian and military police untangled the snarl; the warriors went about their business and the parliamentarians theirs. As Eban's car entered Jerusalem he saw the advanced columns of Colonel Gur's paratroop brigade moving from the south toward Jerusalem in a convoy of buses.

"Like the Battle of the Marne," he remarked to the others in his car.

Jordanian artillery had now zeroed in on northwest Jerusalem, where the Knesset is located. Shells had already hit buildings of the Hebrew University and the National Museum. As darkness fell the Cabinet was called into session in one of the Knesset's air raid shelters. While they waited for Eshkol to arrive they were briefed by Brigadier General Ze'evi of the General Staff. After telling what had happened to the Egyptian, Syrian and Jordanian air forces, he concluded:

"Israel now has the only air power in the Middle East."

At one point during the Cabinet meeting one of the ministers began his remarks:

"I would like to draw your attention to the bombardment of Jerusalem. . . ."

There was no need for anyone to "draw attention." The noise of the bombardment was thunderous, even down here in the shelter. While the battle for Jerusalem was under way that night, Eban and the other

Cabinet members were aware of something the rest of the world might not have understood: to defend western Jerusalem would involve the necessity of capturing eastern Jerusalem, and once the Israeli Army entered the Old City it would be historically and emotionally impossible ever to relinquish it to Jordan again. For Eban and others concerned with foreign affairs it would mean international complications without end. As they discussed the political implications Eban suggested that military considerations should be the only present concern. Eshkol agreed and thereupon announced:

"We are going to take the Old City in order to remove the danger of bombardment and the shelling now being carried on by Jordan."

As Eban was leaving the meeting a Knesset guard loaned him a transistor radio, which he tuned in to some of the Arab stations, over which he heard the "news" that the Israeli Air Force had been destroyed, Egyptian troops were marching on Tel Aviv, Syrian troops on Nazareth, and Jordan was about to cut Israel in half at her narrowest point.

Cables from New York received that evening told how the Egyptian ambassador had protested to the Security Council that Israel had committed "a cowardly and treacherous aggression against my country." France and India were drawing up resolutions calling for a cease-fire and withdrawal. Eban's reaction was "a sense of fatal, historic repetition." Once again, as Israel was breaking out of the circle of Arab aggression, plans were already being made to put her neck back in the noose. He knew that although the rest of the country was exclusively concerned at the moment with the military aspects of the situation, his task was to try to prevent losing the peace that would follow the war. If the international community with any degree of unanimity tried to force Israel back to the lines of June 4, it would mean the loss of all gains or, at best, Israel would be forced into a position of international isolation, boycott and political blockade. The difficulty was that it was normal UN practice (not just in Middle East situations) to couple a cease-fire resolution with a call for a return to pre-bellum lines. It would take a special effort of imagination and intellectual resourcefulness to separate these two concepts in the eyes of the world.

Eban decided he could best perform the herculean task which the situation had forced upon him by going to New York and there making an appeal to world opinion on the inherent righteousness of Israel's resistance and to make sure that the military victory now being won would not be frittered away by a conservative political response. The problem he faced was that the Arabs operated on a policy of "limited liability." If they were to capture any Israeli territory it was inconceivable they would ever give it up, but if Israel captured territory there were always cries of moral indignation and immediate political pressure was applied for its relinquishment. It amounted to: "Heads I win, tails you lose." Eban's task would be to try to break this cycle.

The night was loud with the noise of exploding shells as he made his way home. He found his wife and children in the air raid shelter that had been built into the Foreign Minister's residence. Gila, now eleven, told him excitedly how much she preferred this new world of candles, kerosene lamps, emergency food supplies and a telephone switchboard to her own second-floor room. He broke the news to Suzy that he must leave at once for America.

The battle for Jerusalem was at its height. The hospitals were filling up with wounded. Musrara, the poorest of the city's Jewish quarters, had already suffered much damage and many casualties. Suzy saw him to the front door. As they embraced on the doorstep, then separated, they felt a rush of wind at face level. The policeman on guard later told Suzy a piece of shrapnel had neatly bisected the several feet between their heads.

It took three hours by side roads to get from Jerusalem to Tel Aviv, where Eban and his political secretary, Moshe Raviv, arrived about 11 P.M. They went directly to the Prime Minister's office for a Cabinet meeting and to hear the latest battle reports. The Cabinet authorized a midnight announcement by the Chief of Staff and head of the Air Force. Then there was a long discussion of battle priorities. At 2 A.M. Eban and Raviv went to the Dan Hotel and picked up suitcases. Lod, the international airport, was closed, no international flights were arriving or leaving, so they went to Tel Aviv Airport, where arrangements were made for an Israeli twin-engine plane to take them to Athens. The pilot said he thought he could avoid appearing on the Syrian radar screens if they flew at housetop level until well out over the sea. They took off at 3 A.M. without lights.

As dawn broke, making the Acropolis an object of scarlet beauty, they landed in the Greek capital. After checking all airlines they found the only chance of getting to New York in time to affect the Security Council decision would be if they took one KLM plane from Athens to Amsterdam and then another across the Atlantic. After making reservations they sent cables ahead so that in Amsterdam they were met by the Israeli ambassadors from London, Paris and The Hague. And by a sea of cameras and microphones. It was now no secret that three hundred Arab planes had been destroyed between dawn and dusk. Eban reminded the reporters that nothing like this had ever happened in the history of aerial warfare.

Three hours out of New York one of the stewardesses came from the pilot's cabin with a radio message for Eban. The Security Council debate was in full swing, but no resolution had yet been passed. Eban would be expected to speak as soon as he could get to the UN building. The hospitable Dutch steward and the air hostess cooperated by clearing the little cabin reserved for their own use, setting up a small wooden table, producing a block of paper and then leaving Eban to make his notes in manufactured privacy.

At Kennedy Airport Eban and Raviv avoided the press and drove straight to the Plaza Hotel where they held a fast conference with Ambassadors Michael Comay and Gideon Rafael and other members of the Israeli mission. Then a quick telephone talk with Ambassador Goldberg. At the UN building Eban conferred with Ambassador Hans Tabor of Denmark, the current chairman of the Security Council. India was pressing for withdrawal by Israeli forces to the June 4 positions, which would mean that eighty thousand Egyptian soldiers would be permitted to return to Israel's southern frontier and to control of Sharm el-Sheikh. The Soviet Union, not yet convinced that its Arab friends had lost the war, was in no hurry about a cease-fire. The United States was insisting on a cease-fire without withdrawal.

Soon after Eban's arrival a resolution for a cease-fire and nothing else was passed unanimously. But this clearly was only a respite. Nothing prevented a new resolution of withdrawal being introduced and passed at any time Cairo, Amman, Damascus and Moscow were ready to admit the totality of the Arab defeat.

It was almost midnight when Eban began his impromptu address by saying:

"I have just come from Jerusalem to tell the Security Council that Israel by its independent effort and sacrifice has passed from serious danger to successful and glorious resistance."

For most of the world this was the first outright assertion that Israel had won the war. Then, from the notes he had hastily made on the plane, Eban began weaving his speech. Observing the grave countenances of the Security Council members, he decided to bring the situation home to each of them.

"To understand how Israel felt one has merely to look around this table and imagine a foreign power forcibly closing New York or Montreal, London or Marseilles, Toulon or Copenhagen, Rio or Tokyo or Bombay harbors. How would your governments react? What would you do? How long would you wait?"

Throughout the talk he was calm, whereas the Arab speakers had been emotional to the point of hysteria. He was logically convincing, whereas his opponents had talked largely nonsense. He was factual yet brilliant. It was obvious that he must have thought out what he was going to say under the most difficult circumstances—in the plane, in a taxi, extemporaneously—yet his address was a gem of organization.

In conclusion he talked bluntly about Nasser.

"As he looks around him at the arena of battle, at the wreckage of tanks and planes, at the collapse of intoxicated hopes, might not the Egyptian ruler ponder whether anything was achieved by that disruption? What has it brought but strife, conflict and the stern criticism of progressive men throughout the world? Israel in recent days has proved its steadfastness and vigor. It is now willing to demonstrate its instinct for peace. Let us build a new system of relationships from the wreckage of the old. Let us discern across the darkness the vision of a better and brighter dawn."

It was long past midnight when he got back to his hotel room. It was the next day in Israel. Just before turning out his light he read the latest batch of messages. Because the Arabs had not yet accepted the cease-fire, Israel was still achieving military victories.

President Johnson had let the Israeli mission know he would be able to hold firm against pressure for withdrawal only if there was strong public support for Israel. For this reason, among others, when Eban awoke he was eager to get the reaction to his UN speech. From the New York *Times* he learned that an unprecedentedly large audience had been glued to television and radio sets around the world as he spoke. The Hearst papers said he had "displayed dimensions of true statesmanship," comparing his "eloquence and wisdom" to that of Churchill. A chain of thirty papers in the Middle and Far West said it was "one of the great diplomatic speeches of all time . . . eloquent in its phrasing, brilliantly devastating in its array of facts against an Arab enemy." The Chicago *Tribune* called it "one of the great speeches of modern times" and Ralph McGill, syndicated columnist, said Eban had "cut up the Egyptian delegates with the sword of truth." One West Coast paper said he had "excelled other speakers in about the way Daniel Webster must have excelled all his contemporaries, long since forgotten." One of President

Johnson's principal advisers said the President had heard his UN appearance and thought it "worth several divisions to Israel."

The reaction was almost unanimous throughout the country and when reports on the foreign press came in it was clear that the opinion was universal. It was all very flattering and Aubrey Eban was vain enough to relish this worldwide acclaim. But the main consideration was that if President Johnson needed a pro-Israel public opinion now he surely had it. Just as the Israeli military had achieved success in several notable directions, so Israeli diplomacy now had two accomplishments to its credit: the Arab-Russian attempt to force withdrawal had been met and conquered and massive support had been generated for Israel's action.

But Eban's self-satisfaction was soon destroyed. The next morning he was in telephonic communication with his home and his office in Jerusalem. From them he learned that most Israelis, intoxicated by the military triumph, had remained completely uninformed about what had happened in New York—and little interested. What many had forgotten was that Israel had won impressive military victories before, but had never been able to convert them into a constructive peace. If there was a chance, this time, to get world support for Israel's refusal to withdraw without the fruits of peace, surely this was the most important task to be tackled.

Defeated in battle, the Arabs, supported by their Russian friends, had already commenced the political struggle—a struggle in which the odds were even more against Israel than they had been militarily. But most Israelis, now in possession of the walled city of Jerusalem for the first time in almost two thousand years, occupying all the Sinai desert and the west bank of the Jordan, were in such a state of euphoria and elation that several of Tel Aviv's principal newspapers were saying boldly that Israel ought not to give a thought to the Great Powers or to the Security Council or to world opinion. There was criticism of Eban for having gone abroad and for considering the Security Council meeting important enough to attend and address. Certain isolationist, chauvinistic Israeli elements felt the country should ignore the international community entirely. The Israeli public had paid little attention to his Security Council address. The communications media had given it scant heed. There had been no reports of the eulogistic world reaction. As far as the populace of Israel knew Eban had done a pedestrian little talk to a small, totally disinterested audience.

"It reminds me of Nietzsche's dictum that it is easier to win a victory that to know what to do with it when won," Eban remarked.

Also, not even the cataclysmic events of the past several days had been sufficient to suspend domestic political bickering for long. The knives were out again. The roles played by Prime Minister Eshkol and Chief of Staff Rabin in laying the groundwork for the victory were being ignored, as the public was led to believe that Israel had won a sort of instant triumph, hastily concocted by the unaided skill and magic of those ministers who had joined the Cabinet a matter of hours before resistance began. (This was even more true in the United States than in Israel.)

Eban was eager to get back to Israel as quickly as possible, but he feared that if he departed prematurely a withdrawal resolution might get slipped through.

(Suzy Eban, in a letter to friends in America, wrote: "All the marvellous exhilaration you felt at Aubrey's appearance before the Security Council was never put across here. Here it was only war, life, death, planes, bullets, sniping, the terrible worry about the boys, whose boys? which family? how? with mercy or no mercy? My God, it was awful, quick, violent, intense. You felt you were bursting all the time. The certainty of winning was constant and unwavering. We knew every minute who we were. We are good. Good is a joke. We are special. It is the people and our spirit that makes us win against the Arabs. . . . Gila, as the cease-fire was declared, went to the postoffice to sort out mail and distribute letters on her bike until ten o'clock at night. . . . The house opposite got a shell in the roof. . . . I have visited the wounded from the Foreign Office in the hospitals."[2])

On the day after (Wednesday, June 7, 1967), delegates of the UAR, Syria and Iraq addressed the Security Council without accepting the cease-fire. After hearing Eban the Council adjourned for twenty-four hours, but there was much miscellaneous diplomatic work to be done. It was important to give as much world publicity as possible to the forgery that Nasser and Hussein were trying to perpetrate—that British and American planes, operating from carriers in the Mediterranean, had taken part in the aerial battles of June 5. Fortunately the telephone conversation with Hussein in which Nasser suggested the hoax had been recorded by Israel's communications experts. Also, Eban had to try to persuade the American delegation to drop the idea of returning to conditions imposed by the 1949 armistice agreements and to work, instead, for real peace. Also, there was the embarrassing situation created by the attack on the American signal ship, the *Liberty*, with the loss of so many American lives, a serious diplomatic problem.

On the Evening of June 8 Eban, accompanied by Raviv, set out for Israel. In the plane with them were Theodore White, Washington author, and scores of young Americans, male and female, going to Israel to give whatever service they could. At London a similar group of young British Jews came aboard. Eban spent most of the flight giving out autographs and probing the reason these young people had abandoned careers and comforts at home to rush to Israel's assistance. He summed it up to Raviv:

"I think they suddenly heard voices speaking to them from the forgotten depths of their Jewish past."

As they landed in Israel military activity against Syria was still in progress. Suzy Eban was at the airport to welcome her weary husband. He surprised her by whispering "Happy birthday!" as they embraced.

"I never expected you to remember!" she whispered back.

In his airport press conference he tried to explain the importance to Israel of the political developments. The Jerusalem *Post* next day reported he was "spontaneously cheered by a gathering of airport staff." At the same time he gave what many papers around the world called the first official indication that Israel would refuse to go back to the old armistice lines but would insist on new and secure frontiers.

When Eban reached the Prime Minister's office in Tel Aviv the Cabinet was discussing the Syrian situation. Eshkol filled in his Foreign Minister on what had been happening. In the debate over whether to try to storm the Golan Heights the strongest hesitation had come from Defense Minister Dayan, who feared heavy casualties and the possibility of Soviet intervention, whereas the Mapam ministers, generally the most pacifist, favored the assault in order to relieve their kibbutzim in Upper Galilee from the punishment they had been taking for nearly twenty years. Hawks and doves had temporarily changed their feathers.

Eban was able to make a contribution to the Syrian discussion by reporting that important American officials had hinted to him it would be what they called "funny" if the only country to get off scot-free were to be Syria, who had started it all. He said he had been given the definite impression in Washington that some action against Syria would not be received without sympathy provided it was limited in time. He told his fellow ministers he felt it was wrong to be too squeamish about going after Syria, but he also thought, because of the Soviet link with Syria, Israel should not take too much time to accomplish its objective, otherwise there was the possibility of "Soviet intimidation."

The technicality on which the Golan assault was made was that despite the fact the Syrians had agreed to a cease-fire, Syrian guns were still in action. Eban told the Cabinet he thought they had twenty-four hours in which to achieve their objective without colliding head-on with the Security Council or dishonoring their policy of reciprocal cease-fire. Also, he did not feel the USSR would become involved unless Damascus was threatened.

By nightfall of June 9 Israeli forces had penetrated the Golan Heights at many points. On June 10, as they tried to complete their occupation of the Syrian position, Eban was bombarded with cables from New York. Security Council delegates, who had been reluctant to meet when Israel seemed on the verge of death in late May and early June, had rushed through the darkness to the UN building at 4:30 A.M. on June 10 in response to Syria's call for an emergency meeting. In addressing them Soviet delegate Fedorenko referred to the Israeli "hordes," which caused Eban to remark to the Cabinet:

"A few weeks ago Soviet diplomats thought of us as puny, contemptible pygmies. Now we are like the irresistible hordes of Genghis Khan."

In an attempt to give the USSR the impression that Israel was marching on Damascus, the Syrian General Staff had issued fictitious bulletins crediting Israel with victories hours before they occurred. Soviet threats were uttered in such a loud key that the United States was thrown into its first global alarm since the Cuban crisis. From Washington Eban received hints that Soviet intervention no longer seemed inconceivable and also "dark intimations that hot lines were at work."

Finally, at 1800 hours on June 10 the cease-fire became effective and the Six-Day war came to an end. That same afternoon Soviet Ambassador Chuvakhin, accompanied by his counselor, stormed into Eban's temporary office in Tel Aviv. In a trembling voice and with tears in his eyes he read out a note in sonorous Russian which his associate translated. As Israel forces were "moving toward Damascus" in violation of the cease-fire, the Soviet Union was breaking diplomatic relations with Israel.

Eban's eighteen months of service as Foreign Minister had not included any experience in breaking relations. It was probably just as well, for he replied to the incensed ambassador with an informality that the Russian must have found infuriating, telling him that Israel had no intention of moving on Damascus; that with USSR instigation Syria had been the originator of the war; that if Syrian artillery had not fired from the Golan Heights between June 5 and 10, Israel would have kept the Syrian front quiet. He expressed regret that while in Israel the Soviet ambassador had shown such little understanding of the realities of the situation and expressed hope that someday their relationship could be recemented amicably. Then he wished him personal good fortune, which the Russian ambassador did not seem to anticipate, for his eyes suddenly were full of tears again. The other Communist states, with the exception of Romania, quickly followed the lead of the USSR.

With the guns silent, the Israeli public for the first time began to take interest in the political struggle that was now inevitable. In the Security Council debates Eban had tentatively sketched a policy based on using existing cease-fire lines as a starting point and working toward the objective of peace settlements with Israel's neighbors. He had thus far been acting more on intuition than specific Cabinet decisions. He felt Israel should not regard previous armistice lines as having any meaning, but at the same time it would be wrong for Israel to be swept by such a wave of historic emotion as to regard the new cease-fire lines as the country's permanent boundaries. From his long experience in the world community he was certain that arbitrary and massive annexation would invite international pressure for unconditional retreat to the old lines.

In the Security Council the mortified but angry Soviet Union now introduced a resolution condemning Israel's "aggressive activities" and demanding removal of all Israeli troops behind the original armistice lines.

When a vote was taken Bulgaria, India, Mali and the USSR voted for the first paragraph. The withdrawal demand got also the votes of Ethiopia and Nigeria, but the total was still three short of the required two thirds.

An ironic development now took place. In 1951 the United States, to get around a Soviet veto, devised a procedure whereby the General Assembly can be called into session when the Security Council is deadlocked. It had been used by the United States in the 1956 Hungarian and Suez crises, over the protest of the USSR. Now the USSR used it over American protest.

In the bitter fight that was inevitable in the General Assembly, Israel would be able to count on one vote—her own. The Arab-Soviet bloc could count on forty-five votes for any motion—even a proclamation that the world is flat. To prevent passage of a Soviet resolution Israel needed to line up at least forty-five or fifty votes.

As Eban began to rally support he was beset by a virulent personal campaign at home. He was working around the clock, telephoning and cabling, when the Tel Aviv newspaper *Ha'aretz* published an article demanding appointment of a new Foreign Minister. Just a few days earlier Eban's appointment had been confirmed almost unanimously by the Knesset. Although the paper found no fault with any of Eban's actions to date and confessed that the waiting period had resulted in international support of Israel, nevertheless *Ha'aretz* said it had no faith in Eban's qualifications to carry on. Eshkol was also attacked.

Other papers rallied to Eban's defense and the *Ha'aretz* attack had little domestic effect, but it tended to undermine Eban's strength internationally at a critical diplomatic moment, just as if General Eisenhower's competence to lead the Allied armies had been questioned a few days before the Allied invasion of Europe.

Now that Israel suddenly was aware of the importance of the diplomatic struggle, the press began debating the make-up of the delegation that would represent the country at the General Assembly. It was suggested that Eban should be "accompanied" by other ministers, including Dayan and Beigin. Eban went at once to Eshkol and announced that if he was to carry the burden of the political struggle against the heavy odds Israel faced, he must be "liberated from domestic intrigues."

"It would be as grotesque," he told the Prime Minister, "for two or three ministers to lead a delegation to the General Assembly as it would be for two or three generals to be simultaneously in command of an armored division."

Also, the arrival of a group of Cabinet ministers at the General Assembly would make Israel look divided and somewhat ridiculous to the rest of the world.

"I would not dream of going into Mr. Dayan's map room while he was taking decisions about a military campaign. By the same token he is equally unqualified to hover over me while I seek to manipulate the complex forces on which our political fortunes depend. The leadership of a diplomatic campaign has technical aspects in which specialized experience is needed."

Finally, Eban announced to the Prime Minister that he had no intention of going to the UN himself if other ministers were sent "as watchdogs or as a publicity stunt."

Eshkol agreed and all Israeli newspapers on June 16 carried stories of the decision to put the Israeli delegation to the emergency session of the General Assembly unreservedly under Eban's command. While waiting for the session to begin Eban devised a plan of sending prominent Israelis, including Knesset members and former ambassadors, on special missions to countries whose support was being curried.

From Moscow came word that Premier Kosygin himself would lead the Soviet delegation; that all other Communist countries in the UN would be represented by their heads of government, and the Soviet Union hoped that President Johnson, President de Gaulle, Prime Minister Wilson and other presidents and prime ministers would also attend, thus turning the emergency session into a sort of summit meeting—all for the purpose of forcing little Israel back to the old armistice lines.

On Saturday, June 17 (1967), Eban set off for New York with his chef de cabinet, Emanual Shimoni. In an exclusive interview with Francis Hoffner of *The Christian Science Monitor* just before leaving he served notice that if the General Assembly were to vote 121 to 1 in favor of Israel returning to the old armistice lines Israel would refuse to comply.

"We must not go back to an intermediate situation between war and peace with all its ambivalence and obscurity."[3]

One of the first questions he was asked by reporters when he landed in New York was:

"Is it true there's been a serious split in Israel between the hawks and the doves?"

"Israel is not an aviary!" was his good-humored reply. It was a comment he would use frequently in the months to come, whenever he felt reporters or politicians were exaggerating his conflict with the Dayan-Peres camp.

At the airport he was informed that the speakers inscribed for the meeting of the emergency session on Monday were the Soviet Prime Minister, the Permanent Representative of the United States and the Foreign Minister of Israel. That evening the United States decided that President Johnson would state the U.S. position in a public address Monday morning and the UN debate would be left exclusively to Kosygin and Eban. Washington felt that the David and Goliath implication would have a strong appeal to the chivalry of the American people and probably of the world at large.

Eban realized that such a duel between Moscow and Jerusalem, before so many millions of eyes and ears, would be unique in the history of political disputation. In case he had any doubt about the tremendous responsibility he faced, he received a message from Ambassador Goldberg that the impact which the Israeli cause made on public opinion would determine the atmosphere of the Assembly and would decide the course of American policy.

Kosygin, by coming to New York himself, at the head of a sixty-six-man Soviet delegation (apparently determined to outnumber the Israeli diplomats in almost the proportion Arab soldiers had outnumbered Israeli soldiers), had made certain that whatever happened the result would be drastic, the audience immense. From friends in the communications field Eban learned that on Monday evening all television and radio networks were canceling their entertainment programs and commercials to carry the debate, at a cost of millions of dollars in lost revenue. Also, listeners all over the world would hear by short wave.

The fatigue of recent weeks and the intense consultations since landing in New York prevented Eban from getting to his writing desk until late in the evening of Sunday. As he began formulating what he would tell the Assembly he felt as never before the emotional overtones of the situation. In the thousands of years of Jewish history there was no precedent for this contest between small Israel and one of the world's mightiest powers in a bid for the conscience and imagination of mankind. He was aware that the next day he would live one hour the like of which he had never known before and probably would never know again. It would be one of the most animated hours in the history of the UN. Israel's entire future might depend on how incisive and penetrating an impression he was able to make on the delegates and the rest of the world.

Such thoughts swept back and forth through his mind as he worked into the night, sometimes writing with a pen, sometimes dictating, correcting, redrafting, destroying, expanding, to the despair of a battery of patient secretaries, who kept putting sandwiches and coffee before him.

His original idea was to speak from a few notes, as he had done so successfully to the Security Council, but this would prevent an adequate translation into French, Spanish and Russian, and would make it impossible to supply reporters with an advance release of the text, which is essential if the maximum of publicity is desired.

Late in the evening Ambassadors Harman and Rafael arrived to start going over what he had written. By 2 A.M. he was in a state of despair, for less than half the speech was finished and he was already quite weary. For a moment of relaxation he decided to go over the cables from Jerusalem that had been piling up all evening: Cabinet decisions, a roundup of press comment. The organized campaign against him had apparently died down. Intense expressions of hope and support had come from every part of the country. But in the daily *Ma'ariv* of June 18 there had appeared a letter from an Israeli professor stating that if those who had voted "shamefully" for delay on May 28 had gotten their way, "we should still be waiting helplessly today." It was a stupid communication, for those who voted for delay on May 28 *did* get their way, and a victorious war resulted. It was a venomous attack by an ignorant man, yet Eban's sensitivity is so great, even in moments like this when the task at hand demands his total concentration, that he lost his sense of proportion. Someone else might have shouted profanities, kicked the wastebasket or sent off a collect cable of denunciation to the professor. Instead, Eban let it boil within him until, for a few desperate moments, he contemplated tearing up the draft of his speech and canceling his appearance before the emergency session.

"The impact of this nonsense and malice in the middle of the night, only a few hours from Kosygin, was so physically maddening that I had the absurd idea of not appearing in the General Assembly at all."[4]

But he soon put such thoughts aside and got to work again. At 5 A.M., just as dawn was breaking over Central Park, he committed his final manuscript to the typists and lay down for a few hours' sleep.

At 10 A.M. on Monday, June 19 (1967), President Johnson went on the air addressing a studio audience of educators but actually talking to the world. Eban had been awakened a few minutes earlier and sat in front of his hotel television watching and listening. He considered what he heard "an exercise in lucidity and international courage." Johnson said peace could not be obtained by going back to the fragile and often violated armistice. Withdrawal should be made dependent on peace. Boundaries must be negotiated.

With this encouragement Eban dressed and made his way to the UN, fighting through a forest of television cameras and microphones to the Israeli desk in the General Assembly hall. At his side were Rafael, Comay and other veterans of UN struggles, as well as members of a parliamentary delegation, including Golda Meir. In the hall were ten prime ministers. Almost every other delegation was headed by its Foreign Minister.

The three hundred members of the Arab and Communist delegations applauded loudly as Kosygin walked slowly to the podium. His voice was icy, aloof, monotonous. His eyes seldom left his script as he read his speech without a trace of emotion. His face reflected no more passion than a block of granite. He stood at the lectern like a sturdy, well-fed farmer, holding the two handles of his plow. He bore little resemblance to his predecessor, who twice took off his shoe and banged the table to interrupt other speakers. Yet the opinions Kosygin uttered were fanatical. He accused Israel of almost every crime in the history of human depravity. He demanded not only withdrawal but even payment by Israel of compensation for the damages inflicted by war. He blamed Britain,

America and West Germany for encouraging Israel. He suffered the handicap of speaking a language which few, either in the room or listening remotely, could understand. The translation was halting and without fervor. It was a tedious tirade. He spoke for forty minutes without moving anything but his lips.

Kosygin's suggestion that two and a half million Israelis were a menace to eighty million Arabs and should be punished like a race of subhumans set the stage for the appearance of the defendant. Exactly at noon Kosygin finished and Eban went to the podium. He began in low key.

"The subject of our discussion is the Middle East, its past agony and its future hope."

Soon he was saying:

"I come to this tribunal to speak for a united people, which, having faced the danger to national survival, is unshakably resolved to resist any course which would renew the perils from which it has emerged."

At the end of two minutes he paused, looked over his audience and sensed he had the majority with him. Now he sketched the history of his people through the ages to the days of the holocaust. Then he reviewed the events of the past decade, recounting the mounting crescendo of Arab threats and Israel's attempts to turn away from hostility and get on with its work. In lyrical Churchillian cadences he articulated the anguish and glory of a lonely, encircled nation. Discussing the "disastrously swift" decision of U Thant to withdraw UNEF he asked:

"What is the use of a fire brigade which vanishes from the scene as soon as the first smoke and flames appear?"

He called Nasser's blockade ". . . an act of war, imposed and enforced through armed violence. . . . There is no difference in civil law between murdering a man by slow strangulation or killing him by a shot in the head."

Finally he came to June 5.

"On that fateful morning . . . our country's choice was plain. The choice was to live or perish, to defend the national existence or to forfeit it for all time."

Item by item he listed what the Soviet Union had done to encourage the belligerency of the Arabs.

"As I felt the television cameras closing in on me," he said later, "I thought this was the time to illustrate the direct confrontation between an indignant Israel and a Soviet Union, which, having caused the war, was now placing hypocritical charges against Israel."[5]

He paused for a moment while he searched with his eyes for the desk at which Kosygin and Gromyko were sitting. Then, pointing an angry finger straight at them, he departed from his written text and said in quiet indignation:

"Your Government's role in the stimulation of the arms race, in the paralysis of the Security Council, in the encouragement throughout the Arab world of unfounded suspicion concerning Israel's intentions, your constant refusal to say a single word of criticism at any time of [Arab] declarations threatening the violent overthrow of Israel's sovereignty and existence—all this gravely undermines your claim to objectivity. You come here in our eyes not as a judge or prosecutor but rather as a legitimate object of international criticism for the part you have played in the somber events which have brought our region to a point of explosive tension."

The spectacle of one of the smallest countries in the world pointing an accusing finger at one of the greatest powers of world history sent a wave of surprise through the hall. It even affected Eban himself, for it was almost a full minute before he could go on with his address.

The Soviet-Arab demand that Israel be forced back to where she was on June 4 was answered by Eban with another of his picturesque similes:

"It is a fact of technology that it is easier to fly to the moon than to reconstruct a broken egg."

A minute later he was saying:

"The Arab states can no longer be permitted to recognize Israel's existence only for the purpose of plotting its elimination. They have come face to face with us in conflict. Let them now come face to face with us in peace."

Shortly before Eban concluded, Kosygin rose from his seat and made his way toward the back of the hall, accompanied by several of his aides. Although some reporters considered it a "walkout," others pointed out that Kosygin had sat through the direct indictment of his country and had left when Eban was making hardly debatable generalizations about peace. Also, representatives of other Communist countries remained in their seats. Also, it was exactly 1 P.M. and it was known that Kosygin was to be host at a luncheon for some visiting prime ministers. Eban himself was certain it was not intended as a walkout, yet the fiction persisted in many articles and books. Several reports even said he left the hall when Eban began speaking.

Eban's final words were:

"The Middle East, tired of wars, is ripe for a new emergence of human vitality. Let the opportunity not fall again from our hands."

As he walked from the rostrum there was a crescendo of applause rarely heard in a UN debate. The president hammered in vain for silence. Eban's rebuttal to Kosygin had been like a pin poked into a big red balloon before it had had a chance to do any floating. When he reached his seat his neighbors, Ireland and Italy, held out hands of congratulation.

It was a moment of great personal triumph. Never had the plight of Jews in general and Israelis in particular been articulated so compellingly to such an immense worldwide audience. It was as though all his life until now had been preparation for the hour and twenty-five minutes at the podium where he used all his talents to plead with the rest of the world for justice.

(After the debate Eban gave this characterization of Kosygin: "He was like a surly and rather prosaic bank manager. You could see his eyes glowing with insincerity. He was not impressive even in his malice. He was not formidable, as Khrushchev would have been. He even seemed frightened. The whole world at that time was really rejoicing in the discomfort of the Soviets and the Egyptians. It was like everyone laughing when a big bully falls down. I ended up feeling stupidly sorry for him."[6])

Back at his hotel Eban went to sleep immediately. Four hours later he was awakened by a telephone call from Jerusalem. Prime Minister Eshkol had listened on short-wave radio and wished to convey his emotion. By now such an avalanche of congratulatory telegrams had begun to pour in that the Israeli delegation had to recruit a special staff to handle them. At midnight Eban went to the apartment of Meyer Weisgal and there saw the first editions of the morning papers. Without question Israel's cause was riding on a high crest of world approval.

It would have taken an extraordinary man not to have his ego inflated over what they said. James Reston, associate editor of the New York *Times*, wrote:

"Mr. Kosygin's request that the UN should pretend that two and a half million Israelis were a menace to eighty million Arabs and should be punished like moral monsters set the stage for Israeli Foreign Minister Abba Eban, who talked like a Cambridge don and came through like a tank commander. It is easy, after listening to this debate between Kosygin and Eban, to understand why the Russians are suspicious of free speech. Eban worked through Kosygin's arguments with all the gentility of General Dayan's tanks in the desert."

Hundreds of other clippings that poured in during ensuing days said the same thing in one way or another. Seldom had case-hardened reporters used so many superlatives. Drew Pearson in a column that editors all over the country put on Page One said: "The burst of applause that came at the end of Eban's speech was loud and clear in sound and implication." James Wechsler of the New York *Post* devoted a full column to Eban's performance, writing of his "lyrical Churchillian cadences . . . the finest hour (and twenty-five minutes) of his life." Wechsler said Eban had "articulated majestically the anguish and glory of a people so long under siege . . . with a special passion he cried out against Kosygin's effort to equate Israel's actions with those of the Hitlerites. Rarely has an orator so effectively used the word 'odious' to make a wretched comparison seem utterly repugnant."

Several reporters pointed out the irony that Eban's own people, not having television in their homes, were cheated of seeing him as he twisted the Soviet tail. He got twenty lines in *Pravda*. *Ha'aretz* was not so generous, but the rest of the Israeli press, showing no partisan inhibitions, fully reported the address.

(Suzy Eban, in a letter to friends in America, wrote: "I heard over Voice of America part of Aubrey's speech as he answered Kosygin. I was all with him then, as was most of the country except Rafi. Rafi would eat him alive if they could. *Ha'aretz* simply cut the speech. Never mentioned it. Or even printed part of it. Or told the reactions to it. How vulturous can the vultures be? There is the hour for arms and the hour for the battle of words. Do they feel that wooing world opinion is not to be done?"[7])

There was one man in New York who reacted quite differently than most others to the Eban speech. U Thant, in an unusual move, took the rostrum at the UN to attack Eban's version of the UNEF withdrawal. He was especially infuriated by what he termed "the picturesque simile" about the fire brigade. This in turn led to considerable editorial criticism of the Secretary-General, the Philadelphia *Inquirer*, for example, stating editorially that his attack on Eban "may have sprung from his own guilty conscience, his own realization that he had been wrong in his abrupt withdrawal of the UN force."

However, some diplomatic commentators suggested that Eban had gained nothing by his attack on the Secretary-General and had needlessly hurt his own standing in the UN.[8]

Long after tempers cooled there was still some criticism of Eban. Theodore Draper writing in *Israel and World Politics* said:

"Foreign Minister Eban's analogy between UNEF and a fire brigade may have been effective oratorically but it unwittingly betrayed what was wrong with his reasoning. In no sense was the UNEF comparable to a fire brigade . . . the smoke and flames were made up of overwhelming Egyptian armed forces. UNEF had the alternative of vanishing or fighting fire with fire. . . . In practice UNEF was so outnumbered and outclassed that it mattered little whether it stayed or left, except perhaps to establish a legal point."[9]

Every day Eban's secretary gave him a sampling of the thousands of letters that cascaded in—such a torrent that a force of volunteers was organized to work at mission headquarters opening and sorting. Eventually every person who wrote a letter about either of the UN addresses received a courteous reply.

Some sent money. Some wrote on engraved stationery, some on business letterheads, some on scraps of paper. Many sent poems inspired by Eban's words. Teachers of English wrote about his diction and choice of words. Several asked if he would send them the original manuscript from which he had read. A majority of the letter writers identified themselves as non-Jews. There were suggestions as to what he should say in his next speech. Two men sent twenty- and thirty-page typed speeches, ready for him to deliver. A man in Largo, Florida, wrote: "Don't give up the Suez Canal, even if you don't need it." A man in Albany, New York: "Being a Johnny Nobody and an Irish Catholic to boot, I just had to let you know that what you are doing to help offset the evils of the world is appreciated by all of us." A woman signing herself a Protestant from Kansas City said: "If it weren't for your people my people wouldn't have the Bible." A woman on West 116th Street, New York, suggested that all profit from the Egyptian oil wells now in Israeli hands be set aside for resettlement and education of Arabs displaced by the war. From Freeport, Long Island: "We have our Patrick Henry; Israel has her Eban." There were frequent bitter references to the broadcast by a State Department spokesman who declared at the start of the war that the United States would be "neutral in thought, word and deed." Several Jews and non-Jews criticized Eban for not giving God credit for Israel's military success. From St. Paul, Minnesota: "I am a Portuguese citizen and love my country. However, if I had none and were given the privilege of choosing one I would be proud to be an Israeli." From Milwaukee, Wisconsin: "You are a combination of Demosthenes, Cicero,

Webster and Burke." From a woman in Brooklyn: "Maybe I can help you because I am more down to earth than you are and nearer to the feelings and understandings of the people." From Chicago: "The UN must be a Jewish organization; it never starts on time."

Eban was jolted when he read a letter which began: "Wouldn't you sleep better and enjoy life more if you just told the truth once in a while? Why do you lie, deceive and misrepresent?" Then he glanced at the salutation and noticed it was addressed to "Dear Alex" and was a carbon of a letter sent to Kosygin.

As the days went by and more and more clippings, telegrams and letters poured in it was clear that since the invention of electronic communication made it possible for hundreds of millions to listen to a political debate, and for tens of millions to see as well as hear, few if any other addresses had ever had the impact of this one. It might be years, decades, before anyone else would score such a forensic success. It was Eban's greatest hour of personal triumph and he relished it fully.

Spoken Arts, the organization that had put out the record of Eban reading verses from the Bible, recorded his June 6 Security Council address and made an initial pressing of fifty thousand copies, all proceeds going into the Israel Relief Fund. The sale was so good that they also put out an album of the General Assembly address.

One night in the Oak Room of the Plaza Eban gave his friend Leonard Lyons some comments on the UN. The next day in the "Lyons Den" he was quoted as saying:

"Under the UN Charter, if a man points a gun at your head and says he'll shoot you and if you push the man's gun aside your act constitutes aggression."

Columnist Emmett Watson wrote:

"If he stays around much longer Eban is almost certain to wind up with his own t.v. show."

On the Friday night after his debate with Kosygin, Eban accepted an invitation of the rabbi of Congregation Zichron Ephraim to attend Shabbat services in his synagogue just off Lexington Avenue on East Sixty-seventh Street, directly across the street from the heavily guarded building of the Soviet mission, where Premier Kosygin was staying. On one side of the street flew the Stars and Stripes and Star of David, on the other side the Hammer and Sickle. Almost a hundred photographers, newspaper reporters and radio and television crewmen jammed the block, hoping for an incident.

By the time Eban arrived on foot, having walked the eleven blocks from his hotel, the nine hundred seats were all taken by worshipers who had been required to pass through a police inspection line. Contrary to custom, there was a burst of applause as Eban entered. After delivering his sermon the rabbi introduced Eban as "the voice of Israel." Beginning his own brief address Eban said, "The voice of Israel is getting a little hoarse." Then he compared Israel's recent military success to the victories of Bar Kochba and the Maccabees, adding, "Now the battle is for peace." On leaving the building he was asked by reporters why he had chosen to go to a synagogue in the same block as the headquarters of the Russian mission, to which he replied:

"Why did they choose to rent a building in the same block with my synagogue?"

From the services Eban rushed off for a conference with the Norwegian delegation. By day and by night members of the Israeli mission were working to line up votes against unconditional withdrawal. Eban himself had begun with Secretary of State Rusk, Foreign Minister Couve de Murville and Foreign Minister George Brown. Then he saw the prime ministers of Denmark and Romania. Then the foreign ministers of the Latin American countries, which might hold the balance of power.

After a week of intensive debate Israel's prospects suddenly darkened on June 27 (1967), when news reached New York that the Knesset had voted for certain administrative measures to unite East and West Jerusalem. Eban had indicated to the Israeli Government his own belief that such measures should have been taken on June 18, before the General Assembly convened. They would then have appeared as a direct consequence of the fighting. When this advice was not accepted, the entire Israeli parliamentary delegation in New York, including the Herut party representative, joined in a cable to the Israeli Government urging that their work not be handicapped by any action on Jerusalem until after the General Assembly adjourned.

At the same time on their television screens American audiences were seeing pathetic pictures of Arab refugees, including women and children, trekking eastward across Jordan in flight from the Israeli-occupied west bank.

"I suddenly felt our front crumbling on all sides," Eban said later.

In desperation he cabled Prime Minister Eshkol strongly urging the Cabinet to take remedial steps: first, to make sure that anything that might be represented as expulsion of the Arabs be stopped; second, that Israel reaffirm respect for Jerusalem's holy places; third, to abstain from speeches implying a desire for total annexation; fourth, to return Government House to the UN Truce Organization in order to avoid a new conflict with the Secretary-General.

After a lengthy Cabinet meeting the Government agreed with most of Eban's suggestions, but meanwhile the Arabs were conducting a wild and somewhat successful campaign, exploiting the Jerusalem problem and spreading atrocity stories.

Then King Hussein put in an appearance at the UN. He won much sympathy by renouncing the protocol privileges generally accorded monarchs and having himself introduced merely as "the representative of Jordan." To many he appeared as the pathetic victim of Nasser's conniving, yet he expounded a policy which would reduce Israel to an even smaller geographical entity than she had been from 1949 to 1967.

Early in July it became apparent that the Russian resolution condemning Israel and demanding complete withdrawal and payment of compensation had no chance. Now the fight revolved around a Yugoslav resolution calling for immediate withdrawal to June 4 lines as a first step, after which the Security Council would consider what other steps should be taken.

At this critical moment the French-speaking countries of West Africa, bound to Israel by strong ties of cooperation, agreed to support the Yugoslav resolution, if the one word "immediate" were eliminated.

On Sunday, July 2 (1967), Eban personally rushed around Long Island, Westchester and Manhattan speaking face to face with members of fourteen African delegations. When he discovered that one African country which was expected to vote on Israel's side had no representation at the UN at the time, he cabled Israel's ambassador in that country to use all possible pressure to get the Foreign Minister to make a special trip to New York for the voting. The most influential figure among French-speaking African states was President Houphouët-Boigny of the Ivory Coast, who at the moment was in Europe. Eban cabled Golda Meir, who was attending a convention in Paris, to try to find him. She discovered he was in Germany, a country into which she preferred not to set foot because of profound inhibitions of principle and emotion, but she agreed that the success of the Assembly struggle called for special efforts, which she made. As a result of her meeting with the Ivory Coast President, Israel's position was considerably strengthened.

On the afternoon of July 4 (1967) the emergency session met in a mood of brittle tension. Forty-six countries voted against the Yugoslav resolution, including the entire Latin American bloc, the United States,

Great Britain, most of Western Europe, Israel, Australia, New Zealand, Canada and eight African states. There were only fifty-three votes in favor, far short of the required two thirds. Thus Israel gained one of the most momentous and unexpected political victories of her entire international career.

The USSR now called for a vote on its resolution, which was turned down paragraph by paragraph. The stunned expressions of Gromyko and the Arab ministers gave Eban what he later admitted was "an almost sensual pleasure."

Suddenly the tension of an unforgettable month was over. The Israelis went to their suite at the Plaza where they drank enthusiastic toasts to each other, to the State of Israel and to their friends who had saved them from diplomatic slaughter. When a call finally got through to Jerusalem it was 3 A.M. Middle East time. Arousing the director-general of the Foreign Office from his bed Eban told him the news. He thought at first someone was playing a trick. The general feeling in Israel had been that the Yugoslav resolution would surely be adopted.

30

Negotiate, but Keep Your Powder Dry

AFTER THE EXALTING CONCLUSION of the Six-Day war, and Eban's successful defense in the United Nations, some groups and parties in Israel
suffered a curious malady. As Eban put it, "It was as though something
in the national character made Israel intolerant of her own success."[1]
In the intoxication of victory, some circles became xenophobic and
turned on their own political leaders, with Eban the principal target.
If Israel was so strong, why had she waited two weeks before taking
military action in June? Wasn't this appeasement? Wasn't it reminiscent
of Chamberlain? Rarely had a Cabinet member been so abused by his
own people for his efforts to see whether war was the only answer to
their problems, and to prepare the ground in world opinion if war broke
out. The paradox was that the criticism came after the termination of the
war—after it had been convincingly demonstrated the decision had been
a wise and effective one. As Eban put it: "In most countries people ask
'What went wrong?' In our case people ask with some indignation: 'Why
have things gone so well?'"

Eban could prove that he had been less hypochondriac about the
military prospect than those in Jerusalem who cabled while he was in
Washington about Israel's desperate military plight. Yet he, like all
Israeli leaders, had been haunted by the fear of thousands of casualties,
by the thought that someday he would have to look into the faces of
widows and orphans and answer to them whether he had made every
possible effort to save the national interest without war; and by the
apprehension that if no political work was done ahead of the fighting
Israel would win the war, but lose the peace.

Astonishingly, he was criticized for having gone to Washington at all.
Didn't this show weakness and invite pressure? His answer was that he

kept remembering 1956–57. What if Israel won the 1967 war and then the fruits of victory were snatched away in a few days by the United States joining other nations in an angry reaction, as in 1957, because Israel had not taken Washington into her confidence? It could happen again—indeed, it nearly did. Eban's tactic was to involve the United States in the responsibility of trying to avoid war, so that if the effort failed the United States could not take a resentful postwar attitude. Proof of the wisdom and success of this policy was that this time, after the war, Israel was neither boycotted, blockaded, nor forced to retire from occupied territories, and that American arms continued to flow to Israel. It is easy to guess what would have been said if the United States had reacted badly, as in 1956, and if Eban and Eshkol had been asked why they had not made an attempt to involve the United States ahead of time.

Had 1956–57 been repeated, the Arab world would know for certain that Israel could be provoked or invaded as much as her neighbors pleased. If the attacks succeeded, it would be the end of Israel; if they failed, the outside world would always insist that whatever the Arabs lost be returned to them. The Arabs believed in the law of limited liability. They could gain if they won, and would not suffer penalty if they lost. For Israelis it would be bitter proof that nothing could ever be gained by successful self-defense, and that peace was completely unobtainable. This would have led to a crumbling of morale.

Eban also had to remind his critics that his second consideration had been the USSR. Some of his advisers thought the likelihood of Soviet intervention must at least be taken seriously. Consideration of this possibility meant alerting the United States, the only power with the capacity for deterring Soviet intervention. President Johnson's memoirs fully support Eban's view that the threat of Soviet intervention was real, and was largely averted by the attitude of the United States, to which Eban had addressed himself with such gravity on May 26. After the war, Israelis took it for granted that the USSR had not intervened against them. If more unpleasant possibilities had materialized, would they not have turned on Eban and demanded to know what he had done to alert Washington to the need of localizing the impending war?

Eban argued that his Washington trip made it more certain than it otherwise would have been that Israeli forces would encounter Egyptians and not Soviet soldiers when military action began and, after the victory, Israel would have the political backing which would enable her to resist demands to retire to pre-war lines.

Despite the logic of these arguments, in the months immediately following the victory Eban was the victim of intense rancor in parts of the Israeli press. Some of his trouble was his personal reserve, which kept him from joining or forming cabals or political groups, so that when attacked he could not rely on the spontaneous activation of organized supporters. Another explanation is that his success in preventing an international call for immediate withdrawal worked against him at home. In June 1967 an intensely charismatic climate was created around Moshe Dayan because of the success of the Israeli Army in battle. In July, and thereafter, the spotlight was more on Eban's resistance against Soviet and Arab-Moslem pressures in the international arena. There was some resentment at having to share rather than to monopolize the credit.

The real source of opposition, in addition to the normal political jealousies, was the feeling that Eban represented the consensus in Israel which knew that victory in war was not enough; that the territories were not ends in themselves, but means to be used and transacted in peace negotiations: that, although he favored changes of boundaries in crucial places, like Sharm el-Sheikh, Jerusalem, Golan and the uninhabited Jordan valley, he did not believe that Israel should claim the permanent retention of all or even most of its recently acquired areas.

Whatever the reason, certain segments of the Israeli press kept the anti-Eban campaign alive and on several occasions he and Suzy discussed with a few friends, in the intimacy of their home, "whether the whole thing was worthwhile." The Foreign Ministry, in the years following the Six-Day war, involved an enormous amount of work, the necessity of much arduous and exhausting travel to far places, long separations, little family life and, when at home, the need to be available any hour of day or night for consultations or calls from embassies abroad.

Eban often asked himself whether he had not already done his duty to Israel's revival and would it not be nice to find shelter again in some university, or live simply as a writer and lecturer, or backbencher member of Parliament.

Despite these temptations he carried on, partly because of a basic pugnacious spirit, which he generally concealed behind a deceptively tranquil countenance, and partly because of a feeling that as long as real peace had not yet been achieved there was a great prize toward which he must work.

Buoyed by this belief, Eban rode out the storm and eventually felt he had the silent majority of the Israeli public with him. As proof he cited the applause he often received in public meetings when he mentioned *hamtana* (the waiting); the fact that two years after the war both Golda Meir and General Rabin said that except for the May 28 waiting decision and the diplomatic activity in Washington from May 23 to June 1, it was doubtful whether Israel would have been able to hold firm in the political arena after the war. There was even a 1969 poll showing that 63 percent of Israelis considered the waiting period an act of wise statesmanship, only 24 percent condemning it as an act of hesitancy and indecision.

But there was no resting on laurels for either the Foreign Minister or the country. Eban saw his main postwar tasks as taking all necessary measures to see that Israel was not forced out of occupied territory until her neighbors made peace, and, in the meantime, maintaining a normal structure of international relations. The decisive period was June 1967 to January 1968. The first achievement was the unanimous approval by the Security Council on November 22, 1967, of a resolution which, with all its defects, did make withdrawal conditional on signing a just and final peace agreement, and the establishment of secure and recognized boundaries. In both Washington and London, Eban obtained assurances that, although this was not a blank check to hold forever all occupied territories, it also did not mean a complete return to the old armistice lines.

American ambassador George Ball defined the November 22 resolution as only "a skeleton of principles on which the peace structure could be erected." Immediately after its passage, Eban began efforts he would continue for years to get either Jordan or Egypt to sit down and discuss peace with Israel. Through Ambassador Jarring, he sent to the Arab countries one proposal after another, but they were all ignored. However, by 1971 even Egypt and the USSR had been forced to say what they had refused to say in 1967: that Israel was entitled to peace in return for withdrawal. What Eban called "psychological attrition" was beginning to work.

When the Soviet Union began rearming Egypt with the most sophisticated air, land and sea weapons, the importance of America's support became greater than ever, and Eban made frequent trips in the postwar years to New York and Washington. During the Humphrey-Nixon campaign he paid a final call on President Johnson, who, after insisting that his own officials and members of the Israel Embassy staff leave the room, gave Eban a ribald characterization of the two candidates, then said, in his opinion, whichever one was elected, there would be little, if any, change in American policy toward Israel. He had told Eban in 1968

with great solemnity, in the presence of Ambassador Harman, that nobody except Churchill had ever moved the American people more
deeply by the force of his words. He repeated this eulogy now.

President Nixon took office in January 1969. In March Eban paid him
a visit. It was Israel's first top-level contact with the new Administration
and there was much tension in Israel. As the two former golf partners
greeted each other Nixon said:

"Well, we've both gone up in the world, haven't we?"

Walking through the rose garden Nixon said:

"Your balance of strength will be kept."

A moment later he added:

"Negotiate, but keep your powder dry."

Quickly Eban retorted:

"Mr. President, you give us the powder and we shall keep it dry."

Later Nixon said:

"Of course, you don't have to move until there is peace."

He had made the same remark when visiting Israel before becoming
President, but its reiteration in the White House was of great importance.
American policy since 1967 has not always been to Israel's liking. But it
has had four elements favorable to Israel: the maintenance of Israel's
strength; the dictum of "no withdrawal without peace"; the principle
that no solution must be imposed; and the idea that there must not be a
return to the old fragile armistice lines, but only to negotiated secure
boundaries and peace.

Lyndon Johnson and his representatives had laid down these principles in 1967, and in the first weeks of 1968 Premier Eshkol heard them
formally stated in his meeting with Lyndon B. Johnson in Texas. To hear
Richard Nixon reiterate them in the first weeks of his presidency was
encouraging.

After Eban's White House sessions Ambassador Rabin was able to
report confidently to Jerusalem that Israel would be able to continue
her good relations with the United States through the new Administration as through the old. This was important, for Israel still had traumatic
memories of the vacillations of American policy when Eisenhower took
office and tried to disengage partially from Israel. There had been some
nervous years then and Israel wanted no repetition of that experience,
especially in view of the ominous hostility of the USSR.

The March (1969) White House conferences between Eban, Nixon
and Rogers laid a foundation for subsequent developments in Israeli-
American relations, for Eban was assured that Israel's military strength

would be kept up, that she would not be forced to withdraw without peace and that, although the United States would take part in Four Power consultations, there would be no Four Power agreement which would harm Israel's interests. In all later meetings with Nixon, Golda Meir and Rabin, as well as Eban himself, they would hear this policy often reiterated.

Eban was also concerned during the postwar years about the danger of international isolation, which could have catastrophic political, economic, commercial and psychological effects, so while striving for peace he worked to keep his country's life lines open. His fear was this: the Arabs, unable to defeat Israel on the battlefield, still hoped they might strangle her to death by economic siege and diplomatic attrition. This was the great challenge to Israeli foreign policy. Could Israel maintain, even in victory and occupation, the international links necessary for survival and progress?

Five years after the end of the war, Eban, taking stock, was able to report that Israel, despite some inevitable setbacks, had not only resisted the siege, but had grown stronger in many respects. In spite of being called an "occupier," she had continued diplomatic relations with one hundred countries, and some, such as Romania, Singapore, and some African and Asian nations, had elevated their missions from ministries to embassies. Also, Israel's development role in African and Latin American countries had been maintained. Tourism had increased dramatically, as Israel became a magnet for increased international fascination. More financial aid than ever was flowing in from foreign governments, as well as from Jewish sources.

One of the major elements of Eban's postwar policy was to strengthen Israel's links with Europe. He went to Luxembourg in May 1970 to sign a preferential agreement with the European Common Market which he considered of importance. Although the economic content of the pact might still be slight, when the six nations of the EEC were joined by others including Britain this would create one of the great powers of the world; it was well for Israel to have an official foot in the door. In September 1967 Eban had addressed the Council of Europe in Strasbourg, in what Le Monde called "impeccable French," to urge that a community of sovereign states evolve in the Middle East, with open boundaries and economic integration, as had happened between the former belligerents in Europe after centuries of hostility. In February 1970 he went to Bonn. He began his tour at the Dachau concentration camp, and reached good understandings with Chancellor Brandt and Foreign Minister Scheel. During 1970–71 the foreign ministers of all the Common Market countries, except France, made an unprecedented official pilgrimage to Israel, followed by Britain's Foreign Minister in 1972. In November 1971 Eban had made the first official visit by an Israeli Foreign Minister to the United Kingdom, as the guest of Prime Minister Heath and Foreign Minister Douglas-Home.

In June 1971 Eban called on many African capitals. His tour was followed by the visit to Israel in November of four African presidents, who were persuaded to carry through a policy in the UN much fairer to Israel than in any previously suggested plan. He also cultivated the friendship of Latin America, whose leaders were delighted by his mastery of Spanish.

The death of Prime Minister Eshkol in 1969 brought a domestic political crisis. The newspaper-reading public got the impression Golda Meir was extremely reluctant to accept the premiership. Actually, after taking office she exercised it with eagerness and relish. Her candidacy had not been expected, and it had been thought that the choice lay between Allon and Dayan. The behind-the-scenes maneuvering created considerable personal friction. Some of Eban's supporters were accused of planting stories in the Israeli press designed to prolong the deadlock, in the hope Eban would be chosen as a compromise candidate. If Dayan had won the appointment, it would have meant Eban's exit from the government, for even if Dayan had wanted Eban to continue as Foreign Minister (which is doubtful), Eban himself would probably have refused to remain in the Cabinet. It is no secret in Israeli political circles that although Eban is known to admire Dayan's military attributes, he does not believe that he would be an adequate chief representative of the humane and liberal values for which a Jewish society should stand.[2]

There was never any doubt of Eban continuing as Foreign Minister under Mrs. Meir after she had won the premiership. Yet, soon they were engaged in a controversy which the Israelis, always fascinated by internecine war, followed almost as if it were a soccer match. Since the early Ben-Gurion era, the Government Press Department had been under the Prime Minister's Office, but information abroad had been the responsibility of the embassies and the Foreign Office. One day Mrs. Meir, without previously discussing the matter with Eban, announced to the central committee of Mapai she was going to set up a separate Ministry of Information under Israel Galili, former commander of Haganah. This ministry would centralize information abroad as well as at home. Eban objected, insisting it was vital for a Foreign Minister to have direct supervision of press and public relations abroad. He did not object to an Information Ministry if it confined its responsibility to the home front. The issue was fought in the columns of the entire Israeli press for weeks. At one point there were reports that Eban had threatened to resign. His own version was that he would not be Foreign Minister without control by embassies of the information services abroad; "there is no such thing in the world as a Foreign Ministry which is not in control of its external information services." Eban's attitude seemed to be that since the Prime Minister had committed herself publicly, she would have to get herself out of the political dilemma somehow. There were two or three weeks in which someone had to give in; and she finally did. There was a rare and impressive surge of party and public opinion in Eban's support. As a result, Eban and his Foreign Ministry henceforth had full charge of the foreign press in Israel and Israeli public relations abroad.

After the war, Israel inevitably lost some public sympathy around the world, partly because she was no longer the underdog and therefore no longer an object of pity and apprehension. ("People thought we were on our deathbed. It's normal to think kindly of people in that position. When the patient leaps off the deathbed and shows exaggerated signs of physical vigor, his friends cease to take an interest in him.") Also, the Arabs, supremely inept in public relations during most of Israel's modern life, now began to pour vast funds into the presentation of their case, especially to the American and European public. They were assisted by the New Left, whose spokesmen on hundreds of American college campuses hewed to a blind anti-Israel line.

Eban replied to their assertions by saying:

"If one has to choose between being popular or being alive, we should choose to be alive, because if you are alive you can work hard to reconstruct your popularity, whereas if you are dead you'll be infinitely popular during the funeral oration but the consolation will be short-lived."

After Eban had reorganized the information services under his control, he saw signs of some upswing in public sentiment, even on campuses. For example, at the University of California, Los Angeles, in March 1971, only about one hundred out of eight thousand who listened to him made what he called "obstreperous noises." His own oratorical cradle—the Cambridge Union—twice adopted pro-Israel resolutions against fierce Arab opposition. Polls taken in 1971 showed sympathy for Israel in Western countries still running seven or eight times as high as sympathy for the Arabs. The Arab superiority in UN meetings was an arithmetic fact, but it did not necessarily represent opinion outside the glass house on the East River.

Eban and his Foreign Office had to wrestle with many unusual diplomatic problems in 1968–70 as a result of the series of Arab hijackings that began with the seizure of an El Al plane forced to land at Algiers in July 1968. Delicate negotiating was necessary to save lives and property. Eban was especially angry that "respectable TV stations presented the terrorists not as criminals against humanity but as decent men" and that some statesmen referred to them as "resistance fighters." He said the whole world was to blame in encouraging air piracy by adopting "a forgiving attitude."

There was also a brief diplomatic crisis when Israeli commandos destroyed thirteen planes on the ground at the Beirut International Airport, without causing any loss of Arab life. (This was a reprisal for an Arab attack on an El Al airliner in which two Israelis were killed.)

Shortly thereafter, this exchange took place between a *Time* reporter and the Foreign Minister:

Shaw: Will the adverse international reaction to the Beirut raid affect Israel's policy of retaliation?

Eban: We have no policy of retaliation. We have a policy of survival. If retaliation helps survival, we are for it.[3]

However, it was freely published in Israel that Eban and many other ministers thought it would have been enough to blow up one or two Arab airliners.

Eban was also involved in an internal conflict over withdrawal from occupied territories. Herut and some other extreme groups contended that peace being an illusion, Israel should absorb and formally annex every square foot of territory she had taken. Eban argued this would lose Israel support abroad, especially in the United States; that this, in turn, would make it more difficult for Israel to withstand Arab and Soviet pressure; that the large Arab minority would before long become the majority, and Israel would be swamped and eventually absorbed by those she had beaten in battle. The idea of a state expressing the interests, values and concerns of the Jewish people would be lost. Most of Eban's colleagues agreed with this, but not all of them had the courage to oppose the noisy and militant minority with such blunt arguments. As a result, he became, more than the others who actually shared his opinions, the target of the chauvinists.

When in early 1968 Eban suggested that instead of negotiating directly with the Arabs, the Israelis might agree as a first step to meet them as they did on the island of Rhodes, where the 1949 armistice agreements were reached through the help of a third party, the opposition press became so violent that the number of policemen guarding the Foreign Minister's residence was increased.

Another of his domestic problems was a direct result of his popularity abroad. The fact that hardly any of the one hundred and thirty foreign ministers of the world were as well known in New York, London, Paris and elsewhere as he was and that he was more often on news-paper front pages and television screens than any of his colleagues was resented by some who were as publicity-conscious as he was.

Eban's Achilles' heel is his sensitivity to criticism, especially when he feels it inaccurate, non-objective or too personal. When he is the victim of what he considers an unjust attack he sinks into a deep slough of despondency. Because Israel's political climate is extremely intolerant, he often suffers such torment.

In October 1971, in New York for the opening session of the General Assembly, he appeared as guest on the David Frost television show, taped in New York and broadcast across the country. Near the end of the long and very relaxed interview Frost asked:

"Do you believe now, in 1971, that the search for Nazi war criminals should continue or not?"

"After the Eichmann trial," Eban replied, "I ceased to be interested because the Eichmann drama had its quality of uniqueness. I feel that another Eichmann trial would simply detract from this one. It is il-lustrative. Now I have been to Auschwitz and I have been to Dachau. I have there officiated, which in this case is more moving because I felt that I was representing as it were the collective memories of the survivors and I brought Israel's flag into Auschwitz, which is a terrible feeling that here all the ashes of the millions who were killed and the sense of this sovereign flag would have been their enormous consolation and here I was bringing this flag and their graves were silent.

"This drama of the holocaust I think has its mark on Israel's life today. There's a profound melancholy underneath all the turbulence and vitality and resilience in Israel's life; there is this profound sense of loss and bereavement. But whether some wretched man in Paraguay or in Brazil is brought to justice I think hardly interests me. I think, if found, they should be tried, but I wouldn't get excited one way or another. I don't believe that it matters. What can vengeance do? What can punishment do? This is something that is neither capable of expiation nor even of description. We live with a memory and we have to go on and build some survival, build some consolation for it. So, I don't really care."

Frost then asked Eban for his definition of "an eye for an eye."

"I don't know what you do for a thousand eyes and a million teeth," Eban replied, very gravely, "and the whole proportions are so immeasurable that I would leave it to the law. If the laws of countries still punish Nazi criminals I think that shows a very sound consciousness and an educated consciousness about it, but the fate of the individuals doesn't really interest me and I don't get any consolation from their punishment."[4]

These words, pronounced with deep pathos, stirred the millions who heard them. But when Eban's words were broadcast over Kol Israel a storm broke. One Israeli paper reported that he had "opposed" the pursuit of Nazi criminals, which was not the case, while his intensely moving words about the holocaust were suppressed. The former commander of the Warsaw Ghetto Fighters and the head of a resistance league denounced him, although the former later retracted. In New York, the national president of the United Synagogue of America, the heads of Jewish organizations and the head of the Victims of Nazis League were among many prominent people defending Eban. The Jerusalem *Post* and *Davar*, paper of Histadrut, closely connected with the establishment Labor party, ran editorials castigating Eban.

The tempest continued for more than a month. Late in November, after Eban returned home, the matter went before the Knesset, which spent an entire day in one of the most rancor-filled debates in a long time. Eban defended himself, saying he was shocked by the vehemence; American TV viewers had shown a profound understanding of his statement and had showered him with nothing but praise. Two opposition motions hostile to Eban were finally defeated, 27 to 22, the majority of Knesset members being, as usual, absent. It was an example of Eban's reaction to what he considers unfair criticism, and it was also an example of the virulence of political controversy in Israel.

Eban could draw solace from the attitude of the people he met in the street, and the fact that in some polls, as in the fall of 1971, he received a larger percentage of approval as Foreign Minister than Dayan did as Defense Minister or Golda Meir as Prime Minister.

In the summer of 1970 Richard Crossman, former Labour party Cabinet member, addressed an open letter on the front page of *The New*

Statesman, of which he was then editor, to his old friend Eban, in which he warned:

"The Arabs can survive a decade of Jewish military domination; the Israel you and I believe in can't."

It was a busy summer for Eban, with hijackings and other crises, but he took time from everything else to write an open letter to Crossman combining personal remarks ("Dear Dick, you haven't changed a bit. . . . I well remember the dreams that united us two decades ago") with an able defense of fortress Israel:

". . . you really need not worry lest we shall become Prussia. . . . When you come to visit us you will not find us paralyzed or obsessed by war. . . . You will find a freer movement of men and goods across the whole of the former Palestine area than at any time since 1948. You will be astonished in Jerusalem by an unceasing contact of Jews, Arabs and thousands of all faiths which puts the segregation and fanatical exclusiveness of the Jordanian occupation to shame. You will find a vast flow of visitors to Israel from all over the world. . . . In short, you will find that you are as far from Prussia as you can get in this modern world."[5]

Eban concluded by suggesting that his Socialist friend write his next open letter to Nasser.

Early in 1968, and later, despite strict Israeli censorship of such matters and a tight diplomatic silence by the Foreign Ministry, it was widely reported Eban had had secret meetings in London and elsewhere with King Hussein. This was never admitted officially, and was indeed denied on both sides. But historians may well have to record someday that Eban took part in a dialogue with more than one Arab leader after the 1967 war. On a "Meet the Press" television program in New York in March 1969 this exchange took place:

Pauline Frederick: Mr. Minister, did you or any other Israeli meet with King Hussein of Jordan in the Dorchester Hotel in London last October. . . .

Eban: I haven't met with him in the Dorchester Hotel; it is an interesting hotel. . . .[6]

In the general debate in the General Assembly in September 1969, after pointing out that artillery duels across the Suez had been so constant that no calm dialogue could be heard, Eban suggested October 24, United Nations Day, be proclaimed a Day of Universal Cease-Fire.

"On that day armed action should be halted all over the world; in

Vietnam and in Nigeria, along the Chinese-Soviet border, in all parts of Africa and across the cease-fire lines in the Middle East. When all guns are silent, the leaders of nations will be able, in that solemn and unparalleled tranquillity, to hear the urgent voice of mankind yearning for a world of peace."

In the autumn of 1969, Eban was received in audience at the Vatican by Pope Paul, the first official audience he had ever given an Israeli Cabinet member. It was a gesture toward improvement in relations between Rome and Jerusalem that had been under way for two years. The Arab press protested, understanding the historic significance of the Israeli flag entering the precincts of the Holy See.

About this time Suzy, writing to a friend, gave an indication of the difficulties she was facing in bringing up children in the atmosphere of the Foreign Ministry residence:

"The life we lead! The tensions in the air! The telephones all hours of the day and night. The constant presence of strangers. The constant presence of staff. The police. The people who watch the children as they come in and out of the house. . . ."[7]

In December of 1970 Dewey Stone, then chairman of the Board of Governors of the Weizmann Institute, was seventy and his close friend Harry Levine, treasurer of the Institute's American Committee, was seventy-five. In recognition of their services, a high-level banquet and birthday celebration was organized by the committee. Eban was to have been the main attraction but at the last minute official business made the trip to New York impossible. As a substitute Anne Stone suggested Suzy Eban. At dinner the night she received the cabled invitation Suzy nervously said to her husband:

"Aubrey, I have something I need your consent to."

"It's all right; do it," he replied.

"But I haven't told you what it is," she retorted, a little impatiently.

"You can go and do the talk, Suzy."

When she arrived at the Waldorf-Astoria speakers' table she bore in her hand a manuscript written by her husband, which she intended to read. Maurice Bookstein, one of the Weizmann Institute supporters in America, who sat beside her, asked:

"What are you going to say, Suzy?"

"I have a message from Aubrey," she replied.

"Don't make this a political evening," her dinner companion begged. "Be yourself. Talk as Suzy, not as Eban."

So she tore up the script, borrowed a man's large watch and began her fifteen-minute impromptu speech by saying:

"Good *morning*, ladies and gentlemen. I have just come from Jerusalem. To me it *is* morning and it seems so strange to see all you ladies in such gorgeous gowns and all you gentlemen in formal evening clothes at this hour of the morning." And she paused, while she studied the big watch. Then she added:

"I do not commit the Israel government in what I say. Since ministers often speak without committing the government, wives of ministers should have equal freedom."

Her speech, intimate and personal, received such applause that Aubrey facetiously remarked that he was worried by the competition.[8]

In 1970 Suzy became one of her husband's literary competitors as well. A letter she wrote about her childhood to an American friend received publicity in a New York column, which led a book publisher to ask her to do her autobiography.[9] Instead, she did an article for *The New Yorker* in which she wrote about her Egyptian childhood as she remembered it, in a style as different from her husband's as a poem by Edna St. Vincent Millay is different from the Bible.[10]

William F. Buckley, Jr., had Eban as his guest on his "Firing Line" television program on September 28, 1970. In his column in the *National Review* some days later Buckley wrote:

"It happened that I was with Abba Eban, the Foreign Minister of Israel, walking into the television studio, surrounded by the plainclothesmen who follow Mr. Eban around, when an aide stepped up to say that the radio had just reported the death of President Nasser. Since Mr. Eban was the highest-ranking adversary of Nasser in the United States at that particular moment he paused briefly to absorb the shock. . . . Two minutes later, recording our discussion for television, Mr. Eban was matter-of-factly referring to the 'late President Nasser.' He is a cool one. To be sure, his manner can be irritating. Israel has never been wrong about anything."[11]

On the air Buckley introduced Eban as "probably the best-known citizen of Israel in America" and as "the forensic hero of the year." During a discussion of the moving up of Soviet missiles in the Suez Canal area, Buckley used the word "hawk" and Eban quickly replied:

"I don't know whether a hawk is a complimentary term or not. My experience is that the dove was the only bird in Noah's Ark that knew what it wanted. It went out three times and came back with the olive branch—and discovered dry land."

Late in the show this exchange took place:

Buckley: I assume the death of Nasser was something not anticipated or, for that matter, contrived by your government. Have you been closely, nevertheless, watching domestic developments in Egypt sufficiently to be able to analyze what is likely to happen now?

Eban: It's very hard to analyze because President Nasser occupied such a large place in the life of the country . . . the regime revolved around the person and therefore the vacuum that exists when the person passes on is not like anything that happens in our countries when an office-holder, however eminent, moves on. A change of government is a new opportunity. I expect more realism and less bellicosity from Cairo in the future.[12]

Addressing a typical black-tie-and-evening-gown audience in Washington in the fall of 1970, Eban sparkled with epigrams, some new, some he had used before:

"It is not forbidden for politicians to repeat their errors, but it is not mandatory."

"National suicide is not an international obligation."

"We have peace plans. We only need someone to whom to tell them and a table on which to lay them."

"There are political leaders who never lose a chance to miss an opportunity."

"Every time the Foreign Minister of Egypt opens his mouth he subtracts from the sum total of human wisdom."

"Border clashes, cholera and hijackings appear to be tourist attractions."

"Israel's difficulties are her only possessions nobody has tried to take from her."

"When an ostrich buries its head in the sand to avoid facing unpleasant facts it not only presents an undignified spectacle; it also constitutes an irresistible target."[13]

Almost every year for a quarter of a century Eban had been involved in deciding what Israel's attitude should be toward the two Chinas. Shortly after the revolution and creation of the People's Republic, while Sharett was Foreign Minister, Israel became one of the first countries in the world to recognize Communist China. Ben-Gurion, then Prime Minister, had (and still has) a theory that China will one day become a great power, if not the dominant nation of the world. For this reason, among others, he was eager to create close and friendly relations with Peking. In 1950 Israel voted for the seating of Peking in the United Nations and Sharett told the General Assembly that "it would be unwise for the UN, in disregard of compelling realities, artificially to bolster up a regime of the past, which has lost its hold on the territory and people it claims to represent."

But that was the last time for twenty-one years that Israel voted for the admission of Peking. In 1955 David Hacohen, minister of Israel to Burma, was sent as the head of a delegation to investigate the possibility of commercial and diplomatic relations between Israel and China, but nothing came of it, for reasons never made clear.

From 1951 until 1971 Israel generally abstained when the China question came up in the UN, but in 1954 she voted in favor of a draft resolution calling on the UN *not* to consider the question of representation. Eban at that time in addressing the General Assembly said the postponement for which he was voting "should be used not to lay this burning question aside but rather to prepare for its serious and orderly discussion in conditions likely to bring about a positive result."

In 1966 as Foreign Minister Eban supported a formula which would have acknowledged "both the reality of the Chinese mainland and the reality of Taiwan."[14]

Some of those who favored cementing relations with Peking in the early 1950s felt that Israel's China policy was being dictated by the United States and blamed Eban, then ambassador to Washington.[15]

After almost a quarter of a century of opposing Peking's admission, Israel finally, in 1971, after voting with the United States to consider the matter "an important question" requiring a two-thirds vote, voted for the Albanian resolution seating Peking and expelling Taiwan. But the head of the American delegation, Ambassador George Bush, said that Israel's votes were logical and reasonable, and were no cause for complaint by the United States.

The year 1971 was one of intense diplomatic activity, which succeeded in preserving the status quo, and nothing more. During the first half of the year the American Government permitted a steady flow of Phantom jets to Israel; during the last half the Prime Minister and the Foreign Minister made many trips to plead, urge, beg for resumption of Phantom shipments, without being compelled to make concessions at the expense of Israel's security.

In January (1971), following an annual custom, Eban delivered an address in Arabic over Israel's radio and television, in which he said "we are convinced there was not, is not and there will not be a military solution to the conflict before us." Editorials in Arab newspapers around the Middle East indicated the talk was well listened to.

When the September (1971) session of the General Assembly opened, Adam Malik of Indonesia was elected President, but Eban received one vote. As proof that neither he nor any of his Israeli colleagues was responsible, Eban pointed out that it was Rosh Ha-Shanah (Jewish New Year's day) and by custom no Israelis had gone that day to the UN. Ten delegates called up Eban to hint that they had recorded the single vote in his favor.

In addressing the General Assembly Eban publicly invited Egyptian Foreign Minister Mahmoud Riad to meet him in New York to discuss either a Suez Canal agreement or an over-all peace settlement. The suggestion was ignored, but a few months later Riad was replaced and the prospect of some Egyptian-Israeli talks in 1972 was renewed.

He did see several dozen other foreign ministers, from three continents, and in an interview said Israel was willing to resume diplomatic relations with the Soviet Union "in any form the Russians suggest." It was all a part of his diplomatic dynamism aimed at keeping all Israel's options open. When he first spoke of a possible change in the Soviet attitude to Israel in the summer of 1971, some Israelis criticized his "chronic optimism," but late in the same year it became known that many thousands of Jews were being allowed to emigrate to Israel and that Soviet influences in Cairo had been applied to prevent the threatened renewal of hostilities in 1971.

Eban's view was that no purpose would any longer be served by public debates on the Middle East. The Indo-Pakistan war had revealed the weakness of UN guarantees. Uttering what one reporter called a *cri de coeur* he told his fellow foreign ministers and delegates at the UN General Assembly:

"One of the few things all members of the UN have in common is the ability to discuss each other's imperfections."

After Eban had welcomed the announcement of Nixon's trip to Peking, several Israeli political writers raised eyebrows and wrote again of his perennial optimism, a favorite criticism of those journalistic critics eager to dissect or even disembowel him publicly. Eban's view was that the traditional rivalries of the 1950s and 1960s were being left behind, that new situations were developing and that Israel's alignments should not be static or frozen.

By early 1972 Eban had been Foreign Minister for five years, had been in the Cabinet for nearly thirteen years and had served his country at home and abroad for twenty-four continuous years. Others had had their periods of rest, whether by choice or by necessity. Golda Meir had been out of office three years between being Foreign Minister and Prime Minister. Finance Minister Sapir had left the Cabinet for two years. Ben-Gurion had taken a vacation for two years in the desert during his time as Prime Minister. In Britain, men like Home and Heath, Wilson and Brown had had years in opposition between their years in the government. Eban's burden had been continuous, yet, apart from some days of fatigue and bouts with the common cold, he had been in robust health all these twenty-four years, with hardly a day away from work. The strain was on nerves and emotion, but it rarely showed. What did depress him was the lack of privacy. As a result of El Fatah's terrorist activities, he was rarely able to move abroad without a dozen policemen, secret service agents and detectives on his trail. Always there were guards standing outside his bedroom door. On some trips in the United States the entire first-class section of the plane would be occupied by Eban and his entourage of bodyguards, some in uniform, some posing as ordinary passengers.

Just as Weizmann was never happy without his scientific preoccupation, and just as Ben-Gurion, late in life, felt there was something transitory and fleeting about political life, which required him to read and write in order to gain insight into deeper values and higher truths, so Eban turned more and more to reading and writing for intellectual renewal and revitalization.

In 1968 *My People, The Story of the Jews,* a handsome book on which he had worked for seven years, was published in various languages in the United States, England, Italy, France, Germany, Brazil, Holland and Norway. The reviews were ecstatic, and the book went into nine editions in the English-speaking countries. Eban's friend from World War II days, Nelson Glueck, as critic for the New York *Times Magazine,* called it "A fascinating book, written with knowledge, perception, lucidity, eloquence and passion. . . . It is not an academic exercise in historiography. . . . Everything is seen through the prism of his own tremendous knowledge and deeply reflective and sensitive personality." Other critics were almost as enthusiastic.

Eban admitted that his "vocation had been to explain the Jewish people to a confused and often uncomprehending world. . . . I have come up against the impossibility of understanding and, therefore, of explaining the current Jewish reality without a constant probing of ancient roots. . . . And when all is said and done the Jewish career remains an unpenetrated mystery. The problems can be illuminated, but never solved."

In 1970 Eban finished a shorter work, devoted entirely to the diplomacy of the Six-Day war. It was withheld from publication, temporarily at least, for reasons of diplomatic discretion, by decision of a Cabinet committee. But still another Eban book was in preparation. His love of creative writing was beginning to equal, if not exceed, his interest in expressing himself vocally.

31

The Man Nobody Knows

VERY FEW PEOPLE know Abba Eban. Very few people have ever really known him. He is probably the least understood figure on the international scene. That is the root cause of many of his personal problems and some of his political difficulties. Perhaps Suzy Eban knows him better than anyone else, better than even his brother, sisters and parents, but there are probably facets of his character hidden even from her. One, maybe two, men who have been closely associated with his career have had some deep insight into the inner man. But there are hundreds in Israel and in America who have had daily contact with him for years yet to whom he is a complete enigma.

The public at large knows Eban the articulate platform speaker, or Eban the commanding voice of radio and television, or Eban the polished writer. To them he is brilliant but reserved, intellectual but cold, famous but shy, a man who blushes in an era in which teen-age girls no longer blush, a man who in his middle years can still not tolerate the rules of sociability. People respect him without loving him, agree with him without fully understanding him, criticize him without knowing him. All this is even more true of Israelis than Americans.

There are no footnotes to this chapter, for the pages that follow are based on years of contact with him, an intense study of the mind and heart-workings of the man, and a piecing together of tens of thousands of words of notes taken on tape recorder and scraps of paper while interviewing people on three continents whose lives have touched his on a social, political or personal level. The principal sources for this chapter are listed in the Appreciation at the beginning of the book. Each person contributed something. But because the information and opinions were often given in confidence, no specific accreditation is possible.

The public figure who is best understood is the one whose character, traits and personality are simple and commonplace, bearing at least some relationship to Everyman. Abba Eban's character and personality are not simple, are far from commonplace, are not always understandable and bear no relationship whatsoever to those of the average man.

He is an individualist, which is to his detriment. Yet he is not a non-conformist in the current use of the word. His mind is complex, yet his heart is enormously simple. He is a man of peace in what many consider the most militaristic age in history. He is a man of reason at a time when there is little place in the world's scheme for reasonable men. Most of his political associates and competitors are concerned almost exclusively with what Israel thinks; Eban has always had his mind also on what the world thinks. He is an optimist at times when there seems to be nothing to be hopeful about. He believes in creative dynamism. He is a civilized person who often has to contend with creatures of the jungle. He insists there is nothing intelligent men cannot solve in a moderate manner. Political efforts to him are just as important as military enterprises in assuring national survival. Few people know how warmhearted he can be, because it is not easy for him to show it. He displays this side of his character privately—to only a few.

"Today as I write to you from Jerusalem the guns are silent in Suez. It is time for sane and gentle voices to be lifted up and heard."

This was not oratory. It was not rhetoric. It was the soul of the man speaking.

The reason he appears to talk from the head rather than the heart is because of his innate shyness and his British upbringing, which teaches restraint in the public display of emotion. He has the capacity for compassion and deep concern for people when he is aroused, but he also has the ability to live on a plane remote from the problems and sufferings of others.

A good artist is a perfectionist because his product must be the best he can possibly produce. In that sense Eban has the soul of an artist, for he is never slipshod vocally, in his writing or in his diplomatic creativity. He has, too, the sensitivity of an artist, for most things hurt him more than they would other people. His skin is thin.

He is a man of mild manners at a time in history when this is not considered by most of the West to be a public or a private virtue. Yet he has many impatiences. He is most impatient of stupidity. Fools infuriate him. People who have difficulty coming quickly to the point annoy him, even though he himself is often guilty of circumlocution. Small things of many varieties irk him, yet he is rarely motivated by pettiness.

In international situations he has always displayed consummate courage, even when forced to work in adversity. In human relations he has often been flustered, but never on the public scene. From his mother he inherited an amazingly phlegmatic attitude in times of crisis. Often when he flew from Washington to Israel at a moment of grave international difficulties he would step from the plane at Lod Airport with an air of serenity that gave the assembled reporters and photographers a feeling that everything must surely be all right.

Outwardly he seldom shows any reaction to the bitter disappointments he often experiences. Said one member of his family:

"I think it must be glandular."

He looks like an absent-minded professor removed from the world, but he is much more aware of what is going on, what people are saying and what is important than is generally imagined. His head may be in the clouds at times, yet he is not unobservant of what is happening down below. And it really matters to him.

Early in life he became a mass communications man, always articulate when talking to reporters, but at his best when addressing several thousand people or speaking into a microphone which he knows is sending his voice to millions. His power seems to grow with amplification. No one—not even his mother, wife, sisters—ever heard him say: "I had a wonderful talk with a friend today and I felt enriched by what he said." With very few people does he have "an intimate conversation."

He makes friends slowly because immediately after the introduction a current of cold air seems to be created, although it is seldom intentional on his part. Most people find it difficult to break through this cold wall and get close to him. Also, he is not an easy person to converse with, because he has no use for small talk. In that regard he resembles Ben-Gurion. Eban would not know how to make small talk if commanded on pain of death. He is also handicapped by not being a good listener. He hears only what he wants to hear. He has the uncanny ability of being able to switch his mind off and on at will. Even when he *is* listening he gives the other person the impression he is not. One day an aide gave him two pieces of information that he (the aide) did not consider important but was duty-bound to report. Half an hour later the aide saw two letters already typed by Eban's secretary commenting on the pieces of routine information that he thought the ambassador had not even heard.

Another handicap in person-to-person socializing is Eban's tendency to assume that what he says is of transcendental importance; that whatever the other person says is minor. Although this is often the case, it does not make for good human relations. He also assumes that if there is a difference of opinion it is inconceivable the other person should not accept his (Eban's) point of view. Also, his tendency to monopolize a conversation frequently turns it into a monologue.

At a reception he is quite capable of standing alone, noticing no one, lost in thought, until he is "rescued." At banquets when he is the principal speaker he often finds himself with the podium to his left and on his right the wife of the chairman. At one Bonds for Israel gathering of several thousand people in Washington's Shoreham Hotel the woman on his right was young, beautiful and intelligent. She tried desperately to make pleasant conversation with Eban, in between the usual interruptions by waiters, rabbis, other celebrated guests and auto- graph seekers. With several thousand pairs of eyes upon him, Eban pulled from his pocket the script of the address he would soon deliver and began making corrections, improvements and amendments, while ignoring the chairman's wife.

"I think that's insulting!" someone at Table 3 remarked to the man beside her.

"My dear," came back the reply, "which is more important—for Mr. Eban to listen to what she thinks or for him to polish up a speech that in a few minutes is going to be heard by several thousand people in this room, by hundreds of thousands over radio and television, and read in the press of the world tomorrow by millions?"

Contrary to the public view—that he is cold and aloof—he does have a remarkable capacity for relaxing with a few intimate friends, if they are people who share his gentle irony and sardonic sense of humor. In such company he delights in playing the mimic. His best impersona- tions are of Churchill, De Gaulle and LBJ. As diverse as they were, they come to life as Eban does verbal caricatures of them. The more appreciative the audience the more he relaxes and the more entertaining he becomes. It is one of the greatest pleasures possible to sit with him when he is in such a mood.

Ben-Gurion was well known in Israel for his ability to hate. There were always at least a few people on his list. Some critics said he hated more people than he liked. Eban, by contrast, does not have the ability to hate. He can be momentarily angry with someone and be exceedingly sarcastic. His words can cut like a knife. His humor is not of the Israeli type, but rather of the British variety, sharp and needling. He can also be completely indifferent to a foe.

His face never reveals his thoughts. He does not appear, ever, to be a cynic, or a humorist either. He gets excited inside but seldom on the surface. He never raises his voice. No one has ever heard him shout. When he tells someone off verbally, it is generally done restrainedly, or indirectly. If he ever says a harsh word to anyone, he is immediately so embarrassed that he blushes.

Like any man in public life he has been the victim of sniping, especially by those who are jealous. Speeches and other public statements have been misinterpreted, sometimes intentionally. Reporters have misquoted him. Political rivals have attacked him. He is at his best when he is in a mood to disregard such annoyances. He is at his worst when his armor has been pierced, for then he immediately calls for a stenographer or picks up a pen and counterattacks, showing his victim no mercy.

"Criticism seems to eat him," one close associate said. "He shows it in a very petulant way. He feels he must get in the last word. Often the matter is so petty that it is beneath his dignity to take notice. Yet he does, because of his excessive touchiness. Often after he has written a scathing note to someone, I have tried to persuade him not to send it—urged him to put it in a file for future generations—or for his private pleasure. Or I have said: 'Why don't you talk to him instead?' because I know that he would be much more restrained verbally."

Physically Eban's face is rather long, yet appears to be round, especially on television, perhaps because of the shell-rim glasses he almost always wears. (He takes them off when he is looking closely at fine print.) His smile is friendly but it has a tentative quality. He ambles rather than walks. One of his sisters describes it as "a waddle, rather like that of a penguin." He is awkward in his body movements. He has perhaps the most restless hands in the world. He never seems to know what to do with them. When he is sitting waiting to speak he fusses with his papers, plays with his cuff links, picks up a pencil and taps with it, bites his fingernails, adjusts and readjusts his necktie, puts the cigar in and out of his mouth, doodles on the agenda and plays with whatever objects are on the table in front of him. Once at the podium he often raises and lowers the microphone to the distress of sound engineers, but his words are generally so scintillating that the audience ignores his nervousness.

While holding a press conference or attending a Cabinet meeting or listening to something of importance someone may have come thousands of miles to tell him, he keeps constantly busy with a pencil or pen. Sometimes his doodles are geometrical figures, but more often they are Hebrew words which he crosses out, first with perpendicular lines, then with horizontal lines and finally diagonal lines—an indication of his insatiable desire to be always creating. As soon as the conference is over and he can go back to creating actively he seems happy again.

His restlessness is displayed not only in his inability to sit still for long in one place but his penchant for extensive traveling. "He often invents reasons to go abroad."

His favorite form of recreation is writing. Said an office associate: "He can be having a hectic week with speeches, meetings, an international crisis and suddenly he says, 'I think I'll write an article for Such-and-Such.' I say to myself, 'He's meshugga! With all he's got to do! . . .' After he hands it to me to get it typed there will be corrections and corrections and corrections. He drives us mad! And sometimes he writes on the most petty matters. But how he loves to write!"

Eban's capacity for work is phenomenal. He sometimes keeps going for eighteen or twenty hours at a stretch, wearing out several shifts of stenographers.

His perfectionism compounds the amount of work that he and his staff have to do. One of his office managers said:

"Whatever he writes—a speech, a magazine article or even a memorandum—he corrects many times. There the trouble begins. He will often write out the first draft in longhand and I'll give it to one of the girls to type. When he gets it back he may rewrite it completely. Then there will be a second draft, a third, a fourth, maybe even a fifth. All the time he is correcting, changing, improving. It never seems to be as perfect as he wishes it to be."

He has an almost computer-like power of concentration. If someone comes to him with a problem which he feels deserves his attention—obviously not even his wife bothers him with such problems as whether to wear a pink or a blue dress—and if he feels the problem merits his attention his whole mind focuses on the matter. One can almost see the lights flashing on and off and the machine working. He has the same power of concentration that enables a yogi to lie on a bed of nails. He can concentrate on writing a speech while sitting in an auditorium crowded with people. Once he took a train from New York to Detroit so ill he could hardly stand, but he felt it was important to make the trip, so he worked on the address he was to deliver and postponed being ill until after his appearance.

He is well organized in those areas in which he is vitally interested and shockingly disorganized about whatever he considers minor.

His memory is one of his greatest intellectual assets. He reads photographically, taking in the contents of a whole page in what seems like a single glance, and then stores away the facts, even the phraseology, in the pigeonholes of his mind, ready for instant recall when needed. Often his wife hands him a book and says, "Read that one page." He glances at it and hands it back, almost instantly, to her great annoyance.

"But I asked you to read it!" she will say.

"I did."

If she subsequently questions him, to her perpetual astonishment she discovers that he has almost memorized the page.

Suzy Eban says: "I have never mentioned a magazine article he couldn't discuss. I have no idea when or where he reads them all. He always has a pile of magazines on his bedside table. I really think he reads the top one and then the bottom one and somehow—perhaps by osmosis—knows all that's in between."

He will remember such facts as on what date Nasser made a specific speech, what Gromyko said on a certain occasion, the exact words of a cable from Golda Meir or what he himself said in an address years ago. He remembers only those people who are important to him; not only their names and faces but beautiful anecdotes about them. He remembers anything he hears about language. He remembers details about people who make an impression on him, even if they are bitter enemies. He remembers poems he read in his university days and telephone numbers of once close friends whom he may not have called in years. He not only knows what he has read but can recall where he read it, sometimes even on what page. His English vocabulary is probably ten times that of the man in the street (London or New York) and greater than that of many scholars. He also has such a vocabulary in Hebrew, plus a good working accumulation of words in Arabic, French, German, Spanish, Farsi—seven languages in all. He has as many biblical quotations in his head as Ben-Gurion, as many classical quotations as a Greek professor and almost as many quotations from English literature as Bartlett's. Yet one of his secretaries recalled:

"There isn't an airline in the world that I haven't chased trying to get something he forgot on one of their planes."

Once after his mother had been in Washington for several weeks on a visit he and Suzy took her to the airport and as she was about to get on the plane someone suddenly remembered that all three of them had left her suitcase at the Embassy.

Once Eban went on a one-week speaking tour with George Jessel and Victor Felder. An Embassy aide who accompanied them to be sure there were no minor problems was aware of Eban's forgetfulness and so, in order not to embarrass him, said to all three men the first day:

"I'll keep your room keys in my pocket and give them to you every night when we get back to the hotel."

It became a nightly rite for him to distribute the keys in the lobby, saying:

"This is your key, Mr. Ambassador. This is yours, Mr. Jessel. And yours, Mr. Felder."

It went on like this for four nights. On the fifth night he handed Jessel his key and Felder his, whereupon Eban said, in a perplexed tone:

"Where's *mine?*"

"Mr. Ambassador," the aide replied, "Mrs. Eban will let you in tonight. We're in Washington."

On one occasion he sold the rights to the same book to two competing publishers. Several times he has accepted two speaking engagements for the same hour of the same day.

His unawareness extends to money, about which he is extremely careless. He has no patience with monetary details. In the attic of his home are seventy-nine suitcases. (By the author's actual count.) He likes to shop for suitcases. He also forgets he has an attic. (Suzy says a better example of his forgetfulness is razors. "The other day I discovered he has seven electric razors and nine regular ones. That's because he's always going off and leaving his razor behind or in a hotel bathroom.")

His unawareness also extends to the weather. He rarely cares whether it is snowing, raining, sleeting or the sun is shining. Or knows.

The son of a close friend served as his bodyguard for a whole summer without Eban being aware who he was.

Because he thinks faster than he can possibly speak, it is often a strain for his associates to try to understand orders he gives them, his words telescoping and his thoughts running together. He also often speaks in half sentences and omits saying things he thinks that other person ought to know already.

"We generally have to strain to work it out," one employee said.

He is generous with his time, almost to a fault. If a visitor decides to try to draw him out, the interview may last double the allotted time, to the distress of the secretary who keeps his book.

Normally, unless there is urgent business, he hates to be awakened before 8 A.M. Sometimes, if things are quiet, he will relax between 3 and 4 P.M., reading newspapers. He never takes a siesta nap. His normal retiring time is 2 or 3 A.M.

His love of gourmet food is exceeded only by his craving for sweets of any sort, good, bad or mediocre.

In his early days in the United States he still smoked a pipe, as he had done at Cambridge. Today he has several pipes in his office and at home. As his wife puts it, "He plays around with them occasionally." But now he smokes cigars—for many reasons. A friend told him soon after he came to New York that a pipe is antisocial because you can't offer to share it with someone else.

"Look, Aubrey," he said, "if you're going to puff that villainous smoke into the face of a reporter or a colleague, at least smoke a cigar and offer him one, too."

Eban's own explanation:

"I found that I could never bring all the various elements of pipe smoking together at the same time: the pipe, the tobacco, the pipe cleaner, the matches. There was always at least one of them missing."

He rarely smokes cigarettes, feeling that a cigarette looks foolish in his hand. He sometimes smokes half a dozen cigars a day—always Havanas. When he has a cigar to twirl and play with it gives him something to do.

He is fastidious about hotels. He likes to use the same hotels year after year; this gives him a sense of security and also he is flattered at being recognized by the staff, from manager down. In Jerusalem it's the King David, in Tel Aviv the Dan, in New York the Plaza, in London the Dorchester, in Paris the Raphael.

He has no antipathy for television. When he has time he watches anything political and enjoys a good comedy or even a farce. In the theater he once preferred Shakespeare to anything else but now likes to be amused. ("He has enough heavy stuff in his daily life," Suzy Eban explains.)

Once when asked why he had never learned to play bridge, he said:

"I could learn a new language in the time it would take me to learn bridge."

His favorite colors in clothes are blue and dark gray. He likes to choose his own clothing; it's one of his distractions. After many years of marriage his wife still has trepidation about trying to buy even a necktie for him.

He has a small boy's interest in gadgets. He was once surprised in his hotel room in New York standing for a long time watching the people down on Fifth Avenue through the telescopic finder of his movie camera.

His favorite participatory sport is golf, which he started to play again in Washington after his doctor ordered him to take off fifteen or twenty pounds. But unfortunately he found the golf course cluttered with other diplomats doing the same thing and so it resulted in more talk than golf. He plays golf like an Englishman—blaming his caddy for all his bad shots.

Most Israelis are aware of the biblical scholarliness of Ben-Gurion, but few know how deeply rooted Eban is in his Jewishness. Although Yiddish was not one of the languages of his home, as with so many other Israeli leaders, he can understand it and has an appreciation of Yiddish folk tales and jokes. He learned the Bible by heart, knows all the prayers, can quote long passages from the Talmud and is steeped in Jewish scholarship.

His Israeli colleagues soon learned what his friends at Cambridge discovered about how he compartmentalizes his life.

"There are certain things about his family life which it was important for us in the office to know, but we never found them out from him," an aide said. "His personal secretary would have to hear them from Suzy. He was reluctant to talk to any of us about his family or anything else not in our compartment."

Whether he was stationed in Israel, New York or Washington, he always arranged his trips—no matter to what part of the world—so that he stopped off en route in London. This led to the gossip (Israel is so small a country that gossip has always been one of its favorite recreations) that he had some clandestine romantic attachment in the British capital.

"If you're trying to uncover the real Eban, find out who the girl in London is," one Tel Aviv journalist advised.

It was not difficult.

She rarely meets his plane, but he always telephones her from the airport. He telephones her again from the hotel as soon as he has checked in. He has dinner with her in some quiet restaurant each night he is in London. When he takes her home to her apartment he may stop for a while, until she suggests that he is tired and should get some sleep. Sometimes she has breakfast with him. When he leaves London he always telephones her from the airport just before boarding the plane. Her name is Alida, which will disappoint the gossipmongers.

His mother, being as self-critical as she is, will probably agree with the close associates who say that one disservice his family did him was that no one ever said to him: "You're wrong! Behave yourself! You have made a mistake! That isn't right!" They say that if his mother or someone else had been more critical of him "it might have made it easier for us."

Close associates have used various expressions to describe his supreme egoism: overly self-confident, exceedingly selfish, somewhat narcissistic, given to pomposity, often guilty of intellectual snobbism. They point to his sensitivity about criticism, his desire for an audience, his love of applause, his occasional reference to himself in the third person, his habit of listening to his own voice on a tape recorder, his obsession with personal publicity, his conceit about his own bons mots, his refusal to share credit with others. (Most ambitious public figures have some if not all of these characteristics.)

His sense of humor is not contrived or manufactured just to liven up his public addresses; it bursts forth on even the most solemn occasions. At a Seder in the ambassador's home in Washington one Passover, when the goblet was filled with wine for the fourth and last time, Eban was supposed to read this passage:

"Pour forth thy wrath upon the nations that know thee not and upon the kingdoms that called not upon thy name: for they have devoured Jacob (called Israel) and laid waste his habitation. . . ."[1]

When he came to this passage the ambassador turned to David Gotlin, former Israeli Minister to South Africa, and said:

"Will you please read it? As a delegate to the UN I dare not make such proclamations."

He is most happy when he is engaged in any of three intellectual pursuits: preparing or delivering a speech, writing for a periodical on some current subject (it can even be a letter of protest to an editor) and writing a book.

He has what a friend called "an abc mind." He likes to receive and deliver ideas in some precise pattern or order. He often numbers the points he is making in an address and is happy when other people organize their reports to him in this same manner.

He encourages his subordinates to have ideas, as long as they present them to him clearly and without excess verbiage.

He is impatient with fuzzy thinking, with people who can't express their thoughts succinctly and with those who sprinkle their conversation with clichés. He invented the word "stammers" to describe what he considers the epitome of verbal stupidity:

" 'It is unnecessary to add . . .' When that phrase comes across my desk I send it back to the author marked: 'Then why add it?'

" 'It goes without saying . . .' When someone uses that expression I ask: 'Then why say it?'

" 'It is worth noting . . .' The list is almost without end. Some people don't seem to be able to just start a sentence. They like to say: 'Let it be pointed out at this stage that . . .' All those words can be crossed out without losing anything. Or, 'Another consideration worth bearing in mind . . .' The rest of the sentence, whatever it is, can always stand on its own."

He likes to mimic, with a certain amount of derision in his voice, the speaker who begins: "Governor Simpson, Mr. Horowitz, Mr. Goldberg, Mr. Freudberg, Reverend Clergy, rabbis, senators, former senators, future senators . . ."

At hundreds of fund-raising meetings in dozens of cities he has heard almost the identical Eban introduction, full of clichés and always containing at least once and maybe two or three times the word "eloquent," which soon became his bête noir.

He is not an ordinary man.

32

Into the Future

IT HAS BEEN a crowded life thus far. At fifty-seven he has enjoyed years of international fame, as he has helped fashion a nation and keep its image bright, but it has also been a life full of turbulence, lived in an atmosphere of criticism and challenge.

Of the inner struggles, of the private joys and disappointments, no one will probably ever know. Although he is a supremely self-contained person and rarely reveals himself, either in private conversation with his closest friends or in his most intimate writings, in an interview he has said:

"I am not an entirely contented man. I have a great yearning for certain things which are not attainable while I hold my present office."[1]

In every man who succeeds in public life there is the desire for power of one sort or another. At a time when Eban was winning unprecedented praise and publicity as a diplomat and orator, he began to resent being categorized as "an eloquent spokesman." His yearning then was for a position in which he could do something more than give voice to the policies of others. He saw diplomacy as a game of intelligence and aspired to be the quarterback, calling the signals. He was tired of defending political and military actions of which he sometimes approved and sometimes did not. He wanted to have something to say about how the game should be conceived and played.

Then he became Foreign Minister and entered the field of policy making. He was still not a wholly contented man, for any Foreign Minister is severely inhibited in his statecraft, especially if he is serving under a Prime Minister who has had years of experience in foreign affairs. Yet, it was Golda Meir who graciously said: "Thank God that it was he and not anyone else who got up when Kosygin led the political attack on June 19."

American observers, who study Israeli political polls on the future Prime Minister and see Eban in fourth place, and then predict that he may have reached the zenith of his career, are unaware of a fundamental difference between American and Israeli politics. A short time before Golda Meir was appointed to the premiership her rating in Israeli polls for that job was as low as 3 percent. The party, not the populace, decides who heads the ticket and the infighting for top position can be —and generally is—bitter. The top runners often knock each other off and some compromise candidate gets the place. This happened with Golda Meir and might well happen again. Yet Eban has never as much as hinted that he seeks any higher office than that which he holds. Many years ago, asked what he thought his prospects were for winning the premiership, Eban replied with enigmatic humor:

"I should have to go off and be born in Sejera, some small Polish town or a kibbutz."

(Sejera was a pioneer settlement in Galilee where, for a very brief time, Ben-Gurion and other Jewish immigrants worked the fields.)

Instead, Eban is the product of London, Cambridge and modern Israel. He never spent a day working fields, shoveling manure, digging ditches or milking cows. But the complexion of Israel is changing. Today the vast majority of the voters are no longer from "Sejera, some small Polish town or a kibbutz." There is a higher sophistication and a greater respect for intellectual training.

When shells are falling, Arab armies are on the march and Israelis' face the prospect of possible annihilation, they will probably always feel more comfortable with a former general as their leader, but, lately, more and more Israelis are realizing that war, even if sometimes unavoidable, is not the final answer to their problems; that a modus vivendi must be found so that they and their Arab neighbors can permanently co-exist; that they cannot divorce themselves from the outside world; that even if the day comes when they have all the Phantom jets they can possibly use to defend themselves, there will still be need for political, economic and intellectual universality.

Because of Eban's link with Arab culture, and because millions of Arabs listen when he talks to them in their own language, he will have an overwhelming advantage over most of his colleagues if, and when, there is ever any active peacemaking. He is not associated in the Arab mind with any of the events or statements which have caused their humiliation.

Because he can hold his own in the great battle for world opinion and can meet any other statesman on at least equal terms, he has been able to get the maximum of international support available to Israel in any given set of conditions.

There is no doubt that many millions across the world have a loftier and more positive vision of Israel and the Jewish people through having heard Abba Eban describe his people's experience and ambition.

Starting with no advantage beyond his own capacity and character, he has become a unique figure on the world stage. One of his distinctive contributions has been to remind the Israelis of their lineage and of the special burden they bear—that they must live within their history not their geography—that they must not lose their romanticism, their humanism, their utopian vision. He has incurred the opposition of those who shirk this special burden and want Israel to be just a "normal" country, without any particular conviction or sense of mission. He has had to contend with rival leaders who put all their stress on military valor, unmindful that many successful military societies have been short-lived in their influence and not particularly creative outside the military domain. His message to his own people has been that while Israel may have a destiny of smallness in geography, it has been, can be and should be great in history.

His theme is constant:

"A small nation can achieve stature only in those domains where matter and quantity are transcended by spirit and quality."

No matter what the title before his name, for many years it is certain his presence will be felt across a wide spectum, putting current developments into historic perspective, pricking the conscience of a calloused world, reminding it that man cannot live by guns alone, focusing the clear light of his classical intelligence on the deeper human values, in a manner that makes the rest of us a little less ashamed to be human beings.

NOTES

CHAPTER 1

1. In Yiddish the village was called Yannisheik and in current USSR atlases is listed as Yonishkis or Ionishkis.
2. Yanishki was almost obliterated during World War II, but was subsequently rebuilt.
3. This entire chapter is based on many tape-recorded conversations in England with Mrs. Lina Halper, Mrs. Isaac Eban and other members of the Sacks family, who remember their early years in Yanishki, and also on information supplied by Isaac Don Levine, author and Russian authority, who knew Yanishki intimately in the days when the Sacks family lived there.
4. From material supplied by David Zuckerman, G. Saron and Matthew Pamm, all of South Africa.
5. From an interview with Dr. Sam Sacks, London, 1971.
6. From interviews with anonymous fellow students at Kent Coast College.
7. From *Charlie Chaplin's Own Story, Being the Faithful Account of a Romantic Career*, Bobbs Merrill, 1916, Rare Book Collection, Library of Congress, and *My Autobiography*, Charlie Chaplin, Simon & Schuster, 1964.
8. The stories of life on Kennington Park Road are from tape-recorded interviews in 1970 and 1971 with Dr. and Mrs. I. Eban, Dr. and Mrs. Robin Lynn, Carmel Eban, Dr. Sam Sacks, Dr. Elsie Sacks and Abba Eban.
9. As told by Dr. Elsie Sacks.

CHAPTER 2

1. From a tape-recorded interview with Ruth Lynn, Bath, England, 1970.
2. Ibid.
3. From an interview with Dr. Neville Halper, London, 1971.
4. From a tape-recorded interview with Ruth Lynn, Bath, England, 1970.
5. Rabbi Louis Isaac Rabinowitz later became chief rabbi in Johannesburg, South Africa, then moved to Israel, becoming one of the deputy mayors of Jerusalem.
6. From the Eban Archives, Jerusalem.
7. From a tape-recorded interview with Mrs. I. Eban, London, 1970.
8. As told by Dr. Elsie Sacks, London, 1971.
9. From a tape-recorded interview with Mrs. I. Eban, London, 1970.

CHAPTER 3

1. From an interview with Victor Mishcon, London, 1971.
2. From interviews with various members of Heatid.
3. From a taped interview with Mrs. I. Eban, London, 1970.
4. Brodetsky later became president of Hebrew University, 1949–52.
5. From an interview with Nathan Goldenberg, London, 1971.
6. From a tape-recorded interview with Carmel Eban, London, 1970.
7. From interviews with Mrs. Ruth Lynn in Bath, England, and Israel Schen in Haifa, Israel, 1970.
8. From tape-recorded interviews with Mrs. Ruth Lynn, Carmel Eban and Mrs. I. Eban.

9. From a tape-recorded interview with Mrs. I. Eban, London, 1970.
10. Ibid.
11. From copies of the *Olavian* in the British Museum.
12. From tape-recorded interviews with Mr. and Mrs. N. Doniach, London, 1970.
13. From tape-recorded interviews with Carmel Eban and Mrs. I. Eban, London, 1970.
14. Source confidential.
15. From a tape-recorded interview with Abba Eban, Jerusalem, 1970.
16. From an interview with Moshe Sharett shortly before his death in 1965.
17. Dr. Tabor is now one of the leading physicists at Cambridge University.
18. From interviews with Nathan Goldenberg, Rita Lipton Levy and other onetime officers of the Young Zionist Organizations, London, 1971.
19. From an interview with Dr. David Tabor, Cambridge, 1971.
20. From tape-recorded interviews with Mrs. I. Eban and the Doniachs, London, 1970.

CHAPTER 4

1. From receipted bills in Eban Archives, Jerusalem.
2. From an interview with Abba Eban, Jerusalem, 1970.
3. Ibid.
4. An anonymous interview.
5. Periodical Room, British Museum, and Periodical Room, Cambridge University Library.
6. From daily and weekly newspapers on file in the Cambridge University Library.
7. From interviews with Cambridge graduates who wish to remain anonymous.
8. All information about the Cambridge Union and its debates is either from the Union's present chief clerk, R. S. Thompson, or the chief clerk in the latter part of Eban's undergraduate days, S. A. Elwood, or from the Union's archives, unless otherwise noted.
9. From *Cambridge Graduates,* in the British Museum.
10. From the *Olavian,* Vol. 40, No. 3, British Museum.
11. A "public" school in England is somewhat comparable to a private school in the United States.
12. From Burke's Peerage, British Museum.
13. From *Cambridge Graduates,* in the British Museum.
14. From the *Olavian,* Vol. 41, No. 2, in the British Museum.
15. G. D. Young, *My Visit to Cambridge,* Feb. 15, 1936, issue of *Granta.*
16. From interviews with many Cambridge graduates.
17. From a tape-recorded interview with Abba Eban, Jerusalem, 1970.
18. From the minutes of meetings of the Zionist Federation, 1936–40.
19. From an interview with Ruth Levy, London, 1971.
20. From *Chaim Weizmann, A Biography by Several Hands,* Atheneum, 1963, p. 251.
21. From a tape-recorded interview with Abba Eban, Jerusalem, 1970.
22. From *Ben-Gurion, the Biography of an Extraordinary Man,* Robert St. John, Doubleday, 1959 and 1971, p. 67.
23. Viscount Herbert Samuel was also the first professing Jew to be a member of a British Cabinet. He died in 1963. Standard Jewish Encyclopedia, p. 1,652.
24. From Cambridge and London newspapers of November 3, 1937, in the British Museum and Cambridge University Library, and an interview with Lord Edwin Samuel.
25. From *Cambridge Graduates,* in the British Museum.
26. Namier was knighted in 1952. He died in 1960. From Who Was Who, 1970.
27. From a tape-recorded interview with Abba Eban, Jerusalem, 1970.

CHAPTER 5

1. From the *Olavian,* Vol. 42, No. 3, British Museum.
2. From an interview with Lady Waley Cohen, London, 1971.
3. From a tape-recorded interview with Mrs. Gershon Ellenbogen, London, 1970.
4. Ibid.
5. He was elevated in order to provide a constituency for Ernest Bevin, later Foreign Minister.
6. From an interview with Lady Waley Cohen, London, 1971.
7. From Cambridge daily and weekly newspapers of January, 1939.
8. From an interview with Mrs. Gershon Ellenbogen, London, 1970.
9. From an interview with Carmel Eban, Bath, England, 1971.
10. From *Chaim Weizmann, A Biography by Several Hands,* Atheneum, 1963.
11. From a letter to Joyce Nathan dated September 10, 1939.
12. From a tape-recorded interview with Abba Eban, Jerusalem, 1970.
13. The *Athenia* had been torpedoed with the loss of 118 lives seven days before Aubrey wrote this letter. The *Lusitania* was sunk by a German submarine off the tip of Ireland in 1917, with the loss of 1,198 lives.
14. From a letter to Joyce Nathan dated September 26, 1939.
15. Standard Jewish Encyclopedia, p. 1,510.
16. Leslie Hore-Belisha, Minister of War.
17. From a letter to Joyce Nathan dated January 15, 1940.
18. Ibid.

CHAPTER 6

1. From a tape-recorded interview with Mrs. I. Eban, London, 1970.
2. From an interview with Norman Bentwich, London, 1970, shortly before his death.
3. From an interview with Bernard Lewis, London University, 1971.
4. From a letter to Joyce Nathan dated March 21, 1940.
5. From a tape-recorded interview with Abba Eban, Jerusalem, 1970.
6. Ibid.
7. From a letter to Joyce Nathan dated July 7, 1940.
8. Raphael's ship arrived safely in New York and he spent the rest of the war in Hanover and Tilton, New Hampshire, but another ship, the *Duchess of Atholl,* was torpedoed and after that no more large groups of English children were sent to the United States.
9. From a letter to Joyce Nathan dated August 12, 1941.
10. From a letter to Joyce Nathan dated July 28, 1941.
11. From a letter to Nathan Goldenberg dated August 12, 1941.
12. From a tape-recorded interview with Mrs. I. Eban, London, 1970.
13. From a tape-recorded interview with Teddy Kollek in the mayor's office, Jerusalem, 1970.
14. From interviews with Suzy Eban, Jerusalem, 1970, and correspondence with Cape Town sources.

CHAPTER 7

1. From an interview with Victor Mishcon, London, 1971.
2. *Orde Wingate,* Christopher Sykes, World, 1959, p. 360.
3. From a tape-recorded interview with Abba Eban, Jerusalem, 1970.
4. From a tape-recorded interview with Abba Eban, Jerusalem, 1970.
5. After the establishment of Israel Zaslani changed his name to Shiloah. chief negotiator for Israel of the Rhodes Agreements that brought the 1

war to an end. He was a confidant of Ben-Gurion and is known as the father of Israeli Intelligence, being the first Intelligence chief. Before becoming adviser to Foreign Minister Golda Meir on Iran and Turkey he was minister in Washington under Ambassador Eban during the critical days of the 1956 war. He died in 1959.

6. World Book Encyclopedia, Vol. 20, p. 394.

7. *The Pledge*, Simon & Schuster, 1970, p. 27.

8. Standard Jewish Encyclopedia, pp. 814–15.

9. From a tape-recorded interview with Abba Eban, Jerusalem, 1970.

10. From tape-recorded interviews with Mrs. I. Eban, London, and Abba Eban, Jerusalem, 1970.

11. From a tape-recorded interview with Abba Eban, Jerusalem, 1970.

12. Standard Jewish Encyclopedia, p. 1,327.

13. Standard Jewish Encyclopedia, p. 1,639, and Brit Ivrit Olamit, Jerusalem.

14. From tape-recorded interviews with Abba Eban, Jerusalem, 1970.

15. Ibid.

16. Ibid.

17. From a tape-recorded interview with Teddy Kollek, Jerusalem, 1970.

18. From a tape-recorded interview with Abba Eban, Jerusalem, 1970.

19. In 1972 Allon was Deputy Prime Minister of Israel.

20. From a tape-recorded interview with Teddy Kollek, Jerusalem, 1970.

21. From a letter in the Eban Archives.

22. From a tape-recorded interview with Dr. Neville Halper, London, 1971.

23. Pronounced Glick.

24. One of his spectacular discoveries was the site of Solomon's mines at Ezion Geber. His most important literary work was the four-volume *Explorations in Eastern Palestine*. In 1947 he became president of Hebrew Union College. He died in 1971.

25. All the material on the Eban-Glueck relationship is from a tape-recorded interview with Dr. Nelson and Dr. Helen Glueck at their home in Cincinnati in 1970, shortly before the death of Dr. Nelson Glueck.

26. From tape-recorded interviews with Suzy and Abba Eban and Eileen Ellenbogen, and from "An Ismailia Childhood," *The New Yorker*, December 5, 1970.

27. From *British Foreign Policy and the War*, British Council Lecture Series, 1942–43, in the Eban Archives.

28. From *Controversies on Post-War Reconstruction*, British Council Lecture Series, 1942–43, in the Library of Congress.

29. From the librarian of the Library of Congress, Washington.

CHAPTER 8

1. Unless otherwise noted, all the direct quotations in this chapter are from letters written by Abba Eban to friends, photostat copies of which are in the author's possession.

2. *Orde Wingate*, Christopher Sykes, World, 1959, pp. 469–70.

3. From a tape-recorded interview with Abba Eban, Jerusalem, 1970.

4. From a tape-recorded interview with Norman Bentwich, London, 1970.

5. He later became Sir Iltyd Clayton, K.B.E.

6. From a tape-recorded interview with David Horowitz, Jerusalem, 1970, and from *State in the Making*, Horowitz, Knopf, 1955.

7. The word "ovolimity" does not appear either in Webster's Unabridged or in the Oxford Dictionary.

8. From the full text printed in a special supplement of the *Jerusalem Radio Forum Airgraph Digest*, November 26, 1943.

9. In the Eban Archives, Jerusalem.

10. From a tape-recorded interview with I. Schen, Haifa, 1970.

11. From a tape-recorded interview with Suzy Eban, Jerusalem, 1970.
12. From a tape-recorded interview with Mrs. Dewey Stone, Boston, 1971.
13. Encyclopaedia Britannica, Vol. 2, p. 173, and New York *Times*, December 30, 1950.
14. Thomas died on December 29, 1950, at the age of fifty-eight.
15. From an undated letter to Gershon Ellenbogen and a tape-recorded interview with Nelson Glueck, Cincinnati, 1970.
16. From a tape-recorded interview with Gideon Rafael, Foreign Office, Jerusalem, 1970.
17. Standard Jewish Encyclopedia, p. 58.
18. Standard Jewish Encyclopedia, p. 1,870.

CHAPTER 9

1. From tape-recorded interviews with Dr. Halper and Abba Eban in London and Jerusalem, 1970.
2. Unless otherwise noted, all the direct quotations in this chapter are from letters written by Abba Eban to friends, photostat copies of which are in the author's possession.
3. From a tape-recorded interview with Abba Eban, Jerusalem, 1970.
4. From a tape-recorded interview with Suzy Eban, Jerusalem, 1970.
5. Ibid.
6. The statement was made by Hugh Dalton, then considered the likely Foreign Minister, if Labour won. See *Chaim Weizmann, A Biography by Several Hands*, Atheneum, 1963.
7. From tape-recorded interviews with Norman Bentwich and Abba Eban, Jerusalem, 1970.
8. See Chapter 30 for Crossman's duel of letters with Eban.
9. All quotations in this paragraph are from *Tragedy and Triumph*, by Abba Eban, in *Chaim Weizmann*, op. cit.
10. From a tape-recorded interview with David Horowitz in Jerusalem, 1970, and from *State in the Making*, op. cit.

CHAPTER 10

1. Unless otherwise noted this chapter is based on many tape-recorded interviews with Abba Eban in Jerusalem, 1970.
2. The reports were true. Several years later the Center was moved to Beirut.
3. From a tape-recorded interview with N. Doniach, London, 1970.
4. Bernard Lewis is now professor at the School of Oriental Studies, London University.
5. From a tape-recorded interview with Professor Bernard Lewis at London University, 1971.
6. From an interview with Betty Shiloah, Jerusalem, 1970.
7. From a tape-recorded interview with Teddy Kollek, Jerusalem, 1970.
8. From a tape-recorded interview with Lord Edwin Samuel, Jerusalem, 1970.
9. From an interview in 1971 with Michael Comay, then Ambassador to the Court of St. James.
10. From a tape-recorded interview with Lady Samuel, Jerusalem, 1970.
11. From an interview with Joseph Linton, London, 1971.
12. From a tape-recorded interview with Gideon Rafael, Jerusalem, 1970.
13. From an article written by Abba Eban at the time of the death of Shertok (Sharett), 1965.
14. *Ben-Gurion, the Biography of an Extraordinary Man*, Robert St. John, Doubleday, 1971, p. 113.

CHAPTER 11

1. *Tragedy and Triumph,* in *Chaim Weizmann,* op. cit., p. 286.
2. Ibid, p. 252.
3. The official rate in 1946 was $4.035 to the pound. World Almanac, 1947, p. 404.
4. From interviews in London and Jerusalem with Michael Comay, Morris Rosetti, Joseph Linton, Abba Eban and others.
5. From a tape-recorded interview with Morris Rosetti, Tel Aviv, 1970.
6. *Towards the Precipice,* in *Chaim Weizmann,* op. cit., p. 239.
7. Ibid., pp. 240–41.
8. From a tape-recorded interview with Abba Eban, Jerusalem, 1970.
9. *State in the Making,* op. cit., p. 38.
10. From *Some Social and Cultural Problems of the Middle East,* reprinted from July, 1947, issue of *International Affairs.* Royal Institute of International Affairs, London.
11. *Tragedy and Triumph,* in *Chaim Weizmann,* op. cit., p. 290.
12. Ibid, p. 292.
13. Ibid., p. 293.
14. From tape-recorded interviews with Abba Eban, Jerusalem, 1970.
15. New York *Times,* March 1, 1947, p. 4.
16. *Tragedy and Triumph,* in *Chaim Weizmann,* op. cit., p. 296.
17. From a tape-recorded interview with Abba Eban, Jerusalem, 1970.
18. Ibid.
19. Judge Rosenman is also the editor of the thirteen volumes of *The Public Papers and Addresses of Franklin D. Roosevelt.*
20. Murray Gurfein later became a judge of the U. S. District Court of New York and ruled in favor of the New York *Times* in the case of the Pentagon Papers.
21. From a tape-recorded interview with Suzy and Abba Eban, Jerusalem, 1970.
22. From a tape-recorded interview with Abba Eban, Jerusalem, 1970.
23. Member of a cooperative agricultural settlement.
24. From the destruction of the Second Temple in A.D. 70 to the 1947 UN resolution making Israel's re-creation possible.

CHAPTER 12

1. From a tape-recorded interview with Abba Eban, Jerusalem, 1970.
2. MacGillivray later became the Governor-General of Jamaica.
3. Dr. García-Granados later wrote a friendly book, *The Birth of Israel,* Knopf, 1948.
4. *The Birth of Israel,* p. 172.
5. *Israel, The Establishment of a State,* Harry Sacher, British Book Centre, 1952, p. 83.
6. From *State in the Making,* David Horowitz, Knopf, p. 190.
7. Masaryk died mysteriously the next year. It was never determined whether he was murdered or killed himself in protest against the Communist seizure of his government in February, 1948.
8. *Israel, The Establishment of a State,* op. cit., pp. 83–87.

CHAPTER 13

1. *State in the Making,* op. cit., p. 230.
2. Ibid., p. 232.
3. Ibid., p. 235, and interview with Abba Eban, London, 1970.

4. From an interview with I. L. Kenen (now editor, *Near East Report*), Washington, 1970.

5. From an unidentified source, Eban Archives, Jerusalem.

6. From an interview with Regina Medzini, Jerusalem, 1970.

7. From a tape-recorded interview with Abba Eban, Jerusalem, 1970.

8. He later became President of Lebanon.

9. At various times between 1938 and 1948 Dr. Silver was head of the Zionist Organization of America, the American Zionist Emergency Council, the United Jewish Appeal, the United Palestine Appeal and the Central Conference of American Rabbis. He died in 1963.

10. *Chaim Weizmann*, op. cit., p. 300.

11. *State in the Making*, p. 263.

12. *Chaim Weizmann*, p. 302.

CHAPTER 14

1. From a tape-recorded interview with Abba Eban, Jerusalem, 1970.

2. Ibid.

3. *State in the Making*, op. cit., p. 326.

4. From a tape-recorded interview with Abba Eban, Jerusalem, 1970.

5. From a tape-recorded interview with Chaim Herzog, Tel Aviv, 1970.

6. Said Truman: "I do not think I ever had so much pressure and propaganda at the White House as I had in this instance. The persistence of a few of the extreme Zionist leaders, actuated by political motives and engaged in political threats, disturbed and annoyed me." From *Years of Trial and Hope*, Vol. II, *Memoirs*, Harry S. Truman, Doubleday, 1956.

7. Ibid.

8. From *The Man of Independence*, Jonathan Daniels, Lippincott, 1950.

9. *Chaim Weizmann*, op. cit., pp. 307–8.

10. Greenberg died in 1953 at the age of sixty-four, after having served seven years on the Jewish Agency Executive.

11. *State in the Making*, pp. 332–33.

12. *Chaim Weizmann*, p. 309.

13. Mishmar Ha-Emek is the regional educational center of Ha-Shomer Ha-Tzair, founded by Polish immigrants, which suffered heavy Arab attacks in 1929 and 1936–39.

14. From a tape-recorded interview with Abba Eban, Jerusalem, 1970.

15. *Near East Report*, May 15, 1959.

16. Cable in Eban Archives, Jerusalem.

17. From a tape-recorded interview with Abba Eban, Jerusalem, 1970.

18. *Chaim Weizmann*, p. 312.

19. A Hebrew toast meaning "Here's to life!"

CHAPTER 15

1. New York *Post*, May 28, 1948.

2. From various New York clippings of May, 1948, in the Eban Archives, Jerusalem.

3. New York *Post*, May 28, 1948.

4. *Trial and Error*, Chaim Weizmann, Harper, 1949, p. 480.

5. From Eban's introduction to *Trial and Error*, Schocken Books, 1966.

6. *The First Ten Years*, Walter Eytan, Simon & Schuster, 1958, p. 24.

7. From a tape-recorded interview with Abba Eban, Jerusalem, 1970.

8. "And he said: 'Thy name shall be called no more Jacob, but Israel . . .'" Genesis 32:28.

9. From a tape-recorded interview with Abba Eban, Jerusalem, 1970.

10. *Israel, The Establishment of a State*, Harry Sacher, British Book Centre, 1952, p. 128

11. From a clipping, unidentified, in the Eban Archives, Jerusalem.

12. Ben Hecht died in 1964 and Louis Bromfield in 1956, without ever having been to Israel.

13. Samakh and Majdal are two Palestinian towns.

14. J. B. Glubb, commonly called Glubb Pasha, was a British officer who commanded the Arab Legion of Trans-Jordan for years. He held the rank of captain in the British Army Reserves and until the end of the Mandate was on the staff of the Palestine Government as Assistant Inspector-General of Police. Source: *Israel, The Establishment of a State*, op. cit., p. 207.

15. Romania, Hungary, Bulgaria and Italy were admitted to the UN in 1955; Japan in 1956.

16. From a tape-recorded interview with Abba Eban, Jerusalem, 1970.

17. From a tape-recorded interview with Regina Medzini, Jerusalem, 1970.

18. From a tape-recorded interview with John Shaftsley, London, 1971.

19. Abba Eban Recorded Interview, 1964, The John Foster Dulles Oral History Project, Princeton University, p. 80, quoted with permission of the Princeton University Library and Abba Eban. (Hereafter cited as Princeton Interview.)

20. *Israel, The Establishment of a State*, op. cit., p. 135. *The First Ten Years*, op. cit., pp. 15–16. *Israel and the United Nations*, Manhattan Publishing Company, 1956, p. 59.

21. From an interview with Abba Eban, on tape, 1971.

22. *Israel, The Establishment of a State*, op. cit., p. 308.

23. At that time, one month before the Communist capture of Nanking, Chiang Kai-shek still represented the Chinese mainland.

24. The name of the paper was later changed to the Jerusalem *Post*.

25. From the Eban Archives.

26. *Voice of Israel*, Abba Eban, Horizon, 1957, pp. 27–44.

27. Idlewild had been opened for international business just a few months before this.

28. From a tape-recorded interview with Abba Eban, Jerusalem, 1970.

29. From a tape-recorded interview with Suzy Eban, Jerusalem, 1970.

30. Ibid.

31. From a tape-recorded interview with Mrs. Dewey Stone, Boston, 1971.

32. Native-born Israelis, the Hebrew word literally meaning the fruit of the cactus, very sweet after the prickly shell is removed.

33. From a tape-recorded interview with Chaim Herzog, Tel Aviv, 1970.

CHAPTER 16

1. For several years the New York *Times* insisted on spelling it Sharet.

2. The New York *Times* of March 7, 1949, telling of the name changes, mentioned that Shertok means "little devil," while Sharett literally means "a servant."

3. Interview with Alida Eban, London, 1970.

4. From a tape-recorded interview with Gideon Rafael, Jerusalem, 1970.

5. From a tape-recorded interview with Suzy Eban, Jerusalem, 1970.

6. From souvenirs in the Eban Archives, Jerusalem.

7. Text in the Eban Archives, Jerusalem.

8. From a tape-recorded interview with Suzy Eban, Jerusalem, 1970.

9. Standard Jewish Encyclopedia, p. 613.

10. From letters in the Eban Archives, Jerusalem.

11. From a letter in the Eban Archives, Jerusalem.

12. Ibid.

13. From *The Nation*, December 16, 1950.

14. From a tape-recorded interview with Abba Eban, Jerusalem, 1970.
15. Ibid.
16. Elath, formerly Epstein, had headed the Middle East division of the Jewish Agency from 1934 to 1945 and its Washington political department from 1945 until he was named ambassador in 1948. After nine years at the Court of St. James, he became president of Hebrew University.
17. From an anonymous interview in Jerusalem, 1970.
18. From a tape-recorded interview with Abba Eban, Jerusalem, 1970.
19. Ibid.
20. The Foreign Ministry had not yet been moved to Jerusalem.
21. From a tape-recorded interview with Suzy Eban, Jerusalem, 1970.
22. *Years of Trial and Hope*, Vol. II, *Memoirs*, Harry S. Truman, Doubleday, 1956, p. 162.

CHAPTER 17

1. There are no footnotes to this chapter, because most of the material was supplied by friends and close associates of Suzy Eban, some of whom prefer not to be quoted directly.

CHAPTER 18

1. From a tape-recorded interview with Abba Eban, New York, 1971.
2. From a tape-recorded interview with Abba Eban, Jerusalem, 1970, and from the *Canadian Zionist* of December, 1959.
3. From a tape-recorded interview with Abba Eban, Jerusalem, 1970.
4. From the *World Alliance News Letter* of February, 1951.
5. From a tape-recorded interview with Abba Eban, Jerusalem, 1970.
6. Ibid.
7. From a tape-recorded interview with Suzy Eban, Jerusalem, 1970.
8. *Fulbright the Dissenter*, Haynes Johnson and Bernard M. Gwertman, Doubleday, 1968, pp. 126–27.
9. From a letter in the Eban Archives, Jerusalem.
10. Actually they were Un-American Affairs, Labor and Public Welfare.
11. From a tape-recorded interview with Abba Eban, Jerusalem, 1970.
12. From the Princeton Interview, p. 13.
13. *Einstein, The Life and Times*, Ronald W. Clark, World, 1971, p. 618.
14. *Jewish Chronicle*, October 2, 1959.
15. From a tape-recorded interview with Abba Eban, Jerusalem, 1970, and from *Einstein, The Life and Times*, loc. cit.
16. *Jewish Chronicle*, October 2, 1959.
17. *Einstein on Peace*, Otto Nathan and Henry Norden, eds., London, 1963, p. 571.
18. Ibid., p. 572.
19. From a tape-recorded interview with Abba Eban, Jerusalem, 1970.
20. Princeton Interview, p. 14.
21. Ibid., p. 15.
22. From a tape-recorded interview with Abba Eban, Jerusalem, 1970.
23. On February 2, 1952. See *Moscow and Jerusalem*, Avigdor Dagan, Abelard-Schuman, 1970, p. 64.
24. Ibid., p. 70.
25. From a tape-recorded interview with Abba Eban, Jerusalem, 1970.
26. Also spelled Qibiya.
27. From a tape-recorded interview with Gideon Rafael, Jerusalem, 1970.
28. From a tape-recorded interview with Abba Eban, New York, 1971.
29. From an anonymous interview, Jerusalem, 1970.

30. Memos in Eban Archives, Jerusalem.

31. From a tape-recorded interview with Abba Eban, Jerusalem, 1970.

32. Ibid.

33. The author was present.

34. From the Eban Archives, Jerusalem.

35. All the material on Johnson is from a tape-recorded interview with Abba Eban, Jerusalem, 1970.

36. See pages 106–7, *Israel, The Establishment of a State,* op. cit., pp. 106–7, "Mr. Austin's ideas were admittedly half-baked . . ."

37. From a tape-recorded interview with Abba Eban, New York, 1971.

38. The N.Y.U. citation said the degree was given for "the courage, understanding and diplomacy that catapulted him to leadership in Jewish statehood, for his devotion to the cause of universal understanding and for his inexhaustible effort to further democratic ideals."

39. All the letters from which these excerpts are taken are in the Eban Archives, Jerusalem.

40. *Jewish Chronicle,* October 2, 1959.

41. The Einstein material, unless otherwise credited, is from a tape-recorded interview with Abba Eban, Jerusalem, 1970; from letters written by Abba Eban to his wife, now in the Eban Archives; and from daily newspapers for April, 1955.

42. *Voice of Israel,* Abba Eban, Horizon, 1957, pp. 201–5.

43. From a letter dated April 3, 1955, in the Eban Archives, Jerusalem.

44. From a tape-recorded interview with Abba Eban, Jerusalem, 1970.

45. From *Moscow and Jerusalem,* op. cit.

46. Washington *Daily News,* November 8, 1955.

47. From a tape-recorded interview with Abba Eban, New York, 1971.

CHAPTER 19

1. This chapter, unless otherwise noted, is based on a considerable number of tape-recorded interviews with Abba Eban in Jerusalem, Tel Aviv and New York in 1970 and 1971, and on a tape-recorded interview by Abba Eban for the John Foster Dulles Oral History Project, Princeton University Library, 1964, and on *Dulles over Suez,* Herman Finer, Quadrangle Books, 1964, and on an article by Abba Eban in *The Canadian Zionist,* December, 1959.

2. From a statement by Eban to *The Canadian Zionist,* December, 1959.

3. Called the Sea of Galilee in the New Testament and Lake Kinneret by the Israelis.

4. Princeton Interview, p. 25.

5. Ibid.

6. From a tape-recorded interview with Ben-Gurion, Sde Boker, Israel, 1970.

7. New York *Times,* January 22, 1956.

8. Medzini later became head of the Jerusalem office of the Israel Press Department, spokesman for Prime Minister Eshkol and professor at Hebrew University.

9. From a tape-recorded interview with Abba Eban, Jerusalem, 1970.

10. Ibid.

11. Ibid.

12. Ibid.

13. *Dulles over Suez,* op. cit., pp. 343–44.

14. From a tape-recorded interview with Abba Eban, Jerusalem, 1970.

15. Ibid.

16. Ibid.

17. Ibid.

18. Princeton Interview, p. 38.

19. Ibid., pp. 38–39.

20. Ibid., pp. 37–38.

21. *Dulles over Suez,* op. cit., pp. 391–92.

CHAPTER 20

1. From a tape-recorded interview with Abba Eban, Jerusalem, 1970.
2. Among them Gideon Rafael, Regina Hamburger, Tamar Shoshan, Daniel Levine, Moshe Tov, Emile Najar, Jacob Robinson and Michael Comay.
3. Princeton Interview, p. 39.
4. There was later a Hebrew edition with a glowing introduction by Moshe Sharett.
5. From the *Jewish Criterion* of Pittsburgh, March 24, 1957.
6. From the *Zionist Record* of South Africa, March 8, 1957.
7. From a tape-recorded interview with Abba Eban, Jerusalem, 1970.
8. *Hadassah Newsletter*, November, 1958.
9. Princeton Interview, p. 47.
10. Ibid., p. 32.
11. From the Yiddish word *shnoren*, to beg.
12. From a tape-recorded interview with Mrs. Suzy Eban, Jerusalem, 1970.

CHAPTER 21

1. The quotations in this chapter are from newspaper clippings in the Eban Archives, Jerusalem.
2. From the *Floridian*, Miami, Florida.
3. From an off-the-air transcript of "Open End," with David Susskind, Channel 13, WNTA–TV, New York, March 1, 1959.

CHAPTER 22

1. The facts, figures and impressions in this chapter are principally from British, American and Israeli clippings in the Eban Archives, Jerusalem, from interviews with Israeli and American journalists who covered the 1959 campaign and from interviews with Eban's political allies and opponents, most of whom talked on the understanding that their identity would not be disclosed.
2. From the *Jewish Chronicle* of June 12, 1959.
3. From an interview in Jerusalem, 1970, with one of the journalists involved.
4. From a letter to Alida Eban, July 5, 1959.
5. From the official program in the Eban Archives, Jerusalem.
6. From members of the Gush who do not wish to be named.
7. London *Observer*, August 7, 1959.
8. *Zionist Record*, July, 1959.
9. *Jewish Chronicle*, October, 1959.
10. From a letter to Alida Eban dated September 30, 1959.
11. From a letter to Alida Eban dated July 30, 1959.

CHAPTER 23

1. New York *Times Magazine*.
2. From a letter to Jon Kimche, editor of the *London Jewish Review*, dated December 20, 1959.
3. From a tape-recorded interview with Suzy Eban, Jerusalem, 1970.
4. From a tape-recorded interview with Gideon Rafael, Jerusalem, 1970.
5. From a letter in the Eban Archives, Jerusalem.
6. From an undated letter to Mrs. Dewey Stone.
7. Ibid.
8. Ibid.

9. This quotation is from the verbatim stenographic transcript of President Eisenhower's press conference of January 26, 1960. (Most newspapers carried a somewhat edited version.)

10. From a stenographic, unedited transcript of President Eisenhower's press conference of February 3, 1960.

11. From a tape-recorded interview with an anonymous spokesman, Jerusalem, 1970.

CHAPTER 24

1. The original manuscript of the translation in longhand on Ministry of Education and Culture stationery is in the Eban Archives in Jerusalem.

2. From the Jerusalem *Post* of October 22, 1961.

3. From a clipping in the Eban Archives unidentified as to date and publication.

4. In the Eban Archives.

5. From a letter to Mrs. Dewey Stone dated August 5, 1961.

6. From an undated letter to Dr. and Mrs. I. Eban, London.

7. From the *Rhode Island Herald*, January, 1964.

8. From an interview with Dr. Maurice Shapiro, Washington, 1971.

9. From an interview with Abba Eban, Jerusalem, 1972.

10. From a letter to Eban from Ben Raeburn of Horizon Press, in the Eban Archives.

11. From a letter to Norman Podhoretz dated October 29, 1962.

12. From the New York *Herald Tribune* of September 24, 1962.

13. From a letter to Mrs. Dewey Stone in the Eban Archives.

14. Ibid.

15. From a tape-recorded interview with Abba Eban, Washington, 1971.

CHAPTER 25

1. The next day Ben-Gurion, under pressure from Mapai, agreed to change his mind about resigning from the Knesset.

2. From an undated letter to Dr. and Mrs. I. Eban in the Eban Archives, Jerusalem.

3. *Jewish Observer and Middle East Review*, July 19, 1963.

4. Ibid.

5. From an undated letter to the Stones.

6. From a letter to Anne Stone dated August 3, 1964.

7. From a letter to Anne Stone dated December 14, 1964.

8. From a tape-recorded interview with Abba Eban, Jerusalem, 1970.

9. From a tape-recorded interview with Suzy Eban, Jerusalem, 1970.

CHAPTER 26

1. From a letter to Anne Stone dated November 27, 1965.

2. From a tape-recorded interview with Eli Eban, Jerusalem, 1970.

3. From *Two Years Later*, by Abba Eban, Jerusalem *Post*, June 6, 1969.

4. The remainder of this chapter is based on a series of interviews with Abba Eban in Jerusalem, Washington and New York, in 1970 and 1971.

5. The figures are from the testimony of Rudolph Hess at the Nuremberg trials, as reported in World Book Encyclopedia, Vol. 1, p. 868.

6. The withdrawal of UNEF was protested in Congress, denounced in most of the non-Communist capitals of the world, condemned by such newspapers as the New York *Times* and criticized in their memoirs by both Harold Wilson and Dwight Eisenhower.

CHAPTER 27

1. Unless otherwise noted, the facts and quotations in this chapter were obtained from Abba Eban.
2. As reported by Drew Pearson in "Washington Merry-Go-Round."
3. *The Vantage Point*, by Lyndon B. Johnson, Holt, Rinehart & Winston, 1971, p. 293.
4. Ibid.
5. Ibid.
6. Ibid.
7. *The Six Day War*, Randolph S. and Winston S. Churchill, Heineman, 1967, pp. 69–70.

CHAPTER 28

1. Unless otherwise noted, the facts in this chapter were obtained in a series of interviews with Abba Eban in Jerusalem, New York and Washington, and from others involved in the diplomatic developments of May–June, 1967.
2. From a dispatch by Edwin Roth dated June 4, 1967, in the *Star*.
3. From *The Vantage Point*, op. cit.

CHAPTER 29

1. Unless otherwise noted, the facts and quotations in this chapter were obtained during a series of tape-recorded interviews with Abba Eban in Washington, New York and Jerusalem, 1970, 1971 and 1972, and from newspaper clippings and letters in the Eban Archives, Jerusalem.
2. From a letter to Anne Stone dated June 20, 1967.
3. From *The Christian Science Monitor* of June 19, 1967.
4. From a tape-recorded interview with Abba Eban, New York, 1971.
5. Ibid.
6. Ibid.
7. From a letter to Anne Stone dated June 20, 1967.
8. On August 4, 1967, the Israeli newspaper *Ma'ariv* carried an interview with Gideon Rafael, Israeli ambassador to the UN, in which he was asked whether he thought U Thant made a mistake in handling the withdrawal and replied: "The Secretary-General tried to control the situation and failed, but he cannot be blamed for it. I oppose the tendency which tries to put the blame for what took place in the Middle East on the Secretary-General. . . ."
9. From *Israel and World Politics*, Theodore Draper, Viking, 1968.

CHAPTER 30

1. The facts in this chapter, unless otherwise noted, are from a series of tape-recorded interviews with Abba Eban in Jerusalem and New York, 1970 and 1971, as are also all the direct quotations from Eban, unless otherwise credited.
2. This paragraph is from interviews in Jerusalem and Tel Aviv with many people who have an intimate knowledge of the events discussed.
3. *Time*, January 10, 1969.
4. This is a full, unexpurgated transcript of that portion of the Frost program dealing with war criminals, as transcribed directly from the air by the author.
5. *The New Statesman*, August 14, 1970.
6. From transcript of "Meet the Press" telecast, Vol. 13, No. 11, March 16, 1969.
7. From a letter to Anne Stone dated October 11, 1970.
8. From tape-recorded interviews with Suzy Eban and Anne Stone, 1970.
9. The letter was to Anne Stone, the column was by Leonard Lyons and the publisher was Doubleday.

10. *The New Yorker,* December 5, 1970.

11. From the *National Review,* October 20, 1970.

12. From a transcript of "Firing Line," No. 218, September 28, 1970.

13. From a transcript made by the author at a Bonds for Israel dinner, Shoreham Hotel, Washington, October 11, 1970.

14. Israel's voting record on China and the Sharett and Eban quotes were supplied by the Permanent Mission of Israel to the United Nations, New York.

15. In a report to Prime Minister Moshe Sharett in 1955, David Hacohen wrote: ". . . since every one of our steps toward China is naturally influenced, at least partially so, by our relations with the United States . . ." from *Burma Diary* by Hacohen.

CHAPTER 31

The reason for the lack of notes to this chapter is explained at the start of the chapter.

1. The Haggadah edited by Cecil Roth has this footnote: "Anti-Semites often call attention to this interlude, which they allege to reflect the revengeful spirit of the Jew. How unjust this is may be seen from the fact that precisely this stage of the service is chosen for opening the door that all may know what is taking place. The verses are indeed fierce by modern standards. But the use is not indiscriminate, and the reference is pre-eminently to the overthrow of the Egyptians of old. . . ."

CHAPTER 32

1. From a tape-recorded interview with Abba Eban, New York, 1972.

BIBLIOGRAPHY

ALLON, YIGAL. *The Making of Israel's Army.* Universe, 1970.
———. *Shield of David.* Weidenfeld, 1970.
BEN-GURION, DAVID. *Israel, a Personal History.* Funk & Wagnalls, 1971.
———. *Years of Challenge.* Holt, Rinehart & Winston, 1963.
BURDETT, WINSTON. *Encounter with the Middle East.* Deutsch, 1969.
CHURCHILL, RANDOLPH AND WINSTON. *The Six Day War.* Heineman, 1967.
CLARK, RONALD W. *Einstein, The Life and Times.* World, 1971.
COPELAND, MILES. *The Game of Nations.* Simon & Schuster, 1969.
CRADOCK, PERCY. *Recollections of the Cambridge Union.* Bowes & Bowes, 1953.
CROSSMAN, RICHARD. *A Nation Reborn.* Atheneum, 1960.
DAGAN, AVIGDOR. *Moscow and Jerusalem.* Abelard-Schuman, 1970.
DRAPER, THEODORE. *Israel and World Politics.* Viking, 1968.
DULLES, JOHN FOSTER. *War or Peace.* Macmillan, 1950.
EBAN, ABBA. *My People, The Story of the Jews.* Random House, 1968.
———. *Tide of Nationalism.* Horizon, 1959.
———. *Voice of Israel.* Horizon, 1957.
EBAN, SUZY. "An Ismailia Childhood," *The New Yorker,* Dec. 5, 1970.
EDEN, ANTHONY. *Full Circle.* Houghton, Mifflin, 1960.
EYTAN, WALTER. *The First Ten Years.* Simon & Schuster, 1958.
FERON, JAMES. "That New Boy in the Israeli Foreign Office," New York *Times,*
    April 17, 1966.
FINER, HERMAN. *Dulles over Suez.* Quadrangle, 1964.
GARCÍA-GRANADOS, JORGE. *The Birth of Israel,* Knopf, 1948.
GOLDENBERG, NATHAN. *The Organization of Zionism.* Zionist Federation, 1945.
GRUBER, RUTH. *Israel on the Seventh Day.* Hill & Wang, 1968.
HOROWITZ, DAVID. *State in the Making.* Knopf, 1953.
JOHNSON, LYNDON B. *The Vantage Point.* Holt, Rinehart & Winston, 1971.
KATZ, SAMUEL. *Days of Fire.* Doubleday, 1968.
LAU-LAVIE, N. *Moshe Dayan.* Hartmore, 1968.
LIE, TRYGVE. *In the Cause of Peace.* Macmillan, 1954.
MEINERTZHAGEN, RICHARD. *Middle East Diary.* Cresset, 1959.
NATHAN, OTTO, and NORDEN, H. *Einstein on Peace,* Simon & Schuster, 1963.
PEARLMAN, MOSHE. *Ben-Gurion Looks Back.* Simon & Schuster, 1965.
PERES, SHIMON. *David's Sling.* Random House, 1971.
PRINGLE, HENRY and KATHARINE. "That Witty Young Man from Israel," *Saturday
    Evening Post,* October 20, 1951.
PRITTLE, TERENCE CORNELIUS. *Eshkol of Israel.* Pitman, 1969.
SACHER, HARRY. *Israel, The Establishment of a State.* British Book Centre, 1952.
ST. JOHN, ROBERT. *Ben-Gurion, the Biography of an Extraordinary Man.* Doubleday,
    1959 and 1971.
SHIHOR, SAMUEL. *Hollow Glory.* Yoseloff, 1960.
SLATER, LEONARD. *The Pledge.* Simon & Schuster, 1970.
SYKES, CHRISTOPHER. *Orde Wingate.* World, 1959.
SYRKIN, MARIE. *Golda Meir, Israel's Leader.* Putnam, 1969.
THOMAS, BERTRAM. *Arabia Felix.* Scribners, 1932.
TRUMAN, HARRY. *Memoirs,* Vol. II, *Years of Trial and Hope,* Doubleday, 1956.
WEISGAL, MEYER. *Meyer Weisgal—So Far.* Weidenfeld, 1971.
WEISGAL, MEYER and CARMICHAEL. *Chaim Weizmann.* Atheneum, 1963.
WEIZMANN, CHAIM. *Trial and Error.* Harper, 1949.
WEIZMANN, VERA. *The Impossible Takes Longer.* Harper, 1967.

Index